A COGNITIVE PSYCHOLOGY
OF MASS COMMUNICATION

LEA's Communication Series
Jennings Bryant/Dolf Zillmann, General Editors

For more information on LEA titles, please contact Lawrence Erlbaum Associates, Publishers, at www.erlbaum.com.

A COGNITIVE PSYCHOLOGY OF MASS COMMUNICATION

Fourth Edition

Richard Jackson Harris
Kansas State University

LEA

2004 LAWRENCE ERLBAUM ASSOCIATES, PUBLISHERS

Mahwah, New Jersey   London

Senior Acquisitions Editor:	Linda Bathgate
Assistant Editor:	Karin Wittig Bates
Cover Design:	Kathryn Houghtaling Lacey
Textbook Production Manager:	Paul Smolenski
Full-Service Compositor:	TechBooks
Text and Cover Printer:	Sheridan Books, Inc.

This book was typeset in 10/12 pt. Palatino, Italic, Bold, and Bold Italic.
The heads were typeset in News Gothic Bold Condensed.

Lawrence Erlbaum Associates, Inc., Publishers
10 Industrial Avenue
Mahwah, New Jersey 07430
www.erlbaum.com

Library of Congress Cataloging-in-Publication Data

Harris, Richard Jackson.
  A Cognitive psychology of mass communication /
  Richard Jackson Harris.—4th ed.
    p. cm.—(LEA's communication series)
Includes bibliographical references and index.
ISBN 0-8058-4660-3 (case : alk. paper)
1. Mass media—Psychological aspects. I. Title. II. Series.

P96.P75H37 2004
302.23'01'9—dc22   2004003792

Books published by Lawrence Erlbaum Associates are printed on acid-free paper,
and their bindings are chosen for strength and durability.

Printed in the United States of America
10 9 8 7 6 5 4 3

To four strong women of four generations

My grandmother Anne Roberts Harris (1890–1974),
  who modeled an unconditional love and an exciting intellectual
  curiosity
My mother Helen Sellers Harris (1917–1970),
  who modeled exceptional parenting and was always there for me
My wife Caprice Joan Becker (1955–),
  whose different background and views on media have expanded my
  perspectives
My daughter Natalie Becker Harris (1991–),
  who, with her older brother Clint and twin brother Grady, now
  challenge me in effectively parenting teenagers in media use

Brief Contents

1 Mass Communication in Society: Swimming in the Media Sea **1**

2 Research and Theory in Mass Communication: How We Study Media Scientifically **18**

3 Media Portrayals of Groups: Distorted Social Mirrors **53**

4 Advertising and Marketing: Baiting, Catching, and Reeling Us In **92**

5 Children and Media: More Than Just Little Adults **124**

6 Sports and Music: Emotion in High Gear **151**

7 News: Setting the Agenda About the World **187**

8 Politics: Using News and Advertising to Win Elections **225**

9 Violence: Watching All That Mayhem Really Matters **255**

10 Sex: Pornography, Innuendo, and Rape as a Turn-On **287**

11 Teaching Values and Health: Media as Parent, Priest, Physician, and Moral Arbiter **317**

12 Handling Media: Living With New Technologies and Communicating About Media **352**

Contents

Preface   **xvii**

1   Mass Communication in Society: Swimming in the
Media Sea   **1**
What Is Mass Communication?   **4**
Media Use   **6**
Television   **6**
Radio   **9**
Newspapers   **10**
Magazines   **11**
Computer-Mediated Communication   **12**
Overview of the Book   **14**

2   Research and Theory in Mass Communication: How We
Study Media Scientifically   **18**
Media Research Frameworks   **19**
Looking at Content   **19**
Looking at Exposure   **21**
Looking at Effects   **21**
Theories of Mass Communication   **27**
Social Cognitive Theory (Social Learning, Observational
Learning, Modeling)   **27**
Cultivation Theory   **28**
Socialization Theories   **30**
Uses and Gratifications Theory   **31**
Agenda Setting   **34**
Schema Theory   **35**
Limited Capacity Model   **39**
Cognitive Components of the Media Experience   **39**
Attention   **40**
Suspending Disbelief   **41**

Identification 42
Empathy 43
Suspense 44
Humor 45
Mood Management 48
Media as Perceived Reality 48
The Reflection Myth 48
The Study of Perceived Reality 50
Conclusion 52

3 Media Portrayals of Groups: Distorted Social Mirrors 53
Portrayals of the Sexes 54
The View of Women 54
The View of Men 60
Effects of Gender Stereotyping 63
The Four Stages of Minority Portrayals 65
African Americans 66
How Are They Portrayed? 66
Blacks as Viewers 68
Effects of African American Portrayals 69
Latinos 70
Native Americans 72
Asian Americans 74
Arabs and Arab Americans 76
Gay and Lesbian People 78
Older Adults 80
Persons with Disabilities and Disorders 83
Physical Disabilities 83
Psychological Disorders 84
Occupations 85
Police Officers 86
Lawyers and Courtroom Trials 86
Psychologists and Psychiatrists 87
Farmers and Rural Life 88
College Students 89
Conclusion: So What if They're Stereotyped? 90

4 Advertising and Marketing: Baiting, Catching, and Reeling
Us In 92
Historical Background 93
Types of Ads 94

Psychological Appeals in Advertising 95
  Informational Appeals 96
  Emotional Appeals 96
  Patriotic Appeals 99
  Fear Appeals 100
  Achievement, Success, and Power Appeals 102
  Humorous Appeals 102
  Testimonials (Product Endorsements) 102
  Can Appeals Be Unethical? 103
  A Theoretical Model 104
Cognition and Marketing: Ads as Information to Be
    Processed 105
  Stages of Processing 106
  A Constructionist Framework for Understanding
    Advertising 107
  Deceptive Advertising 108
  Miscomprehension Versus Deceptiveness 108
  True-But-Deceptive Ads (Induced
    Miscomprehension) 110
  Studying Deception Scientifically 112
Sex and Subliminal Advertising 113
  Classical Conditioning 113
  Subliminal Advertising 115
Advertising in New Places 118
  Product Placements 118
  Classrooms and Schools 119
  Advertising on the Internet 120
  Prescription Drug Advertising 122
Conclusion 122

5 Children and Media: More Than Just Little Adults 124
  Children's Use of Different Media 125
    Mental Effort and Social Interaction 125
    Information Extraction and Memory 125
    The Medium and Imagination 127
  Prosocial Children's Television 127
    Sesame Street 129
  Other CTW Projects 132
  Commercial TV Contributions 133
    Science Shows for Children 135
    Channel One 135

Teen Programs **136**
Children's Prosocial Learning from Adult
    Television **136**
Children's Advertising **138**
Differentiating Ads and Programs **139**
Disclaimers **139**
Television, Toymakers, and the Military **140**
Tobacco Advertising and Role Modeling **142**
Media Literacy **144**
Curriculum Development **146**
What Can Be Done in the Home **147**
Conclusion **149**

6 Sports and Music: Emotion in High Gear **151**
The Emotional (Affective) Side of Experiencing Media **152**
What Is Emotion? **152**
Media as Vicarious Emotional Experience **152**
Emotional Expression and Media **153**
Sports **155**
How Television Has Changed Sports **157**
Psychological Issues in Sports and Media **166**
Conclusion **178**
Music **178**
Uses and Gratifications of Popular Music **180**
Content **181**
Effects **183**
Music as a Memory Cue **185**
Conclusion **186**

7 News: Setting the Agenda About the World **187**
What Is News? **191**
Primary Characteristics of a Newsworthy Event **192**
Secondary Characteristics of a Newsworthy Event **195**
News Media as Creating a Perceived Reality **199**
Manipulation of News **200**
The 1991 Persian Gulf War Coverage: Case Study **205**
Effects of News Coverage **208**
The Impact of Different Points of View **208**
Memory for the News **209**
Effects of News on Attributions and Decision
    Making **211**

Responses to Crime Coverage in Media   212
Suicides: Triggered by News?   217
How Media Affect Foreign Policy   217
Conclusion: Fiction Becomes Reality   220
The Docudrama: Fact or Fiction?   221
Limits of Media Influence   222

8   Politics: Using News and Advertising to Win
Elections   225
Closing the Distance Between the Candidate and
the Public   227
Coverage of Political Campaigns   228
What Is Heavily Covered   228
What Is Lightly Covered   231
Interpretation by the Press   233
The U.S. Presidential Debates   235
Candidates' Use of News Media   237
Setting the Agenda   237
Framing the Candidates   238
Creating Pseudo-Events   240
Dealing With Attacks From the Opponent   241
The Need to Be Taken Seriously   242
Case Study: Press Coverage of the 2000 U.S. Presidential
Campaign and Election   242
Election Night Coverage   243
Framing the Electoral Uncertainty   243
Political Advertising   245
Purposes   246
Appeals in Political Advertising   248
Negative Advertising   249
Effects of Political Advertising   250
Television as Cultivator of Political Moderation   251
Conclusion   253

9   Violence: Watching All That Mayhem Really Matters   255
Effects of Media Violence   257
Fear   257
Modeling   260
Sensitization   264
Desensitization   267
Cultivation   269

Important Interactive Factors 269
Catharsis 274
Who Watches Media Violence and Why? 275
Social Factors 275
Individual Differences 276
Longitudinal Studies 277
Research Versus the Public Perception 279
Violent Video Games 280
Helping Children Deal With Violent Media 282
Institutional Solutions 282
Parental Mediation and Media Literacy 283
Conclusion 285

10 Sex: Pornography, Innuendo, and Rape as a Turn-On 287
The Nature of Sex in Media 288
Definitional Issues 288
History of Sex in Media 289
Media Sex Today 290
Effects of Viewing Media Sex 292
Arousal 292
Attitudes and Values 293
Behavioral Effects 300
Catharsis 303
Prevailing Tone 303
Sexual Violence 305
Erotica as Stimulator of Aggression 305
Effects Depend on How the Woman Is Portrayed 305
Individual Differences in Male Viewers 305
Slasher Movies 307
Mitigating the Negative Effects of Sexual Violence 311
Press Coverage of Sexually Violent Crimes 312
Conclusion 314

11 Teaching Values and Health: Media as Parent, Priest,
Physician, and Moral Arbiter 317
Media's Teaching of Values 318
Family Values 320
Family Composition 321
Family Solidarity 322
The Influence of Television on Family Life 325

Religion 328
  Religion in TV Series 328
  Portrayals of Religious Professionals 329
  Religion in the News 330
  Religious Television 333
  Effects of Television on Religion 334
Media Use in Social Marketing 335
  Obstacles to Social Marketing 336
  Considering the Audience 338
  Positive Effects of Social Marketing 339
  Public Health Media Campaigns 341
  Stanford Five-City Multifactor Risk Reduction
    Project 342
  AIDS Awareness Campaigns 343
Entertainment-Education Media 344
  Sample E-E Programs 344
  Effects of E-E Programs 346
Conclusion 349

12 Handling Media: Living With New Technologies and
    Communicating About Media 352
    The Future and New Technologies 353
      The Reach of Media 353
      New Technologies 356
    Influencing the Media 361
      Individual Efforts 362
      Group Efforts 363
    Communicating Media Research Findings to the
      Public 365
    Conclusion: What Is Mass Communication?
      (Revisited) 367

References 371

Author Index 443

Subject Index 461

Preface

A popular movie a few years ago, *The Truman Show,* featured Jim Carrey as a man whose entire life had been a television show, filmed constantly under a huge bubble that was his whole world. His gradual discovery of this situation is personally devastating, and Truman knows he can never be the same again. In a sense he is an exaggerated but apt metaphor for this entire book. Our lives, and all that we know, are far more heavily influenced by the media than most of us realize, even if our whole lives are not completely reducible to a TV show. Although you will not, like Truman, find out through reading this book that you have no identity except as an entertainment figure, you may discover that an amazing amount of what you know and how you behave is a direct product of your interaction with television, radio, print, and computer-mediated communications. In any event, you will probably never look at media the same way again! At least that is my hope.

Some real people are as much media creations as Carrey's Truman. Mourners around the world cried over the death of Britain's young Princess Diana in the late summer of 1997 and over NASCAR driver Dale Earnhardt's fiery crash death in 2001. These were not fake tears; the loss was real. These deaths were a true personal loss for millions of people who had never met Diana or Dale but knew them only as friends through the media. A few years earlier, people had been stunned at the arrest and trial of football great and actor O. J. Simpson for the murder of his ex-wife. Many people truly felt shock and disbelief—how could he have done what he was charged with doing? Simpson's lawyers argued that the saturation tabloid-like coverage of his trial had painted a false media picture of him that had no relation to reality. Even though Simpson was acquitted, many refused to accept that he had NOT committed the crime. The irony, how-ever, was that the picture created by the prosecution was no less a media creation than the original, positive image of the football hero (also entirely a media image). *Where* was the real O. J. Simpson? *Was* there even a real O. J. Simpson? Does anybody know? The media picture became the reality.

Sometimes the media and reality become intertwined in odd ways. The Westport Dry Cleaners in Manhattan, Kansas was suddenly inundated with calls asking for "God" and delivering prayer requests. Why? Because the business happened to have the same phone number as the "God" character in the movie *Bruce Almighty*. Didn't those callers know that wasn't really God's telephone number? Maybe, but if they only meant to harass or play a joke, why not call *any* number and ask for "God"? Why this particular number?

This book initially evolved from my development of the course "The Psychology of Mass Communication" at Kansas State University in the early 1980s. I am grateful to the students in this class over the years for their enthusiasm, inspiration, and challenge; their ideas and dialogue with my material have positively affected the book throughout. More and more I am convinced that the area of mass communication is a marvelous area in which to apply theory and research methodology from experimental psychology and other fields. Media research deals with some of the major activities that occupy our time and addresses problems that people are vitally interested in, such as sex and violence, values in media, and images of different groups.

Trained in the 1970s at the University of Illinois at Urbana-Champaign as a rigorous experimental psychologist studying language, I became interested in applying what I knew about text processing to study the sort of language that people encounter every day. Some research on the cognition of deceptive advertising in the late 1970s first challenged me to think seriously and more broadly about mass media consumption as information processing. It is through this work that the cognitive perspectives on the media came to influence my thinking.

The support of the Psychology Department at Kansas State University and the editors at Lawrence Erlbaum Associates during the writing of all four editions has been tremendous. I cannot imagine a more supportive department in which to teach and do research, nor a more helpful publisher to work with. Karin Wittig Bates has been an excellent editor for this edition. I also greatly appreciate the Fulbright Visiting Lectureships I held in Belo Horizonte, Brazil in 1982 and Montevideo, Uruguay in 1994; these experiences gave me an internationalist perspective that I have tried to bring to this book. Contemporary media are part of an international culture. Although this book relies heavily on U.S. media, since that is what I know best and that is what has been studied the most, the principles are equally applicable elsewhere as I try to suggest with frequent examples from other nations' media.

Although countless present and former students have influenced the ideas on these pages, particular thanks are due to Fred Sanborn, Steven Hoekstra, Jennifer Bonds-Raacke, Elizabeth Cady, John Raacke, Christy Scott, Jason Brandenburger, Andrew Karafa, Chris Barlett, John Berger, Rebecca Schlegel, J. Bret Knappenberger, and Sherry Wright for their helpful reactions and conversations over the years about this material. Also, I thank my parents Dick and Helen Harris for modeling incredibly effective media use in the home I grew up in, long before people were talking about media literacy. Our family media use was often very positive family time. My own media literacy started early with my parents questioning what we saw on television and encouraging me to do the same. Many conversations around the television or the evening newspaper provided some intellectual seeds that bear some fruit in this book. I remember them commenting on negative values, unfair stereotyping, and excessive violence from my earliest days of watching TV. Although TV was a part of our household, so were print media, whose use my parents faithfully modeled. My wife and I now face the challenge of piloting three teenagers through a complex and omnipresent world of media very different from the media of the world we grew up in.

This is the fourth edition of this text and much has necessarily changed. Seldom does the content of a textbook become obsolete so fast as when it deals with the media. Of course there are the predictable changes in what television shows are popular, how Internet use has become widespread, and what changes the latest telecommunications technology has brought. Beyond that, I have done some major reorganization with this edition. The two old chapters on values and prosocial media have been reconfigured into two new chapters, one on children and media (chapter 5), including children's prosocial television, advertising to children, and media literacy, and another on values and prosocial media (chapter 11), including family values, religion, social marketing, and entertainment-education programming. Material on music, a genre of media unfortunately neglected in previous editions of this book, has been included in chapter 6, which has been reconceptualized as a chapter on strong emotional media (sports and music).

Other chapters have some extensive new sections. Chapter 3 has added material on stereotyping of mental illness and therapists and on male body-image media issues. Chapter 4 has a new section on advertising on the Internet, in classrooms, and other unconventional places. Chapter 7 has a new section on effects of news media dwelling on crimes. Chapter 8 has extensive new material on press coverage of the 2000 U.S. Presidential election and its aftermath. Chapter 9 has a new section on the effects of playing violent video games. Chapter 12 has additional material on the Internet and other computer-mediated communications. Throughout the book, readers will find more references to the Internet and World Wide Web and numerous sources from cyberspace. Throughout the book, I have also introduced new boxes with updated material and references to many new research studies that have appeared since the last edition. A large percentage of the references are from the twenty-first century, a strong testimony to the impressive volume of quality research currently being done on media issues. If I have omitted some of your favorites, forgive me; the amount of research and scholarly literature on the media is staggering.

Although overall the book has a *cognitive* perspective—the general framework which has driven my own thinking most strongly—I think you will find the book quite eclectic theoretically, as I think it needs to be. Chapter 2 reviews the major theories that have been used to study mass communication, and these are all referred to throughout the text. I believe that each has something of value to offer, most of them being more useful in some areas than others.

My hope is that reading this book is both a great pleasure and the source of much learning. It will amuse you in places and probably disturb you in others, but I hope it will always be interesting and relevant to your life. Students and teachers, please send me your comments. You can reach me by e-mail at rjharris@k-state.edu. Your reactions are always helpful in improving the book in future editions. Also, please feel free to send me interesting examples to illustrate the principles discussed; maybe I can use them in the classroom or in the next edition.

A COGNITIVE PSYCHOLOGY
OF MASS COMMUNICATION

CHAPTER 1

Mass Communication in Society: Swimming in the Media Sea

Q: What is the most popular leisure activity in the world?

A: Watching television. Every week residents of the United States spend 15 out of their average 39 hours of free time watching television, making it by far the most popular leisure activity. Only work and sleeping take more of our time, and we spend only 2.8 hours reading. Every day people worldwide spend over 3.5 billion hours watching television (Kubey & Csikszentmihalyi, 1990; Numbers, 1997).

Q: When a television is turned on, how often is it for the purpose of watching a specific program?

A: About half the time we turn the TV on for a specific program, and about half the time we just turn it on and then find something. The best and easiest way to start controlling and limiting TV use in your home is to adhere to the rule, "Never turn on the TV *except* to watch a specific program that you have in mind."

Q: What was the most popular U.S. television export of the mid-1990s?

A: *Baywatch*, seen by about 1 billion people in 150 countries every week! ("Most Famous Canadian," 1996). Although such exports may be culturally irrelevant, or even offensive in some places, they do come cheap. According to one estimate, for example, an episode of syndicated *Baywatch* costs $450 to the Namibian Broadcasting Company, compared to $1200 for a local soccer match, and over $2000 for a locally produced drama (Wresch, 1996).

In 2001, 13-year-old Jason Lind of Torrington, CT was hospitalized with second- and third-degree burns after he and a friend poured gasoline on his feet and legs and lit him on fire, in imitation of a stunt seen on MTV's popular show *Jackass*.

People very frequently take portable radios, or even televisions, to the stadium with them when they attend a sports event. When asked why they listen to the play-by-play when the game is going on right in front of them, a common response is, "So I can know what's really happening."

A young news reporter from the British Broadcasting Corporation (BBC) was sent to cover the Vietnam War in 1969. Not being very experienced or knowledgeable about what he was observing, he led off his first televised report of an American attack of a Vietcong stronghold with "My God! It's just like watching television," (Bogart, 1980)

Sandy Charles, a 14-year-old boy, killed and skinned a 7-year-old friend and then boiled the victim's flesh. In the subsequent murder trial, the teen's attorney argued that Sandy believed that he would be able to fly if he drank boiled fat from his victim. He apparently had been influenced by the horror film *Warlock*, which he had seen at least 10 times ("Canadian Case," 1996)

In different ways, these four examples suggest the main theme of this book: that our experience with media is a major way that we acquire knowledge about the world; this knowledge then has consequences in terms of attitudes and behavior. We may call this a *cognitive* approach to mass communication because the emphasis is on the way that our minds create knowledge—indeed, even a mental reality—about the world based on our experience with the media. This mental reality then becomes the basis for various attitudes and behaviors, which have a great impact on our lives. Instead of the media being a more or less accurate reflection of some external reality, it has *become* the reality against which the real world is compared. The media view of the world has become, to many people, more real than the real world itself.

Mass communication in the form of print media has been with us almost since Gutenberg's invention of movable type and the printing press in 1456. However, the nature of mass communication, indeed of life in general, was radically changed in the 20th century by the advent of electronic media, especially television. Television has transformed the day-to-day life of more people in the last 60 years than has perhaps any invention in human history. Radio and print media have been greatly changed by TV as well, although they have by no means been replaced. Watching television is most often reported as people's main source of pleasure, followed only distantly by spending time with friends, helping others, and taking vacations. Besides changing the way we spend our time, television has also revolutionized the way we think and the way we view the world. These effects on our perception and our cognition are particular emphases of this book. The media are not only the magic windows through which we view the world, but also the doors through which ideas enter our minds.

Media are far more than mere conduits of knowledge, although that role is not a trivial one. The act of transmitting that knowledge may itself become the event of note. When the U.S. and Saudi governments and military forces blocked press access to the war front during the Persian Gulf War of 1991, the nature of the war coverage became one of the major news stories of the war. The media were not merely communicating the news; they had *become* the news. In the case of the Vietnam War, scholars, heads of state, and the general public are still debating the role of the media in the declining public acceptance of that war between 1965 and 1973.

We have come a long way from Gutenberg to the thousands of daily newspapers, magazines, television stations, and radio stations in the world today. (See Box 1.1 for further background on print and electronic media.) In this chapter, we introduce the concept of *mass communication* and our use of the media from a cognitive psychological perspective. We conclude the chapter with an overview of the rest of the book.

BOX 1.1
A PRIMER ON ELECTRONIC AND PRINT MEDIA

Mass media have traditionally been divided into two basic types: print and electronic (or broadcast). Print media (i.e., newspapers and magazines) provide information through the production and distribution of paper copies. In contrast to electronic media, print media tend to be more permanent (at least before the advent of widespread video and audio taping) and depend on the literacy of the audience. There are also no channel limits in print media, whereas there has traditionally been a finite number of possible radio frequencies and television channels (though today, these are rapidly increasing in number). There is no inherent limit to the number of newspapers or magazines that may be published. In general, print media lend themselves better to a detailed treatment of subjects than do electronic media.

In contrast to print media, electronic media are technologically more recent, less permanent, and less dependent on formal literacy or accessibility to urban infrastructure. This last point becomes especially crucial in more isolated regions of the world. One can have a portable radio without any access to electricity, schooling, or urban life. Because of their limited channel capacity, radio and television typically are more tightly regulated by governments than are print media (e.g., assignment of television channels by the U.S. Federal Communications Commission [FCC]). The more authoritarian the society, the easier it is for the government to control radio and (especially) television in times that are deemed to be unduly threatening. Although television networks, both private and government owned, tend to be national in scope, they often have influence far beyond their country's borders. One of the major influences in the 1989 democratic revolutions in Eastern Europe was exposure to Western television.

WHAT IS MASS COMMUNICATION?

What makes mass communication *mass?* First, the audience is large and anonymous, and often very heterogeneous (C. R. Wright, 1986). Individual viewers, listeners, readers, or even groups of individuals can be targeted, but only with limited precision. Second, communication sources are institutional and organizational (C. R. Wright, 1986). Some, such as television networks, newspaper chains, wire services, or the conglomerates that own such businesses, are among the largest and richest private corporations. Third, and perhaps most important, the basic economic function of most media in most nations is to attract and hold as large an audience as possible for the advertisers. In one way or another, advertising pays a high percentage of the costs of newspapers, magazines, local TV and radio stations, and commercial television networks like CBS, NBC, ABC, and Fox in the United States; even public television and government-subsidized networks like the Public Broadcasting Service (PBS), Canadian Broadcasting Corporation (CBC), or the British Broadcasting Corporation (BBC) are increasingly subject to commercial pressures.

In spite of all the high-sounding rhetoric about serving the public, the bottom line of commercial mass media is money, which comes from advertisers at rates directly determined by the audience or readership size and composition, which in turn determines the content. Thus, there is tremendous pressure for media to be as entertaining as possible to as many people as possible; this principle also holds for non-entertainment content like news. All of this is not to say that editors and programmers are not concerned about responsibly meeting the needs of the public. They are, but such needs must necessarily be considered within the constraints of the economic realities of the media industry.

Often, economic pressures, and sometimes political and ideological ones as well, influence the content of media. For example, magazines that accept tobacco advertisements print fewer stories about the health risks of smoking than those that have no cigarette ads (Lee & Solomon, 1991; Strasburger & Wilson, 2002). ABC, which is owned by Disney, has killed news stories reflecting negatively on Disney theme parks (Steyer, 2002). See Box 1.2 for a further discussion of both blatant and subtle censorship.

In spite of its mass nature, there is also *communication* in mass communication. In all communication there is a reciprocity, some kind of response from the audience. Although the media user, especially the TV viewer, is often characterized as being extremely passive, mindlessly absorbing the program content, such a picture is far from accurate. Although the meaning a particular program has certainly depends on the content of that program, it also depends on what is in the mind and experience of the viewer. A TV movie dealing with rape will have a very different effect on,

BOX 1.2
THE ISSUE OF CENSORSHIP

A major philosophical and legal issue with regard to media is censorship, which varies greatly across different societies. Prior censorship (i.e., requiring approval of all content before broadcast or publication) occurs in some totalitarian societies, but more subtle forms of censorship exist in all nations. Even in democracies, press freedom has never been absolute, but rather operates within certain constraints. For example, one may not print or broadcast material that is libelous, classified, or obscene, or which incites people to violence or infringes on copyright laws.

In the United States, the FCC assigns channels and issues licenses. Although it has the power to deny renewal of licenses, it has very seldom done so in over half a century of operation. The FCC also enforces application of the Equal Time rule to insure that opposing points of view on controversial issues and political campaigns are aired.

Pressures toward censorship exist, although it may not be called that, especially in the United States, where *censorship* is considered a very dirty word. The National Association of Broadcasters (NAB), a professional organization of radio and television stations, has a fairly rigorous ethical code that it expects its members to adhere to, although court challenges and appeals, an atmosphere of deregulation, and changing social standards weakened adherence to the NAB code starting in the 1980s. Some content that may not be illegal per se may nevertheless not appear on television because it is not in accord with NAB guidelines or because broadcasters fear public outrage (e.g., graphic and explicit sex, violence, or surgery). Also, certain words (e.g., *shit, f****, many racial epithets, and any religious expletives stronger than "Oh, my God!") seldom occur on U.S. prime-time network television. Incidentally, these standards change: 30 years ago we did not hear the words *damn, hell*, or *pregnant*, although we may have heard *nigger, jap*, and other ethnic slurs in the early days of radio or TV.

Real or feared reaction from advertisers is another subtle source of self-censorship. Television networks and stations are very loath to risk offending those who pay the bills for their livelihood. Advertisers occasionally threaten to withdraw their ads in protest. In 1979 General Electric was unhappy with ABC's Barbara Walters' plans to interview Jane Fonda about her antinuclear activism and pulled their ads in protest. However, ABC still aired the interview. Not so noble have been magazines' frequent failure to run articles on the health hazards of smoking for fear of alienating their lucrative tobacco advertisers (M. A. Lee & Solomon, 1991; Strasburger & Wilson, 2002).

A democratic government may exert influence even in cases where it has no formal censoring authority. For example, the British government requested that the BBC not run a scheduled documentary on Northern Ireland in August 1985. This documentary included extensive interviews with IRA and Unionist extremists. The government argued that this gave those whom

---

B O X 1 . 2 (continued)

it called terrorists an undeserved platform and hearing. After extensive discussion, BBC management decided to honor the government's request, although this decision evoked a 1-day strike by BBC employees in protest.

Concern over the public's reaction may be another source of self-
censorship. In 1985, two of the three U.S. commercial networks refused to
run an antismoking PSA that showed a fetus smoking a cigarette in the
womb. Similarly, we see few ads for contraceptives on U.S. television, although they have appeared in magazines for years. In fact, commercials are
the most conservative component of television. Advertisers are extremely
loath to offend viewers; from an economic perspective, the worst sin a broad-
caster can commit is to air something that causes viewers to turn the set off.

---

indeed, a different *meaning* for a viewer who has herself been a rape victim
than for someone else with no such personal experience. A violent pornographic video may incite one man to sexually violent behavior because of
the way his mind interprets and interacts with the content of the video,
whereas another man who sees the same video may be repulsed by it and
show no antisocial behavioral response.

The nature of the media consumption experience must also be considered. Watching television or listening to the radio may be done alone or
in small groups. Reading newspapers or magazines or using a computer
is typically, though not always, a solo activity. The social situation of who
else is watching, listening, or reading and how they react greatly affects the
media consumption experience. Consider the difference between watching
an exciting ball game by yourself or watching it with a group of friends.
Whether someone with whom you are watching a horror film shrieks in
fun, cries in severe distress, laughs, or makes no obvious reaction at all can
affect your enjoyment or level of fear (Zillmann & Weaver, 1996). Within
families, television may either promote family harmony and interaction or
be a divisive force, depending on how it is used (Bryant & Bryant, 2001).

Now let us turn to how we use the various media of mass communication.

MEDIA USE

Television

Although experimental sets existed in the late 1930s, television was essentially unknown by the general public at the end of World War II in 1945.
Although only .02% of U.S. homes had TV in 1946, that figure rose to 9%

by 1950, 23.5% by 1951, and 90% by 1962. By 1980, televisions were found in about 98% of U.S. homes, and that figure has remained constant since that time (Andreasen, 1994). There is an average of 2.2 TV sets in each of those homes (Church, 1996). Although most of the programming over the years has been by networks or local stations, the rapid growth of cable and satellite technology in the 1980s and 1990s greatly expanded the offerings, with a corresponding decline in the network market share. Associated with television sets are video cassette recorders (VCRs), which were in 98% of U.S. households of families with children by 1999 (Jordan, 2001). At the turn of the millennium, 60% of U.S. adolescents and 30% of preschoolers had a television set in their bedroom (Kotler, Wright, & Huston, 2001), and three quarters of American homes had cable TV (Strasburger & Wilson, 2002). Figures for European children were slightly lower overall but varied greatly by country (d'Haenens, 2001).

The television phenomenon is almost as pervasive in developing countries. Even the worst urban slums of the Third World sprout television antennas. In the early years of the 21st century, no place on earth is beyond the reach of television. The number of TV sets per 1,000 people worldwide doubled from 117 to 234 between 1981 and 1997 ("The Faustian Bargain," 1997), although they are hardly distributed evenly across the globe; for example, there were 906 TVs per 1,000 people in the Netherlands and 850 per 1,000 in the United States but only 5 per 1,000 in Bangladesh and 9 in Kenya (Wresch, 1996). As many as 2 to 3 billion people have seen recent Olympic Games and World Cup soccer finals on TV. See Box 1.3 for a look at an anthropologist's views of the stages of a society's acceptance of TV.

The bulk of mass communications research has studied television; the main reason for this is that we spend so much time watching television. A TV set is on in the average U.S. household over 7 hours each day (over 8 hours for homes with cable and subscription services), with the typical child age 8 to 18 watching over 3 hours per day. We spend more time watching television than doing anything else except working at our jobs and sleeping (Roberts, 2000). The average U.S. child sees nearly 15,000 sexual references, innuendoes, and jokes per year, with only 1.1% of those dealing with abstinence, birth control, pregnancy, or sexually transmitted diseases (Strasburger & Donnerstein, 1999). By the time a child reaches the age of 18, he or she has seen 200,000 televised acts of violence (Huston et al., 1992).

Group Differences. The amount of television viewing changes through the life span. It rises sharply between ages 2 and 4, from about 15 minutes to 2.5 hours per day. It then levels off until about age 8, rising again to a peak of around 4 hours a day by age 12 (Liebert & Sprafkin, 1988). It then starts to fall, especially during the high school and college

---

BOX 1.3
STAGES OF TELEVISION IMPACT

Drawing on his studies of television use in several Brazilian communities
with varying lengths of exposure to television, cultural anthropologist Con-
rad Kottak (1990) identified five stages of societal interaction with television.
In Stage, 1 the medium is new and strange and attracts people with glued
gazes—no matter the content. "The medium rather than the message is the
mesmerizer" (Kottak, 1990, p. 139). Stage 2 is usually the next 10 to 15 years,
when people begin to interpret TV's messages and selectively accept or reject them. Due to its high status, television ownership displays conspicuous
consumption and becomes a source of privileged information. In Stage 3, the
community is saturated with television and the length of exposure increases.
By Stage 4, adults have spent their whole lives in a culture permeated by television, whose lifelong impact on members of society is taken for granted.
Finally, Stage 5 occurs with the widespread appearance of cable TV and
VCR ownership. At this stage, there is much more individual control of TV,
in terms of both time shifting and abundant selection of programming. Marketing is increasingly directed at homogeneous segments, not to the mass
audience.

Although Stages 1 to 3 no longer exist in developed countries, Stages 2
and 3 are still present in some isolated sections of Third World nations.

---

years and young adulthood, when people are busy with dating, studying,
listening to music, and rearing young children. There is another rise,
however, in older adult years after one's children are grown. In fact, elderly adults watch more television than most groups. Other groups who
watch television more than average are women, poor people, and African
Americans (Roberts, 2000). It is interesting that many of the groups that
watch the most television are the same groups that are the most underrepresented in TV programming, where characters are disproportionately middle class, white, male, professional, and affluent. We return to this issue in
chapter 3.

Time-of-Day Differences. Television viewing also changes sharply
throughout the day. Typically the largest audience is during "prime time"—
8 to 11 p.m. Eastern and Pacific times in North America (7 to 10 p.m.
Central and Mountain). These are the hours of highest advertising charges
and greatest investment and innovation in programming. The most obvious pinnacle of such efforts may be seen in the prime time "sweeps
weeks" in February, May, and November, in which Nielsen audience size
over a 4-week span is used to calculate advertising charges for the next

several months. These are the weeks when the networks outdo themselves presenting blockbuster movies, specials, and landmark episodes of top-rated series.

Video.   Starting from Sony's slow introduction of $2,000-plus machines into the U.S. market in 1975 (5 years later, less than 1% of U.S. homes owned a VCR), growth took off in the early 1980s until by 1995, 85% of U.S. homes owned a VCR (Hull, 1995). The percentage is even higher (98%) for VCR ownership in households with children (Jordan, 2001). Today many shows are routinely recorded for later viewing (so-called time shifting), with the most-recorded genre being the soap opera, which the VCR has now made available to those who are employed during regular hours.

See Levy (1987) for a discussion of some basic issues in video and Mares (1998) for studies of children's use of video.

Although bitterly opposed to videotaping at first, Hollywood studios have since joined forces to forge a very symbiotic and lucrative relation-ship between movies and video. Videocassette and DVD sales and rentals have brought huge additional income and interest to the film industry. The widespread renting of movies on cassette and DVD has raised some new ethical and legal issues. Although the U.S. film rating system (G, PG, PG-13, R, NC-17) can have some effect in theaters, it has very little in rental stores, where 13-year-olds generally have no trouble renting an R-rated movie. More recently, increasing numbers of films have been produced solely for VHS/DVD distribution, bypassing both theaters and the need to have any rating at all. The more recent introduction of DVDs has been an additional boon to home movie viewing, since DVDs are generally marketed with some additional information (interviews with stars and directors, back-ground information on filming, etc.)

One segment of television still distressed by video technology is adver-tising. Time shifting, which enables viewers to tape TV shows and watch them later while fast-forwarding through the ads, has encouraged new cre-ativity in the ad industry in an attempt to produce ads that viewers will be reluctant to fast-forward through (Harvey & Rothe, 1986; Yorke & Kitchen, 1985). There are also increasing attempts to create ads whose highlights can be noticed while fast-forwarding. It is no accident that the ads have come to look more like the programming, using artsy montage and cinema verité techniques.

Radio

The other major electronic medium—radio—rapidly permeated society in the 1920s much as television would do 30 years later. The current net-work TV format of entertainment programming was borrowed from radio, which reorganized into a primarily music-and-news format in the 1950s following the advent of TV, which co-opted its programming agenda. More than television, radio is highly age- and interest-segmented (top 40, classical, country & western, heavy metal, oldies rock, easy listening, album rock). By late 1996, there were over 12,000 AM and FM radio stations in the United States (J. R. Wilson & Wilson, 1998). Developmentally, radio is little used until preadolescence but becomes a central part of adolescent and young adult culture. Teenagers listen to music on radio or CD 3 to 4 hours per day, more than the 2 to 3 hours per day they spend watching TV (Roberts & Christenson, 2001).

Worldwide, radio is the most available medium. It is crucially important in isolated societies, because it depends neither on literacy nor on the purchase of a relatively expensive television set. Radio receivers are cheap and run well on batteries. Compared to television or print media, programming is very inexpensive to produce, especially talk and music formats. Talk radio, of course, can be anything from ennobling to disgusting. Perhaps the most shocking abuse of radio was the Rwandan station that broadcast calls for genocide and fomented hysteria; these broadcasts culminated in the disastrous Hutu-Tutsi civil war of 1994 to 1995. However, more often radio serves as an important part of the social fabric tying diverse constituencies together. See Box 1.4 for an example of the role of radio in a country sorely lacking in modern infrastructure.

Newspapers

The number of daily newspapers in the United States has been falling for many years, and stood at 1532 in 1995 (Gleick, 1996). The percentage of adults who read a paper daily fell from 78% in 1970 to 59% in 1997, with only 31% of young adults ages 21 to 35 reading a daily paper (Halimi, 1998). In large markets, morning papers are dominant, but afternoon papers are the rule in suburban areas and small cities. Almost half (48%) of all families subscribe to a daily paper (Jordan, 2001). More than television or magazines, newspapers have a local identity and are the preeminent source for local news, advertising, and gossip. Even as the number of dailies continues to fall, the number of weekly newspapers keeps growing, up to 7,654 in 1996 (J. R. Wilson & Wilson, 1998). In the United States, newspapers are almost totally regional, with the exception of *USA Today*, although large national papers are the rule in many nations (e.g., *Guardian* in the United Kingdom and *Le Monde* in France). In spite of their regional character, newspapers are becoming increasingly similar, a trend attributable to a consolidation of media ownership to fewer and fewer sources and also an increasing reliance by most newspapers on a few international wire services like Associated Press (AP), Reuters, and Agence France Presse (AFP) as news sources.

BOX 1.4
RADIO IN NAMIBIA (WRESCH, 1996)

Sparsely populated and largely undeveloped, the southern African nation of Namibia was plundered under German and, later, South African, colonial rule before its independence in 1990. Its only large city is its capital, Windhoek (pop. 150,000).

Public radio has a call-in talk show, *The Chat Show,* from 9 to 10 a.m., where listeners call in with specific complaints about treatment from a business, the government, or the police. The announcer plays a Rogerian therapist kind of role, listening to and summarizing the caller's concerns. After the show ends, station personnel call the government agencies or businesses who received complaints. They record the officials' responses to the complaints and play those back, along with the original complaint, when the second installment of the show airs 3 hours later.

In rural Namibia, radio serves an even broader communicative function. In areas with virtually no phones or mail service, one can relay messages through the local radio station, which will broadcast (free of charge) that a particular listener should, for example, call his grandmother or pick up his textbook for his correspondence course. Even if the intended recipient is not listening, someone who knows him or her usually is and the message gets delivered.

Demographically, the sports section of the newspaper is the most read, and groups who read more newspapers are generally those groups who are light TV viewers: They are older, male, Caucasian, better educated, and have higher socioeconomic status. Newspaper readers are generally engaged in many other activities and like to keep up on the news. They are more likely than non-readers to also watch TV news; it is probably not the case that the increasing use of TV news has been at the expense of newspapers. Those who consume news usually use multiple sources; alternatively, those who do not read newspapers usually do not watch TV news either (Bogart, 1981; Stone, 1987).

Magazines

These are the most narrowly targeted of all the media, having become increasingly so after an earlier period of popular general-interest magazines (*Life, Look, Saturday Evening Post*) ended in the 1960s. An estimated 11,000 magazines were published in the United States in the mid-1990s (J. R. Wilson & Wilson, 1998), mostly devoted to special interests. Magazines combine the newspaper's permanence and opportunity for greater in-depth coverage with television's photographic appeal. Reading magazines is primarily an adult activity, but there are children's magazines such as *Boys Life* and *National Geographic Kids* that are useful in developing children's reading and print media habits. For girls, certain magazines such as *Seventeen* and, later, *Glamour, Vogue, and Cosmopolitan* are an important part of the female adolescent experience and are probably major contributors to the socialization of girls as women in Western society (see chapter 3). The emphasis tends to be on fashion, attractiveness, romance, and sex. There really are no comparable gender-role socializing magazines for boys, although many of them read *Sports Illustrated* and earlier *Sports Illustrated for Kids*.

Computer-Mediated Communication

Not everyone agrees on what other media, if any, are included in mass communication. The boundaries are growing increasingly fuzzy. Cinema, videos, fax machines, the Internet, and the World Wide Web (Kiesler, 1997; Noll, 1996) all have some but not all characteristics of mass media. Movies play a similar role as mass communication in popular culture (Jowett & Linton, 1989), especially now that video technology allows them to be viewed on television.

The capacity for very wide circulation of material on the Internet, as well as through fax networks, allows these systems to act a lot like traditional print and electronic media. As of 2000, 42% of U.S. households had home Internet access. The young are especially frequent users, with 73% of teens ages 12 to 17 being active Internet users (Mastro, Eastin, & Tamborini, 2002). The most common uses of the Internet are for e-mail, playing games, surfing, accessing databases, and interpersonal activities like chat rooms, instant messaging, and discussion groups. A 2003 study by Yahoo! (Weaver, 2003) actually found that people ages 13 to 14 spent more time per week online (16.7 hours) than watching television (13.6 hours).

Sometimes the Internet becomes the primary media source of information. For example, when U.S. President Bill Clinton's grand jury testimony in the Monica Lewinsky case was first released publicly in September 1998, it was released on the web. Although we make some reference to film, video, and computer-mediated communication, they are not heavily emphasized in this book, in part because they are only beginning to be studied empirically. However, readers should bear in mind that they function like mass media in some important ways and are taking rapidly increasing amounts of our time.

In response to requests from parents for some guidance on the appropriateness of media for various ages, the Motion Picture Association of America (MPAA) began issuing ratings of movies in 1968. These have been modified several times since then, and much more recently, similar ratings for television, music CDs, and video games have appeared. These ratings remain controversial, however, and reflect several factors, not all of which appear to be weighted equally. See Box 1.5 for further discussion and study of this issue.

BOX 1.5
**THE MPAA RATINGS: DOES SEX OR VIOLENCE
CARRY MORE WEIGHT?**

Even since their introduction in 1968, the Motion Picture Association of America's (MPAA) ratings for movies have been controversial. Over time, there have been some adjustments, most notably the addition of the PG-13 category in 1984 and the replacement of the pornography-tainted category of X by NC-17 (no one under 17 admitted) in 1990. The ratings are made based on violence, sex/nudity, language, and thematic content. By 2001, over 60% of films submitted were rated R, almost none NC-17, and very few G. Sometimes a rating is negotiable, as when a studio will appeal an R rating or remove or edit an offending scene to obtain the PG-13 rating, often considered the commercially most desirable, since it neither excludes anyone nor has the "kiddie movie" stigma of G and even PG movies. There is widespread belief than many films that previously would have been R are now PG-13 and many PG films would have been PG-13 some years ago.

One specific continuing controversy concerns the relative weighting of the different factors, particularly sex and violence. Although the MPAA denies it, many believe that sexual content carries greater weight than violence. Indeed, many PG and even G movies contain considerable amounts of violence, though a partial nudity scene may earn a film a PG-13 rating. Leone (2002) provided some empirical support for this by finding that scenes present in an NC-17 or unrated versions of a film but removed from the commercially-released R-rated version, were more sexually explicit and graphic than they were violently explicit and graphic.

Perhaps the most overlooked of the four ratings criteria is the thematic one; for example, an Edwardian costume drama *The Winslow Boy*, about a legal challenge to an arcane British family and labor law of the early 20th century, received a G rating, presumably because it had no sex or nudity, no violence, and no bad language. However, it was not a family movie and would have totally bored anyone under 12 (or maybe 16!).

In the final analysis, however, parents must use the movie ratings as part of their own parental mediation. Look at not just the rating but what it is for (most video or DVD boxes give this information). There may be an occasional R-rated movie you would want your 12-year-old to see and some PG-13 movies you wouldn't want your older child to see.

OVERVIEW OF THE BOOK

This chapter has introduced mass communication from a psychological perspective. The next chapter explores, in some depth, the various theoretical bases of research on mass communication, drawing on models from communication, psychology, and other fields. We also examine several psychological constructs important in understanding our interaction with media. The overarching book theme is how we construct meaning from media and how that constructed meaning becomes our perceived reality.

Chapters 3 to 11 are topically organized to explore several specific content areas. Because of the enormous amount of time we spend watching television, as well as the relatively greater amount of research on that medium, this book focuses, though not exclusively, on the TV as a transmitter of mass communication.

Chapter 3 explores the issue of group portrayals in the media. The emphasis here is on how media portray various groups of people and what the effects of such presentations are. We see that media's portrayal of groups may become a stereotyped reality in the minds of the public, especially in cases where the viewer has limited life experience with members of a particular group. Are men and women portrayed in stereotyped fashion? What are the effects of such portrayals on the socialization process of children? Also examined are African Americans, whose portrayals have been more carefully studied than any other group in the history of TV. The portrayals of Latinos, Native Americans, Asian Americans, Arabs, the elderly, gays and lesbians, people with physical and psychological disabilities, and various professions are also examined. What are the effects of unrealistic or even nonexistent portrayals on the public's perception of these groups?

Chapter 4 examines the world as created by advertising. Advertising is a type of information to be processed—one very important way we learn about the world as well as its products. Techniques of persuasion are examined, focusing on various types of psychological appeals, especially as they involve persuasion through the creation of a new reality that then becomes real for the consumer (e.g., a reality full of danger where one needs to buy locks and weapons, a reality where most people are very thin and suntanned, a reality of status-conscious people that one has to continually impress with one's dress and possessions). We examine the cognitive view of advertising, with particular focus on the psychology of deceptive advertising. Next, the issue of subliminal advertising is discussed to see if it is possible to persuade viewers at subconscious level through subtle messages or embedded sexual figures in art work. Finally, we look at the emergence of advertising in new places, such as classrooms, websites, and entertainment programming, and for new products such as prescription drugs.

Although we are concerned with children through most of the book, Chapter 5 focuses particularly on children and adolescents, beginning with developmental issues that affect how children interact with and interpret media, which often is quite different from how adults do so. Children's intentionally prosocial television, such as *Sesame Street*, is examined in terms of its appeals and effects. How children learn positive things from entertainment media is also addressed. The issue of advertising to children is treated in some depth, identifying some surprising and disturbing trends and connections. Finally, the issue of media literacy—how we can help children interact more productively with media—is examined both in terms of curricular development and what can be done in the home.

Chapter 6 looks at two areas of media where emotion is particularly central, namely sports and music. We examine how television not only transmits results and play-by-plays of athletic contests but also influences and changes the ways these sports are played. Rules and practices of sports have been changed by the demands of television coverage, and the nature of media coverage affects the public's interest and tastes in sports. Media coverage can encourage competition, cooperation, gender-role development, hero worship, and the enjoyment of sports violence. The second area—music—is a very important type of media, especially for teens and young adults. The uses and gratifications of music consumption are examined, as well as specific issues like the nature of content in lyrics and how popular music has (and has not) changed over the years.

Chapter 7 examines how the media's coverage of news affects our understanding and attitudes about events in the world. News is perhaps the area where people are most likely to believe that media merely reflect and report the reality that is out there. Drawing especially on agenda-setting theory, we make the argument that such is not the case, that in fact news reporting is by no means such a reality transmission, but is necessarily a somewhat constructed interpretation of reality, based more on what is newsworthy than on what is really important. Simply by choosing what to cover and what not to cover, media are setting an agenda. This necessarily involves only a partial presentation of reality, but this partial reality becomes the basis of our knowledge about the world, even affecting foreign policy.

Chapter 8 continues to examine news by looking at how politicians manipulate media coverage to convey their own intended reality. As practically all of our information about political candidates and officeholders comes through the media, the importance of mass communication in this area can hardly be overstated. Such issues as image building and the construction of an electronic personality are discussed. The impact of televised candidate debates is examined, followed by an in-depth look at the coverage of the extremely close 2000 U.S. Presidential election results and the subsequent vote-counting controversy. A final topic in politics and media concerns the appeals and effects of political advertising, including the controversial negative or attack advertising. Types of appeals in political advertising and their effects on attitudes and voting behavior are examined.

In chapter 9 we look at media violence, the most heavily researched issue of this book. Different effects of televised and filmed violence are examined, including induced fear, modeling, catharsis, reinforcement, desensitization, and the cultivation of fear. In addition, we explore what types of people are drawn to enjoy violent media and what different factors may interact with media violence to enhance or lessen its impact. Long-term effects of watching television violence and recent research on the effects of playing violent video games are also examined. The question of the effects on children of viewing violence turns out to be more complex than is frequently admitted by partisans on either side of this controversial issue, although the weight of the total body of research comes down strongly on the side of demonstrating negative effects. These effects are substantial but usually in interaction with other factors.

Chapter 10 examines the character and effects of sexual content in media, looking at both mainstream media and pornography. The creation and transmission of sexual values through media, as well as the socialization in regard to sexuality and the behavioral effects of media sex, are addressed. Research on the effects of sexual violence, both in pornography and mainstream movies, is considered in some detail, pointing toward the conclusion that viewing sexual violence may be more damaging than viewing either sex or violence by itself.

Turning in a more positive direction, chapter 11 examines the media's teaching of values and prosocial behaviors like positive health behaviors. Although some standards are clearly becoming less strict (e.g., profanity and sexual innuendo and explicitness), others are actually becoming more restrictive (e.g., expressions of racism, sexism, or violence toward women). One area of emphasis is a set of issues loosely subsumed under "family values"; for example, what are the messages from media about family composition and parent–child relationships? Many traditional values, such as family solidarity, patriotism, and abstinence from illicit drugs, continue to be stressed as much as ever. We also examine the topic of religion in media, which in some ways continues to be the most sensitive and taboo topic.

The second part of the chapter deals with explicit attempts to use media to teach skills or persuade people to change their attitudes or behaviors in a more health- or safety-oriented direction. One section discusses principles of social, as opposed to product, marketing. The media's role in public health marketing campaigns to increase prosocial behaviors like stopping smoking, exercising more, or wearing seat belts is also considered. Public service announcements (PSAs) and other social marketing uses of media face greater obstacles in many ways than does commercial advertising. A second part of this section looks at the use of mainstream entertainment media for explicitly prosocial ends (entertainment education), a format very common in developing countries and increasingly so, albeit it in more subtle ways, in Western countries.

Finally, chapter 12 ties together themes from the entire book and explores how we, as consumers in the new millennium, can use the knowledge gained from this book to have a greater impact on the media, including its structure and programming. The contribution of technologically new forms of media, especially computer-mediated communication forms like the Internet and the World Wide Web, are examined. Finally, some ways that we may influence the media, and the way that media report social science research are presented.

CHAPTER 2

Research and Theory in Mass Communication: How We Study Media Scientifically

Q: What was John Hinckley's stated reason for attempting to assassinate U.S. President Ronald Reagan in 1981?

A: He thought that act would cement his relationship with actress Jodie Foster, with whom he was obsessed, although they had never met. (Note: Hinckley's trial found him not guilty by reason of insanity and ordered him to a psychiatric facility.)

Q: The American public believes what percentage of felony defendants uses the insanity plea? How many actually do?

A: The public believes that 37% of defendants plead insanity, while in reality only 0.9% do, most of which are not successful ("Numbers," 1998, January 19).

Q: Why did several people around the country receive hundreds of phone calls each asking to speak with "God" during the summer of 2003?

A: In the movie *Bruce Almighty*, Bruce Nolan (played by Jim Carrey) is contacted by "God" on his cell phone. A particular number is shown, though no area code is given. Hundreds of people around the country called this number locally and asked to speak with "God." In this case, the filmmaker did not follow the usual practice of using 555-prefix phone numbers (which do not exist as real phone numbers).

In some sense everyone is a media critic. Far fewer, however, have real answers to the questions and concerns that are so easy to raise. The answers to many questions about the media come from scientific research. The results from such research are cited throughout this book, but in this chapter we look at some of the theoretical frameworks and constructs behind such research. It is easy to raise concerns about violence in the media; it is more difficult to precisely assess the effects of viewing that violence.

It is easy to bemoan the lack of positive values on TV; it is more difficult to identify exactly what values television does communicate. Our relationship with the media is so profound precisely because it meets some of our deepest psychological needs and contributes to our ongoing psychological development in numerous ways.

In terms of the sheer amount of social science research on media, there is far more study of television than of radio, print, or computer-mediated media. Many of the psychological questions discussed in this book apply equally well to all media, although most have been studied primarily in regard to television. We begin by looking at some general approaches to studying media scientifically and then move on to examining specific theories, drawn primarily from the disciplines of psychology and communication. Next, we introduce several cognitive components of media consumption. Finally, we focus on the construct of perceived reality as a sort of overriding theme for this book.

MEDIA RESEARCH FRAMEWORKS

As well as being of great concern to the general public, the media are also of considerable interest to the worlds of both commerce and science, both of which engage in research using various perspectives to study media (see Heath & Bryant, 1992; Lowery & DeFleur, 1983; McGuire, 1985b; Roberts & Maccoby, 1985, and especially the chapters in Bryant and Zillmann, 2002, for reviews). Much research has been done by or for TV networks, publishers, corporations, or ad agencies for commercial purposes. For example, the Nielsen ratings of the television audience (see Box 2.1) or marketing research studying the public's taste in colas is done for the purpose of increasing the profits of a corporation. The other general type of scientific study is usually performed by independent scientists with the goal of explaining the effects of media and studying their role in society and in people's lives (D. K. Davis & Baran, 1981; Lazarsfeld, 1941). For example, studies of the effects of media violence or analyses of the allegedly sexist content of ads are generally done with no commercial motivation. It is this noncommercial research that is the primary focus in this book.

We begin by examining three general ways of looking at media and then move on to specific theories.

Looking at Content

One very straightforward way to study media is to study its content. This is often an important precursor to research on exposure or effects. For example, there are studies counting the number of characters of different

---

BOX 2.1
THOSE ALL-IMPORTANT RATINGS

The Nielsen ratings are the all-important barometers used to measure the audience size for network television programming in the United States. It is on these ratings that programs, careers, and even broad social trends rise and fall. The A. C. Nielsen Company has for many years selected a sample of American homes to have machines hooked up to their TV sets to measure when the set is on to what channel. It does not measure who, if anyone, is watching the set, how intently they are watching, or what else they are doing at the same time. Another sample of homes, frequently changed, keeps weekly diaries of programs watched. Still others use the "people meter," a remote-control-like device into which the viewer punches in the exact time of the beginning and ending of viewing and information on who is watching. The Nielsen ratings provide two types of information. The rating proper is the percentage of the potential audience that is viewing a program (e.g., a rating of 30 means that 30% of the homes with TVs have that program on). The share compares that program's performance with the competition on at the same time. Network advertising charges are usually based primarily on the Nielsen ratings and shares measured during the three 4-week *sweeps* periods in February, May, and November. Advertising charges are based primarily on the number of homes reached by an ad, adjusted for demographics. For example, a higher proportion of 18–49-year-olds can command higher ad fees. Top-rated prime-time shows could command between half a million and a million dollars per 30-second spot in recent years. The cost for a 30-second spot on the Super Bowl rose from $125,000 in 1975 to around $2 million by 2004. The even more lucrative 15-second spot typically sells for 55 to 60% of the 30-second price. Charges per minute are typically much lower for the non-prime-time slots and cable channels with smaller audiences.

---

racial, ethnic, or gender groups in TV shows. If we are going to argue, for example, that television ads or shows are sexist, then we must carefully define what we mean by *sexist* and then study the ads or shows to see if they fit those criteria. Studies of the effects of sex or violence make use of content-analysis studies to provide data on the prevalence of such themes and changing trends over time. In such research *operational definitions* are crucial. If I do not know how a researcher is defining a sexist portrayal or a violent act, I am not able to interpret their research. There are several important methodological issues involved in content analysis research, one of the major ones being interrater reliability and agreement (Lombard, Snyder-Duch, & Bracken, 2002; Tinsley & Weiss, 2000). For extensive discussions of content analysis as a methodology, see Neuendorf (2002), Riffe & Freitag (1997), and Riffe, Lacy, & Fico (1998).

Looking at Exposure

A second general way to study media is to study the amount of exposure; see Webster and Wakshlag (1985) for a review of methods of measuring exposure. Who reads how many newspapers or watches how much TV and when? Demographic information about different groups of people watching different shows comes from this type of study. This type of information does not fully tap actual exposure, however. Just because the radio or television is on is no assurance that anyone is devoting much attention to it, nor can we conclude that, merely because people are not paying full conscious attention to the source, that they are unaffected by it. Often people are simultaneously doing something else besides listening to radio or watching TV when it is on. Sometimes they leave the room altogether for some periods, especially during commercials. To understand the cognitive processes involved in experiencing media, it is crucial to take seriously the amount and nature of attention devoted to the medium; we return to this issue later.

Looking at Effects

Probably the most common general perspective in studying the media is a search for the *effects* of exposure to mass communication. To the general public, most major concerns about the media probably center on their effects. The nature of these effects can take different forms. These effects can be direct, conditional, or cumulative (Perse, 2001).

With the *direct effects* model, the effects appear quickly and are relatively similar across all audience members. The crudest version of a direct effects model is the *theory of uniform effects.* This model argues that individuals in a mass society perceive messages from media in the same fashion and react to them strongly and very similarly. Media messages are thus magic bullets piercing the mind of the populace. Such a model was used after World War I to describe propaganda effects. Lasswell (1927, 1935) suggested the hypodermic needle metaphor of media (i.e., that viewers were injected with some dubious message that brought out their worst behavior and thoughts). The assumption that media purveyors are evil thought controllers who manipulate everyone in a passive and helpless population in a uniform way is no longer a serious theoretical position among communications researchers but is still implicitly assumed among some strident popular media-bashing critics, who blame the media for most social ills (e.g., Key, 1974, 1976, 1981, 1989; Mankiewicz & Swerdlow, 1978; Winn, 1977, 1987).

With the *conditional effects model,* the media can still have substantial effects, but only under certain conditions or for certain audience members, often in less dramatic form than suggested by the most vocal critics. This is a model of selective effects based on individual differences. Different people perceive the same message differently and respond to it in varied forms. For example, a violent TV program probably will not incite all of its viewers to go out and commit mayhem, but it may reinforce the already existing violent tendencies of a small sample of the viewers and slightly dull the sensitivities of many others. Certain positive or negative aspects of television may affect exceptional children more than normal children (Sprafkin, Gadow, & Abelman, 1992). A major effort of this type of research has been to discover other interactive variables that mediate or moderate the effects. These may be demographic variables classifying the individual or they may be properties of the message or of the context of its reception. The fact that the effects are not uniform does not denigrate their importance. For example, even though a given effect occurs in only 0.01% of the viewers of a certain TV program, that still has an impact on 4,000 people out of an audience of 40 million!

The third model, *cumulative effects*, emphasizes the repeated exposure to media stimuli and suggests that effects are due not so much to a single exposure as to the additive effects of many exposures. For example, a single exposure to a supermodel stimulus may not trigger an eating disorder but repeated exposures to ultra-thin, large-breasted women may cumulatively push a woman in that direction, especially if she likes and identifies with the media models (Harrison, 1997). In looking for any effects of media, we must always keep in mind the importance of cumulative exposure. Most media messages or images are seen or heard dozens, if not hundreds or thousands, of times. Although such exposure is difficult to simulate in a laboratory setting and difficult to control in a field study, there are ways it can be studied. For an excellent collection of papers on measuring responses to media, see A. Lang (1994a).

Behavioral Effects.   There are four general classes of measurable effects. Probably the type most people think of first are behavioral effects, where somebody performs some behavior after seeing someone do it in the media; for example, acting violently, buying a product, voting in an election, or laughing in response to a comedy. This is the particular emphasis among proponents of social cognitive theory (Bandura, 2002), discussed later. Although behavior may be conceptually the most obvious type of effect, it is often very difficult to measure and even harder to definitively attribute a causal role to the media. For example, we can know if somebody sees a certain commercial and we can check to see if that person buys that product, but knowing for sure that he or she bought the product *because* of seeing the ad and not for other unrelated reasons is very difficult to demonstrate. In a case like a shooting at a middle school by a teen who had recently seen a similar scene in a movie, it is very difficult, in either a legal or scientific sense, to demonstrate a cause-and-effect relationship between seeing the movie and the subsequent tragic deaths.

Attitudinal Effects.   A second general class of media effects are attitudinal effects. For example, an ad might make you think more highly of some product or candidate; whether this attitude would be followed up in actual buying or voting behavior is another question. For example, U.S. and Japanese moviegoers viewing the film *Roger and Me* showed a more negative attitude toward General Motors in particular and U.S. business in general (Bateman, Sakano, & Fujita, 1992), but any effects on car buying behavior were less clear.

Although attitudes consist of an intellectual (belief) component (e.g., reasons that you favor one candidate's position over another's), much of the psychological dynamic in attitudes is emotional (e.g., liking one candidate more than another). Sometimes the intellectual and emotional components may be inconsistent with each other, as when most U.S. voters in 1984 disagreed with President Ronald Reagan's positions on issues, but reelected him in a landslide because they liked him and trusted him.

Positive feelings about products or candidates may be taught through the process of classical conditioning, whereby a conditioned stimulus (a product) is associated with an unconditioned stimulus that naturally elicits some positive response. For example, an attractive model paired with some product may engender positive attitudes, especially regarding the emotional component, by associating the product with the sexy model, who naturally elicits a positive response. The precise processes by which classical conditioning occurs in advertising are discussed in more detail in chapter 4.

Media may teach us a whole constellation of attitudes on a given subject. For example, a dramatic TV movie or documentary on AIDS may sensitize people to the illness and make them more sympathetic to AIDS victims. Seeing R-rated horror movies in which women appear sexually aroused by being raped or assaulted may lead viewers to believe that women derive some secret pleasure out of being victims of sexual violence (Donnerstein, Linz, & Penrod, 1987). Attitudes are easier to measure than behaviors and sometimes are of great importance, for they influence behaviors that may follow and influence the way we process future information.

Attitudes may have influence beyond one's opinion on a particular subject. Sets of attitudes may form a sort of mindset through which we view the world. These attitudes color our selection of what we perceive in the world and how we interpret it. The interaction of this knowledge gained from media with our experience in the world can lead to what is called *cultivation* (Gerbner, Gross, Morgan, Signorielli, & Shanahan, 2002; Signorielli & Morgan, 1990). For example, if we accept the cop-show image of large cities being very dangerous places, that knowledge colors our attitudes about cities but also can affect cognitions and behaviors indirectly in ways that can be measured experimentally.

Cognitive Effects.   The third class of effects is cognitive effects, which change what we know or think. The most straightforward example here would be learning new information from media (e.g., facts about chimpanzees from a *National Geographic* article). There are other, more subtle, kinds of cognitive effects. Simply by choosing what news stories to cover, for example, media set an agenda. By covering presidential primary campaigns much more thoroughly than complex but abstract economic issues like the Third World debt crisis or the shift from domestic to export agriculture, the media are telling us that the political minutiae of all those primaries is very important, whereas the other issues are less significant.

Different media may stimulate different types of cognitive processing. In a series of studies comparing cognitive effects of radio versus television in telling stories, children produced more original endings for incomplete stories heard on the radio than they did for stories seen and heard on television. This offers some research support for the intuitive claim that radio stimulates the imagination more than TV does. Children remembered verbal information better from radio but visual, action, and overall information better from television (Greenfield & Beagles-Roos, 1988; Greenfield, Farrar, & Beagles-Roos, 1986).

In some ways radio and newspapers may have more in common cognitively with each other than either does with TV. Both radio and print are largely verbal media, whereas television involves the pictorial dimension as well. There is a positive correlation between the comprehension of a story read from a book and one heard on the radio, but less relationship between a story read and one seen on television (Pezdek & Hartman, 1983; Pezdek, Lehrer, & Simon, 1984; Pezdek & Stevens, 1984). This suggests that skills for extracting information from television are different from those used to extract information from the words of radio or print.

Taking a field study approach to comparing information transmission through different media, Spencer, Seydlitz, Laska, and Triche (1992) compared the public's responses to newspaper and television reports of an actual natural hazard, in this case the saltwater intrusion from the Gulf of Mexico into the lower Mississippi River in 1988. Results found newspapers were better at presenting complex and potentially ambiguous information about possible consequences of the hazard, whereas television was better in communicating material that was relatively simple and in making direct behavior appeals (e.g., buying bottled water). Similar effects of medium were shown on memory for news from the 2000 U.S. political campaign by Eveland, Seo, and Marton (2002).

Although cognitive effects are most often measured by testing the information acquired, other types of methods are also useful. For example, attention to TV may be studied by measuring the time the eyes are focused on the screen (Anderson, 1985: Anderson & Burns, 1991; Anderson & Field, 1991; Thorson, 1994). The amount of cognitive effort required may be assessed indirectly by measuring the reaction time to remember some information and respond (Cameron & Frieske, 1994) or to do some secondary task (Basil, 1994).

Physiological Effects.   The fourth class of media effects, probably the least often measured but being increasingly used, are the physiological changes in our bodies resulting from exposure to the media. For example, sexual arousal resulting from viewing pornography may be measured by heart rate, skin resistance, penile tumescence, or vaginal lubrication (Malamuth & Check, 1980a). Watching a scary movie or an exciting ball game results in physical changes like rapid breathing and heart rate. Even such mundane material as television or radio commercials can induce changes in the heart rate and orienting reflex (Lang, 1990, 1994b), electrodermal responses (Hopkins & Fletcher, 1994), facial electromyography–EMG (Bolls, Lang, & Potter, 2001; Hazlett & Hazlett, 1999), and changes in alpha waves given off by the brain (Reeves et al., 1985; Simons, Detenber, Cuthbert, Schwartz, & Reiss, 2003). See Zillmann (1991a) for a review of the effects of television viewing on physiological arousal.

Caveat: The Third-Person Effect.   A general principle growing out of social psychology is the third-person effect, which can apply to all of the types of effects above. As applied to media, this principle states that (1) people believe that others are more vulnerable to persuasive messages and other media influences than they are themselves, and (2) such perceptions can influence behavior. This principle, soundly supported by research, suggests that people think other people are more influenced by ads, more corrupted by negative media values, or more encouraged to follow antisocial media models than they themselves are. There is even evidence that the third-person effect is larger when dealing with seriously antisocial behaviors, such as violence (Hoffner & Buchanan, 2002; Hoffner et al., 2001). A variety of explanations for this robust finding have been offered, as well as conditions affecting it (see Perloff, 2002, for a review). A sort of self-serving bias, it leads people to underestimate the media's influence in their own lives, even as they loudly decry its corruption of others' lives.

A more general model derived from the third-person effect is the Influence of Presumed Influence Model (Gunther & Storey, 2003). This model postulates that people perceive that some media message has an effect on others and then they react to that perception. These perceived effects may be positive as well as negative. For example, Gunther and Storey evaluated the effect of a radio health campaign in Nepal targeted at health clinic workers. They found that a broader population expected the campaign to affect health care workers, and they, in turn, raised their expectations of their interactions with those workers, with the result that they held more positive attitudes toward those professionals and the quality of their interaction improved. Thus, the message directly affected the perceptions of people other than its target audience, and those perceptions in turn affected the behavior of the target persons.

The Strength of Effects.   Although computing the precise strength of media effects is a very difficult task, there have been some attempts to do so, using techniques like meta-analysis and computation of effects sizes. Such strength measures have been developed for effects of media violence (Wood, Wong, & Chachere, 1991), gender-role perceptions (Herrett-Skjellum & Allen, 1996), and pornography (Allen, Emmers, Gebhardt, & Giery, 1995). Perhaps surprising to some, such studies generally show a small to modest effect size. Effects are almost always stronger in laboratory studies than in field studies or surveys, due to the greater degree of experimental control that reduces random error.

Why aren't the effects of media greater than they are? The major reason is that there simply are so many other influences on behavior, including some that most everyone would expect to be stronger. For example, parents' behavior and values have a greater effect on children's level of violent behavior than violent media do. Personal experience with a particular product has more effect on purchasing behavior than advertising does. Whether one's peers and parents smoke is a better predictor of whether a teen will start smoking than is exposure to tobacco ads. None of this is surprising, however. Personal long-term influence has long been known to be highly influential on all sorts of behavior.

Just because media are not the source of the strongest effects, however, does not mean their effects are trivial. In fact, there is good reason to believe that scientific studies may underestimate media effects, especially for very dramatic types of media. For example, studies of sex and violence, especially with children, do not use extremely graphic violence or pornography as stimuli for ethical reasons. Possible effects of such stimuli are probably greater than those already documented in the research with milder stimuli. Also, effects may not always be linear, although such linearity is often implicitly assumed by researchers and the public. For example, some models of advertising effects are based on a threshold idea, where there are few effects before a certain level of exposure is reached, after which the effect is substantial. Sometimes influences on media effects may have opposite impact and thus cancel each other out. For example, watching violence may cause viewers to believe the world is a more violent place but it may also cause them to stay inside more and thus avoid situations where they may be likely to behave violently. Finally, because media affect different people so differently, it may be the case that a disproportionate amount of the media effect occurs with a relatively small number of audience members, who experience a very large effect, while most others experience little. Thus, group studies will obtain an overall small effect. For a good discussion of this issue in more detail, see Perse (2001).

THEORIES OF MASS COMMUNICATION

Now that we have looked at different media research frameworks and types of effects measured, let us turn to some specific theories that have guided mass communication research over the years. In their current versions, most contemporary theories are heavily cognitive in nature. By this we mean that they view information processing as constructive; that is, people do not literally encode and retrieve information that they read or hear in the media (or anywhere else). Rather, as they comprehend, they interpret in accordance with their prior knowledge and beliefs and the context in which the message is received. Comprehension of a TV program emerges through a continual interaction between the content of the program and the knowledge already in our minds. The mind is always actively thinking about what we see or hear and those thoughts become an important part of the constructive process of comprehension.

Social Cognitive Theory (Social Learning, Observational Learning, Modeling)

This approach initially grew out of stimulus-response behaviorist (S–R) psychology as "social learning theory" by social psychologist Albert Bandura and his associates in the 1960s (Bandura, 1977; Bandura, Ross, & Ross, 1961, 1963; Bandura & Walters, 1963; Tan, 1986). We learn behaviors by observing others performing those behaviors and subsequently imitating them. The relevance to media occurs when the media model becomes the source of observational learning. Over the years this model has increasingly stressed personal agency and cognitive processes.

There are four subfunctions for observational learning from media (Bandura, 2001, 2002). First, someone must first be exposed to the media example and attend to it. Second, he or she must be capable of symbolically encoding and remembering the observed events, including both constructing the representation and cognitively and enactively rehearsing it. Third, the person must be able to translate the symbolic conceptions into appropriate action. Finally, motivational processes develop by internal or external reinforcement (reward) for performing the behavior. For example, a person's violent behavior could be reinforced if the behavior impressed others, or if the person enjoyed the behavior or received a monetary gain as a result.

Social cognitive theory was initially developed in the context of studying the effects of violent media models on behavior (see chapter 9). Although that is still the most studied application, the model has other applications as well, as in the modeling of sexual, prosocial, or purchasing behavior. For example, children randomly assigned to view high-risk behaviors on TV were more likely to later self-report their own tendency to engage in risk-taking behaviors themselves (Potts, Doppler, & Hernandez, 1994). Such reported risk-taking was reduced by viewing a safety educational videotape showing high-risk behavior and its negative consequences (Potts & Swisher, 1998). See Bandura (2001, 2002) for a recent description of the social cognitive model.

Cultivation Theory

This approach looks at the way that extensive repeated exposure to media (especially television) over time gradually shapes our view of the world and our social reality. It was initially developed by George Gerbner and his colleagues in the Cultural Indicators research project at the University of Pennsylvania. See Gerbner, Gross, Morgan, Signorielli, and Shanahan (2002) and Morgan and Signorielli (1990) for overviews of the theory, and Signorielli and Morgan (1990) for a collection of papers using the approach.

One of the major constructs of cultivation theory is *mainstreaming*, the homogenization of people's divergent perceptions of social reality into a convergent mainstream. This apparently happens through a process of construction, whereby viewers learn facts about the real world from observing the world of television. Memory traces from watching TV are stored relatively automatically (Shapiro, 1991). We then use this stored information to formulate beliefs about the real world (Hawkins & Pingree, 1990; Hawkins, Pingree, & Adler, 1987; Potter, 1989, 1991a, 1991b; Shrum & Bischak, 2001). When this constructed world and the real world have a high degree of consistency, *resonance* occurs and the cultivation effect is even stronger.

In terms of methodology, cultivation research usually compares frequent ("heavy") and infrequent ("light") viewers of television through correlational methods. A typical study finds that the world view of heavy viewers is more like the world as presented on television. For example, people who watch a lot of violent TV believe the world to be a more violent place (mean world syndrome) than it really is (Signorielli, 1990). There is also a greater variance of views among the light viewers, suggesting that an effect of watching a lot of TV is to inculcate a sort of middle-of-the-road view. For example, people who watch a lot of TV are less likely to be either extremely liberal or extremely conservative politically, whereas the political views of light viewers run the entire ideological spectrum. Mainstreaming pulls deviants from both directions back to the middle.

The social reality cultivated through mainstreaming takes many forms, including understanding of gender roles (Morgan, 1982; Morgan & Shanahan, 1995; Preston, 1990), political attitudes (Gerbner, Gross, Morgan, & Signorielli, 1984; 1986; Morgan, 1989), estimations of crime risk (Shrum, 2001; Shrum & Bischak, 2001), understanding of science and scientists (Gerbner, Gross, Morgan, & Signorielli, 1981b; Potts & Martinez, 1994), health beliefs and practices (Gerbner, Gross, Morgan, & Signorielli, 1981a), attitudes toward the environment (Shanahan & McComas, 1999; Shanahan, Morgan, & Stenbjerre, 1997), adolescent career choices (Morgan & Gerbner, 1982; Morgan & Shanahan, 1995), effects of prolonged viewing of talk shows (Rössler & Brosius, 2001), and views of the elderly (Gerbner, Gross, Signorielli, & Morgan, 1980) and minorities (Gross, 1984; Volgy & Schwarz, 1980). Cultivation theory has also been applied cross culturally (e.g., Morgan, 1990; Morgan & Shanahan, 1991, 1992, 1995).

There is considerable methodological and theoretical concern about the specific nature of the cultivation process. For example, Potter (1991b) argued that the cultivation effect really involves several components, some of which operate independently. Shapiro (1991) looked at the process of the formation of memory traces from television and its later effects on the construction of one's world view. Tamborini and Choi (1990) looked at the frequent failure of non-U.S. data to strongly support cultivation theory and suggested some reasons for this. Cultivation theory generally focuses on the cumulative effect of many repeated images. However, some images may be far more influential than others. For example, Greenberg's (1988) drench hypothesis says that a highly respected popular TV character at the top of the ratings can have far more impact than a dozen other characters seen and identified with by far fewer viewers.

In spite of being very influential, cultivation theory is not without its critics. Several studies show that careful controls of certain other sociodemographic and personality variables tend to reduce or eliminate cultivation effects (Doob & Macdonald, 1979; Hawkins & Pingree, 1981; Hirsch, 1980; Perse, 1986; Potter, 1986; Wober, 1986). Second, cultivation studies have been criticized on conceptual and methodological grounds, including concerns about response biases and problems with the measuring instruments (Hirsch, 1980; Perse, 1986; Potter, 1986, 1993; Schneider, 1987; Schuman & Presser, 1981; Wober, 1978; Wober & Gunter, 1986). There have also been criticisms of some of the assumptions underlying cultivation theory. For example, it seems to assume, without demonstration, that the messages of TV are essentially uniform (Hawkins & Pingree, 1981) and that viewers accept what they see as perceived reality (Slater & Elliott, 1982). See A. M. Rubin, Perse, and Taylor (1988) for a review of the methodological critiques of cultivation theory and Potter (1993) for a review of conceptual critiques.

To deal with some of these concerns, some have reinterpreted cultivation theory in line with a uses and gratifications approach, stressing the active mental activity of the viewer while watching TV (Levy & Windahl, 1984; A. M. Rubin & Perse, 1987; Weaver & Wakshlag, 1986). Whatever cultivation, in fact, occurs then grows out of the active information processing and the construction of reality performed by the viewer. Another approach has been to stress more cognitive variables, especially the encoding and storage in memory, in an attempt to increase the rigor and predictability of cultivation theory (Shrum, 2002; Tapper, 1995). Finally, considering cultural differences in media and societal factors, and the degree of congruity between the two, can help to predict cultivation in some areas but not in others (e.g., Morgan & Shanahan, 1995).

Socialization Theories

Taking an approach similar to cultivation theory, various socialization theories (see Heath & Bryant, 1992, for discussion) stress how prolonged exposure to media comes to teach us about the world and our role in it. For example, Meyrowitz (1985) and Postman (1982, 1985) argued that children are socialized into the role of adults far earlier in the age of television than had been the case for several hundred years previously. Television is the window through which children learn about the world of adults, which is no longer kept secret from them. The effect of television thus is a homogenization of developmental stages: children become more like adults, and adults become more like children. This has numerous social implications beyond the world of media. For example, children and adults dress more alike, talk more alike, and go to more of the same places. No longer do only children wear t-shirts and only adults swear. Similar blurring of the dichotomies of masculinity-femininity and politician-citizen are also posited and attributed to electronic media, with the effects of increasing androgynous behavior and holding political candidates to personal standards.

Another socialization theory focuses on conditions leading to maximal media socialization influence. Van Evra (1997) argued that the cumulative media effects on children are the greatest when the purpose of viewing is diversion and when they perceive the media content to be realistic, perhaps due to lack of a critical thinking mode present during the viewing. Socialization effects are especially strong on frequent viewers who have few information alternatives and relevant life experience available. For example, a boy who watches lots of sitcoms for entertainment and perceives as realistic the portrayals of ethnic groups with whom he has little personal contact is likely to be heavily affected.

The media, particularly television, are extremely important socializing agents for national and cultural socialization (Rosengren, 1992). Children's perceived reality about the culture they live in is, in part, a media creation. This socialization role of television may be especially crucial in cases where a child lives in a different culture than that into which he or she was born. In an interesting study comparing U.S. and international children residing in the United States, Zohoori (1988) found that the foreign children found TV more interesting, spent more time watching it, identified more with TV characters, and used TV more for learning than did their U.S. counterparts. Consistent with cultivation theory, they also expressed stronger beliefs in the social reality portrayed by television. That is, the perceived reality of TV seemed to them more real, consistent with the fact that they had fewer life experiences in that culture on which to draw. Adult immigrants also draw heavily on television to learn about the United States, both before and after their arrival (Chaffee, Nass, & Yang, 1990). See Box 2.2 for some examples of how three very different societies use television as a socializing agent.

Socialization theories discuss the impact of media in very broad strokes. As such, they have been useful in helping us to appreciate the complexity and pervasiveness of media and their effects. They have, however, been criticized for needing greater specificity and more serious consideration of prevailing social and historical trends. See especially Kubey's (1992) critique of Meyrowitz (1985) for a careful development of this sort of argument.

Uses and Gratifications Theory

The uses and gratifications perspective places much emphasis on the active role of the audience in making choices and being goal-directed in its media-use behavior (Blumler, 1979; Blumler & Katz, 1974; Palmgreen, 1984;

BOX 2.2
MEDIA AS SOCIALIZING AGENTS IN
DIFFERENT CULTURES

Singapore. One of the emerging East Asian economic powerhouses explicitly uses media to further its social ends. Proud of its peaceful multicultural, multiracial, and multireligious society, Singapore censors its television in four areas: racial, religious, moral, and political. No criticism of any race or religion is allowed. No sexual expressions that might offend the Buddhist or Muslim communities are allowed. No religious programming at all is allowed. News of religious or racial strife elsewhere is played down to avoid inflaming latent local grievances. An orderly and harmonious society is deemed to be a higher priority than Western-style political and press freedoms. Singapore's greatest challenge in this effort is likely to be the Internet. The first nation in the world to commit to universal Internet access, Singapore has recently discovered that this laudable goal brings with it many channels of information difficult to control and where attempts to control it produce considerable resentment.

India. A very popular program on Indian television used this modern medium to tell age-old Hindu stories. *Ramayana* uses live actors to dramatize the ancient Hindu epic of the same name. Devout Hindus place garlands and incense on the TV set when the show comes on (Panitt, 1988). This show continues a longstanding tradition, whereby each generation participates in the telling and relearning of the archetypal tales of that culture. The only difference is that the modality has changed from an oral (or written) to a broadcast tradition. Classical Indian song and dance is also very popular in the many movies produced in "Bollywood," India's huge film industry centered in Mumbai (Bombay).

Belize. A small (population 150,000), English-speaking Caribbean country on the northeast coast of Central America, Belize had no daily newspapers or television until a local entrepreneur bought a used satellite dish antenna in 1981, set it up in his backyard, and began selling retransmissions of his pirated signals from Chicago television. Some favorite shows were U.S. sitcoms and Chicago Cubs baseball games. Radio, which was listened to by 95% of the population, aired news mostly from the BBC, *Newsweek,* and the Voice of America. There were seven small weekly newspapers, with mostly local news. Almost all of the media content was foreign, especially from the United States (Snyder, Roser, & Chaffee, 1991) and the U.K., through British Forces Broadcasting Service (Gonzalez, 2001).

Rosengren, Wenner, & Palmgreen, 1985; A. M. Rubin, 2002; A. M. Rubin & Windahl, 1986; Windahl, 1981). The experience and effects of media depend, in part, on the uses one is putting those media to and the gratifications one is receiving from them. For example, the experience of watching a horror film will be very different for someone who is experiencing much empathy with the victim than for someone who is being superficially entertained by the suspense of the plot. Watching CNN *Headline News* or reading *USA Today* may be a very different experience for someone trying to be entertained than for someone trying to be seriously informed on the details of a political candidate's positions.

We may use media for many other reasons besides entertainment or information. Perhaps it is to avoid studying or some other activity. Perhaps it is to escape into a fantasy world or be turned on by a particular sexy star. Maybe it is to find out what everybody's talking about on some popular show. Maybe it is to conform to others who are watching. Sometimes we watch a program we strongly dislike simply to make us feel less alone. For many solo drivers, the radio is a constant traveling companion. What draws different people to consume different types of media may be a critical issue, for example, the factors that cause some people to watch violent pornography. See McGuire (1974), A. M. Rubin (1981, 1984, 2002), and Conway and Rubin (1991) for discussions of psychological motives in uses and gratifications research.

Rubin (2002) identified six current research directions for uses and gratifications research. Some have worked at developing taxonomies of communication motives. Others have compared motives across media, a particularly important area of research in regard to new computer-mediated technologies. A third approach has looked at different social and psychological circumstances of media use (e.g., coviewers, personality, lifestyle, and religiosity). A fourth direction has looked at how one's motives for using media are satisfied or not. A fifth direction has examined the role of individual differences in experiences, motives, and exposure on the media experience. Finally, some have studied measurement issues like the reliability and validity of instruments measuring motivation.

One interesting construct to come out of the uses and gratifications perspective concerns the relationships we have with media figures we have never met. We may think of morning show hosts more as our breakfast companions than as news spokespersons. Evening news anchors are regular dinner guests, not merely people who read the news. It is not unusual for people to respond audibly to a greeting from the tube, as in responding "Hi, Tom" to a news anchor's greeting to start the evening news. This feeling of connectedness with public figures is occasionally dramatically illustrated, such as in the intense worldwide outpouring of grief following the sudden death of Britain's young Princess Diana in a car crash in 1997 (W. J. Brown, Basil, & Bocarnea, 2003). Her loss was a genuinely personal one to millions who knew her only through media. Such *parasocial interactions* (R. B. Rubin & McHugh, 1987; A. M. Rubin, Perse, & Powell, 1985) have many of the characteristics of real interpersonal relationships (Perse & R. B. Rubin, 1989) and are one of the best predictors of television viewing motivation and behavior (Conway & A. M. Rubin, 1991). Parasocial relationships are not limited to real people. When a favorite soap opera character meets her demise, the show's faithful viewers feel a genuine emptiness and loss. Interestingly, there are no social conventions or social support for parasocial grieving, which in fact often is met with outright ridicule. See Giles (2002) for a literature review and proposed model for parasocial interaction. He argues for the importance of specifying the continuum of the relationship between social and parasocial relationships and for identifying the stages in the development of parasocial relationships.

The relationship of media use to mood and personality variables can interact with the reasons for media use. For example, does heavy TV viewing cause people to be escapist, or do factors of temperament and personality cause them to seek escape through heavy TV viewing? Kubey (1986) investigated this issue and concluded that heavy TV viewing is more likely an effect rather than a cause of mood and personality factors. We have uncomfortable and unpleasant feelings and seek an escape from these through television.

Agenda Setting

This theory, which initially grew out of communications research on political socialization (Dearing & Rogers, 1996), defines *agenda setting* as "the ability of the mass media to structure audience cognitions and to effect change among existing cognitions" (McCombs & Gilbert, 1986, p. 4) or, more intuitively, the "creation of public awareness and concern of salient issues by the news media" (Heath & Bryant, 1992, p. 279). The media do not necessarily tell us what to think, but rather what to think *about*. For example, through heavy coverage of such issues in a political campaign, media may tell us that marital infidelity of candidates and whether they smoked marijuana in college are important issues on which to base our vote. Other issues covered in less depth, such as their positions on taxation, are thus positioned as less important. See chapters 7 and 8 and McCombs (1994) for further discussion of agenda setting in regard to news, and McCombs and Reynolds (2002); McCombs and Shaw (1993); Rogers, Dearing, and Bregman (1993); Wanta (1997); and Kosicki (1993) for recent theoretical conceptualizations.

Although it has been explored most fully in regard to news and politics, agenda setting is also relevant to other media issues. For example, in its basic ignoring of religion, mainstream television in the United States is sending a message that spiritual issues are not important factors in people's lives. Soap operas and movies that continually show characters engaging in presumably unprotected casual sex with no apparent concern for consequences like HIV infection or pregnancy are subtly telling us that those concerns are not important.

One way that an agenda can be set is through the use of framing (Entman, 1993; McCombs & Ghanem, 2001; Wicks, 2001). The way a problem is described selects or highlights certain aspects of its reality and neglects or downplays others. This will affect how people respond to it. For example, is some indiscretion described as a "caper," an "affair," or a "scandal?" Jamieson and Waldman (2003) argued that press coverage of the U.S. Presidential election campaign of 2000 framed the candidates as the "lying panderer" (Al Gore) and the "ineffective bumbler" (George W. Bush) and that media and the public noticed details consistent with the frames and neglected details that were inconsistent. See Chapter 7 for further discussion of the framing of the 2000 candidates.

There have been some attempts to integrate agenda setting with other theoretical approaches. For example, Wanta (1997) draws on cognitive and uses and gratifications perspectives to develop a model of agenda setting that focuses more on the individual, rather than the issue, as the unit of measurement. Wanta tested this model and concluded that those most susceptible to agenda-setting effects are those who more actively process information from news media. McCombs, Shaw, and Weaver (1997) extended agenda setting to some new areas, including political advertising, economic news, and comparative effectiveness of television and print media in setting agendas.

Schema Theory

Part of what guides the comprehension and any later memory of information are *schemas* (Brewer & Nakamura, 1984; Rumelhart, 1980; Thorndyke, 1984). The construct of schema refers to knowledge structures or frameworks that organize an individual's memory for people and events. The schema is a general mental construct that acts on all forms of information, irrespective of the mode: visual or auditory, linguistic or nonlinguistic, to which it is exposed. A person holds mental schemas based on past experiences. One consequence of this for information processing is that the individual is likely to go beyond the information actually presented to draw inferences about people or events that are congruent with previously formed schemas (Graesser & Bower, 1990; Harris, 1981; Rojahn & Pettigrew, 1992; M. Singer, 1984). For example, someone with a very negative schema about Mexican Americans might respond very differently to a new TV show set in Latino East Los Angeles than would someone without those prejudices. Much of the content in schemas is typically culture-specific. The schema that members of one culture may hold may cause them to interpret the same story very differently than members of a different culture (Harris, Schoen, & Hensley, 1992; Lasisi & Onyehalu, 1992). Cultural differences must be carefully considered by TV producers in international programming sales (see Box 2.3).

In mass media, activation of a schema in the mind of the audience member may be triggered by some particular information in the program or article. It may also be triggered by the content of certain *formal features* of the particular medium; for example, flashbacks, montage, or instant replays in television or film. Young children do not understand these conventions and will interpret the input literally (e.g., thinking a flashback or instant replay is continuing new action). Part of the socialization to the use of a medium like television is to learn about these formal features and how to interpret them (Abelman, 1989; Bickham, Wright, & Huston, 2001; Calvert, 1988; Huston & Wright, 1987; Kraft, Cantor, & Gottdiener, 1991; Lang, Geiger, Strickwerda, & Sumner, 1993; Rice, Huston, & Wright, 1986; Smith, Anderson, & Fischer, 1985; B. J. Wilson, 1991).

We may speak of learning *scripts* from media (Janis, 1980; Luke, 1987). *Script* here refers to a schema about an activity and is *not* the same as the meaning of pages of dialogue. For example, when we watch a TV drama about a woman who discovers she has breast cancer, we may acquire a script for dealing with that particular situation. The viewer may learn specific activities like breast self-examination, how to tell her husband about her illness, how to seek out information about possible treatments, and how to cope with a mastectomy in terms of her own self-image and sexuality.

Scripts are acquired from the media, among other sources. Through exposure to samples of activities following some script, that abstract script is inferred and gradually becomes a part of our permanent memory (Ahn, Brewer, & Mooney, 1992). This skeleton structure of some activity is then used to interpret future instances of that activity. For example, listeners of a British radio soap opera, *The Archers*, used knowledge of a familiar script from that show to help them remember related material (Reeve & Aggleton, 1998).

The potential consequences of learning scripts from media become especially clear when we consider a situation for which readers have little prior knowledge or scripts from their own life experience. For example, suppose a child's knowledge of dealing with muggers has resulted from watching TV adventure heroes trick and overpower the robber. If that child were to try that script on a real mugger by attempting the same moves as seen on TV, he or she might be considerably less successful than the *NYPD Blue* detectives might be. For another example, consider a TV

BOX 2.3
U.S. CULTURAL IMPERIALISM: FACT OR FICTION?

The rapid diffusion of American movies and television throughout the world in the last few decades has been well documented (Lee, 1980; Tunstall, 1977). Although the United States is the world's largest exporter of television programming, which is the nation's second largest export, studies (M. G. Cantor & J. M. Cantor, 1986; Schement, Gonzalez, Lum, & Valencia, 1984) suggest that no country is able to dominate media today, if indeed this was ever possible. What is actually happening is a globalization of all cultures (Legrain, 2003). McDonald's is becoming popular worldwide, but so are Indian curry, Japanese sushi, and Mexican nachos. Hollywood studios dominate world movie distribution, but film productions are multinational efforts. For example, many top "American" movie stars are not American: Salma Hayek (Mexico); Nicole Kidman, Hugh Jackman, Mel Gibson, and Russell Crowe (Australia); Hugh Grant, Ewan Macgregor, and the entire cast of the *Harry Potter* films (Britain), Sam Neill (New Zealand), Michael J. Fox (Canadian), Antonio Banderas (Spain), and Colin Ferrell (Ireland). Many top Hollywood directors similarly are from elsewhere than the U.S.: Peter Weir (Australia), Stanley Kubrick (Britain), M. Night Shymalan (India), Pedro Almodovar (Spain), Peter Jackson (New Zealand). In terms of music, despite the pressure to record in English, many of international music's biggest sellers are not Americans: Beatles (U.K.), Shakira (Colombia), U2 (Ireland), Björk (Iceland), Nickleback and Avril Lavigne (Canada), Abba (Sweden), and Julio and Enrique Iglesias (Spain).

The United States itself is a market as well as a producer. Many cable markets carry Univisión or channels from the Spanish International Network (SIN), both satellite exports from Mexico. Mexico's Televisa earns millions exporting its soap operas, with some of those sales going to the United States. The British BBC and Granada TV have exported programs to America's PBS for years.

The largest commercial TV networks in the world (e.g., CBS, NBC, ABC, and Fox in the United States; TV Globo in Brazil; Televisa in Mexico) export their programs to dozens of other nations. Millions of people around the world may know virtually nothing about the United States besides what they see on such programs as *Baywatch* or *ER*. How we learn about other groups of people from media is the subject of chapter 3. Some countries, like Japan, Mexico, and Brazil, formerly imported much more American TV than they do today, with most of their programming now being locally produced (Elasmar, 2003). Indeed, some foreign producers are major exporters. Sometimes the television empires fall along linguistic lines. For example, Francophone Africa and French Canada generally buy television from France. American and other non-French sources typically must go through Paris to dub their programs in French before selling to French-speaking markets.

movie dealing with incest. A preteen in the story is being sexually molested by her father and is sufficiently troubled to mention this to a school counselor, a revelation that sets in motion a sequence of events that eventually, but inevitably, brings this event out in the open. Because incest was not taken seriously for so many years, many viewers, including some current or former victims, may have no mental script for how to handle it. In this sense, such a movie, if done sensitively yet realistically, could help victims come forth and seek help. It could provide information on how one may expect to feel about that experience, where to seek help, and, through the context of the drama, could offer a scenario of what the effects of such a revelation might be.

In a more general sense, media fiction may use very abstract scripts such as overcoming adversity. This implicit theme may be reflected in a story about a slave escaping from servitude in the antebellum South, a child learning to cope with alcoholic parents, or a burned-out police officer coming to terms with a vicious crime syndicate (Janis, 1980). Such a script is also used in many human interest news stories.

There is a very general script for stories in Western culture (Kintsch, 1977). This *narrative script* is learned implicitly from the earliest days of young children hearing stories from their parents. Such stories are composed of episodes, each of which contains an exposition, complication, and resolution. That is, the characters and setting are introduced (exposition), some problem or obstacle develops (complication), and that problem or obstacle is somehow overcome (resolution). We grow up expecting stories to follow this general script. Children's stories such as fairy tales do so very explicitly ("Once upon a time there was a___"). Adult stories also follow the same script but often in a more complex fashion. For example, some of the complication may be introduced before all of the exposition is finished or there may be two subepisodes embedded in the resolution of a larger episode.

Television and print media fiction also draw on the narrative script to make their stories more readily understandable. Children's cartoons follow the script very explicitly. Most TV sitcoms and action-adventure shows also do, although perhaps in a somewhat more complicated fashion, for example, two interwoven episodes (subplots), each with its own narrative structure. The use of schemas enhances our information-processing capabilities. Meadowcroft and Reeves (1989) found that children had well-developed story schema skills by age 7, and that such skills led to better memory for central story content, a reduction in processing effort, and a greater flexibility of attention-allocation strategies.

Soap operas traditionally hold an audience by concluding each day's story just before the resolution. Because we have this sense of our narrative script being incomplete, we return the next day or the next week to complete it. This principle of the cliffhanger has been used in some prime-time season finales to ensure the interest and return of viewers for the first show of the next season to learn the resolution.

Even many ads draw upon the narrative script. For example, a nice young fellow is ready to go out on a hot date (exposition), but alas, he has ring around the collar (complication). But his mom and her amazing detergent come to the rescue to wash the shirt just in time (resolution). Because of our familiarity with the narrative script, we are able to comprehend such a commercial readily, which is of course to the advertiser's advantage. Also, because it fits the story structure of many programs, it seems more entertaining and is thus more likely than a traditional sales pitch to hold viewers' attention. The narrative script is a deeply ingrained knowledge structure; Esslin (1982) went so far as to argue that the 30-second story of an unhappy hemorrhoid sufferer has the same dramatic structure as a classic Greek tragedy!

Limited Capacity Model

One of the most influential recent cognitive models is Annie Lang's Limited Capacity Model of media information processing (Lang, 2000). Drawing on basic cognitive psychology, Lang makes two basic assumptions: (1) people are information processors, and (2) the ability to process information is limited. These information processes are sometimes automatic and sometimes controlled, i.e., involving conscious volition. The three major subprocesses are encoding, storage, and retrieval. These may be done partially in parallel, but the processing resources are limited, and heavy allocation to one may result in superficial allocation to another.

One of the automatic selection mechanisms steering the encoding of information is the *orienting response*. When this occurs, as in our attention being captured by the television turning on, more cognitive resources are allocated to encoding the information from that source. Encoding of that information is enhanced, provided that the cognitive load is low. If however, the cognitive load is high, e.g., a set of scenes that rapidly cuts from one location to another, the limited resources will be overwhelmed, and less encoding will occur. Increasing the cognitive load and resources required by speeding up the pace or having more arousing content decreases memory for the controlled processing of verbal content, but not for the automatic processing of visual content (Lang, Potter, & Bolls, 1999).

COGNITIVE COMPONENTS OF THE MEDIA EXPERIENCE

We now turn our attention away from specific theoretical approaches to focus on some different cognitive processes involved in our experiencing media.

Attention

As a prerequisite to any other involvement with media, we must select some information to attend to and process and neglect other information. Although there are many ways, some very sophisticated, of measuring exposure to media (Simons, et al., 2003; Thorson, 1994; von Feilitzen, Strand, Nowak, & Andren, 1989; Webster & Wakshlag, 1985), it is simplistic to assume either that viewers are fully processing everything that they hear on radio or TV or that it is not affecting them at all if they are not paying full conscious attention. The issue is also relevant to other media. For example, how much do we process the typical newspaper or Internet ad as we read through the paper or scan a web page?

Merely measuring when the television is on or how much time we read the magazine is not really enough to tell us how much is being understood or what influence it is having. A big question in the study of television is how much attention viewers are paying to the tube at any given time it is on. Clearly, the TV is often on when it is receiving less than total undivided attention. Research studying people watching television shows that the typical adult or child over age 5 attends to the TV about 55–70% of the time it is on (Anderson, 1985; Anderson & Burns, 1991; Anderson & Field, 1991; Schmitt, Woolf, & Anderson, 2003), depending on the time of day and the type of program being watched. For example, early morning news shows and commercials receive less attention, and weekend shows such as sports and children's cartoons receive more attention. More attention is given to moving images than to static ones (Simons, et al., 2003). Children initially allocate more attention to a difficult segment but quickly reduce attention if the material is beyond their level of comprehensibility (Hawkins, Kim, & Pingree, 1991). Overall, children spend more time attending to "child content" than to "adult content" (Schmitt, Anderson, & Collins, 1999). The most common concurrent activities with TV viewing are socializing and playing (Schmitt, et al., 2003). Clearly, both structure and content factors help determine the amount of attention allocated (Geiger & Reeves, 1993a, 1993b).

Sometimes we may not be looking at the screen very much but may nonetheless be monitoring the sound for items of interest and can redirect our vision toward the screen, if necessary. Even very young children are quite skilled at doing this (Rolandelli, Wright, Huston, & Eakins, 1991).

Attention is also an important issue with newer media technologies. One of the most controversial in recent years has been the cell phone, especially possible distraction effects of using the cell phone while driving. See Box 2.4 for some troubling results from some well-controlled experimental research on effects of talking on the phone while driving.

BOX 2.4
**WHICH IS WORSE: DRIVING WHILE DRUNK OR WHILE
TALKING ON A CELL PHONE? (THE ANSWER
MAY SURPRISE YOU.)**

One of the most popular driving activities in recent years seems to be talking on the cell phone. Is this a dangerous distraction? University of Utah psychologist David Strayer and his colleagues (2004) used a high-fidelity driving simulator to answer this question and their findings are sobering. Compared to a control group devoting all their attention to driving, a group talking on a cell phone missed twice as many red lights, recognized fewer billboards they had driven by, took longer to hit the brake to stop while following another car, took longer to recover speed after passing the car, and had more accidents, in spite of leaving more distance between themselves and the next car.

Some additional conditions helped understand what was going on better. Talking on a non-hand-held phone was just as bad as on a hand-held phone, so it is the cognitive distraction of the conversation, not the motor skill requirement of holding the phone, that is the major problem. Also, drivers listening to the radio or book on tape or talking to a passenger in the car did not differ from the control group, so these conditions do not place strong demands on attention. One does not have to respond to the radio or talking book, and when the other conversant is in the car with you, he or she can also see the driving conditions and make adjustments in the conversation as conditions warrant, such as keeping quiet for awhile. In one study, Strayer got his participants drunk to the minimum blood alcohol level for legal intoxication after they had driven in the control and cell-phone conditions. In the car-following task, students who were legally drunk actually stopped (and later regained speed) *faster* than those talking on the cell phone (though slower than the controls). Thus, talking on a cell phone actually impaired driving *more* than being legally drunk!

This research uses the experimental design of cognitive psychology to address a question of vital social importance. The results support the legislation in some places like New York City to ban cell phone use while driving, although limiting the ban to hand-held units may not completely do the job.

Suspending Disbelief

Like movies or theater, television involves the social convention of the *suspension of disbelief,* in which we, for a brief time, agree to accept the characters we see as real human beings so that we can identify with them to experience their joys and sorrows (Esslin, 1982). We know that two actors are not really married to each other but we agree to suspend our disbelief and accept them as a married couple when we watch their weekly sitcom. Because of the continuing nature of a television series (often several years for a successful show), this suspension of disbelief for television is a far more enduring fantasy than it is for a 2-hour movie or play. Producers in the early days of television may have doubted the ability of the public to suspend that much disbelief. Many of the earliest TV series featured real-life spouses playing TV partners (Lucille Ball and Desi Arnaz, George Burns and Gracie Allen, Jack Benny and Mary Livingston, Ozzie and Harriet Nelson). This phenomenon has been rare since the 1950s, however.

Sometimes disbelief is suspended so long that distinction between fantasy and reality becomes blurred. Although young children have difficulty understanding the difference between actors and the characters they portray (Dorr, 1980; Fitch et al., 1993), this problem is not limited to children. As any series actor knows, adult fans frequently ask an actor playing a doctor for medical advice or hurl epithets at an actress playing a villain on a soap opera. Such fantasies are covertly encouraged by spinoff series, where the same character moves from one series to another (e.g., Dr. Frasier Crane was originally a supporting character on *Cheers*). Children's cartoon or puppet characters like Mickey Mouse, Big Bird, Garfield, Spongebob Squarepants or Barney the Dinosaur may reappear in commercials, toys, and kid's meals at restaurants, all of which support a belief in their reality apart from the show.

Sometimes television may provide such a salient exemplar of an extremely unpleasant reality once the disbelief is suspended. Box 2.5 explores the feared and actual effects of a much-hyped TV movie on nuclear war.

Identification

The emotional involvement that we have watching a TV show depends in part on how much we *identify* with the character, that is, mentally compare ourselves to and imagine ourselves like that character. It is easier to identify with characters with whom we have more experience in common, although that is not a prerequisite for identification. There is a certain universality in most good drama. For example, a huge number of Americans, none of whom had ever been in slavery and most of whom were White, were moved by the landmark 1970s historical miniseries *Roots,* about generations of an African American family starting in slavery. Apparently, the basic humanity of the characters was portrayed so well that viewers could identify emotionally with the characters at some level without having experienced similar situations themselves.

The perceived reality of media is greater if our identification with the characters is such that they become significant persons in our own lives

---

BOX 2.5
NUCLEAR WAR ON TV

One of the most hyped television events of the 1980s was the 1983 ABC-TV movie *The Day After* (TDA), the drama depicting the aftermath of a nuclear attack on the American Midwest, aired in the height of the Cold War. Its anticipation became such a media event in itself that competing CBS'*60 Minutes* took the unprecedented step of covering TDA hype as one of its feature stories 1 hour before the movie's airing. It also became a political event. Antinuclear groups encouraged people to watch it, whereas conservatives decried it as an unfair move in the battle to mold public opinion on arms control issues. Mental health professionals worried over its impact on impressionable young minds and warned people to watch it only in groups and to not allow young children to see it at all. All of the heavy media coverage, of course, insured a large audience, which numbered over 100 million viewers, the largest audience to date for a TV movie.

  Psychologists Scholfield and Pavelchak (1985) studied exactly what impact this controversial film's airing had. Contrary to some fears or hopes, the movie actually did little to change attitudes about arms control and related issues. Arguments such as the possible failure of a deterrence-through-strength policy had been widely discussed in the media and were not really new ideas to most viewers. Many viewers felt that, horrible as it was, TDA's portrayal of the effects of a nuclear attack was actually milder than hype-weary viewers had expected and in fact was somewhat akin to many disaster and horror movies. The movie did have its effects, however. Viewers were more likely to seek information about nuclear issues and become involved in disarmament activities, and they reported thinking about nuclear war twice as often after seeing the film as they had before.

(Potter, 1988). We are more likely to imitate the behaviors or adopt the attitudes of characters we identify with. This has important social ramifications, and that is why there are greater antisocial effects of observing violent behavior by positive good guy characters than by criminal types (see chapter 9).

Empathy

Empathy, the ability to understand and feel what someone else is feeling, may be seen as emotional identification, and it is a very important factor in the enjoyment of media. We enjoy a comedy more if we can feel something of what the characters feel. We enjoy a ball game more if we play it ourselves and can relate to the tense feelings of being at bat with two outs in the bottom of the ninth and our team down by one run. We enjoy a tragic movie more if we can easily empathize with the suffering of another (Mills, 1993).

In the case of media (Zillmann, 1991b), empathy is diminished somewhat by the relatively omniscient position we occupy relative to the characters. We generally know more of what is going on than they do, as when we know that the bad guy is just around the bend waiting to ambush our unsuspecting hero. If we know the final outcome of some behavior, it is often difficult to become as emotionally involved as it would be if we knew as little as the character. Such enjoyment varies a lot depending on the genre, however. Audiences for reruns of sports events are almost nonexistent, whereas audiences for reruns of comedies hold up quite well. Apparently, the loyalty to the characters and show and the empathy and degree of parasocial interaction with them are crucial factors (Tannenbaum, 1980).

Empathy is composed of cognitive and emotional components. Cognitive empathy involves the ability to readily take the perspective of another, whereas emotional empathy involves readily responding at a purely emotional level. M. H. Davis, Hull, Young, and Warren (1987) showed that the level of both of these types of empathy influenced emotional reactions to viewing the films *Brian's Song* and *Who's Afraid of Virginia Woolf?*, but that each type of empathy influenced reactions in different ways.

Empathy has also been conceptualized as a three-factor construct (Zillmann, 1991b). One factor may override another that initially predominated. For example, suppose the initial natural, unlearned response to the victim of violence in a news story or cartoon is one of empathy. This may, however, be overridden by a less empathic response to the next news story, commercial, or cartoon action quickly following. Thus, what might otherwise elicit considerable empathy may not do so, in part due to the sound-bite nature of the medium of television. This could explain why it is so difficult to become caught up emotionally in a TV movie broken up by 2 commercials.

Another approach, not extensively examined in the research, is the extent to which media, especially television, teach empathy to children or could potentially do so, if more sensitivity were given to such issues by writers, directors, and networks (N. D. Feshbach, 1988; N. D. Feshbach & S. Feshbach, 1997).

Suspense

Suspense is usually characterized as an experience of uncertainty whose properties can vary from noxious to pleasant (Vorderer & Knobloch, 2000; Zillmann, 1991c). The suspense we feel in an adventure show or drama evolves as we anticipate the outcome and is maximal if some negative outcome (hero is about to die) appears to be highly likely but not absolutely certain; for example, everything points to disaster with just a slight hope of escape. If the negative outcome either is not very likely or is absolutely certain, there is not much suspense (Zillmann, 1980, 1991c). We experience a high level of suspense, for example, if our hero appears about to be blown up by a bomb, with just a slight chance to escape. Suspense is also heightened by the omniscient status of the viewer; we know something about imminent danger that the character doesn't know, and that knowledge heightens the suspense we feel. The physiological excitation of suspense is relatively slow to decay and may be transferred to subsequent activities (Zillmann, 1980, 1984, 1991c, 1996).

Suspense may be studied either through an examination of suspenseful texts or an analysis of the audience's activities, expectations, emotions, and relationships with the characters (Vorderer, Wulff, & Friedrichsen, 1996). The text-oriented approach examines such factors as outcome uncertainty, delay factors, and threats to the character. The reception approach studies the audience's identification with the character, their expectations and curiosity, their emotions, and their concurrent activities and social situation, which may enhance or detract from the experience of suspense. The fact that both aspects of suspense are important confirm how this experience emerges as the person interacts with the text of the medium to create the emotional experience of suspense.

Humor

One very common aspect of consuming media is the enjoyment that comes from experiencing something funny (D. Brown & Bryant, 1983; Zillmann, 2000; Zillmann & Bryant, 1991). But what makes something funny? Why is one line of comedy so hilarious and a very similar one not at all funny, and perhaps even offensive?

Most comedy involves some sort of incongruity, inconsistency, or contradiction, which is finally resolved, as in the punch line of a joke (Long & Graesser, 1988; McGhee, 1979; Perlmutter, 2000; Suls, 1983; Vaid, 1999; Wyer & Collins, 1992). Neither the incongruity nor resolution by itself is usually very funny. Although the joke "Two elephants got off the bus and left their luggage by the tree" is highly incongruous, it is not particularly funny because there is no resolution. On the other hand, "Two soldiers got off the bus and left their trunks by the tree" has a resolution, but it is not very funny either, because there is no incongruity. Only "Two elephants got off the bus and left their trunks by the tree" has both incongruity and resolution.

The best jokes offer some intellectual challenge, but not so much that we cannot get it or have to work too hard to do so. Some of the most satisfying jokes are very esoteric as in jokes involving knowledge from a particular group, such as a profession. What presents an adequate challenge for one person may not be for another. For example, many children find certain very predictable, even dumb, jokes funny, whereas adults do not. They are simply not novel or challenging enough for adults. Sometimes the relevant in-group may be the viewers of the show themselves; some jokes on *Friends* may be funny only to regular viewers of the show and those viewers may experience solidarity with others as they watch the show.

Another important concept in understanding media humor is the psychodynamic notion of *catharsis,* the emotional release of tension we feel from expressing some repressed feelings. For example, if you are very worried about some problem but talk to a friend and feel better just for having "gotten it off your chest," what you are experiencing is catharsis. Humor is often seen as a healthy and socially acceptable outlet for dealing with some of our darker feelings. For example, we may be able to deal with some of our own hidden sexual or hostile impulses by listening to a caustic comedian or talk-show host insult people or brazenly ask someone about their first sexual experience. We would never say those things ourselves but might secretly want to; hearing someone else do it partially fulfills our need to do so. Catharsis is often invoked to explain why people appreciate racist, ethnic, sexist, or sexual jokes. It is also frequently put forth as a socially beneficial outcome of consuming sexual or violent media, although research has failed to confirm such a conclusion (see chapters 9 and 10).

Social factors can make a lot of difference in the experience of humor (Apter, 1982; Vaid, 1999). Sometimes the presence of others watching with us enhances our enjoyment, particularly for broader, more raucous humor. Although an extreme example, consider watching *The Rocky Horror Picture Show* by yourself versus in a group. The presence of others may genuinely enhance our enjoyment, or we may outwardly appear to enjoy it more due to peer pressure to conform; if we are in a room full of people laughing uproariously at some TV show, it is hard to avoid at least a few smiles, even if we are not at all amused. This is the principle behind the inclusion of a laugh track on some sitcoms. The person who tells the joke is also an important factor. A joke making fun of Mexican Americans may be very funny if told by a Latino but highly offensive if told by an Anglo or an African American.

There are individual and cultural differences in appreciation of humor. Some people prefer puns, others prefer physical humor or practical jokes; still others prefer sexual or ethnic jokes. Also, societal standards change over time. In the very early days of television (early 1950s), *Amos and Andy* could make fun of African Americans as slow-witted; a few years later Ralph Kramden could playfully threaten his wife with physical violence on *The Honeymooners* ("One of these days, Alice, pow, right in the kisser!")

and the audience roared with laughter. Now we have the chance to laugh at more sexual innuendo on TV than we could then, but now Andy and Ralph somehow do not seem quite so funny.

All of these factors affect the dispositional consequences of moral assessment, as theorized by Zillmann (2000; Zillmann & Bryant, 1991). According to this view, the recipient of the humor is a "moral monitor" who either applauds or condemns the intentions of the other character(s). A lot depends on whether that response is positive or negative. For example, a sitcom character who responds to a witty putdown from another character with a retort in kind is implicitly offering approval and the viewers experience humor and liking for both characters. On the other hand, if the recipient character is offended and lashes back at the first character, it sets the stage for an antagonistic relationship, where viewers' emotional support goes to the "good guy" (usually the unfairly wounded party) and roots for the discomfort of the "bad guy." Both paradigms are common in comedy, but the dynamics are different and the experience of viewing is different.

Different cultures find different themes and approaches funny. In North American society, for example, certain topics are off limits or very touchy, at least for prime-time humor (late-night TV and some cable programs are more permissive). Jokes on U.S. TV about racism, feminism, violence against women, or mainstream religion are risky; such humor does exist, but people are likely to take offense and thus producers and comedians are very cautious. On the other hand, a Brazilian TV commercial for a department store chain during one Christmas season showed the Three Wise Men walking to Bethlehem. Suddenly, to a rock beat, they throw open their ornate robes and start dancing in their pastel underwear, featured on sale at the store. It seems unlikely that such an ad would be aired in the United States. See Box 2.6 for some examples of culture-specific humor that ran up against unfunny political realities.

One function of media humor is as a sort of leavening in the context of a more serious offering. A little so-called comic relief in the midst of a serious drama is much appreciated, although if done badly, it runs the risk of being in poor taste and thus offending people. If done well, it can increase motivation and interest and make the characters seem more human. If the humor is too funny, it may distract from the major content. Effects of humor in serious drama are complex and depend on many other factors, including viewer gender, character status (hero vs. villain), and context (King, 2000). This is particularly a concern with commercials. Some of the funniest and more creatively successful TV commercials have not been very effective at selling because the humor overshadowed the commercial message. People remember the gag but forget the product, not a situation that advertisers want!

BOX 2.6
HUMOR IN UNFRIENDLY POLITICAL CONTEXTS

Sometimes political realities conspire against humor. When the producers of *Sesame Street* tried to launch an Israeli version designed to promote harmony between Israelis and Palestinians, they ran into difficulty. Palestinians did not want their Muppets living on the same street as the Israeli Muppets. A later proposal to have the show set in a neutral park foundered on the problem of which side owned the park. In another example, a former president of Zimbabwe, Canaan Banana, banned all jokes about himself after tiring of endless banana jokes. Perhaps the most extreme case is North Korea, where all satire is banned because "everything is perfect in the people's paradise." Still, there are those who resist, as in the case of one enterprising Chinese wit who created a computer virus that destroyed the hard drive of anyone who answered "no" to the question, "Do you think that Prime Minister Li Peng is an idiot?" (What's So Funny? 1997).

Mood Management

Another function of media use, especially entertainment media, is seeking to maintain good moods and alleviate bad ones. People in good moods will seek the least engaging stimulation in order to perpetuate their current state, while people in negative moods will seek stimulation to alter their mood (Potts & Sanchez, 1994). This could help explain why happy people might frequently turn on some mindless sitcom rerun or unhappy people would watch an outrageous comedy that could distract them from their negative mood. Television may also direct attention away from ourselves and how we are failing to meet our ideal standards (Mosalenko & Heine, 2003).

MEDIA AS PERCEIVED REALITY

Now that we have examined some of the research types, theories, and psychological constructs used in the scientific study of the media, let us return for a more careful look at the theme introduced earlier: the reality created by the media.

The Reflection Myth

Often people think of the media as vehicles for reflecting the world around them. News stories report what happened in the world that day. Sitcoms reflect the values, lifestyles, and habits of their society. TV dramas and magazine fiction reflect the concerns and issues that viewers are struggling with. The presence of violence and offensive stereotypes merely reflects the ugly reality of an imperfect world. Advertising reflects the needs and wants that we have. Media, in this view, are a sort of window on reality. This view of media is used in authoritarian societies who attempt to control media and thus control their people's view of reality; see Box 2.7 for what is probably the most extreme modern example of such control.

BOX 2.7
NORTH KOREAN CINEMA AS MANIPULATOR OF REALITY

Surely the most rigidly controlled authoritarian society in the modern world is the North Korean police state ruled by Kim Jong-Il, and earlier his father Kim Il-Sung, since shortly after World War II. As well as being a ruthless dictator, the younger Mr. Kim is also a film fanatic, particularly enjoying American and Hong Kong action and horror films, which he sees at private screenings, although they are not available to his countrymen. He is thought to particularly enjoy the *Friday the Thirteenth* films and gangster movies like *Scarface* and *The Godfather*. All North Korean films are made according to Kim's 1973 book, *The Art of Cinema*, and are overtly for propaganda purposes. They show only a positive image of their country, in fact one of the most desperately poor and plundered in the world. The army is usually the hero who comes to rescue the people. For example, in one film, the army carried buckets of water for miles and joined hands to form a human dam to hold back a flood. Help comes from the army and from working harder, never from foreign nations, the UN, or non-governmental organizations. Kim also had a film made to model another favorite of his, *Titanic*. This film told of the sinking of a North Korean ship in 1945 and even had a love story modeled on the Kate Winslet-Leonardo DiCaprio romance in the 1997 film. Perhaps Kim's most outrageous act was to kidnap the admired South Korean film director Shin Sang-Ok. He captured him and put him to work making North Korean films, among them *Pulgasari,* an imitation of the Japanese *Godzilla,* transformed into an iron-eating lizard who fights with the peasants against their feudal overlords (N. Korean movies' propaganda role, 2003).

Would anybody believe such heavy-handed messages so far removed from reality? Probably so. North Koreans are not allowed to leave their country or have any exposure to foreigners or foreign media, and they have heard this heavy propaganda all their lives. Even Kim Jong-Il hardly even leaves the country; he may very well believe that his beloved American horror and gangster movies portray typical American life.

The reflection view is not the only way to view mass communication, however. It may be that we think certain events and issues are important because the news tells us they are. Sitcoms may portray certain values, lifestyles, and habits which are then adopted by society. TV dramas deal with certain issues that are then considered by the viewers. Stereotypes seen on television implicitly teach young viewers what different groups of people are like, and the presence of much violence on TV teaches that the world is a violent place. Advertising convinces us that we have certain needs and wants that we did not know we had before. In this view, media are not merely reflecting what is out there in the world. Rather, they are constructing a world that then becomes reality for the consumer. This world may be accepted by TV viewers, who are often unaware of such a process happening, as they believe they are only being entertained. Soon the world as constructed by media may become so implanted in our minds that we cannot distinguish it from reality.

Do the media reflect the world or create a new reality? Certainly media do in many ways reflect what is out there in the world. However, they also choose what to tell us about what is out there in the world (agenda setting), and we then accept that interpretation, which then becomes part of our memory and our experience. In this book, we examine how media create a world which then becomes our reality. This cognitive perspective focuses on the mental construction of reality that we form as a result of our contact with print and broadcast media. One's constructed reality often differs substantially from objective reality in ways that one is not always aware of. The plan of this book is to examine various content areas from a cognitive psychological perspective, particularly focusing on the theme of how media create a reality.

The Study of Perceived Reality

Each of the theoretical approaches discussed earlier has something to say about studying the perceived reality that we cognitively construct through interaction with media. For example, agenda setting (McCombs, 1994; McCombs & Reynolds, 2002; Dearing & Rogers, 1996) tells us what is important to think about to begin with. Social cognitive theory (Bandura, 2002) examines how we learn the behavioral component of this reality. Cultivation theory (Gerbner et al., 2002; Signorielli & Morgan, 1990) focuses on the construction of a world view. Uses and gratifications theory (Palmgreen, 1984; A. M. Rubin, 1983, 2002; Windahl, 1981) looks at the uses we make of media and the gratifications they give us, increasingly connecting this research to an examination of the effects of media. Socialization theories stress how this knowledge becomes a part of how we learn what it is like to be an adult member of our society. The Limited

Capacity Model (Lang, 2000) looks at the knowledge structures that we create from exposure to the media.

When we speak of the reality perceived from the media, this is actually a more complex construct than it may first appear. At least two different components are involved (Fitch, Huston, & Wright, 1993; Potter, 1988). The central factor in perceived reality is *factuality*, or *magic window*. This is the belief in the literal reality of media messages. This reality can be conveyed at the level of either style or content. The style of news reporting, for example, may convey a message of factual correctness more strongly than the style of an entertainment program. The content of action-adventure shows presenting a world that is very dangerous may cultivate a view that the world is also like that (Gerbner, et al., 1986, 2002; Signorielli, 1990).

The understanding of factuality develops gradually (Davies, 1997). Two-year-olds do not understand the representational nature of TV images at all and will try to answer a TV person talking to them. By around age 10, children's factuality judgments are essentially equivalent to adults. During the transition period, as they learn to read TV programs, their emotional experience may be affected by the complexity of the plot and also by how realistic they perceive the program to be. For example, Weiss and Wilson (1998) found that the higher the degree of realism attributed to an episode of the sitcom *Full House*, the more concerned elementary schoolchildren were about similar negative emotional events in their own lives. Even relatively mundane factors can affect perceived reality. For example, a larger screen size can lead to greater arousal and involvement of the viewer (Detenber & Reeves, 1996; Grabe, Lombard, Reich, Bracken, & Ditton, 1999; Lombard, Reich, Grabe, Bracken, & Ditton, 2000).

One does not have to believe in the literal reality of media to have it become real for them. A second component of perceived reality is *social realism*, which refers to the perceived similarity or usefulness of the media representation to one's own life, even while recognizing its fictional nature. For example, a viewer with a strong belief that soap operas present very real-life situations would expect more application to their own life than another viewer who feels that soap operas present wildly unrealistic and purely escapist content (A. M. Rubin & Perse, 1988). Shapiro and Chock (2003) found that viewers rely heavily on typicality to judge the social reality of television; the more typical a situation seems, the more real it is judged to be. Because of their much lesser amount of life experience, young children often see greater social realism than adults do in television content, in that they have less with which to compare the media representation to assess its reality. In general, media have greater effects on those who impute a higher degree of social realism to it. This has important consequences whether we are talking about violence, sex, advertising, news or values.

Social realism can be enhanced by the degree to which viewers believe that a character is active in their own lives. In extreme cases there is a tremendous outpouring of grief for these parasocial media friends we have never met, most notably what occurred following the death of Princess Diana in 1997. The character need not even be real. When the network many years ago killed off Col. Henry Blake of $M*A*S*H$ on his way home from Korea, they were deluged with letters from grief-stricken and irate fans who did not appreciate the intrusion of wartime reality into their sitcom. See Fitch et al. (1993) and Potter (1988) for further discussion of the construct of perceived reality.

CONCLUSION

Each of the theoretical perspectives has contributed some helpful insights to the understanding of media and their effects. There has yet to emerge one theoretical approach that adequately captures all aspects, including cognitive, emotional, and behavioral. The rest of this book will take a fairly eclectic cognitive approach, drawing on various theoretical perspectives to approach the study of how media construct reality. In fact, the different theories are not necessarily mutually exclusive in all ways and may in fact be quite complementary. The meaning of something in the media, at either a cognitive or an emotional level, depends on how that information is processed during our experience of interacting with the medium. Each of the theoretical perspectives reviewed in this chapter has something useful to say about the formation of this meaning and its consequences. Elements of the different theories are brought in as appropriate in discussion of the topics in the rest of the book.

The media create a reality for us in many different areas, drawing on different psychological processes as they do so. Next, let us turn to the first set of those perceived realities created by media, namely, our knowledge of what different groups of people are like.

CHAPTER **3**

Media Portrayals of Groups: Distorted Social Mirrors

Q: What percent of teenage girls from Fiji suffered from eating disorders in 1995, before the advent of television to the island nation, and how many after?

A: 3% in 1995. Three years later, 15% did, with another 29% "at risk" for eating disorders. 74% of the teens said they felt "too big and fat." (Goodman, 1999; Numbers, 1999)

Q: How do today's advertising models compare in weight to real women?

A: The models weigh 23% less than the average woman, compared to only 8% less in the 1970s. They are also taller and generally of a very unusual body type (tall, thin, small-hipped). If they have large breasts, they are probably implants, since women of that body type seldom have large breasts (Kilbourne, 1995). All this is happening at the same time as the average women's size has increased from 8 to 14 since 1985! (Kher, 2003)

Q: How many television commercials are targeted at people over 50?

A: Less than 10%, in spite of the fact that this group controls half of the disposable income in the United States.

What do you know about Mexican Americans? Arabs? Jews? Farmers? Schizophrenics? Aging people? One of the major perceived realities that media help create for us involves information about groups of people. Through media we are exposed to a much broader range of people than most of us would ever encounter in our own lives. Not only are media our introduction to these people, but sometimes they are practically the only source of our information about them. Sometimes *everything* that we know about some kinds of people comes from television. Some rural White North Americans have never seen any African Americans or Jews in person.

Many urbanites have never met a real farmer. Most people of the world have never met someone from the United States. In such cases, the media portrayal of African Americans or farmers or North Americans is reality for them. Even in a study done many years ago, children reported that most of their information about people from different nationalities came from their parents and television, with TV becoming increasingly important as the child grew older (Lambert & Klineberg, 1967).

In this chapter we examine primarily the U.S. media image of different groups of people and look at the consequences of such portrayals. The concerns in some of the areas are widely known and discussed (e.g., women, African Americans), and, in the case of some minorities, have been widely examined in research (e.g., Graves, 1980, 1996; Greenberg, 1986; Greenberg & Atkin, 1982; Greenberg, Mastro, & Brand, 2002). Similar concerns about portrayals of other groups have received relatively little attention (e.g., farmers, Arabs, police officers). Although the issue is relevant to all media, television is the primary medium of concern, considering both programming and commercials, as well as movies seen on video or DVD. Although the focus here is on television in the United States, the same principles, if not all the same specifics, hold true for any nation's broadcasting.

Although these issues have been widely discussed and good content analyses performed, rigorous scientific research addressing the effects of group portrayals has been much more scarce. It is difficult to isolate media effects from other influences to establish firm causal relationships. Although all theoretical perspectives discussed in chapter 2 have made their contributions to this area, perhaps the most useful are cultivation and socialization theories. The prevailing portrayal of some groups of people will increasingly come to be the perceived reality in those consumers who partake heavily of the media.

PORTRAYALS OF THE SEXES

To begin with, let us examine gender portrayals. What do media say about what it means to be a man or woman? For reviews of research on gender portrayals, see Durkin (1985a, 1985b), Gerbner (1997), Gunter (1986), and Signorielli (2001).

The View of Women

We have heard a lot in recent years about stereotyping of women by the media, but what, exactly, does content analysis research tell us about the way women are portrayed? Some of these concerns are very familiar, whereas others are more subtle.

Numbers. Perhaps the most basic gender asymmetry is that there are far fewer females than males. Content analyses of characters on television shows in the 1970s, 1980s, and 1990s showed about twice as many men as women in prime time dramas and three to four times as many in children's shows (Fejes, 1992; Gerbner, 1997; Signorielli, 1993; Thompson & Zerbinos, 1995). On ensemble shows of such diverse genres as *Saturday Night Live, ER, Everybody Loves Raymond, Home Improvement, Who's Line Is It Anyway?, Seinfeld, Frasier, Garfield,* and *Sesame Street,* a large majority of the characters have been and continue to be male. The percentage of female characters on U.S. TV only increased from 28 to 36% from 1975–1995, and only 20% of characters ages 45–64 were women (Gerbner, 1997). Until such mid-1980s shows as *Cagney and Lacey, The Golden Girls, Designing Women,* and *Kate and Allie,* shows with all-women lead characters were largely nonexistent in the United States, with very infrequent exceptions like *One Day at a Time* and the arguably sexist *Charlie's Angels* of the 1970s. However, virtually all-male shows have been common through much of the history of television (e.g., *Bonanza, Barney Miller, My Three Sons, Spin City, Simon and Simon, Teenage Mutant Ninja Turtles,* Mickey Mouse and Donald Duck cartoons).

Although women appear almost as often as men as characters in commercials, the voice-over announcer is male 83% to 90% of the time (Bretl & Cantor, 1988; Ferrante, Haynes, & Kingsley, 1988; Lovdahl, 1989), a figure virtually unchanged from the early 1970s (Dominick & Rauch, 1972). Children's cartoon characters are male three times as often as they are female (Dobrow & Gidney, 1998; Thompson & Zerbinos, 1995). Music videos show at least twice as many males as females and tend to reinforce traditional stereotypes (J. D. Brown & Campbell, 1986; Sherman & Dominick, 1986; Sommers-Flanagan, Sommers-Flanagan, & Davis, 1993; Toney & Weaver, 1994; Took & Weiss, 1994; Vincent, Davis, & Boruszkowski, 1987). Photos of men outnumber photos of women everywhere in the newspaper except the lifestyle section (Luebke, 1989). On radio, disc jockeys, news anchors and reporters, musicians, and voice-over announcers all are still overwhelmingly male, although increasing numbers of female voices are being heard (Melton & Fowler, 1987). A substantial minority of news anchors and weathercasters are now women, although far fewer sportscasters are. In a content analysis of guests interviewed on ABC's *Nightline* from 1985 to 1988, Croteau and Hoynes (1992) found that only 10% were women.

Not surprisingly, when children were asked to name their favorite characters on informational TV programs, both boys and girls were more likely to think of male than female characters and remembered more traditionally masculine than feminine behaviors (Calvert, Kotler, Zehnder, & Shockey, 2003).

Physical Appearance.   A second concern is that women are too often portrayed as youthful beauties whose duty it is to stay young and attractive to please their men. Once a woman is no longer so young and attractive, she becomes an object of ridicule. Support for this criticism comes especially from the subtle messages that a woman must not allow herself to age. This message appears especially, although not exclusively, in advertising, the media content with the most stereotyped gender portrayals. Women have become slimmer during the 20th century (Percy & Lautman, 1994), but the weight gap between models and real women is widening. In the mid-1990s, models weighed 23% less than the average woman, a figure up from 8% less in 1975 (Kilbourne, 1995). *Seventeen,* the most widely read magazine among teen girls, devotes two thirds of its editorial content to fashion and beauty topics, with most of the remaining articles about relational topics like finding boyfriends and being popular (K. Phillips, 1993). Wrinkles, gray hair, or a "mature" figure are to be avoided at all costs. At least until recently, women obviously over 30, and especially those over 50, have been grossly underrepresented on television and in all sorts of advertising. When present, they were often seen as stereotyped "old folks" that no one would want to grow up and be like (H. Davis & J. H. Davis, 1985). Women in TV ads are younger than men (70% vs. 40% under 35, respectively), ratios unchanged from the early 1970s (Dominick & Rauch, 1972; Ferrante et al., 1988).

   The idealized portrayal of feminine beauty, especially in advertising, is a highly unusual body type, namely very tall, very thin, and small-hipped. These characteristics co-occur in less than 5% of the adult female population, but models are usually of this type. The other common supermodel characteristic, large breasts, is an attribute so infrequent for this body type that at least one leading scholar in the area concludes that they almost surely must be implants (Kilbourne, 1995). Computerized image construction of models and the use of body doubles, even for very attractive stars, are common. For example, in a prominent movie poster for *Pretty Woman,* what appeared to be actress Julia Roberts was, in fact, composite body parts selected from the best of several models, plus computer graphic enhancement. Some of her sex scenes in the film used body doubles with even more beautiful bodies or body parts (Kilbourne, 1995). For a look at the complex interaction of food, sex, and weight loss, see Box 3.1.

Breast-Feeding.   The breasts are presented on media as sexual organs, even in the context of their intended biological use. Consider the case of breast-feeding, now recommended by virtually the entire medical community as the preferred method of infant feeding. Advertising, and sometimes even photos in feature magazine stories on breast-feeding, show women

---

BOX 3.1
FOOD, SEX, AND WEIGHT LOSS IN THE IDEAL WOMAN
(Kilbourne, 1995)

Two major themes of magazine articles and advertising aimed at women are food and weight loss. Food is often presented as a way to deal with emotional needs (break up with a guy and treat yourself to some ice cream) and is sometimes even presented as a substitute for sex, as when a woman comes close to having an orgasm from eating fine chocolate. Metaphors of addiction and loss of control are commonplace (can't control myself with this candy), sometimes even modeling binge eating (downing a whole quart of ice cream). At the same time, however, women (but not men) are made to feel ashamed or guilty for eating, with supermodel thinness presented as the moral equivalent of virginity, both resulting from keeping one's appetites under control. Never mind the fact that no amount of dieting would turn most women into supermodels. This fear of losing control and losing one's figure is a powerful appeal in the advertising of everything from diet programs to cigarettes. Do such appeals work? With half of teens and adult women on diets, most of which fail, and 75% of normal-weight women thinking they are fat, it would appear that they do.

---

breast-feeding in *very revealing* poses. It would appear that the entire breast must be bared to nurse, when in fact an infant may be nursed in public quite discreetly without revealing the breast. Prospective mothers seeing such images may be turned away from nursing, thinking they do not want to disrobe to that extent in public. Prospective fathers may fear that their wives' nursing entails a sexual seductiveness. Employers seeing such images may be less inclined to allow breast-feeding in the workplace, mistakenly believing it requires considerable undressing and/or sexually revealing poses by nursing women. Advocates of breast-feeding worry that such media images discourage mothers from offering the medically best nutrition for their infants (Dettwyler, 1995).

Concerns of Women. Media women are disproportionately seen as homemakers and mothers, with their business, professional, and community roles downplayed or not represented at all. This is especially true of advertising (Knill, Pesch, Pursey, Gilpin, & Perloff, 1981; K. C. Schneider & S. B. Schneider, 1979), although the range of occupational roles for women in ads has increased (Ferrante et al., 1988). Not limited to the United States, the stereotyping of women in advertisements occurs in many societies (Gilly, 1988).

Women are often seen as dependent on men and needing their protection. Even relatively egalitarian TV families generally show the wife deferring to the husband more often than the reverse, although the behaviors showing this are much more subtle than those of 30 years ago. Women are not seen making important decisions or engaging in important activities as often as men. Advertising often portrays women as terribly perplexed and even obsessive about such matters as dirty laundry or spotted glassware. Women squeezing toilet paper or berating others about soiled clothing also make this point. Early sitcoms showing women playing bridge or gossiping with neighbors all day also illustrate this concern. Newspaper cartoons, particularly strips like *Blondie* or *The Girls*, also frequently show traditional women primarily preoccupied with trivial concerns, although changes do occur even here, as when Blondie started her own catering business in 1991. Brabant and Mooney (1986) found that gender images in Sunday comics had changed little from the mid-1970s to the mid-1980s.

Although we have come a long way from the *Father Knows Best* (1959) dad telling his daughter "Be dependent, a little helpless now and then. The worst thing you can try to do is beat a man at his own game" (Douglas, 1997, p. 24), some of the most gender-stereotyped TV shows are those aimed at children. Often the females in children's shows have been rather frilly and wimpy supporting characters like Smurfette of *The Smurfs*, Baby Bop of *Barney and Friends*, or April O'Neill of *Teenage Mutant Ninja Turtles*, who mainly seem to nurture and support their male colleagues (Crimmins, 1991; Douglas, 1994). Some new shows beginning in the late-1990s, particularly on Nickelodeon and Disney, offered more complex and positive role models for girls (*The Secret World of Alex Mack, Lizzie McGuire, Sister Sister, That's So Raven, Clarissa Explains It All, Buffy the Vampire Slayer*).

Sometimes the power that women do exercise is used in very underhanded and conniving ways, often directly or indirectly involving sexuality. The soap opera businesswoman who sleeps her way to the top is a good example. There are subtle messages that it is not ladylike to confront men (or even other women) directly, but it is perfectly acceptable to deviously trick them. Portraying sexuality as a weapon of power subtly de-emphasizes and even degrades its tender and relational aspects. Even strong female characters like those in *Sex and the City* or *Melrose Place* are very interested in sex and do not hesitate to use it to further their interests. Even relatively powerless victims of possible sexual harassment are often presented as conniving, devious, and manipulative. For example, news media portrayals of various women allegedly involved with President Bill Clinton (e.g., Monica Lewinsky, Paula Jones, Gennifer Flowers) often received this treatment. Female uses of power are not confined to adult media; Lucy, in the cartoon *Peanuts*, dominates the boys through intimidation.

Some current gender differences may be more subtle than those in the past. For example, a content analysis by Zhao and Gantz (2003) found that male fictional TV characters initiated more disruptive interruptions, while females initiated more cooperative interruptions, but only if the interrupter was of higher status than the interruptee and if the conversation was about work. This suggests gender asymmetry in portrayals of the workplace might be more unbalanced than in friendship conversations. See Tannen (1994) for an excellent discussion of language, power, and gender issues in the workplace.

The Superwoman. A more recent concern, focusing on the unrealistic superwoman, is directed specifically at a relatively new media portrayal that has arisen in an attempt to represent modern women more accurately and fairly. Women characters in TV series are often employed outside the home, although only half as often as in real life (34% on TV vs. 67% in reality in 1998). Those who are depicted as employed are most often in professional or managerial positions, and many are also mothers. Although some of these characters are positive role models of professional women, they appear to handle the demands of career, wife, and parent with amazingly little stress and difficulty. Only 8.6% of TV series episodes or characters showed anyone dealing with any kind of job vs. family stress. Real women in two-career families need such positive role models, but they also need some acknowledgment that the great difficulties they experience balancing all of those responsibilities are not abnormal. The supermoms make it look all too easy.

The superwoman myth is also reinforced by advertising. For example, one perfume ad says that a woman can "bring home the bacon, fry it up in a pan, but never let him forget he's a man." In other words, a woman can (or at least should) work outside the home all day, come home and cook dinner for her husband, and still have enough energy left to be sexy for him that evening! Are these realistic messages to send to young girls about what it means to be a woman in today's society? Are these helpful expectations to send to young boys about the women they will eventually marry?

Women and Violence. A final concern is that women are subtly linked with violence, especially as victims of male violence. Some commercials or programs playing on the seductiveness of women also suggest that they are animals to be tamed, something wild to be brought into line by men. A high fashion ad selling negligees by showing a scantily clad woman being playfully attacked by two men, or an auto magazine ad showing a woman in a bikini chained inside a giant shock absorber subtly link sexuality and violence. Perfume ads may stress the wildness, the toughness, and the challenge of women and imply the need for an attack from a man in response to this irresistible fragrance.

Although we may not find Ralph Kramden's (*The Honeymooners*) mock threat of his wife with violence ("One of these days, Alice, pow! Right in the kisser!") as amusing as we did in its 1955 debut, far more graphic instances of violence toward women are common, especially in the so-called slasher films (e.g., *The Texas Chainsaw Massacre, Friday the Thirteenth, Nightmare on Elm Street,* and *Halloween* series) aimed at teenagers and in violent pornography sold to adults. The association of women with violence is a lesser concern on most network television series, although it does occur. When Luke and Laura on *General Hospital* fell in love and married after he raped her, a message was sent to men that, when a woman says "no," she may really mean "yes." In fact, this image of a woman resisting but secretly wanting a man to force himself on her has a long cinematic tradition, including such classics as *Gone With the Wind* and numerous John Wayne westerns. The sex-violence link is also a major concern on rock videos shown on MTV and premium cable channels (J. D. Brown & Campbell, 1986; R. C. Vincent, et al., 1987). Possible desensitization effects of such portrayals are examined in chapter 10.

Although we have so far focused on women, there are also some serious concerns about the media portrayals of men. Although these have received less general attention and scientific research than portrayals of women, unrealistic stereotyping is also a problem here.

The View of Men

Emotionless Beings. The predominant image of men is calm, cool, self-confident, decisive, and emotionless. Although this may be positive in many ways, it sends the message to young boys that this is what men are supposed to be like, and if one cannot deny his feelings or at least keep them all inside, he is not a real man. The Marlboro Man is the quintessential TV man, but many classic TV fathers come in a close second. Who could imagine Ward (*Leave It to Beaver*) or Jim (*Father Knows Best*) shedding a tear? This picture has changed somewhat; modern TV dads like Tim (*Home Improvement*) or Raymond (*Everybody Loves Raymond*) are allowed to cry occasionally, although even they are generally somewhat embarrassed and ashamed to do so. Most men in advertising are looking blankly at no one with a vacant stare (often shielded by sunglasses), whereas women in ads appear to be looking at someone and are often smiling or giving some other hint of what they are feeling.

Physical Appearance. Like women, men are portrayed as young and attractive, but the rules are a little different. Well-developed upper-body muscles are an important part of the ideal male beauty. A study of images of men and women in heterosexual erotic magazines found that photos of women were more sexualized and idealized than photos of men (Thomas, 1986). Also, it is not quite as bad for a man to age as for a woman (H. Davis & Davis, 1985). A little gray hair may make a man look distinguished or possibly even sexy, whereas it just makes a woman look old. It is not unusual to see a man with some gray hair giving the news, sports, or weather, but seeing a woman with gray hair in these roles is more unusual.

In spite of this, the message to stay young is still a strong one for men. One example is baldness. Although a sizable proportion of men lose their hair to a greater or lesser degree starting in their 20s, few sympathetic leading male characters in TV series or even in commercials ever have even the slightest receding hairline. A bald character, when he does appear at all, is usually an object of at least subtle ridicule (e.g., the pompous George Jefferson of *The Jeffersons*, the stupid husband who needs his wife in the commercial to find him the right laxative), or at best a character like the eccentric chap who doesn't believe oatmeal really could have all that fiber. Baldness in a TV series character is most often an indication of villainy, unfashionable eccentricity (e.g., Yul Brynner's King of Siam), or, at best, a sort of benign asexuality (e.g., Capt. Stubing on *Love Boat*). Even middle-aged or elderly male characters usually have full heads of hair. The occasional man who openly wears a hairpiece is the butt of tired old toupee jokes. The few apparent positive exceptions like Kojak, Picard of *Star Trek, The Next Generation*, and some of Ed Asner's characters are clearly middle-aged, if not older.

There is alarming evidence that men are becoming increasingly obsessed with their bodies and feeling increasingly inadequate in comparison to the heavily-muscled media models (Pope, Phillips, & Olivardia, 2000). Just as so many women see an unrealistically thin body as normal, so many young men see a heavily muscled upper body as normal and readily attainable. In one study cited by Pope, et al., over half of a sample of boys ages 11 to 17 chose as an ideal body build a type completely unattainable without steroids. Many men work out regularly in the gym to build up their muscles but may wear full sweats while doing so and take no shower in the locker room afterwards, due to uncomfortableness in having others see their body. Male models of the twenty-first century have far larger "six-packs" on their chest than models of twenty years earlier. Star Wars, Batman, and G. I. Joe action figures of 2000 were far broader in the shoulders, beefier in the chest, and smaller in the hips than their 1970s' counterparts. For example, proportionally, the 2001 G. I. Joe Extreme had a 55-inch chest and 27-inch biceps, the latter over twice as big as the biceps of a fairly athletic real man

(Chamberlain, 2002). In fact, this look would be all but unattainable by real men and certainly not without the use of dangerous anabolic steroids.

Besides the need for bulging "pecs" and "delts," many young men are concerned with other shortcomings of their bodies, including hair (must have plenty of it on your head), height (must be taller than your woman), genital size (need enough bulge under your pants), and even breast size (can't look too large and thus feminine). When these concerns become strong enough to be seriously maladaptive in one's life, one may suffer from Body Dysmorphic Disorder (BDD).

Friendships. Although media images of friendship are common for both men and women, the nature of those friendships is different (Spangler, 1989, 1992). Women show a greater degree of emotional intimacy in their friendships than men do. TV images of male bonding go back to the Westerns of the 1950s, where a cowboy and his sidekick went everywhere together. Sitcom friends like Ralph and Ed on *The Honeymooners*, Andy and Barney on *The Andy Griffith Show*, Hawkeye and B. J. on *M*A*S*H*, or the Chandler-Joey-Ross triad on *Friends* were clearly close emotionally, although that was seldom explicitly discussed, unlike the more overtly emotional women's friendships of Lucy and Ethel on *I Love Lucy*, Mary and Rhoda on *The Mary Tyler Moore Show*, or the women on *Sex and the City*. This gender difference may fairly accurately reflect real life in terms of different communication styles of the sexes (Tannen, 1990). See Box 3.2 for a closer look at the masculine socialization messages in beer commercials.

Domestic Roles. Although men are generally portrayed as competent professionally, they are often seen as bungling nincompoops with regard to housework and child care. TV fathers of year-old infants often do not know how to change a diaper; this is unlikely to be true in even the most traditional real family. Men in commercials often seem to know nothing about housekeeping or cooking and have to be bailed out by their wives, who, in the domestic sphere, are portrayed as very knowledgeable experts. Over the last twenty years there have been periodic TV shows and movies portraying the ineptness of men dealing with small children (*Full House*, *My Two Dads*, *Three Men and a Baby*, *Mr. Mom*, *Daddy Day Care*, *Two and a Half Men*). Although they always learned and grew as persons from the experience, these men's initial ineptitude would seem to suggest that childcare is not a part of the normal male role. In a similar vein, men are often portrayed as insensitive and rough interpersonally (e.g., not knowing how to talk to their children about sensitive personal issues).

In a study of African American Upward Bound high school students' reactions to episodes of *Good Times* and *The Cosby Show*, Berry (1992) found that a majority of the youth found the more authoritarian James Evans

---

BOX 3.2
MESSAGES OF MASCULINITY IN BEER COMMERCIALS

In a content analysis of TV beer commercials, Strate (1992) argued that there is strong socialization occurring about what it means to be a man. Specifically, he claimed that five questions are addressed by such ads:

1. *What kinds of things do men do?* First of all, they drink (although they cannot ever be shown actually drinking on television). This almost always occurs in the company of others in the context of good times. Beer is seen as a reward for a job well done and is a common marker for the end of a work day, such as stopping for a drink with friends after work.

2. *What kinds of settings do men prefer?* Beer is identified with nature and the outdoors, through images like a cowboy, animals, or a clear mountain stream. The second popular setting is the bar, which is always clean, smokeless, and full of polite and non-intoxicated, upper middle-class people. Also, no one ever seems to pay for a drink, either in cash or consequences.

3. *How do boys become men?* Beer serves as a reward for a challenge or an initiation or rite of passage.

4. *How do men relate to each other?* Men relate to each other primarily in groups (interestingly enough, a contrast to the frequent loner image of masculinity). Beer drinking is the shared activity that brings the group together and is never seen as being harmful.

5. *How do men relate to women?* Although women are largely absent in beer commercials, they are occasionally there as rather passive and peripheral accessories. The male group is clearly more important.

Anybody watching sports events or other programming with many beer commercials receives a heavy dose of such messages. Many of these viewers are children. What are boys learning from beer commercials about the use of alcohol and what it means to be a man?

---

of *Good Times* a more positive role model than Dr. Cliff Huxtable of *The Cosby Show,* contrary to what the producers had probably intended. Perhaps James better fit what the youth thought a real man should be like.

Effects of Gender Stereotyping

Although it is relatively easy to describe gender role portrayals on television, the question of their effects is a far more difficult research problem (Durkin, 1985b; Fejes, 1992). Negative or narrow gender images become a serious concern if they are seen as reflective of real life. Although no single exposure to a sexist commercial or sitcom episode is likely to irreparably harm anyone, the huge number of multiple exposures to commercials (100,000 or more ads seen by the time of one's high school graduation) is unlikely not to have some effect, given what we have learned from cultivation and modeling research. In general, effects of repetition are often underestimated; if the same themes about how men and women are supposed to behave and think keep recurring on show after show, that is more likely to be perceived as reality. For example, women may expect men to dominate them and to be relatively insensitive, or men may expect women to be submissive to them and to be preoccupied with their appearance.

Not only may we take the television portrayals of the opposite sex as reality, but we may take the portrayals of our own gender as cues to the ways we should look and behave. When we fail to meet these standards, that failure sets us up for experiencing low self-esteem. For example, a woman who feels frazzled meeting the demands of career, family, and homemaking may feel very inadequate comparing herself to the media superwoman who does it all so well. Similarly, a man losing his hair or a woman losing her youthful figure may feel like a loser when using video bodies as the standard (Myers & Biocca, 1992).

Such concerns are especially important when considering effects on children. Children who are heavy viewers of TV hold more traditional sex-role attitudes (Lemar, 1977; O'Bryant & Corder-Bolz, 1978). This relationship is particularly strong when limited to the amount viewed of sitcoms and soap operas with traditional gender-role orientations (Ex, Janssens, & Korzilius, 2002). Using an argument similar to cultivation theory, Kimball (1986) found that sex-role attitudes of children were less strongly sex-typed than normal in a town with no access to television; however, their attitudes became more stereotypical after the introduction of television. Wroblewski and Huston (1987) concluded that repeated TV appearances of women in traditionally male occupations can lead to more open attitudes in preteen girls toward considering those occupations. Other studies have shown that exposure to advertising portraying women in egalitarian fashion is followed by more accepting attitudes in young viewers (Geis, Brown, Jennings, & Porter, 1984; Jennings, Geis, & Brown, 1980). Botta (1999) found that media variables accounted for 15–33% of the variance in measures of adolescent girls' drives for thinness, body dissatisfaction, bulimic behaviors, and thin ideal endorsement. Women exposed to TV ads portraying women as sex objects judged their current body size as larger and men judged their current body size thinner, compared to control groups (Lavine, Sweeney, & Wagner, 1999). Adolescent girls exposed to TV with conspicuously fat female characters were more likely to exhibit symptoms of eating disorders (Harrison, 2000; Harrison & Cantor, 1997). Obviously we cannot expect any given type of portrayal of the sexes to have a uniform effect on the public. For example, McIntyre, Hosch, Harris, and Norvell (1986) found that less traditional men and women were more sensitive to and more critical of stereotypic portrayals of women in TV commercials, in contrast to more traditional people. Dieting women may react differently to thin media images than non-dieting women (Mills, Polivy, Herman, & Tigge-man, 2002). Men who are more prone to use violence are affected more by sexually violent media (see chapters 9 and 10). Sometimes behaviors related in people's minds (e.g., reading women's magazines and anorexia-risk be-haviors) in fact have different antecedents (Thomsen, McCoy, Gustafson, & Williams, 2002). Parental discussion and mediation can lessen the negative effects of media body-image stereotyping (Nathanson, Wilson, McGee, & Sebastian, 2002). The perceived reality differs across individuals.

Now that we have looked at media's view of the sexes, let us turn to ethnic minorities, starting with a developmental model of the portrayals of minorities in media.

THE FOUR STAGES OF MINORITY PORTRAYALS

A useful model was presented many years ago by Clark (1969), who identi-fied four chronological stages of the portrayals of minorities on television. The first stage is *nonrecognition,* in which the minority group is simply excluded from television. It is not ridiculed; it is not caricatured; it is sim-ply not there. Someone from an alien culture watching the programming would never know that such people even existed in that society. For ex-ample, until quite recently this was largely the position of gay and lesbian people on U.S. television.

The second stage of minority portrayals is *ridicule.* Here the dominant group bolsters its own self-image by putting down and stereotyping the minority, presenting its members as incompetent, unintelligent buffoons. Very early television programs like *Amos and Andy* and characters like Stepan Fetchit or Jack Benny's valet Rochester reflect this stage in terms of portrayals of African Americans. On the current scene, Arabs are a good example of a group at the stage of ridicule; we seldom see positive or likable Arab or Arab American characters on U.S. TV.

A third stage is *regulation,* where minority group members appear as protectors of the existing order (e.g., police officers, detectives, spies). Such roles were typical of the first positive roles open to African Americans in the 1960s; one often sees Latinos in the same types of roles on U.S. TV today.

The final stage is *respect,* where the minority group appears in the same full range of roles, both good and bad, that the majority does. This is not to say that there is never a stereotyped character or that all the characters are sympathetic, but just that there is a wide variety: good and intelligent characters as well as evil and stupid ones.

Now let's turn to looking specifically at the media's portrayal of several particular minorities, starting with African Americans, the minority receiving the most public attention and scientific study for the longest time.

AFRICAN AMERICANS

How Are They Portrayed?

The most studied ethnic group portrayal in U.S. media has been African Americans, who comprised about 12% of the U.S. population in the 2000 census. Until the 1960s, there were almost no African Americans as models in mainstream U.S. advertising (Colfax & Steinberg, 1972; Kassarjian, 1969; see also Box 3.3), and the only African Americans in prime-time TV programming were limited to a few stereotyped and demeaning roles, such as the affable but dim-witted African American friends on *Amos and Andy*. At least, however, the TV series employed African American actors; the earlier radio version of the show had used White actors speaking their interpretations of Black English. The percentage of African Americans among people

---

BOX 3.3
HISTORICAL VIEW OF AFRICAN AMERICANS
IN ADVERTISING

African Americans have been a part of advertising in America as far back as ads for the sale of slaves or return of runaways (Kern-Foxworth, 1994). In the late 19th and early 20th centuries, blacks became common in advertising targeted at European Americans, which in this era included all advertising except that in specifically black publications. Often the portrayals were pictorially demeaning (huge lips, bulging eyes, cannibals, mammy figures like Aunt Jemima) and verbally insulting (brand names like Nigger Head canned vegetables and stove polish). Many of these figures thankfully disappeared quietly, but some of these symbols evolved in interesting ways. For example, Aunt Jemima was first developed in 1889 by Charles Rutt with his introduction of the first ready-mixed pancake flour. In the early years, Aunt Jemima in ads (and her spinoff dolls and personal appearances by various actresses) was right off the antebellum plantation, with her characteristic headdress, uneducated speech style, and subservient behavior. Aunt Jemima gradually became less slave-like over the next 80 years, though the greatest change came in 1968, when she wore more of a headband than a slave bandanna and also appeared younger and more intelligent. Only in 1989, in her 100th year, did Aunt Jemima lose the headgear altogether for the first time (Kern-Foxworth, 1994).

in ads (across all media) rose from .57% in 1949 to 16% in TV advertising in 1986 (Zinkhan, Qualls, & Biswas, 1990).

In the United States, media reflected this prejudiced viewpoint before radio or television were ever conceived. One of the earliest movies was *Uncle Tom's Cabin* in 1903, a film that highly stereotyped African Americans. The controversial film *Birth of a Nation* (1915) presented the Ku Klux Klan as heroic. Such treatment persisted in films for many years (Bogle, 1973). In 1942 the NAACP convinced the Hollywood studio bosses to abandon the characteristic negative roles for African Americans and to try to integrate them into a variety of roles; this agreement did not produce overnight change, but advances did come eventually.

The civil rights movement of the 1960s ushered in significant changes in media (G. L. Berry, 1980). African American models were used in advertising, with none of the feared offense taken by Whites (Block, 1972; Schlinger & Plummer, 1972; Soley, 1983). African Americans also appeared for the first time in leading roles in prime-time TV, most notably *I Spy* (1965 to 1968) with Bill Cosby, and *Julia*, the first African American family drama. In addition, there were African Americans as part of the starring ensemble on 1960s drama programs like *Mission Impossible*, *Peyton Place*, and *Mod Squad*.

In the 1970s and 1980s, there were usually some African American characters on TV, although they tended to be heavily concentrated in sitcoms and largely absent from daytime soap operas and children's programming. Some of these characters were more rounded than early TV African Americans but still retained some stereotypical characteristics, such as the buffoonery and posturing of J. J. on *Good Times* and George Jefferson on *The Jeffersons*. In the 1970s, about 8% of prime-time TV characters were African-American (Gerbner & Signorielli, 1979; Seggar, Hafen, & Hannonen-Gladden, 1981; Weigel, Loomis, & Soja, 1980), with less than 3% in daytime soaps (Greenberg, Neuendorf, Buerkel-Rothfuss, & Henderson, 1982). Comparisons of African American and White characters appearing together in the same show reveal many similarities and some differences, with specifics depending on the programs sampled (Reid, 1979; Weigel et al., 1980).

A landmark occurred with the phenomenal commercial success of *Roots* in 1977. This TV miniseries was based on Alex Haley's saga of his ancestor's forced journey from West Africa into American slavery and later emancipation. Although widely praised for both its artistic and entertainment value and its effectiveness in widely publicizing key aspects of the African American experience, *Roots* was also controversial. Some called it biased for presenting few sympathetic European American characters, whereas others took it to task for making the horrors of slavery acceptable for audiences by transforming a national disgrace into an epic triumph of the family and the American dream (Riggs, 1992). Surprisingly, *Roots* did not open up many new roles for African-American actors, as many had predicted it would.

The current media situation is vastly improved from the *Amos and Andy* days, although some argue that there are still subtle indicators of racism on television (Greenberg, et al., 2002; Taylor, et al., 1995) and still very few realistic portrayals of typical African American life (Riggs, 1992). African Americans are still underrepresented in most TV genres except sitcoms and are largely absent in high-level creative and network administrative positions. Although the phenomenal success of *The Cosby Show* (1984–1992) presumably laid to rest any commercial concerns about Whites not watching Black shows, that show's relevance to the experience of the large majority of less affluent African Americans was hotly debated. Cliff Huxtable and his family were clearly positive role models, but they also enjoyed a lifestyle that was beyond the reach of most African American families (and, for that matter, most of the rest of the population as well).

Although we seldom, if ever, see the racist ads or programming from the pre-civil rights era, some blatantly racist cartoons from as far back as the 1940s are still widely sold in inexpensive video cartoon anthologies; some villains have dark skin, big lips, and even exhibit cannibalistic behaviors. Barcus (1983) found cartoons to be the most ethnically stereotyped of all television genres. Sometimes the bias may be more subtle. For example, two ugly and stupid regular characters in one cartoon are Rock Steady, named after a Jamaican musical genre of the mid-1960s, and Bebop, which was a form of jazz with origins in African American music (O'Connor, 1990).

There are still some biases in news coverage (Entman, 1990, 1992, 1994a, 1994b; Heider, 2000). For example, Romer, Jamieson, and deCoteau (1998) examined 14 weeks of local TV news on three stations in Philadelphia in 1994. They found that people of color (most often African Americans) were disproportionately represented in stories about crime and were more likely to be presented as perpetrators than as victims, relative to the actual demographics from local crime statistics. This finding was replicated in a study of Los Angeles and Orange County CA local news by Dixon and Linz (2000).

Blacks as Viewers

African Americans of all ages watch more television than Whites, even when controlling for socioeconomic status (Graves, 1996; Kern-Foxworth, 1994). They especially watch more sports, action-adventure shows, and news. They watch shows with Black characters and Black-oriented networks like BET and WB in relatively greater numbers than European Americans do (Goldberg, 2002). However, there is no evidence that other groups avoid such shows because of the African American characters (G. Comstock, Chaffee, Katzman, McCombs, & Roberts, 1978; Graves, 1980), even though children of all races tend to identify more with characters of their own race (Eastman & Liss, 1980; Greenberg & Atkin, 1982). Overall, African American children prefer sitcoms, whereas European American children prefer action-adventure shows. Compared to light TV viewers, heavy viewers believe that African Americans and European Americans are more similar, African Americans are more middle class, and racial integration is more widespread (Matabane, 1988). This may be interpreted in terms of cultivation theory to suggest that television mainstreams viewers into the optimistic view that African Americans have "made it" and that segregation and racism are no more.

Effects of African American Portrayals

One focus of research has been on the effects of African American TV portrayals on both European and African Americans (see Graves, 1980; Greenberg, 1986; Greenberg, Mastro, & Brand, 2002, for reviews). Like others, African Americans are more likely to identify with and emulate characters who exhibit personal warmth, high status, and power. Often these models have been White, yet African Americans will readily identify with media Blacks as role models, especially with the more positive ones (Ball & Bogatz, 1970, 1973; Jhally & Lewis, 1992). This can boost children's self-esteem, especially with regular viewing and accompanied by appropriate parental communication (Atkin, Greenberg, & McDermott, 1983; McDermott & Greenberg, 1985). Sympathetic characters like the Huxtable children or the African American teens on *Sister Sister* and *That's So Raven* thus become potentially very important models for young African Americans. Black viewers remembered positive African American TV characters better than they remembered comparable White characters (Appiah, 2002). Studies of White children have shown that prolonged exposure to television comedies or *Sesame Street* with regular African American and Latino cast members influences the attitudes of White kids in a more accepting, less racist direction (Bogatz & Ball, 1971; Gorn, Goldberg, & Kanungo, 1976).

Although everyone identifies more with characters who are perceived to be like themselves on whatever relevant dimensions (Identification theory), being a minority member makes certain attributes more salient (Distinctiveness theory). Thus, one's race is a larger part of one's identity for a person of color in a largely White society than it is for the majority. Similarly, being left-handed, red-headed, or six-foot-six is more salient than being right-handed, brown-haired, or five-foot-nine. Black viewers recalled Black characters better than White characters, while White viewers showed no difference in their recall of White vs. Black characters (Appiah, 2002).

Even a very positive portrayal developed with the best intentions may contribute to misconceptions, however. For example, some White viewers of *The Cosby Show* cited the Huxtables as examples of why affirmative action is no longer necessary (Jhally & Lewis, 1992). If the affluent Huxtables have attained their share of the American dream and they are assumed to be representative of African Americans, then those who haven't made it must not be trying very hard. Consistent with cultivation theory, White heavy viewers of entertainment TV believed that African Americans were relatively well off socioeconomically, although those who were heavy viewers of TV news believed African Americans to be relatively worse off economically (Armstrong, Neuendorf, & Brentar, 1992).

Sometimes TV can unexpectedly reinforce preexisting stereotypes. For example, more traditional White viewers tended to identify with the bigoted Archie Bunker of the 1970s sitcom *All in the Family* and accept his racist views, although less prejudiced people decried these views and found Archie's attitudes offensive or laughable (Surlin, 1974; Tate & Surlin, 1976; Vidmar & Rokeach, 1974; Wilhoit & de Bock, 1976). The same inconsistent reactions were found to the Indian feminist drama *Hum Log* (W. J. Brown & Cody, 1991).

In contrast to this picture of some progress in the portrayal of African Americans, the media image of another American minority of similar size is far less hopeful.

LATINOS

Although Hispanics, or Latinos, are growing very rapidly in numbers (32 million in the U.S. by 2003), they comprise only 2–3% of characters on prime-time TV (Espinoza, 1997, Mastro & Greenberg, 2000; Weaver, 2003a). See Table 3.1. Hispanics are, in fact, several very diverse groups of Americans with ethnic origins in Cuba, Puerto Rico, Dominican Republic, Mexico, Central America, South America, or Spain. Latinos are racially and culturally diverse. Although many Cuban, Puerto Ricans or Dominicans

TABLE 3.1
Ethnic Group Members in U.S. Population and on Prime-Time TV in 2000 (Poniewozik, 2001)

Group	U.S. Population (%)	Prime-Time Characters (%)
African American	12.3	17.0
Latino	12.5	2.0
Asian-American	3.6	3.0
Native American	0.9	0.2
White and Other	71.7	77.8

are racially African American or part African American, most Mexican Americans are mestizos (mixed White and Indian) but seldom African American. Many New Mexicans are purely of Spanish descent, whereas some recent Guatemalan refugees are pure native Americans who speak Spanish only badly as a second language, if at all.

The North American histories of various Latino groups are very different. Although Spaniards have lived in New Mexico since before the Puritans settled in Massachusetts, some Mexicans and Central Americans are very recent immigrants. They are economically diverse, ranging from wealthy Cuban Americans of South Florida or the Spanish New Mexicans of Albuquerque and Santa Fe, to the poor immigrant underclass of southern California and Texas. Latinos are also politically diverse, from the staunchly Republican and conservative Cuban Americans in Florida to the politically liberal Mexican Americans starting to flex their voting muscles in places like Texas and California.

In spite of the small numbers overall, there are several prevailing stereotypes of Latinos in the media (Greenberg, et al., 2002; Ramirez Berg, 1990). The greasy, dirty Mexican bandit appeared in Westerns of the mid-twentieth century and as drug runners in more recent movies. This image also appears in advertising with the Frito bandito of the 1970s or the Taco Bell Chihuahua of the 1990s. A second stereotype is the harlot, the loose woman interested only in sex. A third stereotype is the buffoon or clown, such as Ricky Ricardo of *I Love Lucy* or Rosario of *Will and Grace*. A fifth stereotype is the sensual and musical, but slightly laughable, Latin lover of early films (1920–1945). Finally, there is the mysterious "dark lady" figure. Of the Latinos who appear on American television, characters who were criminals were one and a half times more likely to be Hispanic than European American. Most of the Latino characters were male, and almost no Latino characters appeared on Saturday morning television (Subervi-Velez & Colsant, 1993). Latinos were overrepresented in the criminal justice system, either as police officers or criminals (Dixon & Linz, 2000; Mastro & Greenberg, 2000).

As early as the late 1980s, a few signs suggested that Hollywood and the TV networks were beginning to discover the largely untapped Latino market. Spanish cable channels offered popular options to Spanish-speaking populations. The unexpectedly great commercial success of the films *La Bamba* and *Born in East L.A.* inside and outside of Latino communities allowed several new Hispanic films to be released shortly thereafter, although this trend did not continue.

The success of *Spy Kids* (2001) and *Spy Kids 2* (2002), sort of James Bond movies for kids where the hero family just happens to be Hispanic, may help the overall picture. If adult-oriented films like *Chasing Papi* and *Real Women Have Curves* achieve major box-office success, we will no doubt see more Latino characters. U.S. television has been an even more dismal story. Following the commercial failure of several very short-lived Latino-oriented sitcoms in the 1970s and 1980s, the networks appeared to be wary about more such shows. A few recent shows such as ABC's *George Lopez* and Fox's *The Ortegas* offer some hope. The Nickelodeon bilingual preschool *Dora the Explorer* has become very popular and profitable.

Still, however, in many ways Latinos in media are at a point somewhat similar to that of African Americans 50 years ago (i.e., largely invisible and tending to be in negative or regulatory roles when they do occur). Greenberg and Brand (1994) attributed this at least in part to the low level of minority employment in the broadcast industry, due not necessarily to overt discrimination but more often to the low entry-level salaries that are not attractive enough to the relatively few qualified Latinos, who may have numerous job opportunities. Because decision makers and those at management level are mostly Anglo, it is their world that tends to appear on television.

NATIVE AMERICANS

Clearly the most mistreated groups in the history of the North America, Native Americans were largely the object of extermination campaigns in the 18th and 19th centuries. Today they comprise less than 1% of the U.S. population, with one third living below the official poverty line. Stereotyped negative images have been pervasive in both news and entertainment media throughout U.S. history (Bird, 1996, 1999; Merskin, 1998; Weston, 1996). By far the best known image is the bloodthirsty and savage Indian of old movies and early television. Westerns were one of the most popular genres of television and movies through the early 1960s. Indians were usually depicted as vicious killers and, at their very best, as lovable but simple, slow-witted sidekicks to European American men, for example, Tonto and the Lone Ranger (Morris, 1982). Some of the stereotypical behaviors actually came from others; for example, "scalping" was performed by European Americans on Native Americans rather than the reverse. Later, slightly more serious portrayals of Indian men were most often the "doomed warrior" or "wise elder" characters (Bird, 1999). For the most part, when Westerns declined in popularity, Native Americans disappeared from the screen altogether. When Mastro and Greenberg (2000) did their content analysis of the 1996–1997 prime-time TV season, they found no examples of Native American characters at all! There have very occasionally been the exceptional characters such as those on *Northern Exposure* and *Dr. Quinn, Medicine Woman* in the 1990s.

Although there are 555 officially recognized Native American tribes today, those who have appeared in the media (usually in Westerns) were almost always Plains Indians, and behaviors like living in teepees and hunting buffalo came to be identified with all Native Americans, although they were no more characteristic of the northeastern Iroquois or northwest Tlingits than they were of the English or Africans. The overemphasis on Plains Indian peoples is still seen in a few more recent and otherwise non-traditional films like *Dances With Wolves* (1990), *Thunderheart* (1992), and *Geronimo* (1993). Women seldom appeared, and when they did, they were passive and rather dull background figures. The powerful women in matriarchal societies like the Navajo and Mohawk have never been seen on TV or film. Most media Indians are seen in the historical setting of Westerns; the few modern characters are usually presented as militant activists or alcoholics. There is hardly any Native American news and what does appear is usually about land claims litigation or Indian-run casinos. Without a large national constituency, substantial change may come only from Native American film and television production (Geiogamah & Pavel, 1993).

Given this situation, there is great confusion in the socialization process for Native American children. There is almost a complete lack of non-Plains Indian role models. When Native American children play cowboys and Indians, they are as likely as Whites to want to play the cowboys (i.e., the good guys).

To add to the confusion, one of the few places that Native American ethnic identity appears in mainstream culture is in the names of school and professional sports teams that have nothing to do with their heritage. A currently very controversial issue in many places is the use of Native American names and themes for U.S. sports teams (Atlanta Braves, Kansas City Chiefs, Washington Redskins, Cleveland Indians). Although the most visible examples are names of professional teams, the same issue exists at a local level, where many high schools and colleges use Indian names and mascots. Mostly named many years ago, before much consciousness of ethnic stereotyping existed, such labels probably arose to suggest the strong, fighting, even savage nature associated with the Indian image from Westerns.

Now it is time, argue many, to replace these names with others that do not demean any ethnic or racial group or co-opt and cheapen its cultural symbols (Pewewardy, 1999; Springwood & King, 2001). The issue first came to a head during the 1991 baseball World Series. Fans of the Atlanta Braves had a hand motion called the tomahawk chop to support their team. Critics argued that the use of comparable symbols or names from any other minority group would not be tolerated; could one seriously imagine teams called the Chicago Jews, Washington Wetbacks, or the Dallas Orientals, although we do have the Notre Dame Fighting Irish and the Minnesota Vikings?

As of the early 21st century, many high school teams and a few college teams (though almost no pro teams) had changed their names or mascots, but old traditions die hard. Sometimes circumstances prevail to make change especially difficult. For example, when the controversy arose at the University of North Dakota's "Fighting Sioux" mascot late in 2000, the President convened a commission to study the issue and make recommendations to him. Before its work was complete, however, the school's major alumnus donor, Las Vegas casino mogul Ralph Engelstad, wrote a letter threatening to withdraw his latest $100 million gift for a luxurious hockey arena already under construction if the school dropped the Sioux mascot. Shortly after, the state Board of Higher Education issued a unanimous pre-emptive strike to keep the name, and the money (Brownstein, 2001).

However, others were taking stands. For example, the Portland *Oregonian* (1992), the state's largest daily, the Lincoln (NE) *Journal Star* (2003), and several papers near the University of North Dakota announced they would no longer publish names or nicknames of sports teams that used racial or ethnic stereotypes. The teams would hereafter be referred to only by their city or school. Some radio stations or broadcasters in different places have similar policies. Predictably, many called the whole flap much ado about nothing, but Native Americans were almost uniformly pleased. This controversy is not going away.

The history of oppression of the native peoples is by no means unique to North America. They have been similarly marginalized in Australia, New Zealand, and European-oriented Latin American countries like Argentina, Chile, Brazil, Uruguay, and Costa Rica. An interesting exception to this pattern is Mexico, which, unlike the rest of North America, has always had a very large urban indigenous population. At the time of the Spanish conquest in 1521, the Aztec capital Tenochtitlán was one of the world's most populous cities. In spite of early severe oppression by the Spanish conquistadors, the Indian identity has come to be fused with the Spanish into a unique culture that is the essence of modern Mexico. It is the last Aztec ruler, Cuauhtémoc, not the conquering Spaniard Cortez, who is the Mexican national hero.

ASIAN AMERICANS

The fastest growing minorities in the United States and (especially) Canada in recent decades are Asians, although their immigration history goes back to the large numbers of Chinese brought over to work the railroads in the American West in the 1800s. Japanese emigrated to the United States, as well as to Brazil and elsewhere in large numbers, in the early 20th century. Japanese American U.S. citizens (but not German Americans) on the West Coast were rounded up and put into concentration camps during World War II. Although the official justification was national security, the decision has more recently been attributed to racism. Koreans and Filipinos are coming to America in increasing numbers, some as spouses of U.S. military formerly stationed there. Vietnamese and other southeast Asians came in large numbers following the end of the Vietnam War in 1975. There are also a substantial number of South Asian Americans, from India, Pakistan, Bangladesh, Sri Lanka, and Afghanistan, as well as Iranian refugees from the 1979 Islamic revolution.

Like the Native Americans, there is a long history of media stereotyping of Asians in movies, such as Fu Manchu and Charlie Chan, characters often played, incidentally, by White actors (Iiyama & Kitano, 1982). On television there have been few Asian Americans. The old *Kung Fu* series had the Asian lead played by European American David Carradine. The 1970s and 1980s saw some improvement, with the addition of some minor Asian characters in shows like *Hawaii Five-O* (1968–1980) and *M*A*S*H* (1972–1983), although they were often villains or in stereotyped occupations like Chinese running a laundry or restaurant (Mok, 1998).

Often the villains of choice on entertainment TV follow news events. After the 1989 Tiananmen Square massacre, Chinese officials from the People's Republic of China (PRC) were frequent villains on action-adventure shows. During waves of U.S. concern about Japanese commercial power and ascendancy, Japanese businessmen were portrayed as buying up America in a sort of "yellow scare." Newspaper stories about Asian immigration show headlines like "Asian invasion" or "containing Japan" (Funabiki, 1992). Parallels are drawn between Japanese economic ascendancy and its earlier World War II militarism. As with African Americans, some very tired, old stereotypes live on in children's cartoons in video anthologies. For example, in 1995, MGM-UA Home Video pulled a 1944 World War II-era Bugs Bunny cartoon where Bugs hands out bombs concealed in ice-cream cones to a crowd of Japanese people as he says, "Here you go Bowlegs, here you go Monkey-face, here you go, Slant Eyes, everybody gets one." Prior to the withdrawal, about 800 copies had been sold *in the 1990s!* (What's Up, Doc?, 1995)

Nevertheless, overall, Asian Americans are probably portrayed more positively than most other minorities on U.S. media. In fact, there is one positive stereotype that is increasingly troubling to some Asian Americans: the model minority image of the group that succeeds academically, commercially, and socially. Sometimes this perceived success image is used to ignore problems that the group has or to criticize other minorities for doing less well and thus seeming lazy. Such treatment engenders deep feelings. For example, in the 1992 Los Angeles race riots, some of the major targets of angry African American looters and arsonists were Korean American businesses. For a while, the University of California system and others set an Asian quota, a limit on the number of Asian American students that could be admitted.

ARABS AND ARAB AMERICANS

A much smaller American minority offers a look at a seldom-discussed stereotype, but one that is currently among the most unsympathetic and derogatory portrayals on U.S. media; that is, Arabs and Arab Americans. This stereotype is seen in both news coverage (Suleiman, 1988) and entertainment (Shaheen, 1984, 1992, 1997, 2001).

According to Shaheen, there are several stereotypic ways that Arab men are portrayed, all very negative. One is as the terrorist. Although only a minuscule fraction of real Arabs are terrorists, there are many of these on television, especially since September 2001, or among Arabs identified as Palestinians. A second stereotype of Arab men is the wealthy oil sheik, who is often greedy and morally dissolute. His wealth, often suggested to be undeserved, is spent on frivolities like marble palaces and fleets of Rolls-Royce cars. Sometimes he is portrayed as madly buying up land in America and erecting garishly kitschy homes in Beverly Hills. A third stereotype is that of sexual pervert, often dealing in selling Europeans or Americans into slavery. This is an older stereotype, perhaps originally arising from medieval Christian Europe's enmity against the Muslim infidels, who were, incidentally, primarily non-Arab Turks. Although probably less prevalent than the terrorist or oil sheik portrayal today, this image does appear occasionally. A fourth stereotype is the Bedouin desert rat, the unkempt ascetic wanderer far over-represented on TV, and in advertising in relation to the approximately 5% of Arabs who are Bedouins. Visual images and jokes about camels, sand, and tents are frequent in connection with U.S.-media Arabs.

Arab men are generally seen as villains, a stereotype especially rampant in children's cartoons (e.g., Daffy Duck being chased by a crazed, sword-wielding Arab sheik or Heckle and Jeckle pulling the rug from under "Ali Boo-Boo, the Desert Rat"). More significantly, portrayals of these barbaric and uncultured villains are not usually balanced by those of Arab heroes or good guys. One of the very few positive media models was probably Lebanese American Corporal Max Klinger on *M*A*S*H*. He was a sympathetic and rounded character, yet (especially in early episodes) he dressed in drag and commented about his relatives having unnatural relations with camels.

How about Arab women? They are seen far less than Arab men on U.S. TV and movies, but, when they are seen at all, it is usually as oppressed victims or in highly stereotyped roles such as that of a belly dancer or a member of a harem. The reality about harems, as Shaheen points out, is that they were never common and today are nonexistent in Arab countries. The public veiling of women is presented as the Arab norm, rather than as a characteristic of some, but not all, Islamic traditions. Arab children are practically nonexistent on U.S. television, even though the negative adult Arab stereotypes are perhaps more prevalent in children's cartoons than on any other type of programming. Even as we routinely see African American, Latino, and Asian faces on programs like *Sesame Street*, few if any Arabs appear.

There is also an implicit identification of Arabs with the Islamic religion, although the Muslims among the 65 million Arabs worldwide represent only 12% of the world's Muslims (Shaheen, 2001). As for Arab-Americans, a majority of them are Christian. Islam as a religion is often portrayed as cruel and vicious, in total contrast to the Judeo-Christian faith and civilization. Because most North Americans know very little about Islam except media reports of its extremist fringe, this may easily become their perceived reality about one of the world's major religions. Although many Americans have sufficient knowledge to recognize a Christian cult extremist on TV as very atypical of Christians, they may not have the necessary knowledge to so critically evaluate a media presentation of an Islamic suicide bomber, who is thus taken to be typical of Muslims.

Historically, Arabs may be the latest villains in a long list of many groups who have been maligned by the U.S. media. The vicious Arabs of contemporary entertainment were preceded by the wealthy but cruel Jews of the 1920s, the sinister Asian villains of the 1930s, and the Italian gangsters of the 1950s. Each of these stereotypes has been tempered and balanced as a result of protests from the offended groups and other concerned citizens. Such media portrayals can provide unwitting social support for racist and discriminatory policies and legislation, such as the network of Jim Crow laws and racist practices against African Americans in the century following the American Civil War of 1861 to 1865.

Recent historical events have, at times, encouraged unflattering media portrayals of Arabs: the OPEC oil embargoes of the 1970s, various hostage-taking incidents, the Lebanese civil war, the Iran-Iraq War of 1980 to 1988, the Persian Gulf War of 1991, the Iraq War of 2003, continuing Israeli-Palestinian conflicts, and perhaps most dramatically, the Al-Qaeda terrorist attacks of Sept. 11, 2001. The actual and potential backlash against Arabs and Arab-Americans since the World Trade Center attack stresses the urgency to better understand this group.

The concern is not that there are some negative portrayals of Arabs and Arab Americans. Rather, it is that such portrayals are not balanced by positive portrayals to feed into the perceived mental reality constructed by TV viewers. There is very little programming on Arab culture or society. The Arab world was more intellectually and technically advanced than

Europe in the Middle Ages and gave us many of the basics of modern science, mathematics, and music, but how many Americans know that? Nor do the close family values and other positive features of the Islamic faith and Arab culture receive much press in the United States.

After the Oklahoma City bombing in April 1995, investigating authorities and the general public immediately suspected Arab terrorists, although there was no evidence of such a link. When a pair of European Americans was arrested and later convicted of the crime, there were a lot of embarrassed faces. However, the stereotypes persist on entertainment TV and movies, and still there are almost no positive models. This is not without its consequences. For example, Arab Americans and others charge that Western coverage of the Israeli-Palestinian dispute over the West Bank is severely biased toward Israel due to anti-Arab prejudice.

The concern about stereotypical portrayals of groups is not limited to gender, race, and ethnic groups. Let us look at the media portrayal of a formerly invisible minority.

GAY AND LESBIAN PEOPLE

The Production Code of 1934 formalized the voluntary exclusion of all gay and lesbian portrayals from Hollywood films (Russo, 1981). When television entered the picture 15 years later, the code of silence was maintained, not to be broken until very occasional openings starting in the late 1960s. Norman Lear's *All in the Family* in the early 1970s occasionally dealt with some gay and lesbian themes, a sympathetic drama *A Certain Summer* aired in 1972, but not much else followed until the 1980s.

The advent of AIDS in the early 1980s greatly altered the media perception of gays and lesbians. Although neglected and marginalized at first as a problem of the gay and drug subcultures, the death from AIDS of romantic leading man Rock Hudson in 1985 helped bring AIDS coverage "out of the closet," although it tended to redefine coverage of homosexuality and homosexuals as "epidemic" coverage, with gay people cast in the role of villains carrying the dread disease or as victims of it or both. There were some sympathetic portrayals of gay AIDS victims, though they were almost always male and upper-middle class, as in the 1985 TV movie *An Early Frost*.

By the 1990s, greater numbers of gay, and less often lesbian, characters began to appear in positive roles in television and film, some of them saintly and most of them appearing rather mainstream and being well accepted by their straight friends. Physical contact was rare; a lesbian kiss on the sitcom *Roseanne* was almost vetoed by the network, but Roseanne insisted on it.

BOX 3.4
WHEN LAWRENCE CAME OUT IN THE COMICS
(Lawlor, Sparkes, & Wood, 1994)

For one month in the spring of 1993, Lynn Johnston's popular family comic strip *For Better or For Worse* dealt with the theme of a gay teen, as occasional character Lawrence, a friend of principal family teen Michael, came out to his friends and family on the comic pages of about 1,500 North American dailies. Canadian cartoonist Lynn Johnston drew on the experience of her gay brother-in-law and others as she wrote the story over several weeks. Lawrence initially came out to Michael and later to his parents, who had a very difficult time with the news. His father first threw him out of the house but late relented and offered a grudging acceptance, though not total understanding. There was some predictable negative reaction from the Canadian and U.S. markets. About 40 papers refused to run the strips on this theme, and 16 canceled permanently as a protest of the content. However, the controversy seemed to generate new interest, and the strip experienced unprecedented growth in subscriptions over the succeeding months. In Lawlor et al.'s analysis of almost 2,200 letters received by Johnston, the newspapers, and the distributing syndicate, 70% were positive, many offering poignant personal stories of readers' own experiences. There were, of course, some predictable angry responses, though fewer than had been feared. In any event, it seemed clear that the funnies weren't just for laughing any more.

As recently as 1991, sponsors successfully pressured ABC not to rerun an episode of the drama series *thirtysomething* that had one brief peripheral scene of two minor, nonregular gay male characters sitting in bed with each other (only talking). Such controversy was not limited to electronic media. When the comic strip "For Better or For Worse" had Lawrence, a friend of teenager Michael, come out in 1993, some papers refused to run the strip, although most did (see Box 3.4).

The most publicized gay character in the history of TV was featured in the on-screen coming out of Ellen's lead character Ellen Morgan in April 1997, which coincided with the off-screen coming out of the actress Ellen DeGeneres. Although the coming-out episode set ratings records and was itself the subject of many news stories at the time, the formerly high-rated sitcom was canceled at the end of the following season. Although DeGeneres' next show did not last long, another network sitcom (*Will and Grace*), about a gay man living with a straight woman, became a mainstream hit. Interestingly enough, some of the most daring programming with gay themes came on animated shows, such as *The Simpsons* and *South*

Park. Music videos, the occasional soap opera, and other sitcoms (e.g., *Spin City*) had some prominent gay themes or characters.

How gay rights and gay pride events and issues are communicated via news media is also an important consideration. Gays and lesbians are treated qualitatively differently from ethnic, religious, or other social minorities. For example, Moritz (1995) points out that the Ku Klux Klan and neo-Nazis are not sought out for minority opinions for journalistic balance in coverage of issues concerning African Americans or Jews. However, spokespersons from the political right who would ban and suppress all expression, if not even all discussion, of homosexuality are routinely sought out to present the other side in coverage of gay and lesbian issues. This is one group that it is still socially, politically, and sometimes morally acceptable to publicly despise.

A few studies suggest that positive media portrayals such as Will Truman on *Will and Grace* can be instrumental in improving tolerance and acceptance of gays and lesbians by the broader society. Riggle, Ellis, and Crawford (1992) found that viewing a documentary film about a gay politician led to significantly more positive attitudes toward homosexuals. Bonds-Raacke, Cady, Schlegel, Harris, & Firebaugh, (2004) found that just thinking about a positive media gay or lesbian character of one's choice led to improved attitudes toward gay men. These results suggest a potentially important role for media entertainment in reducing prejudice in this area.

OLDER ADULTS

One of the most underrepresented demographic groups in U.S. media, especially television, has been the older adult (Dall, 1988; R. H. Davis & J. A. Davis, 1985). Although the percentage of the U.S. population over 65 has climbed from 4% in 1900 to 12% in 2000 and is projected to be near 20% by 2100 (Hajjar, 1997), content analyses have shown much lower proportions of characters over 65 in both TV programs and commercials (Cassata & Irwin, 1997; Greenberg, Korzenny, & Atkin, 1979; Hajjar, 1997; Roy & Harwood, 1997). Even the relatively few older people who appeared on TV were not particularly representative of the population. For example, 62% to 70% of the TV elderly in commercials were men, as compared with about 40% men in the over-65 age population (Hajjar, 1997; Roy & Harwood, 1997). A disproportionate number of the TV elderly were in sitcoms, with very few in action-adventure or children's shows. Studies of print media also show underrepresentation and stereotyping in portrayals of the aging (Buchholz & Bynum, 1982; Nussbaum & Robinson, 1986;

J. D. Robinson, 1989). As if that were not bad enough, this age group has the largest portion of television characters treated with disrespect (70% of men, 80% of women) in content analyses (Gerbner, 1997).

Often, the older adult is portrayed as more of a stereotype than a fully rounded character. These stereotypes are of several forms:

1. *Physical and mental weakness and poor health.* Overall, older people on TV are often seen as quite healthy, perhaps even unrealistically so (Cassata, Anderson, & Skill, 1980; R. H. Davis, 1983; Kubey, 1980). Those who are sick, however, are ailing very badly, often seen as infirm, feeble, and some-times senile. Although in terms of numbers of stories, newspapers do the best job of any medium in covering the elderly, a high percentage of such stories are obituaries (Buchholz & Bynum, 1982; J. D. Robinson, 1989)!

Moreover, the elderly are usually sexless. The major exception to this is the other extreme, the so-called dirty old man (or woman), who is pre-occupied with sex and is usually a highly ludicrous character. The very active and healthy senior citizen may be an object of ridicule, such as the grandmother who rides a motorcycle or cruises bars to meet men.

2. *Crotchety and complaining.* This is the narrow-minded older person who is constantly complaining, criticizing, and generally making a pain of him or herself for everyone else. As with the physically weak stereotype, the crotchety complainer is usually at best a laughable buffoon and at worst an object of scorn and derision.

3. *Stereotyped positions and activities.* Older people tend to be seen doing relatively trivial things like playing bingo and sitting in rockers on the front porch. Such identifying symbols of aging are especially common in advertising. For example, a woman in a magazine ad for cookies is placed in a rocker to make sure we recognize that she is a grandmother.

4. *Physically unattractive.* In marked contrast to the unusually attrac-tive young adults on TV, television's elderly are often stoop-shouldered, mousy-haired, badly wrinkled, and wearing long out-of-style dowdy clothing. Such marks may be given to them so that we do not mistake them for younger people. Intentionally or not, it also contributes to their being perceived negatively. Seefeldt (1977) found that elementary school children viewed physical signs of aging as horrifying and saw the elderly as infirm and incapable of doing much.

An interesting class of exceptions to these generalizations can be seen in commercials. Although the elderly are as underrepresented there as in the programs, the characterization is a bit different. The elderly in ads often appear as the young-old, with few of the stereotypic signs of aging except the gray hair, which is almost always there. Although they suffer more health problems than young people in ads, they retain their vigor. It is as if the producers give the character gray hair so we all realize that he or she is supposed to be older, but allow that person to show very few other signs of age that our society finds so distasteful. Baldness, wrinkles, and otherwise general dowdiness are unseemly (R. H. Davis & J. A. Davis, 1985). One content analysis of TV commercials in 1994 found the portrayals of older people to be largely positive (Roy & Harwood, 1997). Still, however, older adults are neglected. Ad agency Grey Worldwide found that less than 10% of U.S. television commercials are aimed at those over 50, in spite of the fact that that group has over half of all the disposable income in the country (Lippert, 2003).

Even in cases where the elderly are portrayed very positively, they tend to be in rather a restricted and stereotyped range of roles. They are almost always in relation to family, very often as a grandparent, but sometimes as the antagonist in a relationship with their adult child. We seldom see an older executive or professional. The older mystery sleuth detectives of *Murder She Wrote* and *Diagnosis Murder* offer a couple of exceptions.

When NBC's sitcom *The Golden Girls* (1985–1992) featured four single women (three widowed, one divorced), aged about 50 to 80, sharing a house in Florida, what was new was the age of the stars. Never before had a sitcom, or perhaps any U.S. TV show, had its regular cast consisting entirely of older adults. There were no precocious children, no smart-mouthed teenagers, no hunks or supermodels, and no angst-ridden yuppie couples, yet the show had consistently high ratings. Nor were the characters the stereotyped TV old ladies. Three of the four were working professionals, and all showed depth of character beyond the typical TV grandma. However, they were criticized for being excessively interested in sex, although that criticism may more reflect discomfort with sexual interest in the mature adult. Also, the humor of the show sometimes perpetuated stereotypes of aging by poking fun at counterstereotypical portrayals (Harwood & Giles, 1992). In spite of the success of *The Golden Girls*, it was not followed by other ensemble shows of older characters. However, as the population ages sharply over the next few decades, a greater variety of portrayals of older adults is practically assured.

In spite of these inadequacies in their portrayal on TV, older people are heavy users of media, especially television. J. D. Robinson (1989) offered a uses and gratifications interpretation of this. A reduction in the number of friends and family seen regularly, perhaps in part due to decreased mobility from health limitations, leads to a proportionately greater reliance on media, especially television, with its high level of redundancy in the visual and auditory modalities. If one sense is impaired, the other may partially compensate. In the case of the sound track, the volume may be turned up, so some elderly TV viewers may actually hear more of what is spoken on TV than what is spoken by other people around them.

PERSONS WITH DISABILITIES AND DISORDERS

Physical Disabilities

Another group that is very concerned about its media image is people with disabilities, either physical or mental (Balter, 1999; Cumberbatch & Negrine, 1991). Disabilities only appear in less than 1% of series characters on TV, compared to 10–20% of the population having some sort of physical disability (Balter, 1999). However, people with disabilities have occasionally appeared, often in the form of the "bitter crip" or "supercrip" stereotypes. In the former, the person with a disability is depressed and bitter due to the disability and other people's failure to accept him or her as a full person. Often such story lines revolve around someone challenging the character to accept him- or herself. Often the character with the disability finds that this self-acceptance miraculously leads to a physical cure, perhaps subtly suggesting that happiness comes only from being physically whole. The supercrip image, on the other hand, is seen in characters like the superhuman and selfless paraplegic who wheels hundreds of miles to raise money for cancer research or the blind girl who solves the baffling crime by remembering a crucial sound or smell that sighted people had missed. Sometimes the two even coexist in the same person, as in *The Miracle Worker*'s Helen Keller, at first bitter and inept, almost animalistic, until she is "tamed" by the saintly teacher Annie Sullivan, after which she goes on to be almost superhuman. A covert message of both of these portrayals is that *individual* adjustment is the key to disabled people's lives; if they only have the right attitude, they will be fine. Factors like prejudice and social and physical barriers of the broader society are underplayed (Longmore, 1985).

Positive images do count. The old TV show *Ironsides* featured the lead detective who worked from a wheelchair. Dr. Carey on *ER* uses a crutch, but it does not define her character. Heather Whitestone, who is deaf, was chosen Miss America in the 1990s. Down syndrome character Corky (played by Down syndrome actor Chris Burke) on *Life Goes On* struck new TV ground for the mentally handicapped. It is not uncommon to see an advertising model in a wheelchair. The teacher in the comic strip "For Better or For Worse" is a positive example of a character who just happened to have a disability requiring her to use a wheelchair. Such portrayals can have substantial impact. When a popular Brazilian soap opera introduced a character who was ruggedly handsome and very sexy but also deaf, interest in learning sign language soared nationwide.

Psychological Disorders

The media image of psychological disorders (mental illness) is also an issue. A content analysis of week-long program samples from 1969 to 1985 showed that 72% of the prime-time adult characters who were portrayed as mentally ill injured or killed others, and 75% were victims of violence (Signorielli, 1989), whereas in reality about 11% of persons with psychological disorders are prone to violence, the same ratio as in the overall population (Teplin, 1985). A comparable bias exists in print media coverage of mentally ill persons (D. M. Day & Page, 1986; Matas, Guebaly, Harper, Green, & Peterkin, 1986; Shain & Phillips, 1991). One of the few truly violent disorders, antisocial personality ("psychopath"), is greatly overrepresented among the media mentally ill (W. Wilson, 1999).

Besides the violent mentally ill person, another stereotype is the person with disorders as object of humor or ridicule (Wahl, 1995). Although mental illness is seldom ridiculed directly, there is frequent use of metaphors that many find demeaning and insulting. For example, in advertising, an ad portrays a straitjacket as appropriate for someone crazy enough to buy the competitor's product; a lawn mower is described as "schizophrenic"; a line of peanuts called Certifiably Nuts is sold by picturing cans of the product wearing straitjackets. Ads describe sunglasses as "psycho," and vicious criminals are labeled "psychotic killers" as if the two words were one. It even creeps into political discourse. In the 1992 U.S. Presidential election campaign, third-party candidate Ross Perot happily told his followers, "We're all crazy again now! We got buses lined up outside to take you back to the insane asylum" (Willwerth, 1993). A popular movie *Me, Myself, and Irene* poked fun at a character labeled as schizophrenic but having the symptoms of Multiple Personality (Dissociative Identity) Disorder. People who have dealt with the tragedies of schizophrenia, depression, or other illnesses find such language and images very hurtful.

A third stereotype is that people with disorders are "a breed apart," that is, totally different from the rest of us (Wahl, 1995). People are presented as being obviously different, unmistakably symbolized by wild hair, disheveled clothing, bizarre behavior, and odd facial expressions. This encourages two inaccurate beliefs: (1) mental illness is immediately identifiable by one's appearance, and (2) people with an unusual appearance are thus objects of suspicion and perhaps fear.

Such attitudes support a stigmatizing of mental illness that discourages people from disclosing their own disorders and perhaps even dissuades them from seeking much-needed treatment. Media discussion of this stigma is perhaps most clearly seen in its role as political poison (Rich, 1997). Traditionally, any seeker of high political office in many countries admits their own use of counseling or psychiatric resources only at their peril. One of the most celebrated political casualties of such prejudice was probably U.S. Senator Thomas Eagleton, the original Democrat Vice Presidential nominee in 1972. He was replaced on the ticket after "admitting" he had been hospitalized for depression some years before. Presidential candidate Michael Dukakis lost ground in 1988 after a *rumor* that he had sought therapy to deal with grief over his brother's suicide some years before. How sad when the desirable seeking of help for problems is considered a moral or character failure! Would someone make a better President if he or she ignored a problem and did not seek help?

Occasionally there are reassuringly helpful images. One of the most influential in recent years was the 2001 Oscar-winning biopic *A Beautiful Mind*, the true story of Nobel Prize-winning mathematician John Nash's descent into schizophrenia and largely successful treatment for it. In spite of some cinematic license (visual hallucinations instead of auditory ones, more successful treatment than is often the case), the illness and its treatment were presented realistically and sensitively. Important issues were dealt with, such as the gradual detachment from reality, the necessity of maintaining medication therapy, and the devastating impact on one's family. Someone watching this film will learn a lot about schizophrenia (though nothing about multiple personality!), as well as being greatly entertained for two hours.

OCCUPATIONS

Finally, in this look at portrayals of groups, our attention focuses briefly on another large area of group stereotyping on television, namely, various occupational groups. Wroblewski and Huston (1987) found that fifth and sixth graders saw television as a major source of information about occupations. The presence of positive media models in certain occupations can greatly increase the numbers of those entering that profession. For example, the number of medical school applicants surged sharply in 1962 to 1963, apparently due to the debuts of the popular medical TV dramas *Dr. Kildare* and *Ben Casey* (M. Goldberg, 1988). The number of journalism students (and unemployed journalists) mushroomed after the Watergate scandal of the early 1970s, when investigative reporters had become heroes. More recently, the number of psychology majors wanting to go into "forensic profiling" has skyrocketed with the advent of movies like *Silence of the Lambs* and TV shows like *The Profiler*. Although the number of such jobs is minuscule, students do not know that. Effects of media portrayals of occupational groups are not always so dramatic, however. We examine a few especially interesting groups and see how the media present these professions.

Police Officers

One important group in regard to stereotyping is police officers. They are especially interesting because (a) police officers are greatly overrepresented in media, especially television, relative to their numbers in the population, and (b) most of us have relatively little intense contact with police in our daily lives. Thus, a high percentage of our knowledge about them is likely to come from television. In fact, heavy TV viewers greatly overestimated the percentage of the population working in law enforcement. Real police officers and trainees see the TV police shows as unrealistic portrayals of their profession (J. Simon & Fejes, 1987).

Lawyers and Courtroom Trials

Some controversy has arisen around the realistic courtroom TV shows like *Divorce Court* and *The People's Court*, as well as the Court TV cable channel. All of these present legal proceedings, either dramatization of real cases (*Divorce Court*) or actual court proceedings (*The People's Court*, Court TV). In *The People's Court* an actual judge presides over small claims court cases where both parties have agreed to have their case settled on the show in lieu of a more traditional setting. The cases were real, as were all parties in those cases.

On the one hand, such shows have been praised for making the court system more available to the public, who now can better understand how this phase of our judicial system functions. In fact, the number of small claims cases has risen considerably since the advent of *The People's Court*, although not necessarily because of that show. Speaking to this point, however, critics argue that many such cases are frivolous. Some judges report that litigants have become more contentious, dramatic, and emotional in court, apparently following the model of the parties on *The People's Court*. Is the public well served by such shows? Do we have a more accurate perception of how courts function, or is our reality colored by some "Hollywoodizing" of the courtroom by the producers of these real-life judicial programs? Even less clear is the impact of newer innovations like Court TV or the extensive broadcasting of sensational trials, such as the O. J. Simpson double-murder trial of the mid-1990s. See Box 3.5 for some thoughts of a prominent lawyer about TV's portrayal of the law as an abstract system.

What is the effect of such shows on people's knowledge and beliefs about lawyers? Cultivation theory would predict that such knowledge in heavy TV viewers would come to approximate the image of occupations

---

BOX 3.5
THE LAW ON TV

Attorney Alan Dershowitz (1985) noted two myths about the law that were very prevalent on popular shows of the time like *Hill Street Blues*, *Cagney and Lacey*, and *Miami Vice*. The first myth is that the law is unambiguous, unforgiving, and controlling, although the people who administer it may be complex, forgiving, or ambiguous. Dershowitz argued that, in fact, real-life law is much more subjective and ambiguous than the shows portrayed. For example, plea bargaining and decisions about bail and sentencing are seldom spelled out precisely in the law, but leave considerable latitude to magistrates and attorneys. This is in contrast to the TV shows, which often presented a judge or attorney's hands in such issues as being completely tied by the law.

A second myth pointed out by Dershowitz is that the Bill of Rights to the U.S. Constitution and Supreme Court decisions like the Miranda rule are to blame for freeing many criminals. A common TV theme is that silly legal technicalities are undoing the valuable work of the police every day. For example, critical evidence is obtained illegally, causing a conviction to be thrown out or overturned, allowing an obviously guilty person to go free. It sometimes may appear as if the Bill of Rights and the Miranda rule are inconsistent with adequate law enforcement. A study done by the General Accounting Office showed that, during the period of the study, only .5% of all serious Federal criminal prosecutions were thrown out because of exclusionary rule violations (illegally gathered evidence). If this frequency had been represented accurately on the TV crime shows, it would have come out to one episode on one show every 2 years!

---

presented on TV. Using this framework, Pfau, Mullen, Deidrich, and Garrow (1995) examined prime-time portrayals of lawyers and the public perception about attorneys. They found that public perceptions were affected in the direction of the TV portrayal, which in this case, interestingly enough, was more positive than expected. It would be interesting to see if the results would replicate in the era following the O. J. Simpson trial and other high-profile trials, which, many argued, portrayed attorneys very badly. Others (e.g., Thaler, 1994) argue that television cameras in the courtroom are turning trials into entertainment, something they have never tried to be before.

Psychologists and Psychiatrists

Another highly stereotyped career in entertainment media are the helping professions, including psychiatry, clinical psychology, marriage and family therapy, and counseling, which are generally not distinguished from each other in entertainment. Sometimes the therapist is a source of humor (*Frasier, What About Bob?*, *The Bob Newhart Show*, various Woody Allen movies). Very often professional boundaries are violated, particularly in the area of having sexual relations with one's patients (*Prince of Tides, Basic Instinct, Eyes Wide Shut*). Other boundary violations include physically assaulting a patient (*Good Will Hunting*), violating confidentiality and making fun of a patient (*Frasier, What About Bob?*), being a socially repressive force (*One Flew Over the Cuckoo's Nest*), and being severely disturbed oneself (*Silence of the Lambs, Anger Management*) (Bischoff & Reiter, 1999; Gabbard & Gabbard, 1999). Is it any wonder that many people who need help are reluctant to seek it if this is their image of those who provide it? There are some positive and realistic images scattered out there. The therapists in *The Sixth Sense* and *The Sopranos* have won high marks, and perhaps the all-time best cinematic portrayal was Judd Hirsch's Dr. Berger in the 1980 Oscar winner *Ordinary People*.

Perhaps even more of a concern than these fictional portrayals are the media therapists like Dr. Phil and Dr. Laura who actually do some semblance of psychotherapy on the air. Although sometimes the therapist is qualified (Dr. Phil has a Ph.D. in psychology from the University of North Texas) and the therapy is well-motivated (Dr. Phil has off-air follow-up therapy for his clients), television is at heart an entertainment medium with all the attendant pressures of ratings. Thus the "therapy" by these real "Frasier Cranes" must first and foremost be entertaining to third parties. This goal is utterly inconsistent with competent psychotherapy, which requires thoughtful reflection, privacy, and freedom from an audience. Amusing one-line zingers, dramatic confrontations, and pat answers do not cut it. If the public learns that this is what therapy is, that may be just as harmful as the distorted fictional portrayals.

Farmers and Rural Life

As a rule, farmers and rural life in general are not highly visible in media, although a few rural TV shows have been among the most extremely stereotyped and unrealistic in the history of the airwaves. In earlier days, it was *The Beverly Hillbillies* and *Green Acres*, then *Hee Haw* and *The Dukes of Hazzard*. All of these portrayed rural people as uneducated, stupid rubes totally lacking in worldly experience and common sense. True, there was also *The Waltons*, perhaps the most popular rural show of all time, but its historical setting detracted from its use as a model of modern rural life. Many, if not most, of the farm shows have been set in rural Appalachia, one of the poorest and most atypical of rural regions nationwide. There is an occasional depiction of the other extreme: the rural refuge of the very wealthy. However, *Dallas* and *Falcon Crest* were as unrepresentative of rural America as *Hee Haw* was, although for entirely different reasons.

This stereotype is not limited to television. Use of Grant Wood's *American Gothic*-type figures in advertising to reach a rural audience reflects an archaic (if ever accurate) stereotype. The popular comic strip *Garfield* occasionally features Jon Arbuckle's farming parents who come to visit wearing overalls and not knowing how to use indoor plumbing and other modern conveniences. Much humor is based on the fact that there is nothing to do on the farm except count the bricks in the silo. The relatively few films set in rural America often have people speaking in southern drawls, even if the setting is Montana or Michigan. Sometimes one sees rather silly farming symbols, such as a tractor driving down Main Street, used to remind us that we are not in a city.

Problems facing the profession of agriculture have typically been underreported in the news, probably because complex issues like the farm debt crisis of the 1980s are difficult to encapsulate into a brief TV or newspaper story. Also, the people involved with producing media in the United States are virtually 100% urban, usually from New York or Los Angeles, with no roots in any rural community.

College Students

Finally, let us consider the occupation of most of the readers of this book. According to movies, television shows, and advertising, how do college students spend their time? Perhaps foremost is drinking lots of beer and partying into the wee hours. Sometimes wildly excessive and destructive behaviors are presented as normal and amusing, for example, a phone company ad targeted at college students showing a fellow passed out on the bathroom floor after celebrating his 21st birthday by binge drinking. By presenting such behavior as normal, such marketing could encourage binge drinking and all its serious consequences. Second, one would think from ads in university newspapers that almost everybody takes a spring break trip to some beach community where there is lots of fun, sex, and alcohol. Where is the studying? Where is the struggle to earn enough money for next month's rent? Where is the volunteer work? Where is the search for a job after graduation?

Does it matter? Some people in some communities have limited personal interaction with college students, and therefore, this media image becomes reality. One student reported that she had trouble finding a summer job back in her hometown because no one wanted to hire college students, thinking they would be constantly partying and would not be responsible workers.

CONCLUSION: SO WHAT IF THEY'RE STEREOTYPED?

The concern about group portrayals may extend to any sort of group; the ones we have discussed are only some of the most maligned and most studied. Many other groups still struggle with achieving a balanced and realistic treatment from television and other media.

We talk a lot in this chapter about rather narrow and negative portrayals from media, especially television. But what is the impact? Although we have already discussed some effects of research in regard to gender and race images, we close here with a couple of controlled experiments (Murphy, 1998; Slater, 1990). Murphy (1998) exposed people to either a gender-stereotypical or counterstereotypical fictional or factual portrayal of a person. Subsequent apparently unrelated judgments about different people were affected by exposure to the previous portrayal. Particularly for men, exposure to the stereotypical portrayals led to less credibility given to different women in sexual harassment and acquaintance rape cases. It did not matter much whether the stereotype was a factual or fictitious person. Counterstereotypical portrayals had the opposite effect, though it was not as strong.

Slater (1990) presented people with information about some social group. The information was attributed to fiction (from a novel) or non-fiction (from a news magazine) and was about a group that was either familiar or unfamiliar to the participants. If the group was unfamiliar, the fictional portrayal actually was *more* influential in forming beliefs than was the nonfictional portrayal, whereas the reverse was true for the familiar group. This suggests the great power of fictional portrayals on knowledge and attitude formation, when life experience with the group in question is lacking.

For most of the groups described in this chapter, media are major, perhaps the predominant, sources of information for most of us. However, they are usually not the only source; there is often at least some reality to temper the media image. Thus, the perceived reality that our minds construct will not be totally taken from media, although it may be very heavily influenced by it. Occasionally, however, media may be the only source of information. Consider the example of prostitutes.

Practically all adults know what prostitutes are and could give some information about them. Few readers of this book, however, have probably ever known a real prostitute. Where does our perceived reality about prostitutes come from? In most cases it comes not mostly, or partly, but *entirely*, from television and movies. The overdressed TV hooker standing on the street corner in the short, short skirt, high heels, and too much makeup is the reality of prostitutes, as far as most of us know. We might describe someone we see dressed this way as looking like a hooker. But is this what hookers really look like, or is it just the way media portray them? Even as the author of this book, I honestly do not know the answer. All I know is what I see on TV.

If I were to meet a woman tomorrow who was identified as a hooker, my media stereotype (schema) would come into my mind to guide the processing of information about this woman. It would not matter if that image was accurate or not. It would be my perceived reality. This is what is happening with children growing up learning from television about groups of people. Many children have had no more personal contact with Arabs, Jews, African Americans, Latinos, farmers, lesbians, or college students than their exposure in the media. This is why stereotypes matter.

CHAPTER 4

Advertising and Marketing: Baiting, Catching, and Reeling Us In

Q: How much advertising are we exposed to in the mass media?

A: About 500 advertisements per day, 182,000 per year, and millions in a lifetime. Every year, we also receive 216 pieces of direct mail advertising (junk mail) and 50 telemarketing phone calls, and see countless billboards and Internet banner and pop-up ads (J. R. Wilson & Wilson, 1998).

Q: How fast are e-mail ads growing?

A: Between 2002 and 2003 alone, the number of unsolicited e-mails grew almost 1900% to 4.9 trillion messages in the U.S. alone (Taylor, 2003). Another source estimated that 14 billion spam messages are sent each day (Sullivan, 2003).

Q: How much does advertising cost?

A: Corporate advertisers paid $1.9–2 million dollars for a 30-second spot on the 2003 Super Bowl. In terms of a regular series, as of late 2002, the NBC comedy *Friends* drew the highest-priced ads, at an average of $455,700 for a 30-second spot (Numbers, 2002).

Q: Where did the National Hockey League the Anaheim Mighty Ducks get its name?

A: From the 1992 Disney movie *The Mighty Ducks*, where Emilio Estevez coaches a pitiful group of boys into a respected team. Later Disney bought an NHL franchise, changed its name to the Mighty Ducks of Anaheim and used the logo from the movie (Harrison, 1999).

The bottom line of media is advertising. With the exception of public television and radio, most network and local broadcasting and cable television are virtually 100% dependent on ad revenues for financial support. Newspapers typically derive around 70% of their revenue from advertising. Magazines sometimes sell subscriptions below cost simply to raise the readership rate to allow them to charge higher advertising rates. The Internet is increasingly dependent on advertising revenue for support. Everything in media except advertising costs money, whereas advertising brings in all the money. This simple fact explains much of the content of the media. Ultimately it is the advertiser, not the audience, who must be pleased.

In spite of the tremendous costs (up to $2 million for a 30-second spot on the 2004 Super Bowl), advertising is still a remarkably efficient way to reach the buying public. Because of the huge size of the audience for highly rated TV shows, the cost per viewer is often in the neighborhood of a quarter to a half a cent per ad. These, of course, only include the purchase of air time; production costs are extra. On a smaller scale, local newspaper and radio ads are far more reasonable in cost but still quite effectively reach the target area of interest to the advertiser. Perhaps the cheapest of all to produce and distribute are Internet ads and spam e-mails, which can show a minuscule response rate and still be profitable.

Advertising makes very heavy use of psychology, and study of this aspect of advertising could easily fill an entire book. This chapter examines certain aspects of the perceived reality created by advertising but is by no means a thorough examination of its effects. After some initial introductory and historical material, we consider some psychological appeals in advertising, followed by a more specifically cognitive examination of ads, focusing on the issue of deceptive advertising, where the perceived reality is at particular odds with objective reality. Next we examine how sexual appeals are used to build a reality of positive feelings and associations about a product. In this section we also consider the issue of allegedly subliminal advertising, which is said to affect us without our awareness. Finally, we examine the many new places for advertising, which has literally infiltrated itself into all corners of our life. It has become increasingly difficult to separate advertising from the more general category of marketing, because, while advertising traditionally has been restricted to mass media, it is increasingly appearing in new places which are not quite media, but are definitely marketing (Stewart, Pavlou, & Ward, 2002).

HISTORICAL BACKGROUND

The earliest known written advertisement was a classified ad from around 1000 BC and was discovered by archaeologists at Thebes, Greece; it offered a whole gold coin for the return of a runaway slave. Advertisements in the true sense of mass communication did not really exist before Gutenberg's invention of movable type in the mid-15th century, however. Newspapers started carrying ads regularly in the mid-1600s. The rapid commercial growth associated with the Industrial Revolution in the 19th century gave great impetus to advertising, as did the rise of magazines during this same period, when transportation infrastructure, especially railroads, allowed distribution of national publications for the first time in a large country. The rise of radio after 1920, television after 1945, cable TV in the 1980s, and the Internet and World Wide Web in the 1990s provided tremendous new outlets for advertising dollars and creativity.

Although there were early experiments with radio by Marconi in Italy in the 1890s and DeForest in the United States in 1906, the first experimental radio station was set up in 1919 in a Pittsburgh garage by some Westinghouse engineers. Station KDKA broadcast the 1920 Presidential election results. There were 30 stations on the air by the end of 1920 and 400 by 1922. Ensuing concerns and debate about how to finance this new medium culminated in the Radio Act of 1927 for licensing and control of radio stations. This piece of legislation endorsed the free enterprise model to pay for radio (i.e., total revenue from the sale of advertising time with no government subsidy). At about the same time, Great Britain made a very different decision in establishing the government-supported BBC. Both of these economic models were carried over from radio to television in the late 1940s and still frame much broadcasting in their respective societies, although the United States now has some public broadcasting and British TV has become more commercialized. One or the other of these two economic models of broadcasting has since been adopted by most of the countries of the world.

TYPES OF ADS

Advertising is the one type of communication most clearly designed to persuade (i.e., have some effect on the hearer or reader). This effect may be behavioral (buy the product), attitudinal (like the product), and/or cognitive (recognize or learn something about the product). Ads may be for particular brands of products but also for services, such as banks, plumbers, or Internet providers.

Frequently, the most direct purpose of an ad is not selling as such but rather image building or good will. For example, when a multinational corporation spends 30 seconds on TV telling us how it provides fellowships for foreign study, it is trying to encourage viewers to think of it as a fine, upstanding corporate citizen. This is done by associating the company with very positive images and dissociating it from negative ones. Image-building advertising is especially prevalent after a corporation or industry has received a public relations black eye, such as the 1989 *Exxon Valdez* oil spill in Alaska. It also is common when a corporation tries to become involved in consciousness-raising on some issue of importance and public interest, such as when a distillery runs an ad encouraging people not to drive drunk. They believe that the good will they achieve by being perceived as taking a responsible public position will more than offset any decline in sales arising from people buying less of their product due to concern about driving under the influence.

A different kind of persuasive media message is the Public Service Announcement (PSA), usually sponsored by some government agency, non-profit organization, or the Advertising Council. Ads by the American Cancer Society or the United Way are examples of PSAs. Historically, the U.S. Federal Communications Commission (FCC) has mandated that stations must offer a certain amount of time free for PSAs but does not usually specify when that time must be aired; thus PSAs frequently air heavily at off-peak hours like late night or weekdays. With the deregulation and weakening of U.S. regulatory agencies in the 1980s, PSAs suffered even more.

A final kind of advertising is political advertising, usually designed to persuade the viewers to support some candidate, party, or issue. In many ways political advertising is very similar to commercial advertising, although there are some important differences. Political advertising is considered in chapter 8 and thus is not further discussed here.

All types of ads try to affect the reality perceived by the consumer (i.e., give us a new image of a product, candidate, or company or make us feel we have a need or desire for some product that we may not have been particularly wanting before). Such processes involve attempts to change our *attitudes*. Our attitudes about products or anything else actually have three components. The *belief* or *cognition* is the informational content of the attitude. For example, Jim prefers Toyota cars because of certain features they have. The *affective* (emotional) content of the attitude is the *feeling* toward that product. Jim prefers Toyotas because he trusts them, likes them, and feels safe with them. Finally, the *action* is the attitude's translation into behavior. In the case of ads, the advertiser typically hopes the final step in the chain to be a purchase. Some ads are designed primarily to influence our beliefs, and others are designed to influence our affect. See Pratkanis and Aronson (1992) for a review of psychological research on attitude change and persuasion. Next, we examine how advertising shapes our attitudes to help us construct a reality.

PSYCHOLOGICAL APPEALS IN ADVERTISING

Any type of media advertising, whether print or broadcast, uses a variety of psychological appeals to reach the viewer. In one way or another, ads attempt to tie the product or service to our deepest and most basic psychological needs. Implicitly, then, the message is that buying the product will do more than give us something useful or pleasant; it can help us be better people as well.

Informational Appeals

Although not the most common type, some ads primarily provide information in an attempt to influence the belief component of our attitudes. A good example of this type would be an ad for a new product; such an ad may explain what that product does and what its features are. As a medium, newspapers are particularly well suited to conveying information in ads (Abernethy, 1992).

Some of the most common belief appeals are exhortations to save money or receive a superior product or service. The feeling that we are getting a good bargain is a powerful motivator in deciding to purchase something. It is so powerful that often the official list prices are set artificially high so that products may be advertised as costing considerably less, when in fact they may have never been intended to sell at the full list price. *Framing* is also very important. For example, advertising a discount or offering a coupon for some amount off the price is more appealing than saying the price goes up after some time, even if the cost you actually pay is the same.

How to word advertising slogans and other information in the ad is an important consideration. In a strongly informational appeal, the advertiser wants to convey as much information as possible in a very short time but not overload or confuse the consumer. Research suggests the optimal answer may not be simple. Although simpler syntactic structures, such as active rather than passive voice, are generally recognized better than complex ones, there are some cases where *moderate* syntactic complexity might be more effective than either very simple or complex (Bradley & Meeds, 2002).

Emotional Appeals

Very often ads appeal to the affective (emotional) component of our attitudes. Influencing emotions is often the best first step to influencing beliefs and, ultimately, behavior. For example, there are many ads that appeal to our love of friends, family, and good times and the good feelings that they bring us. We are asked to call people long distance to affirm our love, buy diamonds and flowers to show how much we care, and drink beer or pop with friends as part of sharing a good time. Such classic slogans as "Reach out and touch someone" or "Friends are worth Smirnoff" illustrate such appeals. Products are an integral part of showing our love and caring for others. The more closely the advertiser can link the product with those natural and positive emotions, the more successful the ad. A baby food company once advertised that it helps babies learn to chew. Such an appeal links the product with a very basic developmental event in the baby's life, thus giving it a much more central role in the child's growth than any mere product, even an excellent product, would have. A car advertises itself as "part of the family," not merely offering something to the family but actually being part of it.

Closely related to family and love appeals is the linking of the product with fun. This is especially clear in ads for soft drinks and beer and anything marketed directly to children. Photography and copy that link images of a product with those of people having a good time at the beach or the ski lodge, or just relaxing at home with friends, encourage people to think about that product whenever they have or anticipate such times. The product becomes an integral part of that activity, and, more importantly, the feelings associated with that activity. Watching a sports event on TV with friends may naturally cause us to seek such a product, which has become part of the event.

Certain cultural symbols have come to evoke warm feelings in viewers, which advertisers hope will transfer to warm feelings about the product. A boy and his dog, grandma baking an apple pie, the national flag, or a family homecoming are examples. Such symbols appear frequently in advertising of all sorts. Connecting one's product with the positive feelings that people have for such symbols can associate a lot of positive affect with that product. Even the name of the product can evoke certain feelings, perhaps connected with a particular culture or country (see Box 4.1).

Perhaps the most effective selling pitch focuses on how the product will affect one's individual psychological well-being and deep-seated personal needs. For example, a camera ad may say, "Look how good you can be" with their product, not simply "Look what good pictures you can take." The product goes beyond providing you with a good product; it actually makes you a better person. When the U.S. Army recruited with the slogan "Be all you can be," it suggested the psychological appeal of *self-actualization*, whereby somebody is motivated to develop their fullest potential.

Sometimes the emotion elicited may change over time. For example, State Farm Insurance recently announced it was retiring its "like a good neighbor" campaign, first introduced by its ad agency DDB Worldwide in 1971. Although the company had an amazing 98% brand name recognition and nearly 70% of Americans could fill in the blank "Like a good neighbor,___is there," younger and more urban consumers increasingly saw a "good neighbor" in different terms. To many of today's young adults, a good neighbor is one who stays on their side of the fence and leaves you

---

BOX 4.1
CHALLENGES AND PITFALLS OF CHOOSING A FOREIGN PRODUCT NAME

If you want to choose a foreign name for your product, how do you do that? The reality is more complicated than simply finding a *real* foreign word in some appropriate language (e.g., French for a perfume, Spanish for a tortilla, Norwegian for skis). It has to be a word that, for example, *looks* French to people who don't know any French. The clothing company *Le Tigré*, for instance, added the accent to the real French word for tiger ("tigre," with no accent). In doing so, they made the word *less* French in fact, but made it *look* more French to English speakers, who know that French has accents and English doesn't. In another example, Häagen-Dazs ice cream may be made in New York, but its foreign-looking name, complete with umlaut, suggests otherwise. Reactions to foreign product names vary a lot depending on the product and the country (Harris, Garner-Earl, Sprick, & Carroll, 1994; Hong & Wyer, 1989, 1990).

Perhaps the area of greatest danger comes in the chance that a brand name means something quite different in the language of a target market. When General Motors tried to market the Chevrolet Nova in Latin America, it didn't sell well, since "no va" means "it doesn't run" in Spanish. Even worse, when marketing its 1970s' Pinto subcompact in Brazil, Ford discovered that "pinto" is a vulgar term for "small penis" in Brazilian Portuguese. For a short time, the Japanese were puzzled why their popular soft drink, Calpis (pronounced "cow-piss") did not sell well in a U.S. test market, where it was a vulgar expression for "cattle urine." Similarly, brand name changes for the American market might be in order for the Iranian detergent called Barf (American slang for "vomit"), the Mexican bread called Bimbo (American slang for "attractive but dim-witted woman"), or another Japanese drink, Sweat.

Sometimes names of products can be changed in the short-term in response to political whims. For example, during the anti-German frenzy of World War I Americans took to calling sauerkraut "liberty cabbage," frankfurters and wieners "hot dogs," and hamburgers "liberty sandwiches." Such silliness is not purely a historical relic. In 2003, after France refused to support President George W. Bush's invasion of Iraq, the U.S. House of Representatives cafeteria began serving "freedom fries" instead of "French fries" (Rawson, 2003).

---

alone, not one who gets involved in your life, as State Farm was trying to suggest (Elliott, 2002).

Often an emotional appeal is centered around the uniqueness of the product or consumer. Interestingly enough, this type of appeal is especially common from the largest corporations, trying to fight an image of large, impersonal, and uncaring corporate institutions. For example, McDonald's "we do it all for you campaign" and Wendy's ads against "assembly-line burgers" illustrate this approach, as does General Motors' "Can we build one for you?" campaign. This is even more apparent in Saturn automobile advertising, which stresses the importance of the individual consumer and, in fact, never even mentions that Saturn is a General Motors product! Wal-Mart uses such appeals very effectively, with its mini-bios of happy families shopping at Wal-Mart and contented employees who love working there. Such marketing not only makes it look like a fun place to shop but also counteracts its image of the megastore that puts all small businesses out of business. Personal attention to the individual is almost always appealing.

Different emotional appeals can work to varying degrees in different cultures. For example, in a content analysis of print ads in Korean and U.S. news and women's magazines, Han and Shavitt (1994) found that American ads more often stressed individual benefits and pleasures, such as standing out from the crowd and being personally happy, while Korean ads more often pitched collective benefits, such as drawing closer to others or making an office work better together. Sometimes a marketing appeal developed in one culture does not translate well to another. For example, when Nissan developed magazine ads to introduce its luxury Infiniti to the U.S. market with several pages of scenes of nature with the name of the car only at the end of the sequence, the approach did not work. In more holistic, collectivist Japan, where people and nature have an inherent connectedness not appreciated in the West, this appeal had worked (Nisbett, 2003). Even different subcultures sometimes call for different marketing appeals (see Box 4.2)

Patriotic Appeals

Appeals to consumers' national pride are common in ads. They were abundant during the quadrennial Olympic and World Cup events, as well as events like the U.S. Bicentennial (1976), the French Bicentennial (1989) or the Columbus Quincentennial (1992). The nationality of the manufacturer is of minor importance. Toyota is just as likely as General Motors to use an American patriotic appeal to sell cars in the United States. Volkswagen in New York salutes U.S. Olympic victories and McDonald's in Dublin helps raise money for the Irish Olympic team. In terms of advertising themes, patriotism is where the market, not the home office, is.

Sometimes particular international events have their repercussions in advertising. Shortly after the Soviet invasion of Afghanistan in late 1979, a strong wave of anti-Soviet sentiment swelled up in the United States. One Turkish vodka manufacturer began a campaign of "Revolutionary vodka without the revolution" (i.e., buy our vodka and still get imported

---

BOX 4.2
ADVERTISING TO LATINOS

The largest ethnic minority group in the United States as of 2002 were Latinos, with 32 million in 2003 and a projected 56 million by 2020. The $800 billion they spend annually on goods and services has started to attract major advertising attention recently and helped to integrate Hispanic tastes and culture into the national mainstream.

In 2002, NBC bought the second-largest Spanish-language network, Telemundo, for $2.7 billion. Some magazines publish Spanish-language versions (e.g., *People en Español*) and Spanish-language TV and radio are widely available in all major U.S. markets. However, the Latino audience also watches much English-language programming and a large percentage are bilingual and bicultural.

Procter and Gamble aired a Crest Toothpaste commercial in Spanish during the 2003 Grammy Awards Ceremony. Many companies, including Pepsi and Nike, have used some Spanish in their mainstream TV ads. Kraft Foods now sells a milk-based Jell-O (O Gelatina Para Leche), a Kool-Aid flavor "Aguas Frescas," and a lime-flavored mayonnaise. Pepsi and Nestlé sell fruit drinks with flavors like mango and tamarind, and Nabisco began selling three Latin American cookie brands in the United States in 2003 (Weaver, 2003a).

---

quality without supporting those dirty communists). Still, when nationalism crosses the line to tasteless jingoism, it may become commercially counterproductive, as when a small-town U.S. restaurant published an "Iranian coupon—good for nothing," or when some advertisers took heavy-handed Japan-bashing approaches during times of high feeling against Japanese trade practices. After the terrorist attacks of September 2001, advertisers were extremely cautious about doing anything that might appear to be capitalizing on those events, but we still saw an increase in public symbols like the Statue of Liberty or the new "heroes" like firefighters and emergency personnel in advertising. Public outcry against excessively mean-spirited patriotic appeals backfires on the advertiser in ways that tend to discourage such campaigns, at least in their most blatant form.

Fear Appeals

These involve some kind of threat of what may happen if one does not buy the product (e.g., a scenario of a child trying unsuccessfully to phone parents when in danger because the parents don't have call waiting). Selling home computers by asking parents "You don't want your child to be left behind in math because you wouldn't buy him a computer, do you?"

is a subtle but powerful emotional appeal to guilt and fear. Somewhat less subtle are appeals involving the safety of one's children, such as when one car manufacturer showed an apparent sonogram of a fetus in utero as the most important reason to buy its car. Such appeals to parents, playing on their love for and responsibility toward their children, are common and probably highly effective. Psychological research on persuasion shows that fear appeals have varying effects. The conventional wisdom in both social psychology and advertising for many years has been that there is an optimal level of fear at which persuasion is the strongest. A weaker appeal will be less effective, but if the fear induced becomes too strong, the ad may turn people off and make them defensive, in which case they tune out the message. As Rotfeld (1988) pointed out in a careful review paper on fear appeals and persuasion, however, there is no consistency in the research on this point (see also King & Reid, 1990, regarding fear appeals in PSAs). It is hard to draw firm conclusions because what each researcher has defined as a strong, moderate, and low fear appeals has varied widely, and there has typically been little assurance that the participants in the studies have viewed the appeals similarly to the researchers. Indeed, sometimes ads are viewed hugely differently by different segments of the audience, some of whom may be highly offended; see Box 4.3 for a particularly controversial example. Fear appeals in ads can be effective, but exactly which ones are most effective is not yet entirely clear.

BOX 4.3
BAD TASTE OR BRILLIANT MARKETING?

A Nike ad that ran during the 2000 Summer Olympics became very controversial. The ad showed a horrified 1500-meter Olympian Suzy Hamilton running from a masked pursuer wielding a chainsaw. She escapes him due to her superior running shoes and her own athletic ability. Nike defended the ad as one that empowered women and celebrated their strength. Critics assailed it as insensitive "glorified rape fantasy" making light of violence toward women. NBC dropped the ad in response to complaints (Fussell, 2000).

Some other ads that have been pulled after consumer complaints include a pair of Bungee jumpers where one survives because he is wearing Reeboks, a Just for Feet ad where a barefoot African runner is tackled by White westerners who put shoes on his feet, and various Calvin Klein ads with apparent preadolescents in sexual positions that appeared to many to be uncomfortably close to child pornography.

What do you think? Are these creative artistic endeavors or tasteless insensitive marketing? One thing that is not in dispute, however, is that all these ads were noticed.

Achievement, Success, and Power Appeals

Another popular theme in ads is striving to win, whether the prize be money, status, power, or simply having something before the neighbors do. A candy ad may blatantly say "Winning is everything," picturing a chocolate Olympic-style medal, or it may more subtly suggest that only the people who use the particular product have really arrived. The idea that using some product enables us to be a winner is a powerful appeal, whatever the prize. Even an appeal to pure altruism in a PSA can use such an appeal, by calling on us to achieve a "moral victory."

Humorous Appeals

Humor is often used as an effective selling tool in ads. The audiovisual possibilities of television offer a particularly rich set of possibilities for humor, although there is much humor in print and radio advertising as well. Indeed, some humorous ad campaigns have become classics of popular culture (e.g., Alka-Seltzer's "I can't believe I ate the whole thing" campaign of the 1960s, the Wendy's "Where's the beef?" of the 1980s, or the Budweiser frogs of the 1990s). Radio's "see it on the radio" campaign drew on people's ability to use visual imagery to imagine a humorous situation described only through sound (Bolls & Lang, 2003).

One caution regarding the use of humor concerns its distractibility potential. Some humor clearly attracts attention and increases motivation and general positive feeling about the product or service. Sometimes humor in ads may lead to improved memory for the content (Furnham, Gunter, & Walsh, 1998). However, sometimes a very funny spot may be so entertaining that it detracts from the advertiser's message. Viewers may remember the gimmick but forget what product it was selling (Gelb & Zinkhan, 1985).

A related concern in regard to humorous ads is the *wear-out factor.* Any ad campaign depends on repeated presentations to reinforce its message. However, if an ad appears too often in too short a time, its effect may wear out and even become counterproductive by turning people off due to overexposure. Humorous ads have a shorter wear-out time. They become older, more tired, and more annoying faster than other ads (Pechmann & Stewart, 1988).

Testimonials (Product Endorsements)

In the *testimonial* ad, some identified person, such as a well-known entertainer or athlete, offers a personal pitch for some product or service. This person may clearly be an expert in the particular field or no more informed than the average person. Social psychological research on persuasion shows that we are more likely to be persuaded by a prestigious and respected figure, even if that person has no particular expertise in the area of the product being sold (Hass, 1981; T. B. Heath, Mothersbaugh, & McCarthy, 1993; Kahle & Homer, 1985). We tend to trust that person more due to our parasocial relationship (Alperstein, 1991; Giles, 2002), and the positive associations and feelings we have about him or her may be transferred in part to the product, thus transforming that product's image (Walker, Langemeyer, & Langemeyer, 1992). When 1996 Presidential candidate Bob Dole later became a pitchman for Viagra, the trust we felt for Dole and his long years of public service in the U.S. Senate transferred to the anti-impotence medication.

One advantage of testimonials is that it often allows fairly precise age targeting. Bob Dole and Eminem clearly reach a different age demographic. Sometimes a product can be identified so strongly with a particular age group that others might be less interested. For example, Daimler Chrysler originally tried to market its 1930s-retro look PT Cruiser to young adults. However, their baby boomer parents bought the car in droves and it later became identified with that generation. Similarly, the small, economical Toyota Echo appealed not to young buyers but to their parents. The same was true for the Saturn Vue SUV and the boxy Honda Element. In spite of these cars being pitched to them, the young adults instead preferred sportier cars like the powerful Dodge Stratus, Mitsubishi Lancer, and Hyundai Tiburon (Fonda, 2003). An age-connected image can be hard to crack. High median ages of buyers for Buick (63) and Cadillac (55) make a strong youth appeal in marketing difficult. General Motors once tried to market against this image by advertising a certain model was "not your father's Oldsmobile." Apparently its success was limited; GM stopped making Oldsmobiles altogether shortly afterwards.

Can Appeals Be Unethical?

Just because an ad appeals to genuine human emotions does not mean that it is necessarily appropriate in a broader ethical sense. One of the most controversial international media campaigns centered around the selling of infant formula as an alternative to breast milk in poor countries. Although it was sold as being healthier than mother's milk, the fact that it was often mixed with unsafe water and/or in dirty containers actually led to a far greater danger of disease than using breast milk, to say nothing of the added expense to already desperately poor families. Concern over the alleged social irresponsibility of such media campaigns led to a worldwide boycott of Nestlé products (Fore, 1987).

The nearly ubiquitous presence of television around the world has led to numerous advertising campaigns whose appeals have come under fire on grounds of social responsibility. Poor children often spend what little money they have on expensive junk food and soft drinks rather than on wholesome school lunches, thanks in part to the influence of advertising. Even though 40% of Mexico's population has no access to milk, poor people are increasingly starting the day with a soft drink and a Ganso (a sort of Mexican Twinkie), in part due to massive TV ad campaigns of Coca-Cola and Pepsico, who sell more products in Mexico than in any other country outside of the United States (Ross, 1992). American tobacco companies are increasingly turning to developing countries as markets, finding less knowledge of health risks, fewer limits on smoking, and less stringent advertising restrictions. The percentage of smokers in China, for example, has skyrocketed in recent years. How the commercial demands of television and other media confront the real world of desperate poverty leads to many questions about media transmission of values. Is it the media's responsibility to promulgate a more culturally sensitive set of values?

A Theoretical Model

Although advertising may be studied from a variety of theoretical perspectives (see chapter 2), one of the most useful in recent years has been the Elaboration Likelihood Model (ELM) (see Petty, Priester, & Briñol, 2002, for a recent formulation). The ELM was initially developed to account for situations where full attention to processing was lacking but yet some influence might still be occurring, i.e., exactly the situation with the typical exposure to advertising.

The central distinction in ELM is the postulation of two distinct routes to persuasion, the central and the peripheral. The central route involves effortful cognitive processing, where we bring to bear our conscious thought processing and relevant information retrieved from long-term memory. Arguments of the persuader are thoughtfully evaluated to determine their merits, and a conclusion is arrived at.

In contrast to the central route is the peripheral route, which does not have to involve conscious effortful processing. In fact, in the real world of responding to ads, it is neither possible nor desirable to bring the cognitive resources to perform central processing on every TV commercial or billboard. Peripheral processing tends to make an initial, often affective, response to one aspect of the message. For example, we like a commercial because of the familiar rock music sound track, or we dislike one because it features our most hated comedian. When the likelihood of active cognitive elaboration is high, the central route predominates; when it is low, the peripheral route does. When our involvement with a product is low, the peripheral route tends to dominate.

BOX 4.4
AD AS SOCIAL STATEMENT: CASE OF UNITED
COLORS OF BENETTON

One of the most controversial international ad campaigns of recent decades has been the United Colors of Benetton campaign begun by the trendy Italian clothing company in 1989. Instead of picturing the product, Benetton ads present powerful visual images of social issues. Some of these, such as the Hasidic Jew and the Palestinian embracing or the loving family cradling the near-death AIDS patient, suggest uplifting possibilities. Others, such as a burning car or guerrilla fighter holding a human leg bone, are more troubling. Still others, such as a Black woman nursing a White baby, a Black and a White hand handcuffed together, or a rack of vials of blood with names of world leaders on them, are merely striking and vaguely disquieting.

Why such a campaign? In part, it seems to be a personal statement of company President Luciano Benetton and creative photographer Oliviero Toscani. Benetton has long been politically active and was a member of the Italian Senate. Toscani has been a fierce critic of advertising and its promotion of consumerist values. United Colors is clearly a product of their social beliefs. Still, the ads have greatly increased attention to their products and discussion of their ads and have probably helped lead to large increases in sales during this period. Critics, however, are troubled by the apparent exploitation of social problems to sell trendy clothing. The framing of social issues as products seems to demean or commodify them. Various United Colors ads were banned, or proposed for banning, in different North American and European countries in the 1990s (Tinic, 1997).

Thus far we have primarily focused on the general psychological appeals in ads. In any real ad, of course, there may be multiple appeals. Sometimes it is not entirely clear what appeal is being used (see Box 4.4). Although psychological appeals in advertising have been studied from a variety of perspectives, we now turn more specifically to the cognitive perspective and its application to advertising.

COGNITION AND MARKETING: ADS AS INFORMATION TO BE PROCESSED

The cognitive approach to advertising considers an ad as information to be processed (Shimp & Gresham, 1983; Thorson, 1990). A broadcast commercial or print ad is a complex stimulus, involving language (presented orally or in writing) and, for print and TV, pictorial stimuli as well. Television is a particularly complex medium, because it contains both the visual and auditory modalities. Typically, there is a close relationship between the audio and video portion of a TV commercial, but this is not always the case, such as when a disclaimer is presented only in writing across the bottom of the screen (Kolbe & Muehling, 1992). The question of how the consumer processes and integrates information from the verbal and visual components of TV commercials is a complex and important issue in itself (G. Cook, 1992; M. P. Gardner & Houston, 1986; Percy & Rossiter, 1983; Shanteau, 1988).

Stages of Processing

When we perceive and comprehend an ad, there are eight stages of processing involved in understanding and acting upon it (Shimp & Gresham, 1983). First of all, we must be *exposed* to the ad. Second, we choose to *attend* to it, perhaps selectively perceiving some parts more than others. Third, we *comprehend* the message. Fourth, we *evaluate* the message in some way (e.g., agree or disagree with it). Fifth, we try to *encode* the information into our long-term memory for future use. Sixth, some time later we try to *retrieve* that information. Seventh, we try to *decide* among available options, such as which brand to purchase. Finally, we *take action* based on that decision (e.g., buying the product). If any one or more of the stages is disrupted in some way, overall comprehension or impact of the ad may suffer.

These eight stages are involved in our processing of every aspect of the ad. Even something as simple as the choice of a name or slogan for a product can have important ramifications for processing, depending on the nature of that name or slogan. For example, the memorability of a name may vary depending on various characteristics. A name that lends itself to an interactive logo or mental image may be remembered due to its amenability to organizational working memory strategies called *chunking*, which leads to a greater number of possible avenues of retrieval from long-term memory (Alesandrini, 1983). For example, a basement waterproofing sealant named Water Seal once used a logo of a seal (animal) splashing in water in the middle of a seal (emblem). This choice of a name allowed information about the product name (Water Seal), its use (sealing), and its sound (/sil/) to be unified into one visual image that is easy to remember.

Characteristics of the ad may affect how much attentional resources are allocated to processing the ad. A major challenge to advertisers, especially in the age of VCRs, channel-surfing, and pop-up Internet ads, is to grab the attention of viewers. For example, Bolls and Lang (2003) found that highly imageable radio ads draw more attention than less imageable ones, perhaps because of the extra cognitive effort expended in comprehending them.

The context in which an ad appears also will affect how well it is processed and remembered. For example, Furnham, Bergland, and Gunter

(2002) tested students' memory for a beer commercial embedded in a popular prime-time British drama segment *Coronation Street*. The target ad was remembered better if it appeared as the first ad in the commercial cluster than if it had been later. They also found that similar program content (characters drinking in a pub) which appeared just after the break led to improved recall of the beer ad compared to a control group, but that the same content before the ad led to poorer recall of the ad. This may have been due to cognitive interference of the program content with the ad, although recall was also good when the program had characters drinking both before and after the commercial break.

One of the most common types of entertainment programming on television involves high levels of violence (see chapter 9). Perhaps surprisingly, however, Bushman (1998) found that violent programming actually *reduces* memory for the commercials in those shows. (See Bushman & Phillips, 2001, for a meta-analysis in this topic.) In attempting to explain this finding, Bushman suggests one reason may be that watching violence raises one's physiological arousal by making people angry and putting them in a bad mood. An angry mood can prime aggressive thoughts, which in turn may interfere with retrieval of the ad content. Negative moods are known to interfere with the brain's encoding of information. Also, the effort taken to try to repair the bad mood may distract from attending to and processing the ad. Thus it may be that advertisers are not getting as much "bang for their buck" with violent programming as with nonviolent programming. This also suggests that other material being processed during violent entertainment might not be retained as well. Also, the use of such a context runs greater risks of substantial portions of the audience being offended by the material (see Box. 4.3). Thus, perhaps students shouldn't study while they watch violent entertainment.

Sometimes the stimulus may be altered in ways that do not substantially affect its processing. One interesting phenomenon called *time compression* involves compressing a 36-second ad into 30 seconds by playing the ad at 120% of normal speed, an acceleration small enough that it is not readily detected and does not produce a higher pitch or other noticeable distortion. Studies of the reactions to such ads (e.g., Hausknecht & Moore, 1986; D. L. Moore, Hausknecht, & Thamodaran, 1986) show different effects at different stages of processing (e.g., reduced attention and evaluation, two processes that ultimately influence persuasion).

A Constructionist Framework for Understanding Advertising

The cognitive principle known as *construction* argues that people do not literally store and retrieve information they read or hear, but rather modify it in accordance with their beliefs and the environment in which it is perceived. The encoding and later retrieval of information about the product is guided by knowledge structures called schemas (see chapter 2). A schema is a knowledge structure or framework that organizes an individual's memory of information about people and events. It accepts all forms of information, irrespective of the mode—visual or auditory, linguistic or nonlinguistic. The individual is likely to go beyond the information available to draw inferences about people or events that are congruent with previously formed schemas (Graesser & Bower, 1990; Harris, 1981; Harris, Sturm, Klassen, & Bechtold, 1986; Kardes, 1992; Stayman & Kardes, 1992).

For example, a commercial for Lucky Soda might depict a group of dripping, smiling young adults running on a beach and opening a cooler filled with pop. In bold letters at the bottom of the screen are the words Get Lucky. The slogan, along with the picture, evokes a schema from memory, a schema containing information about such events, based on the viewer's experience. This schema helps the viewer draw inferences to fill in information about the scene, as well as ascribe meaning beyond what is specified directly in the ad. In this example, the readers' beach party schema lends a sense of coherence and meaning to a scene that is otherwise incomplete in letting them know exactly what is happening, has happened, or is about to happen. The viewer uses the schema to infer information not specifically stated in the ad, such as (a) the people have been swimming, (b) the temperature is hot, (c) the people are thirsty, and, most importantly, (d) drinking Lucky makes the people happy and playful.

Deceptive Advertising

One issue of great concern to the general public is the issue of deceptive, or misleading, advertising. This relates directly to the theme of perceived reality of media and is at heart a cognitive question. The comprehension of an ad may be tested to determine whether the consumer constructs a meaning at variance with the facts, that is, is deceived (Burke, DeSarbo, Oliver, & Robertson, 1988; Harris, Dubitsky, & Bruno, 1983; Richards, 1990). Ads may deceive either by increasing a false belief held by a consumer or by exploiting a true belief in ways designed to sell the product (J. E. Russo, Metcalf, & Stevens, 1981). This issue is examined in some depth in the following section as an example of an advertising issue eminently amenable to a cognitive analysis.

Miscomprehension Versus Deceptiveness

From a cognitive perspective, the question is much more complex than merely determining the literal truth or falsity of the ad itself. I. L. Preston and Richards (1986; see also Preston, 1994) made a helpful distinction between *miscomprehension* and *deceptiveness*. Miscomprehension occurs when the meaning conveyed to the hearer (perceived reality) is different from the literal content of the message. Deceptiveness, on the other hand, occurs if the conveyed meaning is inconsistent with the facts about the product, regardless of what the ad states. Studies examining comprehension and miscomprehension of ads and other information from media have shown high rates of miscomprehension, typically 20% to 30% of the material misunderstood in some way (Jacoby & Hoyer, 1987).

If both the literal and conveyed messages are true, then there is neither miscomprehension nor deceptiveness. If the literal message is false but is conveyed to the consumer as true, there is deceptiveness but no miscomprehension. For example, if an ad states an incorrect price for a product and we believe it, we have been deceived but have not miscomprehended the ad. The hearer constructs a meaning not consistent with reality, but not because he or she misunderstands the ad. Such advertising is clearly both illegal and bad business and is thus fairly unusual, with the possible exception of ads for weight-loss products and diets. An FTC study of weight-loss advertising (Sommerfeld, 2002) found that nearly 40% of the ads contained claims that were almost surely false, such as "You will lose 30 pounds of fat the first week." Although there is no scientific evidence supporting over-the-counter supplements as leading to sustained weight loss, Americans spend over $33 billion each year on these products and services. People are so eager for a quick fix for losing weight that does not require them to decrease calorie intake or increase exercise that such outrageous claims continue to sell products.

It is also possible to miscomprehend without being deceived. An ad may state a claim that is literally false, but we comprehend it in some nonliteral way that is consistent with reality, and thus we are not deceived. For example, claims like "Our cookies are made by elves in a tree," "A green giant packs every can of our vegetables," or "At this price these cars will fly out the door" are unlikely to be comprehended literally; thus a miscomprehension leads to *not* being deceived. Generally, the U.S. Federal Trade Commission (FTC) and the courts have allowed advertisers to assume some degree of intelligence in the consumer. This issue involves an interesting psychological, and occasionally legal, question of how much intelligence may reasonably be assumed; according to a 1983 policy statement interpreting earlier legislation, advertisers may assume that the consumer is acting reasonably (Ford & Calfee, 1986). See Box 4.5 for a discussion of photographic conventions that you may or may not think are deceptive.

Assuming that an ad does contain factual, rather than purely evaluative, information, determining whether an ad is either deceptive or miscomprehended is not the same as assessing its literal truth value. Truth

---

BOX 4.5
THE CREATIVE WORK OF FOOD STYLISTS

People called food stylists prepare food for photography and try to make it look as good as possible. Sometimes the realities of the studio conventions call for surrogate munchies, and what you see in the ad may not be the real thing. For instance, ice cream may be mashed potatoes covered with chocolate sauce, because ice cream melts too fast under hot studio lights. The head on beer is often shampoo or soap suds, because real beer bubbles do not last long enough for photography. White glue is added to milk to make it look whiter and creamier, and roasted chickens are spray-painted golden brown to look like they've been in the oven for hours—but aren't wrinkled (J. R. Wilson & Wilson, 1998). Pancakes are sprayed with Scotch-Gard to keep the syrup from soaking in so you can see it run appetizingly down the sides of the pancake. Pieces of cereal may be glued into white cardboard in a bowl so they won't ever get soggy.

These conventions have been justified on the grounds that the literal falseness actually presents the product less deceptively and more honestly than literal truth (e.g., real ice cream would look like creamed soup, not ice cream, whereas mashed potatoes look like ice cream). Some cases, however, have been more questionable and sometimes have been disallowed by the FTC or the courts. For example, how many marbles should be allowed in the bottom of a soup bowl to buoy up the solid ingredients before it should be considered deceptively suggesting more solid ingredients than are really there? How about the shaving cream commercial where the sandpaper being shaved was actually loose sand grains on clear plastic? The razor would in fact shave sandpaper, but only fine sandpaper, not coarse. Because fine sandpaper looked like regular paper on TV, the advertiser used the sand grains on plastic. This particular case was argued in the courts for years (I. L. Preston, 1975).

---

may be considered a legal or linguistic question, which may be resolved by examining external reality. Miscomprehension, however, is a function of the understanding of the consumer and is thus basically a question of information processing. As such, it is covert and unobservable and must be inferred from an assessment of someone's understanding of an ad. One may be deceived by an ad that is either true or false in some objective sense; the deception may or may not result from miscomprehension.

True-But-Deceptive Ads (Induced Miscomprehension)

The type of advertising claim that is potentially the most damaging is the statement that is literally true, but miscomprehended, thus deceiving consumers by inducing them to construct a meaning of the ad that is inconsistent with reality. Such statements may be either evaluative or factual statements that imply something beyond themselves. We have long recognized the inferential nature of information processing, and studies on inference strongly suggest that, in order to derive the meaning of a statement, people typically interpret beyond what is explicitly stated. When applied to advertising, the consumer may be led to believe things about a product that were never explicitly stated (e.g., an ad states that a mouthwash fights germs and the reader infers that it destroys germs).

There are several different types of linguistic constructions that may deceive the consumer without actually lying. Such claims may invite the consumer to infer beyond the information stated and thus construct a stronger interpretation. This inference-drawing tendency draws on our knowledge in the form of mental schemas discussed earlier and is a natural component of our information-processing system.

One common class of true-but-potentially-deceptive claims are hedge words or expressions (e.g., *may, could help*), which considerably weaken the force of a claim without totally denying it, e.g., "Scrubble Shampoo *may help* get rid of dandruff *symptoms*," "Rainbow Toothpaste *fights* plaque," or "*Although I can't promise to make you a millionaire by tomorrow,* order my kit and you too *may* become rich."

Another common type of linguistic construction that may imply false information is the elliptical comparative, e.g., "The Neptune Hatchback gives you *more*," "Fibermunchies have *more* vitamin C," or "Powderpower laundry detergent cleans *better*." Comparative adjectives or adverbs necessarily involve some sort of standard to which something is being compared. When a product merely says it gives *more*, the statement is largely vacuous without knowing the basis of comparison (more than what?). As long as anything true could be used to complete the comparative, the statement cannot clearly be considered false. However, our minds tend to construct the most plausible basis of comparison, not necessarily the most accurate.

Often a causal relationship may be implied when no more than a correlational one in fact exists. Making further inferences beyond what is stated directly increases the active cognitive processing by the consumer, which in turn typically improves memory. One particular technique is the juxtaposition of two imperatives, as in "Help your child excel in school. Buy an Apricot home computer" or "Shed those extra pounds. Buy the Blubberbuster massage belt." In neither of these cases does the ad state that buying the product will have the stated effect, but the causal inference is very easy to draw.

Such a cause-and-effect relationship may also be implied in a more general sense. For example, consider a radio commercial for diet pop where a young woman talks about using and liking the product. Then, at the end of the ad, we hear a male voice saying, "And I like the way it looks on her too." Listeners may infer that drinking that product will cause female listeners to be more attractive to men, although the ad never states that directly.

Something unfavorable may be implied about a competitor's products or services, without stating it directly. Although direct false statements about the competition are usually not tolerated, false implications are less clearly proscribed. For example, consumers may infer from some statements like "If we do your taxes and you are audited by the IRS, we will accompany you to the audit" or "Our company gives refunds quickly if your traveler's checks are lost or stolen" that competing companies do not provide the same service, whereas most in fact do so.

Reporting of scientific evidence in incomplete fashion may also imply considerably more than what is stated. In reporting results of surveys, "Three out of four doctors recommended Zayer Aspirin" would not be false if only four people were questioned. Claiming that "2,000 dentists recommended brushing with Laser Fluoride," without reporting the sample size or "In a survey of 10,000 car owners, most preferred Zip" without reporting the number responding is seriously incomplete and potentially misleading. Our minds fill in the missing information in ways favorable to the advertiser.

Comparative advertising may employ very selective attribute comparisons to imply a much more global impression. For example, "The Egret Pistol has more front-seat leg room than a Ford Taurus, more rear-seat headroom than a Nissan Maxima, and a larger trunk than a Toyota Camry" may imply that the car has a more spacious interior on most or all dimensions than any of the competitors, which is not necessarily a warranted inference from the given statements.

Studying Deception Scientifically

In experimental studies, people do in fact make the invited inferences described and remember the inferred information as having been stated in the ad (e.g., remembering that a toothpaste prevents cavities when the ad only said it fights cavities). This is a stable finding that occurs with a variety of dependent measures (Burke, DeSarbo, Oliver, & Robertson, 1988; D. M. Gardner & Leonard, 1990; Harris, Pounds, Maiorelle, & Mermis, 1993; Harris, Trusty, Bechtold, & Wasinger, 1989; Richards, 1990; J. E. Russo et al., 1981). Burke et al. (1988) even developed a computer-based measurement technique for assessing the deceptive effects of advertising claims.

Training people not to make such inferences is very difficult, because the tendency to infer beyond the given information is so strong. However, a training session that has participants individually analyze ads, identify unwarranted inferences that may be drawn, and rewrite ads to imply something more or less strongly, does have some significant effect in teaching them to put a brake on this natural inference-drawing activity (Bruno & Harris, 1980). Such research has direct application to the preparation of consumer-education materials, including some media literacy programs (see chapter 5).

Sometimes changing the wording of an ad may induce highly different interpretations, although it may not neatly fit the deception model. For example, consider a meat advertised as "75% lean" versus one that is "25% fat." Consumers evaluate the former more favorably than the semantically identical latter wording (Levin & Gaeth, 1988). The positive frame leads us to construct a more positive image of the product. One type of currently popular advertising, where one must carefully watch the wording, is ads that appeal to environmental consciousness (see Box 4.6).

Now we turn to some noncognitive aspects of advertising, focusing on the use of sex to sell and more generally on the question of whether we can be persuaded by messages we are not even aware of, so-called subliminal advertising.

SEX AND SUBLIMINAL ADVERTISING

One of the most common types of appeals in advertising is sex. Although some products such as perfume and cologne are sold almost exclusively through sex appeals, practically any product can be marketed through associating it with a beautiful woman or man. The sexual association and allure, and even more, the overall good feelings engendered, then become a part of the perceived reality of that product for many consumers.

Classical Conditioning

A psychological process called classical conditioning sheds some light on how sex in advertising can affect us. Classical conditioning is the process discovered by Ivan Pavlov, who studied the physiology of hunger in dogs in the early years of the 20th century. In his studies he noticed a curious fact: his dogs would often start to salivate merely at the sight of an empty food dish. Given that there is no natural connection between plastic dishes and drooling, why did they do this? Pavlov eventually decided that they had been classically conditioned. This process became one of the cornerstones of experimental (especially behaviorist) psychology and is as important for consumers of ads as it was for Pavlov's dogs.

BOX 4.6
GREEN ADVERTISING

One of the most recent kinds of social responsibility appeals in advertising has been regarding the environment. Being able to advertise one's product as being biodegradable, organic, or otherwise conserving the earth's resources is a popular concern and would seem initially to be a socially responsible position. In fact, the emphasis in green advertising is much more on the means of production and on the consumption process (Iyer & Banerjee, 1993), presumably because that is where the environmental impact is at issue. However, this may not be the best way to reach the consumer.

Green advertising has suffered from a problem of low credibility; consumers apparently are not believing its claims. Sometimes the scientific reality is more complex than what is presented in the ad (T. M. Smith, 1998). For example, one popular kind of trash bag advertised that it was made of biodegradable plastic. Although this sounds good, once a sealed bag of contaminants is in a landfill, it may actually be better for the environment if it is *not* biodegradable, rather than slowly decomposing over several years, gradually releasing toxic content into the groundwater system. Some such products rely on the sun to initiate the decomposition process, and it is not at all clear how much sun the typical bag buried deep in a landfill would receive.

Sometimes some guidelines can be helpful to consumers. For example, in October 2002, the U.S. Department of Agriculture implemented legal definitions of "organic" foods. If a label says "100% Organic," that must mean that all the ingredients contain no synthetic pesticides, herbicides, chemical fertilizers, antibiotics, hormones, or artificial preservatives. "Organic" means that at least 90% of the ingredients meet or exceed the USDA specifications, while "Made with Organic Ingredients" requires only 70% (Bjerklie, 2002). Do you find such guidelines helpful in your shopping?

An *unconditioned stimulus* (UCS) naturally, without learning, elicits an *unconditioned response* (UCR). For example, meat (UCS) naturally produces salivation (UCR) in a dog. Similarly, the sight of a gorgeous woman (UCS) naturally elicits mild sexual arousal or at least some positive feelings (UCR) in most heterosexual males. At this point in the process, there is no conditioning. The conditioning occurs when the UCS is *paired* (associated) with the *conditioned stimulus* (CS), which does not normally elicit the UCR. For example, Pavlov's dog dish (CS) was associated with meat (UCS), just as the attractive model (UCS) is associated with a product (CS) in a commercial. There may be some natural and obvious connection between the model and the product, such as a perfume ad that suggests a woman will attract sexy men if she wears that fragrance, or there may be no intrinsic connection at all, such as the beautiful woman who merely appears next to the steel-belted radial tires repeatedly.

After enough association of the UCS and the CS, the CS by itself comes to elicit the *conditioned response* (CR), which is very similar to the UCR. Just as Pavlov's dogs eventually began to salivate (CR) to the empty food dish (CS), so may we have positive feelings (CR) about the tire (CS) when we see it without the gorgeous model. This basic classical conditioning paradigm is the psychological process being employed by most ads using sexual stimuli.

Ironically, sometimes advertisers themselves may be loath to be associated with certain stimuli that they feel evoke strong negative responses in a large segment of the population. For example, condom manufacturers are wary of becoming too closely associated with the gay community for fear of alienating potential heterosexual customers.

Subliminal Advertising

Although we could look at classical conditioning as a subliminal effect in the broadest sense, people are more likely to worry about subliminal persuasion, especially as applied to advertising. In the late 1950s several popular press articles reported a study by advertising expert James Vicary wherein he reported increasing the sales of Coke and popcorn in a New Jersey theater by flashing the messages "Eat popcorn" and "Drink Coke" for a few milliseconds every 5 seconds during a movie. Although the research was never published and in fact was admitted by Vicary in 1962 to have been a complete fabrication and was only intended to increase his advertising agency's business (Pratkanis, 1992), the public became very alarmed, and the FCC and the National Association of Broadcasters (NAB) outlawed the practice. Excited about its prospects, a few radio stations even started broadcasting subaudible messages like "Isn't TV dull?" and "TV's a bore" (Haberstroh, 1994).

Even today, large numbers of people continue to uncritically accept the existence of subliminal persuasion, in spite of there being no credible scientific evidence for its existence or effectiveness. *Subliminal* means below the threshold of conscious perception; by definition, if something is subliminal, we are not aware of it. Such stimuli may be a subaudible sound message in a store ("Don't shoplift"), a very brief visual message in a movie or TV show ("buy popcorn"), or a visual sexual stimulus airbrushed into an ad photograph (S-E-X spelled in the crackers or sex organs drawn in the ice cubes). What are the alleged effects of such stimuli? Do they, in fact, work to sell products?

A helpful distinction to bear in mind in considering this problem is the difference between establishing the *existence* of some subliminal stimulus and demonstrating that such a stimulus has some *effect*. Books like Wilson Bryan Key's *Subliminal Seduction* (1974), *The Clam-Plate Orgy* (1981), *Media Sexploitation* (1976), and *The Age of Manipulation* (1989) focus on demonstrating the existence of subliminal messages and sexual implants, but they give few arguments to demonstrate any effects that such stimuli have. Such authors often implicitly assume that showing its existence also entails that it has an effect. This assumption is completely unwarranted, however. Although there is some reputed evidence of an effect (Cuperfain & Clarke, 1985; Kilbourne, Painton, & Ridley, 1985), much of the so-called evidence is anecdotal or open to other interpretations. In fact, there is little evidence that subliminal messages affect people very much (see Merikle & Cheesman, 1987; T. E. Moore, 1982, 1988; Pratkanis, 1992; Pratkanis & Greenwald, 1988; and Saegert, 1987, for reviews).

Moore (1982) identified three types of stimuli: subliminal visual perception, subaudible speech, and embedded sexual stimuli, and carefully examined research evidence on possible effects in each. Moore concluded that there is only a little evidence, although it is far from compelling and not directly related to advertising anyway, that subliminal stimuli may in some cases have a weak positive effect of a general affective nature (i.e., they make us feel a little better about the product, probably due to classical conditioning). However, there is virtually no evidence for any effects of subliminal stimuli on *behavior*. Saegert (1987) looked at the very few studies that seem to suggest effects and argued that other interpretations are possible. The conclusion at this point seems to be that subliminal stimuli may exist on occasion but that their effects are minimal or nonexistent. Subliminal advertising seems to be a perceived reality in the mind of much of the public, but not an actual reality that stands up to scientific scrutiny. The same is true for subliminal learning tapes (Greenwald, Spangenberg, Pratkanis, & Eskenazi, 1991; Merikle, 1988; Merikle & Skanes, 1992). One new area not yet receiving much scientific or public attention is the possibility of presenting subliminal visual stimuli via computer, such as on web sites.

Similar issues are involved in heated controversies over subliminal messages in rock music. In 1990, the family of two teenage suicide victims in Nevada brought suit against the group Judas Priest and CBS Records, on the grounds that subliminal and backmasked messages on the album *Stained Class* had directed the boys to take their own lives; the judge ruled against the family (J. R. Wilson & Wilson, 1998). Another concern has been allegedly satanic messages recorded backwards into certain rock music recordings. See Box 4.7 for details of a careful research program designed to test for effects of such stimuli.

BOX 4.7
SATANIC MESSAGES IN ROCK MUSIC?

Periodically one hears the claim that some rock music contains embedded messages recorded backward. Although no one claims that these messages can be consciously perceived easily when the record is played forward, concern has been expressed that there may be some unconscious effect unbeknownst to the listener. Furthermore, some have even been concerned that such messages may be satanic and have caused legislation to be introduced in several states that would call for warning labels about such messages to appear on album jackets.

Psychologists John Vokey and Don Read of the University of Lethbridge in Alberta were contacted by a radio announcer for information about this phenomenon. They first made the point that the *existence* of such embedded messages does not presuppose any *effect* of such messages on the listener. The evidence presented by concerned members of the public is highly anecdotal and often debatable but nearly always speaks to the existence issue, not the effects issue.

Vokey and Read (1985) conducted a careful series of studies designed to test the effects of such messages, assuming for the moment that they exist (an assumption that is not at all established, but we will leave that for now). When verbal messages on tape were played backwards, research participants showed no understanding of the meaning; identifying the sex or voice of the speaker was about all that they could perceive. Next, they tested for *unconscious* effects by giving a spelling test where some of the words were homophones (*read, reed*). A biasing context sentence (*A saxophone is a reed instrument*) was played backward, but listeners were no more likely than a control group to write *reed* instead of *read*. When backward messages were played and subjects were merely asked to assign the statement to the category Christian, satanic, pornographic, or advertising, based on its content, they could not do so at greater than chance level. The only time that people ever perceived and reported anything at greater than chance level was in one study where the experimenter picked out words in advance and asked the participants to listen for them. Only under conditions of such strong suggestibility could people comprehend anything from the backward messages.

Vokey and Read's studies clearly demonstrate that, even if backward messages do exist in albums, it is highly unlikely that they could be having any effect on the hearers. This conclusion is all the more striking considering that in their studies there was no competing forward message like the music in rock albums. In at least a couple of cases, proposed record-labeling legislation was withdrawn based on results of this research.

ADVERTISING IN NEW PLACES

In recent years advertisers have had to scramble harder and harder to attract and keep our attention. Although ads seem to be everywhere, we have more technology to delete or subdue them (e.g., muting or fast-forwarding videos, using delete keys and spam filters for e-mail ads). In response, the advertisers have become more and more clever in placing ads in places we can't ignore, sometimes even in places where we don't realize they are ads. This section of the chapter looks at several of these.

Product Placements

When your favorite actor in a TV show or movie drinks a Pepsi, smokes a Marlboro, or uses a Sony Walkman, is the choice of a brand coincidental? Hardly. The manufacturer has probably paid thousands of dollars through a placement agent or somehow contributed to the film or TV show as part of a deal to have those products used. For example, Nokia paid to have Jennifer Aniston use one of their cellular phones in *Friends* and producers of *The Saint* actually shot *after the film wrapped* and used several scenes featuring Volvo's latest model, in response to Volvo's offer of an ad campaign that promoted the car and the film together (Gornstein, 1997). Ramses Condoms paid over $10,000 to feature its product in *Lethal Weapon II*, while Safetex paid around $15,000 to have Julia Roberts pull a Gold Circle condom out of her boot while sitting on Richard Gere's desk in *Pretty Woman* (J. R. Wilson & Wilson, 1998). James Bond films are some of the most blatant and ubiquitous uses of product placements, including Visa card, Avis car rental, Smirnoff vodka, Ericsson cell phones, British Airways, Omega watches, Heineken beer, L'Oreal makeup, and Mercedes automobiles (Rimmer, 2002). The reality-based TV shows like *Survivor* and *American Idol* have brought product placement to new heights, with their many scenes of the "cast" using the products.

Often the payment for such positioning is more subtle than a flat fee for appearance of the product. For example, Plantronics placed its headsets in *Minority Report* and *Die Another Day* in 2002 by paying "marketing dollars" for costs toward promotion of the film (Rimmer, 2002). This way film advertising, trailers, and merchandising can promote both the product and the film at the same time.

Do product placements work? After Elliott used Reese's Pieces to lure the alien from his hiding place in the family's backyard in *E.T.* in 1982, sales of the candy increased by 65%. Mars had initially declined an offer to use M&Ms in this role (Rimmer, 2002). Although there has not yet been a lot of research on effects of product placements, one study showed research participants a 20-minute clip from the movie *Die Hard*, where the lead character either smoked or did not smoke; those who saw him smoking found him more appealing than those who saw the nonsmoking clip (Gibson & Maurer, 2000).

Variations on product placement are becoming more numerous and more creative. In 2002, cosmetics giant Revlon cut a deal with ABC to have a part on three months of the soap opera *All My Children*, where the story line had a protagonist spying on a rival firm (Eisenberg, 2002). The digitally animated movie *FoodFight!* features a supermarket coming to life, where the "good brands" like Twinkie the Kid, Charlie the Tuna, Mrs. Butterworth, and Mr. Clean battle the evil "brand-X" products for control of the store (Eisenberg, 2002).

There are even product placements within other ads (Elliott, 2002b). For example, a Toyota ad featured a Sony Vaio laptop computer inside the car to highlight its feature of a 110-volt outlet inside the car, at the same time burnishing the prestige of both products. Sometimes the juxtaposition can be more humorous for purposes of attracting attention. For example, Chevrolet featured a TV commercial with the two "lonely Maytag repairmen" cruising around in a Chevrolet.

Guests on talk shows may even be product placements of a sort. For example, drug companies sometimes pay celebrities like Lauren Bacall, Kathleen Turner, or Rob Lowe for pushing their products on talk shows (Eisenberg, 2002). Sometimes these guest appearances were not noted as paid appearances.

Is there an artistic or ethical problem with product placements? If the script, the blocking, and the editing are driven by motivation to show a product rather than artistic and script-driven concerns, there may be a compromise of artistic quality. Particularly troubling is the case of the modeling of the use of unhealthy or dangerous products, such as tobacco or alcohol. For example, although instances of smoking on U.S. TV are very low (far lower than the 25% or so of the population who smoke), smoking is far more common in movies and its incidence has not fallen in the last forty years. Much of this difference is attributed to product placement of tobacco in movies.

Classrooms and Schools

As school districts and universities become increasingly financially strapped, they are turning to private industry to provide funds that public entities do not have. One sort of arrangement is the sales contract where a school agrees to exclusively sell one brand of soft drink, for example, on its campus for some period of time in return for a substantial sum. For example, one university concluded a contract with Pepsico to sell only Pepsi drinks on campus in return for $5 million dollars for the university library.

At a time when journal subscriptions and library hours were being cut, $5 million dollars was a big help.

Public schools have long had corporate tie-ins, like the Pizza Hut Book-It campaign, where an elementary school child receives a coupon for a free Personal Pan pizza from Pizza Hut if they complete an agreed-upon number of pages of reading per month. Sometimes if everyone in the class meets the requirements, the whole class gets a pizza party at the end of the semester. Children are encouraged to read, and Pizza Hut socializes a new generation of customers for its restaurants.

Sometimes there are required sales quotas to actually receive the money. For example, a Colorado Springs, Colorado school district was somewhat behind on its agreement with Coke to sell 1.68 million bottles of Coke products. Not wanting to risk losing the $8 million, 10-year contract, the district administrator moved vending machines to more accessible areas, encouraged principals to allow drinking Cokes in class, and generally exhorted staff and students to drink more Coke products as a way to support their school (Labi, 1999).

Advertising has become a fact of life in schools. School buses sell advertising space, high school athletic scoreboards have ad panels, students watch the commercials on daily news summaries on Channel One or CNN Headline News, and Taco Bell and Pizza Hut sell their products in the school cafeteria (Wartella & Jennings, 2001).

Sometimes ad money can go to other good uses. The bottled-water maker Evian refurbished a run-down public swimming pool in the London suburb of Brixton and tiled the bottom with its brand name, which just happens to be highly visible for passengers arriving and leaving from nearby Heathrow Airport (Eisenberg, 2002).

Advertisers are forever finding new places to put ads; see Box 4.8 for some of the newest and most creative.

Advertising on the Internet

One of the fastest growing areas of advertising is the Internet, although that has provided some challenges to marketers as well (Schumann & Thorson, 1999). The pop-up, pop-under, and banner ads familiar to us on most web sites tend to be as annoying as they are ubiquitous. The more salient they are, the more annoying. The ads that pop up and are hard to get rid of risk alienating the potential market, yet the advertiser has to get people's attention. The most explosive growth of ads on the Internet in recent years has come in the form of spam, or e-mail advertising, which grew almost 1900% in the U.S. between 2002 and 2003 alone, to 4.9 trillion pieces of mail (Taylor, 2003). Many of these are for cheap loans, weight-loss products, Viagra and other drugs, computer cartridges, and most distressingly,

---

BOX 4.8
CAPTIVE MARKETING

The advertising industry is forever finding new places to hawk its wares. Some of the newest agencies, with names like Flush Media, Cunning Stunts, and Captivate Network, take advantage of places where people find themselves necessarily looking at a flat surface for entirely unrelated reasons. One of the most potentially profitable of these new "captive marketing" sites are public restrooms. Print ads or even video screens are appearing above sinks, urinals, and inside toilet stall doors in restrooms. The user is captive for a minute or so, a building owner can make some profit off the otherwise no-income-producing restroom, and very precise gender-targeted marketing can occur. Another popular new advertising site is the elevator, another non-revenue-producing space where both the advertiser and building owner can now make a profit. Increasingly, we are also seeing video ads in theaters, airplanes, buses, taxis, and even golf carts (Orecklin, 2003).

Sometimes we meet marketing where we least expect it. Big Fat Promotions of New York has hired people to pose as bar customers and talk up certain drinks to the clientele, mothers to talk up a laundry detergent at their children's ball games, and commuters to play with a certain PDA on the train home from work (Eisenberg, 2002). A British agency even rents college students' foreheads to display corporate logos of semipermeable color transfers made from vegetable dye. These last about a week, and students receive $6.80 an hour for the 3-4 hours a day they are visible to other students. Cunning Stunts spokesperson Nikki Horton reports reaction from financially struggling students has been "overwhelming" (Payne, 2003).

---

breast- and penis-enlargement products, pornography, and solicitation of sexual encounters. How to screen out the spam has been a major challenge of e-mail providers and programs in recent years. Some are even questioning whether the huge volume of spam will soon begin to make e-mail not worth the trouble (Sullivan, 2003).

How effective are Internet ads and how do people respond to them? Social psychologist Brad Sagarin and his colleagues have conducted some research to begin to answer that question (Sagarin, Britt, Heider, Wood & Lynch, 2004). First of all, they found an extreme version of the third person effect (Perloff, 2002); almost everyone thought that they themselves paid no attention and were not affected at all by Internet ads. In fact, although they found the ads annoying, most people seemed willing to go along with the "exchange" of putting up with the ads in exchange for free Internet use. However, Sagarin et al. found some subtle ways that people were affected by Internet ads in ways unbeknownst to them. For example, the ads did sometimes distract users doing a problem-solving task, even though they did not remember paying attention to them.

Perhaps the most troubling aspect of computer-mediated advertising is the advertising of pornographic materials and solicitations through web site advertising and through e-mail. Offers to sell products to augment penis or breast size, improve sexual potency, view sexually explicit photos, and, most disturbingly, meet sexual partners, come frequently and routinely by mass mailing to e-mail accounts. Many children have such accounts, especially through free providers like Hotmail, Yahoo, or Juno, and regularly receive such e-mails. Spam filters help some but do not screen out everything. Although the threat of porn on the Internet is often magnified to an irrational frenzy, the threat is real, and the legal system and social norms have not caught up with technology in figuring out how to deal with it. Child pornography in particular has become much easier to circulate via the Internet and e-mail, in spite of being illegal almost everywhere.

Prescription Drug Advertising

Although not a new place for advertising, one of the fastest growing areas of advertising, in terms of type of product, is the pharmaceutical industry. Emerging from being almost nonexistent at the start of the 1990s to an estimated $1.7 billion spent on TV advertising alone in 2000, the hawking of prescription drugs is a major growth industry (Belkin, 2001). Fourteen percent of prime time shows in the U.S. advertise prescription drugs, while half of adult prime-time programming and 43% of popular teen shows have ads for over-the-counter drugs (Christenson, Henriksen, & Roberts, 2000). A 1997 loosening of requirements which formerly had required including all consumer warnings in every ad, greatly facilitated this trend. One positive effect of this change is some increased empowering of the public to learn about these drugs and request them from their physicians. While this probably has brought needed treatment to some who would otherwise remain undiagnosed, it also has quite likely brought unneeded treatment to some looking for a quick fix to all of life's problems. Although a physician's prescription is usually still necessary, this is sometimes obtained without a consultation, particularly with drugs purchased over the Internet.

CONCLUSION

This chapter is in no way a comprehensive review of the psychological effects of advertising or even of all issues relevant to the perceived reality of advertising. Rather, the emphasis is on looking at a few areas where advertising attempts to create a reality within our minds that is conducive to purchasing a product. We are taught positive emotional associations about the product through classical conditioning or association of the product with positive experiences in our past. Natural information-processing tendencies like drawing inferences and invoking knowledge schemas to interpret ads are used by advertisers to encourage us to draw certain inferences and interpretations. Knowledge of the way that the mind processes information allows the advertiser to produce ads designed to encourage us to construct a meaning favorable to the advertiser's ends. On the other hand, knowledge of such processes also allows consumers to take steps to be less manipulated. One important issue in advertising that we have not yet examined is advertising to children, which is looked at in the next chapter, along with some tips on how to handle media influence within the family (media literacy). Advertising is not going to go away and, in fact, will keep finding new places to ensconce itself.

CHAPTER 5

Children and Media: More Than Just Little Adults

Q: What is the most watched educational television program of all time?
A: *Sesame Street,* on the air continuously with new episodes since 1969.
Q: What are the two most important attributes of television shows for children 6 to 11?
A: Comprehensibility and action. These were the most valued attributes by both Dutch and U.S. children (Valkenburg & Janssen, 1999).
Q: How many 7th to 12th grade smokers preferred Camel cigarettes *before* and *after* the Old Joe smooth character ad campaign began in 1988?
A: Less than half of one percent chose Camels before Old Joe. Two years later, 33% did (DiFranza et al., 1991).
Q: What ages were deemed appropriate for "Forward Command Post," a bombed out dollhouse with smashed furniture and bullet holes in the walls, and "Burnout 2: Point of Impact," an auto racing video game of scenes of gruesome car crashes, including one where a man's head goes smashing through the windshield?
A: Forward Command Post was recommended for children 5 and up, and Burnout 2 was rated appropriate for 6-year-olds (Herbert, 2002).

Much of the concern about media involves their effect on children, and much of the research cited so far in this book has been done on children. However, in this chapter we look at some aspects of child and adolescent development that are particularly important for understanding the effects that media have on young people. We begin with the way children use different media. Next we look at children's prosocial television and its effects. Next, following up on the last chapter, we examine advertising directed at children, one of the fastest-growing advertising markets. Finally, we examine attempts to teach children about media at home and in other settings, that is, media literacy. We may not be able to completely shield our children from media, but there is much we can do to mitigate its negative effects.

CHILDREN'S USE OF DIFFERENT MEDIA

Mental Effort and Social Interaction

Although fiction occurs in both written and television format, children recognize at an earlier age that books are fiction (Kelly, 1981); television *looks* more like real life. Thus, the perceived reality based on television is more easily confused with reality itself than is the printed construction of reality. The medium itself affects how the child can extract information from that medium and represent it in memory (Salomon, 1979, 1983, 1987). In general, television involves a lower amount of invested mental effort (AIME) than print media, although this varies with age and type of program (Bordeaux & Lange, 1991; Salomon, 1984). Lower socioeconomic status and minority children are even more likely to accept the television reality as accurate than are white middle-class children (Dorr, 1982).

Greenfield (1984) offered an insightful discussion of the historical development of media in regard to the psychological processes engaged by each medium. The invention of print several centuries ago permitted for the first time the widespread physical storage of information. People who had acquired the skill of literacy thus had access to vast amounts of information previously unavailable except through oral tradition. Literacy also had a social implication, in that it was the first medium of communication that required solitude for its effective practice (Olson, 1994).

Critics of television who fear that its advent has isolated children from social interaction are in fact concerned about an earlier effect of the onset of print media; television only continued the requirement of physical isolation, but it did not initiate it. In fact, research has shown no relationship between the amount of television watched and time spent in interpersonal activity.

More recently, concern has focused on the use of the Internet and World Wide Web. Fears of web surfers being socially isolated, perhaps even socially inept, sound amazingly like concerns expressed in the early days of print and later in the early days of television. In a very provocative book, Reeves and Nass (1996) argued that we interact with computers, televisions, and other media much more similarly to the way that we interact with other people than most of us realize. For example, we treat computers with politeness and emotion and perceive them as having personalities.

Information Extraction and Memory

In some ways radio and newspapers may have more in common cognitively with each other than either does with TV. Whereas both radio and print are heavily verbal media, television involves the pictorial dimension as well. There is a positive correlation between the comprehension of a story read from a book and one heard on the radio, but less of a relationship between a story read and one seen on television (Pezdek & Hartman, 1983; Pezdek & Stevens, 1984). This suggests that skills for extracting information from television are different from those used to extract information from the words of radio or print. Studies of television show that children derive more information from the visual component than from the verbal one (Hayes & Birnbaum, 1980), although the high degree of redundancy between the two generally aids comprehension. Overall, material presented via television was better understood than the same story presented via radio to second- and sixth-grade children (Pezdek, Lehrer, & Simon, 1984), and it was consistently remembered better, regardless of reading proficiency (Gunter, Furnham, & Griffiths, 2000). Presentations on television led to fewer later novel ideas from the child than did the same presentation on radio (Valkenburg & Beentjes, 1997). Thus, television is a very efficient way to transmit information to children, suggesting both greater potential and greater concern regarding this medium.

Beagles-Roos and Gat (1983) had children retell a story heard on the radio or seen on television. The style of the retold stories differed in an interesting fashion. Retold TV stories contained more vague references, such as the use of pronouns without identifying the referent, the use of definite articles ("*the* boy...") without first introducing the referent, and other forms presupposing more shared information with the hearer. Retold radio stories provided more information, much as a radio sports play-by-play provides more information than a televised play-by-play. Having children write a story from either TV or real life, Watkins (1988) found that the amount of television the child watched determined how elaborate and complex the TV story was. Greenfield (1984) suggested that one subtle effect of watching a lot of television could be to learn a verbal style that is relatively vague in reference, much like talking face-to-face. In both cases, much shared knowledge may be assumed, and thus less must be explicitly explained. With radio and print, however, the language must be more explicit to compensate for the lack of a pictorial component.

Baggett (1979) found that adults recalled information from either a silent movie (*The Red Balloon*) or a constructed spoken version equally well, whereas young children remembered the silent film version better. This visual advantage in memory may be part of the appeal of television. Although it decreases somewhat with age, it is a natural characteristic of our cognitive processing system, rather than one that is subtly induced by television exposure. The visual continues to have some advantage even with adults, however. In delayed testing a week later, Baggett found that the adults also showed better memory for the visual than the verbal story.

The Medium and Imagination

Although media, especially television, have the potential to stimulate or reduce children's creativity and imaginative play, overall there is much more evidence for some type of reduction effect (Valkenburg, 2001). Certainly creative play can be stimulated by watching certain TV shows, especially educational TV, but facilitated creativity does not appear to be a general effect. *Sesame Street* and especially the slower paced *Mister Rogers' Neighborhood* have been shown to stimulate imaginative play (J. L. Singer & D. G. Singer, 1976; Tower, Singer, & Singer, 1979), whereas action-adventure shows are associated with the lowest imaginative play scores (J. L. Singer & D. G. Singer, 1981).

Reductions in creativity or imaginative play could come for several reasons. First of all, there is some evidence that television watching displaces more creative play and interferes simply by replacing that activity. Other possible explanations remain possibilities but have as yet garnered less general support (Valkenburg, 2001). TV may induce passivity, which is inconsistent with imagination and creativity, or the rapid pacing of children's programs does not allow time for reflection and imagination. Finally, the highly visual nature of television may be so salient that it may distract from processing ideas creatively, a type of thinking that may be easier with print or radio presentation. J. L. Singer and D. G. Singer (1981) found that preschool children who watched more TV were less likely to have an imaginary playmate and showed lower scores on imaginative play.

One sometimes hears the claim that radio is the medium requiring the most imagination, due to the need to mentally fill in the missing visual aspect. A fascinating study reported in Greenfield (1984) had children complete interrupted stories told via radio or television. Results showed that radio stories evoked more novel elements in the imagined story endings than did the televised versions of the same stories. For a thorough review of the medium of radio and its effects, see MacFarland (1990).

Does watching television interfere with the development of reading skills or fantasy play? It probably depends on what activity television is replacing. See Box 5.1 for a look at several hypotheses about the effects of television on reading.

PROSOCIAL CHILDREN'S TELEVISION

Given children's massive exposure to media, primarily television, it is all but inconceivable that they are not learning anything from it. Understanding children's perceived reality and what they are learning from TV requires careful examination of both the content of the programs and the

---

BOX 5.1
DOES TELEVISION INTERFERE WITH READING?

A common concern of many parents is that their children watch too much television and do not read enough. Beentjes and van der Voort (1989) identified several hypotheses about the effect of watching TV on reading and looked at the support for each of them.

A *stimulation hypothesis* argues that watching television stimulates or enhances reading. Not a theory that is widely held, only two small pieces of evidence support it, namely reading subtitles on foreign TV (see Box 12.2) and reading a book directly based on a TV show after watching the show (see Box 5.3).

More widely believed and scientifically studied is some sort of *reduction hypothesis*, with TV watching having a negative impact on reading. There are five variations of this hypothesis. First, the *passivity hypothesis* (e.g., Healy, 1990) argues that TV causes children to become more mentally lazy and less prepared to invest the mental effort necessary for reading. Although it is true that TV requires less mental effort than reading (Salomon, 1984, 1987), viewers are far from totally passive. A second variety of reduction hypothesis is *concentration-deterioration*, which says that TV weakens a child's ability to concentrate. There is really no support for this either. The least promising of the reduction hypotheses is probably the *retardation hypothesis*, which argues that TV deteriorates or rots the brain. The active verbal and visual information processing required in watching TV or any other medium makes this untenable. The *anti-school hypothesis* argues that TV leads children to expect school to be as entertaining as *Sesame Street* or *Barney and Friends* and, when it is not, they lose motivation. This is a difficult hypothesis to study empirically, and the evidence that does exist is inconclusive.

Finally, the *displacement hypothesis* argues that television hurts reading but only when it takes away time from reading. Although all the research is not entirely consistent (Koolstra & van der Voort, 1996; Mutz, Roberts, & van Vuuren, 1993; Ritchie, Price, & Roberts, 1987), this hypothesis has the most support. If children watch TV instead of reading, it may diminish their reading skills. If they watch TV in addition to reading, there probably is no detrimental effect on reading. Regarding fantasy play, watching nonviolent TV programs does not interfere with children's fantasy play, but violent shows reduce fantasy play (van der Voort & Valkenburg, 1994). Overall, TV appears to stimulate day dreaming but reduce creative imagination (Valkenburg & van der Voort, 1994).

---

cognitive processing that the child is capable of at different developmental stages. Here, however, we focus on some specific projects designed to teach through television.

Although there had been some specifically educational children's shows on the U.S. commercial networks since the early 1950s (e.g., *Ding Dong School, Romper Room, Captain Kangaroo*), by the mid-1960s there was increased interest in developing more children's television programming that would be commercial-free, explicitly educational, socially positive, and of high technical quality. In the United States, the Corporation for Public Broadcasting was founded in 1967, followed by the PBS in 1970. The artistic and technical quality of children's programming greatly improved in this period, particularly with the founding of the Children's Television Workshop (CTW) in 1968, initially supported by both public and private funds.

Sesame Street

The next year saw the debut of *Sesame Street*, one of the most important television shows of all time. Although it was only the first of several such shows, *Sesame Street* is still by far the most successful and popular young children's show worldwide; it is seen in 130 countries with 19 different adaptations. As appropriate, it has been translated into many languages but is always locally produced and adapted to local culture (Fisch et al., 1999; Gettas, 1990). Its original stated purpose was to provide preschoolers with an enriched experience leading to prereading skills. With its urban and multicultural setting, the program was especially targeted at so-called disadvantaged children who often entered school less prepared for reading than their peers. In fact, however, the show appealed to children across the social spectrum. Regular characters like Big Bird, the Cookie Monster, Oscar the Grouch, and Bert and Ernie have become part of almost everyone's childhood.

What the Show Is Like.   The technical quality of *Sesame Street* has been consistently very high, using much animation, humor, and movement. There is a pleasing mixture of live action, animation, and puppet/muppet characters. Recognizing that commercials are familiar and appealing to young children, *Sesame Street* draws on many technical characteristics of ads (e.g., "This program has been brought to you by the letter H and the number 6."). More recently the influence of music videos is apparent in the many segments that use that format. The segments are short, so as to not lose even the youngest viewers' interest. In fact, even some infants under 1-year-old are regular watchers. Practically all people now reaching adulthood in many societies of the world have had some exposure to *Sesame Street*, and many have had very heavy exposure. In many markets it is shown 3 to 4 hours per day on PBS affiliates, and much more is available on video and DVD. In some weeks, 70 to 80% of 2- to 5-year-olds see it at least weekly, making it by far the most watched educational TV program in history.

There is also much wordplay and satire to amuse adults watching with their children or listening in the background. A rock band of insect muppets sings about nutrition in the song "Hey Food," which just happens to sound a lot like the Beatles' "Hey Jude." There is also spoofing of its own network, PBS. The segment "Monsterpiece Theatre" featured a smoking-jacket-attired Cookie Monster ("Good evening. I'm Alastair Cookie.") introducing classics about numbers and letters, including "The Old Man and the C," "1 Flew over the Cuckoo's Nest," and "The Postman Always Rings Twice." In its own version of *Lethal Weapon 3*, Mel Gibson and Danny Glover duck a falling concrete number 3. Children are introduced to operatic music at the all-bird Nestropolitan Opera with conductor Phil Harmonic and lead tenor Placido Flamingo. Popular adult stars frequently put in guest appearances: Jay Leno, Glenn Close, Candace Bergen, Barbara Walters, Phil Donahue, Paul Simon, Robin Williams, and even the mayor of New York all visited *Sesame Street*. Adults who had earlier watched the show as preschoolers frequently have the feeling seeing *Sesame Street* as adults that there are a lot of nuances that they had missed earlier, unlike shows like *Barney and Friends* or *Mister Rogers' Neighborhood*, which have little intrinsic appeal to adults. This appeal is not accidental; children get more out of *Sesame Street* if their parents watch and discuss it with them, and the producers know that.

The intentional use of a multiracial, multiethnic, multiclass, and increasingly gender-balanced cast ensemble has set a valued social model for children as well; it provides a far more diverse and positive multicultural modeling than most of what is offered by commercial television. Among the human characters on the show, there have always been substantial numbers of women and members of diverse ethnic groups, who go about their business of being human, not particularly being members of some social group. Sometimes the teaching is more focused. For example, there is a heavy drawing from various Hispanic cultures, including Spanish and bilingual English-Spanish songs, such as "Somos Hermanos/We are Brothers." On another occasion, the characters from *Sesame Street* took a trip to the Crow Reservation in Montana to learn about that particular Native American culture. There have also been visits to Louisiana to learn about Cajun culture and food and zydeco music.

Effects of Watching Sesame Street. Besides being the most watched young children's TV show of all time, *Sesame Street* has also been the most extensively evaluated show, in terms of research. We turn now to some of the effects of watching *Sesame Street* (Fisch, 2002; Fisch & Truglio, 2000; Huston, Wright, Rice, Kerkman, & St. Peters, 1990).

As most parents realize, children's attention and interest level while watching *Sesame Street* is high; preschoolers really do like the show. In terms of more substantive effects on learning, there is solid evidence for short-term effects, in the sense of vocabulary growth and the acquisition of prereading skills and positive social skills and attitudes, such as showing evidence of nonracist attitudes and behavior (D. R. Anderson, 1998; Ball & Bogatz, 1970; Huston & Wright, 1998; Rice, Huston, Truglio, & Wright, 1990). Those who watched *Sesame Street* also spent more time reading and doing other educational activities and needed less remedial instruction (Fisch, Truglio, & Cole, 1999; Zill, 2001). Longer term effects are less clear, with some early studies showing that the advantages of watching *Sesame Street*, compared to a control group not watching it, disappear after a few months or years (Bogatz & Ball, 1971). However, more recent longitudinal research has shown that heavy viewing of *Sesame Street* in preschool years is positively correlated with school grades in English, math, and science, even with early language ability and parental education level controlled (Huston, Anderson, Wright, Linebarger, & Schmitt, 2001; Huston & Wright, 1998).

Some interesting qualifications of these effects have been found. The positive effects are stronger if combined with parental discussion and teaching (T. D. Cook et al., 1975). This suggests that, among other functions, the program can serve as a good catalyst for informal media education within the family. Another interesting finding is that, at least initially, *Sesame Street* helped higher socioeconomic status children more than lower socioeconomic status children (Ball & Bogatz, 1970). Thus, the show had the ironic effect of actually increasing the reading readiness gap between the higher and lower socioeconomic status children, when its stated goal had been to decrease that gap. However, this result should not have been unexpected, because any kind of intervention generally most helps those who are most capable to begin with and thus more able to take full advantage of what it has to offer.

There were also positive social effects. Minority children watching *Sesame Street* showed increased cultural pride, confidence, and interpersonal cooperation (Greenberg, 1982) and more prosocial free play (Zielinska & Chambers, 1995). Also, after 2 years of watching *Sesame Street*, White children showed more positive attitudes toward children of other races (Bogatz & Ball, 1971; Christensen & Roberts, 1983).

Although widely praised, *Sesame Street* does have its critics (e.g., Healy, 1990; Winn, 1977, 1987), who mostly fault its encouragement of passivity and short attention span, as well as its slighting of language skills by the necessarily highly visual nature of television. However, these criticisms are mostly general criticisms of television, with little recognition of the differential quality of programming. See D. R. Anderson (1998) for a careful discussion and refutation of specific claims of these critics.

BOX 5.2
SESAME STREET DEALS WITH DIFFICULT ISSUES

One of the most remembered segments in the history of *Sesame Street* was the death of Mr. Hooper in 1983. When the human actor playing Mr. Hooper passed away, the producers decided to have the character die as well. They used the segments around his death to teach three specific points they believed all viewers would accept: (1) Mr. Hooper died, (2) He is not coming back, and (3) He will be missed. In order not to offend any viewers with particular religious beliefs (or lack of them) regarding any afterlife or reasons for the death, no mention was made of heaven or hell. Evaluation research showed that half of preschool viewers' parents reported discussing death with their child after watching the critical episode. A few years later the show dealt with the human characters Luis and Maria falling in love, getting married, and having a baby. Teaching goals for this sequence were for the children to understand points like: (1) people can love each other even when they argue, (2) a baby grows inside its mother's body, and (3) the baby can move inside the womb. A 1990s' proposal to deal with divorce through Snuffy and Alice's parents divorcing was scrapped and never aired after a pilot version showed that viewers did not understand that the parents still loved their children and that the children would continue to see their dad after the divorce (Fisch, et al., 1999).

Sesame Street is still going strong in its fourth decade. New material is continually being created, but there is also a heavy reusing of old material, and old and new segments appear together in the same show. Preschoolers are not bothered by reruns; in fact, the familiarity makes them more attractive. Although often at the forefront of dealing with social issues (see Box 5.2), there are some areas about which *Sesame Street* has remained silent. For example, there generally is little treatment of religion or religious holidays and there are no gay or lesbian characters. In 2002 producers were contemplating whether to introduce an HIV-positive character.

OTHER CTW PROJECTS

In the fall of 1971, CTW launched a second major program, *The Electric Company* (TEC), which used much of the successful *Sesame Street* format but was aimed at improving the reading skills of older children (around second grade). TEC was heavily used in the schools as well as at home. Evaluative research (Ball & Bogatz, 1973) found that viewing TEC led to improved scores on a reading test battery in children who had watched in school, but there was no improvement in a control group who had merely watched TEC at home. This suggests that the show was helpful in teaching reading, but primarily so in conjunction with the experiences offered in the classroom by the teacher and the curriculum. Never as popular as *Sesame Street*, TEC later operated in reruns and was finally canceled in 1986.

There have been other CTW projects (e.g., *Feeling Good; The Lion, the Witch, and the Wardrobe;* and *Square One TV*), as well as independently produced prosocial programs like *Where in the World is Carmen Sandiego?, Mister Rogers' Neighborhood, Ghostwriter, Barney and Friends, Freestyle, Vegetable Soup,* and *Infinity Factory*. Many of these shows have produced demonstrable positive effects. For example, when preschoolers watch Barney, the purple dinosaur that anyone over 6 loves to hate, they show better manners than a control group not watching Barney's show on manners (Singer & Singer, 1998). In a move some may find ironic, television has even been used to teach children about literature and to encourage reading (see Box 5.3). In the light of increased difficulties in obtaining funding for such shows, some have criticized the newer programs, especially, for being more entertaining than educational, a situation brought about by economic pressures to attract an audience. For reviews of these programs and their effects, see Chen (1994), Fisch (2002), and Mares and Woodard (2001).

COMMERCIAL TV CONTRIBUTIONS

The 1990 Children's Television Act, requiring all broadcast stations in the United States to provide educational programming for children, was clarified by the 1996 interpretation of this law by the FCC, which required each station to provide a minimum of three hours a week of educational and informational programming for children (Kunkel, 1998). Since that time there has been a substantial increase in commercial educational programming for children.

The most extensive single project has been the cable channel Nickelodeon's $30 million investment in new children's programs (D. R. Anderson, 1998). The preschool shows have been popular and have shown some promising initial evaluation research results. *Allegra's Window* uses puppets and humans to emphasize social problem solving in a continuous half-hour story. *Gullah Gullah Island* features a real human family from a little-known American culture, the Gullah of the South Carolina sea islands. The shows are shown as part of a commercial-free block. *Spongebob Squarepants* is an animated show aimed at children but, like *Sesame Street*, has a subtext of more mature humor that appeals to teens and preteens.

Blue's Clues, aimed at preschoolers, features a human character with an animated dog (Blue) in an animated world. Every episode invites the viewers to help solve the day's mystery, for which Blue has left

---

BOX 5.3
USING TELEVISION TO ENCOURAGE READING

Using a television show to encourage reading? Surely that is an oxymoron and a lost cause? A couple of popular PBS shows think otherwise. The book review show, *Reading Rainbow*, hosted by *Star Trek's* Levar Burton, reads stories to children, accompanied by compelling illustrations and live-action photography and followed by Levar's visit to a setting described in the story. Near the end of the show other books are read or reviewed in briefer fashion. Does it matter? Sales of books featured on *Reading Rainbow* jumped 150% to 900% and a survey of librarians found that 82% reported children asking for books featured on *Reading Rainbow* (Fisch, 2002; Wood & Duke, 1997).

Another PBS show, *Wishbone*, takes a different approach to literature. Wishbone is a wisecracking terrier owned by 12-year-old Joe Talbot. Every week Joe and his friends David and Samantha experience various challenges of growing up. The gimmick is that a parallel abridged dramatization of a work of great literature is interspersed with Joe's adventures, and a costumed live dog Wishbone is always a lead character in the literary play within the play. Usually there is some thematic parallel between the contemporary and literary story. As if that were not enough, each half hour ends with a brief how-to segment on how the special effects of the literary segment were filmed. Children are captivated and inspired to seek featured books from the library, or even buy the paperback *Wishbone* versions of the classics (expanded from the TV show but greatly condensed from the original work). As with most successful kids' shows, there are spinoff products of software, card games, and plush toys (some of Wishbone in costume as Romeo, Odysseus, or Robin Hood!).

Can the same phenomenon happen with adults? Although acclaimed novelist Toni Morrison won a Nobel Prize in 1993, that was nothing compared to having her novel *Song of Solomon* selected as the second offering of the Oprah Book Club in December 1996. Although Morrison, who seldom watches TV, had never heard of the Oprah Book Club, she quickly realized its importance. Within months, a million copies of the selected novel sold, and paperback sales of her other novels jumped about 25% (P. Gray, 1998)! Author Jonathan Franzen responded ambivalently to a tentative offer to feature his novel *The Corrections*; Oprah promptly withdrew the invitation and left Franzen out in the cold. When Oprah announced in 2002 that she would be discontinuing her book club in a few years, publishers and authors emitted a collective gasp.

---

her pawprint in three places as clues. Her human sidekick frequently "needs help" and asks the audience questions and waits for them to answer, in order to more actively involve the child in creative problem solving. The same episode is shown five days in a row, in order to better empower the child to make use of all the clues; research shows that attention is maintained at a high level, at least through three episodes (82% of the time looking at the screen), after which it drops to around the level of attention to entertainment programming (Anderson, Bryant, Wilder, Santomero, Williams, & Crawley, 2000). Research showed that viewers of *Blue's Clues*, compared to a non-viewing control group, did better on several measures of cognitive development (Anderson et al, 2000; Crawley, Anderson, Wilder, Williams, & Santomero, 1999).

Science Shows for Children

Although science shows for children are not new (Marlon Perkins' *Wild Kingdom* and *Mr. Wizard* appeared in the 1950s), one of the earliest modern science shows was the CTW project, *3-2-1 Contact*, which debuted in 1980 with the goal of teaching scientific thinking to 8- to 12-year olds. It attempted to help children experience the excitement of scientific discovery and to encourage all children, particularly girls and minorities, to feel comfortable with science as an endeavor (Mielke & Chen, 1983).

More recently, PBS' *Kratts' Creatures* and *Zooboomafoo* feature young adult naturalist brothers Martin and Chris Kratt as they go romping over the world in their quest to see interesting creatures and teach young viewers how important it is to preserve these species and their habitats. The Kratts not only observe; they participate. They climb trees with the monkeys, wallow in the mudhole with the elephants, and slither through the forest with the snakes, but always being respectful of the animals' space. The Kratts' childlike marveling at the wonder of nature, whether it be the massive invasion of Costa Rican beaches by sea turtles to lay their eggs or the discovery of the habits of a backyard urban raccoon, sells children on the wonders of zoology and conservation.

A somewhat different, and even higher energy approach, is taken by *Bill Nye, the Science Guy*, another PBS program offering a wide variety of high-tech, high-action science demonstrations, with a generous helping of wisecracks thrown in. There is modeling of conducting experiments in many settings. The commercial offering *Beakman's World* takes a similar approach. Both shows effectively counter the image of science as being difficult, stuffy, and generally uncool.

See Fisch (2002) for an excellent review of educational effects of children's prosocial television programs.

Channel One

One of the most controversial efforts in prosocial children's TV has been Channel One, a service of daily news for secondary school students.

Offered directly to schools at no charge since 1990, Channel One was in about 40% of all middle and high schools in the United States by 1997 (Bachen, 1998). Channel One, owned by K-III Communications since 1994, has been controversial since its inception, primarily because of its inclusion of 2 minutes of commercials, whose sales support the 10 minutes of news in the program. Although commercials are hardly new to teenagers, the captive audience nature of the school experience caused particular concern. Evaluation research (see Bachen, 1998, for a review) suggests a small positive effect of learning about events in the news. Some research shows that students report a greater desire to buy the advertised products, relative to a control group (Greenberg & Brand, 1993). Interestingly, another potential but seldom expressed concern about Channel One is the possibility for abuse by some future producers who might choose to set a particular political agenda or offer a very biased view of the news to this young captive audience.

Teen Programs

One of the most positive changes to come from the proliferation of cable channels has been greater amounts and quality of positive programming targeted at preteens and early adolescents. These programs, particular prevalent on Nickelodeon and Disney cable channels, are the most extensive attempts ever on commercial TV to develop quality older children's programming. Such shows as *Lizzie McGuire, The Amanda Show, That's So Raven, Boy Meets World, Even Stevens,* and *Sister, Sister* are immensely popular with 11 to 15-year-olds. These shows model behavioral scripts of dealing with difficult situations common to that age, for example, bullying, trying to be popular, maintaining friendships, and relating to parents and siblings. They present interesting and humorous characters in amusing situations, but with a refreshing lack of bad language, sexual overtones, or violence. See Box 5.4 for a look at how teen shows portray friendships.

Children's Prosocial Learning from Adult Television

Although children's television is important, a large majority of what children watch is not television produced for children but rather programs produced for a general audience of primarily adults. Can children learn prosocial attitudes and behaviors from general television? At least one study suggested that they can. Rosenkoetter (1999) had first, third, and fifth graders watch episodes of the family sitcoms *The Cosby Show* and *Full House* and then tested them for comprehension of the moral lessons

---

BOX 5.4
TEEN FRIENDSHIP ACCORDING TO DISNEY

One of the most popular early teen shows as of this writing is Disney's *Lizzie McGuire*, centering on a lovable though klutzy 14-year-old and her family and friends. Lizzie faces challenges of growing up, dealing with peers, and surviving with her mouthy and pretentious younger brother Matt. Her parents are kind and supportive, if a little dim-witted and clueless in the classic sitcom tradition. Lizzie's long-time best friends are Miranda and David ("Gordo"). This trio hangs out together in and out of school. One interesting aspect of Lizzie's support system is that, of her two best friends, one is a boy and one is a girl. Gordo is not a boyfriend, though a couple of scripts tested the waters of some mutual attraction between Lizzie and Gordo. Although perhaps unusual that a middle-school girl would have a boy as a best friend, it is actually a very common configuration in TV shows, books, and movies targeted at teens and pre-teens. Consider the *Harry Potter* trio of classmates Harry, Ron, and Hermione or films like *Big Fat Liar* (2002) where Jason and Kaylee go on an adventure in Hollywood together to exact revenge on a ruthless film producer who stole Jason's script idea. Although no doubt one reason for these cross-gender friendships is commercial, i.e., attracting both the boy and girl audiences, it also may serve a useful prosocial function. This prevalent model communicating that you can have close friends of the opposite sex with no romantic or sexual component is a positive social model for an age where preoccupation with coupling is strong. It is also interesting in this world of media saturated with sex and sexual innuendo that there is this common model of such friendships. Go, Lizzie, Gordo, and Miranda!

---

contained in the shows. The large majority at all ages comprehended the lessons from the *Cosby* episode, and about half did so from the *Full House* episode. How many hours of prosocial sitcoms children watched was a moderate predictor of first graders' actual prosocial behavior, as judged by their parents, although this difference was less with the older children.

If children can learn antisocial behaviors, such as violence, from media, can they also learn prosocial behaviors? The answer would appear to be "yes." Potts and Swisher (1998) exposed children ages 5–8 to a safety educational videotape, in which child actors engaged in dangerous recreational behavior from which they suffered injuries and later enacted alternative safe behaviors. Watching this video decreased the children's willingness to take physical risks and increased their identification of injury hazards, as measured by pre- and post-tests.

CHILDREN'S ADVERTISING

One of the most important media concerns in regard to children is tele-vision commercials aimed specifically at children, such as those aired on Saturday morning, after-school shows, and child-oriented cable channels like Nickelodeon and Disney (McNeal, 1999). We must keep in mind, how-ever, that children's programming constitutes only a minority of the hours of TV that children watch, although the percentage of that time filled with commercials has increased in the United States since the 1980s. "Kidvid" represents only about one-quarter of the viewing time for 6-year-olds and a mere 5% for 11-year-olds. The rest of the many thousands of commercials that a child sees every year are seen on general programming (i.e., prime time and daytime offerings such as game shows, soap operas, and syndi-cated sitcom reruns). Increasingly a sizable market, children under 12 years of age spent $23.4 billion in 1998, in contrast to only $2.2 billion thirty years earlier (McNeal, 1999). Teens spent another $155 billion in 2000 (Salamon, 2001). In addition, they influence an estimated $188 billion of their par-ents' purchases (McNeal, 1998). Thus children are not a trivial market, and advertisers take them very seriously!

Turning now to kidvid ads specifically, about 80% of them advertise products in only four categories: toys, cereal, candy and snacks, and fast-food restaurants (Kunkel & Gantz, 1992). Only 3% of the ads were for healthy foods. Almost half of the food ads (43%) are for breakfast cere-als, and 20% plugged fast food restaurants (Bower, 2002). The toy ads are many but highly seasonal, being primarily concentrated during the pre-Christmas season, with numbers much lower during the rest of the year.

Children's ads are technical marvels, full of color, movement, and ani-mation, with most of them emphasizing how much fun children can have with the product. Special visual and sound effects are common and cap-tivating. The pace is fast. Even less hard information is presented than in adult ads, and there is even more of a global association of the product with fun times. There is lots of alliteration (e.g., Crazy Cow, Kit Kat) and word plays (e.g., "fruitiful", a character yodeling "Cheerio-ios"). The most common theme is fun (27%), followed by taste and flavor (19%) and prod-uct performance (18%). In contrast to adult ads, appeals based on price, quality, nutrition, or safety accounted for less than 1% of kids' ads each (Kunkel & Gantz, 1992).

Valkenburg and Cantor (2001) identified four stages that a child goes through in understanding advertising. During the first two years of life, the child primarily notices bright and colorful television images (many of the best of which are commercials) and starts asking for products seen on TV as early as 18 months to 2 years of age. In the preschool years (2–5), children understand TV literally and are very vulnerable to its appeals. By the third stage (ages 5–8), they have somewhat more competence and begin to develop strategies for negotiating with parents over purchases. In the last stage (ages 9–12) the child makes the transition to more adult styles of consuming. Within this sequence of development, there are several issues of concern.

Differentiating Ads and Programs

One major concern about children and commercials is that very young children do not discriminate between commercial and program content and do not understand the persuasive intent of ads or the economics of television. Although children can identify commercials at a very early age, this identification seems to be based on superficial audio and video aspects rather than on an understanding of the difference between programs and commercials (Raju & Lonial, 1990). Preschool children have little understanding that commercials are meant to sell products. Depending on how such understanding is tested, elementary school children show various stages of development of the understanding of the purpose of ads (Bever, Smith, Bengen, & Johnson, 1975; Dorr, 1980; Martin, 1997; Robertson & Rossiter, 1974; Sheikh, Prasad, & Rao, 1974; Stephens & Stutts, 1982; Stutts, Vance, & Hudelson, 1981; Ward, Wackman, & Wartella, 1977). The insertion of video and audio separators to mark the transition between program and commercials has not made this discrimination easier (Hoy, Young, & Mowen, 1986; Stutts et al., 1981). Perhaps the separators are just too brief to be noticed, or perhaps they look much like the adjacent programming. Discriminating between ads and programs is especially difficult if a primary character in the show is also the spokesperson in the ad, a situation called host-selling (Hoy et al., 1986; Kunkel, 1988).

As they grow older, children show increasing understanding of the selling purpose of ads (see Martin, 1997, for a meta-analysis). Only about a third of 5- to 7-year-olds understand this purpose, but almost all do by age 11 (Blatt, Spencer, & Ward, 1972; Robertson & Rossiter, 1974; Ward et al., 1977; Wilson & Weiss, 1992). Typical explanations of middle elementary children center around the truth (or lack thereof) of the material; however, not until late elementary school is the distrust based on perceived intent and an understanding of the advertiser's motivation to sell the product. Among demographic groups, African Americans and lower socioeconomic class children tend to be the most trusting and least critical of ads (Wartella, 1980; Young, 1991).

Disclaimers

A particularly interesting issue in children's advertising is the question of disclaimers, those little qualifying statements like "partial assembly required," "batteries not included," "action figures sold separately," or "part of a nutritious breakfast." For obvious reasons these are seldom the central focus of the commercial. In fact, the disclaimers often occur in vocabulary far beyond the age of the target viewer and often occur only in writing superimposed at the bottom of the screen. This is completely lost on a prereading child and probably on an older child as well, because the colorful activity in the background is so much more enticing and interesting. In a content analysis, Kunkel and Gantz (1992) found that over half of the commercials aimed at children had some sort of disclaimer, with 9% having two or more. These usually appeared as an adult voiceover or in small print at the bottom of the screen at the end of the ad (Muehling & Kolbe, 1999). Unlike the rest of the ad, most of the disclaimers used adult terminology. Most preschoolers do not understand such terminology (Stutts & Hunnicutt, 1987), although some disclaimers were less difficult to understand than others.

Incidentally, disclaimers and other fine print information flashed at the bottom of the TV screen are not limited to children's ads. A content analysis of prime-time TV ads overall found two thirds of them contained some sort of disclaiming "footnote" (Kolbe & Muehling, 1992).

Television, Toymakers, and the Military

Although not the first such instance, in 1983 Mattel's popular He-Man toy made the move to television (*He-Man and the Masters of the Universe*) and within a year became the second best-selling toy in the country (Diamond, 1987). This successful marketing approach has been massively copied since then and has raised a new issue in regard to children's TV ads, namely, the commercial-as-show phenomenon. In succeeding years, dozens of television shows were linked to toys in some way, e.g., *The Transformers*, *She-Ra: Princess of Power, Teenage Mutant Ninja Turtles, Power Rangers*, and *The Care Bear Family*. Toy companies, TV networks, video game makers, and even restaurants routinely promote the toys and their tie-ins together (Pecora, 1997). One of the most successful was the Pokémon craze of the late 1990s. Although beginning as 150 cartoon characters in a Japanese Nintendo game, Pokémon was simultaneously launched in the U.S. and elsewhere in 1998 as a TV cartoon series, collector card series, video game, and toy merchandise. This was shortly followed by a Warner Brothers movie, Burger King kids' meal toys, children's clothes, and other merchandise (Strasburger & Wilson, 2002). Thus the toy industry, a $20 billion industry in the U.S. alone, and television have been wedded almost as significantly and profoundly as have been sports and TV (see chapter 6).

This marriage raises several concerns. Critics have argued that children's programming is driven too much by the marketability of associated toys rather than by the quality of the shows (Carlsson-Paige & Levin, 1990; Kline, 1992). Toy and broadcasting executives defend the policy by arguing that creative animated shows are preferable to tired syndicated sitcom reruns. Still, producers of non-toy-related children's programming report difficulty funding and selling their products. Programming is increasingly initiated around an existing (or soon to be marketed) toy. Although merchandising toys from successful TV shows has long been practiced (*Mickey Mouse Club, Sesame Street*), until the 1980s, the show came first, not the toy. That is no longer the case.

There is also some evidence that the combination of toys and TV shows that feature the toys have an inhibiting effect on imaginative play, especially for older children able to play more creatively than the toy's use in the show's context (Greenfield et al., 1993). While the toy-show connection may help the youngest children see play possibilities, in the older children it restricts their play options to what is suggested by the show.

The toy-television alliance has also helped to produce increasing marketing segmentation by gender (Carlsson-Paige & Levin, 1990). The violent shows and accompanying toy weapons and action figures (never called "dolls" if marketed to boys) are sold to boys, whereas girls are offered the soft, cuddly shows and toys like *My Little Pony* and *Rainbow Bright* and Barbie dolls. Successful boy toys may be repackaged and sold to girls, as in pink Barbie jeeps and computers or the "Adorable Transformables" that change from a dog into lipstick instead of from a car into a robot. Although food ads are likely to portray boys and girls together, ads for toys are usually gender-segmented, most often selling action figures or video games to boys and Barbie dolls and such to girls. Also, the type of interactions was different; ads to girls showed cooperation 80% of the time, while only 30% of the ads to boys did so (Larson, 2001b).

The huge success of boy-oriented action figures, as well as violent video games, has led to another odd but troubling alliance. Toymakers such as Hasbro regularly work with the military in developing new battle toys (Hamilton, 2003). The new offerings closely follow world events. Firefighter and police action figures sold well after Sept. 2001. Shortly after, action figures like "Delta Force Sniper" and "Marine Force Recon" sold well. Dragon Models sells "Josh Simon," a "Desert Nuclear, Biological, Chemical Trooper," and Army National Guard "Homeland Security Amy." The U.S. Army has developed a video game "America's Army," where players work as a team to conduct missions and raids. As well as being entertaining, it just might be useful as a subtle recruiting tool (Carlson, 2003).

Perhaps more surprising is that this military-toymaker alliance is not one way. The Pentagon looks to toymakers for inspiration in developing new weapons, which new military recruits who have grown up with those toys can use very naturally. Pentagon spokesperson Glenn Flood says that the

M-16 rifle was based on a Mattel toy, quick-loading assault weapons were inspired by super-soaker water guns, a Marine Corps remote-controlled truck called the Dragon Runner is guided by a keypad modeled after a Sony PlayStation, and unmanned robotic vehicles use gaming control panels from electronic games (Hamilton, 2003). The Institute for Creative Technologies, founded by the U.S. Army in 1999, brings together computer scientists, video game manufacturers, the entertainment industry, and the army to cooperatively develop "immersive " (i.e., highly realistic) training simulations. This high degree of realism is important both in military training and in video games, an issue we return to in chapter 9.

Many of the toy-related shows, especially those targeted at boys, are highly violent in nature. This in itself is not new; children's cartoons have always been the most violent shows on TV, in terms of numbers of violent incidents (see chapter 9). A particular concern with the newer shows, however, is that the availability of toys makes it easier to act out the violence modeled by the cartoon characters. Whereas children have always played war games of sorts, in the past they have usually had to employ their imagination to make a stick into a sword or a cardboard cutout into a gun. In so doing, they also developed their creative capacities.

A plastic Uzi or AK-47, however, can only be used to play killing people and thus requires no particular imagination. The more highly defined the violent purpose of the toy, the more it directs the child's play in a violent direction, even in a child who might not otherwise be inclined toward violent play. It also encourages the child to look on the real thing as just a toy (Carlsson-Paige & Levin, 1990). There are many serious consequences of the failure to distinguish toy weapons from the real thing: children using toy guns have been killed by police officers who thought they were about to be fired upon with real weapons. For this reason, in some jurisdictions such realistic-looking toy guns (but, curiously, seldom the real ones) have been banned.

Sometimes the wedding of toys, violence, and advertising goes to amazing lengths. For example, a popular toy for Christmas 2002 was a bombed out dollhouse with bullet holes and smashed furniture. An Easter 2003 promotion in which Easter baskets included military action figures and weapons was withdrawn from Wal-Mart and K-Mart after public complaints. Even a neo-Nazi group has joined the fun, with a game called Ethnic Cleansing, where players run through a rotted city killing African Americans, Latinos, and Jews (Carlson, 2003).

Tobacco Advertising and Role Modeling

A final area of particular concern with marketing to children and teens is tobacco advertising, especially advertising that is allegedly aimed at nonsmoking youth. Tobacco is the most heavily advertised product in the

United States ($4 billion business in the mid-1990s), all this in spite of a ban on broadcast advertising since 1971 (Strasburger, 1995)! Almost all smokers start in their teens, most often at ages 11 to 13 and almost never after age 20. Magazines are the major outlet for tobacco advertising, and those publications that accept it have less coverage of health-related issues than those which do not accept such ads. Tobacco companies have become more creative in marketing, however. Sponsorship of sporting events, logos on shopping carts and baskets, and designer clothing and tote bags advertising the brand names are common and (at least as of early 2004) perfectly legal in the U.S.

Movies are a particular concern. In spite of a huge drop in smoking among U.S. adults between 1960 and 1990 (down from over half to about 25%) and of smoking by TV series characters (down to 2% by the early 1980s), the rate of smoking in movies has remained constant and is about three times the rate of smoking in the population. This may be in part due to product placements, which the tobacco industry claims to have discontinued; for example, Philip Morris reportedly paid over $350,000 to have Lark cigarettes smoked in the James Bond movie *License to Kill* (Strasburger & Wilson, 2002). Various studies showed tobacco use in 85–90% of the most popular movies in the 1990s, cutting across all genres of film (Roberts, Henriksen, & Christenson, 1999). Even over half of the animated G-rated movies issued from 1937–1997 featured smoking, and many of these old films are still classics viewed by millions of modern children (Strasburger & Wilson, 2002).

There is increasing evidence that smoking by characters in movies, especially if they are admired characters and actors, can lead youth to start smoking (Distefan, Gilpin, Sargent, & Pierce, 1999; Sargent et al, 2001; Tickle, Sargent, Dalton, Beach, & Heatherton, 2001). Teens perceive smoking in films as common and an accurate reflection of reality, seeing it as a model for dealing with stress, developing of one's self-image, and as a marker of passage into adulthood (McCool, Cameron, & Petrie, 2001). As long as the "hot stars" like Gwyneth Paltrow, Reese Witherspoon, Brad Pitt, and Ben Affleck smoke onscreen, this behavior is likely to be modeled by their adoring fans.

There is evidence of a causal relationship between advertising and tobacco consumption (Tye, Warner, & Glantz, 1987) and huge profits from sales of tobacco to minors and to those who became addicted to tobacco as minors (DiFranza & Tye, 1990). Tremendous criticism was leveled at the Joe Camel character used to sell Camel cigarettes in the 1980s. At one time he was recognized by 98% of adolescents, though by only 72% of adults. This occurred at the same time that sales of Camels to minors were skyrocketing from less than half of one percent to a third of the youth cigarette market (DiFranza et al., 1991)! Selling the image of smoking as cool and the "in thing" to do pays off. Children who believe that smoking will enhance

---

BOX 5.5
ADVERTISING REGULATION, THE FCC, AND THE FTC

In the United States, the watchdog agency overseeing advertising is the Federal Trade Commission (FTC). The FTC was established in the early 20th century during the trust-busting era of increasing concern over abusive monopolistic practices of large corporations. Its sister organization, the Federal Communications Commission (FCC), oversees radio and television and was set up primarily to deal with such issues as assigning frequencies and channels and insuring access and fair practices.

There have usually been stricter regulations and laws regarding children's advertising than for commercials aimed at adults. For example, drug advertising aimed at children has usually been prohibited. In the late 1970s the FTC was probably at its most aggressive as a proconsumerist organization, in such issues as deceptive advertising and children's ads. This changed in the early 1980s, with increasing deregulation and the pro-business philosophy of the Reagan administration. For example, in 1983 the FCC abolished its children's TV guidelines and in 1984 it lifted the limits on allowed commercial time per hour. In the 1980s the FTC became far less aggressive in pursuing claims of misleading advertising based on the implication of a false claim. In the 1990s the pendulum started to swing the other way, as can be seen in the Children's Television Act (1990) requiring broadcasters to air some educational programming ratings for television shows. The FCC later interpreted the 1990 act to require at least three hours of "educational and informational" programming per week (Steyer, 2002).

---

their popularity or attractiveness are 4.7 times more likely to smoke than children who do not believe that (DiFranza et al., 1991).

Advertising to children has always been regulated more than advertising to adults, but the extent of the oversight has varied considerably depending on the political whims of the time (see Box 5.5). Whatever the government or industry regulation, there is still a tremendous need for media literacy in the home and elsewhere. We look now at the practical concern of what may be done to help children deal better with media to which they are inevitably going to be exposed.

MEDIA LITERACY

There is increasing recognition of the need for a higher level of media literacy in modern society. Media literacy may be defined as the "ability to access, analyze, evaluate, and process media" (Steyer, 2002, p. 195). Its goals are to teach children to use media consciously and selectively and to think critically about media messages and images. Media literacy may be conceptualized in different ways, including as a public policy issue, an educational curriculum issue, as tips for parents, or as an area of scholarly inquiry from a variety of disciplinary perspectives (Christ & Potter, 1998). Although there were consumer media-education movements as far back as the 1970s, interest has greatly increased since then (Alvarado, Gutch, & Wollen, 1987; J. A. Brown, 1991, 1998; D. G. Singer & J. L. Singer, 1998). See Potter's (2001) textbook for the most comprehensive recent formulation of media literacy.

Consistent with recent theory and research on mass communication, the contemporary emphasis in media literacy is more on empowerment of choice rather than protection from some pernicious influence. Realistically, no one can be completely shielded from media and popular culture; they are omnipresent and enduring parts of our lives. Rather, we must learn to live with not only traditional print and electronic media, but also with all the new technologies of mass, personal, and computer-mediated communication (Dorr & Kunkel, 1990; Ganley, 1992; Mundorf & Laird, 2002), including what is popularly known as cyberspace (Borden & Harvey, 1997; Kiesler, 1997; Noll, 1996). See chapter 12 for more discussion of new technologies. In all of this, the purpose of media literacy is to give us more control over our interpretations from media (Potter, 2001). We need to teach our children that they are not powerless pawns of media.

Different scholars identify different types of media literacy. Meyrowitz (1998), for example, suggests three. *Media content literacy* focuses on characters, themes, information, behaviors, and so on. *Media grammar literacy* looks at learning the formal features of each particular medium. For example, as children mature and experience more TV, part of the perceived reality naturally arising from that experience is a knowledge of how to interpret the cuts, fades, dissolves, and general montage techniques used in the editing of film to make a TV show. Very young children may misinterpret things that they see on television because they fail to understand these techniques. The third type of literacy, *medium literacy,* involves learning the specific conventions, modalities, and processing requirements for using each particular medium. Messaris (1994, 1997, 1998) argues that there are specific conventions of visual literacy that require different skills and understanding than what is required for understanding purely verbal media. For example, television to some extent and especially some computer-mediated communications like hypertext on the World Wide Web are notoriously nonlinear in character, in contrast to radio and print.

Media literacy can be carved up in a different way into four inter-related dimensions, each of which must be developed, and each can be thought of as a continuum (Potter, 2001). The *cognitive* dimension involves, thinking, knowledge, and mental processes. It draws heavily on one's knowledge structures. Some examples of such cognitive knowledge are understandings of formal features of a medium (e.g., a TV exterior shot of a house followed by a cut to an interior shot suggests that the room is inside the house pictured just previously) or structural understandings like knowing that companies buy commercial time on TV shows to sell products. The *emotional* domain concerns the emotional response to media. For example, we understand that suspenseful movies make us anxious and understand the techniques used to evoke that feeling (e.g., scary music, certain editing techniques). The *aesthetic* dimension involves appreciating the content from an artistic point of view, such as understanding certain TV genres as a group or appreciating the style of a certain director. Finally, the *moral* domain concerns comprehending the underlying values portrayed by a particular medium, show, or episode. For example, action-adventure shows and movies may convey that the use of violence is acceptable against "bad guys," and soap operas may convey that prevailing sexual values involve considerable promiscuity.

Curriculum Development

Numerous attempts have been made to develop curricula for use in schools to help children become more critical viewers of television. These programs have been more widespread in places like Australia, Canada, and the United Kingdom than they have in the United States. For an extensive review and careful evaluation of some of these projects, see J. A. Brown (1991) and Potter (2001). Such curricula have been developed by school districts, universities, religious organizations (e.g., U.S. Catholic Conference, Media Action Research Center), private companies (e.g., The Learning Seed Co., Television Learning, Ltd.), United Nations/UNESCO, and other governmental or public interest groups (e.g., Scottish Film Council, Western Australia Ministry of Education, National Congress of Parents and Teachers). See Buckingham (1993, 1996, 1998) for active programs in the United Kingdom.

Although even a superficial examination of the different media literacy curricula is beyond the scope of this book, as an example we briefly examine an early program developed by Dorothy and Jerome Singer and their colleagues at Yale University starting in the late 1970s. They offered eight lessons to be taught twice a week over a 4-week period to third-, fourth-, and fifth-grade children. Topics included reality and fantasy on TV, camera effects, commercials, stereotypes, identification with TV characters, and violence and aggression. Evaluation studies showed sizable increases in knowledge in the experimental group, particularly at immediate testing. The program was then extended to kindergarten, first-, and second-grade children; extensive pilot testing suggested that such children could be taught considerable amounts about the nature of television through such a curriculum (J. L. Singer & D. G. Singer, 1981; D. G. Singer & J. L. Singer 1983; D. G. Singer, J. L. Singer, & Zuckerman, 1981; D. G. Singer, Zuckerman, & J. L. Singer, 1980).

A second sample project is that of Dorr, Graves, and Phelps (1980). Their materials used taped TV excerpts and group discussion, role playing, games, and teacher commentary. One emphasis was on the economic bases of the broadcasting industry, stressing, for example, that the bottom-line purpose of television is to sell advertising time to make money. A second emphasis, very much in line with the theme of this book, stressed how TV programs vary greatly in realism. It encouraged children to critically evaluate the reality of each show in several ways. In evaluative research, Dorr et al.'s (1980) curriculum was shown to engender a questioning attitude about television and skepticism about its accurate reflection of reality.

A third project was an 18-lesson, 6-month classroom intervention for third and fourth graders (Robinson, Saphir, Kraemer, Varady, & Haydel, 2001). This program was designed to reduce television, videotape, and video game use, which would thus lead to fewer effects of those media on the children. It succeeded in doing so, and also in reducing the number of children's reports of requests to parents to purchase advertised toys, especially in the children who reduced their TV and video use more. However, it did not affect the parental reports of toy purchase requests, compared to a control group. Still, this suggests that it is possible to reduce television and video consumption and such reductions can have other positive effects.

What Can Be Done in the Home

Media education should not be limited only to the classroom, however. Whatever the negative effects of television on children, they can be mitigated, and perhaps even redirected to positive changes, through dialogue in the home leading to the development of so-called "receivership skills" (Ploghoft & Anderson, 1982). Such *parental mediation*, as it is called, can take any of three general forms (Nathanson, 1999). *Active mediation* involves talking with children about television. This mediation may be either positive (e.g., endorsements of content) or negative (e.g., condemnation of content). It may be fully intended as mediation (strategic mediation) or only thought of as irrelevant conversation (nonstrategic mediation) (Buerkel-Rothfuss & Buerkel, 2001). *Restrictive mediation* involves setting rules and limits on television viewing. *Coviewing* involves watching television with children. These categories are not mutually exclusive and in fact often co-exist in a family. For example, parents may limit children watching certain shows and may coview others with their children, while making both positive and negative active mediation comments. All of these types of mediation probably occur in all families at some point, but parents would be well-advised to recognize their mediation or be more intentional about it.

Although it is obviously not possible to do all the mediation one might like to, even occasional mediation by parents may be helpful. As the family watches television together or discusses shows previously watched, conversation may occur about deceptive advertising, stereotyped group portrayals, antisocial values, or excessive sex or violence. Parents can question children about their reactions to what is on TV, thus better understanding the perceived reality constructed by the child. They may comment about their own reactions, thus providing a balance to what may be a skewed portrayal on TV. For example, parents could voice their concern about a violent scene and share that they remember being scared by such scenes as a child (Nathanson & Yang, 2003).

Parental mediation has measurable effects. Johnsson-Smaragdi (1983) found some evidence that family interaction, especially for children around 11 years old, was facilitated by television viewing, at least when it was seen as an important family interactive activity. Negative active mediation can induce a mistrust of television, lower levels of aggression and skepticism toward television news, while positive active mediation is related to positive attitudes toward television and improved understanding of cognitively complex material (Austin, 1993, 2001; Austin, Bolls, Fujioka, & Engelbertson, 1999; Austin, Pinkleton, & Fujioka, 2000; Nathanson, 1999). Even sibling coviewing, without parents, may have some positive effects, e.g., in reducing fearful responses to suspenseful programs (B. J. Wilson & Weiss, 1993).

Television may be used as a catalyst for discussion of important issues within the family. Although it may be difficult for a parent and child to discuss topics like sex or drugs, it may be easier in the context of discussing a TV program on that theme. Even if the program is not particularly well done or consistent with the family's values, it still may serve as a relatively nonthreatening catalyst for discussion. Parents should take advantage of such opportunities.

Television need not be an antisocial medium that isolates one family member from another (the "shut-up-so-I-can-listen" model). It can be an activity that brings them together to watch as a family, but also to talk about the content and other topics that it leads to (the "hey-look-at-this" model). It can help family members learn each other's reactions to many topics and situations. It can be a stimulus to cognitive, emotional, and personal growth. All of this is not to say that it *will* be such a positive influence, just that it *can* be. The more carefully that programs are selected and the more intentional the parent is about discussing the content, the better the outcome. Austin, Roberts, and Nass (1990; see also Desmond, Singer, & Singer, 1990, and Nathanson, 1999) developed and tested a model of how parent-child communication about TV and its portrayals can affect the children's construction of reality. Social, cultural, and family structure variables also have a role in determining the effect of family interactions on the impact of TV on children (Greenberg, Ku, & Li, 1992; J. C. Wright, St. Peters, & Huston, 1990). For an excellent general book to help parents guide their children through the decisions and challenges of television, see Chen (1994), and for the specific issue of dealing with fear induced in children by violent media, see Cantor (1998).

One final point regarding parental mediation and discussion of media within the family should be stressed. It is difficult to have much mediation of any sort if the children or teens are usually watching TV or using computers in their own room. Keeping the major media hardware, especially the television set, in public areas of the house is an important way for the parents to keep some control on what children watch but also will allow many more opportunities for parental mediation. If a parent laments their child or teen's amount of TV or program choices and the lack of control the parents have over this, they have contributed greatly to that problem by allowing personal television sets in bedrooms. Although many people relent and allow this in response to the frustration of dealing with arguments among kids over what to watch, those disagreements can themselves be positive times of learning valuable negotiation skills.

CONCLUSION

In this chapter we have looked at several issues specifically involved with children's and teens' use of media. We continue to discuss these in the rest of the book as we look at specific content-oriented topics, such as violence, sex, sports, or news. With many of these issues, most notably violence, it is the effects on children that most concern people. Even as we study these disturbing effects of antisocial material in media, however, we need to remember the great positive potential of media for children. The enormous impact of *Sesame Street* and other prosocial programs designed to help children must not be forgotten. With the growth of cable TV and computer technologies, there is more positive programming and information for children than there has ever been before. Parents and the broader society need to learn how to deal with this media smorgasbord and how to help our children navigate through its darker sides.

BOX 5.6
**USING SUPERMAN AND WONDER WOMAN TO TEACH
LANDMINE AVOIDANCE IN CENTRAL AMERICA**

How can children in war-torn lands be taught how to avoid the lethal land mines that remain long after the war has ended? A part of the Organization of American States' (OAS) De-mining Assistance Program in Central America involved the distribution of over 600,000 copies of special *Superman y la Mujer Maravilla* comic books in schools in Honduras, Guatemala, and Nicaragua. In this collaborative project of UNICEF, D.C. Comics, and the U.S. Army's Southern Command, Superman grabs Diego just before he steps on an antipersonnel mine, while Wonder Woman (La Mujer Maravilla) saves little Gabriela from a mine in a stream where she is washing clothes. A similar comic book had been successful at alerting children to landmines in the former Yugoslavia in 1996 (Mesmer, Baskind, & Lerdau, 1998).

Sometimes media can be used in innovative prosocial ways to help children deal with particular concerns or dangers in a specific context. See Box 5.6 for a program using comic books to teach children about avoiding landmines in post-civil-war societies. Using media for prosocial purposes for adults, including the broader issue of the media teaching values, will be examined in chapter 11.

CHAPTER 6

Sports and Music: Emotion in High Gear

Q: What event captures the largest TV audience in the world?

A: The opening ceremony of the 1996 Summer Olympics was seen by an estimated 3 billion viewers worldwide (Wulf, 1996)! World Cup Soccer competition draws up to 2 billion viewers watching some part of the multigame series (Real, 1989)! The most-watched single show in U.S. TV history was the 1993 Super Bowl, seen by an estimated 133.4 million viewers, about half the nation's population.

Q: How did the advent of golf tournaments broadcast on TV significantly slow play on actual golf courses?

A: Amateurs suddenly felt they had to bend over and line up their putts as they had seen the pros do on TV, even though they often had no idea what they were doing.

Q: What percentage of popular songs mentioning alcohol present its use as having no consequences to the user?

A: 91%. Only 9% mentioned any negative consequences (Roberts, Henriksen, & Christenson, 1999).

Although emotion is a major component of many, if not most, types of media use, there are some domains where both what we feel in response to consuming the media and how we express that feeling are particularly central to the experience. This chapter looks at two of those content areas, sports and music. Before beginning to examine them, let's look a little at the psychology of emotion.

THE EMOTIONAL (AFFECTIVE) SIDE OF
EXPERIENCING MEDIA

What Is Emotion?

We cannot observe emotion directly; we do not see anger or hear happiness. We see violent behavior and feel angry; we hear laughter and feel happy. Emotions themselves are internal states and must be inferred from behavior. This can be tricky because sometimes the obvious inference is not the correct one. We may see someone crying over a TV movie and infer that they feel sad, when in fact they might be crying for joy or in anger, or for that matter, they might have an allergic condition where the crying does not reflect emotion at all. The behavior we observe is not the emotion felt inside by the person behaving.

Emotions are an integral part of the appreciation of media, especially radio and television. Perhaps no kind of programming hooks into emotions more strongly than music and sports, but many other genres of shows do so as well, including action-adventure shows, soap operas, game shows, and comedies. What we feel while watching or listening is a central part of the whole psychological experience. If the emotional aspect is absent, we miss an important dimension of the experience. Consider the unsatisfying experience of watching a ball game between two teams when you have little knowledge of the teams and no interest in who wins.

There are two components of emotion: the physiological and the cognitive. When we are aroused, there are certain changes in our bodies, such as increased heart rate, sweating, and changes in electrodermal (skin) measures. We also *think* about our feelings and attribute causes and interpretations to them. For example, if you feel very hyped up just after being offered a new job, you would interpret the same state of bodily arousal differently than you would if you had just consumed 10 cups of coffee or had just escaped from the clutches of a crazed killer. Thus, the emotions we feel are a product of both our bodily state and our cognitive appraisal of that state (Schachter & Singer, 1962; Zillmann, 1983, 1991a).

Media as Vicarious Emotional Experience

Watching a crime show on TV allows us to experience some of the emotion felt by the characters without putting ourselves in any physical danger. Thus we can become aroused safely through this *vicarious* experience, that is, experiencing the emotion through someone else's experience. This indirectness allows us to focus on the excitement of a police show or the humor of a sitcom. If we actually experienced those situations in real life, the danger or embarrassment might overpower the positive aspects and they would not be nearly as much fun as they are on TV (Tannenbaum, 1980).

Many emotions are enjoyable to experience vicariously. Many comedies show people in embarrassing situations that are more humorous when happening to someone else. TV characters may do things we would like to do but have moral or ethical proscriptions against. We can, however, with a clear conscience, watch others have extramarital affairs, verbally insult their boss, or drive recklessly. One programming genre where participants are particularly encouraged to be highly expressive emotionally is the game show. In fact, a major screening characteristic for participants is high emotional expressiveness. The producers want bubbly, emotive, expressive contestants who yell, scream, and hug.

Occasionally, a particular live media event is so emotionally compelling as to make a lasting impact, for example the collapse of the twin towers of the World Trade Center after the Sept. 2001 terrorist attacks. When the U.S. space shuttle Challenger exploded in January 1986, this event was seen live at the time on TV or later that day by 95% of the population of the country (J. C. Wright, Kunkel, Pinon, & Huston, 1989). In a study of the reactions of schoolchildren to the event, Wright et al. found strong evidence of emotion evoked by the tragedy, especially among girls, reflecting the gender stereotyping of girls admitting to feeling more emotion.

Emotional Expression and Media

Mainstream North American and Northern European societies often discourage direct expression of intense emotions. Television, however, sets some new rules that are more flexible. It is more acceptable to yell and shake your fist at a referee in a ball game on TV than to do the same at your boss. Although sports is probably the only arena in some societies where adult men may show physical affection toward other men without intimations of homosexuality, some of the same license is transferred to viewing sports on television. Thus, two men may playfully slap each other or even embrace after watching a spectacular play in a televised ball game.

The social situation of watching TV also makes a difference in our cognitions and experience. Watching a ball game or scary movie might be very different by yourself versus at a party with friends. There might be more expression of emotion in the group. The scary movie might be scarier alone and funnier with the group. Even though the stimulus of the TV show is the same in both cases, the experience, especially the emotional experience, may be quite different. The social experience of teenagers going to a horror film together is often very different than one might predict purely from considering the content of the film; for example, they may laugh at graphic horror (Oliver, 1993; Tamborini, 1991; Zillmann, Weaver, Mundorf, & Aust, 1986).

Children may learn from TV, helpfully or otherwise, how to deal with and express emotions they feel in various situations. Some years ago, young children learning to play tennis cursed and threw their racquets in imitation of John McEnroe, whose antics on the court were carried on TV as a model for dealing with frustration in sports. In an even more serious case, if TV regularly portrays men who feel frustrated with women as expressing such feelings through violence (battering or rape), children may learn that these antisocial ways of dealing with those feelings are acceptable.

There is ample evidence of *emotional contagion*, whereby we unconsciously mimic and synchronize our language and behavior to those of someone around us (Hatfield, Cacioppo, & Rapson, 1992, 1993). This mimicking and synchronicity then leads to an emotional convergence with the person being mimicked. Such persons may be from the media as well as in real life. Sometimes some TV and radio take advantage of this process by intentionally eliciting and manipulating negative emotions for their own ends of entertaining and promoting a particular agenda. See Box 6.1 for some of the most egregious and outrageous examples of this emotional manipulation.

BOX 6.1
TALK SHOWS THAT ELICIT AND MANIPULATE NEGATIVE EMOTIONS FOR ENTERTAINMENT

1. Radio talk-show host Rush Limbaugh, heard by 20 million Americans daily, regularly made misogynist jokes, calling feminists "feminazis who look like rhinoceroses." WABC's Bob Grant calls welfare mothers "maggots." The audiences cheer (Mattussek, 1995).
2. In a 1995 episode of the *Jenny Jones* show, guest Jonathan Schmitz was told he would soon meet his secret admirer who had a crush on him. The mystery person turned out to be another man, Scott Amedure, who spoke of fantasies of tying Schmitz in a hammock and spraying him with whipped cream and champagne. Schmitz was very distraught and 3 days later was arrested for killing Amedure. He told the police that the embarrassment from the program had eaten away at him (Gamson, 1995).
3. *Ricki Lake* hosted confrontational guests on talk shows with titles like "Get Real, Honey, Your Boyfriend Is a Dog," "Pack Your Bags or You'll Wish You Were Dead," "I Want to Tell My Cheating Boyfriend It's Now or Never," and "You're the Rudest Thing Alive, and I'm Sick of Your Attitude" (Zoglin, 1995). *Jerry Springer* aired shows "I Won't Let You Sell Your Body," "Pregnant Bad Girls," and "Guess What, I'm a Man!"

(J. Collins, 1998). Yelling, screaming, crying, and even hitting other guests were allegedly encouraged.

4. Shauna Miller from Livermore, CA appeared on the *Richard Bey Show* after being told she would be reunited with someone from her past. Expecting it to be an older brother she had never met, Shauna was surprised to see her younger brother's fiancée, with whom she had been feuding. The younger woman began yelling at her, and making all sorts of accusations, apparently having been encouraged to do so by program staff (Bellafante, 1995) .

5. Nikki and her new husband Chico appeared on the *Jerry Springer Show* without being told what the producers really had in mind. During the taping it was revealed that Chico was still seeing his old girlfriend Mindy and also had a male lover, Rick. Both of them were on the show with the couple, and Mindy even assaulted Nikki. The audience was encouraged to show contempt for them. "It's white trailer trash! I love it!" said an 81-year-old farmer from Oregon (J. Collins, 1998). The show offers to pay for counseling for guests afterward, but few accept the offer.

6. One episode of *The Maury Povich Show* featured a group of teens who lived together in a one-bedroom apartment. Jason was in love with Calvin, who was having an affair with Jason's twin sister Jamie, who was also the mother of a three-month-old. Jamie was interested in Scott, who had had sex with at least Calvin and Tiffanie, who walked onstage holding Jamie's hand. The audience enjoyed name-calling and criticizing the teens and questioned their sexual orientations and morality (Gamson, 1995).

Are such programs freak shows that exploit guests and bring out the worst in the audience, or are they legitimate formats to hear people's stories that we would otherwise not hear (but perhaps should)? By the way, in case you ever wondered where these shows find these people, there is a National Talk Show Guest Registry, a database of thousands of people who tell stories or have problems they are willing to vent about on the air.

Although emotion is present in virtually all types of media, we now turn to examining in more detail two domains of media where the emotional response is absolutely central, namely sports and music.

SPORTS

Media sports are a part of everyone's consciousness today, even those who have no great interest in sports themselves. Events like the Super Bowl and the Olympics have become cultural phenomena that touch the lives of many people and not just regular sports fans. An estimated 3 billion people (half the population of the planet) saw the opening ceremony of the 1996 Summer Olympics in Atlanta (Wulf, 1996). Over one third of all network programming on broadcast television involves sporting events (Bryant & Raney, 2000). The media, particularly television, are the way we learn about sports. Our perceived reality about particular sports is largely a media creation. In the case of sports not played locally, media may be the *only* source of information. The marriage of sports and television is so accepted and taken for granted today that it is easy to overlook the enormous influence that television and other media have had on the games themselves. See Box 6.2 for a look at sports and media in the days before TV.

BOX 6.2
SPORTS AND MEDIA BEFORE TELEVISION

In spite of the recent profound effect of television on sports, the marriage of athletics and the media is not a new relationship. The first sports story in an American newspaper appeared in 1733, when the *Boston Gazette* reprinted a British press story on a boxing match in England. The first British sports publication appeared in 1801, followed by the first U.S. sports periodical in 1819. Oddly titled *The American Farmer*, it included primarily results of hunting, fishing, shooting, and bicycling matches, plus some essays on the philosophy of sport. U.S. newspapers began regular reporting of sporting events in the 1850s, especially cricket and horse racing, followed by baseball in the 1860s, when Henry Chadwick invented the box score and the batting average, thus allowing fans to compare present and past performance much more easily (Rader, 1984). By 1890, most major daily newspapers had established sports departments. Sports journalism has continued to occupy a strategic place in print media. The sports pages are the most widely read section of newspapers.

Magazines were a late entry to sports media but quickly became an important player. *Sports Illustrated* has been a top-circulation magazine since its 1954 inception. Many newer and more specialized magazines fulfill interest in particular sports, including some covering sports that receive relatively little coverage in newspapers or television (*Dirt Bike, Cycle News, National Dragster*). On the whole, readership of sports magazines tends to be heavily male and disproportionately middle class and well educated, although this varies some according to the sport.

With the advent of broadcasting, new horizons were opened to sports reporting. Baseball games were broadcast on radio almost from its inception. The Dempsey-Carpentier fight was broadcast from Jersey City in July 1921. One month later, pioneer Pittsburgh radio station KDKA broadcast a Pirates-Phillies game live. The first regular play-by-play season programming of baseball and football was in place by 1925, although for some years it was primarily the World Series that was carried play-by-play. Some apparently live play-by-play broadcasts as late as the 1950s were in fact re-creations by a local sportscaster reading Morse code transcriptions over the telegraph and ad-libbing a commentary about a far-off game, such as future U.S. President Ronald "Dutch" Reagan's re-creations of the Chicago Cubs' games for Des Moines station WHO.

The first sporting event to be televised was the Berlin Olympics of 1936, which was broadcast only to the area immediately around Berlin. The first TV sports in the United States came in 1939, with the live broadcast to the 200 TV sets in greater New York of a Columbia-Princeton baseball game and the Lou Nova-Max Baer boxing match (Guttman, 1986). Widespread TV ownership had to wait, however, until after World War II (1939–1945). Early television technology was such that only sports with a small and fixed arena of action worked well on the screen. Boxing and wrestling thrived on 1940s and 1950s TV, whereas baseball, basketball, and football became far more popular later, with the advent of technology allowing multiple cameras, zooming, panning, and instant replays.

This section is in two major parts and begins with a look at the influence of media, especially television, on the games themselves. Secondly, we examine several psychological issues related to sport (e.g., competition, violence, gender, hero worship) and see how media have become formative influences in our perceived reality about sports and playing sports.

How Television Has Changed Sports

Audiences for major sporting events are among the largest for any programming, and television has become an integral part of the financing of most professional sports as well as technically amateur sports such as the Olympics and college football. Although sports have been seen on television almost since its inception, TV was relatively unimportant to sports before the late 1950s, when professional teams began to see television as a potentially lucrative source of revenue. This revenue source was considerably more stable, with greater potential for increase, compared to ticket sales and other more traditional revenue sources. Usually broadcast on weekend afternoons, TV sports offered a chance to greatly increase the audience at traditionally low-viewing times. However, the great popularity of sports led to prime-time broadcasting of games as well, most notably ABC's *Monday Night Football*, the many evening baseball games, and the Olympics. The advent of popular all-sports cable channels like ESPN and Fox Sports has further increased the amount of TV sports available. Over the years, the television audience has become considerably more important than the stadium spectators, and sports have changed much more to adapt to the needs and desires of TV and its viewers than to the fans in the stadium. For economic reasons, the perceived reality of the TV audience has come to be more important than the reality perceived by the fans in the stadium. Sportscasting has become so important that there have even been scientific studies of sportscaster language (Kuiper, 1995).

Social Changes and the Growth of Sports and Media.   Although television greatly affected sports in its early years, there were other profound social changes occurring during that time that played into sports-media growth. In the post-World War II years after 1945, unparalleled economic prosperity fueled a building boom and a massive migration from the central cities to the new suburban areas (Coontz, 1992). The suburbs were far more dependent on the automobile, signaling the shift from primary dependence on public transportation to private cars. Soon this led to the construction of better highways and freeways and the decline and even loss of public transportation.

With all of these changes came a privatization of leisure. As more people owned their own homes, with more space inside and lovely yards outside, their recreation and leisure time was increasingly centered around the home or, at most, the neighborhood. One major activity of this home-based leisure was watching television. No longer did one have to ride the trolley to the theater to watch a movie; similar entertainment was available for free and more conveniently from television. The same was true for watching sports. The fact that most of the ballparks of the time were ancient edifices in decaying and dangerous parts of town with little parking and few modern conveniences did nothing to help stem this tide of change. The rise of auto racing as a local spectator sport and softball and later soccer as participant sports also provided competition for professional baseball attendance.

Probably the biggest change in sports thanks to TV is simply the fact that many more people participate in many more sports than they used to, following exposure to these sports on TV. Team owners' early fears that radio (and later TV) would keep people from attending games in person proved, at worst, a temporary problem. The potential financial bonanza from selling television rights only gradually came to be fully appreciated (Guttman, 1986; Lever & Wheeler, 1993; Powers, 1984; Rader, 1984; Whannel, 1992).

The New Look of Games.   Television has changed sports in a myriad of ways. There is much more color in sports than there used to be. Before TV, tennis balls were always white. For centuries a sport of the elite, tennis was brought to the masses by television coverage of major tournaments.

Before TV, football stadiums had less colorful end zones. Female cheerleaders, even chorus lines of precision marchers, replaced the pre-World War II male yell captains at college football games. Uniforms are more colorful, with players' names written on the backs for TV audiences to read. Increasing numbers of domed stadiums have lessened the number of boring rain delays that play havoc with TV programming. Computer graphics technology has allowed for lively and colorful scoreboards. Hockey changed the center line from a solid to a broken line to be seen better on television.

Technological Changes. Continuing technical advances in broadcasting have affected sports. One of the most dramatic is the instant replay, first seen in 1963. The same play can be seen over and over at different speeds, from different camera angles. Technical advances allow the editing and delayed broadcast of lengthy events with interpretation added and uninteresting sections deleted; such techniques have been used especially effectively with TV coverage of the Olympics. The growth of cable and satellite technology has greatly increased the available hours of sports programming, most notably through the founding of the USA network in 1975 and ESPN in 1979. Although both networks later expanded to include other types of programming, with the USA network eventually becoming mostly nonsports, the 1990s saw the rise of ESPN-2, Fox Sports, and more pay-per-view television for major events like boxing matches. Recent expanded opportunities for sports coverage have given some publicity to sports long considered too minor and unprofitable to broadcast (see Box 6.3).

The Telegenic Factor. Some sports are much more naturally suited to commercial television than others. Baseball, with its many half-inning divisions, is a natural for commercial breaks. Football and basketball have fewer structured breaks, but the frequent time-outs and foul calls help somewhat. The continuous action and low scoring of hockey and soccer make them relatively poorer TV sports. Some have suggested this to be why soccer, by far the most popular spectator sport worldwide, has never caught on in a large way in the United States. Soccer lacks a focus of attention like the area between the pitcher and home plate in baseball or the opposing lines in football. The ball often flies off in unexpected fashion, making TV close-ups in the wrong places worthless. However, this lack of TV friendliness is not an entirely satisfactory explanation, because soccer (often called football outside the United States) is seen on TV daily in dozens of countries. The quadrennial World Cup series is the most-watched professional sporting event worldwide, with an estimated viewership of up to 2 billion (Real, 1989). Sometimes a bit of the action is lost due to commercial breaks, but there are also increasing experiments with alternatives like windowing, where we see, for example, the game in the middle of the

---

BOX 6.3
NEW SPORTS AND NEW TEAMS COMING TO A CHANNEL
NEAR YOU

The effectively limitless expansion of cable television has opened new possibilities for televised sports. The Classic Sports Network showed there was
an audience for watching old classic ball games (interested in watching the
1960 World Series or the 1990 Super Bowl again?). College Sports Television
(CSTV) devotes 24 hours a day to college sports, particularly the so-called
minor sports not already captured by the major networks, ESPN, and Fox
Sports Net. Thus, for the first time, a broader audience can see football or
basketball from largely unknown conferences, as well as all sorts of collegiate sports previously absent altogether from television, including baseball,
lacrosse, track, soccer, volleyball, and others. (Gregory, 2003a).

Sometimes the major sports price themselves out of a major network TV
market and newer sports can take their place. For example, after NBC lost
$300 million on the last two years of its contract with the NBA, it replaced
them with the much more affordable Arena Football League (AFL) in 2003.
This gave a much-needed boost to the indoor football league, which had
been around since 1987, but had languished without major TV exposure
(Gregory, 2003b).

---

screen and an ad around the edges or across the bottom, or the ad on most
of the screen with the game in a window in an upper corner.

In spite of what one might think, some of the most popular sports in
terms of attendance are not particularly popular on television. Two of the
top American sports in gate receipts are NASCAR auto racing and horse
racing, yet, until quite recently, they have been seen by large audiences on
TV only in the very top contests like the Indianapolis 500 and the Big 3 of
thoroughbred racing (Kentucky Derby, Preakness, and Belmont Stakes).
There are also considerable regional differences in sports interest (see
Box 6.4).

Institutional Changes.   There have been some dramatic structural
changes in the institution of sport due to television. For example, the 59
baseball minor leagues in the late 1940s were down to about 15 leagues
30 years later. The chance to see major league baseball on television all
over the country largely destroyed the appeal and thus the financial vi-
ability of the minor leagues. A parallel development occurred with the
soccer leagues in Great Britain after the onset of TV. Even the attendance
at American pro football and major league baseball was at first reduced
by regular TV broadcasting (blacking out TV in local markets moderated

BOX 6.4
GEOGRAPHICAL DIFFERENCES IN SPORT

There are huge international differences in what sports are popular, both in terms of participation and TV watching. The two most popular TV sports in the United States do not command much worldwide interest. Baseball is very popular in some of East Asia (especially Japan and Taiwan), the Caribbean, and northern Latin America as far south as Venezuela but remains largely unknown in Europe, Africa, and most of Asia and South America. There are a few occasional exceptions, such as the professional Italian league, and there are some indications that interest in baseball is spreading into Europe and southwest from Japan into east Asia.

Football is big in the United States and Canada but practically nowhere else, although the name *football* is often used for soccer, with *American football* referring to the U.S. variety. Some current efforts to export it to Western Europe are having modest success. Bicycling as a major sport has long been immensely popular in France and Italy; the fact that the American Greg LeMond won the Tour de France several years beginning in 1986 was completely unprecedented and helped to increase interest in the event and the sport in the United States. In Britain and some former Commonwealth countries like India, Pakistan, some Caribbean nations, east Africa, and South Africa (but nowhere else), cricket is popular. Bullfighting is popular on the Iberian peninsula and Northern Latin America but nonexistent elsewhere.

Even within the United States and Canada there are considerable regional differences in sports preferences. Throughout Canada and the extreme northern United States, hockey is the major sport. U.S. hockey teams depend heavily on Canadian talent. Even at the college level, hockey far eclipses football and basketball in quality and popularity at schools like the University of Maine and the University of North Dakota, which regularly send their graduates to the NHL. Although college football is popular all over the United States, it is particularly so in the Midwest and South; in Canada and elsewhere outside the United States, big-time collegiate sports are nonexistent. Basketball is most popular on the U.S. mid-Atlantic coast and especially in the state of Indiana, a unique state which begins interscholastic competition in elementary school and regularly draws college recruiters from all over the country. Women's field hockey is popular in the Northeast U.S., as is jai alai in south Florida. Obviously, winter sports like ice skating and snow skiing are more popular in colder climates.

There is some tendency for television to lessen these regional differences, as people become exposed to sports not played in their community. The increasing popularity of soccer in the United States, especially among youth, and American football in Europe testifies to this.

this trend somewhat), but the huge financial bonanza of selling TV rights ultimately far more than compensated, eventually actually increasing stadium attendance through the interest generated from seeing the games on television. The old American Football League (AFL) was saved from bankruptcy in 1964 by NBC's offer of $42 million for a 5-year TV contract (Guttman, 1986).

In spite of the rampant growth of sports and television, there does seem to be a saturation point. For example, the formation of the United States Football League in the early 1980s and the XFL twenty years later were colossal failures. There are also signs of tedium and lower than expected ratings as division playoffs and tournaments extend the seasons of different sports longer and longer. People often tire of baseball by late October or NBA (basketball) and Stanley Cup (hockey) playoffs still going on in June. Audiences for some major sporting events have been declining; although 56% of the viewing audience saw the 1980 World Series, only 25% saw the 1997 Series.

College Football.   In college football, the National Collegiate Athletic Association (NCAA) severely restricted the TV broadcast of games in the 1950s, in spite of some disgruntled schools and legal challenges on antitrust grounds. With the advent of very lucrative TV contracts in the early 1960s, far more games appeared on television, although this primarily enriched the few very strong teams and conferences and weakened many others. This trend was accentuated by the post-season Bowl games, which sold TV rights for multimillion-dollar deals as early as the 1960s. Power conferences like the Big Ten, Big Twelve, and Pacific Ten depend on Bowl appearances to recruit strong talent and Bowl receipts to finance their programs. The proliferation of post-season Bowl games and by now almost universal corporate sponsorship (Tostitos Fiesta Bowl, Jeep-Eagle Aloha Bowl, Southwestern Bell Cotton Bowl, Insight.com Bowl) has opened new advertising and revenue opportunities. By the early 21st century, interest and attendance at some Bowl games had shown signs of declining, and there was growing controversy about bowl-team selection processes.

Although TV has brought big-time college football into the lives of many who never would have attended a game, it has been at the cost of heavily, even crassly, commercializing the football programs of the major schools, leaving them amateurs in name only. It has also drawn a large TV audience in part at the expense of small college and high school football, whose supporters often prefer to watch top-rated teams on TV instead of attending a local game in person. In recent years, increasing numbers of top college players bolting to the high-paying NFL before the end of their collegiate eligibility also concerned college teams. More and more critics are claiming that major men's sports, especially football, are compromising what the university should be all about (e.g., Sperber, 2001).

Pro Football.   Although college football had been around and popular since the 19th century, pro football was more like an athletic footnote on the U.S. sports scene before the age of television. When Pete Rozelle became NFL commissioner in 1960, the entire staff consisted of three people (Rader, 1984); by 1984 the same headquarters occupied five entire floors of a Park Avenue skyscraper. Pro football learned how to deal with television more adeptly and in a more unified fashion than did baseball. NFL commissioners Bert Bell and his successor Pete Rozelle negotiated craftily and with the support of the owners, using local blackouts often enough to preserve stadium audiences but not so often as to engender fan resentment. The close-up focus of television, coupled with interpretation by the sportscaster, served to make a previously opaque and uninteresting game fascinating to large numbers of new fans, who now were able to follow what was happening with the ball.

One of the most brilliantly marketed ongoing media events of all time has been the Super Bowl, which began in January 1967 after the merger of the NFL and the AFL the year before. By the early 1970s, the Super Bowl had overtaken the baseball World Series and the Kentucky Derby in TV audience size in the U.S. Unlike these other events, the Super Bowl was a creation of television, not a preexistent institution adapted to the new medium. Super Bowl Sunday practically became an annual January holiday, complete with ebullient media hoopla weeks in advance. The games themselves were frequently watched in over half of U.S. households, in spite of a string of very uneven and unexciting games during many of those years. The broadcast in itself became the event; what happened in the game was almost irrelevant. By the 1980s, major advertisers, paying top dollar for ad time, launched new ad campaigns with commercials presented for the first time during the game; this annual advertising debut became a significant spin-off media event. Networks alternated the privilege of broadcasting the game. A whole series of satellite events sprang up, such as numerous televised parties and pre- and post-game specials. This large audience is sometimes even used for other purposes, such as collecting "Souper Bowl" food donations for food banks and consciousness-raising about the rise of wife-battering during and after the Super Bowl. Wenner (1989) even argued that the Super Bowl pre-game show is a vehicle for subtle political socialization.

The Olympics.   Some immensely important sporting events, in terms of their TV impact, are the quadrennial summer and winter Olympics. Although these games have occurred in modern times since 1896, interest in them has soared exponentially since their broadcast on television worldwide. Olympic committees have been selling broadcast rights ever since the 1960 Rome games, and the Olympics have become totally dependent on television financially, a status that gives them a professional character that they never had before (Seifart, 1984). NBC paid a record $1.27 billion package deal for the rights to televise the 2000 Summer and 2002 Winter games.

Due to the traditionally amateur status of the Olympics, TV has popularized sports that have not otherwise been sources of large revenues. Most notable here have been all women's sports, which have received a tremendous boost from Olympic coverage. Certain sports that have little audience elsewhere are very popular in the Olympics (e.g., gymnastics and ice skating). In such minor sports, television serves an important educational function: people learn about new sports from watching the Olympics. Sometimes this translates into their own participation in these activities. The Olympics have produced many heroes, including Nadia Comaneci, Bonnie Blair, Kristi Yamaguchi, Florence Griffith Joyner, Carl Lewis, Brian Boitano, Scott Hamilton, Bruce Jenner, Sarah Hughes, and Mary Lou Retton. Olympic stars, through the catalyst of TV, can be catapulted to athletic or show business stardom, to say nothing of economic security.

Sometimes the commercial pressure to pay back the enormous cost of the broadcasting rights may lead to low-quality television, with a high total ad time (up to 20 minutes per hour) and poor placement of ads (e.g., while hockey goals are being scored or figure skating scores are being announced). Olympic Organizing Committees have altered schedules so two top-rated hockey teams would not have to play each other until the finals. Starting with Calgary in 1988 and Barcelona in 1992, the games were lengthened to include three weekends of prime sports broadcasting time.

As with sport in general, emotional aspects of the athletes are often highlighted, leading to some criticisms that broadcasting the sport has become subordinate to televising the tearjerker (Carlson, 1996). More likely, this trend may reflect attempts to increase the numbers of women viewers. Probably the most notorious case of such soap opera coverage was the Nancy Kerrigan—Tonya Harding feud ("Dueling Figure Skaters") of the 1994 Winter Games. Harding and her boyfriend were implicated in a knee-bashing sabotage attempt against Kerrigan. This nasty side issue almost eclipsed the actual skating competition, although it ironically delivered a record boost to the figure skating audience.

A more common melodramatic theme is that of the triumph of the human spirit over adversity. During the 1996 Atlanta Games, NBC dug up, according to one count, about 140 heart-wrenching family melodramas and broadcast them (Carlson, 1996). Often they were brief, like diver Mary Ellen Clark's cancer-stricken father meeting her at poolside. Sometimes they were more extended. Belorussian gymnast Vitali Scherbo, winner of six gold medals in 1992, stopped training for months to care for his wife

Irina after her serious car accident. As she slowly started recovering, she insisted Vitali return to training for 1996. He did, but only received a bronze medal for group effort. NBC, however, celebrated the family by taking Irina and their daughter back to the crash site for an emotional visit. Is this sports coverage?

For all the fun of the Olympics, there still is a certain aura of seriousness in the media coverage. Occasional more light-hearted treatments can raise some eyebrows; see Box 6.5 for some unconventional aspects of local coverage of the 2000 Summer Games in Sydney.

Olympic coverage may be used to further the host country's political or economic goals. South Korea used the 1988 Seoul Summer Games to showcase its economic progress. Viewers learned during the 1992 Summer Games that residents of host city Barcelona speak Catalan, not Spanish, and identify more with their autonomous region of Catalonia than with the nation of Spain. Many former Soviet republics competed for the first time as independent nations in 1992 or 1996, the first year that every single independent country in the world, all 197 of them, had some presence at the Summer Games (Wulf, 1996). Coverage is not the same in all places. The way that the Olympics are broadcast may also reflect the national and cultural values of a nation. See Box 6.6 for an interesting contrast of U.S. and Brazilian Olympics coverage.

So far we have looked at how the media have changed the various sports themselves and the reality about them that we perceive. Next we examine several psychological factors that are directly affected by the perceived reality of media sports.

BOX 6.5
OLYMPICS AS SITCOM

Certain steps were taken to liven up the games during the 2000 Summer Olympics in Sydney, Australia. For example, during the baseball games, every foul ball (even the grounders) was accompanied by sound effects of breaking glass. Beach volleyball had its own comic host, "Lifeguard Dave," who worked the crowd like a stand-up comedian. Roy Slaven and H.G. Nelson, late-night hosts of *The Dream*, ran Greco-Roman Olympic wrestling coverage to a sound track of Barry White love songs and commentary pondering why large men would try to grope and mount each other. The show's mascot "Fatso the Fat-Arsed Wombat" became so popular that Olympic athletes all wanted to pose with it, until the I.O.C. requested that they stop doing so. Does such coverage enhance or detract from the Olympics? (Luscombe, 2000)

BOX 6.6
A CASE STUDY IN SPORTS MEDIA COVERAGE
AND CULTURAL VALUES

How do national social and cultural values affect media coverage of sports and sports heroes? The answer may be more substantial than we realize. Consider the following comparison from Kottak (1990) of U.S. and Brazilian media coverage of their respective medal winners in the 1984 Olympics.

First, although Brazilian media overall gave less Olympic coverage to its own competitors than did the United States, there was also a much greater emphasis on team sports and victories by Brazilian media, whereas the U.S. media spent much more time on individual human interest stories of participants (e.g., skater Dan Jansen's sister dying just before his 1988 Winter Games competition). In contrast, Brazilian swimming medalist Ricardo Prado was lauded by his media for his stellar performance but only in the context of much criticism of the team's overall poor showing. Brazilian athletes were blamed by their media for poorer than expected performance, whereas U.S. athletes were praised for fine attempts and empathized with for disappointing showings. The theme of the underdog triumphing was prominent in U.S. media, whoever the winner. Brazilian media gave scant coverage to their own runner Joaquim Cruz's surprise gold medal, although U.S. media ran a human interest story on his rise from a humble upbringing in the slums to stardom. Pratfalls and slips were covered heavily in Brazilian media, typically in a humorous vein, not the heartbreak angle more common in U.S. Olympic coverage. Brazilian Olympic athletes reported being extremely worried about how the audience back home would judge their performance.

Why the difference? Kottak argued that, even though the United States in many ways embodies more competitive values than does Brazil, U.S. sports coverage is rife with the American cultural theme of the striving and success of the individual. The individual person and his or her efforts are celebrated and seldom criticized, even if the results are disappointing. Everyone has a chance, and even the lowliest individual can rise high through valiant individual effort. Brazilian media, on the other hand, reflect a more stratified and less mobile society where no one is expected to rise in the social hierarchy. Thus, people do not see hard work as being efficacious in raising one's social status, and it may even be seen as a threat.

Psychological Issues in Sports and Media

Why do people seek to consume sports media, and what is the nature of that experience psychologically? In some ways it is like other media consumption, but in other ways it is unique. On TV, only sports (and in a very different way, news) is live and unrehearsed with the outcome unknown. This is very different from the rather predictable, formulaic nature of most entertainment programming and advertising. In this section we examine several aspects of the sports media consumption experience, with the major emphasis being on the medium of television.

Sports Media Consumption as a Social Event. More often than for other TV programming, part of the reality of the experience of sports media consumption involves the presence of others (Rothenbuhler, 1988). Friends gather at someone's home or patrons congregate in a bar to watch a big game. Often the game seems more enjoyable in a group than it would be watching alone, with the presence of others rooting for the same team somehow seeming more important than having coviewers while watching a movie, a sitcom, or the news (Wenner & Gantz, 1989). The expression of emotion, discussed later, may be part of the reason. Also, watching with a group partially re-creates the stadium situation of watching the event in a crowd.

One interesting aspect of the social reality of TV sports viewing is the eating and drinking that accompany the viewing. People eat and drink more watching sports than watching other events on TV, especially when viewing in groups, but the range of what they consume is fairly narrow. The food is most often junk food, snacks, or perhaps hot dogs, and the drink is typically soft drinks or beer. In short, we eat and drink the same sort of substances at home that we might consume if we were in attendance at the stadium. It seems somehow odd to have coffee and croissants while watching the Chicago Bears and the Green Bay Packers or to savor a fine red wine while watching the heavyweight boxing championship fight. One increasingly thorny issue in regard to food and drink involves the advertising and promotion of alcohol at university athletic contests (see Box 6.7).

Sports is the type of television most often consumed in a social context. Who the others watching with you are and how much you enjoy the game help determine what the experience of viewing is like. For example, watching a sporting event alone, with a group, or with one's family or significant other leads to different uses and gratifications (Bonds-Raacke & Harris, 2004). Wenner and Gantz (1998) identified five levels of motivations for watching sports, in decreasing amount of emotional involvement. First is the fanship dimension, focusing on the thrill of victory and identifying strongly with the players. Second, the learning dimension involves acquiring information about the game and the players. Third, the release dimension involves "letting off steam," relaxing, and eating and drinking. Fourth, companionship involves watching to be in the company of others who are watching; such motivations are especially important in the case of family or significant others. Finally, the filler dimension, the least emotionally involving, involves watching to pass the time or because one is bored.

BOX 6.7
ALCOHOL ADVERTISING IN COLLEGIATE SPORTS

As colleges and universities becoming increasingly concerned about alcohol abuse among students, especially binge drinking and the role of alcohol in crimes like rape and domestic violence, the lucrative advertising contracts between breweries and university athletic departments are drawing closer scrutiny. Although most schools do not sell alcohol in their athletic facilities, and many prohibit fans from bringing alcohol into the games, those same fans often see lots of beer advertising inside the stadium or coliseum. The income from such advertising is not trivial. For example, the University of Minnesota-Twin Cities signed a 3-year contract for $150,000 with Miller Brewing Company in 1994, giving the brewery the right to install advertising signs in university athletic arenas and to use the university mascot, the Golden Gopher, in its advertising. When that contract expired in 1997, a similar offer of $225,000 was rejected by the university on ethical grounds (Naughton, 1998).

   Although only a few major universities (e.g., Brigham Young, Baylor, University of North Carolina-Chapel Hill) refuse all alcohol ads in sports arenas and on radio broadcasts of games, increasing numbers, like Minnesota, are clamping down. However, private facilities, like post-season bowl arenas, are a harder sell. The Big Ten and Pacific Ten conferences failed to persuade the city of Pasadena to ban beer sales at the 1998 Rose Bowl game; officials remembered that 30,000 beers were sold at the 1997 Rose Bowl game (Naughton, 1998)! What is your school's policy on alcohol advertising and college sports?

Competitiveness and Cooperation.   Obviously, one of the major psychological components of sports is competition and the achievement of victory. Part of the perceived reality of TV sports also involves this desire to win, a drive which is learned early through the media. This strong competitive drive can easily overshadow the learning of teamwork and cooperation. The natural socialization process of child development often involves an identification and support for certain sports teams and individuals. Who this will be is often, although not necessarily, determined by geographical considerations. We most often root for the local team, the team of our school, or the team our family has supported, perhaps for generations. Still, major teams have fans all over. The hapless Chicago Cubs have supporters who have never been near Wrigley Field, and Roman Catholics throughout North America cheer for the University of Notre Dame's football team.

   Competition may come in the form of nation versus nation in international competition. The U.S. hockey team's upset victory over the Soviet

Union in the 1980 Winter Olympics was especially savored in a nation angry and frustrated by the Soviet invasion of Afghanistan a few weeks before. The World Cup, with one team per nation, becomes a national competition, during which the business life of certain soccer-happy countries in Western Europe and South America takes a de facto holiday. When the Toronto Blue Jays made the baseball World Series in 1992, all Canada celebrated, in spite of the fact that there were no Canadians on the team. The first-time entry of independent former Soviet and Yugoslav nations like Lithuania, Estonia, Croatia, and Slovenia into the 1992 Olympics was a time of intense national pride. Such sports nationalism can occasionally degenerate into antisocial extremes. Colombian soccer star Andrés Escobar was assassinated upon returning home from World Cup play in 1994, apparently by a fan angry and ashamed of his weaker-than-expected performance on the field.

The reward in sports is generally for winning, with very few kudos, endorsements, or dollars for coming in second, much less third or tenth. In carrying so many more sports into so many lives, television has certainly, at least indirectly, encouraged competitiveness. With the star mindset that focuses on individuals, television lavishes attention and acclaim on the winner, whereas it often virtually ignores everyone else. This helps to construct a reality for viewers that coming in first is what is important. Athletes are not interviewed after the game for doing their best or being good sports. Sports metaphors carry over into our speech and thinking in many other areas of life, such as relationships. A fellow goes on a date and scores, gets to first base, or strikes out. A woman complains that men see women as conquests or trophies. Parents feel like losers if their child is not accepted to a prestigious college.

Often the star mentality of television and the entertainment business in general affects the presentation of sports in the media. Individual plays of the superstars are exalted and glorified by the sportscasters more than, for example, shows of fine teamwork. Coverage tends to focus on the outstanding athlete, much as coverage of religion tends to focus on the pope or stories about government focus on the president. This extolling of the individual may subtly undermine the importance of teamwork and cooperation for the viewer, especially the young viewer.

A very different, and subtler, way that competitiveness can manifest itself in the sports viewer is in the accumulation and exhibiting of copious, seemingly endless, sports trivia and statistics. Sportscasters encourage this through their endless recitation of such information during radio and TV broadcasts, in part probably to fill the time when there is no play or commercial to air. The computer has made it even easier to amass and retrieve these figures. Such statistics have become part of the reality of media sports. Even young children seemingly unable to remember much in school may recite voluminous facts about RBIs, passes completed, and shooting percentages.

Sports Violence. Although the appeal of violent sports goes back to ancient times (Guttman, 1998), recent concern is expressed over the way that media, especially television, tend to heavily focus on, perhaps even glorify, the occasional brawl or fight on the field. In a sense, this is an auxiliary competition to the primary one being played. Although no sportscaster celebrates or even condones serious tragedies like player or fan deaths, the camera and media attention immediately shift routinely to any fight that breaks out either in the stands or on the field. When results of that game are reported later on the evening news, it is more likely to be the brawl, not the play of the game, that is chosen as the sound bite of the evening. Even if fighting is clearly condemned by the sportscaster, the heavy coverage given to the fight conveys a subtle agenda-setting message of its own. The perceived reality to the viewer, especially a young one, may be that the winner of the brawl is to be admired as much as the winner of the game itself, because temper tantrums, rudeness, and racket-hurling are more photogenic and lively than self-control and playing by the rules (Tavris, 1988).

Do people really enjoy watching sports violence? In a study of response to sports aggression, Bryant (1989) found that avid sports fans do enjoy watching rough and even violent sporting events, especially under certain conditions. Inherently more violent people enjoy sports violence more. The more one dislikes the victim of the violence, the more that violence is enjoyed. Bryant reported a study where highly prejudiced Whites greatly enjoyed seeing a race car crash where a Black driver was killed. Violence that is morally sanctioned, that is, presented as acceptable or even necessary, is enjoyed more and seen as more acceptable than violence presented as unfair or out of line (Beentjes, van Oordt, & van der Voort, 2002). Such moral sanctioning may come from several sources, including the rules and customs of the game, the tone of the commentary of the sportscaster or sportswriter, and even the reactions of other fans. The more of these conditions that are present, the more the viewer enjoys the violence. Overall, however, the higher the level of violence in a game, the greater the fan enjoyment, especially for men (Bryant, Zillmann, & Raney, 1998).

There is also some evidence of negative behavioral effects from watching aggressive sports. Fans leaving a college football game (J. H. Goldstein & Arms, 1971) or wrestling or hockey events (Arms, Russell, & Sandilands, 1979) scored higher in hostility and aggressiveness than control fans who had watched a swimming meet. It did not matter if one's team won or lost or if the aggression was stylized (wrestling) or spontaneous (hockey). Although these studies have not been replicated with fans who are television spectators, the results are provocative and suggest that the presence of aggressiveness may be more important than merely the element of competition.

Sometimes sports competition has had some extreme and tragic consequences. In 1969, Honduras and El Salvador fought the so-called soccer war, precipitated by a particularly bitter soccer game. In 1985, 39 people in Brussels died, and 450 were injured, in a deadly brawl among fans watching a championship soccer game between Liverpool, England and an Italian team. Such incidents have caused fans to be screened with metal detectors, nations to exchange information on the most violent fans, and heavily armed soldiers to stand guard in the stadium between the seating areas for fans of the opposing teams. These security measures have come to be part of the reality of sport, although those watching on TV need not be so inconvenienced.

Emotional Benefits.   Although there are clear benefits from participating in sports, those benefits are somewhat less clear when it comes to consuming sports through media. Obviously, physical health and fitness are not enhanced by watching ball games on TV and may even be hindered if watching takes up time that the viewers would otherwise spend exercising. Emotionally, the picture is a little less clear. The tension reduction or emotional release called *catharsis* may result from physical exercise where we release stress through muscular and aerobic exercise. Some psychologists in the *psychodynamic* tradition dating back to Sigmund Freud argue that catharsis may also be achieved through substitute activities. Although research has not supported the value of a cathartic release of aggressive feeling through watching sports, there is still widespread belief among the general public that such a process exists (Tavris, 1988).

There clearly is often a lot of emotion felt while consuming media sports. Zillmann, Bryant, and Sapolsky (1979) proposed a disposition theory of sportsfanship to describe such feelings. The enjoyment we experience emotionally from witnessing the success or victory of a competing individual or team increases with the degree of positive sentiments and decreases with the degree of negative sentiments we feel toward that party. The reverse is true for what we experience when we witness a failure or defeat. The more we care about a team's success, the more emotional satisfaction we feel when they do well and the worse we feel when they do badly. Thus, it is hard to become emotionally involved, or sometimes stay interested at all, in watching a game between two teams that we know or care little about.

Still, feelings about the competitors are not the only determinants of emotional response to sports. As with any drama, the degree of perceived conflict is crucial. A game that is close in score and hard-fought in character evokes more emotional reaction, regardless of team loyalty, than one where the final victor is never in doubt or one where the participants appear not to be trying very hard. As with other kinds of drama, unpredictability and suspense are important (Zillmann, 1980, 1991c). A close basketball game settled at the final buzzer carries the viewer along emotionally throughout its course. A game whose outcome is known is less likely to be of interest to watch in its entirety. How many ball games are ever rerun on television? How many people watch a videotaped ball game of which they already know the final score? However, a few people may actually prefer the predictable to the uncertain; see Box 6.8.

Gender Roles and Bias. Throughout the history of media sports, male sports have received much more coverage than female sports, with estimates indicating that as much as 95% of sports coverage is of male sports

---

BOX 6.8
PERFECTIONISM, PROBABILISM, AND SPORTS FANATICISM

Why are some people rabid sports fans, whereas others could not care less? It does not seem to be particularly related to their personality, because even meek and nonassertive people can be extremely competitive watching sports. The author's personal theory, completely untested, suggests a possibility.

Like statistics, sports is a very probabilistic venture. One can make all kinds of odds on who will win the game or the race, but they are only that—odds. If Team A is better on most relevant criteria than Team B, it will probably win. Probably but not necessarily. Once in a great while even the most invincible team is knocked off by a lowly challenger. The expansion underdog team Florida Marlins even won the 1997 and 2003 baseball World Series.

On the one hand, this uncertainty is part of what makes sports exciting to watch. On the other hand, uncertainty is handled very poorly by some people, particularly perfectionists. Perfectionists think in all-or-none terms: either they win (succeed) or they are a total failure. Perfectionists like predictability; if one side is objectively better on all relevant criteria, they should win—always. Unlike most people, perfectionist sports fans may prefer a 55–0 shellacking by their football team to a close victory.

More often, perhaps, perfectionists are not that drawn to watching sports at all. It is too unpredictable and it hurts too much when their side does not win. It may not be that they do not care who wins. They may care too much.

(Coakley, 1986; Fink, 1998). Also, attendance at men's events is higher than at women's events. The nature of the relationship between coverage and fan interest is complex, however. Does the heavier media coverage of male sports merely reflect the reality of greater fan interest in men's sports, for whatever reason, or is the greater media coverage a cause of greater fan interest in men's sports?

Some major media sports, most notably football and baseball, are virtually male only, without parallel female teams for the media to cover. In other sports, such as pro golf, tennis, and basketball, there are parallel women's leagues and competition. Only in professional tennis and the Olympics does the media coverage of women's competition even approach the attention given to the men, however, and both of these cases are fairly unusual, in that competition for both sexes occurs in the same structured event (e.g., Wimbledon or the Davis Cup includes both men's and women's matches, whereas the PGA and LPGA or NBA and WNBA are separate and unequal events). In the reporting about female athletes that does occur, the coverage is asymmetrical, with women being described in less powerful and success-oriented language (Duncan, Messner, & Williams, 1990; Messner, Duncan, & Jensen, 1993). They are more likely than men to be called by their first names and have their strengths described ambivalently, e.g., "small but so effective," "big girl," "her little jump hook" (Duncan, 1992). They are also more likely to be described in terms of their attractiveness, while male athletes are described in terms of their athleticism (Kane, 1996).

The Olympics are an instructive and somewhat atypical instance. Both the summer and winter games are heavily covered by television, often with both live coverage and extended edited excerpts broadcast a few hours later at more convenient local times. Because of this edited nature of the coverage, women's events receive nearly as much coverage as men's events, but overall numbers of minutes and quality of coverage still favors the men (Billings & Eastman, 2003). Interest in women's Olympic sports has been high for many years, and women superstar athletes such as Jackie Joyner-Kersee, Bonnie Blair, Sarah Hughes, Kristi Yamaguchi, and Dorothy Hamill have become genuine heroes and every bit as popular as the men.

Sportscasting and sports reporting is probably the last and most stubborn bastion of male supremacy in the journalism industry. Although female news anchors and reporters, meteorologists, and even editors are increasingly common and accepted, the female sportscaster or sports reporter (covering men's sports) is still highly exceptional. Not until 1993 was the first woman pro baseball announcer hired (Sherry Davis by the San Francisco Giants). Whether this absence reflects the public's true dislike or distrust of women reporting men's sports or merely an unfounded industry fear is unclear. Clearly, the problem is deeper than highly publicized but bogus pseudo-issues such as the issue of sending female sportscasters into men's locker rooms for post-game interviews. (No reporters of either gender are sent into women's locker rooms after the games; couldn't that model work for the men as well?)

Although not nearly as dichotomous as in the past, boys are still encouraged to participate in all kinds of sports more than girls are. Less obviously, the same asymmetry applies to media consumption of sports. Boys are encouraged by their parents (usually their fathers) to watch games on TV as well as to play catch and shoot baskets in the yard. Not only the playing of sports but also the watching of sports on TV has become a part of the male socialization role. The boy who is not particularly interested in spending his time this way, but whose father is, often receives subtle or not-so-subtle messages that such lack of interest does not measure up and perhaps even calls into question his masculinity. Consuming media sports together has become a part of the reality of many father-son relationships, and some father-daughter ones.

One advantage for men watching sports is that this is probably the one arena where they are most free to express emotion. Men watching a ball game together, somewhat like the players themselves, may relatively freely express feelings and even touch one another. In mainstream Anglo North American society this is practically the only time when most men feel comfortable publicly embracing. Many heterosexual men probably never in their lives hug another man outside their family, or perhaps inside it as well, except in the context of playing or watching sports. For this reason, if for no other, sports are important.

In the past, girls were often given messages, especially after reaching puberty, that participation in sports was tomboyish and unfeminine and could be a serious liability in attracting a man. In recent decades, however, this has changed considerably, and girls and women are increasingly allowed to be athletic and sexy at the same time. Less and less is it considered surprising or inappropriate for women to watch ball games or to know more about sports than their men, although TV audiences for most sporting events are still, by a large majority, male. Another important variable in effects of media coverage may be whether a sport is "lean" or "nonlean" (Harrison & Fredrickson, 2003). In lean sports such as gymnastics, diving, or cross-country, weight and appearance are more important for success, whereas in nonlean sports like basketball, tennis, golf, track and field, volleyball, or softball, they are less relevant. See Creedon (1994) for a collection of readings about women, sports, and the media.

Racial Bias. Although a majority of American players in the NFL (60%) and NBA (80%), as well as lesser but substantial numbers in other sports and the Olympics, are African American, their numbers are far smaller in administration, for example, 7% of front office personnel in the NFL and NBA, 1 out of 28 NFL head coaches, 6 out of 27 NBA head coaches (Lapchick & Rodriguez, 1990; J. Stein, 1997b). In 1997–1998, 7.8% of NCAA head football coaches were black, in contrast to half the players (Suggs, 1999). Basketball was slightly better, with 16.4% of head coaches for men's teams and 10.6% for women's being African American.

A few content analysis studies of play-by-play broadcasting suggest that racist stereotypes are being at least subtly reinforced by sportscasting. For example, in a content analysis of 12 NFL games in 1976, Rainville and McCormick (1977) found that White players, as compared to African Americans, were more often described in terms of positive physical characteristics, as causal agents, and in terms of past positive accomplishments. Jackson (1989), looking at NFL and NCAA men's college basketball commentary, found that 65% of comments about African American football players pertained to physical size or ability, compared to 17% for White players. On the other hand, 77% of comments about White football players stressed their intelligence, leadership, or motivation, and only 23% of comments about African American players did (63% vs. 15% for basketball players). Similar findings occur for European sports media, where athletes of African, Asian, or Latin American descent are often admired for their "natural athleticism" but more often than white Europeans are described in terms of group stereotypes, such as "Latin temperament," "Pakistani religious fanaticism," or "superior African muscularity" (Blain, Boyle, & O'Donnell, 1993).

In light of such figures, it is interesting and particularly disturbing that sports are apparently widely perceived by young men of color as a route out of poverty and the urban underclass (Edwards, 1987), although research has shown no relationship between participation in sports and subsequent educational or occupational mobility for African American males (Howell, Miracle, & Rees, 1984).

Hero Worship. Media coverage of sports has enhanced, or at least altered, the perceived reality of the hero. Sports stars have long been heroes emulated by youth, but the age of television, and to a lesser extent other media, has changed this role somewhat. On the one hand, Michael Jordan may be seen by many more people on television than was previously possible. On the other hand, the close scrutiny of television shows the faults as well as the nobler aspects of a potential hero.

Children emulate their TV sports heroes in some very traditional ways, but also in some new ways. A child may imitate not only his hero's great shooting but also his temper tantrums or drug use. Nor is emulation of athletes limited to children. Long-time golfers report that play on golf courses slowed noticeably after major golf tournaments began to be televised in the 1960s. This occurred primarily because amateur golfers started lining up their putts and imitating other behaviors they saw the pros do on TV, no matter that the amateurs may not have understood what they were looking for when lining up that putt.

Fans develop significant parasocial relationships with sports figures. Sometimes this can be very traumatic, as seen in the outpouring of grief following the crash death of NASCAR driver Dale Earnhardt in 2001. Half the country was dumbstruck with grief and could barely discuss it; the other half said "Dale Who?" Rapidly expanding from its Southeastern U.S. base to become one of the fastest growing North American sports, NASCAR adherents are very loyal, especially to their favorite drivers. Earnhardt was a true hero, and his death was a troubling loss to many.

One particular area of concern in regard to hero worship has been the use of drugs by sports stars and the resulting effects on youth (Donohew, Helm, & Haas, 1989). The widespread cocaine use by baseball and basketball stars in the 1980s seemed somehow worse than such use by other citizens, even by other public figures, because sports figures are heroes to youth. This has caused persons and institutions like the commissioner of baseball, the NCAA, and the NBA to be tougher on drug users among their athletes than they might otherwise be. The hero status is often used more directly to discourage drug use, as when Earvin "Magic" Johnson was hired to do an antidrug testimonial PSA, several years before he tested positive for HIV and became a spokesperson for AIDS awareness and safer sex (see Box 6.9).

A substantial benefit of hero status is lucrative product endorsement contracts for the major stars. For Olympic athletes this is often the critical part of their financial support, allowing them to pursue their amateur career. For wealthy professional athletes it is more like the icing on the already rich cake. These endorsement campaigns lead to an even greater media presence, as that person becomes familiar as a spokesperson in advertising for that product. Sometimes a single individual may endorse several different products in different classes. A certain wholesome and unblemished status is required, however. After NBA star Latrell Sprewell assaulted and threatened his coach in December 1997, he was immediately dropped from his Converse shoe endorsement contract (J. Stein, 1997b). When former Romanian Olympic gymnast hero Nadia Comaneci emigrated to the United States, the fact that she was openly and unapologetically living with a man married to someone else apparently rendered her worthless to advertisers for endorsements.

Another aspect of emulating athletic heroes is seen in the area of fashion. Thanks to the influence of television, we not only want to act like the stars but we want to dress like them also. Dress of different sports becomes chic at different times and places. Jogging clothes became high fashion, not

BOX 6.9
SPORTS HEROES WITH THE AIDS VIRUS

In the 1990s, there were increasing numbers of revelations of sports heroes who tested positive for HIV, the AIDS virus. Perhaps the most celebrated case was pro basketball's superhero Earvin "Magic" Johnson, who resigned from the Los Angeles Lakers at the height of his career in late 1991, announcing that he had tested positive for HIV. A widely recognized athlete of tremendous talent, as well as a positive role model for youth, Johnson's announcement was greeted with a massive outpouring of public sympathy. Moreover, he was appointed by former President George H. W. Bush to an advisory committee on AIDS policy (Johnson later resigned in disgust at a perceived lack of government commitment to AIDS) and embarked on a heavy schedule of speaking engagements to youth about the importance of safe sex and traditional values. Receiving heavy media coverage for several weeks, Johnson admitted that he had been quite promiscuous as a single man before his recent marriage, and it was this activity that had presumably infected him. Interestingly, this violation of traditional morals did not seem to significantly affect his superhero status (including lucrative commercial endorsements), as an admission of homosexual relations surely would have. How many products have you seen openly gay Olympic diver Greg Louganis endorse?

In the wake of Magic Johnson's revelations, the media carried a number of stories about the sexually promiscuous lifestyles of some male professional athletes, and many athletes became vocally concerned about possible physical contact with HIV-infected opponents during a football or basketball game. Still, there seemed to be considerable moral ambiguity about such behavior; during this same period, former basketball great Wilt Chamberlain publicly boasted of having had sex with 20,000 different women. Although clearly practicing exceptionally unsafe sex, as well as behavior laden with moral issues, Chamberlain did not lose his hero status. Even a celibate but gay superstar athlete probably would not have been treated half as well.

A very different situation occurred around the early 1992 revelation by retired tennis great Arthur Ashe that he was HIV positive, as a result of a blood transfusion with tainted blood during heart surgery in the early 1980s. Although Ashe had known of his infection for over 3 years, he only chose to reveal the fact publicly after a USA Today reporter had discovered the information and told Ashe that he intended to make it public. Unlike Johnson, Ashe was retired and no longer a public figure and had acquired the HIV virus through means above moral reproach. Although public response to Ashe's announcement and his death in early 1993 was uniformly sad and sympathetic, the question remains about whether the privacy of Ashe and his wife and daughter or the public's right to know was more important.

only for nonjogging adults, but even for infants who cannot even walk! Clothing manufacturers make large sums selling high fashion clothes for tennis, skiing, or bicycling to folks who have never played those sports and who have no intention of ever doing so. Some people wanting to learn to ski first buy the latest ski fashions and only later the skis and poles.

In spite of television's enhancement of sports heroes, some (e.g., Coakley, 1986; Rader, 1984) have argued that today's sports heroes are not on the same pedestal as past stars like Willie Mays, Johnny Unitas, Jesse Owens, or Stan Musial. The huge salaries and fast-track living seem to separate such persons from us and encourage their narcissistic and hedonistic tendencies rather than the righteous and humble characteristics that we at least used to think our heroes possessed. The intrusive eye of television focuses on a ballplayer not only when he makes that glorious play, but also when he is petulantly fuming on the sidelines or selfishly proclaiming that he cannot make ends meet on two million a year. No matter that all of us have our selfish and petulant moments; we like to think that true heroes do not, and the age of television makes it harder to maintain that fiction.

Conclusion

Media reporting sports events are doing more than reflecting the reality of that game. Television in particular has changed the very sports themselves. Television has also changed the way that our minds consider these sports and the way our hearts react to them. TV sports is a world all its own, a world often only imperfectly related to the sports in the stadiums, coliseums, or racetracks. When people think of sports, they are most likely to first think of watching television. The perceived reality of sports acquired through television is thus what sports become for most people. Just as media are our knowledge source about groups of people, social values, or products for sale, so do they tell us about sports, how to play them, how to watch them, and how to feel about them. The very high level of coverage also sets a clear agenda that sports are important. Sports fans consider what the sportscaster says, not what they observe with their own senses, as authoritative; thus people take their radios and even their small televisions to the stadium, so they can know what is "really happening."

Now let us turn to a second media domain which plugs in very centrally to our emotions, namely, the world of music.

MUSIC

Listening to popular music is one of most preferred leisure activities worldwide by young adults, occupying between two and a half and five hours per day for the average teen (Strasburger & Wilson, 2002). Since the advent of rock and roll in the 1950s, the latest artists, whether it be Elvis Presley, the Beatles, Metallica, Pink Floyd, or Eminem, have been immensely popular with teens but thought scandalous by their parents. Popular music has also always been associated with dancing, going back at least to the charleston in the 1920s, which raised eyebrows of parents in its time. When Elvis appeared on *The Ed Sullivan Show* in the 1950s, he had to be photographed from the chest up, so that his gyrating hips would not arouse teens beyond their control or excessively offend their parents.

Pop musicians have often been at the forefront of fashion. When the Beatles came to America from Britain in 1963, the "long hair" created an immense stir, but within a few years much of the male population was wearing their hair at least that long. Punk and heavy metal rockers may have scandalized people in the early 1980s by wearing earrings, but 15–20 years later body piercings in all sorts of places were widespread.

Beginning in the early 1980s, music developed a visual component. Music Television (MTV) began in 1981 by playing promotional videos made by the record companies. Discovering that these ads had very wide appeal, the cable channel played more and more music videos and grew until it become a youth icon. MTV Europe was formed in 1987. MTV grew to be both a barometer and a leading trend-setter of the youth culture market. Some have argued that the demand for access to world popular culture was a major reason for the democratic revolutions in Eastern Europe in 1989–1991, that it was "not so much the failure of the Marxist systems but rather the inability of these systems to deliver Big Macs, Levis, and rock music. Karl Marx in his political theory never anticipated the problem that 'I want my MTV' could create for decision makers in socialist countries" (Orman, 1992, p. 282). In recent years MTV has evolved to include other kinds of teen-oriented programming, such as the stunt program *Jackass* and its annual spring break marathon. Other music video-oriented channels, notably VH-1 and Black Entertainment Television (BET), have arisen to provide more music video programming.

About half of all music videos are performance videos, where the singer or group performs a song in a studio or concert setting. A concept video, on the other hand, tells a story, which may go beyond the lyrics of the song. Concept videos contain many special visual effects and also make heavy use of sex, dance, and sometimes violent themes.

The heavy influence of American and British groups has been a major factor in the ascendance of the English language as the worldwide language of popular culture. However, there is also much rock music in numerous other languages. It is a fact, however, that international stars need to record in English to break into the U.S. market. Whereas South Americans, Europeans, or Africans will listen to music sung in a language they don't

---

BOX 6.10
AFRICAN POP MUSIC AND DEMOCRACY

Ivorian pop music has long been quite political. When a 1999 coup by General Robert Gueï took over, it announced the overthrow of the Ivory Coast President with reggae superstar Alpha Blondy performing a song and then introducing the new president. Singer Tiken Jah Fakoly was even more identified with the revolution, having been an advisor to Gueï's forces. The singers also act as liaisons between media and law enforcement agencies (Lee, 2000). Ivorian anthems have been used by political forces elsewhere. For example, Tiken Jah Fakoly's "We've Had It" was taken up by protesters in Madagascar and his "The Country's in Trouble" became the opposition anthem in Chad's 2000 election (Médioni, 2002).

Nigerian singer Fela Anikulapo-Kuti, founder of the Afrobeat style, found an international audience before his death in 1997. His son Fema Kuti founded a movement against corruption and regularly writes editorials in song, most of which are censored in Nigeria. Afro-funk singer Angélique Kidjo emerged as the most popular person in her native Benin in a poll asking who they would prefer as President. Not interested in politics, she nonetheless has integrated Afro-Brazilian and African traditions to support democracy in Africa, as well as entertaining large international audiences (Médioni, 2002).

---

understand (often English), it is commonly believed that North Americans will not do so. There is also increasing cross-national, and cross-genre influences as almost every musical style becomes more international (Hutcheon, 2002). Formerly very local music now has found international audiences. Indian sitar music, Jamaican reggae, Brazilian samba, Irish Celtic ballads, Louisiana zydeco, and Caribbean salsa are listened to worldwide. New hybrid styles are continually emerging and finding large audiences. For example, Afro-Colombian cumbia blends African percussion, European melodies, and Andean flutes and accordions. Nigerian Afrobeat combines traditional African beats with American funk. See Box 6.10 for examples of how music has political power in Africa.

Uses and Gratifications of Popular Music

Popular music, indeed all music, appeals to the emotion in many different ways (Strasburger & Wilson, 2002). There are many uses and gratifications that we receive from music. For one thing, music is physiologically arousing. The body is "pumped up" in response to many kinds of music, although individual tastes vary. Music can induce pleasant mood states of different sorts and it can reduce feelings of anxiety and generally lift the spirits. Indeed, music is frequently used as a tool for mood management (Knobloch, 2003).

Music is also used to fill silence and fill in background noise, either at home or driving a car. Thus, it can relieve boredom. It also has a social function, being a natural background or a part of talking with friends, partying, or other recreation. Roberts and Christenson (2001) make the point that it is difficult to definitively separate social and solitary uses of music. Teens may often listen to music by themselves but for reasons that serve social relationships. For example, music may remind one of an absent friend and relieve loneliness. This is what Roberts and Christenson call "quasi-social."

Music can also serve to help define one's self-identity and facilitate one's entry into some group. Within a high school, for example, one group listens to rap, one to heavy metal, another to country music, and so on. The music can be an agent of socialization to bring the teen into the subculture by influencing how they dress and act. This musical culture is not necessarily restricted to one's culture of origin. For example, many popular musical genres (e.g., jazz, blues, rap, hip hop) had their origin in the African-American community but have wide appeal beyond that subculture. Many continue to be amazed at the current popularity of rap, with its urban Black origins, with affluent White suburban teens.

Finally, music in adolescence, along with its accompanying dancing, serves as a marker of separation from adults. Part of its appeal is frankly that adults dislike it and don't understand it. This phenomenon repeats itself with rap and heavy metal today as it has in the past with rock and roll in the 1950s or the charleston in the 1920s. Even something as simple as a teen turning on the radio in the car or house serves as a separation from parents. If the radio is on, he doesn't have to talk to his parents.

Music is powerful material, and anything powerful can be very threatening. See Box 6.11 for some examples of how music has threatened the status quo throughout history.

Content

Perhaps surprisingly, the most common theme in music lyrics over the last fifty years is being in love, although the lyrics are more sexually explicit than they used to be, for example, expressing love as lust (Hansen & Hansen, 2000). There was an increase of violent and misogynistic themes starting in the 1990s, especially in rap, punk, and heavy metal. Increasingly these themes became more mainstream, as seen when bad boy rapper Eminem (Marshall Mathers) received Grammy and Oscar awards in the early 2000s.

BOX 6.11
MUSIC AS A THREAT
(Taruskin, 2001)

Music has often been a threatening force and sometimes can produce a violent reaction. Perhaps the most extreme example of a backlash against music was seen in the brutal regime of the Taliban in Afghanistan (1996–2001), which sought out musical instruments, cassette tapes and videos, and cassette players and burned them in public pyres. Musicians caught playing were beaten with their instruments and then imprisoned. Other puritanical authoritarian regimes also opposed music. Believing it had hypnotic or addictive effects, theocratic ruler Ayatollah Khomeini banned music from TV and radio in Iran after the Islamic Revolution of 1979.

Such extremes have also been seen in Western church and secular tradition as well, however. Plato's *Republic* was highly suspicious of music as taking hold of the soul. In the history of Christianity, there have been many religious leaders suspicious of music, including such diverse company as St. Augustine, St. John Chrysostom, and various conservative Protestant groups.

Music also derives power and threat from its culture of associations. For many years the German nationalist composer Richard Wagner was not performed in Israel (by custom, not by law). When composer Daniel Barenboim broke this taboo in 2001, the decision was very controversial and many Israelis found his choice insensitive.

The advent of music videos in the early 1980s offered a new outlet for women to be presented as sex objects and ornamental decorations, much as they had long been portrayed in much advertising and many entertainment genres. Music videos also provided more opportunities for the intertwining of sexual and violent themes.

One content concern with popular music has been the promotion of drug use. Roberts, Henriksen, and Christenson (1999) analyzed the lyrics from the 1000 most popular songs in 1996 and 1997. They found that 17% of the songs overall had reference to alcohol and 18% to illicit drugs. With rap, however, figures were much higher (47% for alcohol and 63% for illicit drugs). Furthermore, any mention of negative consequences of drug use was rare; only 9% of songs mentioning alcohol mentioned any negative consequences of its use. Tobacco was rarely mentioned, although more often in rap and hip-hop than other genres.

These antisocial themes were generally higher in music videos than in the lyrics themselves, especially in rap videos (DuRant, Rich, Emans, Rome, Allred, & Woods, 1997). For example, Jones (1997) found the following percentages of themes in rap videos: guns (59%), drug use (49%), profanity (73%), grabbing (69%), alcohol use (42%), and explicit violence (36%).

Content analysis itself does not tell the whole story, however. The interpretation of that content is important, and different ages do not always interpret lyrics in the same way (Hansen & Hansen, 2000). For example, teens see less sex and more love than adults do in the same lyrics (Rosenbaum & Prinsky, 1987). Girls often see a sexy woman as a powerful figure, whereas boys see her as a plaything. Children will interpret a concept video more literally than a teen or adult will. Often teens did not fully understand the lyrics anyway (Desmond, 1987, Greenfield, et al., 1987; Strasburger & Wilson, 2002).

There may also be a socially positive side to even fairly extreme lyrics. For example, some have argued that rap music has a positive social role, being a voice for a very marginalized and disenfranchised group, at the same time empowering young black males and drawing the attention of their plight to the broader society (Krohn & Suazo, 1995; McDonnell, 1992).

These lyrics or videos probably serve to prime ideas and serve as cues to retrieve related knowledge. If a teen watches lots of videos that portray women as sexual playthings, for example, that will prime gender-role memories and attitudes consistent with that type of schema. This in turn will guide future attention and information processing, directing attention toward exemplars that confirm such beliefs and away from those which are inconsistent with it. For example, Gan, Zillmann, & Mitrook (1997) found that sexually enticing rap videos primed a negative stereotype for African American women in White viewers, and that this negative schema was subsequently used to evaluate other Black women in more negative ways.

Effects

Parallel to popular judgments about media violence, people often take an extreme position on popular music, either damning it as the cause of all moral collapse in society or dismissing the criticisms as "no big deal." Although it is difficult to do well-controlled research on causative effects of music consumption, we do know something about its effects.

There is clear research support for arousal, that is, music does arouse us emotionally, even though specific tastes differ greatly and what is pleasant for one person may be aversive for another. It also can clearly affect mood (Ballard & Coates, 1995). Although a possible causative role is not entirely clear, there is some evidence that a preference for heavy metal music, in particular, may be a marker for alienation, psychiatric disorders, risk-taking, and/or substance abuse in adolescence (Strasburger & Wilson, 2002), in that heavy metal is disproportionately preferred by teens with these conditions.

Reactions to music can depend on one's prior knowledge, experiences, and prejudices. Fried (1996, 1999) conducted a couple of very interesting experiments on reactions of adults of various ages to music lyrics. The lyrics to an old Kingston Trio folksong "Bad Man's Blunder" from the 1960s were pretested and shown to be not recognized as a folk song and equally credible as country or rap music. The lyrics, very similar to the controversial Ice T "Cop Killer" rap of 1992, tells of a young man who intentionally shoots and kills a police officer and shows no remorse for it. The written lyrics were identified as being from an artist named "D. J. Jones" and were then shown to European-American and Hispanic adults in public places like malls and coffee shops. The key manipulation was that half were told it was a country music song and half that it was a rap song, two genres identified as surprisingly similar by some text analyses (Armstrong, 1993; Noe, 1995). Participants were then asked to rate the lyrics on seven attitude scales like "I find these lyrics offensive" and "This song promotes violence, riots, and civil unrest," from which a composite score was created.

Results showed that adults over 40 rated the lyrics much more negatively when they were identified as rap than when they were identified as country. Adults under 40, however, showed no difference as a function of the genre attribution and produced much more positive ratings overall. A second analysis, partitioned by whether the participants had children instead of by age, showed that adults with children rated the allegedly rap lyrics more negatively than the allegedly country lyrics, but adults without children showed no difference. Clearly the reactions are not only to the presented lyrics but also to prior knowledge and attitudes about the musical genre. In the case of older adults and adults who are parents, rap is far more negative. Fried (1999) offers several possible explanations for these findings. One invokes a subtle racism, where the rap music is associated with the urban Black culture, which has negative associations, especially with violence, for White and Hispanic parents. Another factor is familiarity, where the less familiar is more threatening. The older adults were probably less familiar with rap as a genre than with country. In any case, these studies show that we bring considerable emotional baggage when we respond to music.

There is also evidence of desensitization effects of music. For example, exposure to violent rap videos can lead to greater acceptance of violence in dating situations and lower academic aspirations of young African-American teens and college students (Johnson, Adams, Ashburn, & Reed, 1995; Johnson, Jackson, & Gatto, 1995). Watching rock videos with antisocial themes led to greater liking of antisocial behavior (Hansen & Hansen, 1990b).

See Box 6.12 for an example of the use of music in attempts to gain international influence.

BOX 6.12
POP MUSIC IN THE SERVICE OF DIPLOMACY

Who is the largest distributor of Arabic-language popular music in the Middle East? It is Radio Sawa ("Together"), and it will probably surprise you to know that Radio Sawa is funded by the United States government in its efforts to woo the hearts and minds of young adult Arabs. Radio Sawa is the successor to the Voice of America Arabic service, a seven-hour-daily news service on shortwave radio that was little more than U.S. political propaganda with little popular appeal even for those few who could receive it. Designed by Norman Pattiz after intense local market research, Radio Sawa broadcasts on FM and sometimes AM with a 24-hour format of eclectic popular music from the Arab world, the U.S., and elsewhere. There are also two hourly news segments (a 10-minute segment with correspondent reports and a 5-minute headline segment), as well as PSAs on topics like drugs, drunk driving, and AIDS. In an attempt to win local appeal, announcers use local Arab dialects and broadcast local news, weather, and traffic reports. Of course, the most controversial aspect is the news, this being a part of the world with a high level of distrust and dislike of the U.S. government. What do you think of Eminem and Britney Spears being an integral part of the U.S. diplomatic message to the Arab world? Radio Sawa has its headquarters in Dubai and is broadcast to Jordan, Qatar, the UAE, Kuwait, Bahrain, Djibouti, and Cyprus, with access from these places to Iraq, Egypt, Palestine, and elsewhere. (Gubash, 2002).

Music as a Memory Cue

Music turns out to be an excellent cue to memory, with melody providing an additional possible retrieval route beyond the words themselves. In many societies, extensive oral traditions have been handed down for generations through music, with the melodies serving to help encode the verbal information and preserve it in the collective memory (Rubin, 1995). Marketers have long known that musical jingles can aid memory for products advertised (Yalch, 1991). Songs can also be powerful cues for remembering the events of one's life (Cady, Harris, & Knappenberger, 2004; Schulkind, Hennis, & Rubin, 1999). People strongly associate certain songs with their senior year in high school, a long road trip with friends, or driving to work at a certain job. The popularity of oldies radio stations and classic rock in general is no doubt due to the highly effective triggering of personal memories by these songs. Cady, et al. (2004) found that, when college students were presented with a list of songs popular during certain eras of their lives (e.g., preschool, middle school, high school), most could easily recall a personal memory associated with that song. For the most part these were very pleasant memories, with the earliest ones being the most pleasant and the more recent ones being more vivid.

CONCLUSION

Nothing elicits more emotion from most people than an exciting ball game between two teams they care about or listening to a song that they really love or hate. Although very different in many ways, sports and music do have this in common. The triggering of emotions by media can be very powerful. If you have any doubt about this, think back to a song you associate with some significant event in high school and the most exciting ball game that you watched in the last few years. A flood of memories and feelings should be quickly yours!

CHAPTER 7

News: Setting the Agenda About the World

Q: What does the public think is most wrong with news reporting?
A: According to a 1997 Roper poll, 82% thought reporters were insensitive to people's pain when covering disasters and accidents. Other complaints were mentioned by no more than 64% (Valente, 1997).
Q: How has TV news coverage changed in recent years?
A: According to a study by the Center for Media and Public Affairs of over 135,000 U.S. network evening news stories during the 1990s, an average of fewer than 100 were about murder in 1990–1992. During, 1993–1996, that number jumped to 352 (excluding the heavy O. J. Simpson murder trial coverage). In 1997–1999, the number jumped to 511. All of this occurred during a decade where the actual homicide rate steadily declined to its lowest point in 1999 (Farhi, 2001)!
Q: How many children are frightened or upset by news stories on television?
A: 37% of children between kindergarten and 6th grade, according to a survey of their parents by Cantor and Nathanson (1996). The typical minute of network news in the United States is seen by an estimated half a million children aged 2 to 11.

If there is one area of media that people are most likely to uncritically accept as reflecting reality rather than constructing it, that area is probably the news. People watch, read, or listen to news to find out what happened in the world that day. However, the perceived reality often diverges quite dramatically from the real world, where much more happened than can be reported in any day's news program or publication. Even the most earnest attempt to accurately and fairly represent the day's events requires producers and editors to select which items to cover, how prominently to cover them, and in what manner to cover them. The typical daily newspaper, for example, only selects 25% of the daily wire service material to print (McCombs, 1994).

These choices necessarily involve some *agenda setting* (see chapter 2); that is, telling us what is important (McCombs, 1994; McCombs & Reynolds, 2002; McCombs & Shaw, 1993; Dearing & Rogers, 1996; Watt, Mazza, & Snyder, 1993). Agenda setting tells us what to think *about*, what is important. It does not necessarily tell us what to *think*. The news is not a reflection of the day; it is a "set of stories constructed by journalists about the events of the day" (McCombs, 1994, p. 11). When the months-long U.S. presidential primary elections are given massive media coverage, the public receives the implicit but unmistakable message that these campaigns are important. Likewise, when stories receive little coverage, a message is communicated that they are not important. Those in power know this well. For example, when the Israeli government closes the West Bank to reporters, it is hoping that the ensuing lack of coverage will cause the problems there to be perceived as less important. See Brosius and Kepplinger (1990); Demers, Craff, Choi, and Pessin (1989); and Edelstein (1993) for different measures of agenda setting in regard to news.

News programming is put in an especially tricky position by the economic realities of the mass communications industry. Even though news divisions are separate from entertainment divisions at the U.S. television networks, and news clearly has the primary function to inform rather than entertain, the success of news is determined by ratings every bit as much as is the success of a sitcom or movie, and that increases the pressure to entertain. Similarly, a newspaper or magazine must try to maximize its advertising revenue, which is closely related to the number of subscriptions. In deciding what news to include in a publication or broadcast, pressures clearly exist to tell people what they want to hear and what will entertain them, in order to keep them coming back and to keep advertisers happy. If the public does not want to hear that its leaders are conducting an unjust war or if major advertisers do not care to see news coverage of their product being harmful, those pressures are unlikely to be ignored (Lee & Solomon, 1991; Steyer, 2002).

Understanding the psychology of media news requires an examination of the nature of the medium itself as it transmits news. After some introductory comments on recent trends in coverage and consumption, this chapter examines what news is, in a psychological sense, and how the perceived reality about world events is constructed from reading or watching news reports. The rest of the chapter examines effects of consuming news, including effects on memory, decision making, behavior, and even foreign and domestic policy.

Thinking about contemporary news coverage requires us to take a close look at television news. Much newer than print journalism, it has its roots in the movie newsreel of the early to mid-20th century. With such news shorts, which were shown in theaters before feature films, the audience experienced an immediacy with distant world events, even if often delayed several weeks, that had never been possible before. This use of moving visuals to convey the news brought about the new technique of *montage*, the juxtaposition of images for dramatic effect. Reporters and editors can reassemble the ingredients of the reality to best express what they perceive as the essence of that reality. Montage allows the telling of a news story using many of the dramatic techniques from drama and fiction writing to make the event more compelling and entertaining. Such techniques open the door for other elements of fiction to enter as well.

Although news has been on television from its early days, the TV coverage of John F. Kennedy's assassination and funeral in November 1963 firmly established television as a serious, if not the predominant, player in news coverage. All other programming was pre-empted for three days as the country sat glued to their TV sets. There was even an unexpected surprise when the assassination of the alleged assassin Lee Harvey Oswald by Jack Ruby was captured on live TV from the basement of the Dallas police station! In the next 5 years, the U.S. TV news audience jumped 50%, the sharpest increase ever. By 1977, 62% of all adult Americans watched at least one newscast per weekday, making television the major source of news in the United States. In recent years, however, the network share has fallen. In the nineties, the audience for national news on the three major U.S. networks fell from 60 to 30% (Farhi, 2001), with much of the loss going to cables news channels like CNN and Internet news sources. However, local news, including weather and sports, is especially popular and is crucial for local stations in establishing their unique identity in the community, because the large majority of programming is either network initiated or syndicated, both of which are identical regardless of the local station. See Box 7.1 for further discussion of weather reports and reporters.

One interesting recent trend is for increasing numbers of people, especially young adults and teens, to get their news from late-night comedy programs like *The Tonight Show, Saturday Night Live, The Daily Show with Jon Stewart,* and *Politically Incorrect.* In 2000 over one-third of Americans under 30 reported such shows to be their *primary* source for news and almost 80% said they sometimes or regularly got political information from such entertainment sources (Williams & Delli Carpini, 2002). It is sobering to think that large numbers of citizens are getting their news primarily from parodies of the news!

One significant change has been a precipitous drop in the amount of international news coverage in the U.S. in the last twenty years, in part due to budget-cutting reductions of expensive foreign correspondents. Just between 1989 and 1995, the number of minutes of stories on the ABC, NBC,

BOX 7.1
TV WEATHER FORECASTS: MORE THAN TELLING
IF IT WILL RAIN

Local news anchors, sportscasters, and weathercasters are extremely important to local TV stations in establishing their signature and identity in their market. Although a large majority of programming on commercial television is either network or syndication, local news is one of the few programs where a local station has control of all aspects of the programming. A popular team of local anchors can bring an extremely helpful ratings boost that greatly raises the visibility of that station in the target market.

A seemingly indispensable part of all local news shows, as well as some national ones, is the weather forecaster. Although all U.S. weathercasters use essentially the same data, those gathered by the National Weather Service, clearly not all weathercasts are equal. Although increasing numbers of weathercasters are trained in meteorology, some are more performers than reporters. NBC's Willard Scott did the weather on the *Today Show* dressed in various costumes and always with panache. Early TV events like a Chicago weatherman giving his Thanksgiving forecast to a turkey, a Milwaukee weathercaster puppet named Albert the Alleycat delivering the forecast, and crumpled falling confetti to signify snow being predicted are things of the past. High quality computer graphics now allow even small local stations to give a weathercast of high technical quality, a far cry from 1950s weatherman Bill Carlsen, who squirted his map with shaving cream to show snow. (Garelik, 1985).

Although weathercasts are often seen as the frivolous or soft side of the news (the first on-the-air newswomen were the "weathergirls" of the late 1950s), often the subject is deadly serious. Forecasts and warnings of tornadoes, hurricanes, and floods can mean the difference between life and death. Although the National Weather Service issues the watches, warnings, and advisories, often the local weathercaster does additional interpretation as to how strongly to advise precaution. A wrong judgment call in such a situation can have tragic consequences.

and CBS evening news broadcasts from foreign correspondents dropped from 4,032 minutes to 1,991 minutes, less than half that number. Where is this air time going? In 1995, the network evening news broadcasts spent 1,591 minutes on the O. J. Simpson murder trial, compared to 418 minutes on the bombing of the Oklahoma City federal building, and 318 minutes on the civil war in Bosnia (Moeller, 1999). Think about the agenda that is being set as to what is important.

One of the greatest unknowns in the next decade or so will be the role of Internet. Already an important and popular source of news, the

Internet web pages for various newspapers, networks, wire services, television stations and other sources are read by millions daily. There is some indication that this may be particularly at the expense of newspapers, although some of the most widely visited sites are newspaper sites, some of which (e.g., *The New York Times*) have free e-mailing services available with news summaries and links to complete stories. See Gunter (2003) and Tewksbury (2003) for thorough discussions of Internet news.

TV news reporters, especially network news anchors, become trusted friends in our lives. They may be a part of our mealtimes, almost like having the news anchor as a regular dinner guest. We invite them into our homes through our choice to turn on the TV to a particular channel. It is not unusual for people to audibly respond to a greeting, such as responding "Hi, Tom" back to NBC news anchor Tom Brokaw as he signs on with "Good evening." They become substitute friends in a sort of parasocial interaction (Giles, 2002; A. M. Rubin, Perse, & Powell, 1985), as discussed in chapter 2. There is a sense of solidarity with them. As one person explained such a relationship, "I grew up watching him. I guess I expect him to be there when I turn on the news. We've been through a lot together" (Levy, 1982, p. 180). That feeling of being through a lot together captures very well why news anchors are far more important people in our lives than merely folks who read us the day's events. Even with local news, if one of the anchors is married or has a baby, it becomes one of the news stories that evening. There is no equivalent relationship with newspaper editors or writers.

WHAT IS NEWS?

Jamieson and Campbell (1992, p. 31) defined *hard news* as "any report of an event that happened or was disclosed within the previous 24 hours and treats an issue of ongoing concern." The event itself need not be recent (although usually it is) but it must involve some new revelation or previously unknown connection. Revelations of Abraham Lincoln's suffering from depression, Franklin Roosevelt's previously unknown extramarital affair, or the discovery of the asteroid crater that probably led to the extinction of the dinosaurs 65 million years ago have all been news in recent years.

In contrast to hard news are *human interest stories*, which touch universal concerns and are less tied to place and time. These features are most prevalent on so-called slow news days (such as weekends) and may include anything from a farmer in west Texas who planted 1959 Cadillacs tail-fin-upward in his field to the heartwarming story of a poor Mississippi sharecropper whose nine children have all graduated from college (most with advanced degrees), to the mildly titillating story of a brothel madam with a master's degree.

Primary Characteristics of a Newsworthy Event

Jamieson and Campbell (1992) identified five qualities of a newsworthy event. They may not all be present in every story, but no doubt several of them will be for each hard news story. The more of these characteristics a story has naturally, the more likely it is to be heavily covered in the news. An understanding of these qualities goes a long way toward explaining why certain events receive so much coverage and certain others so little.

Personalization.   First, a newsworthy story is personalized—it is about individuals. This allows audience identification with the person and may make a dauntingly complex event easier to comprehend. It lends itself well to photography and the interview format, which works well on either TV or print, but it may be at the cost of oversimplifying (and possibly distorting) complex events and overemphasizing stars such as the president, the Pope, a serial killer, or a terrorist looking for a media platform.

Drama and Conflict.   Second, a newsworthy event is dramatic and conflict-filled, even violent, in the pattern of entertainment TV. Shots of police beating protesters makes more exciting news copy than a debate among politicians about the economy. With its emphasis on conflict, this tendency helps to ensure coverage of opposing views but, on the negative side, may overemphasize the confrontational and violent nature of the story. Very infrequent violent events may be assumed by viewers to be the norm. Nonviolent events may be neglected, and very important issues not conducive to drama, conflict, or personalization may be grossly underreported. Complex economic stories like the Third World debt crisis or changing interest rates are often covered only in the context of specific conflicts growing out of those problems. See Box 7.2 for coverage of a less dramatic but very important story.

There is some reason to think that the emphasis on conflict has escalated in recent years. In a very provocative book, *The Argument Culture: Stopping America's War of Words*, sociolinguist Deborah Tannen (1998) argues that American society at all levels has become more confrontational and argumentative in recent decades, with this contentiousness seen in the press, politics, the legal system, and even in family and interpersonal relationships. At least for the press, Tannen traces much of this back to Watergate in the 1970s, where investigative journalism did indeed play a strongly, and constitutionally important, adversarial role in rooting out the scandal in the Nixon administration. She worries that the mindset has never really changed and news media, as well as office holders, continue to believe they must attack and challenge at every opportunity. Thus one sees, for example, candidates for office or nominees for cabinet positions

---

BOX 7.2
NEWS COVERAGE OF NUCLEAR WAR THREATS

Although a terribly important story, nuclear war is an ongoing continual threat that does not have many of the characteristics of a newsworthy story on a day-to-day basis. D. M. Rubin and Cummings (1989) conducted a content analysis of network news coverage of three stories related to the nuclear threat that appeared in 1983, in the last high point of the Cold War threat. The first was the proposal of the new scientific theory of nuclear winter, which proposed that a nuclear war would trigger enough fires to send up enough smoke, dust, and soot to block 95% of the sun's light in many latitudes, to be soon followed by a huge disruption of the ecosystem and growing season and the possible destruction of all humanity. The second event was the televising of the fictional ABC movie *The Day After* about a Soviet nuclear attack on Kansas; this became the highest rated TV movie up to that time. Embraced by the antinuclear movement and attacked by conservatives, its impact was weaker than either group predicted (Scholfield & Pavelchak, 1985). The third story was the continuing public discussion by members of the Reagan administration about the possibility of fighting and winning a limited nuclear war.

Compared to what one might expect about their importance, D. M. Rubin and Cummings (1989) found coverage of these three stories to be minimal and offered four possible explanations for this slighting. It may be that TV journalism had accepted that life could not survive a nuclear exchange; additional evidence was thus uncritically embraced and ignored. The nuclear winter story and the message of *The Day After* was "not so much displaced. . . . as smothered by uncritical acceptance" (Rubin & Cummings, p. 49). A second, more paternalistic possibility is that TV news had decided that viewers were too threatened and emotionally unable to handle any more discussion of this issue. Third, it is possible that TV journalism had decided that nuclear weapons were here to stay and thus should not be politicized by arousing controversy. In support of such a view is the fact that the network cut a line from *The Day After* which stated that the justification for the Soviet attack was the U.S. movement of Pershing missiles, and also the fact that there was very little questioning of the Reagan administration's assumptions about nuclear war. Finally, the paltry coverage may have been due to the fact that TV has acquired only a limited inventory of images for communicating the horror of nuclear war, such as computer graphics, writer landscapes, file footage of Hiroshima and Nagasaki, Pentagon film of missile tests, or scenes of everyday life with a voice-over intoning the consequences of nuclear war.

In conclusion, the "coverage of these events in 1983 was fatalistic, overly respectful of government, visually unimaginative, and politically neutralized. The strongest impression of the image of nuclear war on television news in the Reagan years was of no image at all" (Rubin & Cummings, 1989, p. 56).

subject to unprecedented intense scrutiny of all aspects of their personal lives. Sometimes this is so intense that highly qualified people withdraw from consideration rather than subject themselves and their families to such treatment.

Action.   The third characteristic of a newsworthy event is that it contains action and some observable occurrence. This often becomes the hook on which to hang what is essentially a more abstract story. For example, trends in inflation may be covered by interviews with specific consumers shopping and expressing their views on rising prices. Important stories that do not have such a convenient hook or discrete encapsulating event receive less attention. For example, the dramatic shift in the Third World over the last 50 years from domestic-food producing to export agriculture is a profound change, but it is seldom mentioned in the news because it is not easily symbolized by discrete events or manifest in crisis points.

Novelty and Deviance.   The fourth characteristic of hard news is that it is novel or deviant. Contrary to the "late breaking news" metaphor, most news is not particularly surprising. For example, much political and economic news is covered by the normal beat reporters who know in advance that certain speeches will be made, votes taken, or meetings held. Events outside this predictable range of news will stand a better chance of being covered if they are novel, with chances of coverage increasing as the events get more strange and bizarre. A junkie being shot to death in New York City may not be big news, but a Sunday school teacher killed in a Satanic ritual in rural Saskatchewan is.

An event may be deviant in different senses (Shoemaker, Chang, & Brendlinger, 1987; Shoemaker, Danielian, & Brendlinger, 1987). *Statistical* deviance refers purely to the frequency of an event, with highly unusual events being the most deviant. *Normative* deviance involves the degree of violation of social and legal norms. Pritchard and Hughes (1997) offer evidence from an analysis of homicide reports that normative deviance is a more important component of newsworthiness than is statistical deviance. Finally, *potential for social change deviance* refers to how much the existing status quo is threatened, a type of deviance very high in terrorist events like the 1995 Oklahoma City bombing of a federal office building or, most extraordinarily, the September 11, 2001 attacks on the World Trade Center and the Pentagon.

Link to Ongoing Themes.   Finally, events are more likely to be covered in news if they are linked to themes of ongoing current interest. Some of these themes are deep seated, almost archetypal, at least within a given society. For example, the first theme, *appearance versus reality*, has always been a common theme in literature and drama. News stories about deception and hypocrisy make good copy; the Watergate scandal of 1972 to 1974, which eventually led to the resignation of President Richard Nixon, was one of the hottest news stories in the nation's history. Second, *big versus little* is a powerful theme, nicely captured by some of the crusading stories on *60 Minutes* or *20/20*. Closely related is *good versus evil*, a moral framework often imposed on news stories (e.g., the brave consumer vs. the evil polluting corporation, righteous America versus the evil dictator). The fourth theme is *efficiency versus inefficiency*, commonly used in stories such as exposés of government or corporate waste or mismanagement. Finally, the *unique versus routine* highlights the unusual.

Besides these underlying, archetypal themes we also have cyclical themes such as the quadrennial presidential elections in the United States and seasonal, holiday, and weather themes. For example, we know we will see the Pope saying midnight mass on Christmas, the groundhog looking for his shadow every February 2, and local news reporters in the spring in the Midwest telling us how to protect ourselves from tornadoes. Such events appear in the news because they fit the cyclical themes, in spite of having few of the other characteristics of newsworthy events.

Secondary Characteristics of a Newsworthy Event

Inoffensiveness.   Besides the five basic characteristics of newsworthy events, there are four other, more specific pragmatic characteristics that are required for a story to receive much coverage. A story must be *inoffensive* or at least not blatantly offensive. Sometimes such concerns about taste keep a story from receiving coverage it would otherwise have. For example, the press was very slow to pick up on reporting on the AIDS epidemic in the early 1980s, in part because they balked at mentioning the most common way to acquire the disease, namely, anal intercourse (Meyer, 1990). After the terrorist attacks of 2001, the U.S. press only very cautiously addressed the issues of how U.S. foreign policy might have contributed to a climate spawning radical Islamic terrorism. Mainstream media concluded that most of the country did not want to hear that our policies might be at least partially responsible for those horrible events.

Credibility.   Second, a serious story must be perceived as *credible*. An occurrence so bizarre that readers or viewers would not believe it is less likely to be reported, at least by the mainstream press (Meyer, 1990). Although this requirement may sometimes have the salutary effect of weeding out tabloid-style oddities such as Elvis sightings at K-Mart, it may have a less benign effect, such as when news media self-censor a story that they do not believe their public would accept or want to hear, such as a report that a very popular and respected leader has been involved in corruption.

"Sound Bites." Third, a story must be packageable in small pieces, fit for a 45-second TV news story or a short piece in the newspaper. A story that fits this packaging demand is much more likely to receive coverage than one that does not. The importance of this sound bite requirement is often underappreciated by those wishing their work would receive more coverage, such as scientists and others less than skilled in explaining their work to journalists in small, easy-to-digest pieces. Although the sound bite is often seen as a creation of television, some have argued that the pithy sound bite, whether or not it was actually uttered by its supposed author, has actually been with us for a long time (Wernick, 1996). For example, Louis XIV's "L'état, c'est moi" ("I am the state"), Julius Caesar's "Veni, vidi, vici" ("I came, I saw, I conquered"), or Harry Truman's "The buck stops here" have a lot in common with Ronald Reagan's "Just say no" to drugs or George W. Bush's "the axis of evil" reference to nations harboring terrorists or making weapons of mass destruction. The size of these bites has been decreasing; the average length of a TV news story about a U.S. Presidential election campaign declined from 43 seconds in 1968 to 9 seconds in 1988 (Hallin, 1992). Although television news deals in very short pieces, some media offer alternatives. In the case of newspapers, the trend over the last century has been to print longer stories with more interpretation, relative to pure reporting of the facts (Barnhurst & Mutz, 1997).

The Local Hook. A final secondary characteristic of newsworthiness is the local hook, the connection of the story to the community of the reader, viewers, or listeners. At the local level, a newspaper or TV/radio station will be much more likely to cover a national or international event if it has a local angle (e.g., a local resident caught in a foreign uprising, the closing of a local plant because of Mexican economic policy). On a national level, the hook in the United States may be a current policy debate in Washington or the presence of U.S. troops abroad. Sadly, some very important stories are downplayed or missed altogether because of the lack of an obvious local hook. U.S. media in particular are notorious for extensive foreign coverage during an immediate crisis, but very little before or after. Consequently, for the average person some crises seem to emerge suddenly out of nowhere, because they have not been aware of some smoldering issues. Also, after the immediate crisis, the all-important follow-up period receives little coverage. For example, the Afghanistan invasion of Fall 2001 to oust the Taliban regime received extensive coverage, but the following period of "nation-building" did not. The press had moved on to preparations for invading Iraq to oust Saddam Hussein. After that was accomplished in March–April 2003, the protracted and challenging aftermath almost dropped off the radar screen. See Box 7.3 for an extended example of American news coverage from the same part of the world a generation earlier.

BOX 7.3
COVERAGE OF THE IRAN HOSTAGE CRISIS
(J. F. Larson, 1986)

The fact that Iran's 1979 Islamic revolution came as a surprise to many Americans was in part attributable to the nature of news coverage prior to that time. From January 1972 to October 1977, U.S. network news coverage of Iran accounted for only about 1% of all international news stories. Of those stories that did occur, only 10% originated from Iran itself, the others being wire service stories or overseas reports about Iran filed from another country. The two dominant themes of those stories were oil and arms sales, exactly the focus of U.S. government relations with Iran during that period. Although there were occasional hints of discontent, such as demonstrations against the Shah, the autocratic but pro-U.S. Iranian ruler, no consistent attention was paid to the developing unrest. Professional writings by foreign policy experts during this period also showed little understanding of grassroots discontent in Iran (Mowlana, 1984).

From November 1977 to January 1979, U.S. reporting on Iran changed considerably. The Shah's visit to Washington in November 1977 evoked an anti-Shah demonstration quelled by tear gas across the street from the White House. After this newsworthy event, attention began to be paid to flaws in the Shah and his regime. In 1978, all three TV networks placed correspondents in Teheran, which resulted in over half of the stories on Iran originating from there and focusing on antigovernment demonstrations, strikes, and marches. After the departure of the besieged Shah in January 1979, TV served as the major communication between the exiled Islamic leader Ayatollah Khomeini in Paris and the fragile caretaker government in Teheran. After the return of Khomeini to Iran in February, U.S. news focused on Iran, especially its implications for the United States. From April to October, however, coverage of Iran on U.S. TV dropped off sharply.

After the Iranian seizure of dozens of American hostages at the U.S. embassy in Teheran on November 4, 1979, however, coverage increased dramatically, comprising nearly one third of all international news stories in 1980. Television, and to a lesser extent, newspapers, became major channels of communication between the two governments, as all diplomatic and commercial channels had been broken. Iran allowed an NBC interview with hostage William Gallegos and even took out a full-page ad in the *New York Times* to print the text of a Khomeini speech to America. U.S. media also covered the hostage families, early release of some hostages, the death of the Shah in Egypt in July 1980, and the effect of the hostage crisis on the 1980 U.S. Presidential election. The safe release of the hostages on Ronald Reagan's Inauguration Day in January 1981 received heavy coverage, but subsequent stories on Iran that year originated elsewhere or occasionally from correspondents from other nations who were stationed in Iran. For an analysis of the media in Iran before, during, and after the revolution, see Beeman (1984).

This strong desire to play up a local connection and make the story relevant to readers can sometimes end up distorting the news (Goldberg, 2002). For example, when the media discovered the problem of the homeless in the 1980s, the homeless individuals actually interviewed were very articulate, usually white, often professional people down on their luck, in short, just like the majority audience. Never mind that the majority of the homeless had substance abuse and/or major mental illness problems and often were people of color. In another example, when AIDS started to receive wide coverage in the late 1980s, it was the relatively few heterosexual, non-drug-user AIDS victims who were interviewed. Just as with the homeless problem, the media believed that viewers would be most interested in the problem (thus higher ratings) if they felt it was a threat to themselves. Thus the media chose "representative" individuals most like the majority audience in order to make the story connect with the most viewers. The result, however, was that many people were far more worried about contracting AIDS or becoming homeless than was warranted. At the same time, the real problems of what to do with the homeless mentally ill after state institutions closed and how to stop the spread of HIV among IV drug users and gay men not practicing safe sex received little attention.

The surest way to obtain coverage of one's activities is to imbue them with these primary and secondary newsworthy characteristics. The more of these an event has, the more likely the media will be to show interest. Possessing these characteristics does not necessarily ensure that the event is important, but it does ensure that the perceived reality will be a newsworthy event. For example, the murder trial of O. J. Simpson in 1995 had all of the newsworthy characteristics. It focused on one person who was greatly admired but was accused of committing a very violent act. It centrally related to many of the cultural themes (big vs. little, right vs. wrong, appearance vs. reality). The fact that the entire trial was televised also helped to ensure saturation coverage for several months. See Box 7.4 for an interesting argument from Aristotle to explain the public fascination with the Simpson trial.

One group who, unfortunately, knows all about how to stage a newsworthy event, are terrorists. This is why they are particularly fond of large public symbolic targets, like the Pentagon, World Trade Center, and government buildings, especially in well-known places like New York City, London, Paris, or Washington. They know there will be more news coverage there and likely more damage and deaths, due to the denser population.

Now that we have seen what makes a newsworthy event, we examine how the media create the story that is news.

BOX 7.4
ARISTOTLE'S EXPLANATION OF INTEREST
IN THE O. J. SIMPSON TRIAL

Although written around 400 BC, Aristotle's *Rhetoric* offers some arguments about three elements needed to move an audience. Although Aristotle was talking about theater, Stonehill (1995) argued that these elements (*pathos*, *logos*, and *ethos*) also fit television and help to explain the intense public fascination with events like the O. J. Simpson trial of 1995. Pathos, the emotional appeal, was very high in this murder case, with overtones of sex, race, and deceit. Logos, the intellectual component, appeared in the mystery of whodunit but also in other questions such as why the low-speed chase occurred and what all the DNA evidence meant. Finally, ethos is charisma, celebrity, or authority, which was of course very high in this case of the trial of a previously loved and respected public figure. Stonehill even argued that this case might be one of the highest ever on these three Aristotelian dimensions.

However, not long after the Simpson trial faded, other high-profile events captured the media's and the public's sustained attention. The tragic death of Britain's Princess Diana in August 1997 and the Clinton-Lewinsky sex scandal of 1998 likewise went off the charts in pathos, logos, and ethos— and press coverage. Aristotle was right!

NEWS MEDIA AS CREATING A PERCEIVED REALITY

The term *media* suggests that mass communication mediates between the audience and some objective reality that actually exists somewhere out there in the world. In Western culture, at least, we assume that such an external reality exists. More than with any other domain of media content, people tend to assume that news conveys objective reality to us in a clear and unbiased form. However, news writers and producers communicate their interpretation of that world reality through both their choice of topics and the amount of coverage they give (agenda setting). News is a "frame that delineates a world" (G. Tuchman, 1978).

> TV is a storytelling medium. It abhors ambiguities, ragged edges, and unresolved issues. The effect all too frequently is to impose upon an event or situation a preconceived form that alters reality, heightening one aspect at the expense of another for the sake of a more compelling story, blocking out complications that get in the way of the narrative. (Abel, 1984, p. 68)

Although choices of media coverage are usually motivated from a sincere desire to present news stories to the public in the most complete and

BOX 7.5
NEWS REPORTER OR NEWSMAKER?

In their desire to make "an invisible truth visible, dramatic, and entertaining" (Bogart, 1980, p. 235), media occasionally go too far. In 1966, CBS helped to finance an armed invasion of Haiti in exchange for exclusive TV rights of the event; the invasion was aborted by U.S. Customs. The next year a U.S. soldier cut off the ear of a dead Vietcong soldier; it later came out in his court martial that he did so after being offered a knife on a dare by a TV news cameraman (Lewy, 1978). There were numerous accounts of TV news crews in the 1960s arranging for protest demonstrations or drug parties to be staged again for the cameras if the original event was not caught on camera. Janet Cooke lost her Pulitzer Prize in 1981 after admitting that her article, "Jimmy's World" was not based on a real Jimmy, but rather on different people who contributed to the composite Jimmy. NBC faked a crash test in 1993 to show that a car it believed to be dangerous would explode. In 1998, Stephen Glass, writer for the *New Republic* and other magazines, was found to have fabricated all or parts of dozens of investigative journalism articles, even including a totally fictitious story about a cult that worshiped George Bush, Sr. (Lacayo, 2003). Writer Jayson Blair and two editors lost their jobs at the *New York Times* in 2003 after numerous articles of Blair's turned out to be fabricated or plagiarized from other sources.

   At other times, news journalists may become newsmakers in more positive ways. For example, Egyptian President Anwar Sadat's historic trip to Israel in 1977 was arranged not by the United Nations or U.S. State Department diplomats, but by CBS News anchor Walter Cronkite. It was Cronkite who persistently called Sadat and Israeli Prime Minister Menachem Begin to arrange their eventual meeting (Weymouth, 1981).

accurate way possible, there are occasional instances when the construction of reality goes beyond the bounds of what most would consider acceptable (see Box 7.5).

Manipulation of News

Aside from the constraints of being newsworthy, sometimes other forces inside and outside of government impinge on journalists in ways that affect the reality of the news they create.

   Direct Censorship.   In countries with prior censorship, material must be submitted to government or military censors for advance approval before being aired, or the government owns and controls all news media.

In such cases, a very selective piece of reality may be offered, so much so that history may be substantially rewritten. For example, Russian citizens' views of the West were for many years very heavily colored by news stories about American crime, racism, homelessness, and imperialism that appeared in the Soviet press. Even if very little in these stories was actually untrue, one's overall perception was grossly distorted if, for example, crime was believed to be the rule rather than the exception.

Direct censorship can come in other ways. Azerbaijan's government owns the printing company all newspapers must use; it refuses to print those it doesn't like. Malaysia and Singapore have laws forbidding discussion of topics that may become divisive (religion, inter-ethnic violence or anything that might make the government look bad). Belarus evicted the newspaper *Pahonya* from its offices and moved it to a building with no water or sewage service. Later, the tax auditors levied a large fine against the paper (Martz, 1998).

Intimidation. Sometimes journalists are bullied by forces which may or may not be connected to any government. For example, when the editor of Tijuana's newspaper *Zeta* wrote against the local drug cartel, he was visited by a team of assassins. Although he survived and continued to write, not everyone would have had the courage to do so. When Zairean freelance writer Jean Mbenga Muaganvita wrote a series of articles on then-strongman President Mobutu Sese Seko, he was arrested and held incommunicado, and soldiers raped his 14-year-old daughter when they searched his home (Martz, 1998). Noted Colombian investigative journalist Fabio Castillo was fired by Bogotá's *El Espectador* after implicating a government minister in a bank corruption scandal. Although the paper claims he was let go purely for financial reasons, the fact that the minister under suspicion mysteriously received an advance copy of the article before publication suggests otherwise (Rosenberg, 2003). Many journalists have been killed in recent years in Algeria, Mexico, Colombia, India, Cambodia, and other places.

Blocking Access. Certain news stories may be effectively censored purely through blocking the access of the media to the scene of the story. For example, during the apartheid era in South Africa, journalists were often forbidden to enter the black townships. Similar policies by the Israeli government have sometimes kept the press out of the West Bank during times of Palestinian unrest. In both cases, the governments involved clearly hoped that public attention to the problem would wane if compelling images could no longer be obtained for publication or broadcast.

Probably the clearest and most controversial examples of blocking press access have come in the coverage of recent regional wars. Working on the conventional (although dubious) wisdom that unrestricted press coverage lost the Vietnam War for the United States, Britain in 1982 and the United States in 1983 forbade the press from accompanying troops in the island wars in the Falklands/Malvinas and Grenada, respectively (Strobel, 1997). The same policy was followed by the United States in the 1989 invasion of Panama to oust dictator Manuel Noriega. Only much later did the public learn that casualties were far higher than originally reported, including the nearly total destruction of a large poor neighborhood in Panama City. The most widespread case of censorship through blocking access was exercised by the United States, Saudi Arabia, and their coalition allies in the six-week Persian Gulf War against Iraq in 1991. Coverage of this war is examined in more depth as a case study later in the chapter.

Indirect Censorship. In some nations, it is an official crime to broadcast material that is in any way against the interests of the state. Such vague legislation is available for use according to the political whims of the current rulers. At other times, the government and large business interests are so close that politically suspect TV stations and newspapers cannot get the advertising they need to survive. Even in most democratic countries, the government issues licenses for TV and radio stations. Sometimes these are withheld or delayed for political reasons. Some countries require journalists to be licensed, a practice consistently condemned by the International Press Institute as threatening freedom of the press. In other cases, the supply and distribution of newsprint is controlled by the government and may be allotted according to political considerations.

Manipulation by Timing. Even in a thriving democracy with constitutional guarantees of a free press, there are limits on news. Release of classified information damaging to national security is not permitted, although just how broad this doctrine should be has been the subject of many court challenges. In many other ways, however, the government manipulates, although does not control, the press. For example, U.S. President Gerald Ford's pardon of ex-President Richard Nixon for any Watergate-related crimes was announced on a Sunday morning. In 1992, former President George Bush pardoned Iran-contra defendants on Christmas Day. All of these unpopular policies were announced at times of the week likely to receive the least possible coverage and attention. Often, government sources strategically leak stories about upcoming policy to gauge public reaction (trial balloon). If the reaction is negative, the policy need never be officially announced and the government will not be blamed for proposing it.

Media Self-Censorship. Sometimes censorship is self-imposed by the media. Often this is due to pressure or fear of pressure from advertisers or

parent companies. The largest commercial TV networks give limited attention to major corporate changes involving themselves or to any story reflecting unfavorably on their parent company, such as ABC TV and Disney
(Lee & Solomon, 1991; Steyer, 2002). It is well-documented that magazines
that accept tobacco advertising publish fewer stories about the health risks
of smoking than do magazines that do not accept tobacco ads (Strasburger
& Wilson, 2002). Advertiser pressure can lead to self-censorship. For example, the *San Jose Mercury News* published a lengthy consumer story in
1994 on "how to buy a car," including tips on negotiating with dealers and
information on dealer incentives and money holdbacks and using the in-
voice to figure the actual cost of the car. In response, the Santa Clara County
Motor Car Dealers' Association pulled $1 million of advertising. The editor
published a letter apologizing for the article and extolling the paper's longstanding partnership with the local car dealers. There have been no further
in-depth stories dealing with auto dealership issues (Lieberman, 2000).

Sometimes newspapers or the TV networks are in possession of information that they choose not to reveal for some reason. Sometimes this may
be information about troop movements, but it may also be information
that some government official has lied. The press may conclude (rightly
or wrongly) that the public just does not care to hear certain highly negative news about their country or government. For example, when the
Soviet Union shot down a Korean commercial airliner in 1983, the Kremlin
made the predictable Cold War charge that it was an American spy plane.
Although this claim was widely reported in the United States, it was practically never taken seriously. In a careful analysis of the coverage of this
issue by *Time, Newsweek,* and *U.S. News & World Report,* Corcoran (1986)
concluded that all three publications, with an estimated combined readership of around 50 million, followed a virtually identical Reagan administration party line of anti-Soviet diatribe and paranoia (see also Entman,
1991). Outside of the United States (e.g., in reputable British publications
like the *Guardian*) available evidence supporting the theory that the airliner
was on a spy mission was fully examined and seen to be a credible explanation, though it was never either verified or discredited. Why was this
perspective not heard in the United States? It was not due to government
censorship but perhaps was due to the press sensing that the U.S. public did
not want to seriously consider (or perhaps would not believe) such a claim.

In the Watergate scandal of the early 1970s, the press chose to call President Nixon and other high U.S. government officials liars only after a
considerable period of time and after compelling evidence had been presented. In the mid-1980s, the press was very hesitant to directly expose
the very popular President Reagan's communication of misinformation
about Soviet involvement in Nicaragua. Only after the revelation in late
1986 that the Reagan administration had been sending arms to Iran with

the profits being diverted to the Nicaraguan right-wing contra rebels did the press seem to give itself permission to seriously criticize the president. Finally, the Washington press corps long knew of the Reagan administration's disinformation campaign in attributing a Berlin disco bombing in 1985 to Libya's Muammar Qaddafi, but said nothing.

Consolidation of News-Gathering Organizations.   Although not exactly manipulation of news as such, another concern in determining the perceived reality of world events is the increasing consolidation of news-gathering organizations. Skyrocketing costs, plus the undeniable logic of efficiency, mandates a pooling of resources. Clearly, not every newspaper, news magazine, and TV and radio station can afford to have its own reporter in every potential news spot in the world.

This consolidation, however, has reduced news gatherers to a very small club. In terms of newspapers, most news copy in most newspapers comes from a very few sources, especially the wire services of Associated Press (AP), Reuters, and Agence France Presse (AFP). Only a very few large dailies have their own wire service (*New York Times, Los Angeles Times*). In terms of television, the U.S. commercial networks of ABC, NBC, CBS, Fox, and CNN, have enormous influence worldwide. A few other major networks, such as the BBC and ITN in the United Kingdom and Brazil's TV Globo, take large pieces of the remaining pie. These few sources have enormous impact on our perceived reality of distant events. For example, even in stridently anti-American regimes, a large percentage of the news copy comes from the AP wire service. A small number of sources is not in and of itself cause for alarm. Large organizations like the AP or CNN take great pains to present diverse and balanced viewpoints, and it is strongly in their interest to be perceived by all as fair and unbiased. Still, however, the potential influence of any of these sources on people's knowledge worldwide is sobering.

Another consequence of the financial realities of international news reporting is a greatly decreased number of foreign bureaus and correspondents. For example, by 1996 CBS was down from 20 to 4 major foreign bureaus (Tokyo, Moscow, Tel Aviv, London), with ABC having 8, NBC 7, and CNN 20. Although this reduction does not preclude a news anchor or Washington correspondent from reading a foreign story accompanied by visuals from file footage or freelance or government sources, the number of minutes of news stories on the three major networks from correspondents posted at foreign bureaus fell from 4,032 to 2,763 just between 1989 and 1994 (Strobel, 1997). Although 45% of news time on U.S. network news was international in the 1970s, only 13.5% was international by 1995 (Moisy, 1997). The quality of the remaining foreign stories probably fell as well.

Now that we have looked at how the media mediate between the reality of the news and the reports we receive, we examine such processes in operation in an extended case study of the reporting of the 1991 Persian Gulf War.

The 1991 Persian Gulf War Coverage: Case Study

For 6 weeks beginning January 16, 1991, much of the world was at war for the stated purpose of ousting Saddam Hussein's Iraq from its occupation of neighboring oil-rich Kuwait. Until the war's last week, the primary activity was an almost continuous U.S.-led air assault on Iraq and its forces in occupied Kuwait. This air war and one week of ground assault succeeded in ousting Iraq from Kuwait, although that country and much of Iraq lay in ruins. Conventional wisdom in government and the military was that uncontrolled press coverage of the Vietnam War (1964–1975) had contributed to the loss of (a) the war itself, the only war ever lost by the United States; and (b) public support for the war. This widely accepted but unsupported conventional wisdom led to the press in the Gulf War being kept on a very short leash, using the Falklands/Grenada model, as part of a tightly managed campaign where imagery was a prevailing concern. Referring to the sympathetic media coverage, former Reagan White House staff member Michael Deaver commented: "If you were going to hire a public relations firm to do the media relations for an international event, it couldn't be done any better than this" (M. A. Lee & Solomon, 1991, p. xv).

To start with, reporters were put in pools. The numbers of persons in these pools grew during the war, up to around 200 during the ground campaign in the last week. The stated purpose of these pools was to protect journalists and prevent allied forces from being overwhelmed by reporters. Stories were subject to censorship, ostensibly to prevent the leaking of troop movement information helpful to Iraq. However, sometimes stories were held up for days, and in some instances the Pentagon actually announced the story first at its briefings.

There were total blackouts at the start of the air and ground campaigns, as well as a ban on photos of coffins of killed U.S. soldiers arriving home at Dover Air Force Base. Far from hiding from the press, however, military spokespersons held daily briefings in Riyadh, Saudi Arabia at central command and at the Pentagon. These briefings were filled with facts and figures, such as the number of missions or the number of Iraqi Scud missile sites destroyed. The talks were illustrated with colorful maps and other visuals. Those holding the briefings were friendly and cooperative and appeared to provide much information. They were, however, very cautious in their estimates of Iraqi damage, apparently to avoid excessive optimism and thus hold expectations to a point that could be very easily exceeded.

Beyond their informative function, the media were used by the military to help the coalition confuse the Iraqis. For example, reporters were frequently taken to the area near the southern Kuwaiti border with Saudi Arabia but not to the western border area where the real build-up for the ground invasion was occurring. Pools were taken to cover practice maneuvers for an apparent sea assault on Kuwait, an assault that never came but was rather used to divert attention from the planned ground thrust from the west. The CIA planted a false story of 60 Iraqi tanks defecting early in the war, with the hope of encouraging actual Iraqi defections.

Although they occasionally complained, the media (especially in the United States) were remarkably compliant, even obsequious, in their acquiescence to military censorship. They continually marveled over the technological prowess of new weapons, not bothering to question the accuracy of claims of very high percentages of hits on military targets with few civilian casualties. Long after the war, missile accuracy was revealed to have been much less than reported at the time.

Experts interviewed on TV news programs almost always supported Bush administration policy. Voices of dissent were only heard in minimal coverage of antiwar protests, typically portrayed as the domain of lunatic fringe elements. The experts interviewed were almost entirely White men, whereas polls showed that minorities and women were less likely to support the war. Iraqi leader Saddam Hussein was continually demonized and compared to Adolf Hitler, whereas prior U.S. support for him in the Iran-Iraq War of 1980 to 1988, as well as serious human rights abuses of coalition partners Saudi Arabia, Syria, and Kuwait, were downplayed or ignored. The U.S. military's use of fuel-air bombs and white phosphorus was almost never mentioned (M. A. Lee & Solomon, 1991).

Why was the press, in many ways so diverse and independent, so unquestioning of the military and of the Bush Administration? Partly, of course, it was because they were denied access to the real story. That cannot explain the high degree of cheerleading and uncritical support, however. Journalists were probably themselves highly supportive of the coalition effort; even the most strident critics of U.S. policy had little sympathy or support for the brutal Saddam Hussein. Just as the military and political powers were planning policy in reaction to the myth that the Vietnam War was lost because the press had had too free a hand, the media were determined not to allow themselves to be criticized as they had been in Vietnam. They were not going to be made the scapegoats for a war if it was less than a rousing success. They were not going to allow themselves to be called unpatriotic. This concern may not have been unrealistic; the little independent coverage that did occur sometimes elicited angry cries of traitor. For an interesting propaganda analysis of the Gulf War, see Jowett (1993).

In spite of efforts to discourage it, there was some independent (i.e., nonpool) coverage of the war. Most visible was CNN's Peter Arnett, the only Western journalist left in Baghdad after the start of the air war. Arnett transmitted daily stories and photos to Western media. These were subject to Iraqi censorship and were always identified as such. This led to some charges of Saddam using Arnett for his own ends and of his being duped by Iraqi propaganda. Arnett's reports did, in fact, show numerous photos of destruction caused by Allied bombings, the only photos then available of such damage. Some called this unfair and unpatriotic, even going so far as to picket CNN's headquarters in Atlanta or write angry letters to the editor in newspapers.

There was other independent coverage, however. For example, Patrick Cockburn of the British *Independent* reported at the time how the air strikes were less successful than announced (M. A. Lee & Solomon, 1991). A massive oil slick unleashed by the Iraqis occupying Kuwait was reported by an independent British ITN crew a full two days before the pool reporters arrived (Zoglin, 1991). During the 6 weeks that the war lasted, there were increasing attempts by journalists to go out on their own. In one case, a CBS crew was actually captured and held by the Iraqis for a few days. If the war had lasted longer, there probably would have been greater numbers of independent reports.

Media coverage of the Gulf War continued to be debated and analyzed for many years (e.g., Iyengar & Simon, 1993). Aside from the obvious controversy around the whole censorship issue, other concerns arose. CNN became recognized as the preeminent news source and received kudos from widespread segments of electronic and print journalism. World leaders watched CNN, including George Bush and Saddam Hussein, to learn what was happening. Other TV networks carried CNN footage. To whatever extent that CNN may have boosted the fortunes of those promoting the war, the reverse may have been even more true with longer lasting effects (Zelizer, 1992). See Greenberg and Gantz (1993) and Mowlana, Gerbner, and Schiller (1993) for sets of readings on press coverage of the Persian Gulf War.

Postscript: The Iraq War of 2003.   The second coalition assault on Iraq, this time in 2003 with the stated intent of removing Saddam Hussein's government and preventing him from using weapons of mass destruction, provided an interesting contrast in terms of media coverage. This time the press was much less confined; in fact, they were invited to accompany U.S. and British troops marching into Iraq from Kuwait. These so-called "embedded" reporters sent daily stories back from the front lines. They at least had the appearance of telling a fuller story about the war than what was seen in 1991. These reporters generally had good relations with the troops they traveled with and were given fairly wide access to potential stories. Access was much less restricted than it had been in the 1991 war, although at least one maverick reporter (Geraldo Rivera) was evicted for divulging too much about troop locations.

EFFECTS OF NEWS COVERAGE

Long after the events reported in the news, what is remembered is the coverage. "The reality that lives on is the reality etched in the memories of the millions who watched rather than the few who were actually there" (G. E. Lang & Lang, 1984, p. 213). Now let us turn to examining the impact and effects of consuming news coverage, including memory for the news, its effects on decision making and other behaviors, and the effect of news reporting on foreign policy. Before we begin to look at effects directly, however, we need to examine how our point of view can affect our interpretation of news.

The Impact of Different Points of View

Part of the reason that people in different nations tend to perceive the same situations so differently is that the reality they construct in response to news is so different. Not only does the reporting of such events in the media vary in different places, but even more basically, the interpretation of the same events differs, depending on the knowledge and experience of those who hear or see the news. To illustrate, we look at a few case studies.

In late 1991, the beating of African American motorist Rodney King by some White Los Angeles police officers happened to be captured on videotape by an onlooker. The ensuing criminal trial of the officers resulted in a verdict of not guilty on most charges of police brutality in April 1992. The country was generally outraged at the verdict that seemed to go so against what appeared to be obvious excesses shown repeatedly on the news. Resulting civil disturbances and riots in Los Angeles and elsewhere brought to the forefront issues of race relations and urban decay. For our purposes, however, what is most interesting is the different reactions of African Americans and European Americans to the verdict. They did not differ in their general appraisal (most found it shocking and unfair). They did differ, however, in how *typical* they saw such a verdict. Most Whites saw it as an exceptional, although disturbing, miscarriage of justice. Most African Americans, used to receiving the short end of institutional justice and services, saw the outrageous verdict as more typical; thus their response was far more impassioned. The same news story and the same video sequence had a very different meaning for the two groups because of their different experience.

Many of the most intractable and chronic world conflicts have at their heart a gigantic divergence in point of view, a chasm that causes the two sides to interpret the same events totally differently. They also consistently fail to appreciate how differently other people view the same events. For example, during the Cold War (1945–1990), the Soviet Union and Western nations viewed each other through their own biases (Hirschberg, 1993). Israelis and Palestinians, Tutsis and Hutus, Serbs and Croats, and Northern Irish Catholics and Protestants see themselves besieged and oppressed by the other. When the West moved to expand NATO, for example, that looked much more threatening from Moscow, who saw it as an aggressive move. From their perspective, it looked like preparation for war to the east. When the United States moved hundreds of thousands of troops to the Persian Gulf and invaded two countries (Afghanistan in 2001 and Iraq in 2003) to remove unfriendly regimes, neighboring countries quite reasonably wondered if they would be next, even if that concern seemed ridiculous to many Americans. See Box 7.6 for a more extended example of the sharply divergent points of view of Islam and the West on political, social, and religious issues.

Memory for the News

News offers an interesting case to test people's memory in a real-world setting, with obvious applied, as well as important theoretical, import (Graber, 1989; McCombs & Reynolds, 2002; V. Price & Czilli, 1996). News stories in all media are most typically fairly short, self-contained pieces. S. L. Schneider and Laurion (1993) studied metamemory for radio news, finding that people's assessment of what they had remembered from news was fairly accurate. In the case of television, however, the information involves more than the verbal content. The simultaneous presence of both the visual and auditory information provides the potential of their either complementing or interfering with each other in the processing of and memory for news content. In general, memory for visual themes is better than memory for verbal themes (Graber, 1990), and overall memory is better if there is a close fit between the video and the audio component, such as when the video illustrates exactly what was being described by the reporter. When the relationship is less clear or when the video and audio portions evoke different previous information from the viewer's memory, comprehension and memory for the new information suffers (Grimes, 1990, 1991; Mundorf, Drew, Zillmann, & Weaver, 1990). Memory for persons in the news can also be affected by the viewers' social attitudes, e.g., Whites' being overly likely to identify an African American

---

BOX 7.6
THE COGNITIVE GULF BETWEEN ISLAM AND THE WEST

Islam as a religion is very poorly understood in the West, a fact especially troubling to Muslims, given the historical connection of their faith through Abraham to Christianity and Judaism. Events of the last 30 years, particularly the heightened terrorist threat of the new millennium, bring a new urgency to bridging this gap. There are some fundamental differences in the faiths and associated cultures that both sides would do well to understand. It is very much against Islam to criticize the theology of Judaism or Christianity, which are seen as part of the foundations of Islam, although considerable criticism of Western politics is permitted. In a similar vein, it is acceptable for Christians to make gentle jokes about Jesus, but in Islam there exist strong proscriptions against discussing the personal life of Mohammed or even of having any pictorial representations of him. Intellectual debate and disagreement about his actions is quite acceptable but anything personal or disrespectful is not. Finally, Islam is not all monolithic, any more than Christianity is. Muslims are very offended when the media portray some radical Islamist terrorist as a typical Muslim.

There is also a fundamental difference between Islam and the West in the relationship between church and state. Most Muslim countries accept some degree of theocracy, although the degree varies. Thus, insulting Mohammed is an insult to all Muslim nations and all Muslims, even those not practicing their faith. This is somewhat like nonreligious Jews' abhorrence of anti-Semitism, although there is no real parallel in Christianity, which has much less nonreligious cultural identity than does either Judaism or Islam.

One of the most basic beliefs in western Europe and especially in North America is the separation of church and state, a belief whose deep ideological character and ramifications are not well understood by Muslims. In the West, it is unacceptable for someone's religious beliefs to infringe on another person's political freedom. Although it is a political belief, this tenet is highly ideological, almost religious in character, especially in the United States. Furthermore, the Western democratic tradition of free speech is also practically like a religion to most people in the United States and the European Union. The treatment of women is seen in the West as a political right, not a religious decision, although most Western religions support equality of the sexes as well. (Easterbrook, 1989).

---

as a criminal suspect than a White person (Gibbons, Taylor, & Phillips, 2004; Oliver & Fonash, 2002). Assuming the video and audio portions are congruent, children remember news presented in a televised form better than news presented in a radio or print form, even if the print form contained illustrations (Walma van der Molen & van der Voort, 2000). See

Graber (1988) and Gunter (1987) for discussions of memory for broadcast news.

How the visual and auditory portions might interact and possibly interfere with each other is an important theoretical and practical issue. A particularly interesting type of case occurs with an emotionally intense visual shot, the sort that frequently accompanies news stories about wars, accidents, famines, or riots. Its effect on memory turns out to be complex. An intense emotional image, such as a shot of the bloody disfigured body of an accident or war victim, actually inhibits memory for verbal information presented just prior to that picture (Christianson & Loftus, 1987; Loftus & Burns, 1982; Newhagen & Reeves, 1992). However, material presented during or after the intense image is remembered shortly afterward as well as or, in the case of material presented after the image, sometimes even better than, material not accompanied by an intense image. It also makes a difference exactly how memory is measured (Brosius, 1993).

In a careful experimental study manipulating the presentation of televised news stories with or without an accompanying visually intense image, Newhagen and Reeves (1992) found that, 6 weeks after exposure, memory for factual information and topics was better for stories without the compelling visual image, but that memory for the visual images themselves was better in cases where they had been emotionally compelling. Apparently, what happens cognitively is that the intense emotional image disrupts the rehearsal in working memory of the immediately preceding information, much as a moderate head injury can produce retroactive amnesia for events just preceding the impact. However, the intense picture is itself highly memorable and may enhance memory for following related information by serving as an organizational schema for construction of a memory representation. Thus, a TV news editor deciding whether and when to show a bloody shot of accident victims should recognize that the decision has ramifications for viewers' memory of material in that story.

Effects of News on Attributions and Decision Making

Comprehension of the news has implications beyond memory. How the news is reported can affect our knowledge about the topic. For example, Gibson and Zillmann (1994) found that readers of a magazine news story about carjacking evaluated the problem as both more serious and more frequent if it had contained an extreme example (victim killed in the crime) than if the example had been less extreme (victim injured little or not at all). N. B. Brown and Siegler (1992) found that the amount of media coverage of a country predicted people's rated knowledge of that country and also its estimated population. Countries receiving more media coverage were believed to be more populous than those receiving less coverage. Tewks-bury (1999) found that viewers' goals in watching TV news and their exper-tise on the topic affected how carefully and systematically they extracted information from the news story.

Another issue is the effect of media publicity on juror decision making. There are two general concerns here. One regards specific pretrial public-ity about a case. Jurors' exposure to information about a particular case affects verdicts (see Carroll et al., 1986, for a review). For example, lurid pretrial information about a rape or murder case increases the likelihood of a conviction vote. This knowledge is not erased by a judge's direction to disregard the information. A second concern involves general pretrial publicity and jurors' exposure to information about other cases involving similar issues.

To test this second type of effect, Greene and Wade (1987) asked students to read a news magazine story about either (a) a heinous crime—the rape of an elderly woman, or (b) a miscarriage of justice—the wrongful conviction of a man for a rape to which someone else later confessed. A third group of students was not given any story to read. In a second phase of the study, which was presented as an unrelated experiment, the research participants acted as jurors, reading an excerpt from a different court case and deciding on a verdict.

Reading about the prior case did affect their verdicts. Compared to the control group, twice as many (20% vs. 10%) who had read of the unre-lated heinous crime said that the defendant in the second case was defi-nitely guilty. Although 57% of those reading about the prior miscarriage of justice called the new defendant probably not guilty, only 25% did so after reading about the heinous crime, probably due to having that very available instance in their memory (cf. Tversky & Kahneman, 1973). In the real world, jurors' prior exposure to such examples is all but impossible to control, because such cases receive wide media coverage. A powerful example can do much to drive future information processing and behavior (Zillmann, 2002).

Responses to Crime Coverage in Media

Several recent books, most notably Barry Glassner's *The Culture of Fear: Why Americans Are Afraid of the Wrong Things* and Joel Best's *Random Crimes: How We Talk About New Crimes and New Victims*, address the question of the effect of media's coverage of crimes on the public perception of different dangers.

How News Distorts the Reporting of Dangers. Best (1999) identified three unwarranted, yet widely believed, assumptions about so-called "random" violence. First of all, violence is believed to be *patternless,* with everyone equally likely to be a victim. However, the facts are otherwise. Young adult men, especially if they are nonwhite, are much more likely to be victims than anyone else (except for women as rape victims). Second, violence is seen to be *pointless,* i.e., perpetrated for no apparent reason. On the contrary, there is almost always some motive for violent crime, although the rare exceptional cases where there is not receive heavy coverage. Finally, violent crime is perceived to be *getting worse,* while in fact most violent crime rates in the U.S. have been falling since the early 1990s. If violent crime rates are falling and violent crime is not patternless or pointless, why do most people believe otherwise?

One reason is that very often in crime reporting, scenarios substitute for facts. Vivid cases are reported without reference to a base rate of incidence for that type of crime. The vivid case is thus made to appear typical, perhaps representing an "epidemic." For example, Glassner (1999) looks at the trendy crime of "road rage" beginning in the early 1990s. We suddenly started hearing about people being shot at on the freeway for no apparent reason and people became afraid to do their regular driving. However, when looking at bases rates instead of vivid cases, Glassner finds that five drivers died from road rage crimes in the years 1993–1998, amounting to less than one-thousandth of the 250,000 road deaths from 1990–1997; 85 times as many motorists died from drunk drivers. This sloppy use of statistics confuses instances with rates, sometimes forgetting that instances often go up because of more people but the rates go way down, as we see in rates of violent crimes or airline crash victims.

Since the 1960s, the volume of commercial air flights has more than doubled but the accident rate is down 85%, with the probability of dying in an aircraft crash about one in four million. Yet people are typically much more afraid to fly than to drive, which is statistically much more dangerous.

The chance of being killed by a coworker at work is about one in two million, even less if you are not in a couple of particularly dangerous occupations like taxi driving or mining. The chance of your child being killed at school was actually *less* in 2000 after highly covered tragedies like the Columbine High massacre in 1999 than it was in 1990.

One of the biggest fears of the 1970s was the fear of tainted Halloween candy (Glassner, 1999). Glassner cites a 1985 article, which concluded there had been *no* deaths or serious injuries from strangers' candy and only a few reports of minor cuts from sharp objects in bags, most of which were hoaxes. The only two documented cases of deaths from Halloween candy were one case where candy was laced with heroin by the child's family to fool police on the cause of the child's death and another where the child's father poisoned candy with cyanide to collect life insurance money on his child.

In a similar vein, Glassner argues that the trendy rohypnol "date rape drug epidemic" of 1996–1998 in the U.S. was overblown. The actual number of rapes committed by tainting someone's drink with rohypnol was actually very small. Glassner notes that the drug had formerly been commonly used to get high and in fact was legal and available by prescription in most countries. Only in the U.S. was any "epidemic" ever reported.

One of the most sensationalized crimes is child abduction. For example, a *USA Today* headline in 1994 screamed "MISSING CHILDREN: A FEARFUL EPIDEMIC." CBS' *48 Hours* set up a mock abduction to show how easily children could be lured out of a mall store by a stranger needing help finding his dog, even though there was no evidence such a crime had ever happened! In a 1997 show on child abductions, Geraldo Rivera scared us with the following:

> This isn't a commentary, this is reality: They will come for your kid over the Internet; they will come in a truck; they will come in a pickup in the dark of night; they will come in the Hollywood Mall in Florida. There are sickos out there. You have to keep your children this close to you [gestures with fingers]—this close to you. (Glassner, 1999, p. 64)

Although the few celebrated cases receive publicity on milk cartons and the local news, most missing children are runaways, not kidnap victims, and most of the small minority that are true abductions are by noncustodial parents in child custody disputes. In fact, only 1.3% of child abductions are by nonfamily members (Numbers, 2001). Nevertheless, parents drag their children to the mall to be fingerprinted or have dental identification implants with apparently no thought to the fear and insecurity they might be inducing by telling their child they are doing so in case they are abducted and murdered, their remains could be identified.

There are other impacts of such reporting, beyond the fear induced in the public. Typically, some vicious stranger is blamed for the crime, instead of bad policies creating conditions increasing its likelihood. Thus, we worry about encountering the crazed gunman on the freeway but don't think much about policies that allow anyone to buy a deadly weapon without even a background check or the lack of a social support network that leaves inner-city youth nowhere to turn but drugs and crime. Sometimes there are major financial interests who have reason to profit by fomenting irrational fears of crime. For example, large political donations from pharmaceutical companies may discourage elected officials' criticism of legal drug abuse, especially when it is easier to focus on illicit drug abuse, whose purveyors have no powerful legislative lobby, nor do they contribute to political candidates.

Another effect of such reporting is to malign certain social groups by association. For example, Glassner argues that the crack cocaine "epidemic" of 1980s in the U.S. really amounted to an attack on urban African-American neighborhoods. Although crack cocaine was widely condemned as a major cause of crime, the use of cocaine powder, the form more often preferred by suburban whites, was not. In fact, in the late 1980s, the U.S. Congress mandated penalties 100 times as severe for possession of crack as for powdered cocaine.

There are other examples of blaming the victim. For example, single mothers (especially teens) are often blamed for many modern social ills, seldom noting that the teen birth rate was the highest ever in the 1950s and in fact has shown a decline since the early 1990s. Absent fathers are also sometimes blamed, implicitly suggesting that everything would be fine if only they had not abandoned their children. In a similar vein, working mothers are sometimes blamed for all problems their children have, or baby boomer parents are chided for being too tolerant of their own kids using drugs because they feel guilty and hypocritical about their own "youthful indiscretions." Glassner argues, however, that these are not real problems, only media angles.

Just as there are problems that we worry about too much, so Glassner argues that there are others that we may not worry about enough. Although we worry a lot about illegal drugs, we think much less about the mixing of alcohol and prescription drugs, which is very common in overdose cases. The abuse and overdose of prescription drugs sends more adolescents to emergency rooms than the use of cocaine, heroin, marijuana, and LSD combined. Drug abuse by physicians and the elderly is a huge problem, however its full extent is unknown. In terms of drugs and rape, the fact that alcohol is involved in a very large number of date rapes sometimes gets lost in the hysteria over the "date-rape drug" epidemic.

In terms of violence, Glassner also argues that we are worrying about the wrong things. Although middle class communities remain very safe places, some poor communities are extremely dangerous. The high chronic violent crime rate in minority communities receives far less media attention than a single sensational crime in a middle-class part of town. The ready availability of guns in the U.S. has led to far higher rates of death from handguns in the U.S. than elsewhere. More teen suicide attempts succeed today than formerly because more (60%) use guns. Is there a cost to inducing disproportionate fear in children by overreacting to extremely rare crimes like child abduction? The author once noted another dad at a parent soccer meeting for a second-grade team speak out strongly against putting the child's name on the back of the soccer jersey because "then someone could call him and kidnap him."

Another area where we worry about the wrong things concerns medical risks. For example, in almost all cases, the danger from not receiving a vaccine is far more than the danger of an extreme side effect of the vaccine. Before 1949, 7,500 kids died from whooping cough and 265,000 were sick annually, whereas the actual deaths from DPT vaccine were zero or almost so (Glassner, 1999). During a vaccine scare in the U.K. that led to a 40% drop in immunizations, 100,000 whooping cough cases appeared over 8 years. Japan had a tenfold increase in cases and a threefold increase in deaths after a temporary ban on the vaccine. Much better would be to worry about tobacco as the cause of so much death and illness or the high percentage of auto accident deaths that involve alcohol.

Sometimes what appear to be strong concerns for safety may have the opposite effect due to a failure to consider base rates. For example, periodically one hears calls for requiring the use of child safety seats in airplanes for children under two. Although this might occasionally save a child's life, it most likely would cost far more, because the extra expense (children under two can now fly free on their parent's lap) would send many people to the much more dangerous travel mode of driving instead. Finally, calls to allow disconnection of airbags in cars have often followed the very rare deaths of children, usually infants, in car seats in the front seat. In fact, airbags have saved many lives, and allowing motorists to disconnect them would almost surely cost some, whereas the risk to children can be better dealt with by putting children, especially infants in car seats, in the back seat.

Lowry, Nio, and Leitner (2003) examined the reasons for a jump from 5% to 52% in terms of the percent of the U.S. public who believed crime to be the "most important problem" facing the country. From looking at TV news broadcasts and crime statistics from 1978–1998, they concluded that network TV news variables accounted for four times as much of the variance in public perceptions as did actual crime rates! One of the best individual predictors was the sheer amount of time devoted to crime stories. Coming from the cultivation theory perspective, Romer, Jamieson, & Aday (2003) found that the amount of exposure to crime-ridden local TV news was a good predictor of the amount of fear and concern about crime. Busselle and Shrum (2003) found that people recalled media examples very readily, especially for classes of events where one's life experience was limited (e.g., murders, drug busts, and courtroom trials). In a series of experimental studies, Berger (1998, 2000) found that exposure to base-rate information (e.g., information about population increasing faster than associated crime rates) led to lower apprehension and perceived victimization risk in men (though not in women) compared to those receiving only frequency information (e.g., reports of increasing numbers of crimes over time).

Thus, it is clear that the way crimes are reported has a huge influence in the way we think about specific crimes and the likelihood of ourselves being victimized.

Suicides: Triggered by News?

A very different approach to studying the effects of news stories was taken by sociologist David Phillips (Bollen & Phillips, 1982; D. P. Phillips, 1977, 1984; D. P. Phillips & Carstensen, 1986), who used archival data to study the role of media news in triggering suicides. This research examined the hypothesis that news coverage of suicides encourages others to take their own lives.

Phillips' basic method was to examine correlations of media reports of suicides with changes in the rates of actual suicides. For example, Phillips and Carstensen (1986) examined 7 years (1973–1979) of such relationships by looking at 12,585 actual teenage suicides in relation to TV news reports and feature stories about suicide. They found that there was a significant increase in suicides 0 to 7 days after such a news story. This increase was correlated ($r = .52$) with the number of news programs carrying the story. This correlation was significant only for teen, not adult, suicides, and was stronger for girls than for boys. The experimenters concluded that the news stories (either general feature stories or reports of actual suicides) do in fact trigger teen suicides. In their article, Phillips and Carstensen discussed and refuted several possible alternative explanations of their findings, although the findings remain controversial. See Joiner (1999) and Kessler, Downey, Milavsky, & Stipp (1988) for arguments against the "suicide contagion" hypothesis.

How Media Affect Foreign Policy

News media, especially television, can even affect foreign policy and foreign relations (Gilboa, 2002; J. F. Larson, 1986). The transnational character of media news gathering necessarily involves it in policy making issues. The sharing of wire service stories and TV footage is common. Reporters in a foreign locale depend on local facilities to transmit news stories home, and often they must cope with local censorship or interference with such coverage. Governments sometimes try to manipulate our perceived reality by limiting the coverage. For example, Saudi Arabia has prevented Western reporters from covering repression of women and non-Islamic religions in its country.

Diplomatic Negotiations.   The presence of the press makes private or secret negotiations between governments more difficult. Diplomats negotiating sensitive issues must also then consider the implicit third party of public opinion in the negotiations. With television, it is especially hard to keep secret talks secret. Although such public scrutiny has probably placed some highly desirable curbs on corruption and extralegal chicanery, it has also made legitimate secret negotiations in the public interest much harder to keep secret.

Compelling Images.   The availability of relevant and appropriate video material affects the choice of stories. This clearly leads to overcoverage of some photogenic issues and undercoverage of others that are less so, thus covertly setting the agenda toward some issues. It also favors coverage from places where networks or wire services have correspondents on site, which historically for U.S. media has meant primarily Western Europe, with many other places covered firsthand only if there is a current crisis (J. F. Larson, 1984).

A particularly compelling visual image can galvanize world opinion and may affect foreign policy decisions. The picture of a lone person standing in front of a line of tanks in Tiananmen Square in Beijing in 1989 helped to increase the world's condemnation of the Chinese government's squelching of the pro-democracy movement. In the late 1960s, Pulitzer Prize-winning photos of a Vietcong prisoner being shot in the head and a naked little girl running from U.S. bombing in Vietnam helped to turn U.S. public opinion against the continuation of that war.

Some have worried that the policy of the United Nations sending military forces to oversee relief efforts in Somalia in 1992 to 1993 was a direct product of reactions to the grotesque images of starving children broadcast worldwide. Although such images probably played a role, Strobel (1997) argued that the media more followed the agenda of government rather than set it. Although the power of media, especially television, to convey emotions and a sense of intimacy may be necessary for U.S. action, it is not in itself sufficient in the absence of government resolve. Although the U.S. government appeared to be sending troops to Somalia in response to press and public outcry, there were comparable grisly images from Bosnia in late 1992 and Rwanda in spring 1994 that did not result in U.S. military intervention. Strobel argued that in these cases there existed a firm government policy against intervention, a position absent in the Somalia situation, and thus the press coverage had less policy impact. See Gilboa (2002) for a discussion of research on the nature and impact of media on foreign policy decisions.

Media and Government.   In fact, television networks and major wire services usually follow or reinforce government policy, at least implicitly

(J. F. Larson, 1984). This occurs not due to slavish conscious adherence to official policy by media, but rather because so many of the sources for most stories are inside governments. Also, the newsworthiness of individual people ensures that policy makers and spokespersons tend to be followed by reporters more than trends and background are. For example, summit meetings between world leaders are massively covered in the press, even when it is known in advance that little of substance will emerge.

Media sometimes even participate in foreign policy by serving as a direct channel of communications between government officials or policy elites in different nations. The press may thus become an "intervening actor" in mediation between nations or factions. For example, CBS news anchor Walter Cronkite's role in bringing Israel's Begin and Egypt's Sadat together in 1978 (see Box 7.5) was pivotal. On several occasions, Ted Koppel of ABC's *Nightline* used his program to bring together parties to start talking to each other. In some crisis situations, media may actually know more than governments and may thus reverse the usual government-to-media flow of news. During the 1991 Persian Gulf War, both U.S. President Bush and Iraqi leader Saddam Hussein regularly watched CNN to learn what was happening in the war. Furthermore, they both used the network to send messages to the other side, since that was the fastest and most reliable means of communication.

Policy problems may be created or exacerbated by lack of media attention to basic processes of social and cultural change in developing nations. The bias in international news coverage by U.S. sources toward greater coverage of developed nations and those of obvious present geopolitical importance has long been known. Western Europe, Japan, and Russia receive heavy coverage in the United States, whereas Africa, Latin America, and much of Asia are largely invisible (J. F. Larson, McAnany, & Storey, 1986; McAnany, 1983). Only in a crisis or when events thrust the United States into immediate involvement does the focus shift to such places, as was seen in Iran in 1979 (see Box 7.3), Iraq in 1990 to 1991, Somalia in 1992, Bosnia in 1993, Rwanda in 1995, Afghanistan in 2001, and Iraq in 2003. Thus the perceived reality is heavily ahistorical, with no background provided for understanding the puzzling present events.

The Vietnam War.   Media can change public perceptions about foreign affairs, particularly when they convey new visual information and when such information is repeatedly presented over a long period of time. The dramatic change in U.S. public opinion about the Vietnam War from 1965 to 1969 is perhaps the most dramatic example. As well as being the first war lost by the United States, the Vietnam conflict was the first television war. This aspect is sometimes cited as a major reason why the war lost support among the American people to an extent never before seen in the

United States. Although there were many other reasons for the lack of public support for the Vietnam War, the fact that the public could see the horrors of war every night while they ate dinner brought home the reality of how violent and deadly it truly was. The romantic ideals that some soldiers traditionally have taken to war, and that some family members back home have clung to, simply could not continue to be embraced. This war (like all others) was hell, but this time everybody could see it firsthand. The effect of bringing such wars into our living rooms has been a hotly debated topic, however; see Cumings (1992) and Strobel (1997). Some (e.g., Strobel, later in this chapter) argue that the role of the media in changing public opinion about Vietnam was far less influential than generally believed.

Terrorism. Although a terrorist incident is often a highly newsworthy story in terms of the characteristics discussed earlier in this chapter (Weimann & Brosius, 1991), terrorism stories place a difficult set of pressures on the media. Wittebols (1991; see also Herman & Chomsky, 1988; Herman & O'Sullivan, 1989) distinguished between *institutional* and *grievance* terrorism. Grievance terrorism challenges the powers that be and actively seeks media to advance its cause and publicize its side of the story. For example, radical Islamist groups killing journalists in Algeria or Irish Republican Army terrorists placing bombs in London or Belfast are grievance terrorists. On the other hand, institutional terrorism has the purpose of maintaining the status quo and generally shuns media coverage, even actively threatening those who try to cover it. For example, paramilitary death squads in El Salvador in the 1980s or Bosnian Serb paramilitary groups attacking Muslim and Croat homes in the Balkan war of the early 1990s represent institutional terrorism.

The most likely trap that media fall into with grievance terrorism is excessive coverage that risks legitimizing or glamorizing the terrorists, a frequent criticism of coverage of terrorism in the 1970s and 1980s. Since that time, the press has learned a bit better how to handle terrorists. On the other hand, the risk with institutional terrorism is failing to cover it at all, or failing to identify those really responsible for it, assuming that such responsibility can even be determined. See Alali and Eke (1991), Paletz and Schmid (1992), and Picard (1993) for further examinations of media coverage of terrorism.

CONCLUSION: FICTION BECOMES REALITY

The media as media have become news in themselves. The weekly top-10 Nielsen ratings are reported on TV news and in newspaper wire services and feature stories. Certain blockbuster TV entertainment shows become news events in themselves, receiving coverage throughout print and broadcast media. For example, the last new *Seinfeld* episode in May 1998 and the coming out episode of *Ellen* in April 1997 were major news stories. The annual publication of the *Sports Illustrated* swimsuit issue is announced on the news in all media. The release of blockbuster movies like every new Harry Potter or Star Wars film is a major news story.

The Docudrama: Fact or Fiction?

Sometimes the line between the genres of media news and fiction becomes blurred. A particularly controversial form is the docudrama, a fictional story based on real events. Although it is certainly not new to take some historic events and build a story around them, embellishing where facts are unavailable or undramatic (Shakespeare did it all the time), there is greater concern with such recent TV dramas and miniseries based on spectacular crimes, political and international figures, and other stories. Such programming is popular with the networks. On one weekend in January 1993, CBS, NBC, and ABC all aired premier TV docudrama movies based on the story of Amy Fisher, the "Long Island Lolita" teen prostitute who only months earlier was accused of trying to kill her alleged lover's wife. All three movies did at least reasonably well in the ratings.

Docudramas are growing ever more timely and difficult to distinguish from news. In one sweeps week in late May 1993, networks aired TV movies about the first World Trade Center bombing (February 1993), Hurricane Andrew (August 1992), and the siege of the Branch Davidian cult in Waco, Texas (April 1993). The latter script was written and came to the screen in record time. From the initial shootings of federal agents in late February to the final FBI assault on the compound on April 19, the country waited for news of how the siege would be played out. All the while, the TV movie was in production, with the script being written and rewritten in response to each day's news. The movie aired on May 23, only 34 days after the real death of its lead character David Koresh and dozens of his followers. For millions of people, that script's interpretation of the Waco events became reality. There may be limits on what the media believes the public will find acceptable. For example, at least as of late 2003, there have been no docudramas released about the terrorist attacks of September 2001. Entertainment based on events that horrible carries a risk of being perceived as profiting from a catastrophic tragedy.

Producers are hungry for such deals and have few compunctions about changing the facts to suit entertainment needs. For example, when

North American peace worker Jennifer Casolo was approached about a movie contract about her experiences working in El Salvador in the 1980s and being falsely arrested for being a revolutionary, the producers wanted her permission to make two changes in the story. They wanted her to (a) be actually guilty instead of innocent, and (b) fall in love with one of her captors. Unimpressed, Ms. Casolo turned down a lucrative offer. Is art imitating life, is life imitating art, or are they both the same?

In fact, the whole genre of the docudrama is merely a continuation of filmed interpretations of the past. In a fascinating study of cinematic stories of American historical events, historian Robert Toplin (1995) argues that films such as *Mississippi Burning, Sergeant York, JFK, Bonnie and Clyde, Patton,* and *All the President's Men* all significantly distort the historical record but yet at the same time convey a sense of the time and place to many people who would never be reached by purely historical writing. Although there is often an underemphasis on examining the underlying motivations for the behavior of historical figures (Hoekstra, 1998), the dramas are compelling and make events of the past accessible to many people. How does one balance the distortion of the historical record with the advantage of telling more people an important story? See Box 7.7 for a detailed comparison of fiction and reality in one recent docudrama.

Limits of Media Influence

We must be careful not to attribute a larger role in the perceived reality of our world to media than is appropriate. Although TV and other media are very important sources of news, some research (e.g., Gunter, 1987; J. P. Robinson & Davis, 1990) suggests that television is not a very effective way of acquiring news information.

Using the Vietnam War as an example, critical media coverage, starting around 1967, followed public opinion, rather than preceded it. The change in public opinion away from supporting the war occurred similarly for both the Korean (1950–1953) and Vietnam (1963–1975) wars and was more due to increases in U.S. casualties and a prolonged stalemated situation than to the nature of news coverage (Strobel, 1997). Although the worry that news coverage is influencing neutral people is widespread, such influences may be exerted less often than we believe (Perloff, 1989). Even if the media have less power to influence policy than is often believed, the fact that many policy makers firmly believe in that power can itself affect policy, most notably in the careful restriction and censorship of military operations since 1980, in order to avoid "another Vietnam."

BOX 7.7
CASE STUDY OF THE DOCUDRAMA *AMISTAD*

One of the movie hits of the winter 1998 film season was Steven Spielberg's *Amistad*, the previously little-known story of a rebellion by 53 kidnapped Africans aboard a Portuguese slave ship in 1839. They killed all but two of their captors. Double-crossed by these two sailors, who kept sailing to America at night, the Africans ended up in a Connecticut jail. However, their cause was taken up by Christian abolitionists, who hired ex-President John Quincy Adams to argue their case up to the U.S. Supreme Court, which eventually released them. The movie left out or downplayed certain major protagonists and enhanced the roles of others or combined them into fictional composites (e.g., Morgan Freeman's character). J. Q. Adams' (Anthony Hopkins) stirring speech to the U.S. Supreme Court never happened, according to *Amistad* historian and film consultant Clifford Johnson. The Africans' earlier attorney Roger Baldwin is portrayed as a more minor and inept character than he in fact was. Abolitionism as a movement almost disappears in the film, except for the abolitionist Lewis Tappan, who is played as a hypocrite with a more minor and far less noble role than the historical Tappan had. The central driving role of Christianity in the lives of the abolitionists is largely absent, in keeping with the general invisibility of religion in American popular culture (see chapter 11). Still, for all its rewriting of history, the film *Amistad* brought this important but previously largely unknown incident to the consciousness of millions in a way that historians could never hope to do (W. Goldstein, 1998; A. Schneider, 1998).

In a curious footnote to the controversy over this film, an egregious historical error has come to light. The revolt's leader Cinqué, portrayed as a hero in Spielberg's film, has been identified in several sources as having later returned to Africa and himself become a slave trader. In a bit of bibliographic sleuthing, *Amistad* historian Howard Jones traced the historical source of this claim to several history textbooks by Samuel Eliot Morison in the 1950s and 1960s. The sole source cited in these texts is a 1953 novel *Slave Mutiny* by William Owens. Apparently, several historians adopted Morison's interpretation without checking primary sources. Although novelist Owens apparently reported seeing some document somewhere confirming Cinqué's role as a slave trader, researchers at the Amistad Research Institute could find no record of such activity (Hot Type, 1998).

Even if news is not quite the preeminent influence it is sometimes heralded to be, it occupies a major place in the popular imagination. The coverage of news has itself become news, sometimes bigger news than the event being covered. On the eve of the Iowa presidential caucuses one year, a voter in the studio was asked if she planned to attend the caucus and thus participate in the selection of a nominee for president. Her reply was to look around the studio and say, "Oh, I guess so, but I hate to miss all the excitement here." In other words, the act of reporting had become the newsworthy event, eclipsing the event being reported. This example suggests the continuation of this discussion in the context of the specific area of politics, which is the subject of chapter 8.

CHAPTER **8**

Politics: Using News and Advertising to Win Elections

Q: In general, what is the most common type of television news content across different cultures?

A: Politics. It comprised between 25% and 40% of all news stories of each nation in a cross-cultural study of television news in the United States, Japan, Germany, Russia, Italy, India, Colombia, and China. This was more than economic, social, cultural, military, or crime stories (Straubhaar et al., 1992).

Q: How much is spent on political campaigns in the U.S.?

A: The 2000 Presidential election, the most expensive ever, cost $3 billion in combined expenses for all candidates, parties, and interest groups. (Johnston, 2001).

Q: What was the average length of stories on U.S. network TV news during the Presidential campaign of 1968?

A: 42 seconds (Hallin, 1992)

Q: What was the average length in 1992?

A: 8 seconds (Gibbs, 1996)

Politics and the media have long been intimately involved with each other, with media strongly setting the agenda that politics is very important. Although television has made some drastic changes in the nature of that relationship, the connection itself is not new. Print media have long covered political campaigns, and the level of political rhetoric has sometimes been far more vicious than it is today. For example, the U.S. presidential campaign of 1884 saw Democrat Grover Cleveland's alleged fathering of an illegitimate child as a major campaign issue ("Hey, man, where's my pa?" "Gone to the White House, ha, ha, ha!"). For another historical example, see Box 8.1 for more on the political use of the media by abolitionists in pre-Civil War United States.

BOX 8.1
ABOLITIONIST MEDIA CAMPAIGNS IN THE
19TH CENTURY

One of the major political and philosophical issues in 19th-century America was slavery, a controversy so divisive that it played a major role in leading to the calamitous American Civil War (1861–1865). Historical novelist John Jakes (1985) identified several ways that the Abolitionists successfully used pre-electronic media to gradually turn the nation's thinking against slavery. Abolitionism was a rather extreme position in its early days of popularity in the 1820s, in that it advocated the end of all slavery, on moral grounds, not merely proscribing its extension to the new Western territories. The Abolitionists ran their own newspapers and had supporters in the editors' chairs at many publications. Probably the most famous was William Lloyd Garrison's *Liberator,* begun in 1831. There was also Frederick Douglass' *North Star,* Horace Greeley's New York *Tribune,* and even a children's newspaper called *The Slave's Friend.*

Several books were also tremendously influential. Narratives of escaped slaves became popular in the 1840s, with the preeminent example being Frederick Douglass' autobiography. Far eclipsing all other books, however, was Harriet Beecher Stowe's *Uncle Tom's Cabin* (1852), written more out of religiously motivated concern for the treatment of slaves than of any political conviction or true egalitarian sentiment (Stowe favored sending freed slaves back to Africa). In fact, the novel was based on only one short visit to a Kentucky plantation and contained very condescending portraits of African-Americans. Still, it had substantial political impact.

Highly newsworthy events that received wide coverage and polarized already strong opinions helped lead the nation to war. Public meetings led by White clergymen or escaped slaves drew increasing crowds. Protests over the Fugitive Slave Law allowing Southern slaveholders to hunt and retrieve runaway slaves in the North occasionally led to dramatic, even violent, reaction. Garrison once burned a copy of the U.S. Constitution, calling it "a covenant with death and an agreement with hell." In 1859 Abolitionist John Brown and 21 followers tried unsuccessfully to seize arms from the federal arsenal in Harpers Ferry to arm a slave rebellion. He was caught, tried, and hanged, but coverage of the trial split the country more sharply than ever.

Still, from the first tentative and fragmented radio reporting of Warren Harding's U.S. Presidential victory in 1920 to today's framing of whole campaigns around the use of television news and advertising, broadcast media have transformed political campaigns beyond recognition from Grover Cleveland's days. Franklin D. Roosevelt (1933–1945) was perhaps the quintessential radio president; his lofty mellow tones electrified listeners in ways that watching his body in a wheelchair could never do. In recent decades, candidates have had to deal with the visual aspect of television, and some of them have done so only grudgingly.

CLOSING THE DISTANCE BETWEEN THE CANDIDATE AND THE PUBLIC

Meyrowitz (1985) argued that television coverage has forever changed politics by decreasing the distance between the politician and the voter. Although it is no longer necessary to cross the wide gulf between oneself and the voters by being an imposing physical presence in a crowd or an accomplished orator, it is now imperative to know how to use the more intimate medium of television to one's advantage. Analysts of various political persuasions have acknowledged that U.S. Presidents Ronald Reagan and Bill Clinton were highly effective television politicians, as was John F. Kennedy in an earlier period. Other recent presidents and candidates, such as George H. W. Bush, Gerald Ford, Al Gore, Richard Nixon, Michael Dukakis, Jimmy Carter, Robert Dole, and Walter Mondale, have been criticized for less effective use of television.

Because of TV, political audiences are not as segmented as they used to be. A candidate cannot deliver one speech to an audience of factory workers and a contradictory address to a group of lawyers, because both may be reported on the evening news, particularly if reporters perceive any inconsistency. A single unfortunate statement or behavior may have a lasting contaminating effect through the magic of television transferring that one place to all places. For example, Democratic presidential candidate Edmund Muskie was the front-runner for his party's nomination in 1972 until he was seen on television shedding a tear in New Hampshire in response to an editor's unfounded attack on his wife. This reaction, however noble and loyal, was then interpreted as weakness and may have cost him the presidential nomination. Nixon Agriculture Secretary Earl Butz' private racist joke, which became public, and Reagan Interior Secretary James Watt's insensitive comment about a group containing "a Black, a Jew, and a cripple" had costly career effects because of the instant widespread dissemination of the comment.

Richard Nixon may have never fully realized why the Watergate tapes of White House conversations were so damning and ultimately forced him to resign from the U.S. Presidency in 1974 in the face of certain impeachment. Meyrowitz (1985) suggested that Nixon was evaluating those tapes as private conversations rather than as public statements. In private most people say some things on occasion that they would not deem appropriate for a public forum, due to language (e.g., profanity), content (e.g., prejudicial or judgmental comments), or style (e.g., imitation of someone). Limited to the private world, such conversations may not be unusual. As public discourse, however, they appeared highly inappropriate, insensitive, and even shocking. Electronic media technology has broken down that public-private barrier by bringing formerly private discourse into the public world. No longer can a public figure assume that private comments will forever remain private.

In this chapter we begin by looking at the news media coverage of political campaigns, including televised candidate debates. Then we examine how politicians can manage the news coverage that their campaign receives. This is followed by an extended case study of the media coverage of the closest Presidential election in U.S. history. Next we take a careful look at political advertising, when candidates pay to say exactly what they want. Finally, we briefly look at the cultivation theory thesis that television cultivates a political moderation in heavy viewers. Politicians consistently hope to use media to create a favorable reality about themselves in the public mind. The examples discussed are primarily from the United States, because that is the area known best to the author and the one most studied by scholars examining politics and the media. Most of the principles discussed, however, are also applicable elsewhere.

COVERAGE OF POLITICAL CAMPAIGNS

In most nations of the world, the media strongly set the agenda that politics is a very important concern. Political campaigns, candidates, and issues, especially at the national level, receive heavy coverage. Looking at this coverage more closely, however, reveals that some aspects receive more coverage than others.

What Is Heavily Covered

Certain aspects of political campaigns are inordinately heavily covered and others lightly covered, in large measure depending on how newsworthy they are, in the sense discussed in chapter 7. First, major pronouncements receive press attention, especially formal announcements of intent to run for office or to withdraw from a race. Other types of strong statements, like a strident attack on an opponent, also have high visibility.

Second, any type of major blunder, even if substantially inconsequential in the long run, receives wide attention. Candidate Gary Hart's apparent overnight tryst with model Donna Rice and his challenge to the media to 'follow him' ensured saturation coverage and led to his temporary withdrawal from the Democratic presidential race in the spring of 1987. When he later re-entered the race, his campaign never really caught on. One of the most notorious blunders was President Gerald Ford's statement in the 1976 presidential debates about Poland being a "free country." Although this was clearly in error, and so acknowledged shortly after by Ford, the press did not let the country forget. Vice-President Dan Quayle (1989–1993) (and later President George W. Bush) became legendary for his wrong word choices. Sometimes the public may weigh these blunders less than the media; a series of allegations in early 1998 about President Bill Clinton's dalliances with several women received heavy, almost tabloid, coverage but did not seem to hurt his popularity very much. For a case study of a very outrageous and offensive set of campaign misstatements that did alienate the public, see Box 8.2.

Third, any kind of colorful response to a political speech or event captures coverage. Cheering masses or angry demonstrations draw cameras. In many countries, rulers of questionable legitimacy regularly pay people to attend a speech and "spontaneously" cheer. Likewise, protests against

---

BOX 8.2
WOMAN-BASHING IN CAMPAIGN DISCOURSE:
AN OUTRAGEOUS CASE STUDY

Although politics in most countries has been long dominated by men, women are entering in record numbers, having held the top elected positions in Great Britain, Norway, Turkey, Pakistan, India, Sri Lanka, Israel, Iceland, Argentina, Bolivia, Nicaragua, New Zealand, the Philippines, and elsewhere. Still, in many places a candidate's being a woman remains a liability. In 1990, Texas Republican gubernatorial candidate and political novice Clayton Williams seemed to bring insensitivity to new depths in his campaign against Democratic state treasurer Ann Richards. First he vowed to bring back the days when "a man was a man" and "a woman knew her place was not at the top of the Democratic ticket." Later at a cattle roundup, he commented that bad weather was like rape, "If it's inevitable, just relax and enjoy it," a comment that drew shocked widespread condemnation from people concerned about violence against women. Slow to learn, Williams went on to insult Mexicans and Mexican-Americans by saying that during his youth, crossing into Mexico and "being serviced by prostitutes" was part of a healthy male's coming of age. Aides of Williams called Richards an "honorary lesbian" for supporting gay rights (Carlson, 1990). Do such tactics work? Although Williams began over 10 points ahead of Richards, he became an acute embarrassment to Texas Republicans and lost the election.

a leader are carefully orchestrated primarily for the TV cameras, not for the speaker. The Filipino democratic revolution of 1986 was greatly aided by television coverage of the protests against Ferdinand Marcos' apparent stealing of the election. This revolution was broadcast around the world and the lesson was duly noted. In the summer of 1987, widespread and broad-based popular protests in South Korea were televised over the world and soon forced President Chun Doo Hwan to agree to popular elections for President and a return to democracy. Televised images of anti-Soviet protests in the Baltic nations and elsewhere in 1990 and 1991 helped to hasten those states' independence from the crumbling Soviet Union. Protesters worldwide routinely have sets of posters and banners in several languages to display as appropriate, depending on which nation's camera crew is present. The media audience is the most important one.

Fourth, meetings of a candidate with important people receive press coverage. This is particularly important for candidates without wide experience in some areas. For example, U.S. presidential aspirants with little foreign affairs background often make visits to foreign leaders, in order to be seen on the evening news shaking their hand and conferring.

Finally, and probably most importantly, any aspect of a campaign that emphasizes the "horse race" receives coverage. Poll results are reported widely and promptly, as are predictions by experts and any event that "upsets" the relative standings of the "players." In the 2000 U.S. Presidential campaign coverage, 71% of the news stories were concerned with the horse race, rather than the issues (Lichter, 2001), while fewer than a third of the TV news stories mentioned any issue at all (Jamieson & Waldman, 2003). The number of poll-related stories and the relative prominence of such stories have risen greatly in the last 40 years (Craig, 2000), with the agenda increasingly set that what is important in the campaign is primarily the change in poll results since the last report.

What are the effects of such preoccupation with who's ahead and who's behind? Relatively unknown candidates suddenly perceived as serious contenders or frontrunners receive a rapid and substantial increase in coverage. At least in primary elections, they do not necessarily even have to win; a simple "better-than-expected" showing is often enough for a media victory. Dark horse anti-Vietnam War candidate Gene McCarthy's surprisingly good showing in the New Hampshire Democratic primary in 1968 was instrumental in President Lyndon Johnson's surprise decision not to seek renomination himself. Right wing Patrick Buchanan's surprising (although not close to winning) showing in the 1992 New Hampshire Republican primary catapulted him from a fringe extremist candidate to someone that the media apparently perceived as a serious challenger to incumbent President George H. W. Bush.

This heavy coverage of horse races has probably encouraged the proliferation of more and earlier contests. With the New Hampshire Presidential primary established by law *as two weeks before the earliest primary of any other state*, that state ensures the continued attention and economic development benefits of all the media coverage. Other states such as Iowa have attempted an 'end run' by having non-primary caucuses or statewide straw polls earlier. These contests end up drawing considerable coverage, often starting close to a year before the general election. Most primary states have moved their primaries earlier in recent years so as to have some say before the contest is decided. The primary system has now become so front-loaded that the two major candidates are usually effectively chosen by March or April, 7 to 8 months before the general election in November! This extensively protracted campaign period is a major reason for both the rapidly escalating cost of campaigns and the public's weariness of them. They simply last too long, a fact almost everyone acknowledges but no one knows quite how to fix.

The race aspect that is covered the most heavily of all is, of course, the result of the actual election. There is a lot of concern that knowledge of the results, or predicted results, in the case of network projections of winners, may actually affect the outcome of the election by influencing voters who have not yet gone to the polls. See Box 8.3 for further discussion of this issue.

What Is Lightly Covered

Just as some aspects of political campaigns are heavily covered, so others are relatively lightly covered. Candidates' qualifications in intangible, but highly important, ways are relatively difficult for the press to cover. What has someone gained from being governor of Texas or senator from Tennessee, for example, which would help in being president? Very abstract issues such as character are in one sense extremely important but in another sense very difficult to assess. Coverage that does occur tends to focus on superficial, though not necessarily irrelevant, indicators of integrity (or more often lack thereof), like marital infidelity or shady business dealings. Although there was much talk early in the 1992 presidential campaign of Democrat Bill Clinton's apparent extramarital affair some years before, the exact relevance or irrelevance of this to his possible performance as president was never clarified (and perhaps could not be).

Also relatively lightly covered are positions on issues, especially complex ones. Television news especially is ill-suited to detailed presentations of positions on complex issues like the economy. Print media can do much better, as in publication of a candidate's lengthy position paper on some issue. However, few people read such reports; they listen to television's

BOX 8.3
PUBLIC OPINION POLLING AND ELECTION RESULTS

Started by newspapers in the 1800s but greatly refined recently, public opinion polls are an integral part of modern political life most everywhere. The famed Gallup Poll began in the 1930s and held a margin of error of 4% in the period of 1936–1950, but this had fallen to .3% by 1984. It is larger if there are three, instead of two, candidates, as in 1980 when the Carter-Reagan-Anderson contest produced a margin of error of 4.7%.

One of the most notable errors in polling history occurred in the *Literary Digest* presidential poll in 1936. Mailed to auto and phone owners in the heart of the Great Depression, the poll came back favoring Republican Alf Landon, who in fact lost to incumbent Franklin Roosevelt by a huge landslide. The poll, so inaccurate due to a skewed sample of more affluent than average voters, was such a point of disgrace that it helped lead to the demise of the magazine.

One particularly controversial issue concerns the broadcasting of election results and projection of winners before the polls have closed in all states. In the days of paper ballots, no substantive results could be obtained for several hours anyway, but that is no longer the case. Four studies done many years ago assessed West Coast voters' exposure to election results and projections before they voted (Fuchs, 1966; Lang & Lang, 1968; Mendelsohn, 1966; Tuchman & Coffin, 1971). These studies show only modest exposure to the projections and very small proportions indicating changing their vote or deciding not to vote (1%–3%). Still, these studies were done before the widespread use of exit polls and, in any case, many elections are decided by very close margins.

Since these studies were done, sampling techniques have improved and networks today take exit polls by asking voters as they leave the polling places which candidate they voted for. Assuming appropriate sampling and truthful responses, exit poll results can highly accurately project winners before the polls close. Networks, in a race to scoop the competition, routinely have declared projected winners in races with only a tiny percentage of the votes counted (less than 10%). Although this may be scientifically sound, based on the statistics of representative sampling, it may convey a troubling message to viewers. If results can be obtained with only 5% of the votes in, it may not seem to an individual voter that a single ballot can make much difference. The United States has consistently had one of the lowest voter turnout rates in the world, not infrequently less than half of the qualified voters. There is not much incentive to go and vote after you have already heard the results on television.

30-second interpretation of it, which may focus on peripheral aspects that are more 'newsworthy.' Some candidates and incumbents have written scholarly books or papers carefully outlining comprehensive positions on complex issues; such positions may be vitally important to predicting their performance in office, yet they are difficult to cover adequately in the media, especially on television. A 200-page treatise on economic issues simply does not translate well to a 20-second news story. Most TV campaign coverage is even shorter than that; the length of an average TV political news story fell from 43 to 9 seconds from 1968 to 1988 (Hallin, 1992).

Interpretation by the Press

When issues such as economic ones are covered, they tend to be seriously distorted. For example, early in the 1992 Democratic presidential primary campaign, major rivals Bill Clinton and Paul Tsongas had both written extensive, detailed, and well thought out economic programs for the country. What one heard about these from the media was that Clinton favored a modest income tax reduction for middle income Americans, whereas Tsongas did not, calling Clinton's proposal a "gimmick." What we did not hear, however, was that almost the entire economic programs of Tsongas and Clinton, except that relatively minor point, were very similar and each offered a reasoned viable alternative to the programs of Republican incumbent George H. W. Bush. Because of the media's highlighting of differences (remember, conflict is more newsworthy), the truth suffered.

Sometimes the political and general culture of a society will affect how certain aspects of a campaign and other political news are covered. Perhaps the most striking example of this is the response to sex scandals of high officials (see Box 8.4 for a historical view). When reports of dalliances of President Bill Clinton with several women began to surface in early 1998, the domestic and international press did not quite know what to make of it. On the one hand, allegations and rumors were reported in great detail, along with rampant speculation of how the President may have lied about these affairs, possibly to the point of a legally impeachable offense. Even as the public soaked in this saturation, tabloid-like reporting, a curious thing happened. The President's popularity in the polls actually increased to some of his highest levels. Many constituencies were in a quandary. Opposition Republicans were presented with an opportunity for political gain but one with definite risks. If they succeeded in impeaching and removing the Democratic President Clinton, they would have an incumbent President Al Gore (as Vice-President, he would be Clinton's replacement) to face in the next election, instead of an inexperienced challenger. Likewise, more

---

BOX 8.4
PROMISCUOUS PRESIDENTS: HOW MUCH DO WE WANT TO KNOW?

Although President Bill Clinton's (1993–2001) alleged extramarital adventures received far greater coverage in the late 1990s than had indiscretions of his predecessors in earlier times, they are by no means unprecedented for U.S. Presidents. With a few exceptions, notably Grover Cleveland's alleged illegitimate child who surfaced in the 1884 campaign, relatively few people knew of such liaisons and those who did either did not care or chose not to make them issues. For example, John F. Kennedy (1961–1963) and Lyndon B. Johnson (1963–1969) were long rumored to have had affairs but the press refrained from pursuing the specifics too aggressively. Somewhat earlier, Warren Harding (1921–1923) and Franklin D. Roosevelt (1933–1945) were known to have mistresses but both also had strong wives highly respected in their own right. Woodrow Wilson (1913–1921) was widowed while in office and later married Edith Bolling Galt, with whom he had been rumored to have had a long-term relationship. The second Mrs. Wilson later was essentially de facto President after her husband became physically incapacitated, a condition hidden from the public by Mrs. Wilson. Founding Father Thomas Jefferson (1801–1809) became a widower early in life but later apparently had a long-term relationship, including children, with one of his slaves, Sally Hemings. Although historians still sharply dispute the veracity of these claims, it may have been as hard for the public of Jefferson's time to accept that he might have had a long-term caring relationship with a Black slave as to accept he had children by her.

Perhaps most potentially controversial, and least well-known, are recent claims that the U.S.'s only bachelor President, James Buchanan (1857–1861), was a homosexual who lived with a senator from Alabama, a disturbing piece of news that, when discovered by his fiancée Anne Cole, led to her suicide. It is also possible that the married James Garfield, killed after being in office only months, had frequent homosexual flings (Hurst, 1998). If the press had not shown some restraint, how might these stories have played out? Is the public better off knowing or not knowing?

---

liberal constituencies were embarrassed by the apparently sexist, insensitive behavior by the President who had done more to show professional respect personally and advance the cause of women legislatively than had any of his predecessors.

The international press responded through their own cultural lenses. Several Middle Eastern countries (especially Iraq, but also others) presented Bill Clinton as a sort of immoral clown totally unfit for his office. They mused at how such a powerful country could permit such an irresponsible person to hold office. On the other hand, many Western European nations wrung their journalistic hands at how a puritanical nation was threatening to destroy a highly successful Presidency over details of his private life, which should remain private and have no bearing in evaluating his public performance in office. Only a few years earlier, the state funeral of former French President François Mitterrand prominently featured both his wife and his longtime mistress, and the children of each, among the mourners.

The U.S. Presidential Debates

An exception to television not dealing well with complex candidate positions would seem to be the U.S. Presidential candidate debates, first in 1960 (Kennedy vs. Nixon), and regularly since 1976 (Ford-Carter), 1980 (Carter-Reagan), 1984 (Reagan-Mondale), 1988 (Bush-Dukakis), 1992 (Bush-Clinton-Perot), 1996 (Clinton-Dole), and 2000 (Bush-Gore). See Hinck (1992) and Kraus (1962, 1977, 1988, 1996) for analyses of these debates. Here the candidates have a chance to put forward their positions in more detail than usual for television and, most importantly, in perhaps the only forum where partisans of the other candidate will actually listen to them.

Still, however, the debates are typically analyzed by both media commentators and the public in terms of superficial appearances and performances. Polls and scholars showed that Kennedy "won" in 1960 with those who watched on TV, while Nixon "won" with those who listened on radio (Kraus, 1996). Gerald Ford "lost" the 1976 debates because of his Poland remark. Reagan "won" the 1980 and 1984 debates because he seemed friendly and trustworthy and stuck to generalities; the only exception was the one debate that he "lost" because he became too bogged down in facts where he was not comfortable, eloquent, or accurate. Bill Clinton "won" the third 1992 debate, which involved talking directly to audience members, a format at which he excelled. Third-party candidate Ross Perot impressed viewers in the first debate with his pithy, down-to-earth, no nonsense replies; by the third debate, however, these aphorisms seemed to many as shallow, hackneyed, and lacking in substance.

Debate Coverage. The media mediate between the debate itself and the viewers' interpretation of it. There has consistently been much criticism of presidential debate coverage as being too superficial. However, Kraus (1988) argued that such critics often fail to accept the reality of debates and campaigns. In spite of their stated intent, people expect the debates to produce winners and losers. They are an integral part of a candidate's campaign designed to produce a winner. The debates are part of a society that loves a contest and expects to be constantly entertained by television.

The specific format of a particular debate is whatever the candidates themselves decide, because they must agree and will only agree to what they think will help them.

Most of this is not really new. The Lincoln-Douglas debates of 1858 in Illinois are often seen as a prototype of pure political debate, but in fact they actually were much more like today's presidential debates than we often realize. Candidate Abraham Lincoln manipulated the press and used the occasion to launch his national platform and campaign for the presidency in 1860. At least today technology allows the accurate recording of a debate; Lincoln-Douglas relied on the biased memories of each side.

The horse-race type of debate coverage has always predominated. In a study of the 1980 debates, Robinson and Sheehan (1983) found that CBS and UPI (a former newspaper wire-service, now defund) both devoted more space to horse race aspects than to any other, and 55% to 60% of the coverage failed to contain even one sentence about an issue. This type of coverage of debates is in fact very natural and predictable and totally consistent with other political coverage and what makes an event newsworthy (see chapter 7).

In a careful review of the 1996 debates and their predecessors, Hart and Jarvis (1997) conclude that, despite their problems, the presidential debates have been a positive influence on the political process. "Debates cut through some of the campaign baloney, ground political discourse a bit, sharpen points of difference, make the candidates at least faintly introspective, and restrain overstatements" (p. 1120). Even if they do not do any of these to the extent we might hope for, they do so to a substantial degree. As for how presidential debates have changed between 1960 and 1996, Hart and Jarvis conclude that the major longitudinal change has been a decreasing certainty and more tentativeness of statements and an increasingly conviviality and sociability. This may be due to what Hart (1994) called the "phenomenology of affect" engendered by the highly intimate medium of television, whereby everything and everyone on television strives to connect more with the viewer at the emotional level.

Effects on Viewers.   What are the effects of the debates on the public? To begin with, at least the presidential debates draw large audiences, although far less recently than in their early years (60% of homes in 1960 vs. 26% in the last debate of 2000; Jamieson & Waldman, 2003). They are regularly followed by polls about the candidates' debate performance. Campaign handlers know this and carefully plan to try to make a strong impact first. One very important, although fairly intangible, function is to activate the electorate. "Televised presidential debates may be unparalleled in modern campaigning as an innovation that engages citizens in the political process by building large audiences, creating interest and discussion among voters, and influencing voter decisions" (Kraus, 1988, p. 123). The research is inconsistent in regard to the effects of debates on actual voting. They certainly reinforce and crystallize existing attitudes and may actually influence votes. One 1983 study cited by Kraus showed that 58% of people said that the debates were more helpful in deciding their vote than were TV news reports or TV political ads.

There is one additional thorny problem of the televised debates, and that is how to handle third-party candidates. Presumably one would not want to include any and all fringe candidates, most of whom typically have minuscule popular support. In the case of a viable third-party candidacy, however, it becomes awkward. For example, in 1980 centrist Independent John Anderson showed strong support in early polls. However, to be included in the televised debates, both other major candidates would have had to accept his participation. Because one did not, it was only a two-way debate, and Anderson's fortunes fell sharply after this exclusion. A different solution was reached in 1992, with populist billionaire third-party candidate H. Ross Perot. Perot had a substantial minority of the electorate supporting him, and Democrat Bill Clinton and Republican George H. W. Bush apparently both thought that the damage to them from Perot's debate presence would be less than the public relations damage if they were to exclude him, so Perot participated in a set of three-way debates. Conventional wisdom was that Perot "hung himself" in this format, to which he was not well-suited. When Perot ran again in 1996, incumbent President Clinton and Republican candidate Robert Dole felt strong enough to exclude Perot from the debates.

Following the precedent of the presidential debates, increasing numbers of local candidates now conduct televised debates. Now let us turn to looking at how candidates can use the media news coverage to their advantage. Later in the chapter we look specifically at political advertising and its effects.

CANDIDATES' USE OF NEWS MEDIA

Setting the Agenda

Campaign strategists devote considerable energy to examining how to most effectively use news coverage to create a positive and electable image of their candidate. This is both much cheaper and more believable than using advertising. Use of the news for political gain can be done in many different ways, some of which are an integral part of the daily life of newsmakers. For example, an elected official may have more or fewer news conferences, depending on the desire for coverage. An incumbent has considerable advantage over the challenger in such matters. For example, while Democratic presidential candidates were squabbling among themselves in early summer 1972, Republican candidate (and incumbent president) Richard Nixon captured media attention with his historic trip to China. His landmark voyage opened up the world's largest country to the West and contrasted sharply to the petty bickering of his Democratic opponents attacking each other in their primary campaigns. Ronald Reagan tried to divert media attention from the unfolding Iran-contra scandal in early 1987 by becoming more active and outspoken in seeking an arms control agreement with the Soviet Union. His historic trip to Moscow in spring 1988 contrasted to the Democratic primary squabbles going on at the time.

In any political system, but especially in totalitarian ones, it is not uncommon for a leader to whip up support and mute discontent by emphasizing or even provoking a foreign "enemy." Iraq, under Saddam Hussein, and Iran, under the Ayatollah Khomeini, periodically invoked the American "bogey man" to distract from dissatisfaction with failing domestic policies and political repression, whereas Argentina's military government in part provoked the Falklands/Malvinas War with Britain in 1982 to unite the country and mute criticisms of the economy and its own major human rights abuses. In the Cold War era, right-wing dictatorships used to blame all of their problems on communism, whereas communist states blamed the American CIA or international capitalism.

Candidates help to set an agenda by telling us what issues are important in the campaign. Ronald Reagan in 1980 and 1984 told us that it was important to "feel good" about America, and that struck a responsive chord in a nation weary of inflation, Watergate, and international terrorism. The same appeal by George H. W. Bush in recession-weary 1992 failed to resonate with voters who did not "feel good" about their economic distress. In 1984 Walter Mondale tried unsuccessfully to argue that honesty was an important issue, even to the point of saying that he might have to raise taxes. It is a reality that, in setting the agenda in terms of issues, candidates must consider not only what they believe is important, but also what they believe the public wants to hear.

Framing the Candidates

Pinocchio and Dumbo.   Candidates can come to have a prevailing image that becomes the frame through which their actions are viewed. For example, in the 2000 U.S. Presidential election, Democrat Al Gore came to have the "lying panderer" or "Pinocchio" frame, while Republican George W. Bush had the "inexperienced dolt" or "Dumbo" frame (Jamieson & Waldman, 2003). Bush was seen as more trustworthy and Gore as more knowledgeable. Such frames may evolve from the media's attempt to play amateur psychologist and identify and explore the candidates' character. All too often, however, the deep probing of character and its potential effects on qualifications for office do not occur, leaving the frame with a life of its own with everyone interpreting the candidates' actions simplistically around it.

Because of the Pinocchio frame, Al Gore's statements were scrutinized much more carefully than George Bush's for possibly misleading information. For example, Gore was often chastised for claiming to having invented the Internet. His actual statement, made in an interview with CNN's Wolf Blitzer, was, "During my service in the U.S. Congress, I took the initiative in creating the Internet" (Jamieson & Waldman, 2003, p. 48), reflecting that he had in fact played a large role in securing funding for expanding that new system. Once the word "invented" became a part of that statement, however, there was no correcting it. Because of the well-known principle of thought, the confirmation bias, we tend to seek, notice, and remember information consistent with our prior beliefs and forget or ignore information incongruent with those same beliefs.

On the other hand, George Bush's malapropisms like "misunderestimate" were given much more attention than Gore's. The confirmation bias is also at work here with both journalists and the public. Bush's, but not Gore's, speech errors were front-page news, as was his poor performance on an impromptu test of naming world leaders.

These frames are reinforced not only by many journalists but also by comedians. David Letterman and Jay Leno continually poked fun at Bush's intelligence and speech and at Gore's exaggerations and stiffness. Since the early nineties, TV comedy and talk shows have become increasingly important formats not only for what they say about the candidates but also as expected venues for the candidates to visit. In recent elections, visiting Jay Leno and MTV has been as necessary as visiting the Iowa caucus and New Hampshire primary. Some have argued that this development only goes to show that political news, and perhaps news more broadly (e.g., John Stewart's satirical news "The Daily Show"), has become subordinate to entertainment and just another part of television's overriding aim of entertaining its audience (Taylor, 2000).

Changing Frames. Sometimes for various reasons a frame may become undesirable or cease to be useful. One of the most dramatic illustrations of this occurred in the U.S. in 2001. Although the dim, inexperienced "Dumbo" image of George W. Bush persisted several months into his Presidency, the terrorist attacks of September 11, 2001 changed all that. Suddenly, we did not want Dumbo or the Sheriff of Mayberry leading us in those tragic times where difficult decisions had to be made. Overnight, the descriptions of Bush in the press radically changed. His speech errors were no longer noted. He was described with new language, like "elo-quent," "thoughtful," and a "strong leader." Many wrote about how the President had been transformed by September 11, but there are some good arguments that it was actually the reporters who had been transformed (Jamieson & Waldman, 2003). Comedians also changed; Bush was the butt of 32% of all late-night jokes in 2001 up until September 11, but only 4% thereafter.

Although the predominant frame before the attacks was Dumbo, after-wards we did not want to think of our leader in that way, so the idealized frame of the wise and strong leader took hold. Using the confirmation bias, reporters and the public noted Bush's statements and behaviors that fit this new image and neglected those congruent with the old Dumbo frame.

Creating Pseudo-Events

In case normal news coverage is not enough, "pseudo-events" may be cre-ated to capture media coverage and, in effect, produce many hours of free advertising. For example, when Bob Graham ran for governor of Florida in 1978, he began as an unknown state legislator with 3% name recog-nition and 0% of the projected vote. How he overcame this was largely due to his "work days" project. During the campaign he worked for 100 days doing different jobs around the state, one job per day, apparently to learn the demands and needs of different sectors of the electorate. These were heavily covered by the media and worked greatly to Graham's ad-vantage, in spite of the obvious self-serving motivation behind them. He defused some of the predictable criticism of opportunistic gimmickry by dressing appropriately and actually working a full eight hours on each job. The first nine days were done before the media were invited in, so Graham had time to fine-tune his procedure. Photos from the work days were of course used in his campaign advertising, but, more importantly, they were also widely covered *as news*. In his speeches he made refer-ences to insights he had gained from these days, and he continued them intermittently after becoming governor, all in all confirming the impres-sion that he had actually learned from them and was not merely dealing in transparent political grandstanding. All in all, it was a brilliant exam-ple of the use of news media for one's own political gain; no amount of paid advertising could have bought what he gained for free in the news coverage.

Some new opportunities for pseudo-events appeared in the U.S. begin-ning in 1992 with the advent of "talk-show politics." Candidates Clinton, Bush, and Perot all were interviewed on MTV, "Larry King Live" and other entertainment talk shows. In fact, these programs opened new avenues for the candidates to present themselves as "real people" who were very approachable. Lasting images remained from some of these appearances. When amateur musician Clinton donned sunglasses and played the saxophone with the band on "The Arsenio Hall Show," the contrast of the energetic and hip young baby-boomer candidate with the aging and cautious George H. W. Bush and the stodgy and curmudgeonly Ross Perot was striking.

Creating pseudo-events can backfire, however. In 1988, modest-sized candidate Michael Dukakis sat in a tank to try to project a "strong on defense" image but instead looked more like a small turtle sticking his head out of a large shell. Likewise, Ivy Leaguer George Bush Sr.'s occasional attempts to don cowboy boots and eat pork rinds to appear like a "true Texan" did not always ring true. His son George W. Bush came across more believably in this role.

Dealing With Attacks From the Opponent

In the 1992 Democratic primary campaign, candidate Bill Clinton had been accused of an extramarital affair that allegedly occurred years before. The forum he chose to respond to this was a *60 Minutes* TV newsmagazine interview where he and wife Hillary admitted that there had been "problems" in their marriage but said that those had been worked through and they were thoroughly reconciled. It was a masterful combination of confession and avoidance of admitting critical information. Clinton's story of how his daughter Chelsea hugged him after hearing of the accusations melted people's hearts. They were ready to forgive, interpreting what they saw on TV as sincere repentance and love for family. Shortly after the interview, the alleged affair ceased to be a campaign issue. It is hard to see how it could have been so effectively refuted and defused in a traditional press conference or political beat reporting interview. Later, when confronted with other allegations of personal and real estate scandal, Clinton apparently forgot his own lesson and did not meet criticism so directly.

How a political candidate responds to attacks from the opposition can be very important. Although an attack left unchallenged may be believed uncritically by the electorate, an overly vicious or petty response may actually engender support for the opponent. An incumbent has less flexibility than a challenger in handling attacks. In some cases it may be better to ignore or brush off an attack than to "dignify" it with a response, such as challenger Ronald Reagan's oft-repeated "Well, there you go again" response to President Jimmy Carter in the 1980 debates. On the other hand, an incumbent's attack on a challenger is not always so easily dismissed by the latter. Candidate Reagan's criticism of President Carter in 1980 for the failure to bring home the Iranian hostages became a substantive one, in spite of the fact that neither he nor anyone else offered any idea of what could be done to free them.

There always exists the danger of a backlash of sympathy for the opponent if an attack is perceived as too unfair. This tends to keep potential mudslinging in check. However, sometimes this fear may also suppress useful dialogue. For example, in the 1988 Democratic primary, other Democrats were somewhat reluctant to squarely attack Jesse Jackson, the only African-American candidate, for fear of being labeled racist. However, this caution also led to their being less public debate about Jackson's platform. If a candidate is not attacked by opponents, the perception is of a less-than-serious campaign. In fact, if a candidate is far ahead in the polls, he or she usually refrains from attacking the opponent, because an attack only tends to legitimatize that opponent.

The Need to Be Taken Seriously

For lesser-known candidates, the most difficult aspect of the campaign is convincing the media to take them seriously. If the public and the media do not perceive someone as having a realistic chance of winning, the public acceptance or rejection of that candidate's stand on issues or themselves as persons is largely irrelevant. Although polls showed that large numbers of Americans favored the positions of moderate Independent candidate John Anderson in the 1980 presidential race, less than 10% eventually voted for him, largely because they felt that he had no chance of winning. In 1992, early summer polls showed Ross Perot's support substantial enough to conceive of his winning the presidency. However, his support gradually waned by November, although he still acquired a larger share of the vote (around 20%) than any other third-party candidate in modern times. When he ran again in 1996, he failed to do as well. Because no one besides a Republican or Democrat has been elected President in the United States since 1848, people perceive such an eventuality as highly unlikely, a social perception that can quickly become a self-fulfilling prophecy.

CASE STUDY: PRESS COVERAGE OF THE 2000 U.S. PRESIDENTIAL CAMPAIGN AND ELECTION

The historic 2000 Presidential election on November 7 was perhaps the closest race in U.S. history. Republican George W. Bush and Democrat Al Gore were virtually tied in both electoral and popular votes the morning after the election. For the next 36 days, the outcome was uncertain as the controversy swirled around the count in the state of Florida. The election was only finally declared decided on December 12, after a close decision by the U.S. Supreme Court that favored the claims of George Bush. After this decision, Al Gore conceded; but it probably will never be definitively established which candidate actually won Florida, where the popular vote was within one hundredth of one percent, with the winner receiving the entire electoral vote. The role of the press in covering this election and the post-election process was carefully examined in an illuminating book by Jamieson and Waldman (2003).

Election Night Coverage

Premature Overconfident Projections. On election evening, the networks early projected Florida first for Gore and later reversed themselves and called it for Bush. Around 10:15 they retracted both and placed the state (and thus the whole election) back into the undecided category. Several smaller states were also very close and undecided until well into the next day or days. At 2:20 a.m. the networks called the election for Bush but retracted this call at 3:50 a.m. When networks made projections that turned out to be accurate (as most were), they tended to take credit for their skill. However, when they had to retract their projections, as they did repeatedly with the Florida presidential returns, they tended to blame "bad data," even though all networks were drawing on basically the same data, from the Voter News Service (VNS).

As the election results became increasingly uncertain as more returns came in, which is the opposite of the usual trend, reporters and pundits struggled in their interpretation. There was numerous discussion about "egg on their faces" and "eating crow," as well as extended discussions of possible scenarios ("if Gore wins these three states, he could still lose Florida and win . . ."). Some of this discussion was accompanied by the startlingly low-tech graphics of network analysts and anchors drawing scribbles on paper with a crayon and holding them up to the camera!

Framing the Electoral Uncertainty

Jamieson and Waldman (2003) argue that, during the next five weeks, the prevailing frame for discussing the outcome of the election gradually came to increasingly favor Bush over Gore, although the objective data coming in over that time did not necessarily do so. The three possible frames, each drawing on true information, would be that (1) Gore had won the popular vote and was ahead in the electoral vote, and the final outcome in the Electoral College was uncertain, (2) Bush was ahead in the key state that would decide the final electoral vote and thus was the presumed victor unless Gore's campaign proved otherwise, or (3) Neither candidate was ahead nor held an advantage over the other. In the news coverage over the next five weeks (especially the critical Sunday morning network news shows), the bias favoring the second frame with Bush's victory did not immediately emerge after Election Night but rather did so gradually, as Bush's campaign people managed the media more effectively than Gore's people. See Wicks (2001) for discussion of the idea of framing of news events.

First of all, Republicans began to frame the post-election hand recount as flawed and unfair. The Bush camp framed the initial machine count, which showed him ahead by a few hundred votes out of several million cast, as legitimate and the subsequent statewide hand recount as suspect and unreliable. The latter was always referred to as a "recount" rather than with such terms as "full count," "complete count," or "hand count." Attempts to force a recount were described as attempts to "overturn the results." Also, the Bush campaign talked openly of challenging Gore's winning results in other close states like New Mexico, Oregon, Wisconsin, and Iowa, but Gore's camp did not aggressively do so.

Perhaps the most telling reframing came in the decisions about the legitimacy of the overseas absentee ballots, which came in late and had to be counted by hand. Gore attempted to have those strictly evaluated, with those not meeting specified criteria (such as containing a postmark no later than Election Day) thrown out, while the Bush campaign framed those ballots as "military ballots" (which only some of them were) and questioned the patriotism of those trying to "disenfranchise" the voting of our "brave men and women defending our country." Both sides insisted on strict adherence to the law only when it favored their candidate. In the case of the absentee ballots, whose legitimacy was decided very idiosyncratically in each county, the Bush frame of casting Gore's adherence to the law as an attack on the patriotism of the military came to be adopted by the news networks, who came to see Gore's moves as illegitimate and as a desperate attempt to overturn the election results favoring Bush. Thus, 680 questionable votes were accepted and counted, even though some had no postmark, or a postmark after Election Day, and in some cases were from people who had already voted. These may well have determined the election, where Bush's final certification of victory was only a 537 vote margin.

The frame of Bush as the apparent winner and Gore as the stubborn loser became the prevailing network news frame by late November. Frequent photo shots of Bush supporters holding "Sore Loserman" signs parodying the Democratic "Gore Lieberman" placards supported this frame. When Bush starting naming people to his cabinet but Gore did not, this perception of the inevitability of a Bush victory was only further reinforced. Implications of "stealing the election" were raised for Bush only three times in the five weeks of Sunday news shows but were mentioned 12 times in connection with Gore. Also, 20 out of 23 times the word "concession" appeared in a question over these weeks; it was applied to Gore.

The contest was finally ended 36 days after the election when the U.S. Supreme Court ruled to halt the further counting of votes, arguing that the petitioner Bush would be "irreparably harmed" by continuing the count and "casting a cloud upon what he claims to be the legitimacy of his election" (Jamieson & Waldman, 2003, p. 127). The vote was 7–2 that there were constitutional problems with the state-court-mandated recount and 5–4 to halt the count and declare Bush the victor. Two of the original seven majority had thought there were possible ways to correct the problems with the recount; a bare majority of five believed there were not. After the ruling in Bush vs. Gore, Al Gore promptly conceded the election.

Once Bush had been declared the victor and especially after he assumed office on January 20, 2001, the press seemed eager to assert his legitimacy and downplay a consideration of the possibility that the wrong man may have assumed the Presidency. In fact, there were two media recounts in 2001 of the Florida votes, designed to answer the question for the historical record. The first, by the *Miami Herald, USA Today*, and Knight-Ridder, produced eight sets of results, depending on the standard used to judge acceptability of ballots; five of these favored Bush and three favored Gore. The second, more comprehensive, recount was conducted by the Associated Press, the *New York Times, Washington Post*, and the *Wall Street Journal*. This count produced 44 separate results, 22 favoring Bush and 22 favoring Gore! Because these were not available until shortly after the terrorist attacks of September 11, 2001, their release was not trumpeted with much fanfare to a press and country too traumatized from terrorism to consider it might have made a mistake at the last Presidential inauguration. The fact remains, though, that we will never definitively know which candidate actually received more votes in Florida and thus actually "won" the election.

Now that we have considered the use of news for one's political advantage, let us now consider the most direct form of political media, namely political advertising. Although political advertising has much in common with advertising in general (see chapter 4), there are also some important differences (Thorson, Christ, & Caywood, 1991).

POLITICAL ADVERTISING

One of the major political issues of our time is the rapidly escalating costs required to run for office, in large part due to the increased purchase of television time and hiring of media consultants. In the 1996 U.S. Presidential election, incumbent Bill Clinton spent $98.4 million on television advertising, while opponent Robert Dole spent $78.2 million! (Devlin, 1997). In the 2000 election, candidates spent almost two billion dollars on TV advertising, almost two-thirds of the total campaign finance dollars (Steyer, 2002). Although the arguments of the campaign finance reform debate are outside the scope of this book, we want to examine the purposes and effects of political advertising, whose aim is to affect the perceived reality of that candidate in our minds.

Purposes

Name Recognition. What are the purposes of political advertising? A primary one for lesser-known candidates and those campaigning outside of their previous constituency (e.g., a senator or governor running for president) is simply awareness and recognition of their name. Voters must have heard of a candidate before they can be expected to have any image of or attitude about that candidate. Name recognition is the perennial problem of "dark horse" challenger candidates for any office. In this sense, the goal of political advertising is not unlike the goal for advertising a new product on the market.

Agenda Setting. Political advertising also sets the agenda on issues by conveying to us what issues we should feel are particularly important (Schleuder, McCombs, & Wanta, 1991). Obviously a candidate will try to highlight those issues where he or she is strongest. For example, an incumbent president with several foreign policy successes but economic problems at home is going to try to position foreign policy as a major issue in the campaign, whereas the opposing candidate may try to set the agenda toward domestic issues. Sometimes such decisions are not so clear-cut. For example, Democrats in 1980 had to decide whether to make age an issue in regard to Republican Ronald Reagan, who would be the oldest president ever elected. On the one hand, they stood to gain if voters became concerned that 69 was too old to begin the job. On the other hand, they stood to lose if voters perceived them to be too mean spirited and unfairly attacking a nice older gentleman fully capable of competently functioning in office. For better or worse, Democrats chose not to make age an issue, a strategy adhered to in 1984 against a then 73-year-old Reagan. For the same reason, 50-year-old Bill Clinton did not make challenger Bob Dole's 72 years an issue in 1996.

Schleuder et al. (1991) argued for a spreading activation memory model (e.g., Collins & Loftus, 1975) of agenda setting. For example, if a person is primed by exposure to a prior story about the economy, associations from that initial concept will travel in one's memory to activate related information on that topic to a more conscious level than other information.

Thus, the agenda is set that this issue is important when it comes to processing later information such as a political ad. In this model, either a prior ad or a news story could serve a priming function and set the agenda for interpreting a subsequent ad. Thus, a candidate must be concerned about an ad appearing immediately following a news story that inadvertently sets a different agenda. For example, a candidate weak on economic issues would not want his or her ad to follow a news story about gloomy economic indicators.

Image Building. Political advertising also seeks to convey an image of a candidate, or perhaps reinforce, soften, or redefine an existing image. This construction of an image is done especially effectively by television, which communicates nonverbal as well as verbal behaviors. One effective way to communicate an image is through eliciting emotional responses in the viewer (Englis, 1994). The widespread use of media consultants testifies to the importance of image. Polls are taken by a candidate's campaign staff to determine what issues voters are concerned about and what aspects of their own and the opponent's campaigns attract or trouble them. Then the candidate's image is tailored accordingly.

Some studies of candidate image have focused on general affective traits or personality or social attributes and compared the image a voter has with actual voting behavior (Anderson & Kibler, 1978; Nimmo & Savage, 1976). More situational approaches have demonstrated a relationship between voters' ratings of candidate behaviors and voting preference (Husson, Stephen, Harrison, & Fehr, 1988). Another approach has been to study how voters use their cognitive schemas (see Chapter 2) to form an image of a candidate, which subsequently affects their evaluation (Garramone, Steele, & Pinkleton, 1991). Lau (1986) argued that there are four general schemas that people use to process political information: candidate personality factors, issues, group relations, and party identification. Many voters fairly consistently use one of these schemas more than the others.

There are limits, of course, to what a media campaign can do; an urban candidate may never look comfortable and convincing astride a horse making a political ad for the rural West. Also, one cannot assume that all voters will understand an ad in the same way. The image that different members of the public construct in response to the same ads may be strikingly different because of their unique experiences and political predilections. What one viewer sees as a sincere interest in common people looks to another as incredible hokeyness and opportunism.

Issue Exposition. Occasionally, ads develop a candidate's position on issues. Such ads are most conducive to print media, particularly direct mail ads, but there is the high probability that a large majority of voters will not read such material. Of course, due to the mass nature of media communication, even a minuscule percentage of the population reading a newspaper ad might be considered a success for the candidate. If the appeal is simple, even a TV spot can effectively communicate a candidate's position, perhaps even more successfully than a televised debate (Just, Crigler, & Wallach, 1990).

Fund Raising. Finally, ads may be used to raise money. Ross Perot included toll-free phone numbers for contributions in his advertising during his 1992 and 1996 third-party campaigns for the U.S. Presidency. Such ads, which are a major expense, may also directly attract money to meet those expenses. Of course, they also do so indirectly by keeping the candidate's name in the public consciousness, a prerequisite for any successful fundraising.

Appeals in Political Advertising

Political ads use most of the same types of appeals' as discussed in chapter 4 on advertising. Psychological appeals are very common. Basic appeals to security come out both in the "strong national defense" and "law and order" appeals. Fear appeals can be especially powerful in political advertising. For example, in George H. W. Bush's infamous "Willie Horton" ad of the 1988 presidential campaign, viewers were encouraged to fear that Democratic opponent Michael Dukakis would let dangerous criminals go free, citing the example of Massachusetts felon Willie Horton, who had been released on parole and then committed murder. The fact that Horton was an African-American subtly played to White fears about Black crime and may have reinforced racist stereotypes of African-American men. Fear appeals, in general, are most often used by incumbents, playing on voters' fear of the unknown quality of what the challenger's work in office would be like.

Patriotic appeals are of course especially common in political advertising, with certain symbols like the American flag very commonly present, even for state and local races. Certain other patriotic symbols like familiar public buildings in Washington, D.C. the Statue of Liberty, and national historical symbols are widely used.

Family and affiliation appeals are seen in the typical family campaign ad photo of a candidate with smiling supportive spouse and children, as if being married or a parent somehow qualified one to hold public office. It is interesting and ironic that an occupation virtually guaranteed to take enormous amounts of time away from family is so heavily "sold" with such family appeals. Using only pure logic, one might argue that an appeal from an unmarried, childless candidate who could say, "I have no family responsibilities; I'll spend all my time in office working for you" would be the most successful. However, such an appeal would probably be a dismal failure.

Testimonials are often used, sometimes by famous endorsers such as a senator or president plugging for the local candidate, or by the man or woman in the street saying how much they trust a candidate to look after their interests in Washington. A popular president or other office holder of one's party is eagerly sought for testimonial purposes; an unpopular one may be an embarrassing liability for their party's candidates for other offices.

Negative Advertising

The issue of how stridently and directly to attack the opponent in advertising is a major question that all political campaigns must deal with. Attacks on the opposition may be highly effective *if* they are perceived as fair. Regardless of their factual merit, or lack of it, if they are perceived as mean-spirited "cheap shots," they can disastrously boomerang against the candidate (Garramone, 1984, 1985; Merritt, 1984). Fear of such a scenario sends shivers up the spines of all politicians and often causes them to not take chances in this area, as seen in the Democrats' decision not to make Ronald Reagan's or Bob Dole's age issues.

It is not clear how much negative advertising has increased. By some counts (Kaid & Johnston, 1991), negative advertising increased in the 1980s over the 1970s to about one third of the TV ads in the presidential campaigns. Others, such as the Campaign Discourse Mapping Project (Jamieson & Waldman, 1997), conclude that attack ads have been roughly constant in percentage since 1960. Others argue that the outrage at negative advertising that was common in an earlier era has become much more muted since about 1988, as voters apparently have accepted some degree of mudslinging and even falsifying the opponent's record as normal (Jamieson, 1992). Still others argue that it is not even conceptually clear what a negative political ad is (Richardson, 2001).

Attacks may be strong without being direct or even mentioning the opponent by name. For example, in 1964 incumbent President Lyndon Johnson ran a TV ad (shortly afterward withdrawn due to complaints) showing a little girl in a field of daisies. Suddenly an atomic bomb explodes and we hear Johnson's voiceover: "These are the stakes: to make a world in which all God's children can live, or go into the dark" (Devlin, 1987). Republican candidate Barry Goldwater was never mentioned, but the ad clearly played on viewers' fears of his hawkishness.

Does negative advertising work? The answer seems to be yes and no. Research suggests that negative ads are remembered well, even if they are not necessarily well-liked (Faber, 1992; Garramone, 1984; Garramone, Atkin, Pinkleton, & Cole, 1990; Johnson-Cartee & Copeland, 1991). For example, in a study of responses to TV commercials used in the 1988 Bush-Dukakis presidential campaign, Newhagen and Reeves (1991) found that people judged negative ads more unfavorably than positive ads, yet they remembered them better. Such a finding is quite consistent with the widespread negative attitudes about negative political advertising and the perception that such ads apparently work (Kaid & Boydston, 1987). Negative emotional ads are remembered better than positive emotional ads, perhaps due to their greater use of automatic, as opposed to controlled, cognitive processing (Lang, 1991, 2000) and peripheral rather than central processing (Petty, et al., 2002). There is also evidence that negative ads engender cynical attitudes (Schenk-Hamlin, Procter, & Rumsey, 2000). It may also be important whether the negative message is embedded in a positive or negative context. Messages that contrast with their context are recalled better (Basil, Schooler, & Reeves, 1991).

Whether negative ads affect voting behavior is less clear (Faber, 1992). It may matter what the source of the negative message is, whether the focus is issue- or person-oriented, what point in the campaign they are used, and what sort of response is made to the negative attack. In a study of effects of ads in the 1996 Presidential general election campaign, Kaid (1997) concluded that negative ads did affect the voters' image of the candidate in intended ways, and that this in turn affected voting behavior. In a study of a U.S. Senate race, Lemert, Wanta, and Lee (1999) found that attack ads by a Republican candidate, coupled by a pledge from the Democrat not to use negative advertising, led to a lower voting rate by Republicans but not Democrats. Negative ads, in the framework of comparing the two candidates directly, may be the most effective way to produce attack advertising. One study showed such comparative negative ads reduced preference for the targeted candidate without much backlash against the sponsoring candidate (Pinkleton, 1998).

Effects of Political Advertising

The effects of political ads, as well as other forms of political communication in media, can be of several sorts (Biocca, 1991; Chaffee & Choe, 1980). The study of such effects has come from the perspectives of political science, political advertising, social psychology, and communication.

In spite of the perception that the overriding intent of political ads would appear to be to cause attitude change in people, relatively few political ads actually change anyone's mind, in the sense of causing them to switch loyalties from one candidate to another (Blumler & McQuail, 1969; Comstock et al., 1978; Cwalina, Falkowski, & Kaid, 2000). This is not to say that they are ineffective, however. They frequently help crystallize exist-ing attitudes by sharpening and elaborating them. For example, perhaps someone was slightly leaning toward Al Gore for president in 2000 because of his leadership as vice-president under Bill Clinton. Political advertising for Gore may help 'flesh out' that attitude, by providing more informa-tion about his positions, past performance in office, and general intangible impressions about the candidate. In a related vein, political advertising may reinforce existing attitudes in voters to 'keep in the fold' a voter who is leaning toward a candidate but not strongly committed. Such an atti-tude that is reinforced is more likely to translate into voting on Election Day and greater resistance to an opposing candidate's attempts to change that attitude. Political strategists are always concerned about reinforcing "soft" support from voters who are leaning toward their candidate but not strongly committed. Many ads are targeted at such people.

Sometimes political advertising may actually convert a voter from one candidate to the other, but this is quite rare and did not increase sub-stantially with the advent of television (Boiney & Paletz, 1991; Comstock et al., 1978; Lazarsfeld, Berelson, & Gaudet, 1948; Berelson, Lazarsfeld, & McPhee, 1954, for pre-TV studies). Of course, because many elections are decided by a tiny fraction of the vote, such swing votes are not unim-portant.

Reactions to political advertising may depend on the bond that the voter feels with the candidate (Alwitt, Deighton, & Grimm, 1991). Such an atti-tudinal bond may be based on an objective belief ("I like his program for the economy") or a subjective emotion ("I feel good about him") criterion. Sometimes the two may be opposed, as in the case where there is objective bonding in terms of agreement with the candidate's positions on issues but passionate opposition on more emotional levels. Also, an image-oriented ad may have a different impact than an issue-oriented ad. For example, Geiger and Reeves (1991) found that candidates were evaluated more fa-vorably after issue ads than image ads, but visual memory for the candi-date was better following an image ad. See Faber (1992), Jamieson (1992), Johnson-Cartee and Copeland (1997), and Kaid and Holtz-Bacha (1995) for reviews of political advertising and its effects.

TELEVISION AS CULTIVATOR OF POLITICAL MODERATION

Before leaving the topic of politics and media, let us examine the ar-gument of one group of researchers who believe that television, in a very general sense, shapes our political attitudes and perceived reality about politics in some subtle ways. Using cultivation theory, Gerbner,

---

BOX 8.5
TELEVISION AND IDEOLOGY: BRAZILIAN CASE STUDY

Does television serve to indoctrinate or perpetuate political and social ideologies? The answer is a complex one with no easily generalizable answer. A
case study of the Brazilian "telenovela" (soap opera) is an instructive example. In developing countries television is typically controlled largely by the
economic elites, often with close political ties to right-wing ideologies. This
was true in military-ruled Brazil in the 1970s, when the huge Globo communications network thrived and rose to become the world's fourth largest
TV network of the time, after the big three in the United States. Globo came
to be acclaimed for its high-quality programming, which was exported to
dozens of countries around the world. The most popular shows, both do-
mestically and for export, were the telenovelas, which typically aired for an
hour 6 nights a week for a period of several months. Somewhat like a very
long mini-series, they had a fixed ending, after which they were replaced by
another novela.

During the 1980s, however, the content of some of the novelas came to
reflect some politically left themes. For example, *Isaura the Slave* was set in
colonial Brazil and strongly condemned racism and slavery. *Malu, Woman*
showed the struggles of a divorced woman and had a strong feminist message. *Roque Santeiro* told of a small town controlled by political bosses who
stopped at nothing to maintain power. *Wheel of Fire* told of a business executive who repented of past corruption. It featured characters who were
torturers, rulers, and guerrillas during the years of military rule (1964–1985).
Formerly shunning television as a tool of the capitalist elites, leftist artists
like *Roque Santeiro's* author Dias Gomes, a self-described Marxist, later realized the potential of television, particularly through a large and powerful
corporation like TV Globo, to reach far more people than theater, films, or
print media could ever hope to. At the same time, Globo's corporate executives began realizing the immense profitability of television programs that
deal with some of these progressive themes (Bacchetta, 1987).

In the years since, Globo has continued to dominate Brazilian TV, selling
80% of the nation's television ad time in the seventh largest advertising
market in the world (Amaral & Guimarães, 1994). In addition, its programs
are exported worldwide and many of the nation's newspapers are part of its
communications empire.

Gross, Morgan, and Signorielli (1982, 1984, 1986) examined the relationship
between television viewing in general and political attitudes. Using data
gathered for several years in the late 1970s and early 1980s by the National
Opinion Research Center in their General Social Surveys (NORC/GSS),
Gerbner et al. (1984) looked at the correlation of the amount of TV viewing

(and other media use) and political self-designation on a liberal-moderate-conservative dimension.

Frequent TV viewers were most likely to label themselves as moderate politically, whereas frequent newspaper readers labeled themselves conservative and heavy radio listeners labeled themselves liberal. This relationship was quite consistent within various demographic subgroups, especially so for the conservatives and the moderates. Among light viewers, there was consistently greater difference of opinion between liberals and conservatives on several different specific issues than there was between the liberal and conservative heavy viewers. Gerbner et al. (1982, 1984, 1986, 2002) argued that television, with its mass market appeal, avoids extreme positions that might offend people and thus by default it cultivates middle-of-the-road perspectives.

Nor is this cultivation limited to North American culture, although the specific effects may differ in different places. Morgan and Shanahan (1991, 1995) found that Argentine adolescents who were heavy TV viewers were more likely to agree that people should submit to authority, approve of limits on freedom of speech, and believe that poor people are to blame for their own poverty. In a country having recently come through a repressive military dictatorship, it appears that television "cultivates views that provide legitimacy to authoritarian political practices" (Morgan & Shanahan, 1991, p. 101). See also Morgan (1989, 1990) for other applications of cultivation theory to international settings. For an interesting comparison of the 1988 presidential elections in France and the United States, see the readings in Kaid, Gerstle, and Sanders (1991). For a comparison of effects of political advertising in France, Germany, and Poland, see Cwalina, et al. (2000).

Television may interact with political ideology in other ways to subtly support or undercut existing structures in a society. The social and commercial realities of television may sometimes produce politically strange bedfellows. see Box 8.5 for an interesting example.

CONCLUSION

Our perceived reality of the political world is largely a product of the media. The role of the media, especially television, in politics will continue to be hotly debated. The loudest critics will decry how TV has corrupted the democratic process and reduced political discourse to banal superficialities. Its defenders will point to the technical marvels and improved dissemination of information that technology has allowed us to use in the political process. For example, the Internet has come to have a role in political campaigns (Selnow, 1997).

BOX 8.6
**WATCHING *THE WEST WING* MAKES PEOPLE LIKE THEIR
REAL PRESIDENTS BETTER**

It is not only political news and political advertising that affect our political
attitudes and help construct our political reality. A clever study by Holbert,
Pillion, Tschida, Armfield, Kinder, Cherry, and Daulton (2003) showed that
entertainment may also prime political attitudes. The show they chose was
NBC's drama *The West Wing*, set in the White House of a sympathetic fictional President played by Martin Sheen. Using a pretest-posttest design,
they found that Missouri students who watched an episode of *The West
Wing* in February 2002 afterward showed an increase in perception of positive character traits of both sitting President George W. Bush and former
President Bill Clinton. Apparently watching and thinking about a positive
example of a President, even a fictional one, helped cause one to see the real
Presidents more positively.

There is a consistent historical trend of people being the most critical of
the newest medium or newest uses of old media. "If one goes back through
the history of press criticism, a distinct pattern emerges: the most modern
medium is always regarded as the most issueless, the most frivolous—first
in print, then daily press, then radio, then television . . . newest medium
attracts the loudest complaints" (Robinson & Sheehan, 1983, cited in Kraus,
1988, p. 88). In recent years there have been loud criticisms of candidates'
using talk-show TV formats in campaigning. We may expect even louder
outcry about the political use of the Internet that has begun to take hold in
recent years (Jacques & Ratzan, 1997; Whillock, 1997).

What is certain, however, is that media do create a political world that
is the basis of most of our perceived political knowledge and subsequent
political behavior, such as voting. That role is not likely to change, so it behooves us to understand it better. "With these technological advances, both
the sending and receiving of political information changed. Our thinking
about political events changed. What constituted political reality for us was
not the influence of a political event alone but the interpretation (often, the
alteration) of the event by the mass media, especially television" (Kraus,
1988, p. 8). Even entertainment media may affect political attitudes, see
Box 8.6. The almost-tied 2000 U.S. Presidential election, whose true outcome will never be known, reminds us of the potentially very high stakes
of constructing that political reality in a responsible fashion.

CHAPTER **9**

Violence: Watching All That Mayhem Really Matters

Q: What is the overall conclusion from the research about the effects of watching media violence?

A: Of the 3,500 research studies conducted since 1950 studying the effects of watching media violence, all but 18 (i.e., 99.5%) show negative effects of violent entertainment. (Grossman & deGaetano, 2001).

Q: How many murders has the average child seen on TV by the time he or she finishes elementary school?

A: Eight thousand, plus 100,000 other acts of violence (Huston et al., 1992). If they happened to have seen the film *Die Hard 2*, they saw 264 murders in that movie alone!

Q: How many hours per week do eighth graders spend playing video games?

A: Boys spend 4.2 hours and girls 2 hours, mostly at home (Funk, 1993a).

Although specific figures depend on our precise operational definition, the reality of media, especially television and film in the United States, Japan, India, and elsewhere, is a highly violent world. Around 60% of American TV programs and 90% of the movies on TV contain some sort of violence (National Television Violence Study, 1997). On U.S. television, there are 14 violent acts per hour on children's programming (Strasburger & Wilson, 2002), and children's programming overall has the most violence, much of which is trivialized, glamorized, and sanitized (Wilson, Smith, Potter, Kunkel, Linz, Colvin, & Donnerstein, 2002). Considerable violence even occurs in programming we do not immediately associate with aggression, such as news, music videos, and even commercials aimed at children. Also, the large majority of video games (85%) are violent (Funk, 1993b; Provenzo, 1991).

How about the retort that media violence only reflects an imperfect world that is very violent? Yes, there is violence in the real world but much less than what is in the media. According to FBI statistics, about 87% of real crimes are nonviolent, but only 13% of crimes on reality-based TV entertainment are. For murder, the contrast is even stronger; only 0.2% of crimes reported to the FBI are murders, whereas 50% of the crimes on TV are murders (Bushman & Anderson, 2001; Oliver, 1994). We have already seen in chapter 7 how the sensationalist news reporting of unusual but grisly crimes leads to people hugely overestimating their occurrence in reality (Best, 1999; Glassner, 1999).

Consistent with the definition of most researchers, violence is defined here as behavior causing intentional physical harm to another individual. Excluded from this definition are accidental injury, vandalism of property, and various behaviors sometimes called "psychological" or "verbal" aggression, including emotional abuse and the "alternative aggressions" often used by girls to intimidate other girls by threatening to withdraw relationships (Simmons, 2002). These issues are all very important and deserve serious study in regard to media images. However, they have not received much study as yet, whereas the presentation of physical violence has been the subject of intense research scrutiny for the last half century. Although the term is not always used precisely, *aggression* is the internal motivation behind the *violent* behavior. Acts of violence may be observed directly; the motive of aggression must be inferred from those acts.

Violence on television has long been a contentious political issue, and there has probably been more psychological research on the topic of violence than on all other topics in this book put together, by one estimate between three and four thousand studies (Grossman & deGaetano, 2001; Huston, et al., 1992). This chapter makes no claim to comprehensively review all of that literature; thorough reviews and discussions in varying detail are available elsewhere (e.g., Donnerstein & Smith, 1997; Dubow & Miller, 1996; Geen, 1994; Huston, et al., 1992; Murray, 1999; National Television Violence Study, 1997; Paik & Comstock, 1994; Smith & Donnerstein, 1998; Sparks & Sparks, 2002; Wood, Wong, & Chachere, 1991). This research has been conducted particularly within the social learning and cultivation frameworks, although other perspectives have also been useful. Often the discussion of the scientific issues has been clouded and colored by the economic or philosophical perspectives of those involved, and much of the popular writing on the topic has taken the form of either (a) polemical and unfounded media bashing, or (b) a defensive *apologia* to support one's economic self-interest, in either case often ignoring the large body of research that is reality available. In either type of argument, crucial distinctions among diverse types and contexts of violence and among different populations are often lacking.

In considering the effects of media violence on society, we must not make the mistake of imagining media to be the only factor, or even the major factor, which contributes to violence in society. Negative social conditions like poverty, racism, crowding, drugs, parental neglect, availability of weapons, and the underclass subculture doubtlessly contribute far more than television. Negative family and/or peer role models also have substantial effects. Even if media violence is responsible for only 5% to 15% of societal violence, as estimated by some researchers (Sparks & Sparks, 2002; Strasburger, 1995), that is still important. Because of the nature of mass communication, even a very small effect of media can be substantial in terms of numbers. For example, suppose a violent movie could be shown to cause .001% of the viewers to act more violently. Although the percentage may be minuscule, .001% of an audience of 20 million is still 200 people!

We approach the study of media violence in this chapter by looking at the various effects of the violent view of the world presented in media. This study of the perceived reality of media violence focuses on the psychological processes involved and the weight of the evidence supporting the existence of those effects. Later in the chapter we look at individual differences among those who are attracted to or repelled by media violence and longitudinal studies probing for long-term effects. Next we look at one of the newest areas of concern, violent video games. Finally, we address the question of what may be done to provide balance to this violent perceived reality and thus mitigate the negative effects of media violence.

EFFECTS OF MEDIA VIOLENCE

Most of the public concern and scientific study of the perceived violent reality of media centers around the effects of viewing televised violence. The effect that many think of first is modeling, when people imitate violent behavior that they see on television. However, this is only one of several effects. The research on the different effects has been driven by diverse theoretical frameworks (see chapter 2); for example, studies of behavioral effects have most often been driven by social learning/cognitive theory, and studies of attitudinal effects often draw on oncultivation theory. The following section examines several different effects of media violence in turn and the evidence supporting each of them. We begin with what is perhaps the most immediate effect of viewing violence: Watching violence induces fear.

Fear

Much of the research on fear responses to violent media comes from the laboratory of Joanne Cantor (1996, 1998a, 2002), who concludes that "transitory fright responses are quite typical, that enduring and intense emotional disturbances occur in a substantial proportion of children and adolescents, and that severe and debilitating reactions affect a small minority of particularly susceptible individuals of all ages" (Cantor, 1996, p. 91). Overall, there is a correlation between the hours of television viewed and the prevalence of symptoms of psychological trauma like anxiety, depression, and posttraumatic stress (Singer, Slovak, Frierson, & York, 1998).

Fear-Inducing Images.   Different categories of stimuli and events differentially produce fear responses in viewers of different ages. Distortions of natural forms (e.g., monsters and mutants) are very scary to preschoolers but typically less so to older children. Depictions of dangers and injuries (e.g., attacks, natural disasters) are more scary to upper elementary school children than to preschoolers, in part because the older children are cognitively able to anticipate danger and its possible consequences and thus be fearful *before* the actual event occurs. The older the child, the more able he or she is to think abstractly and be frightened by seeing situations of endangerment to others. Sometimes two siblings viewing together may be afraid of very different aspects of a movie, or one, not necessarily the younger, may be afraid while their sibling is not. For example, consider two brothers watching a movie about a benevolent alien visiting from outer space. The preschooler may be afraid of the fantastic form of the alien, while the older child may be afraid during the scenes where he recognizes that the friendly alien or sympathetic humans may be in potential danger from others. Alternatively, the younger child may not be afraid at all—in fact, he may love the cute little alien—and may not be able to think abstractly enough to understand why his brother is afraid of the potential endangerment.

Responses to Fear.   Cantor and Oliver (1996; see also Cantor, 1998a, 2002) identify some principles to predict fear responses in children. First, the older the child, the more that a character's behavior, relative to appearance, is important in predicting fear responses, although all children will be more fearful of an ugly than an attractive character. Second, as children grow older, they become more responsive to realistic dangers and less responsive to fantasy dangers in the media. Third, and closely related, the older the child, the more able he or she is to be afraid of increasingly abstract dangers. In fact, very young children tend not to be very afraid of abstract threats. For example, fear responses to a 1980s movie about nuclear war in the heartland of the United States found young children to be the least afraid and adults the most afraid (Scholfield & Pavelchak, 1985), with the number of parental reports of their children discussing the movie with them increasing with the age of the child (Cantor, Wilson, & Hoffner, 1986).

When they are afraid of watching something scary, preschoolers tend to cope by using non-cognitive strategies like eating, drinking, covering their eyes, or clutching an object. School-age children tend to use and respond well to cognitive strategies like verbal explanations, reminders of the unreality of the situation, or instructions to think about the danger in a new, less threatening way, provided that the explanation is at an appropriate level. It is, however, quite difficult to totally reason away a strong media-induced fear in a young child.

Several studies (Cantor & Oliver, 1996; Harrison & Cantor, 1999; Hoekstra, Harris, & Helmick, 1999) found that practically all young adults were able to readily remember an incident of being extremely scared by a movie as a child or teen. At least the memories, and perhaps some of the effects as well, are long lasting. Some effects reported are general fear/anxiety, specific fears (e.g., fear of swimming after seeing *Jaws*), sleep disturbances, and nightmares. See Box 9.1 for some actual memories reported by Cantor's participants.

Sometimes self-report may not be a completely adequate measure of induced fear. For example, Sparks, Pellechia, and Irvine (1999) found that certain "repressor" personality types reported low levels of negative affect in response to watching a 25-minute segment from the horror film *When a Stranger Calls* but high levels of physiological arousal, as measured by skin

---

BOX 9.1
MEMORIES OF BEING SCARED BY MOVIES SEEN
AS A CHILD

Joanne Cantor, in her research on the inducement of fear by violent media, has interviewed and tested hundreds of young adults about their memories of being scared by a movie seen in childhood. Here are two actual accounts of these experiences, from Cantor (1998b, pp. 9–10).

> "After the movie [*Jaws*], I had nightmares for a week straight. Always the same one. I'm in a room filled with water with ducts in the walls. They would suddenly open and dozens of sharks would swim out. I felt trapped with no place to go. I would usually wake up in a sweat. Occasionally I'll still have the exact same dream. The movie didn't just affect me at night. To this day I'm afraid to go to the ocean, sometimes even a lake. I'm afraid that there will be a shark even if I know deep down that's impossible."
>
> "I watched [*Friday the Thirteenth, Part 2*] when I was 14 years old and it scared me so much that I couldn't sleep for a whole month. I was scared of the name Jason and I hated standing under a thatched roof. At night I needed a night light so I could see everything around me. I was very conscious of the smallest little noise, I had nightmares about knives, chainsaws, blood, screams, and hockey masks. I was very jumpy. This kind of slaughter film still has these effects on me."

conductance. In a similar vein, Peck (1999, as cited in Cantor, 2002) found that in general women's verbal reports of fear in response to watching scary scenes from *A Nightmare on Elm Street* were more intense than men's, but in some cases men's physiological responses were more intense than women's, if the victim in the scene was male. Thus, it is possible that in some circumstances some people either cannot or do not accurately report their fear experienced, and we cannot assume that self-reports of fear are completely adequate.

Brain Correlates.   Some exciting recent work with brain imaging suggests that our brains respond differently to violent and nonviolent stimuli (Liotti, Murray, & Ingmundson, in press; Murray, 2001). Children ages 8–13 watched 18-minute violent (boxing segment from *Rocky IV*) or nonviolent (National Geographic documentary or *Ghostwriter* children's literacy TV program) video segments while functional magnetic resonance imaging (fMRI) mapped their brain activity. Although both videos activated certain brain regions involved in visual and auditory processing, only the violent film activated parts of the amygdala and right cerebral cortex involved with arousal, threat detection, and unconscious emotional memory. This suggests a brain basis of the fear response from violent video and suggests that areas such as the right hemisphere and amygdala, known to be involved with other kinds of affective responding, are also active while watching violent media. Such emotional memories often endure long after the associated cognitive memories have faded, thus explaining why someone might be afraid of swimming in the ocean years after seeing *Jaws*.

Clearly, violent media do induce fear in viewers, and what type of image induces the most fear varies greatly depending on the age and cognitive developmental level of the child or adult. However, any expression of fear by a child should be taken seriously by the parent or caretaker, not ignored and never belittled. Even if the danger is very unreal or even silly to an adult, the fear is very real, and that is what the child must deal with. See Cantor (1998b) for an excellent guide for parents on this subject.

Modeling

Research on modeling comes primarily out of social learning (social cognitive) theory (Bandura, 1977, 2002), which applies principles of learning to social situations. See Tan (1986) for details on the application of social learning theory to media violence and Bandura (2002) for a recent theoretical formulation.

How Modeling Works.   In this view, people see a violent act in the media and later, as a result, behave more violently themselves than they otherwise would. For this to happen, first the relevant behavior of the model must be *attended to*. Second, it must be *retained,* somehow encoded into memory in some form, as it is being analyzed and interpreted through cognitive processing. Whether the learned behavior is later actually *produced* by the viewer will depend on many factors, such as motivation and the strength of prevailing inhibiting factors.

The process of modeling may actually teach new behaviors, much as one might learn a new athletic skill by watching a teacher demonstrate it. When a teenager opens fire on his classmates a few days after seeing a film with a similar scene in it, he may not have known or thought to behave that way before seeing the film. This would appear to be a particularly grisly example of the common phenomenon called *observational learning*. A well-documented example is the notorious New Bedford gang rape case of the mid-1980s, where several men raped a woman on a pool table in a bar (later the basis of the movie *The Accused*). The rapists had recently seen a movie with a barroom gang rape scene in a nearby theater. See Box 9.2 for the story of some especially tragic cases where legal charges were filed against media for teaching violent behaviors.

More often, however, it is not the specific behavior itself that is learned from the media. A second process by which modeling can work is where watching media violence produces *disinhibition*, that is, it reduces the normal inhibitions most people have against performing violent behavior. For example, watching a movie with scenes of street fighting might produce disinhibition by weakening a viewer's usual proscriptions on fighting. The viewer already knows how to fight, and the medium cannot be blamed for teaching that behavior. However, TV may be breaking down the normal inhibitions that we would otherwise have against engaging in violence. Thus, actual violent behavior may occur in the future with less provocation than would have been necessary to evoke it prior to the disinhibition.

Disinhibition may also occur through the teaching of more accepting attitudes toward violent behavior. Although most people are raised with the general belief that violent behavior is bad (specific circumstances where it might be acceptable may vary), exposure to repeated media violence may break down these normal attitudinal inhibitions against thinking violence is acceptable. This change toward a more accepting attitude about the appropriateness of using violence to settle disputes may subsequently and indirectly lead to violent behavior, although such a causal connection is very difficult to empirically demonstrate unequivocally.

Most of the concern with modeling effects of TV violence assumes that persons may become violent in their own behavior in a somewhat different way than the media model; that is, the effect generalizes beyond the specific behavior demonstrated in the media. For example, watching a war movie may disinhibit violent behavior generally, and a viewer may subsequently

BOX 9.2
ARE MEDIA CRIMINALLY LIABLE FOR EFFECTS
OF VIOLENT CONTENT?

From time to time, lawyers defending perpetrators of violent crimes who appear to have been affected by television have used rather creative defenses, which inevitably come up against First Amendment freedom-of-speech issues. Consider the following: Ronald Zamora, 15, killed his 82-year-old neighbor in a robbery attempt after she discovered Zamora and threatened to call the police. What was particularly unusual was that the defense attorney argued for temporary insanity at the time of the crime, arguing that Zamora was "suffering from and acted under the influence of prolonged, intense, involuntary, subliminal television intoxication" (Liebert & Sprafkin, 1988, p. 127). He further argued that the shooting was a TV-learned conditioned response to the stimulus of the victim's threatening to call the police. Television was thus an accessory to the crime. In the end, however, the jury failed to accept this reasoning, and Zamora was convicted on all counts and sentenced to life.

A second case involved 9-year-old Olivia Niemi, who was assaulted and raped with a bottle by three older girls and a boy. Four days before, a TV movie, *Born Innocent*, had been aired, showing a scene of a girl being raped with a plumber's plunger. Olivia's mother then sued NBC for $11 million for alleged negligence in showing the movie in prime time. Her lawyer argued for vicarious liability and claimed that the movie had incited the children to criminal activity. After a series of appeals and countersuits, the case was finally thrown out when a judge ruled that the plaintiff had to prove that the network had intended its viewers to imitate the violent sexual acts depicted. However, when NBC aired *Born Innocent* as a rerun, it aired at 11:30 p.m. and with most of the critical rape scene edited out (Liebert & Sprafkin, 1988).

Such cases are not unique to television. The magazine *Soldier of Fortune* ran the following classified ad:

> FOR HIRE: U.S. Marine and Vietnam veterans. Weapons specialists with jungle expertise for high-risk assignments in the United States or overseas. Call___.

Texan Robert Black hired a former marine through this ad, with the assignment of murdering his wife. Her surviving family brought suit against the magazine for negligence and was awarded $9.4 million in damages in a federal court case (Brockhoff, 1988). The legal basis of the judgment was that the magazine should have known that its offer included illegal acts such as murder. How much responsibility does a publisher or broadcaster have to anticipate such consequences of its messages?

punch or kick another person but not necessarily start shooting with an AK-47 exactly as happened in the movie. This generalized type of modeling is far more common than the modeling of a very specific behavior.

Sometimes the nature or timing of the response can be taught through media. For example, Grossman (1996, 1998) argued that violent TV and movies, and especially violent video games, train children to shoot without thinking at the appearance of certain stimulus. The normative behavior in many video games is to shoot as soon as some target appears, with the fastest reaction the most optimal. Thus, the child playing video games, Grossman argues, is learning to shoot first and ask questions later. Does this learned shooting behavior transfer to other situations? Grossman (1998) cited one of the boys charged in the 1998 Jonesboro, Arkansas schoolyard shootings who had little if any experience shooting real guns but a lot of experience playing video games. He and his buddy were good enough shots to hit 15 people with 27 shots from a distance of 100 yards! Research on video games is discussed later in the chapter.

There are other, even more indirect ways in which modeling may occur. Violence may alter the general affective (emotional) responsiveness of the viewer, which could in turn lead to violent behavior. It may also raise the overall arousal level, which could prime the person for (among other behaviors) violence. Now let us turn to some of the research done to test the modeling hypothesis and to identify the conditions under which modeling occurs.

Basic Social Learning and Field Research. The best-known early research studying modeling of media violence was social psychologist Albert Bandura's Bobo doll studies (Bandura, 1965; Bandura, Ross, & Ross, 1963; see also Hicks, 1965). In a typical Bobo doll study testing modeling, Bandura had young children watch someone else behave aggressively toward a large plastic inflatable doll. The child's own behavior with the Bobo doll was subsequently observed. Studies of this type consistently demonstrated that children imitated violent behavior previously observed in a live model. Most important for our purposes, the same effect was found when the aggressive model was on film rather than live (Bandura, et al., 1961; Nelson, Gelfand, & Hartmann, 1969; Rosencrans & Hartup, 1967; Walters & Willows, 1968).

Many laboratory studies have replicated these effects over the years and have demonstrated generalization to other behaviors. For example, participants who had seen a series of violent films were more likely to respond negatively to a research assistant in an "unrelated" study who had written insulting comments on a questionnaire they had completed (Zillmann & Weaver, 1999).

264   9. VIOLENCE

Although these experimental studies were important, they were not without criticism. Primarily, they were attacked for being too artificial and of questionable generalizability to the real world. However, later research moving away from the laboratory also found corroborative evidence for modeling (Huesmann, Lagerspetz, & Eron, 1984; Joy, Kimball, & Zabrack, 1986; Lefkowitz, Eron, Walder, & Huesmann, 1977; Leyens, Camino, Parke, & Berkowitz, 1975; Parke, Berkowitz, Leyens, West, & Sebastian, 1977). The rates of violent crimes rose in societies following the introduction of television with its steady diet of violence. For example, although the homicide rate for White Americans and Canadians rose 93% and 92% respectively between 1945 and 1974, it declined by 7% in the same period for White South Africans, living in comparable economic conditions, except for the lack of television, which was not introduced in South Africa until 1975 (Centerwall, 1989a, 1989b, 1992, 1993; Joy, Kimball, & Zabrack, 1986). After the introduction of TV, the homicide rate rose there as well. Centerwall rules out other explanations like economics, age, firearm availability, and civil unrest as causing these changes. Thus, there is evidence that modeling media violence is not purely an artificial laboratory phenomenon.

Sensitization

Sensitization is a sort of reverse modeling effect, whereby viewers react so strongly to seeing some violence and have such a traumatized perceived reality that they are actually *less* likely to imitate it as a result. This is most likely to occur with very extreme violence and might be the reaction, for example, of someone who has never seen anything stronger than a G-rated Disney movie to seeing a graphically violent R-rated film. The behavioral tendency away from violence might arise from either the arousal of anxiety about the violence and/or the arousal of empathy for the victim of the violence. For example, Tamborini, Stiff, and Heidel (1990) used physiological and questionnaire measures to conclude that people who most dislike watching graphic violence (i.e., those who are most sensitized) are those who score high in the empathy dimensions of wandering imagination, fictional involvement, humanistic orientation, and emotional contagion. That is, these people can more easily imagine themselves in the position of the victim of the violence and vicariously experience the negative emotions that person would feel. Someone who cannot easily do this would also be aroused but would be more likely to enjoy the violence, because the negative emotions would not be so strongly felt.

It is likely that the strongest sensitization effects could come from very graphic violence that is clearly understood as real (i.e., the news). Sometimes producers face a difficult decision as to whether to air an extremely violent scene from a news story (see Box 9.3 for some especially compelling

BOX 9.3
EXTREMELY VIOLENT NEWS IMAGES

Sometimes television networks or stations or print media are faced with a difficult decision about whether to air a graphically violent news photograph. One of the most agonizing decisions came in July 2003 after the deaths of deposed Iraqi dictator Saddam Hussein's sons Oday and Qusay in an assault by the U.S military on a fortified house in Mosul, Iraq. At this point, Iraq was occupied by U.S. and U.K. forces but Saddam was apparently still alive and in hiding. The two sons were notoriously hated and feared for perpetrating crimes of incredible cruelty. Although the United States generally had a policy of not releasing photographs of people killed in military action, it decided that at least the Iraqi public needed concrete evidence that the hated brothers were really dead. Thus the gruesome photos of the dead brothers were published.

Sometimes cameras happen to capture an unintended gruesome image. Local media photographers covering a routine 1987 news conference by Pennsylvania Treasurer C. Budd Dwyer captured the unexpected image of Dwyer putting a pistol in his mouth and pulling the trigger, killing himself instantly. Network news, TV stations, and newspapers then faced the decision of whether to run the grisly sequence. Most TV stations chose not to air the tape or did so only to the point of Dwyer placing the gun in his mouth. A few TV stations and newspapers carried pictures of what happened after that, saying it was "an important historical event" and should be covered. In a 1993 case, a Florida woman being interviewed by a television crew in a park in broad daylight was suddenly accosted and shot several times by her estranged husband. Although the unexpected murder photos later provided important legal evidence, networks were faced with the decision of whether or not to air the footage on the news. Many (including CNN) did so.

The public has a right to know, but how much does the public have a need or right to know *and see explicitly?* The answer is obviously an ethical and policy question, although one study suggested a positive effect of learning at least some gory details. College students who read a newspaper report of a wife-battering incident rated it more seriously and rated the batterer more negatively if the victim's injuries were described in detail, compared to a situation in which they were not explicitly described (Pierce & Harris, 1993). These descriptions, however, were much less graphic than the pictorial images described above.

examples). Once in a while they may be unable to block the image, such as if it comes in the form of a political ad, which may not legally be censored. Although product and political advertisers generally are loathe to offend, once in a great while a political candidate may desire to. In the fall 1992 U.S. election campaigns, several anti-abortion candidates for Congress and

---

BOX 9.4
HOLLYWOOD GOES TO VIETNAM

The 1966 pro-military film *The Green Berets* starred John Wayne in a stylized epic with good guys and bad guys. By 2 or 3 years later, such a simplistic approach to Vietnam rang very shallow and false. A very few years after *The Green Berets,* sentiment in the United States had turned completely around, and whatever glory there had ever been to the Vietnam War had rapidly disappeared. The 1974 Oscar-winning documentary *Hearts and Minds,* by Peter Davis, was very graphic and carried such a strong antiwar message that some newspapers refused to publish reviews of the film. Although the last U.S. troops left Vietnam in 1973 and Saigon fell in 1975, there were practically no commercially successful film images of Vietnam before 1978, when *The Deer Hunter* and *Coming Home* picked up seven Oscars between them. Both of these (along with *Apocalypse Now* in 1979) carried a strong antiwar message and reflected the country's disgust with the war in Vietnam, a wound that had just started to heal.

That healing was not complete in 1986, when Oliver Stone's graphic and realistic *Platoon* and Sylvester Stallone's live-action comic book *Rambo: First Blood Part II* appeared. Both were huge successes, but *Platoon* was the greater commercial gamble, having taken years to acquire the necessary funding. The Pentagon refused to help the producers, although it enthusiastically aided the makers of the heroic *Top Gun,* on the grounds that it wanted to ensure a realistic portrayal of the military! Widely hailed as a critical success (including winning the Best Picture Oscar), *Platoon* astounded everyone with its huge commercial success as well. It was then followed by a spate of realistic Vietnam films like *Gardens of Stone, Casualties of War, The Hanoi Hilton,* and *Full Metal Jacket,* none of which received close to *Platoon's* critical or commercial success.

By 1988, the wounds of Vietnam had healed enough to allow the production and modest commercial success of the first Vietnam War TV series (*Tour of Duty*) and big-screen comedy *Good Morning, Vietnam.* A comedy about Vietnam would have been unthinkable much before that time. Not too long later followed another Oliver Stone antiwar film, *Born on the Fourth of July,* the biographical story of gung-ho soldier turned antiwar protester Ron Kovic.

---

other offices chose to air photos of what they said was an aborted fetus. Their explicit goal was to offend viewers, or rather to show them how offensive abortion really is. Such tactics are risky, however, because viewers might be even more offended by their decision to use such an image.

Although sensitization effects are hard to study scientifically for ethical reasons, general sensitization effects are probably not too widespread and do not occur nearly as often as their opposite, desensitization (see below). In general, situations for which one can posit sensitization effects can often be interpreted equally plausibly in terms of desensitization. For example, people have argued that daily news broadcasts of the Vietnam War sensitized us to the horrors of war and eroded public support for that conflict, in contrast to previous wars. On the other hand, others have argued that the same news broadcasts desensitized us to war, and thus we now are not as bothered by seeing images of other conflicts (see chapter 7). See Box 9.4 for a history of the treatment of the Vietnam War in films.

Desensitization

Although public debate about the effects of TV violence typically worries primarily about increases in violent behavior, there may be far more pervasive attitudinal effects, especially in the area of desensitization. The basic principle here is that viewing a steady diet of violence in the media makes us less sensitive to it, more jaded, and less aroused and bothered by it. We become so used to seeing people wasted, blown apart, or impaled that it no longer particularly troubles us. For example, after seeing a violent TV show, sixth graders were less sensitive to violent images in a subsequent film than were children who had seen a nonviolent film first (Rabinovitch, McLean, Markham, & Talbott, 1972). Desensitization is typically measured experimentally through physiological and/or attitudinal measures.

How Desensitization Works. Desensitization may be seen as a straightforward example of classical conditioning (see Fig. 9.1). The normal,

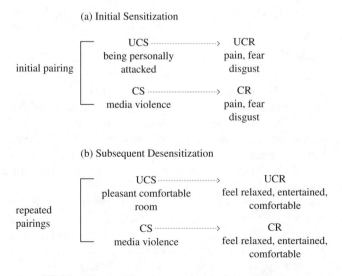

FIG. 9.1. Desensitization as classical conditioning.

unlearned responses to being physically hurt include pain, fear, and disgust. The first time one sees media violence, it probably evokes such negative emotional responses, due to its similarity to real violence (Fig. 9.1a). Such a single occurrence may actually produce sensitization as discussed above.

What happens with repeated viewing of violence in comfortable surroundings is quite different, however (Fig. 9.1b). Suppose, for example, that the normal, unlearned response to sitting at home in one's easy chair is feeling relaxed and happy. When this is repeatedly paired with violence on TV and movies, vicarious violence in a pleasant home context gradually becomes associated with that situation and itself comes to be seen as entertaining, pleasant, and even relaxing. The natural association of filmed violence and real-life violence has been weakened as the new association of video violence with recreation is strengthened. We repeatedly see violence without experiencing pain or hurt ourselves and thus the normal negative responses to it weaken. Given what we know about classical conditioning in psychology, it is unlikely that such frequent and repeated exposure to stimuli could *fail* to have a substantial effect. In the adolescent subculture, part of the male gender-role socialization has been for a boy to desensitize himself so that he can watch graphic violence and not appear to be bothered by it (Harris, et al., 2000; Mundorf, Weaver, & Zillmann, 1989; Tamborini, 1991; Zillmann & Weaver, 1996; Zillmann, et al., 1986). Demonstrating desensitization to violence thus becomes a way to impress a date.

Consequences of Desensitization. What are the implications of people becoming desensitized to violence from the media? Becoming jaded to news of war and violence will cause such stories not to bother us so much anymore. Even if we never come to actually like violence or behave violently ourselves, we may not dislike it nearly so much; it does not seem all that serious. This has important implications for behavior. For example, Drabman and Thomas (1974, 1976) had 8- to 10-year-old children watch a violent or nonviolent film and later watch younger children at play. When the younger children started to get rough, the older children who had watched the nonviolent film called an adult sooner than did the older children who had watched the violent film, thus showing some generalization of the desensitization effect.

One of the major areas of concern with desensitization has to do with tolerance of violence toward women. Male college students who viewed a series of slasher horror movies later showed less empathy and concern for victims of rape (Linz, Donnerstein, & Penrod, 1984). Sexual violence is one of the major current concerns among media researchers studying violence; we examine this aspect of violence in some detail in chapter 10.

Cultivation

Another type of attitudinal effect in regard to violence is cultivation. As discussed in chapter 2, George Gerbner and his colleagues argue that the more exposure a person has to television, the more that person's perception of social realities will match what is presented on TV (Gerbner, Gross, Morgan, Signorielli, & Shanahan, 2002; Signorielli & Morgan, 1990; Weaver & Wakshlag, 1986). In fact, cultivation theory was first developed in regard to studying media violence. In contrast to modeling, cultivation attributes a more active role to the viewer, who is interacting with the medium, not being passively manipulated by it. Nevertheless, there is a coming together of the viewer's outlook and that of the medium, whereby the person's perceived reality gradually approaches that of the TV world.

Cultivation theory is best known for its research on the cultivation of attitudes related to violence (Gerbner, Gross, Morgan, & Signorielli, 1980; Gerbner, Gross, Signorielli, & Morgan, 1986). Such studies show that frequent viewers believe the world to be a more dangerous and crime-ridden place than infrequent viewers believe it to be. The world of TV shows 50% of characters involved in violence each week, compared to less than 1% of the population per year in real life. This cultivation effect could be due either to TV teaching that this is what the world is like or to the fact that more fearful people are drawn to watching more TV. If it is the former, and cultivation theorists believe it is, TV can induce a general mindset about the position of violence in the world, completely aside from any effects it might have in teaching violent behavior. Finally, cultivation theory speaks of television teaching the role of the victim. From watching a heavy diet of crime and action-adventure shows, viewers learn what it is like to be a victim of violence, and this role becomes very real to them, even if it is completely outside of their own experience.

The effects of media violence just discussed are not presented as an exhaustive list but rather as general classes into which most proposed effects fall. Occasionally an effect falls outside of those classes, however; see Box 9.5 for some interesting evidence of violent media causing amnesia in viewers.

Important Interactive Factors

Now that we have looked at the major effects of watching media violence, it is time to examine the major moderating variables that affect how much the violent behavior will be modeled or the attitudinal effects of desensitization, cultivation, or fear will be induced. Consistent with the conditional effects model based on individual differences discussed in chapter 2, a violent model does not affect everyone the same way under all circumstances.

BOX 9.5
DO VIOLENT IMAGES CAUSE AMNESIA?

Amnesia is not on the typical lists of effects of media violence, but just such an effect has been proposed (Christianson & Loftus, 1987; Loftus & Burns, 1982; Newhagen & Reeves, 1992). It has been known for some time that a physical injury to the brain can result in a loss of memory for events immediately preceding the impact. For example, the shock of one's head flying against the headrest in an auto collision may lead to amnesia for events immediately preceding the impact. It is as if the brain had not yet had time to transfer the event from short-term to long-term memory. Loftus and Burns (1982) demonstrated that such an effect may also occur solely from the mental shock of seeing graphic violence on the screen. Research participants saw a 2-minute film of a bank robbery, in either a violent or nonviolent version. In the violent version the fleeing robbers shot their pursuers and hit a young boy in the street in the face, after which he fell, clutching his bloody face. The nonviolent version was identical up to the point of the shooting, at which point the camera cut to the interior of the bank. Measured using both recall and recognition measures, people seeing the nonviolent version of the film remembered the number on the boy's t-shirt better than those seeing the violent film, although the shirt was shown the same amount of time in both. A second study ruled out the possibility that the effect could have been due to the unexpectedness or surprisingness of the shooting.

Numerous important variables heighten or attenuate effects like modeling or desensitization. Violent media do not affect everyone in all circumstances in the same way.

Model Attributes.   First, several *characteristics of the violent model* are important. People are more likely to imitate or be disinhibited by viewing the violent behavior of an attractive, respected, prestigious model than by one who does not have such qualities. Also, the more deeply we identify and empathize with a model, the more likely we are to imitate that person (Huesmann, Lagerspetz, & Eron, 1984; Huesmann, Moise-Titus, Podolski, & Eron, 2003). These points suggest that violence by the characters we admire and identify with is a stronger influence than violence by the bad guys. This has important ramifications for assessing effects of action-adventure and police shows.

Reinforcement of Violence.   Whether or not the violence is *reinforced* in the plot is also a very important moderating variable. One of the central principles of operant conditioning, and indeed of all psychology, reinforcement refers to any event that follows a response and increases the probability of that response occurring again. The connection (contingency) between the response and the reinforcement is learned; thus the response is made in anticipation of receiving the reinforcement. A dog learns to fetch a stick because he is reinforced with a dog biscuit when he performs the act. A girl does her homework each night because she is reinforced by being allowed to watch TV after she is finished. After learning has occurred, responses continue to be made for some period of time without the reinforcement, until they gradually diminish and are finally extinguished altogether.

If acting violently appears to pay off for the violent character (in money, power, relationship, etc.), it is thus reinforced in the context of the story. Research suggests that reinforced violence is more likely to desensitize or be modeled than nonreinforced or punished violence (e.g., Bandura, 1965). Krcmar and Cooke (2001) found that 4- to 7-year-olds thought unpunished violence in a video clip was more right than punished violence. In a typical TV story line, violence by the hero is more likely to be rewarded (reinforced) than is the violence of the villain, although the latter may have been reinforced for much of the show. Model characteristics and reinforcement suggest that a particularly troubling type of violent perpetrator is the child or teen. Content analyses show that, compared to adult models, child violent models in media are more attractive and less likely to be punished or experience other negative consequences of the violence (Wilson, Colvin, & Smith, 2002); both of these characteristics make modeling by the viewer and other effects more likely.

Finally, media, rather than reinforcing behavior or tendencies to behave in certain ways, may reinforce certain values about the use of violence. For example, characters on action-adventure TV shows and movies frequently use violence to settle interpersonal disputes. As such, they are subtly reinforcing the value that violent behavior is a realistic and morally acceptable manner of dealing with conflict, a value that may become part of the viewer's perceived reality. Children seeing a fantasy movie clip ending in violence later rated a different story with violence as more morally correct than children seeing the same clip but without the violence (Krcmar & Curtis, 2003). When sportscasters legitimatize sports violence as necessary or regrettably acceptable in the context in which it occurred, or when an athlete receives only a slap on the wrist for assaulting another player, such treatment reinforces violence as a way of dealing with the stresses of the game.

Perceived Reality. Another important moderating factor is whether the violence is seen as real or make-believe, that is, the degree of perceived reality (van der Voort, 1986). There is some evidence of stronger effects of violence that is perceived as real than of violence that is perceived as unreal. Although children's cartoons are by far the most violent genre of TV show, the violence is also the most stylized and unrealistic. Some studies (e.g., Feshbach, 1976) show cartoon violence to have less negative effect than more realistic violence.

In understanding the perceived reality of violent television, it is important to consider the child's cognitive understanding of television at any given time (e.g., Cantor, 1998b, 2002; Cantor & Sparks, 1984; Gunter, 1985; Sparks, 1986). A very young child might think that a violent death on a police drama actually shows someone dying, rather than merely an actor pretending to die. Children who believe such staged violence to be real are often more disturbed by it than those who understand the convention of acting. The greater the perceived realism of media violence, the more likely that aggressive behavior will increase (Huesmann, et al., 2003). Continuing this line of reasoning, the most difficult forms of TV violence for children to deal with are probably news and documentaries, because violence on these programs is real and not staged. Beyond the issue of perceived realism, the whole area of how the viewer interprets the violence is very important; such variables often account for more of the variance than stimulus factors manipulated by the experimenter (Potter & Tomasello, 2003).

Personality Characteristics of the Viewer.   Research has also generally found larger modeling and other effects in people more naturally inclined toward violence in terms of personality (Heller & Polsky, 1975; Parke, et al., 1977), although this result has not been found consistently (e.g., see Huesmann, Eron, Lefkowitz, & Walder, 1984). Violence in the media may reinforce dispositional violent tendencies already present in the viewer, although it is not the *cause* of those tendencies. The more that such tendencies are reinforced, the more likely they are to manifest themselves in behavior. Regrettably, the lack of uniform effect on viewers has often been used to argue that there is no substantial impact of media violence. As suggested previously, however, a modeling effect on even a tiny percentage of the population may be cause for serious concern. The fact that people less naturally inclined toward violence do not respond as strongly as those more inclined toward violence is not an argument that media violence has no effect!

Another important factor in moderating the effects of media violence perceived by the viewer may be the thoughts that one has in response to viewing media violence (Berkowitz, 1984). Those thoughts may focus on the suffering of the victim, the triumph of the violent person, the relation of the violence to one's own experience, and so on. Depending on the nature of these thoughts, their mediating role in facilitating violent behavior may vary substantially. For example, someone who is overwhelmed by the suffering of the victim is probably less likely to behave violently than one who identifies strongly with a heroic and attractive James Bond (McCauley, 1998). See Dorr and Kovaric (1980), Tamborini (1991), and Goldstein (1998) for discussions of individual differences in reactions to TV violence.

Arousal. Next, the variable of *arousal level* of the viewer is important. A person who is already physiologically aroused for whatever reason is more likely to engage in violence after seeing a violent media model than is a nonaroused person (Tannenbaum, 1971, 1980). The arousal may come from the film itself, given that violent films tend to be emotionally arousing and exciting, or it may come from some prior and unrelated source, such as the manipulation in some experiments that makes one group of participants angry before exposing them to a violent media model (e.g., Berkowitz, 1965; Hartmann, 1969; Zillmann, 1978). See Zillmann (1991a) for a review and discussion of the media and arousal issue. This issue of the interaction of arousal and a violent model becomes important when considering sexual violence, which is examined in chapter 10.

Age and Gender. In terms of *age* and *gender*, modeling effects typically increase up to about ages 8 to 12 and slowly decrease thereafter. After this age, children have developed their own viewing set and are better able to separate video experience from reality. Although boys consistently both watch more violent TV and are themselves more violent than girls, there is no clear evidence of a stronger modeling effect as such on either boys or girls, at least not before about age 10 (Hearold, 1986).

Context of Violence. One contextual variable that has not yet been studied very extensively is the embedding of graphic violence in a humorous context. For example, violent characters can utter humorous wisecracks, a laugh track can accompany violent scenes, and acts of violence can be presented with humorous consequences. Sometimes technical or editing devices can serve to reinforce violence in such a context. For example, when the hero in the film *Natural Born Killers* drowned his girlfriend's father in a fish tank and killed her mother by tying her to a bed, dousing her in gasoline and burning her alive, a background laugh track encouraged us to see this brutality as humorously entertaining, reinforcing positive responses within the viewer. One empirical study of the effects of viewing wisecracking heroes and villains in a violent action film (*The Hitman*) found a different pattern of results in men and women (King, 2000). The presence of humor in the hero increased distress in women but not in men, while their reactions to a subsequent nonfiction film showed the reverse effect. There are also a high number of acts of violence on comedy shows, especially in scenes of farce (Potter & Warren, 1998).

This embedding of violence in comedy is a specific instance of the broader situation of violent behavior being reinforced by virtue of its occurrence in a context that is overall very reinforcing. For example, because viewers may choose to identify more with the glamorous opulence of *Beverly Hills 90210* than the gritty seediness of *NYPD Blue*, violence on the former show may have a greater effect, even if the actual violence is less in quantity or graphic specificity. However, this effect may be mitigated by the fact that the more realistic shows may have a greater impact than the less realistic ones due to their greater relationship to the viewers' own experience. Thus, we see that many factors are at work in determining modeling effects.

We turn now to a final apparent psychological effect of violence: catharsis.

Catharsis

The notion of catharsis extends all the way back to Aristotle's *Poetics*, where he spoke of drama purging the emotions of the audience. In modern times, however, the notion was developed largely in psychoanalytic theory. According to Freud, the id, ego, and superego are locked in battle, with anxiety resulting from id impulses trying to express themselves and, in so doing, coming into conflict with the moralistic superego. The threatening unconscious impulses like sex and aggression are repressed from consciousness but may cause anxiety when they creep back. These repressed impulses and the anxiety that they produce may be dealt with directly by overt sexual or violent behavior or indirectly through some sublimated substitute activity, such as watching others act sexually or violently on television.

The emotional release called *catharsis* comes from venting the impulse (i.e., expressing it directly or indirectly). This emotional purging has been a notoriously difficult concept to operationally define and test, but it has continued to have a lot of intuitive appeal and anecdotal support (e.g., people report feeling better after watching a scary movie). Catharsis theory does, however, make one very clear prediction about the effect of TV violence on behavior, a prediction that is eminently testable and exactly opposite to the prediction of modeling theory. Whereas modeling predicts an *increase* in violent behavior after watching media violence, catharsis theory predicts a *decrease* in such behavior (S. Feshbach, 1955). If the substitute behavior of watching the violence provides the emotional release that would normally result from someone actually acting violently, then violent behavior should decrease after watching media violence. Thus, the two models are clearly and competitively testable. When such tests have been done, modeling theory has been supported (e.g., Siegel, 1956), whereas catharsis theory seldom has. In spite of consistent failures to be supported by scientific evidence over many years (Bushman, Baumeister, & Stack, 1999; Geen & Quanty, 1977; Zillmann, 1978), catharsis continues to occupy a prominent but undeserved place in the conventional wisdom about the effects of media violence.

Later refinements of catharsis theory were proposed (S. Feshbach & Singer, 1971). It may be that the media violence elicits fantasizing by the viewer, and that fantasizing, rather than the media violence per se, is what leads to catharsis. Another version of catharsis theory argues that watching media violence reduces one's arousal level, and thus one is less prone to violence. There is evidence that a reduction of arousal level is associated with decreased violent behavior. Third, TV violence may elicit an inhibition response, which puts a brake on tendencies toward violent behavior. This is very similar to a sensitization hypothesis. None of these explanations, however, has offered a serious challenge to the overall conclusion that viewing media violence leads to increases in violent behavior.

WHO WATCHES MEDIA VIOLENCE AND WHY?

Another approach to studying media violence has been to examine what attracts viewers to violence and why some are attracted much more than others (Fenigstein & Heyduk, 1985; Goldstein, 1998; Sparks & Sparks, 2000). What is it that is appealing about violence as entertainment? Some answers that have been suggested are its novelty, sensory delight, and the violation of social norms. It also may have some social utility, for example in allowing the display of mastery of threats or dependence on a loved one (Zillmann & Weaver, 1996).

Social Factors

In an historical sense, very violent films, especially horror films, have generally been the least popular during wartime and have shown very strong popularity during times of overall peace accompanied by high degrees of social unrest.

In terms of gender socialization in adolescents, Zillmann and Weaver (1996) developed and tested a model of the role of social motives in consuming horror films. Specifically, they argued that preadolescent and adolescent boys use horror films to develop mastery over fear and to perfect their displays of fearlessness and protective competence. Girls, on the other hand, use the same films to develop their displays of fearfulness and protective need. While girls actually enjoy the films less than boys do, both find them socially useful as they learn the still very traditional gender roles in dating, whereby the boy is the fearless protector and the girl the dependent and fearful party. The boy's expression of boredom or amusement in response to graphic violence is thus a statement of his apparent mastery over fear. This mastery then may actually mediate a feeling of pleasure. This pleasure, however, was much greater in the presence of a fearful young female companion than in the presence of a fearless female companion who expressed less dependence. Young men, compared to women, are much more desirous that their date not know how scared they felt while watching a scary movie (Harris, et al., 2000).

Individual Differences

Several researchers have examined the relationship between personality factors and preference for violent media (e.g., Haridakis, 2002). One of the most-studied trait in this regard is empathy. Although empathy is itself a multidimensional construct (M. H. Davis, et al., 1987), it is generally correlated negatively with preference for violent media, especially strongly for the cognitive components like perspective taking and fantasy empathy. Tamborini (1996) has developed a complex cognitive-motivational model of empathy as a predictor of reactions to viewing violence. Empathy may be evoked to different degrees by certain editing techniques and formal features. For example, extended close-ups of faces encourage empathic responses more than rapid-fire wide-angle camera shots. In terms of a path analysis, Raney (2002; see also Raney & Bryant, 2002) argues that the elicitation of empathy may evoke sympathy for the victim of violence, which in turn predicts lesser enjoyment of the violence.

Another personality variable studied in relation to violent media consumption is sensation seeking (Zuckerman, 1994, 1996), the "seeking of varied, novel, complex, and intense sensations and experiences, and the willingness to take physical, social, legal, and financial risks for the sake of such experience" (Zuckerman, 1996, p. 148). Sensation seeking is positively correlated with a preference for viewing violence (Krcmar & Greene, 1999), although the relationship is tempered by the degree of alienation experienced and by the fact that high sensation seekers tend to prefer real-life over vicarious experiences and thus tend to be lighter-than-average TV viewers overall (Slater, 2003).

Another individual difference variable studied is psychoticism. Men (though not women) scoring high in psychoticism found violence more acceptable to solve an interpersonal problem after seeing very violent contemporary action films like *Total Recall* and *Die Hard II*, though not after seeing "old-style" violence or horror-film violence (Zillmann & Weaver, 1997). This suggests that personality factors can interact with certain kinds of violence but not others.

LONGITUDINAL STUDIES

Although literally hundreds of studies have shown some psychological effects of media violence, most of those have been short term and in the laboratory, often using the methodology of showing participants a film and subsequently measuring their behavior or attitudes in some way. Although these findings are important, they do not directly address the long-term cumulative effects of watching hundreds of hours of violent television as recreation throughout one's childhood. There have been a few studies that have addressed this issue, most notably those by Rowell Huesmann and Leonard Eron and their colleagues.

Longitudinal studies over ten years in the United States and Finland provided the first evidence of a causal relationship between real-world viewing of TV violence through childhood and violent behavior as a child and a young adult (Eron & Huesmann, 1984; Eron, Huesmann, Lefkowitz, & Walder, 1972; Huesmann & Eron, 1986; Lefkowitz, et al., 1977; Pitkanen-Pulkkinen, 1981). Through careful design and control of other variables, Eron et al. (1972) and Lefkowitz et al. (1977) concluded that they could rule out other plausible third variables, such as dispositional violence, as being the cause of both violent TV viewing and violent behavior. Huesmann and Eron's research has shown that the amount of television watched at age 8 is one of the best predictors of criminal behavior at age 30, even after controlling for individual aggressiveness, IQ, and socioeconomic status. Those who were heavy TV viewers in preadolescence were also more likely to more severely punish their own children many years later than were those who watched less TV during the critical years of ages 8 to 12. Watching more TV in adolescence did not seem to matter.

In a 3-year longitudinal study, Huesmann, Lagerspetz, and Eron (1984) further explored the role of several intervening variables on the relationship between viewing media violence and violent behavior in U.S. and Finnish children in elementary school. The study collected a mass of data between 1977 and 1980 from the children, their parents, the children's peers, and the school. Data gathered included measures of TV viewing, attitudes, behaviors, ratings of self and others, and family demographics. A few of the highlights are presented here.

As had been found in many other studies, there was a positive correlation between violent TV viewing and peer-rated aggression, which was stronger for boys than for girls and for U.S. people than for Finns. The overall level of violent behavior was also higher in the U.S. children. One of the most striking results for both samples was the strong correlation of violent behavior and self-rated identification with the violent TV model, especially for boys. The best predictor of later violent behavior was the interactive product of violent viewing and identification with the violent character. There was no evidence that violent TV affects only those children naturally more predisposed to violent behavior or that children who fantasize more were affected any differently. Neither were there particular effects of level of parental violent behavior or parents' TV viewing on children's violence.

The most recent longitudinal research presents the strongest evidence yet that exposure to media violence from ages 6 to 10 predicts violent behavior in young men and women in early adulthood (Huesmann, et al., 2003). Following up on children first tested in 1977–1978 (Huesmann & Eron, 1986), all of the same persons who could be found (about 60% of the original sample) were tested as young adults from 1992 to 1995. Data were obtained on their adult TV violence viewing and their adult aggressive behavior, the latter obtained from self-reports, spouse/significant other reports, and archival crime and traffic-violation data. Results showed that childhood TV violence viewing was a significant predictor of adult aggressive behavior. These effects were strongest if there was strong viewer identification with the aggressive model and if the perceived realism of the violence was high. Unlike the earlier longitudinal studies, the 2003 study found these predictive effects for both men and women. The effects persisted even when the factors of socioeconomic status and intellectual ability were controlled. These results were replicated by another 17-year longitudinal study of 700 children (Johnson, Cohen, Smailes, Kasen, & Brook, 2002).

Although the evidence from longitudinal and other studies has consistently supported the existence of significant negative effects of viewing media violence, studies that look at multiple contributors to societal violence typically estimate that media account for 10% to 15% of the variance in the dependent measure (Perse, 2001; Sparks & Sparks, 2002). Some critics tend to dismiss the media component in the face of the 85% to 90% of the variance attributable to other factors. In fact, however, this 10% to 15% range is neither surprising nor is it insignificant. In any complex social behavior, there are naturally going to be multiple causes. In the case of interpersonal violence, there are numerous known strong causes such as parental teaching, poverty, drugs, gangs, absent parents, easy access to weapons, and decline in family values, all of which clearly contribute greatly to this problem. Thus, it would be surprising, indeed completely incredible, to expect media to account for half of the societal violence! Its importance is further demonstrated when we realize that media may be one of the easier causes of societal violence to change. There are also some good reasons to think the contribution of media to societal violence may be underestimated by these studies (Perse, 2001).

The clearest conclusion about the mass of research on the effects of media violence requires taking a convergent validation approach. Any study taken by itself is subject to some criticism in terms of methodology, inter-pretation, or ecological validity. When looking at the big picture, however, the weight of the evidence clearly falls on the side of violent media hav-ing several negative behavioral and attitudinal effects, especially modeling and desensitization. These effects typically are not uniform and frequently are moderated by other variables, but they do seem to be causal in nature. The "no effects" or "no clear picture yet" conclusion is simply not ten-able scientifically, although it is surprisingly the view that is increasingly presented in popular news reporting.

RESEARCH VERSUS THE PUBLIC PERCEPTION

Bushman and Anderson (2001) conducted a meta-analysis of over 200 stud-ies of the effects of media violence, collectively involving over 43,000 par-ticipants. They concluded that the evidence for negative effects of media violence is strong and its strength is increasing, especially in the post-1990 research. Overall, effects are larger for experimental ($rs = .25$) than corre-lational studies ($rs = .10–.15$), as one would naturally expect, but the trend is the same. Interestingly enough, however, during this same period when the research evidence on the negative effects of media violence was becom-ing stronger, the popular news reporting of the same research erroneously suggested that these effects were becoming weaker.

What are some possible reasons for this serious deviation from real-ity? Bushman and Anderson suggest three. One, the media industry has a considerable vested interest in denying a strong link, since they make enormous profits from selling violence. Television networks, movie stu-dios, cable channels, and sometimes print media outlets as well, are part of the same huge conglomerates with considerable pressure to maintain or increase their audience size for their advertisers. A second reason sug-gested by Bushman and Anderson is what they call a "misapplied fair-ness doctrine." One of media's strongest abiding principles is fairness—presenting all sides of an issue. This causes media to look very hard for an opposing view, e.g., pro- vs. con-opinions on the negative effects of media violence. The resulting presentation of both sides of this issue leaves the reader/viewer with the mistaken impression that research opinion is more or less evenly divided on the issue. This scrupulous attempt to be fair ends up obscuring the fact that, although there are two sides of opinion on the issue (violent media do or do not cause violent behavior), the overwhelm-ing majority of scientific opinion comes down on the negative effects side. Finally, Bushman and Anderson argue that the research community has often failed to advocate its position with strength and clarity. Researchers by training are very cautious and conservative about overgeneralizing the effects of their research, and most have no training and little or no experience in talking to the press.

VIOLENT VIDEO GAMES

One of the newest forms of media violence, video games, is causing great concern among both scholars and parents, especially since the discovery that certain celebrated teen killers like the Columbine High assassins of 1999 were apparently obsessed with very violent video games. Unlike TV, movies, or print violence, video games are interactive and allow the viewers to *participate* in the violence as aggressors themselves (Grodal, 2000). Video games are particularly popular with college students, with about 70% reporting playing them at least "once in awhile." Although men and women play video games equally often, in terms of uses and gratifications, men are more likely to play for fun (45%) and women because they're bored (33%). Gaming is more social for men, with 51% of men but only 34% of women believing that gaming improves their friendships, contrary to the alienated social misfit image sometimes associated with video games. Interestingly, more women than men (60% vs. 40%) reported playing computer and online games like Diamond Mine and Tetris, perhaps in part because they don't require the player to choose a character (Weaver, 2003b).

Probably the major concern with video games is the high level of violence. For example, Grand Theft Auto 3 allows you to commit carjacking and murder police officers as you drive through a virtual criminal playground of Liberty City. You can pick up a prostitute and take her to a dark alley. She takes your money (as the car rocks excitedly) but you can get it back by killing her. In Postal 2, you become a paranoid psychopath and kill hostile people, with no penalty for shooting innocent bystanders. Once someone is wounded, you can stand above them while they beg for mercy and then shoot them (Crockett, 2002). Night Trap features vampires who attack scantily dressed young women and drill them through the neck with a power tool. Splatterhouse 3 features a man wearing a hockey mask who uses meat cleavers and knives to attack flesh-eating monsters (Strasburger, 1995). Quake II features a machine that consumes humans and spits them out in bits and pieces. A French video game by BMG Interactive called on players to become public enemy number 1 by stealing, murdering, and drug trafficking. Paris' largest police union called for the game to be banned (Hamilton, 1998). In Carmageddon, one tries to knock down and kill innocent pedestrians. In Duke Nukem, the shooter shoots posters of scantily-clad women and then moves to murdering female prostitutes, who are often naked and tied to columns pleading "Kill me, kill me." In Outlaw Golf, players build their skill by punching their caddies in the stomach and smashing car windows. Players of Manhunt stalk gang members trying to kill them before they kill you.

Media violence research and its theories have guided the more recent research on the effects of playing violent video games. Following predictions from social learning/cognitive theory (Bandura, 2002), game players learn shooting behaviors from playing the video game and imitating violent characters in the game. Children behave more aggressively after playing a violent video game than a nonviolent one (Anderson & Morrow, 1995; Bartholomew & Anderson, 2002; Bushman & Anderson, 2002; Kirsch, 1998; Lightdale & Prentice, 1994). Playing violent video games also raises the overall arousal level, thus raising physiological indicators like heart rate and priming the person to behave violently with relatively less provocation than would otherwise be the case (Anderson & Dill, 2000; Ballard & Wiest, 1996; Fleming & Rickwood, 2001; Panee & Ballard, 2002). Playing violent video games can also engender hostile expectations, leading one to expect that others will respond aggressively (Bushman & Anderson, 2002).

Sherry (2001) and Anderson and Bushman (2001) independently conducted meta-analyses of 25–35 studies conducted between 1975–2000 on the effects of violent video game play on violent behavior. Results showed a consistent effect of playing violent video games leading to more violent behavior, stronger for fantasy and realistic-violence games than for sports games. Violent video games also increase physiological arousal and aggressive affect and cognitions. Interestingly, Sherry (2001) found that the effects became less the longer the games were played, unlike findings from TV violence research exposure. See Griffiths (1999) and Bensley and Van Eenwyk (2001) for reviews of the literature on the effect of playing violent video games on violent behavior.

The type of video game of perhaps the greatest concern does not yet have too much empirical research as to its effects, but the need for this is great. These are the first-person shooter games, located in arcades, where the player controls interactive guns that they have to learn to hold, aim, and fire at a moving target. In House of the Dead, players fire at zombies and monsters that attack. In Time Crisis 3, the game has a kickback function to simulate the feel of a real weapon. The player also has a foot pedal that can control when the character takes cover to reload or steps out and shoots. In Play Station's Operation Desert Storm, the player shoots Iraqi soldiers. Home video systems are increasingly able to add features to approach the arcade game level of realism. For example, some games have a built-in vibrating system called a rumble pack, which vibrates the controller whenever a bullet is fired. The expectation is only for these games to become more violent and more realistic with improvements in technology in coming years. The games will be more easily customizable, where one can scan in photos of one's school, neighborhood, or "enemies." Even back

BOX 9.6
WHO SHOOTS BETTER, SOLDIERS OR VIDEO GAMERS?

In studying historical battles, military psychologist David Grossman (1996) discovered that there was often more posturing than killing. For example, 90% of the muskets picked up from dead and dying soldiers at the Battle of Gettysburg in 1863 were loaded, over half of them with multiple loads. This was surprising, considering that it took 19 times as long to load a musket as to fire one. Such findings suggest that there was a lot of loading and posturing by basically decent young soldiers who could not bring themselves to actually fire their weapons. A later study (during World War II) asked soldiers what they did in battle and found that only 15% to 20% could bring themselves to fire at an exposed enemy soldier. Once the military discovered this, they set out to improve this record through training involving classical and operant conditioning, desensitization, and a heavy dose of brutalization. Their results worked. In the Korean War, 55% of the soldiers were willing to fire, and over 90% were in the Vietnam War.

Grossman (1996, 1998; Grossman & DeGaetano, 1999) argues that we are doing the same thing with video games and violent movies, except that we start much younger. Teaching people to shoot immediately in response to the sight of the enemy is not always good soldiering or good police behavior, but it is successful video game playing. Associating brutal killing with entertainment greatly lessens the distress and inhibitions we normally have about such behavior, and that is what is going on all the time with teens watching a steady diet of graphic horror movies as regular amusement. "We have raised a generation of barbarians who have learned to associate violence with pleasure, like the Romans cheering and snacking as the Christians were slaughtered in the Colosseum" (Grossman, 1998, p. 5).

in 1999, the computer of one of the Columbine High assassins contained a customized version of Doom, where the killer had scanned in photos of his school and classmates he despised so he could practice killing them.

Do first-person shooter games teach anything more than the military and police training do? See Box 9.6 for some surprising research from military psychology about how eager and effective soldiers have been in battle.

HELPING CHILDREN DEAL WITH VIOLENT MEDIA

Institutional Solutions

The V-Chip. Given the probable negative effects and influences of violent television, what can a parent do, short of prohibiting viewing altogether? Prohibition would not be totally successful, anyhow, because children see TV at friends' homes and may rent violent videos and movies. Even as the V-chip mandated by the Telecommunications Act of 1996 has become standard practice (Price, 1998), it must be programmed in each TV set to block out the violent shows, as determined by the rating. To the surprise of many, the V-chip has been little used. The reasons for this are not clear, but is probably a combination of ignorance of its presence, lack of knowledge about how to program and implement it, and a reluctance to block out a large number of programs of possible interest to the parents.

MPAA Television Ratings. First implemented in the late 1990s as a parallel to the more familiar movie rating systems, the TV ratings attempt to specify appropriate age (e.g., TV-14 not suitable for children under 14) and sometimes information as to the nature of the questionable content (sex, language, violence). These ratings continue to be the subject of criticism and refinement in attempt to make them more useful.

Parental Mediation and Media Literacy

Classroom Training. Although mitigating the effects of TV violence has not been the major thrust of the research, there have been some interesting findings that speak to this issue. Huesmann, Eron, Klein, Brice, and Fischer (1983) developed a treatment designed to change children's attitudes about violent TV. One hundred sixty-nine first- and third-graders who watched a lot of violent TV were exposed to two treatment sessions over 2 years. The first session involved showing children TV film clips and having them discuss the violence and alternative nonviolent realistic ways that the problems could have been solved. Neither the treatment session nor a control group session discussing other aspects of TV had any effect on the children's own violent behavior or on their belief about the reality of TV violence.

However, a second intervention nine months later with the same group had children develop arguments about the negative effects of TV violence, write a paragraph on the topic, and make a group video with everyone reading his or her essay. This treatment (but not the control) led to reduced violent behavior and a weaker relationship between aggression and violent TV viewing. In terms of attitudes, the treatment had a substantial effect on children's responses to two questions ("Are television shows with a lot of hitting and shooting harmless for kids?" and "How likely is it that watching a lot of television violence would make a kid meaner?"). The mitigation effect was strongest in children who identified least with the violent characters, suggesting the important role of identification with the aggressive model.

More recently, Robinson, Wilde, Navracruz, Haydel, and Varady (2001) tested a 6-month training session for third- and fourth-graders and their parents designed to reduce television, video, and video game use. Children were encouraged to watch no TV or video for ten days and stay to a one-hour-per-day regimen thereafter. Children also received lessons on various aspects of media literacy and parents were encouraged to help their children follow the schedule and to encourage the family to do likewise. Compared to a control group, the experimental group showed less peer-rated aggression and observed verbal aggression.

Systematic Desensitization.   A somewhat different approach by Wilson and Cantor and their colleagues draws on an application of classical conditioning. They used systematic desensitization techniques to reduce children's fear reactions to scary media presentations (B. J. Wilson, 1987, 1989; B. J. Wilson & Cantor, 1987; B. J. Wilson, Hoffner, & Cantor, 1987). For example, before watching a scary movie about lizards, children of ages 5 to 10 either (a) saw a live lizard, (b) saw the experimenter touch a live lizard, or (c) had no exposure to a live lizard. The group where the experimenter modeled touching the lizard led to the most reduction in negative emotional reactions and interpretations (B. J. Wilson, 1989).

The successes of Huesmann and Wilson and their colleagues in mitigating the effects of TV violence through training is encouraging if for no other reason than that it shows that this antisocial learning is subject to alteration by new learning. This is especially encouraging, because violence as a dispositional behavior trait is known to be remarkably stable over time (Huesmann, Eron, Lefkowitz, & Walder, 1984; Olweus, 1979).

Personality Development.   Another approach to mitigating negative effects of media violence is suggested by the individual differences research of Tamborini and his colleagues (Tamborini, 1991, 1996; Tamborini & Stiff, 1987; Tamborini, et al., 1990; Tamborini, Stiff, & Zillmann, 1987; see also J. Cantor, 1991, and McCauley, 1998). If certain types of personalities (e.g., highly empathic) find graphic violence distasteful and disturbing, and others (e.g., sensation seeking, Machiavellian) find it pleasantly arousing, cultivating empathic qualities in one's children and discouraging Machiavellianism and sensation-seeking presumably should help in ensuring that they will not find viewing violence to be pleasurable. Similarly, encouraging psychological identification with the victims and not the perpetrators of violence should decrease the enjoyment level of violent TV.

See Cantor and Wilson (2003) for a thorough review of strategies to reduce negative effects of media violence in children.

CONCLUSION

What, then, may we conclude from this mass of research on media violence inside and outside of the laboratory? Although no single study by itself is definitive in establishing the deleterious effect of TV violence on children, the evidence overall strongly converges on the conclusion that media violence does have harmful effects, especially on children, primarily in three areas. After exposure to media violence, there is an increase in fear, violent behavior, and desensitization (Huston, et al., 1992). The laboratory research generally has yielded stronger conclusions than the field studies, which is exactly what would be expected (e.g., Dubow & Miller, 1996; Friedrich-Cofer & Huston, 1986; Huston, et al., 1992; Strasburger, 1995; Wood, et al., 1991). The majority of the opinion clearly concludes that there is strong evidence of those three negative effects. Even in the unlikely event that the effects turn out to be somewhat more restricted than most would argue today, considerable cause for concern is still present.

Although most of the longitudinal field studies have shown a significant positive correlation between viewing televised violence and subsequent aggressive behavior, such correlations have typically been small in magnitude (e.g., Pearson r correlations between .15 and .30, accounting for 2% to 9% of the variance). The fact that this amount is small, however, should not be surprising. Social learning theory, for example, would predict such a modest effect, because television is, after all, only a small part of the matrix of influences in people's lives (Perse, 2001; Tan, 1986). It is, however, clearly one of those influences.

The effects of media violence, however, do not fall equally on all viewers. Some people are affected more than others, and some portrayals of violence and some shows have more effect than others. In proposing policy, either legislative regulation or network industry guidelines, such distinctions must be considered. All violence is not equally harmful to all people. This is the challenge to those implementing the V-chip and industry ratings.

Another issue that complicates policy-setting questions is the fact that violent themes are very widespread in media. Certainly most prevalent in entertainment TV programming and films, violence is also widespread in cartoons, news, song lyrics, and other places we do not always think about when discussing media violence (see Box 9.7).

The debate over the effects of media violence has been strident and heated and probably will continue at that level. Predictably, the networks and television industry in general have refuted the conclusions of much of the behavioral research. The negative effects of TV may not be quite as widespread and serious as suggested by the strongest critics, but neither are they anywhere nearly as benign as suggested by the apologists. We

---

BOX 9.7
OTHER MEDIA SUPPORT FOR VIOLENCE

When we talk of violence in media, we typically think of television entertainment, movies, and possibly news. However, there are many other media
messages that violence is cool, okay, or at least not too bad. Consider the
following:

1. *Music.* Popular music, especially rap and heavy metal, have many violent themes. A very popular song on the U.S. pop charts in late 1997 was
"Smack My Bitch Up" by the dance band Prodigy. A popular gangsta rap
lyric "Know the Game," from Mobb Deep, said, "Hitman for hire, who's
the next to expire/Shoot it up in black attire, hit you wit the rapid fire/The
stainless bisket will leave your brain smoking/Your whole frame broken
and clothes soaken, head blown open" (Bullard, 1998).

2. *Sports.* In a December 1997 practice, Golden State Warriors' leading
scorer Latrell Sprewell assaulted coach P. J. Carlesimo by throttling him on
the neck and, a few minutes later, yelling, "I'm going to kill you. You better
get me off this team, or that's what I'm going to do." Although this earned
him the longest NBA suspension in history (1 year) and the immediate loss
of a lucrative endorsement contract with Converse, there was still much
discussion in the press of how Carlesimo had provoked Sprewell and was
insensitive. Sprewell's suspension was later shortened, but even so, he was
punished more severely than other NBA hotheads, such as basketball superstar Charles Barkley, who earlier had spat on a fan and thrown a man
through a plate-glass window (J. Stein, 1997b). Still, many wondered what
other job would allow someone to return to work at all after assaulting the
boss and threatening to kill him.

3. *Advertising.* A Minnesota physician examined the commercials shown
during 15 baseball playoffs and World Series games in 1997. He found 104
violent commercials, 67% of them promoting movies or other TV programs.
Half of them showed guns and about one quarter showed knives (Colburn,
1997).

---

must go beyond both blaming the media for all violence and exonerating
media from having any responsibility for it.

We have not yet seriously addressed one of the types of media violence
causing the greatest concern today (i.e., sexual violence). We examine this
issue and research on the problem in detail in the next chapter after a look
at sex in the media.

CHAPTER **10**

Sex: Pornography, Innuendo, and Rape as a Turn-On

Q: How many teen girls read women's magazines?

A: Almost 86% of 12- to 15-year-old girls read *Seventeen*, while 53% read *Teen* and 50% *YM*. For 16- to 19-year-old girls, 56% read *Seventeen*, 49% *YM*, and 31% *Cosmopolitan* (Walsh-Childers, Gotthoffer, & Lepre, 2002).

Q: How many sexual references does the average U.S. child see per year?

A: Nearly 15,000 sexual references, innuendoes, and jokes per year. Only 1.1% of these deal with abstinence, birth control, pregnancy, or sexually transmitted diseases (Strasburger & Donnerstein, 1999).

Q: Although violent men are sexually aroused by viewing an explicit rape or sexual assault scene, normal heterosexual men are generally not turned on by watching a rape scene *unless what* occurs in the scene?

A: If the woman is portrayed as enjoying and being turned on by being raped, normal men are aroused by it (Malamuth, 1984; Malamuth & Check, 1983).

Some of our major sources of information about sex come from media (Sutton, Brown, Wilson, & Klein, 2002). Everything from the mildest innuendo on a network sitcom to the most explicit pornographic video can contribute to our perceived reality of what sex is all about and what people expect from it. According to a 1998 Time/CNN poll (Stodghill, 1998), 29% of U.S. teens identified television as their principal source of information about sex, up from 11% in 1986. Somewhat more (45%) mentioned friends as the major source, but only 7% cited parents and 3% cited sex education. Another study found 29% of boys rated pornography as their most significant source of sex education (Check, 1995). In other studies, 90% of Toronto boys (mean age = 14) and 60% of the girls had seen at least one pornographic movie, and 43% of U.S. males saw at least one sex magazine in a year (Russell, 1998). One of the newest media sources of sex is the Internet, which, in addition to the numerous pornography sites, has numerous informational sites that are widely visited (Cooper, 1998; S. N. Wilson, 2000). We are continually learning more about sex and modifying our constructed reality of its nature. How we act on that information may have serious consequences for our lives and the lives of others. In this chapter we first examine how sex is presented in the media and then turn to the research on the effects of exposure to that material. Toward the end of the chapter, we focus on one of the most controversial varieties of media sex, namely, sexual violence.

THE NATURE OF SEX IN MEDIA

Definitional Issues

Whenever we speak of sex in the media, we must clarify what we are including. There is a class of media (at least in the United States) explicitly labeled erotic, pornographic, or sexually explicit, which comprises magazines, videos, films, and Internet web sites. These materials have typically been marketed separately from nonsexual media and have been at least somewhat restricted from children, although this is becoming increasing difficult to do, especially with the Internet. A 15 billion dollar annual industry in the U.S., pornography brings in far more money than professional sports, performing arts, theater, or all other Internet commerce. Video porn alone brings in $4 billion per year, with 11,000 new titles released annually (compared to only 400 from Hollywood), with 750 million video/DVD rentals per year ("Naked Capitalists," 2001, May 20). An estimated 100,000 adult pornographic web sites take in around one billion dollars annually, and porno films are ordered by business travelers in hotel rooms ten times as often as standard films (Sigesmund, 2003).

Traditionally, these media have been recognized as being for sexual purposes only and without recognized literary or artistic merit, although there are signs that pornography is becoming more mainstream (Sigesmund, 2003). Porn film stars are becoming more widely known, and several recent feature films have dealt with the porn industry (*The People vs. Larry Flynt, Boogie Nights, Wonderland*), and TV series like Fox's *Skin* and Showtime's *Family Business* feature porn producers as the major characters. More than anything else, however, the widespread private availability of pornography on the Internet has spread its influence. Interestingly enough, as the new technology has spread sexually explicit media in unprecedented ways, some traditional sex media, notably magazines, have fallen on hard times. Most porn magazines have lost 10% circulation per year since the mid-1990s. For example, *Penthouse* has fallen from 5 million copies a month to under 1 million (Sigesmund, 2003).

Scholars have found it helpful to distinguish between *sexually violent* material, which portrays rape and other instances of physical harm to persons in a sexual context, and *nonviolent sexual* material, which may or may not depict *degradation, domination, subordination, or humiliation. Nonviolent and nondegrading material* typically depicts a couple having vaginal or oral intercourse with no indication of violence or coercion. Research has consistently shown more negative effects from viewing sexual violence than from the nonviolent, nondegrading material, with intermediate results from the nonviolent degrading material. *Child pornography* portrays minors and, although illegal to produce in the United States and many other places, still circulates widely through foreign magazines, personal distribution, and the Internet. For obvious ethical reasons, there has been little scientific research on its effects.

Of course, sex occurs in many other media outlets besides these explicitly sexual materials. For example, it is rampant in advertising, particularly for products like perfume, cologne, and after-shave, but also for tires, automobiles, and kitchen sinks. Sex in media is not limited to explicit portrayals of intercourse or nudity, but rather may include any representation that portrays or implies sexual behavior, interest, or motivation. However, the major focus in this chapter is on the more explicit materials, although not necessarily limited to what is generally called pornographic. Some of these other issues were discussed in chapter 4 on advertising. Because the term *pornographic* is highly value-laden but scientifically imprecise, we instead generally refer to such materials as *sexually explicit*.

History of Sex in Media

Sexual themes in fiction have been around as long as fiction itself. Ancient Greek comedies were often highly sexual in content, such as Aristophanes' *Lysistrata*, an antiwar comedy about women who withhold sex from their husbands to coerce them to stop fighting wars. Literary classics like Chaucer's *Canterbury Tales* and Shakespeare's *The Taming of the Shrew* are filled with sexual double entendres and overtly sexual themes, some of which are missed today due to the archaic language and the classic aura around such works. Throughout history, the pendulum has swung back and forth in terms of how much sexual expression is permitted in literature and how explicit it may be.

Since the advent of electronic media, standards have usually been more conservative for radio and television than for print, because it is easier to keep sexually oriented print media from children than it is radio or TV.

With the advent of widespread cable and videocassette technology, a sort of double standard has arisen, with greater permissiveness for videocassettes and premium cable channels than for network television, on the logic that premium cable and rented movies are invited into the home, whereas network programming is there uninvited whenever a TV set is present. Of course, the most difficult access issue is the ready availability of sex on the Internet and how to restrict its access to minors. Pornography filters have some success, although they raise free speech issues and sometimes restrict unintended sites (e.g., breast cancer information); also, porn site owners are often one step ahead of the screeners in designing sites to avoid the filters.

Media Sex Today

Content analyses show that sexual innuendoes and, less often, behaviors are rampant, very frequently occurring in a humorous context. In 2000, 68% of overall U.S. TV programming (75% of prime-time) contained sexual content, with higher rates in movies (89%), comedies (85%), and soap operas (80%) (Kunkel, Cope-Farrar, Biely, Farinola, & Donnerstein, 2001). More of the programs contained *talk* about sex (65%) than actual sexual *behavior* (27%). Only 1.1% of these instances referred at all to abstinence, birth control, or consequences of sex like pregnancy and STDs (Strasburger & Donnerstein, 1999). Media references to premarital and extramarital sexual encounters far outnumber references to sex between spouses, by at least 6:1 (Greenberg & Hofschire, 2000) and as high as 32:1 in R-rated movies (Greenberg et al., 1993). A 1995 content analysis of soap operas showed some increase since the seventies and eighties of themes of negative consequences of sex and rejection of sexual advances (Greenberg & Busselle, 1996).

Sex in media is one area where we clearly accept some limits on freedom of speech, and that fact is generally accepted. The sharp differences of opinion come in deciding just where those limits should be. Few are arguing that a network sitcom should show frontal nudity or child prostitutes, although it is highly unlikely that the producers would ever care to do so. One important issue in discussion of where the limits should be is the age of the viewer or reader. There is far more concern about the effects of sexual media on children than on adults. Even a highly libertarian person might not want their 6-year-old surfing porn sites on the Internet or reading *Hustler*, whereas even a morally very conservative person would be less alarmed about adults viewing X-rated videos than about children seeing them. The whole area of the effects of sexual media on children is a difficult area to study for ethical reasons; however, there are some ingenious ways to probe their effects without actually

---

BOX 10.1
STUDYING EFFECTS OF SEXUAL MEDIA ON CHILDREN

One empirical question we would like to know the answer to is almost impossible to study for ethical reasons: What is the effect of sexual media on children? Who is going to approve their young child watching pornography, or even an R-rated movie, for research purposes? Nevertheless, we all know that children do see sexual media. One clever methodology to examine this problem involves the use of the retrospective method which entails questioning adults about their memories of watching sexual content as children. The researchers are not exposing the child to any questionable stimuli, merely asking them about material they have seen on their own. Cantor, Mares, & Hyde (2003) asked 196 college students to remember an exposure to sexual media between the ages of 5 and 12 or during the teen years. Almost 92% could do so, 39% remembering something seen between the ages of 5 and 12 and 61% age 13 and over. Most often (79%) the content was R or NC-rated movies, and 80% were viewed with someone else (only 17% with parents, however). Disgust, shock/surprise, interest, and embarrassment were the most common emotional responses remembered (21% to 25% each), with sexual arousal (17%) and avoidance (14%) the most common physical reactions. Memories from younger ages (5–12) tended to focus on salient sensory aspects like nudity, kissing, and sexual noises, while the older memories focused on dialogue or themes like rape or same-gender sex. Overall, men's memories were more positive and more often focused on physical aspects. While there is no way to verify the accuracy of these students' memories, the vividness of memories years after the exposure testifies in itself to the powerful effect of seeing this sexual content relatively early in life.

---

presenting children with stimuli that many of their parents would object to (see Box 10.1).

Explicit sexual materials have traditionally been designed by men and for men. As such, they have a distinctly macho and hypermasculinized orientation. Although all varieties of heterosexual intercourse are shown, there is typically little emphasis on associated foreplay, afterplay, cuddling, or general tenderness. Women are seen eagerly desiring and participating in sex, often with hysterical euphoria. There is little concern with the consequences of sex or the relational matrix within which most people find it. Quite recently, there has been some increase in sexual materials with more emphasis on relationship, pre- and postcoital behaviors, and the woman's point of view generally, developed primarily to be marketed to women (Mosher & Maclan, 1994). However, these comprise only a minuscule part of the market worldwide. Although men are much more active seekers and users of sexual material than are women, this cannot necessarily be attributed to greater intrinsic male interest in sexual media; it may merely reflect the pornography industry's extreme slant to the traditional male perspective.

Media are clearly major sources of information about sexual issues that we use to construct our reality of what sexuality and sexual behavior and values are all about (Dorr & Kunkel, 1990; Fabes & Strouse, 1984, 1987; Strouse & Fabes, 1985; Wartella, Heintz, Aidman, & Mazzarella, 1990). To better understand this perceived reality, let us examine some effects of viewing sex in the media. How do we change after exposure to such material?

EFFECTS OF VIEWING MEDIA SEX

Although many people might wish it otherwise, sex—even very explicit sex—apparently does sell. Sexually oriented media, print, broadcast and internet, are highly profitable, and this fact has ramifications for all media. However, since this economic issue is not the focus of this book, we turn now to the various psychological effects (see Gunter, 2001; Harris & Scott, 2002; Linz & Malamuth, 1993; Lyons, Anderson, & Larson, 1994; and the papers in Greenberg, Brown, & Buerkel-Rothfuss, 1993, and Zillmann and Bryant, 1989, for reviews of the literature on the effects of viewing sexual media).

Arousal

A fairly straightforward effect of sex in media is sexual arousal, the drive that energizes or intensifies sexual behavior. Sexually oriented media such as magazines and videos do arouse people sexually, both in terms of self-rating of arousal level and physiological measures such as penile tumescence (Eccles, Marshall, & Barbaree, 1988; Malamuth & Check, 1980a; Schaefer & Colgan, 1977), vaginal changes (Sintchak & Geer, 1975), and thermography (Abramson, Perry, Seeley, Seeley, & Rothblatt, 1981). Overall, men tend to be aroused by sexual media more than women are (Malamuth, 1996; Murnen & Stockton, 1997), although there is some evidence that women may be more aroused by sexual media developed by and for women and thus not portraying sex from an extreme hypermasculine fantasy (Mosher & Maclan, 1994; Quackenbush, Strassberg, & Turner, 1995). Sexual violence is particularly arousing to sex offenders and much less so to normal men, unless the victim is portrayed as being aroused by the assault; these findings are discussed in more detail later in the chapter.

Sexual arousal to stimuli not naturally evoking such a response may be learned through classical conditioning. This process could account for the vast individual differences in what specific stimuli arouse people sexually. Through our different experiences, we have all been conditioned to different stimuli through their associations with those we love. Because of its association with a particular person, someone is aroused by a certain perfume or cologne, type of clothing, or specific behaviors.

Contrary to what one might expect, the degree of arousal is not necessarily highly correlated with the degree of explicitness of the media. Sometimes one is actually more aroused by a less sexually explicit story than a more explicit one (e.g., Bancroft & Mathews, 1971). Censoring out a sex scene may actually make a film more arousing, because viewers can fill in their own fantasies. Sexual arousal is highly individual. When people are allowed to use their own imaginations to construct the ending of a romantic scene, they are more likely to construct a reality that is more arousing to them personally than if they view someone else's idea of what is arousing. There is some validity to the old truism that the most important sex organ is the brain.

Attitudes and Values

A large class of effects of media sex has to do with effects on attitudes and values. We clearly have come a long way from the days where Lucy and Ricky Ricardo on *I Love Lucy* had to have twin beds and referred to her expectant state as "having a baby," never as "pregnant," but there are still firm standards that no network or mainstream cable TV shows dare cross, such as frontal nudity or explicit sexual intercourse.

Standards for television are more conservative than for radio, which is in turn more conservative than the recording industry. These differences are especially clear in terms of rock and rap lyrics. When Mick Jagger and the Rolling Stones appeared on *The Ed Sullivan Show* in the 1960s, they had to change the line "Let's spend the night together" to "Let's spend some time together." When Jagger performed this line, he did so with exaggerated gesture and body language to communicate his attitude about the censoring. Concern has continued ever since, such as when a song moves from the more permissive radio to the more conservative television, as in the case of MTV. Some of the strongest rap and heavy metal lyrics never even make it to radio, but are widely available to youth on CD or the Internet.

In exploring sexual attitudes and values, we now turn to four specific value issues.

Sexual Details in the News.   How explicit should the media be in re-porting news of sex-crime trials? When is the public's right to know over-shadowed by its right to standards of good taste? When does reporting turn into voyeurism? Consider some examples.

A small city is the scene of a child sexual molestation trial involving a prominent businessman and two 13-year-old boys. Each day's court proceedings are reported in great detail in front-page stories in the local newspaper, always identifying the accused but never the boys. Sexually oriented entertainment involving pornography and alcohol in the man's home was described in detail, along with extensive direct quotes from the testimony: "He rubbed our butts in the shower," "He called me to where he was sitting and told me to play with his penis," "He also made me [and the other boy] lay on the floor and have oral sex with each other while he watched." Other episodes such as the man asking the boys to reach inside his underwear and squeeze his penis hard were also explicitly described.

Predictably, this coverage provoked some community comment, al-though even the most outraged people nevertheless always managed to read the articles. Although no one defended the events that had occurred, some argued that young readers should not be exposed to such explicit descriptions in the newspaper. Others countered, however, by saying that such events are serious and need to be reported in detail to show everyone how horrible they are and thus increase commitment to ensure that they would not happen again. Both sides made strong value-oriented justifica-tions about their positions on publication of this information.

In the early 1990s there were two celebrated date-rape trials of men of some notoriety. In the first, John and Ted Kennedy's nephew William Kennedy Smith was accused of raping a single mother at the Kennedy estate in Palm Beach, Florida. In the second trial, boxing heavyweight champion Mike Tyson was accused of raping a Miss Black America con-testant whom he had met and invited to his hotel room. Both trials were broadcast on cable (with faces of victims blanked out) and were heavily covered in all the news media. In both trials, the basic legal question was whether there was consent. Viewers heard questions like, "Did you ejacu-late into her mouth?" and "Did you have an erection?" and the answers to them.

One of the most celebrated cases of sexually explicit language in the news came with the release in September 1998 of U.S. President Bill Clinton's grand jury testimony in the Monica Lewinsky case. The critical legal, and potentially impeachable, question here was whether the Presi-dent had perjured himself in grand jury testimony about the specific sexual behaviors. The videotapes and news commentary on them had the look of both high political drama and sleazy tabloid reporting. Parents were in a quandary as to how to explain these matters to their children. Many lamented the depth to which news reporting had fallen, but no one quite knew what to do about it. Such a story involved the leader of the free world in a possibly impeachable offense and thus could not be ignored.

Although such sexually explicit language would never be accepted on prime time entertainment programming, because these stories were news their use was less controversial. Still, however, it caused some concern, especially insofar as many people watch TV news and read the newspaper for entertainment purposes.

Premarital Sex. Having sex before marriage is openly discussed on TV news and entertainment shows today, at least superficially. However, it is often traditional values that are affirmed in the end, especially in story lines involving youth. A teenager may openly consider having sex with a boyfriend or girlfriend and discuss it openly with family and friends. In the end, however, more often than not, the teenager decides that he or she is not ready and chooses to abstain. Even when the decision is affirmative, however, there is considerable moralizing and prior discussion of the behavior, often with parents. Moreover sometimes there is clear regret afterwards. In such cases, traditional values are more or less affirmed.

In contrast to this moral angst of teen decisions about premarital sex, between adults it appears to be a nonissue. Dramatic TV shows and movies seem to presuppose a norm of early sexual activity on the part of adult dating couples, usually with little if any concern about either moral propriety or protection against pregnancy or sexually transmitted diseases. Premarital sex is often portrayed as accepted and noncontroversial with little indication of either party struggling with the decision. In fact, there is seldom any discussion by either party about whether that is right, whether it is too soon in the relationship, and so forth. Only in story lines with adolescents does it seem to be considered a moral issue. Premarital sex is thus treated very conservatively in regard to teens and very permissively in regard to adults. See Box 10.2 for a very unusual case where a sitcom story line involving the consequences of premarital sex caused a national political furor.

Extramarital Sex. In television and movies, extramarital sex is a common occurrence; the 9,200 scenes of suggested sexual intercourse shown each year on TV occur 5 to 32 times as often outside of marriage as inside of it (Greenberg, et al., 1993; Kunkel, et al., 2002). Depending on the situation, it may be treated farcically or seriously. If treated seriously, it may carry the implicit message that adultery is okay, or at least that it does not have terribly serious consequences, or it may convey the message that adultery

---

BOX 10.2
THE VICE PRESIDENT VERSUS *MURPHY BROWN*

On May 18, 1992, the sitcom *Murphy Brown* aired what turned out to be a more memorable than expected season finale featuring the birth of the baby of single female news anchor Murphy Brown. The day after the TV birth, then-U.S. Vice President Dan Quayle made a political speech lamenting the nation's poverty of values. In this speech he referred to the bad example set by character Murphy Brown in "having a child alone, mocking the importance of fathers, by bearing a child alone, and calling it just another lifestyle choice" (Dan Quayle, 1992, p. 20). Aside from the irony of this comment coming from a leader very outspoken in his opposition to legal abortion, the comment was interesting in highlighting the depth of emotion evoked by a sitcom portrayal. President George H. W. Bush, network executives, and many political leaders and columnists (and of course many humorists) commented extensively on the issue in subsequent weeks. What was it about Murphy Brown having a baby that inspired so much feeling? Why didn't these critics complain about all of the sex on soap operas or, for that matter, all of the real children born out of wedlock every day to single parents far less capable than Murphy Brown?

Although Quayle's detractors chided him for making such a big deal out of a sitcom plot, they too may have missed the point. So what if Murphy Brown is not a real person, and no one ever had actual sex to produce that fictitious baby? A TV character has a reality and an impact on real people that most real people do not. In some sense, both the vice president and his critics were affirming the thesis of this book.

Nor did the story end there. On the fall 1992 premiere of *Murphy Brown*, the plot revolved around new fictitious mom Murphy seeing a real news report of Dan Quayle criticizing her moral example. Her office is besieged with reporters asking for reactions. Although staying secluded for awhile, Murphy eventually made an on-air editorial response to the vice president. Subsequent news reports told of the fictional program's response to the real criticism by Quayle. Quayle even sent a real baby gift of a stuffed Republican elephant to the fictitious baby. Fantasy and reality had never become so blurred.

---

has serious repercussions for all concerned. The effect on viewers may be very different in these two cases. If treated farcically, it may discourage taking seriously the consequences of marital infidelity.

The first shows that come to mind are soap operas, where adultery is a frequent theme, even an accepted way of life for many of the characters. In terms of values, both approval and condemnation come through at different times. A sympathetic character who is trapped in an unhappy marriage uses an affair as a relatively healthy outlet for her needs. The inevitable pain and hurt resulting from the adultery may or may not be dealt with in the plot line to any significant degree.

What is the perceived reality constructed from viewing such shows? In a study of cultivation effects of soap opera viewing by college students, Buerkel-Rothfuss and Mayes (1981) found that heavy viewing of soap operas was positively correlated with higher estimates of the percentages of people having affairs, divorces, abortions, and illegitimate children, although it was unrelated to their perception of how many people were happily married. Bryant and Rockwell (1994) showed effects of heavy viewing of sexually oriented TV shows on adolescent's moral judgments. Other research using a uses and gratifications approach showed that the motives and purposes of viewing must also be considered (Carveth & Alexander, 1985; Greenberg, et al., 1982; Perse, 1986). The perceived reality constructed from such shows apparently depends not only on the program content, but also on the viewer's motives and uses of the medium, as well as parental values and parent-child discussion and co-viewing.

Just as extramarital affairs are presented as common, sometimes marital sex is actually denigrated. For example, one episode of the family sitcom *Married With Children* had the father eye his wife dressed very seductively and say, "Geez, if I weren't married to you, I'd really be turned on about now!" The message is clear: sex *within* marriage is boring, uninteresting, or otherwise devalued. The good stuff lurks elsewhere.

AIDS Education and Birth Control. Although we accept great amounts of implied or semi-explicit sex on TV, even after the onset of AIDS in the mid-1980s, birth control ads were for a long time seen as too controversial for most U.S. television, although such ads had appeared regularly in magazines for years. It is as if the action of having sexual intercourse is acceptable if done in the heat of a passionate moment, but that *planning* for it is somehow unseemly or dirty. This communicates a potentially dangerous reality! The teen pregnancy rate is far higher in the United States than in any other industrialized country, and such rates elsewhere fell dramatically after media campaigns that included televised birth control ads. It is an interesting paradox that all sorts of nonmarital sex, much of which would clearly be against the personal values of most Americans, were considered acceptable for story content, but that the use of birth control, a practice consistent with the values and practice of most citizens, was seen as too controversial to advertise or to even mention in story lines. Thus, we see another paradox of fairly extreme permissiveness in regard to nonmarital media sex coexisting with extreme conservatism in regard to birth control and protection. Why are premarital and extramarital sex so acceptable but birth control and a reasonable concern about acquiring sexually transmitted diseases not?

The spread of AIDS has heightened the discussion of such issues. As AIDS spread beyond the gay and drug cultures in the late 1980s, the general population in many countries became concerned and alarmed. The common introduction of AIDS education into schools suggests that fear of AIDS (and death) was gradually becoming stronger than fear of exposing children to sexual information. In terms of media, the advertising of condoms had cautiously crept into some cable channels like MTV and some large markets by the late 1990s. In terms of entertainment programming, story lines continued to portray very casual attitudes toward nonmarital sex and its consequences, especially among adults. Although there have recently been increasing numbers of story lines indicating some concern about AIDS or the use of protection (so called safe sex), that is still much more the exception than the rule.

One concern is a desensitization to certain expressions of sexuality deemed by others to be inappropriate. For example, sitcoms showing teenagers considering being sexually active may contradict and thus weaken family-taught values that prohibit premarital sex. Car magazines selling shock absorbers by showing a bikini-clad woman held in mock bondage by a giant shock absorber may desensitize readers about violence toward women.

Sometimes the media may actually change one's values or attitudes, rather than merely desensitizing or reinforcing an existing one. It may be that teenage boys watching one of the *Home Improvement* sons as he considers having sex with his girlfriend may also come to adopt those values. This is especially likely to happen if the TV characters holding those values are respected characters with whom viewers identify. Sexual promiscuity by a prostitute character is less likely to influence the values of a viewer than promiscuity by a respected suburban wife and mother.

Another concern about the effects on values and attitudes is that sexually oriented media may encourage people not to take sexual issues as seriously as they should. When a sex magazine has a regular cartoon called Chester the Molester featuring a child molester, many argue that this is an inappropriately light treatment of an extremely serious subject. A *Penthouse* story "Soothing Private Ryan" featured a barmaid putting a condom over the private's privates, in a spoof of the serious war movie *Saving Private Ryan*. One article in a sex magazine aimed at male teenagers was entitled "Good Sex with Retarded Girls"; this too is open to such criticism. Although few would be likely to argue that sex should never be comedic, there are for most people *some* sexual subjects that do not seem appropriate for light treatment.

Sometimes a comedic treatment of sex can send a serious message. When the father on *Married With Children* chastises his daughter for receiving a bad grade, he is relieved because "at least it was in sex education." Ironically, this sexually permissive sitcom confirmed a very conservative, and in this case unfounded, belief that knowledge about sex and contraception leads to promiscuity. When a car ad features two women discussing whether men drive big cars to compensate for the size of their penises ("I wonder what he's got under the hood"), they send a message about what is important about men in the eyes of women (Leo, in Strasburger, 1995).

One type of value of particular concern involves attitudes toward women. One of the major criticisms of traditional pornography is that it is antiwomen in an ideological sense. It is usually women, not men, who are the playthings or victims of the opposite sex. Although this concern spans the gamut of sexual content in media, it is particularly leveled at sexual violence. What are teenage boys first learning about sex going to think that women want when they see a picture of a jackhammer in a woman's vagina as the opening photo to a story called "How to Cure Frigidity"? When *Hustler* magazine runs a photo spread of a gang rape turning into an orgy, showing the women appearing to be aroused by the assault, what is being taught about women and their reactions to forcible sex? Research examining this question is discussed in detail later in the chapter.

Finally, in regard to values and attitudes, people sometimes complain that media sex, especially the more explicit varieties, removes some of the mystique, some of the aura, from what is a very mysterious, almost sacred, activity. This argument holds that sex is very private and more meaningful and more fun if it is not so public. This is a hard concern to articulate, and even harder to refute or test empirically, but it is one often expressed.

Research on Media Effects on Sexual Attitudes.   Several studies have shown effects on attitudes and values about sex as a result of exposure to nonviolent sexually explicit materials. After seeing slides and movies of beautiful female nudes engaged in sexual activity, men rated their own partners as being less physically endowed, although they reported undiminished sexual satisfaction (Weaver, Masland, & Zillmann, 1984). In another study, men reported loving their own mates less after seeing sexually explicit videos of highly attractive models (Kenrick, Gutierres, & Goldberg, 1989). Men who saw a pornographic video responded more sexually to a subsequent female interviewer than those seeing a control video, although this result only held for men holding traditional gender schemas (McKenzie-Mohr & Zanna, 1990). All of these studies show significant attitude changes after a very limited exposure to sexual media.

Using a paradigm of showing participants weekly films and testing them 1 to 3 weeks later, Zillmann and Bryant (1982, 1984) found that participants seeing the sexually explicit films overestimated the frequency of sexual practices like fellatio, cunnilingus, anal intercourse, sadomasochism, and bestiality, relative to perceptions of a control group seeing nonsexual films. This may reflect the cognitive heuristic of *availability*, whereby we judge the frequency of occurrence of various activities by the ease with which we can generate examples (S. Taylor, 1982; Tversky & Kahneman, 1973, 1974). Recent vivid media instances thus lead to an overestimation of such occurrences in the real world and a perceived reality substantially at odds with actual reality.

Using the same methodology that was used in their 1982 and 1984 studies, Zillmann and Bryant (1988a, 1988b) found effects of this perceived reality on attitudes about real people. Participants seeing the explicit films reported, relative to a control group, less satisfaction with the affection, physical appearance, sexual curiosity, and sexual performance of their real-life partners. They also saw sex without emotional involvement as being relatively more important than the control group did. They showed greater acceptance of premarital and extramarital sex and lesser evaluation of marriage and monogamy. They also showed less desire to have children and greater acceptance of male dominance and female submission. Results generally did not differ for men versus women or college students versus nonstudents.

The medium may make a difference. Dermer and Pyszczynski's (1978) male participants were told to think about their mates before reading some explicit passages about a woman's sexual fantasies. They later rated their own partner as more sexually attractive. This inconsistency with the Zillmann and Bryant results may be due to specific procedural aspects of the research, particular materials used, or psychological differences in responses to print versus video material. Nonpictorial descriptions of sex in words in the print medium (e.g., the *Penthouse* Advisor column) may be more conducive to fantasizing about one's own partner, whereas photographic sex may encourage unfavorable comparison to that person.

The sexual material need not be explicit or graphic to affect attitudes. Bryant and Rockwell (1994) found that, compared to controls, teenagers who watched a heavy diet of highly sexual prime time programs showed an influence on their judgments of the degree of sexual impropriety or of how much the victim had been wronged, although these effects were greatly attenuated by a clear and well-defined family value system, active critical viewing, and open discussion within the family.

Behavioral Effects

Teaching New Behaviors.   A second large class of effects is effects on behavior. On the one hand, sexual media may actually teach new behaviors.

As part of sex therapy, a couple may buy a sex manual like *The Joy of Sex* in order to learn new sexual positions or behaviors that they had not tried before. New behaviors are not always so benign, however. One issue of *Penthouse* contained a series of photographs of Asian women bound with heavy rope, hung from trees, and sectioned into parts. Two months later an 8-year-old Chinese girl in Chapel Hill, North Carolina, was kidnapped, raped, murdered, and left hanging from a tree limb (*New York Times*, 1985, cited in Final Report, 1986, p. 208). Of course, such examples are not commonplace, and definitively demonstrating a causal relationship in such cases is difficult, but the juxtaposition is nonetheless disturbing.

Disinhibition of Known Behaviors. Erotic material may also disinhibit previously learned behavior, as when the viewing of TV's treatment of premarital sex disinhibits a viewer's inhibition against engaging in such behavior. Watching a rape scene where a woman is portrayed as enjoying being assaulted may weaken some men's moral prohibitions on committing such a crime. This is of particular concern given some evidence suggesting that a surprisingly large number of college men reported that they might commit rape if they were sure they would not be caught (Check, 1985; Malamuth, Haber, & Feshbach, 1980).

Sex Crimes. One of the main concerns about a behavioral effect of viewing sexually explicit materials is that such viewing may have a relationship to sex crimes. There have been many studies looking at rates of crimes like rape, exhibitionism, and child molestation, relative to changes in the availability of sexually explicit materials. Drawing scientifically sound general conclusions has been difficult, however. Court (1977, 1982, 1984) argued that there is in fact a correlation between availability of sexually explicit materials and certain sex crimes. Court claimed that earlier studies, especially the Kutchinsky (1973) study claiming a drop in reported sex crimes in Denmark after liberalization of pornography restrictions in the 1960s, were not really valid, due to an inappropriate lumping of rape with nonviolent acts of voyeurism, indecent exposure, and homosexual sex.

Most Western nations have experienced a large increase in both the availability of sexually explicit media and the rise in reported rapes in the last 30 years. However, Court (1984) presented some data from two Australian states that showed a sharp increase in rape reports in South Australia, but not Queensland, after state pornography laws were liberalized in South Australia in the early 1970s. A comparable downturn in reported rapes occurred temporarily in Hawaii between 1974 and 1976 during a temporary imposition of restraints on sexually explicit media. For an interesting apparent counterexample, see Box 10.3.

BOX 10.3
PORNOGRAPHY IN JAPAN (ABRAMSON & HAYASHI, 1984;
DIAMOND & UCHIYAMA, 1999).

Japan is an interesting and unusual case study of a society with wide availability of sexual media, but very low rape rates. Sexual themes in art and society go back centuries to ancient fertility religious objects and wood block prints called *ukiyo-e*. Although some restriction and censorship occurred after the Meiji Restoration in 1868 and even more under the U.S. occupation that began after World War II ended in 1945, sexuality continued to be a strong theme of Japanese society and one not associated with shame or guilt. Although there are specific restrictions on showing pictorial representations of pubic hair or adult genitalia anywhere in Japan, there is no restriction of sexual media to certain types of magazines, bookstores, or theaters, as occurs in the United States. Thus nudity, bondage, and rape occur regularly on commercial television and popular movies and magazines, including in advertising. Films often portray very vivid scenes of rape and bondage. In recent years, a market has surged for magazines featuring pictures of naked schoolgirls. It is legal in Japan for men to have sex with children over 12, and some schoolgirls earn extra money from prostitution or catering to men's sexual fantasies in Tokyo's image clubs. Some have attributed men's rising interest in child sexuality to their feeling increasingly threatened by women's growing sophistication and demands for equality (Lolita in Japan, 1997).

Why, then, is the incidence of reported rapes so much lower in Japan than elsewhere (2.4 per 100,000 vs. 34.5 in the United States, 10.1 in England, and 10.7 in Germany)? Abramson and Hayashi (1984) argued that the answer may lie in cultural differences. Japanese society emphasizes order, obligation, cooperation, and virtue, and one who violates social norms is the object of shame. Also, sex is not compartmentalized relative to other segments of society as it is in the United States. Others have suggested that rape in Japan is more likely to be group instigated, perpetrated by juveniles, and greatly underreported by victims (S. Goldstein & Ibaraki, 1983).

Firmly establishing a causal relationship between the availability of sexually explicit media and the frequency of rape is extremely difficult, due to the many other relevant factors that cannot be controlled, including the different varieties of sexual material, changes in social consciousness about reporting sexual assaults, and changing norms sanctioning such behavior. Although some have argued from the evidence that an increase in sex crimes follows greater availability of pornography (Court, 1984) and others have argued that there is no such demonstrated relationship (Kutchinsky, 1991), there has been no recent support for an explanation that greater availability of sexually explicit media decreases the rate of sex crimes. See Bauserman (1996) for a review.

Catharsis

Another alleged effect of media sex is catharsis, that emotional release so important to psychodynamic models of personality (e.g., Freud). Applied to sex, the catharsis argument says that consuming media sex relieves sexual urges, with the magazine or video acting (perhaps in conjunction with masturbation) as a sort of imperfect substitute for the real thing. A catharsis argument was used some years ago by civil libertarians to support appeals for lessening restrictions on sexually explicit material (e.g., Kutchinsky, 1973). The research support for catharsis as a function of viewing media sex is meager if not totally nonexistent, however (Bushman, Baumeister, & Stack, 1999; Comstock, 1985; Final Report, 1986). In fact, exposure to sexual media typically energizes the sex drive and leads one to do more to fulfill it, not less. Still, however, as we saw with the violence research, the popular belief in this scientifically discredited process remains strong.

Prevailing Tone

The perceived reality of media sex and the effects of sex in media are not entirely due to the nature of the material itself. They also depend on the context of the material and the context in which the person sees it. This diverse collection of variables is called the *prevailing tone* (Eysenck & Nias, 1978).The nature of this prevailing tone can make an enormous difference in the experience of consuming sexually explicit media.

One of the relevant variables of the prevailing tone is the degree of playfulness or seriousness of the material. Even a highly explicit and potentially controversial topic may not be particularly controversial when presented seriously. For example, a documentary on rape or a tastefully done TV drama on incest may be considered perfectly acceptable, whereas a far less explicit comedy with the same theme may be highly offensive and considered too sexual. What is really the concern in such cases is not the sex as such, but rather the comedic treatment of it. A second factor in the prevailing tone is the artistic worth and intent. We react very differently to a sexually explicit drawing by Picasso versus one in *Hustler* magazine. Shakespeare, Chaucer, *The Song of Solomon* in the Bible, and serious sex manuals like *The Joy of Sex* are seen to have serious literary or didactic intentions, and thus the sex therein is considered more acceptable and even healthy. One interesting issue in this regard is how to respond to something of clear artistic worth that was written at a time when standards differed from what they are today. For example, should Rhett Butler's forcing his attentions on Scarlett O'Hara in *Gone with the Wind* be seen as rape or as the noncontroversial romantic moment that it appeared to be in 1939? In fact, the theme of a man continuing to press his sexual desires against a woman's clearly stated wish that he stop, today legally defined as rape, was a common theme in films in the mid-twentieth century.

The relation and integration of sex to the overall plot and intent of the piece is another part of the prevailing tone. A sex scene, even a mild and nonexplicit one, may be offensive if it appears to be thrown in merely to spice up the story but having no intrinsic connection to it. Something far more explicit may find greater acceptance if it is necessary and central to the plot. Sex scenes in a story about a prostitute may be much less gratuitous than comparable scenes in a story about a female corporate executive. Sex, of course, is not the only common gratuitous factor in media; for example, contemporary TV shows and movies frequently insert car chases and rock video segments only tangentially related to the plot.

The context of the viewing also influences the experience and effect of sex in the media. Watching an erotic film may elicit different reactions, depending on whether you watch it with your parents, your grandparents, your children, by yourself, in a group of close same-sex friends, or with your spouse. It can be seen as more or less erotic or arousing and more or less appropriate or offensive.

The cultural context is also a factor. Some cultures do not consider female breasts to be particularly erotic or inappropriate for public display. We recognize these cultural differences and thus, at least after the age of 14, most readers do not consider topless women from some exotic culture in *National Geographic* photos to be the slightest bit erotic, sexual, or inappropriate. Even in Western culture, standards have changed. In much of the 19th century, knees and calves were thought to be erotic, and the sight of a bare-kneed woman would be as scandalous, perhaps even as sexually arousing, as would a topless woman today. As societies go, North America overall is a bit more conservative in allowing sexual expression than many Western European or Latin American cultures but far more permissive than most Islamic and East Asian cultures.

Finally, the expectations we have affect our perception of the prevailing tone. Sex is less offensive and shocking if it is expected than if it appears as a surprise. Seeing a photo of an orgy may be less shocking in *Hustler* magazine than if one were to suddenly encounter it in *Newsweek*. The stimulus may be the same, but the perceived experiential reality of the fact of seeing it would differ considerably in the two cases.

We now examine that potent combination of sex and violence in the media: sexual violence.

SEXUAL VIOLENCE

Although neither sex nor violence in the media is new, the integral combination of the two has become more prevalent in recent decades. Cable,
video, and Internet technology have greatly expanded the capability of
privately and conveniently viewing sexually explicit material. Although
many people are not willing to seek out and visit theaters that show such
films, the chance to view such material safely and privately in one's own
home makes it much more accessible. Another old familiar genre, the horror film, has recently evolved into showing frequent and extensive scenes
of violence against women in a sexual context (see readings in Weaver &
Tamborini, 1996). These films are widely viewed by teens and preteens, in
spite of their R ratings. With all of these media, the major concern is not
with the sex or violence in and of itself, but with the way the two appear
together. The world constructed in the mind of the viewer of such materials
can have some very serious consequences. Let us turn now to examining
some of the effects of viewing sexual violence.

Erotica as Stimulator of Aggression

Links between sex and aggression have long been speculated upon, particularly in the sense of sexual arousal facilitating violent behavior. The
research has been inconsistent, however, with some studies showing that
erotic materials facilitate aggression (Baron, 1979; Donnerstein & Hallam,
1978) and others showing that they inhibit it (Donnerstein, Donnerstein, &
Evans, 1975; White, 1979). The resolution of this issue apparently concerns
the nature of the material. Sexual violence and unpleasant themes typically facilitate aggression, whereas nonviolent, more loving and pleasant
soft-core explicit materials may inhibit it (Sapolsky, 1984; Zillmann, Bryant,
Comisky, & Medoff, 1981).

Effects Depend on How the Woman Is Portrayed

Men who see films with scenes of sexual violence later showed a more
callous attitude toward rape and women in general, especially if the women
victims in the film were portrayed as being aroused by the assault. In
terms of sexual arousal, men were aroused by the sexual violence only if
the victim was shown to be aroused but not if she was not so portrayed
(Malamuth, 1984).

Individual Differences in Male Viewers

Other studies examined convicted rapists and found them to be aroused by
both rape and consenting sex, whereas normal men were aroused only by

the consenting sex (Abel, Barlow, Blanchard, & Guild, 1977; Quinsey, Chapman, & Upfold, 1984). An important exception to this occurred if the victim was portrayed as enjoying the rape and coming to orgasm; in this case normal U.S. and Japanese male college students, though not women, were equally or more aroused by the rape than by the consenting sex (Malamuth, Heim, & Feshbach, 1980; Ohbuchi, Ikeda, & Takeuchi, 1994). Malamuth and Check (1983) had men listen to a tape of a sexual encounter with either (a) consenting sex, (b) nonconsenting sex where the woman showed arousal, or (c) nonconsenting sex where she showed disgust. Where the woman showed disgust, both dispositionally violent and nonviolent men were more aroused, in terms of both self-report and penile tumescence, by the consenting than the nonconsenting (rape) scene. However, when the woman was portrayed as being aroused, the nonviolent men were equally aroused by both consenting and nonconsenting versions, whereas the violent men actually showed more arousal to the nonconsenting (rape) version. Similar results were obtained by Malamuth (1981) using video stimuli.

Some situational variables can affect arousal as well. For example, normal men were more than normally aroused by a rape scene if they had been previously angered by a female confederate (Yates, Barbaree, & Marshall, 1984). Also, alcohol consumption can decrease sensitivity to victim distress and thus allow greater arousal to sexual violence (Norris, George, Davis, Martell, & Leonesio, 1999).

Can such effects transfer to new situations? Donnerstein and Berkowitz (1981; see also Donnerstein, 1980) showed men a sexually violent film where a woman is attacked, stripped, tied up, and raped. In one version of the film, the woman was portrayed as enjoying the rape. Afterward, participants were given a chance to administer electric shocks to a confederate of the experimenter, one who had earlier angered them. Men who had seen the film where the woman enjoyed being raped administered more shocks to a female confederate, but not to a male. This suggests that the association of sex and violence in the film allows violent behavior to be transferred to the target confederate in a new situation.

Most of this research has been conducted on men. However, a few studies examining women have shown behavioral effects of increased aggression toward other women (Baron, 1979) and desensitization effects of trivialization of rape and acceptance of rape myths and more traditional gender-role attitudes (Malamuth, Check, & Briere, 1986; Mayerson & Taylor, 1987; Schwarz & Brand, 1983; Zillmann & Bryant, 1982).

Conclusions.   In a meta-analysis of studies examining the relationship of exposure to pornography and the acceptance of rape myths, Allen, Emmers, Gebhardt, and Giery (1995) conclude that experimental studies show a consistent positive effect between pornography exposure and rape myth acceptance, while nonexperimental studies show only a very small positive or nonexistent effect. The relationship was consistently stronger when the pornography was violent rather than nonviolent, although some experimental studies obtained effects in both cases.

Several conclusions emerge from the sexual violence research (see Pollard, 1995, for a review). One is that a critical aspect of the perceived reality of sexual violence is whether the woman is seen as enjoying and being aroused by the assault. Far more undesirable effects occur in normal men if the woman is shown as aroused than if she is seen to be terrorized. This media portrayal of women as being turned on by rape is not only a distasteful deviation from reality, but also a potentially dangerous one. A second important conclusion is that sexually violent media often affect men very differently, depending on their propensity to use force in their own lives. Convicted rapists and other men prone to use violence in their own lives are more likely to become aroused or even incited to violence by sexually violent media, especially if the woman is portrayed as being aroused by the assault.

Slasher Movies

Sex + Violence in Mainstream Movies. Because the studies discussed so far in this section used very sexually explicit materials that would be considered hard-core pornography, many might consider them beyond the limits of what they themselves would be exposed to. However, sexual violence is by no means confined to pornographic materials restricted from minors. Hundreds of mainstream R-rated films are readily available to teenagers anywhere, in theaters and especially on video and DVD. There are the highly successful series like *Halloween, Child's Play, Friday the Thirteenth, Scream, Nightmare on Elm Street, Scary Movie,* and *I Know What You Did Last Summer,* as well as many single films like *The Texas Chainsaw Massacre* (1974 or 2003 versions) and *The Blair Witch Project.* Many are extremely violent with strong sexual overtones. Even the 1995 James Bond movie *Goldeneye* featured a villainess who seduces men to have sex with her and then crushes them to death. It also contains scenes of seduction with very violent mutual battering as a sort of foreplay. In some countries, rape and other acts of violence against women are even more standard entertainment fare (see Box 10.4).

Although most of these films have R ratings in the United States, others are released unrated to avoid the accompanied-by-parent restriction of R-rated movies. Because few restrictions apply in video stores, the rating is not a major issue. The viewing of such films is widespread among youth. Oliver (1993) found that punitive attitudes toward sexuality and traditional attitudes toward women's sexuality were associated with high school

---

BOX 10.4
RAPE TO SELL, INDIAN STYLE

The nation producing the largest number of movies annually is India. Many of these use rape scenes as major audience draws. The great Indian epics *Mahabharat* and *Ramayana* have demure heroines who are nearly raped but are indeed rescued from their attackers by their own virtue. This pattern also appears in Indian movies featuring the same type of heroine. But the women characters who are portrayed as more independent, corrupt, immoral, or even morally ambiguous must suffer their fate, which is more typically blamed on their lifestyle rather than on the attacker. A 1989 film, *Crime Time*, advertised: "See first-time underwater rapes on Indian screen." One popular Indian actor, Ranjeet, has enacted over 350 rape scenes in 19 years of film acting (Pratap, 1990).

There is some call for change from women's groups and others. Bharatendu Singhal, chairman of the Central Board of Film Certification, announced his intent in 1990 to force producers to remove much of the titillation from the rape scenes, although filmmakers lobbied for his removal from the post. Curiously, verbal suggestiveness is more frowned upon than overt violence. A 1993 movie *Khalnayak (Evil One)* stirred up controversy when prominent film actress Madhuri Dixit clutched her breast while singing "What's beneath my blouse?" (Maier, 1994).

Does this state of affairs reflect society or help mold it? Over 8,000 rapes, half against poor and lower-caste women, are reported yearly in India, although that is probably a small fraction of the rapes that occur. Occasionally a rape case even comes to trial. A policeman in Bihar accused of raping 18 women was acquitted by a judge, who felt that the women were so poor that they could have been bribed to file a false complaint (Pratap, 1990).

---

students' greater enjoyment of previews of slasher films. Some have noted a trend toward stronger, less victimized female characters in recent films like *Urban Legend, I Know What You Did Last Summer,* and *The Bride of Chucky.*

The major concern with such films is the juxtaposition of erotic sex and violence. For example, one scene from *Toolbox Murders* opens with a beautiful woman disrobing and getting into her bath, with the romantic music *Pretty Baby* playing in the background. For several minutes she is shown fondling herself and masturbating in a very erotic manner. Suddenly the camera cuts to the scene of an intruder breaking into her apartment, with loud, fast-paced suspenseful music in the background. The camera and sound track cut back and forth several times between these two characters until he finally encounters the woman. He attacks her with electric tools, chasing her around the apartment, finally shooting her several times in the head with a nail gun. The scene closes after she bleeds profusely, finally lying on the bed to die with the sound track again playing the erotic *Pretty Baby*.

Effects of Viewing Slasher Films.   Linz, Donnerstein, and Penrod (1984; see also Linz, 1985; Linz, Donnerstein, & Adams, 1989) examined the effects of viewing such films. Male college-student participants were initially screened to exclude those who had prior hostile tendencies or psychological problems. The remaining men in the experimental group were shown one standard Hollywood R-rated film per day over one week. All of the films were very violent and showed multiple instances of women being killed in slow, lingering, painful deaths in situations associated with much erotic content (e.g., the *Toolbox Murders* scene described earlier). Each day the participants filled out some questionnaires evaluating that film and also completed some personality measures.

These ratings showed that the men became less depressed, less annoyed, and less anxious in response to the films during the week. The films themselves were gradually rated over time as more enjoyable, more humorous, more socially meaningful, less violent and offensive, and less degrading to women. Over the week's time, the violent episodes in general and rape episodes in particular were rated as less frequent. A similar study by Krafka, Linz, Donnerstein, and Penrod (1997) tested women and did not find the same effects on perception. Although these data provide clear evidence of desensitization in men, there is still the question of generalization from the films to other situations.

To answer this question, the same people participated in what they thought was an unrelated later study (Linz, et al., 1984; Krafka, et al., 1997; Weisz & Earls, 1995). For these experiments, they observed a mock rape trial at the law school and evaluated it. Compared to control groups seeing nonsexual violent or sexually explicit nonviolent films, both men and women who had seen the sexually violent films (regardless of whether a man or a women was the rape victim) rated the female rape victim in the trial as less physically and emotionally injured. These results are consistent with those of Zillmann and Bryant (1984), who found that massive exposure to sexually explicit media by jurors resulted in shorter recommended prison sentences for a rapist. Such findings show that the world we construct in response to seeing such movies not only can be at variance with reality but also can have dire consequences when actions are taken believing that such a world is reality.

Conclusions.   Not surprisingly, this study and others by the authors along the same line (see Donnerstein et al., 1987, for a review) have caused considerable concern in the public. They have also caused considerable scientific concern. Some of the major effects have not been replicated in

later work (Linz & Donnerstein, 1988), and there have been some methodological (Weaver, 1991) and content (Sapolsky & Molitor, 1996) criticisms.

The sharp distinction that Donnerstein and Linz made between the effects of violent and nonviolent pornography has been called into question
(Weaver, 1991; Zillmann & Bryant, 1988c). Research findings have been
somewhat inconsistent in each area; Zillmann and Bryant argued that Linz
and Donnerstein were too quick to cite failures to reject the null hypothesis as support for the harmlessness of nonviolent pornography. Check
and Guloien (1989) found that men exposed to a steady diet of rape-myth
sexual violence reported a higher likelihood of committing rape themselves, compared to a no-exposure control group, but the same result was
found for a group exposed to nonviolent pornography. There is considerable controversy, both scientific and political (see Box 10.5), about the use
and interpretation of data from particular studies. See Pollard (1995) for a
review of pornography and sexual aggression.

BOX 10.5
THE PORNOGRAPHY COMMISSIONS, OR WHY SCIENCE
AND POLITICS DON'T MIX

A commission was established by U.S. President Lyndon Johnson in 1967
to analyze (a) pornography control laws, (b) the distribution of sexually
explicit materials, and (c) the effects of consuming such materials, and to
recommend appropriate legislative or administrative action. It funded more
than 80 research studies on the topic, providing important impetus to the
scientific study of sexually explicit material. The final report three years later
recommended stronger controls on distribution to minors but an abolition
of all limits on access by adults. The latter recommendation was based on
the majority conclusion that "there was no evidence that exposure to or use
of explicit sexual materials play a significant role in the causation of social
or individual harms such as crime, delinquency, sexual or nonsexual de-
viancy or severe emotional disturbance" (U.S. Commission on Obscenity
and Pornography, 1970, p. 58). Although the composition of the commission
has been criticized for being overloaded with anticensorship civil libertarians, its majority conclusions were rejected anyway by the new administration of Richard Nixon, who declared, "so long as I am in the White House
there will be no relaxation of the national effort to control and eliminate smut
from our national life" (Eysenck & Nias, 1978, p. 94).

Some years later, a second commission was formed. U.S. Attorney
General Edwin Meese charged this commission in 1985 to assess the nature,
extent, and impact of pornography on U.S. society, and to recommend
more effective ways to contain the spread of pornography, clearly stating a
political position. One of the major conclusions of the commission dealt with
the effect of sexual violence: "the available evidence strongly supports the

hypothesis that substantial exposure to sexually violent materials bears a causal relationship to antisocial acts of sexual violence, and for some subgroups, possibly the unlawful acts of sexual violence" (Final Report, 1986, p. 40).

Groups like these commissions typically have both a scientific and a political agenda (Einsiedel, 1988; Paletz, 1988; Wilcox, 1987). Sometimes, even if there is relative consensus on the scientific conclusions, there is often strong disagreement about the policy ramifications. For example, Linz, Donnerstein, and Penrod (1987) took exception with some of the conclusions drawn by the 1986 commission from those researchers' own work demonstrating deleterious effects of sexual violence. Linz et al. (1987) argued that the commission's call for strengthening obscenity laws was not an appropriate policy change based on the research, because it ignored the strong presence of sexually violent themes in other media not covered by such laws.

Nor are such political-scientific hybrids unique to the United States. During the same period, the Longford (1972) and Williams (B. Williams, Report of the Committee on Obscenity and Film Censorship, 1979) commissions in Great Britain issued reports, followed a few years later by the Fraser commission in Canada (Report of the Special Committee on Pornography and Prostitution, 1985). The major conclusion of these commissions was that there is a lack of conclusiveness of the research to date. Do such commissions serve a useful purpose?

Mitigating the Negative Effects of Sexual Violence

The results from the research showing strong desensitization effects are disturbing, especially given the widespread viewing of horror films by children and young teens and the overall increase in sexually violent media. Some studies have developed and evaluated extensive preexposure training procedures to attempt to lessen the desensitizing effects of sexual violence (Intons-Peterson & Roskos-Ewoldsen, 1989; Intons-Peterson, Roskos-Ewoldsen, Thomas, Shirley, & Blut, 1989; Linz, Donnerstein, Bross, & Chapin, 1986; Linz, Fuson, & Donnerstein, 1990). These studies have typically shown mitigating effects on some measures and not on others. Linz, et al. (1990) found that men were most strongly affected by the information that women are not responsible for sexual assaults perpetrated upon them. There is evidence that desensitization can be reduced by introducing information about rape myths and the inaccuracy of media portrayals *after* people have seen some of the sexually violent media. At least some participants were more impressed with such arguments *after* they had felt themselves excited and aroused by the film and had seen specific examples to illustrate the point of the debriefing/mitigation information. In the

---

BOX 10.6
ETHICS OF SEXUAL VIOLENCE RESEARCH

The more potential harm that is identified from viewing sexually explicit, especially sexually violent, materials, the more questions are raised about the ethics of doing research by exposing people to such materials (Malamuth, Feshbach, & Heim, 1980). Although we have clearly learned some valuable information, what will be the cost of this knowledge in terms of the lives of the research participants? This issue has been taken seriously by Malamuth, Heim, and Feshbach (1980) and others, who have offered an extensive debriefing, complete with information on the horrible reality of rape and the complete unreality of the victim enjoying it. They even included a discussion of why the myth of enjoying being raped was so prevalent in sexually violent media. Some studies have included evaluations of such debriefing sessions and shown that, compared to a control group not in the experiment, debriefed people showed less acceptance of rape myths (Donnerstein & Berkowitz, 1981; Malamuth & Check, 1980b). It is, of course, unethical to have an ideal control group that views the sexual violence in the experiment but is not debriefed!

---

context of having seen such a film, the specific points of the sensitization training have greater impact. See Box 10.6 for further discussion of ethical issues in such research.

Using a different approach, B. J. Wilson, Linz, Donnerstein, and Stipp (1992) measured the effect of seeing a prosocial TV movie about rape. They found that, compared to a control group, people viewing the film generally showed heightened awareness and concern about rape. However, not all groups were so affected. Unlike women and young and middle-aged men, men over 50 had their preexisting attitudes reinforced and actually blamed women more for rape *after* seeing the film. This suggests that the attitudes and experiences of the target audience of interventions must be carefully considered.

Although the discussion of sexual violence so far has dealt with effects of fictional portrayals, there is another type of material with this content, namely, news coverage of sexually violent crimes. This too is part of our exposure to sexually violent content.

Press Coverage of Sexually Violent Crimes

The way that the press covers crimes like rape can subtly support the rape myths. For example, even severe violence may sometimes be described in terms of passion or love. When a man kills his ex-wife and her boyfriend, the press calls it a "love triangle." When a man shoots and kills several coworkers, including a woman that refused to date him, it is called a "tragedy of spurned love." When a man kidnaps, rapes, and strangles to death his estranged wife, the press reports that he "made love to his wife, and then choked her when he became overcome with jealous passion" (Jones, 1994). Does love really have anything to do with such crimes?

Benedict (1992) identified several problems with the press coverage of sex crimes. To begin with, there is a gender bias of the writers, reporters, and editors covering such crimes. They are two or three times more likely to be male than female, usually crime and police reporters. There is also a gender bias of language, with women always more likely than men to be described in terms of their physical appearance and sexuality. Some rape myths are subtly supported by describing rape as a sex crime due to unfulfilled sexual need. Less often do we encounter rape presented as an act of torture, although that perspective is more likely to be used in reporting of wartime rapes. For example, when mass raping of Bosnian women occurred in the Bosnian civil war of the early 1990s, it was reported as an act of war, as torture, and there was no description of the victims' attractiveness or dress or flirtatious behavior.

In her content-analysis studies of numerous newspaper reports of several high-profile rape cases, Benedict (1992) identified two common rape narratives, both of which distort and trivialize the crime. The most common is the *vamp*, a sexy woman who incites the lust of a man, who then cannot control himself and rapes her. A second narrative is the *virgin*, the pure and innocent woman attacked by a vicious monster, who is often portrayed as crazed and who often has darker skin than the victim. Benedict identifies several factors that increase the likelihood that the press will use the vamp narrative, i.e., blaming the victim. She is more likely to be described with the ramp narrative if (a) she knew the assailant, (b) no weapon was used, (c) she was young and pretty, (d) she showed deviation from traditional sex roles, and (e) she was of the same or lower-status race, class, and/or ethnic group as the rapist. The more of these conditions that hold, the more likely it is that the reporting will conform to the vamp narrative; the fewer of them that hold, the more likely it is that the case will be told as a virgin narrative.

Why does such bias occur? Benedict in part blames the habitual pressure of deadlines but also our emphasis on victims of crimes. While this is in part a well-meaning sympathy, it also taps into a desire of reporters and all of us to reassure ourselves that such acts will not happen to *us* because *we* don't behave like that. Thus, the behaviors and attributes of the victim are highlighted. There is less emphasis on the rapist, especially in the vamp narrative, and not much examination of the societal forces that drive men to behave in such violent ways. Such biases can have consequences. When a Texas grand jury in 1993 refused to indict a man for rape because his quick-thinking victim had convinced him to use a condom, the public outcry forced a reconsideration.

One particular touchy issue is the question of whether to publish the names of victims of rape and similar crimes. Although some have argued for doing so (e.g., Gartner, 1991), most journalists have continued to respect the privacy of victims. For an eloquent argument for preserving such privacy, see Pollitt (1991).

CONCLUSION

What may we conclude from the research on the perceived reality and effects from viewing sexual media? First, it is useful to make a distinction between violent and nonviolent sexual media, although this distinction may not be quite as important as Linz and Donnerstein have argued. While there are some negative effects of nonviolent material, especially on attitudes toward women (Weaver, 1991; Zillmann & Bryant, 1988a, 1988b), the research is particularly compelling in the case of sexual violence. Sexual violence is arousing to sex offenders, naturally violent men, and sometimes even to normal men if the woman is portrayed as being aroused by the attack. For reviews and meta-analyses of results from numerous experimental studies on the effects of viewing sexually explicit media, see Allen, D'Alessio, & Brezgel, 1995; Allen, Emmers, Gebhardt, & Giery, 1995; Bauserman, 1996; Gunter, 2001, 2002; Harris & Scott, 2002; Lyons, Anderson, & Larson, 1994; Malamuth & Impett, 2001; Pollard, 1995; and Strasburger, 1995.

Repeated exposure to sexual violence may lead to desensitization toward violence against women in general and greater acceptance of rape myths. Not only does this suggest that the combination of sex and violence together is considerably worse than either one separately, but it also matters further what the nature of the portrayal is. If the woman being assaulted is portrayed as being terrorized and brutalized, negative effects on normal male viewers are less than if she is portrayed as being aroused and/or achieving orgasm through being attacked. Perhaps more than any other topic discussed in this book, this is an extremely dangerous reality for the media to create and for us to accept as real. There is nothing arousing or exciting about being raped, and messages to the contrary do not help teenage boys understand the reality of how to relate to girls and women.

Not all the themes of sexual aggression against women are limited to specifically sexual material or even very violent movies. These images are even found in mainstream television. For example, in a content analysis study, Lowry, Love, and Kirby (1981) found that, except for erotic touching among unmarried persons, aggressive sexual contact was the most frequent type of sexual interaction in daytime soap operas. Some years ago

---

BOX 10.7
NORMATIVE PORNOGRAPHY THEORIES

Two of the most prominent researchers on sexual media, Linz and Mala-muth (1993), have talked about how various normative theories have guided research and may be lurking behind the scientific evidence. First is the *conservative-moralist* theory. This position, very prominent in Anglo-American history and culture, sees public portrayals of sex as disgusting and offensive. However, they are at the same time arousing and are seen as very threatening if the sex occurs outside of monogamous relationships. There is an implicit belief that a heavy emphasis on sexual gratification and permissiveness leads to behavior that undermines other moral beliefs about woman and sexuality and ultimately to the decay of family and other traditional societal structures. This position would tend to encourage re-search on sexual arousal and what materials produce it and how exposure to sexual materials undermines traditional attitudes and can affect later reactions.

A second normative theory is the *liberal* theory, which believes that sexual depictions trigger fantasies but that these fantasies are not acted out and thus no one is hurt. They may even be socially beneficial through liberating a person's excessive prudishness. Liberals believe that if sexual behavior (and the viewing of it) is kept private, then the government should not restrict or regulate what is best left to the marketplace of ideas, which will adjust to changing social standards. The liberal theory would tend to more highly value research on physical and behavioral effects of sexual media in the real world rather than in the laboratory. It would also favor media literacy education and counteracting antisocial messages with competing messages rather than through legislative restriction.

The third and most recent normative theory is *feminist* theory, which views pornography as a powerful socializing agent that promotes the sexual abuse of women and the social subordination of women as a group. Feminist-inspired research tends to focus on the arousal, or lack of it, of women in rape scenes. It also tends to look more at attitudes than behaviors, including differences between men with or without a propensity to rape.

Linz and Malamuth recognize that each normative theory has inspired some useful research, but they stress that we must recognize researchers' ideological positions when we evaluate their conclusions and the place of their studies in the matrix of overall media effects research.

---

a story line of *General Hospital* focused on the rape of one main character by another. Although the woman first appeared humiliated, she later fell in love with the rapist and married him. *Newsweek* reported that producers and actors in soap operas believe the increase in sexual aggression in that genre has attracted more male viewers, who "started watching us because we no longer were wimps. When a woman was wrong, we'd slap her down" (Soap operas, 1981, p. 65).

Such images appear in other media as well. A content analysis of detective magazines found that 76% of the covers depicted domination of women, whereas 38% depicted women in bondage (Dietz, Harry, & Hazelwood, 1986), all of this in a publication never even considered sexual, much less pornographic! Studies of rock videos (Hansen & Hansen, 1990a; Zillmann & Mundorf, 1987) show that sexual content is highly appealing but that violent content is not. Although sexual violence may have the negative effects just discussed, it may not even be enjoyed. The effect of parental warning labels about sexual content on CDs and tapes is not entirely clear, but in one study (Christenson, 1992) these labels seemed to decrease appeal to middle school students. However, these sexually violent themes are pervasive in much media and no quick fix of stricter pornography laws or warning labels will make them go away entirely.

The reality of some of these media is that men dominate women and even brutalize them. Moreover, the women are sometimes portrayed as being sexually turned on by being raped or tortured. That is the message about how men treat women, but what is the cost of this message on those in the public who may not realize that this picture deviates so significantly from reality?

On such an emotionally charged topic as pornography, we need to be aware of our own biases and ideology that we bring to the topic. Even the scientific research can be directed, in part, by the researchers' ideology (see Box 10.7).

Finally, just as people believe that *other people* are influenced more in general by media than they are themselves, the so-called *third-person effect* (Perloff, 2002; Gunther, 1991), people believe that others are influenced more by pornography than they are (Gunther, 1995). This is exactly what people believe about the effects of advertising (Gunther & Thorson, 1992) and news coverage (Gunther, 1991; Perloff, 1989). It always affects the other guy, not ourselves.

CHAPTER 11

Teaching Values and Health: Media as Parent, Priest, Physician, and Moral Arbiter

Q: How much of television can be considered educational TV?

A: According to former FCC chairman Nicholas Johnson, "All of it. The only question is, what is it teaching?"

Q: What percentage of fictional TV characters have an identifiable religious affiliation, compared to what percentage of actual Americans who claim a religious affiliation?

A: While 89% of Americans claim some religious affiliation, only 5% of TV characters do, and most of them are on just a few shows (Skill, Lyons, & Larson, 1991).

Q: What was the effect of NBC *Today* anchor Katie Couric undergoing a colonoscopy on national television in March 2000?

A: According to a study in the *Archives of Internal Medicine*, colonoscopy rates in the U.S. jumped over 20% after the nation saw the inside of Katie's bowels on TV. With colon cancer almost always curable if detected early but still the second leading cause of cancer deaths, Katie undoubtedly saved many lives. Incidentally, this was not an idle publicity stunt; Couric's husband had recently died at 42 from colon cancer and Katie was determined to save others the heartbreak that her family had suffered (Bjerklie, 2003).

Much of this book has focused on rather problematic perceived realities gleaned from the media: worlds of excessive violence, deception, stereotyping, or sexual promiscuity. However, media can be used in more positive ways. In this chapter we examine some of this potential, where the media are intentionally or otherwise used to produce or encourage socially positive outcomes. We begin by looking at the issue of values very generally and how the media can be a teacher of values, with a particular focus on values about family and the image of religion in media. Next, we will look at public service media campaigns to teach improved health behaviors. Finally, we examine the use of entertainment media such as prime-time television and movies to teach explicit prosocial lessons.

MEDIA'S TEACHING OF VALUES

One of the concerns often raised about the role of media in society is their role as teachers of values, "passing the social heritage from one generation to the next" (Lasswell, cited in G. Tuchman, 1987, p. 195). What the precise content of this social heritage is continues to be debated, however. Although relatively few print media stories or radio or TV broadcasts have the explicit purpose of teaching values, values are being taught implicitly, particularly by television. Here we define *values* very broadly as attitudes dealing with any topic where there is a moral dimension, i.e., a readily perceived right and wrong position.

On the one hand, the media may be seen as mirroring the values of the society in which they occur. If sexual values support promiscuity in a society, this will be reflected in its media; if certain religious values predominate in a society, they will also prevail in its media. On the other hand, the media may be seen as a catalyst for value change in a society. Values in the media may not exactly reflect those prevailing in society but may serve, not necessarily by design, as a force for moving society's values in a new direction. This is, of course, exactly the concern of media critics who argue that U.S. television and cinema most strongly reflect the values of the New York and Los Angeles communities where most programming originates and thus tends to cultivate those values in the rest of the country.

Taking a different approach, critics sometimes argue that media have a responsibility to lead society in the direction of more prosocial values; for example, after the terrorist attacks of September 11, 2001, there were calls for media to promote ethnic harmony and not inflame passions against Muslims out of anger over the al-Qaeda attacks. Some countries take a much stronger position; in multicultural Singapore and Malaysia, for example, media are censored and not allowed to say anything that might encourage intergroup animosity.

We often hear laments that television and film are so much more permissive today than they used to be ("Oh, if we could just have back the good old days of *Ozzie and Harriet*, *The Donna Reed Show*, *The Brady Bunch*, and *Leave It to Beaver* when family values were solid"). Clearly, in many respects Western media are more permissive today than they used to be, although the situation is far from anything goes. In fact, there are some ways in which media are less permissive and stricter today than they were 50 years ago. Perhaps most prominent among the restrictive trends is any content or language that could be considered racist or sexist. The early TV hit sitcom *Amos and Andy* was considered too racist even to show in reruns as early as the mid-1950s; today it would be extremely offensive and inappropriate, if not downright grotesque. Racist jokes simply are not acceptable in U.S. prime time media, except possibly from a very bad character in a drama.

Any real or implied violence against women, unless it is critically examined in a dramatic context, is another very touchy area. Ralph Kramden in *The Honeymooners* shaking his fist in his wife's face and angrily saying, "One of these days, Alice, pow, right in the kisser!" was hilarious in 1955. Today it strikes modern viewers as offensive and inappropriate, much as a sitcom father swearing profusely or having a homosexual experience might have seemed in the mid-1950s. Rhett Butler persisting in his sexual overtures to Scarlett O'Hara in spite of her saying "no" in *Gone with the Wind* could be defined as rape today, although it was considered romantic in 1939. In fact, there is good reason to believe that the golden age of the 1950s was not quite the way people often remember it (see Box 11.1).

Although most of the concern and study of values has focused on television and film, print media and radio are by no means uninvolved in value issues. Newspaper editors are continually faced with questions of how much information to print about crime victims. Radio stations must worry about listener response to song or rap lyrics that go too blatantly against prevailing social values, e.g., Prodigy's "Smack My Bitch Up," rapper Ice-T's "Cop Killer," Intelligent Hoodlum's "Bullet in the Brain" (about killing a police officer), or many selections by Eminem.

In this section we look at how media are involved in teaching or reinforcing values, particularly in the areas of family values and religion. These areas are offered as examples and are not meant to be an exhaustive discussion of values with which media are involved. Also, each of these two areas actually includes several more specific issues. Most of the comments primarily reflect media in the United States and may or may not be directly applicable to other nations, but all nations have some important media values issues.

Media transmission of values is perhaps the most difficult area of this book in which to do solid, well-controlled empirical research. Although there is much discussion of the effect of media on social values, there is much less good research that offers definitive answers. There has been some content and effects research, however, and some of that will be examined in this chapter. In terms of the theoretical perspective, probably the cultivation theory (Gerbner et al., 2002; Signorielli & Morgan, 2001) and uses and gratifications approaches (A. M. Rubin, 2002) have been most

---

BOX 11.1
THE REAL STORY OF THE GOLDEN AGE OF THE 1950s

Critics of modern media and society in the United States often lament that we have lost the solid family values of the 1950s, the last decade of television before all the social upheavals of the 1960s. Historian of the family Stephanie Coontz (1992, 1997) looks more carefully at this alleged golden age and finds that all was not in fact as golden as we remember it.

Coontz argues that the 1950s was a decade unlike any before or since. First, it was an era of unparalleled economic expansion; there was more growth in real wages in any year of the 1950s than in the entire period 1980 to 1995. Birth rates skyrocketed, approaching the rate of India. Even under the Republican Eisenhower administration, there was greater federal government support for families than there has ever been before or since. With the GI Bill paying college tuition, large amounts of money available for first home purchases and education costs, and numerous jobs available building interstate highways, expanding infrastructure and heavy industry, the 1950s were one of the very few eras in U.S. history when a large number of families could thrive on a single income. The divorce rate was lower than in the years that followed but also lower than what had proceeded: one third of the pre-World War II marriages had ended in divorce or abandonment. There was also a massive shift in family structure. People were moving to the suburbs and farther away from extended families, thus putting all of their energy into the nuclear family, a model reinforced by the cheery sitcoms of the time. Not everyone was prospering, however. Most minorities were largely excluded from the American dream. Rates of domestic violence, crime, incest, and child abuse were high but denied, since their principal victims were racial, ethnic, and gender minorities. A larger percentage of children were living in poverty than do today. Coontz argues that the 1950s are a time we could never return to if we wanted to, and she questions whether we should even want to.

---

useful in generating and guiding research. As certain consistent values are repeated in a variety of specific instances, they then cultivate those values in the consumer. How strongly those values are cultivated may sometimes depend on the consumer's particular uses of the media and what gratifications they are obtaining from that use.

FAMILY VALUES

Family values is an often-heard phrase in social and political discourse, but it has different meanings to different people, because there are many value issues that relate to the family and the relationships among its members. For reviews of research on the effects of media on family values, see D. Brown and J. Bryant (1990), Gunter and Svennevig (1987), Pitta (1999), and especially the fine collection of papers in Bryant and Bryant (2001).

Family Composition

A content analysis of 630 U.S. network TV shows featuring families over 45 years from 1950 to 1995 showed that overall about 55% of the children were boys, and that families were almost exclusively white until the 1970s, with African Americans the only significant minority since then. The proportion of traditional nuclear families fell from 38% to 25% of the total families from the 1950s to 1960s but has remained constant since the 1960s. The number of extended family configurations has increased (18% to 26%), and the number of childless families has declined (24% to 12%). Single-father families have always outnumbered single-mother families on TV, but the reverse is true in real life (Robinson & Skill, 2001). Divorced major characters did not appear until the debut in 1975 of *One Day at a Time*, featuring a divorced mother and her two teenage daughters, although divorced adults have been fairly common on TV since that time.

How are families portrayed on television? Family-interaction patterns showed more harmonious conflict-resolution behaviors in traditional than in nontraditional families (Skill, Wallace, & Cassata, 1990). Working-class families are far rarer on TV than upper middle class families and they show more distressed and less happy relationships than the middle and upper classes do (Douglas, 2001). Sibling relationships are overall positive, though less deep and meaningful than in real life (Larson, 2001). The psychological health of TV families in the 1990s was rated quite high in the categories of cohesion, adaptation, and communication skills, suggesting some positive role modeling (Bryant, Aust, Bryant, & Venugopalan, 2001).

In recent decades, most often both parents in TV families have had careers outside of the home, or one parent brings his or her career into the home. However, a major departure from reality is the way that modern TV families appear to manage career and family demands so successfully and effortlessly that the difficulties inherent in managing two-career families are glossed over, if not totally ignored (Heintz-Knowles, 2001). There are few appearances of child care providers or day care; more often than not, one of the employed parents is completely available at home. The spheres of home and career on TV are presented as separate domains which seldom intersect and as such is a "misrepresentation of the lives of most American adults, but it can send powerful message to viewers struggling with these collisions, and to their employers and colleagues" (Heintz-Knowles, 2001, p. 197).

These content analyses show that TV family portrayals present a very positive picture overall. Family members are most likely to be of traditional gender-role orientation, and children tend to be very precocious. Interactions among family members are most often cooperative and helpful. Where conflict exists, most often between siblings, it is generally handled positively and resolved by the end of the half-hour. The use of power in families is usually reasonable, with mutual concern and respect as predominant values. Family happiness is not related to financial status, with family unity being stronger for middle-class than for wealthy families (Comstock & Strzyzewski, 1990; M. S. Larson, 1989, 2001a; Robinson & Skill, 2001; Skill, 1994; Skill, Robinson, & Wallace, 1987; Skill & Wallace, 1990; Skill, Wallace, & Cassata, 1990).

Even in the context of traditional families, some of the patterns of interaction have greatly changed from the more authoritarian days of *Father Knows Best* and *Leave It to Beaver*. Parents and children are much more likely to talk out differences, often complete with yelling and immature behavior on both sides. See Box 11.2 for two examples from popular sitcom episodes illustrating just how much parent-child relationships have changed.

Family Solidarity

Perhaps the most pervasive of the family values on TV is family solidarity (loyalty, support, and love for one's family). This is most clearly seen in the family sitcom. The basic message here, as true for *The Simpsons* and *Everybody Loves Raymond* in the early 21st century as it was for *Leave It to Beaver* or *Father Knows Best* 40 to 50 years earlier, is that one's family is more important than money, power, greed, status, or career advancement. Even the most irreverent family shows teach a family cohesiveness that tends in the final analysis to strongly affirm traditional values; for example, when *The Simpson's* dad Homer lost his job, the whole family pitched in to help save money.

One may ask if such family solidarity is a realistic reflection of our society. It clearly is for many families and just as clearly is not for many others, whose troubled family dynamics would more typically be characterized by vicious backstabbing, betrayal, and generally putting oneself above other family members. Still, even those families might agree that the sitcom characterization is a worthy ideal to hold up as a model, even if it is not totally realistic. Maybe this is a socially helpful model to portray and can help offer some useful new cognitive scripts to viewers in dysfunctional families.

BOX 11.2
CASE STUDIES OF MODERN FAMILY RELATIONS

Case 1: An episode of the 1980s sitcom *Family Ties* presented a story in which high school senior Alex Keaton anticipates his 18th birthday by withdrawing from family responsibilities and interaction. The final blow comes when he goes with some friends to a bar, defying his parents' plans for a family birthday dinner. His mother Elyse drives some distance to retrieve an embarrassed Alex from this peer gathering. After they arrive home, both are seething with anger. After Alex sarcastically yells at his mother about his right to do as he likes now that he is an adult, she responds in only slightly more controlled fashion, "you have complained to me, grunted at me, lectured to me, and presented me with ultimatums [but never] even come close to talking with me." She accuses him of canceling out on family dinner plans "without a moment's thought to *my* concern." Gradually growing contrite, Alex eventually acknowledges, "I'm sorry I wasn't more sensitive," and both acknowledge that they have made mistakes in dealing with each other. When Alex asks "How do we figure out who's right and who's wrong?" Elyse responds that there is no absolute right or wrong and then offers a startling statement about contemporary parent-child relations: "It's my job as a parent to set boundaries and it's your job to negotiate the changes."

In this scene, fairly typical of family shows of the last 20 to 25 years, the morally serious transgression of the child is not disobedience but *insensitivity.* If there are troubles in the family, the parents have probably made mistakes as well as the children. Parent-child interactions are to be negotiations, not decrees followed by obedience. Even though traditional family solidarity and family values are in many ways affirmed today as they have always been on TV, the specific nature has changed somewhat.

Case 2: The 1990s workplace sitcom *Spin City* featured an episode where Mike, a big-city mayor's political damage control assistant, has to deal with rumors of the mayor's extramarital affairs. After finally tracking down the mayor in the middle of the night in a hotel room with a woman, he is surprised to find his own mother coming out of the bathroom.

Although Mike is surprised and distressed to find his mother as the object of his boss' latest sexual escapade, it is the sitcom distress of the awkward situation that stands out, not the moral outrage of a son who has been devastated by discovering his mother in circumstances sons do not imagine their mothers in. Although dialogue earlier in the same episode had made clear Mike's close relationship to and respect for his mother and his basic contempt for the dalliances of his employer, his chagrin at the discovered tryst has no moral dimension or outrage at all. It is just merely another momentarily awkward situation.

Family solidarity may occur in groups other than biological families. Television shows which feature a group of friends, for example, *Friends*, *That 70s Show, Seinfeld, Sex in the City*, and *Beverly Hills 90210*, basically uphold the group of friends as the de facto family unit. Typically, the loyalty to this social family is even stronger than to one's biological family, which the featured group has apparently replaced for these particular characters. Another common setting for both sitcoms and dramatic shows is the workplace, which essentially becomes a surrogate family (e.g., *ER, Spin City, NYPD Blue, Scrubs, Cheers*). The strong message in these shows is always love your coworker (even if you really don't) and put his or her needs above your own. This, more than traditional family solidarity, is more tenuously tied to reality.

One aspect of workplace solidarity is probably a direct consequence of the TV series format. This is the way that characters are so intimately involved in the personal lives of fellow workers, employers, and employees. Although real-life coworkers may sometimes be close friends, such intimacy is not typically, and it is almost unheard of in the real world for *all* of the workers in a unit to be close personal friends. Yet this is the typical case in television land. For example, when one character delivers her baby, the entire crew from the office is on hand. In real life this would not only be unlikely, but probably obtrusively inappropriate and unappreciated, even if for some reason it did occur.

Perhaps even more of a deviation from reality is the way that this workplace solidarity is extended to the clients of a professional. For example, one of the doctors on *ER* might spend his day off to find a lost family member of a patient or to smooth out a domestic quarrel that he believed was interfering with the recovery of the patient. In real life, physicians seldom do this sort of thing and might be considered derelict in their duty at the hospital if they did. Still, such an image of a professional is appealing because that is what we want to *think* our doctor would be like. Even if I have never been a patient in a hospital, it comforts me to feel that a doctor I might have would be as caring as Dr. Carter on *ER*.

Before leaving the subject of family solidarity, we should consider one important class of apparent exceptions to this theme, namely soap operas and similar movies and miniseries. The mean-spirited and self-serving backstabbing between family members would seem to be as opposite as it can be from family solidarity. It is interesting to note that there was a period of great popularity of nighttime soaps like *Dallas* and *Dynasty* in the 1980s. However, in the years since, the nighttime soap genre with its dueling family members has all but disappeared in the United States, although the workplace dramas and family sitcoms are as strong as ever. Of course, daytime soaps remain popular, even more so due to the time-shifting capabilities of the VCR. Also, in much of the world, soap opera-type shows remain the most popular type of program (e.g., the telenovelas of Latin America), although shows in some of these cultures depict strong family cohesion. See Pingree and Thompson (1990) for a discussion of the nature of the family in daytime soaps and Liebes and Livingstone (1992) for a comparison of British and U.S. soap operas.

The Influence of Television on Family Life

Does television add to or detract from the quality of family life? The conventional wisdom is that TV has a negative influence, but that conclusion is by no means certain or simple. In some instances, family TV viewing can be a positive time of family discussion and interaction, including commenting on the programs or laughing and crying together. In other instances, it can be very negative, for example, if it induces quarreling among family members over what program to watch or whether to turn off the set. Particular conflicts may occur around certain events such as mealtimes, bedtimes, or children's disagreement with parental prohibitions of certain programs.

A uses and gratifications approach to studying family TV use looks at motivations for watching, which may vary greatly depending on the program or the individuals' moods. For example, Kubey (1986) found that divorced and separated people watch TV more when they feel down and alone than married or other single people do, perhaps due to their use of TV for solace and comfort to replace a lost relationship.

Men and women may view television watching differently. For example, men and boys are more likely to control the remote and channel-surf; this behavior is often the source of TV-based marital conflict (Gantz, 2001; Walker & Bellamy, 2001). The gender difference is stronger with older than younger couples, although younger people do more channel surfing in general. In terms of uses and gratifications, women saw TV viewing as more of a social activity and were also more likely to be doing other activities (e.g., housework) concurrently, whereas men were more likely to devote full attention to the program. Men saw TV watching as "earned recreation," whereas women saw it as a "guilty pleasure," a distraction from homemaking duties (Morley, 1988).

Working within one's home to have television viewing enhance, rather than detract from, family life is a major challenge for families. See Chen (1994) for some excellent advice for families in this regard. Other value issues that parents should take note of include abstract but pervasive values such as affluence (see Box 11.3) and more specific ones, such as tobacco and alcohol use and abuse (see Box 11.4).

Does television have a fascination with affluence, even opulence? What subtle messages are sent to middle-class and poor viewers? This is most blatantly seen in voyeuristic shows like *Lifestyles of the Rich and Famous, Who Wants to Marry a Millionaire?*, or *A Current Affair*, the saturation news coverage of such stories as the O. J. Simpson trials (1995–1996) and the death of Princess Diana (1997), and the continuing fascination with entertainment personalities in both tabloid and mainstream media. Seeing all this glitz and glamor may lead viewers to assume that such lifestyles are realistic aspirations for themselves. Even sitcom families, although generally not super-rich, typically live in very large, well-decorated homes rich in splendor and space—especially striking given the great amount of time that the wage-earners spend at home instead of on the job.

Why are affluent people so interesting to watch? There is some evidence that hard economic times bring on more escapist stories of the perils of great wealth, as seen in the many movies of wealthy people that were popular during the Great Depression of the 1930s, in contrast to many movies and TV shows about poor people popular during the affluent 1950s. People like to watch rich people and their fine trappings like sports cars and fancy clothes, but also like to be reminded that these people have serious problems too, preferably more serious than their own. Maybe this is reassuring.

Still another factor is that the producers of television and films themselves tend to be rather affluent, mostly from southern California. The media grossly over-represent the world of those who produce the programming, which tacitly presents this world as far more typical of overall American life than it really is. Most shows are set in Los Angeles or New York, few in Tennessee or South Dakota. Some research suggests that exported programs of glitz and glamor may be cultivating negative images of Americans in viewers elsewhere (Harris & Karafa, 1999; Kamalipour, 1999). Popular TV programs dwelling on the rich are by no means a uniquely North American phenomenon; many developing countries' domestic shows also present such affluent lifestyles. For example, the telenovelas of Mexico and Brazil present characters with income levels and lifestyles wildly beyond the reach of most of their nation's viewers.

Some very deeply held values center around substance use and abuse. Perhaps the greatest change in this area since the early days of TV is in the attitudes and behavior about smoking. Like many early TV characters, Lucy and Ricky Ricardo smoked cigarettes regularly in the old *I Love Lucy* show of the 1950s, sometimes at the specific request of the tobacco company sponsor. With very few exceptions, however, regular characters on TV series have not smoked since the 1960s, clearly out of a health concern over a possible negative effect on youth seeing admired TV characters smoking. Although this certainly reflects the great decline in the percentage of adult smokers since 1960, it may have also contributed to that decline. Even among teens, smoking is much less cool than it used to be, and television may be part of the reason for that. Curiously, however, the same trend is not apparent in movies, where characters smoke far more frequently; this is probably due in part to product-placement agreements with tobacco companies to feature those products (see chapter 4). Recent indications of a possible rise in teen smoking have focused more attention on such media models.

In regard to alcohol, the most widely abused drug, the United States has seen decreasing acceptance of alcohol abuse since the mid-1980s and 1990s. Although social drinking remains at high, although at modestly reduced levels, and alcoholism as a disease and a social problem is still rampant, attitudes about excessive drinking are much less tolerant in the United States than previously. The drunk is not so much an object of humor as of pity or disgust. Portrayals of drinking on TV have had to, at least implicitly, take note of this. Whether TV has been a factor in producing this societal change in values or whether it is merely reflecting what has been caused by other social forces is unclear at this point. One area of recent concern is binge drinking among college students. This is perhaps encouraged by, for example, university newspaper stories about people celebrating their 21st birthdays by visiting several bars until totally drunk, or by a telephone or credit card company ad showing a fellow passed out on the bathroom floor with "Happy 21st" written below. Is this just reporting reality or is it legitimizing dangerous antisocial behavior?

Finally, TV shows today are careful not to show illicit drug use by respected characters. Adults or teens may occasionally be shown using drugs, but it is nearly always presented as wrong. This mindset even carries over into news; when conservative U.S. Supreme Court nominee Douglas Ginsburg admitted in 1987 to past marijuana use, the media treated this as a very serious issue, ultimately culminating in the withdrawal of the nomination, even though polls showed that most Americans thought past marijuana use should not disqualify one from the Supreme Court. As the baby boom generation, who came of age in the 1960s and 1970s, began to move into leadership positions, however, reactions started changing. In 1992, Democratic Presidential nominee Bill Clinton admitted to trying marijuana once as a graduate student in 1969. This was greatly covered in the media (especially a rather curious statement that he "didn't inhale").[1] However, the public did not hold this transgression against Clinton; he won the election.

[1]When questioned later about the apparently self-serving "I didn't inhale" comment, Clinton explained that, having never smoked tobacco, he did not know how to inhale. This explanation, however, received very little coverage in the copious news coverage of this issue.

RELIGION

Perhaps no topic is so intimately tied up with values as is religion, the second general topic considered in this chapter. Gallup polls consistently show the United States to be by far the most religious industrialized country in the world (over 90% of Americans believe in God; over 40% attend religious services weekly), yet religion has often been one of the most touchy and neglected areas in media. When Beatle John Lennon said offhandedly in 1966 that their group was more popular than Jesus, many were highly offended. Even subsequent clarifications or apologies of sorts failed to mollify critics. Out of fear of controversy, religion often becomes invisible in media, especially television and popular movies, or rather invisible except for the overtly religious programming, which is most typically viewed primarily by those already of that faith. Let us examine several aspects of religion in the media.

Religion in TV Series

Generally speaking, religion plays almost no significant role in the lives of entertainment series characters. Even very traditional families hardly ever mention going to church or believing in God. They also, however, rarely mention that they do *not* go to church or that they do *not* believe in God. It appears that producers are loathe to offend anyone either by identifying their favorite TV characters with a particular faith or by saying that they have none. Action-adventure shows have virtually no mention of religion either, with an occasional exception of having an extreme religious fanatic or terrorist as a villain.

This absence of religious themes probably reflects (a) TV producers' and writers' relative lack of involvement with religion themselves, compared to most Americans, and, most importantly, (b) an implicit recognition that religion is a very touchy subject and one where people are easily offended. Perhaps they fear that Protestants and Jews will stop watching *Home Improvement* if the Taylors are identified as Catholic or that atheists and agnostics will lose interest in *Friends* if Chandler and Monica became born-again Christians. For a collection of readings of how different Christian groups use media, see Stout and Buddenbaum (1996).

In a content analysis of 100 episodes of U.S. prime time network entertainment TV, Skill et al. (1991) found only 5% of the characters with an identifiable religious affiliation, compared to 89% of the U.S. population. Over half of those identified characters were Roman Catholic, with the rest Protestant, cult members, or New Age adherents. There were no Jews, Muslims, or any other religions represented. A large proportion of those few that were represented appeared on a few episodes of particular shows,

---

BOX 11.5
THE MOST RELIGIOUS SITCOM

By most estimates, the prime-time show on American TV that takes religion the most seriously is the irreverent animated sitcom *The Simpsons*. Unlike almost any other TV family, the Simpsons attend church weekly, pray before meals, self-identify as Christians, and generally find spiritual issues important in their lives. To be sure, the sharp-edged show satirizes the foibles of religion, as it does just about everything else, but Homer and Marge and the kids return to God in prayer and trust time and again. They attend Springfield Community Church (no denomination specified). Neighbor Ned Flanders is a somewhat rigid evangelical Christian, but he is more than the totally hypocritical caricature that most prime-time evangelical Christians are reduced to. If Bart Simpson prays before dinner, "Rub-a-dub-dub. Thanks for the grub," he is not unlike many of our own children. When Marge tells God she will be a better person and give the poor something they really like, not just old lima beans and pumpkin mix, it strikes a familiar chord.

Why do the producers of *The Simpsons* believe they can endow their sitcom family with a spiritual dimension while almost no other TV writers do? Is there something about the animated format that makes this less risky? Or is Matt Groening the only writer who has dared to try?

---

particularly a few non-specific "God" shows like *Touched by an Angel*. For more on the surprising candidate for the most religious sitcom, see Box 11.5. As Skill et al. (1991) found that adherents to religions other than Christianity are, as a whole, seldom seen on TV. When they are present, they are often stereotyped. Jews may be stereotyped by name, occupation, and perhaps by speaking a particularly irritating New York dialect. In the news they seem to appear especially in stories about the Holocaust, particularly as protesting against something that they view as disrespectful to Holocaust victims, or in reaction to U.S. or Israeli government Middle East policy. Muslims, who are usually Arabs, appear as suicide bombers or arrogant oil sheiks, with limousines and harems in tow (see chapter 3). Members of some Eastern religions appear as airhead airport panhandlers or ascetic navel gazers, on the very rare occasions that they appear at all.

Portrayals of Religious Professionals

Except for explicitly religious programming like the *Billy Graham Crusades*, *The 700 Club*, or the Christian Broadcasting Network, religious professionals are greatly underrepresented on U.S. television. When they are shown, they are often, at best, rather saintly but shallow characters, and, at worst, vicious hypocrites hiding behind their clerical collars. In many early Westerns, there was a man of the cloth, often a significant supporting, although seldom a lead, character. Historically, one of the most rounded and developed religious characters of long-running U.S. prime time TV history was Father Mulcahy on $M^*A^*S^*H$. Compared to the cardboard clergy making occasional cameo appearances on other shows, Mulcahy was interesting and complex, yet compared to practically every other character on the later $M^*A^*S^*H$, he was rather shallow.

A more insidious religious type is the fanatical cult preacher. These characters are very extreme and very evil. Such characters have to be very perverted so as not to evoke any sympathy or any criticisms about the program saying negative things about a real man of God. Such characters became especially popular after such news stories as would-be messiah David Koresh leading the Branch Davidian cult to a fiery death in 1993 in Waco, Texas, or the cult members who committed suicide in 1997 after believing that extraterrestrials would carry them off in the wake of the visit of the spectacular Hale-Bopp comet.

The success of the show *Touched by an Angel* in the mid-1990s caught the networks' notice of the public's interest in spiritual themes, even if in somewhat generalized and romanticized form. The fall lineup of 1997 shows featured several sitcoms and dramas with explicitly religious themes and characters. The most controversial, and most critically acclaimed, was *Nothing Sacred*, about a young Catholic priest struggling with his own humanity. Although created by a Jesuit priest and praised by critics like novelist priest Father Andrew Greeley, *Nothing Sacred* drew the wrath of the conservative Catholic League for showing a member of the clergy being attracted to a woman friend and counseling a woman considering abortion to follow her conscience (J. Stein, 1997a). Remembering that Reverend Donald Wildmon's American Family Association campaign against *NYPD Blue* had scared away enough advertisers to force the network to sell ad time at bargain-basement rates for a top-rated show, the networks took notice (Perkins, 1997). In the end, however, what probably killed *Nothing Sacred* was its sacrificial time slot opposite the top-rated *Friends*.

Religion in the News

Although, in general, religious news has traditionally been underreported in the United States, relative to its importance, a look at what is reported reveals some interesting trends.

What Is Covered. Religious news that is centered around an individual person receives relatively heavy coverage, following the star model of political news coverage (see chapter 7). Travels and pronouncements of the Pope, for example, are rather easy and predictable to cover, much more so than comparable Protestant or Jewish happenings that are less focused on a particular person. One exception to this is a flamboyant TV preacher, particularly one with extreme views. Fundamentalist sects, radical mullahs, and especially bizarre cults receive more coverage than mainstream religion, because they are more often focused on a charismatic individual with controversial views.

When religious events are covered by TV news, they tend most often to focus either on Roman Catholicism, whose colorful pageantry and identifiable newsmakers (especially the Pope) make good photogenic copy, or on Protestant fundamentalism, whose dogmatic theology and contentious political activism make good controversy-ridden stories, especially when centered around a charismatic individual. Groups of mainline Protestants politely discussing multiple points of view on social welfare, or Reform Jews examining different degrees of support for Israel may be just as important but less photogenically newsworthy.

The Televangelism Scandals.   Some changes in religious news coverage started in 1987 with several key events. Early that year Oral Roberts announced that God had told him He would "call Oral home" if several million dollars were not donated to his Tulsa ministry and hospital before a certain date. The subsequent revelation that popular TV evangelist Jim Bakker had had a sexual liaison with a secretary several years before was sharply at odds with the pious image that he and other televangelists sought to portray. This was followed by discoveries of financial mishandling of Bakker's PTL Ministries funds and of the extravagant lifestyle of Bakker and his wife Tammy. The ensuing public name-calling among evangelists Bakker, Jerry Falwell, Jimmy Swaggart, and others had more the character of soap opera family feuds than what people had come to expect from the electronic pulpits. The subsequent tryst of Jimmy Swaggart and a prostitute hardly cleaned up the image. Unlike many earlier religious stories, these were widely reported in the media and widely ridiculed by comedians. The media apparently decided in this case that comedy about religion, even scathing and derisive comedy, was acceptable, even though almost unprecedented in the United States.

The Role of Religion in Secular News Stories.   Although religion is sometimes simplistically presented as the basis of what are actually much more complex social problems (e.g., Northern Ireland, Palestine, Lebanon, India), in other cases the importance of religion is missed altogether. A prime example of this is the role of religion in the revolutions that brought down the communist regimes of eastern Europe in 1989 to 1991.

In Poland the Roman Catholic church had been the only legal forum for political discussion for years and, as such, had been the focus of dissent. Neighboring rebellious Lithuania, the only former Soviet republic with a majority Roman Catholic population, was the first to challenge Moscow and demand its independence. In Romania, the revolt against the brutal regime of Nicolae Çeauçescu began with a protest after a reformed church service in Timişoara, a western city near the border of less-censored, already-democratizing Hungary. The protesters were gunned down, but an outraged Romanian nation responded with a force that ended in the televised execution of the hated dictator and his wife on Christmas Day, 1989.

Probably most dramatic, however, was the situation in the old German Democratic Republic (GDR), where 40% of the officially atheistic country were practicing Lutherans, ironically a much larger percentage than in free West Germany. The weekly protests in Leipzig that led to the fall of the GDR government and its hated symbol, the Berlin Wall, in November 1989 had actually begun the previous summer with a weekly Monday night prayer meeting at a Lutheran church. Its numbers grew weekly from a handful of members who quietly picketed after the prayer meeting to a mass protest of thousands filling the streets. The church was given so much credit for the peaceful revolution that the Leipzig city government later hung a huge banner that read WIR DANKEN DIR, KIRCHE ("We thank you, church").

In the U.S. media, very little was said about the role of religion in these democratic revolutions. Why not? It was probably not a conspiracy of silence, but rather simply an oversight by people for whom religion was not very important in their own lives. Perhaps also, they were not used to seeing politics and religion interact in this very different way than they do in the United States. Another possible factor was some uneasiness regarding how to present the role of religion to a society used to having the religious sphere completely separate from the secular sphere, as it is in the United States.

In a somewhat different type of situation, religious dimensions of the news are sometimes ignored or underplayed when they become politically awkward. For example, when the U.S. media were patriotically drumming up support for wars against Iraq in 1991 and again in 2003, much was made of Iraqi leader Saddam Hussein's admittedly brutal dictatorship, but few stories mentioned that he did allow considerable freedom of religion and that Iraq was one of the few Arab nations with a sizable Christian minority. Moreover, U.S. ally Saudi Arabia rigidly forbade the practice of any religion but Islam, even to the extent of not allowing Christian and Jewish U.S. soldiers stationed there to privately practice their own faith.

Why are the mainstream media so reluctant to cover religious news and religious dimensions of secular news? Hoover (1998) suggests six mistaken beliefs. First is the belief that as societies become more modern and advanced, they necessarily become more secular and less religious; this tenet seems to be widely believed in American intellectual life. Second is the belief that religion is fundamentally a private matter and thus largely outside the realm of public discourse, including journalism. Third, religion makes claims outside the empirical realm of what is knowable and concrete. Journalism is "all about verification and sources, but religion is fundamentally unverifiable" (Hoover, 1998, p. 29). Fourth, religion is thought to be complex and thus hard to cover in a brief media piece. Fifth, religion is controversial and coverage, however careful and objective, is likely to offend someone. Finally, there is the misunderstanding that the First Amendment to the U.S. Constitution forbidding the establishment of a state church somehow implies the complete separation of church and state.

There is an interesting minority view in contrast to the view of the media as predominantly secular. Silk (1995) argues that several themes with their origins in religion actually pervade many secular news stories in ways that may not always be apparent. Some of these themes are applause for good works, embracing of tolerance, contempt for hypocrisy, appreciation of faith in things unseen, and concern about religious decline. These themes, while generally positive and socially useful, appear in coverage of news stories and are common themes in the small amount of explicitly religious general entertainment media (e.g., *Touched by an Angel*).

Religious Television

In the United States, although in few other places, explicitly religious programming is a multimillion-dollar business (Bruce, 1990; Hoover, 1988; Peck, 1992), produced and distributed totally separately from other television programming. This is consistent with the separation of religion from other aspects of American life. Religious books are sold in separate bookstores from secular books, religious music is typically recorded by different artists and marketed separately from other music, and religious television is produced by religious networks. Although largely a U.S. phenomenon, there is some international growth of TV evangelism, especially in Latin America and most notably in Guatemala, the first majority Protestant country in Latin America.

Although there was some Christian broadcasting in the early days of radio and television, the modern electronic church really began with Billy Graham's TV specials starting in 1957. These were later followed by Rex Humbard, Oral Roberts, Jerry Falwell, Robert Schuller, Jimmy Swaggart, Pat Robertson's *700 Club*, and Jim and Tammy Bakker's *PTL Club*. These took a variety of formats and emphases, including Robertson and Bakker's talk-show format, Falwell's emphasis on politics, and Roberts' focus on spiritual healing. All except Schuller were theologically evangelical or fundamentalist, with a heavy emphasis on evangelism (Hoover, 1988). In spite of its evangelistic emphasis, however, Christian TV attracts few non-believers and, in fact, serves mainly to reinforce the existing beliefs of its viewers (Fore, 1987).

The TV evangelism scandals of 1987 to 1988 were watershed events in the history of religious broadcasting. They seemed to confirm what critics of televangelism had been saying for some time, but now were allowed to say much more publicly. Fundraising for all TV ministries, even those un-tainted by scandal, became more difficult. The media reality of the sullied preacher, long suspected by many skeptics, became the perceived reality for many. Although this negative attention faded over time, some of the lost respect was never regained.

Effects of Television on Religion

It may be that the mere presence of television as a medium has altered all religion in subtle but profound ways, so much so that the perceived reality about religion will never be the same again. In his provocative book, *Amusing Ourselves to Death*, Neil Postman (1985) argued that television has radically reshaped practically everything about our lives. One domain that has been greatly changed is religion, in ways that go far beyond the Sunday broadcasts and the TV evangelists. Postman argued that, because TV is, at heart, entertainment, then the preacher is the star performer, and "God comes out as second banana" (p. 117). Although Christianity has always been "a demanding and serious religion," its TV version can acquire its needed share of the audience "only by offering people something they want" (p. 121), which is hardly historical Biblical Christianity. Furthermore, Postman argues, TV is such a fundamentally secular medium that religious TV uses many of the same symbols and formats (e.g., *The 700 Club* was modeled after *Entertainment Tonight*).

Thus, TV preachers are stars who are attractive and affluent just like movie stars. Worship on TV is not participatory; the audience can sit at home and absorb, but cannot have the corporate worship experience of group singing, praying, or liturgy. Although a church may be considered holy ground where people act with reverence, there is no comparable sa-cred space when watching church on TV at home, where one can sit in dirty underwear drinking beer and eating pizza during the sermon.

Postman (1985) argued that, as more and more religious services are broadcast on TV and as pastors are more acquainted with the television medium, the "danger is not that religion has become the content of tele-vision shows but that television shows may become the content of re-ligion" (p. 124). Pastors become concerned about providing the kind of worship conducive to television, even if the service is not being televised.

Congregations subtly expect to be entertained, even amused. Worship services have jazz music, rap liturgy, and computerized multimedia presentations. One church ran a full-page ad touting its contemporary Saturday evening service called "Church Lite" for college students who wanted to sleep in on Sunday. Other churches use Sunday school curricula like *The Gospel According to the Simpsons* or *The Gospel According to Harry Potter.* A Baptist church in Arkansas hired Wacky World Studios in Tampa for a $279,000 makeover of a former chapel into "Toon Town," with buzzers and confetti that explode during joyful celebrations like baptisms; the Sunday school attendance doubled (Labi, 2002). Is this a creative reaching out to people in mission or selling one's soul on the altar of popular culture? The answer is not always obvious.

Places of worship have no particular sacred character, because one can worship through TV while at home. One congregation worships regularly in a former roller rink, another in an old laundromat, whereas yet another rents space on Sunday mornings in a large university classroom. There is no sense of the sacred, as was found most strikingly in the magnificent cathedrals of Europe. Thus, behavior in the house of worship is no different than it is anywhere else. Has television contributed to this change? For a stimulating set of readings about media, religion, and society, see Hoover and Lundby (1997).

Some have argued that the big retail chains such as Wal-Mart have an undue but unrecognized control on religious media and popular culture more generally; see Box 11.6.

The media have tremendous potential, much of it as yet untapped, for inducing and encouraging positive social change. Now let us turn to media attempts to intentionally change behavior in socially positive ways through marketing healthy and safe behaviors, drawing on the model of marketing products.

MEDIA USE IN SOCIAL MARKETING

A traditionally underemphasized but currently booming area of marketing is *social marketing*, which involves the selling of socially and personally positive behaviors to ensure or improve one's health or safety (Atkin & Arkin, 1990; Backer, Rogers, & Sopory, 1992; Brown & Walsh-Childers, 2002; Flay & Burton, 1990; M. E. Goldberg, 1995; Manrai & Gardner, 1992; Wallack, 1990). Many social critics, researchers, and practitioners long concerned with selling products are now turning their attention to selling healthy, safe, and socially positive lifestyles. Mass media are a major, although not the only, component of a social marketing campaign. The perceived reality of the medium is intended to be a catalyst for some behavior or attitude change.

BOX 11.6
IS WAL-MART OUR MEDIA VALUES GATEKEEPER?

The growing economic power of retail giant Wal-Mart and other discount chains has led to concern about their influence on public values and taste. In 2003, Wal-Mart alone accounted for over 50% of the sales of best-selling albums/CDs, over 60% of best-selling DVDs and 40% of the best-selling books. Over one-third of all music sales was through the big chains, with 20% of the total from Wal-Mart alone. Because they sell so many of the best-selling items, Wal-Mart and other chains do not carry a broad assortment, a policy that leaves music, books, or films that have limited or esoteric tastes or are at all controversial left behind. For example, they sell no albums with parental warning labels, a policy that excludes Eminem and most hip–hop artists. They also sell huge amounts of Christian music, videos, and books. The *VeggieTales* videos of animated vegetables teaching Bible and morality lessons only received widespread exposure after Wal-Mart started selling them. The publisher of the *Left Behind* series of apocalyptic Christian novels credits Wal-Mart with turning one of its novels into the best-selling book in the country. Country music sells well at Wal-Mart, as do Christian writings and popular books by politically conservative authors. Is this trend a positive development in "controlling smut," as some have argued, or a disturbing market force steering popular culture in a politically conservative, rural-oriented, evangelically Christian-flavored popular culture? (Kirkpatrick, 2003).

Although theory building in this area has not been extensive, Manrai and Gardner (1992) have developed a model to explain how the differences between social and product advertising predict a consumer's cognitive, social, and emotional reactions to social advertising. Hornik and Yanovitzsky (2003) argue that a theory of prosocial media effects is essential in designing such campaigns.

Obstacles to Social Marketing

Although selling good health or safety is in many ways not unlike selling soap or automobiles, there are some difficulties that are particularly acute for social marketing. Social and product advertising differ in several important ways, most of which lead to greater obstacles facing public health and other social advertisers, compared to commercial advertisers (M. E. Goldberg, 1995; Manrai & Gardner, 1992).

First, social ideas tend to have a higher degree of both shared benefits and shared responsibilities than products, whose use is entirely an individual choice. For example, some (perhaps most) of the benefits of recycling household waste will be to society, not to the individual. Those individuals may view society as also having much (or most) of the responsibility for the problem. Thus, motivating (selling) the social message will be more difficult than selling a product with benefits to the individual.

Second, the benefits that do exist with social marketing tend to be delayed and/or intangible. Often there is a great physical, or at least psychological, distance between the consumer and the product. Selling toothpaste can stress how much sexier your breath will be for that big date tonight. Selling the idea of quitting smoking has a much less immediate payoff. Teenage smokers think much more about looking cool with their friends this weekend than dying from lung cancer or emphysema in 30 to 40 years. Young, healthy adults do not typically feel much urgency to sign an organ donor card; the need is very distant psychologically. Often in social marketing, the consumer is not all that opposed to the message and may even support it; they simply do not feel the immediacy of it and thus are not particularly inclined to make an effort to act on the message.

Third, the social marketing campaign may be very complex, compared to what is typically involved in commercial marketing. Particularly in regard to health, the beliefs, attitudes, and motives for unhealthy practices are deeply rooted and highly emotion laden and thus very resistant to change. For example, trying to convince women to self-examine their breasts for lumps flies against their enormous fear of cancer and the potential damage to one's sexual self-image by the contemplation of possible breast surgery. Convincing people to wear seatbelts when they have driven for 50 years without doing so is not easy. People are particularly resistant to change if anxieties occur in response to unrealistic but prevalent fears, such as the fear of being declared dead prematurely in order to acquire organs for transplantation (Harris, Jasper, Lee, & Miller, 1991; Shanteau & Harris, 1990). The complexity of the interaction of individual motives for behavior, the social context of that behavior, and the news media coverage and prosocial appeals can be very difficult to conceptually and theoretically unravel (Yanovitzky & Bennett, 1999).

Fourth, social marketing messages frequently face strong opposition, unlike product advertising. This opposition may be social, as in the adolescent peer group that encourages and glamorizes smoking and tanned bodies, or it may be organized and institutional, as when tobacco companies threaten to withdraw advertising from magazines that carry articles about the dangers of smoking. Social marketing campaigns are often poorly funded compared to product advertising, and they often face opposing forces that hold enormous economic and political power. For example, the Tobacco Institute, the oil industry, and the National Rifle Association are tremendously powerful lobbies set to oppose media messages against smoking, alternative energy sources, or handgun controls, respectively. PSAs, whether print or broadcast, often are noticeably poorer in technical quality and appear less frequently than commercial ads because of budget limitations. Although radio and TV stations air a certain number of unpaid PSAs, they generally do so at times when they are least able to profitably sell advertising. We see many PSAs during the late late movie and very few during the Olympics or *ER*. Thus, specific demographic groups cannot be targeted by PSAs as well as they can by commercial advertising.

Fifth, social marketers often set unrealistically high goals, such as changing the behavior of 50% of the public. Although a commercial ad that affects 1% to 10% of consumers is hugely successful, social marketers often have not fully appreciated that an ad that affects even a very small percentage of a mass audience is a substantial accomplishment. Persons preparing social marketing campaigns are often less thoroughly trained in advertising, media, and marketing than are those conducting product ad campaigns.

Finally, social marketing appeals are often aimed at the 15% or so of the population that is *least* likely to change. These may be the least educated, most traditional, oldest, or most backward segment of the population, precisely the people least likely to stop smoking, start wearing seatbelts, or request medical checkups. Just as political media strategists target advertising at the few undecided voters, so might social marketing better target those people most conducive to attitude and behavior change in the intended direction, rather than the group that is least likely to ever change at all.

Considering the Audience

Knowing the audience well and targeting it as specifically as possible is as helpful selling health as it is soap or beer. Targeting a reasonable audience, not the ones least likely to change, and setting realistic goals and targets are useful. Trying to see the issue from the audience's point of view will make a more convincing message. Frequently social marketers are fervently convinced of the rightness of their message and fail to see how anyone else could view the issue differently. Self-righteousness tends not to be convincing. The attitudes, desires, motivations, and reasonable beliefs of the audience may be used to drive the character of the message. A serious consideration of what kinds of psychological appeals will be the most effective in motivating the particular target audience will be helpful. For example, when targeting adolescents with their strong sense of invulnerability and focus on other people for approval and comparison, forcing them to focus on the message and elaborate its meaning more deeply can be successful in reducing risk-taking behavior (Greene, Krcmar, Rubin, Walters, & Hale, 2002). To focus an appeal on some behavior being stupid if it appears adaptive within the target person's world (e.g., driving dangerously) or from the framework of their personality (e.g., as a sensation seeker), that appeal is likely to fail (Morgan, Palmgreen, Stephenson, Hoyle, & Lorch, 2003; Nell, 2002; Stephenson, 2003). Perceived realism and relevance to one's life are also important (Andsager, Austin, & Pinkleton, 2001).

The age of the child in the target group is vitally important to consider when designing the media intervention. For example, in testing anti-smoking posters, Peracchio and Luna (1998) found that 7 to 8 year olds responded best to a picture of a dirty sock labeled "gross" next to an ashtray full of cigarette butts labeled "really gross." The 9 to 10-year-olds responded best to pictures of dead insects with a message saying smoking is chemically equivalent to spraying yourself in the face with insecticide, while 11-year-olds responded best to a poster of a car's tailpipe with written copy asking why you would smoke if you wouldn't suck car exhaust.

Focusing on specific behaviors that the audience may change one small step at a time is often more useful than a general exhortation aimed at changing attitudes. People may know very well that they should stop smoking or start wearing seat belts. What they most need are more specific realistic behaviors that can be used to meet that end. Often, existing motivation may be harnessed and channeled to build confidence in taking appropriate specific actions. Merely exhorting people to stop smoking may be of limited use. Showing a PSA of a young child smoking and talking about how cool he looks, just like Daddy, might reach the smoking parent more effectively. Telling people that many others are doing the bad behavior may boomerang by legitimatizing the unwanted behavior (see Box 11.7)

Positive Effects of Social Marketing

In spite of the obstacles, social marketing media campaigns do have some clear positive effects. The first effect is an altered perceived reality that includes a heightened awareness of the problem. Virtually everyone in North America is aware of the health dangers of smoking or not wearing seat belts; such was not the case 40 years ago. Unlike 20 years ago, most people today are aware of the need for organ donors (Shanteau & Harris, 1990), largely due to media publicity.

A second positive effect is making the problem more salient, thus increasing receptivity to other influences in the same direction later. Even though a particular PSA may not immediately send a person to the doctor to check a suspicious mole for possible melanoma, that person may

---

BOX 11.7
HOW TO CONVINCE PEOPLE NOT TO STEAL PETRIFIED
WOOD FROM A NATIONAL PARK

Social psychologist Robert Cialdini (2003) has discovered that some types of appeals are more effective than others in discouraging environmental theft. He performed a very clever field experiment in Arizona's Petrified Forest National Park, which suffers from a loss of 14 tons of petrified wood stolen by visitors each year. Cialdini tested the relative effectiveness of two types of signs posted at entrances to visitor walking paths. The descriptive-norm appeal read "Many visitors have removed petrified wood from the Park, changing the natural state of the Petrified Forest" and was accompanied by pictures of three visitors taking wood. The injunctive-norm sign stated "Please don't remove the petrified wood from the Park, in order to preserve the natural state of the Petrified Forest" and was accompanied by a picture of one person stealing a piece of wood with a red circle and bar through it over his hand. Results showed that theft of specially marked pieces of petrified wood over five weeks was higher (7.9%) in the vicinity of the descriptive-norm signs than it was around the injunctive-norm signs (1.7%). Why the difference? Cialdini argues that the descriptive approach, although trying to impress on visitors the enormity of the theft problem, in fact may be legitimatizing it by suggesting "everybody does it."

---

pay more attention to a later message on that topic and may be a little more careful about excessive exposure to the sun. An eventual behavioral change may actually be a cumulative effect from several influences. This, of course, makes it very difficult to scientifically measure precise effects of particular media campaigns.

A third effect is the stimulation of later conversation with one's family, friends, or doctor. Publicity about the dangers of smoking may encourage supper table conversation between parents and teenagers who are being encouraged by peers to smoke. Although a decision not to smoke may result more from the personal interaction than directly from the message, the latter may have partially laid the groundwork for the discussion. Sometimes media publicity may be responded to too strongly. By the early 1990s, pediatricians were being warned against overdiagnosing Lyme disease. A high level of media publicity over the preceding few years was leading patients to ask about this illness and physicians to be quicker to diagnose it. In the psychological realm, the explosion of diagnoses of child sexual abuse in adults with very common and non-specific symptoms in the 1990s, led to huge controversies in the counseling field (Loftus & Ketcham, 1994).

A fourth effect of social marketing campaigns is the generation of self-initiated information seeking. Someone may seek additional information on some topic as a result of interest being piqued by media attention to that issue. They might ask the doctor about it on their next visit; they might read a newspaper article on the topic that they would have passed by before.

Finally, prosocial media campaigns can reinforce positive existing attitudes and behavior, such as encouraging the ex-smoker to try hard not to succumb or reinforcing someone's feeling that he or she really should see a doctor about some medical condition. Often people know what they should do but need a little encouragement to actually do it.

Now we examine one of the major domains of social marketing campaigns, public health.

Public Health Media Campaigns

Breslow (1978) identified three methods of risk-factor intervention in medicine. *Epidemiological* intervention involves identifying the characteristics correlated with increased frequency of the disease and taking steps to alter those characteristics. For example, cardiovascular risk factors like smoking, obesity, cholesterol level, physical inactivity, and hypertension are first identified, followed by screening people using blood pressure and blood chemistry tests.

Environmental intervention involves changing the environment in a healthier direction. For example, legislation restricting smoking in public places or reducing industrial emissions into the air or water, and adding fluoride to drinking water illustrate such interventions. Adding air bags to cars, substituting canola oil for coconut oil in fried foods, and selling lower fat milk also manipulate the environment.

The third type of intervention, *educational* programs, often involves media and is of most concern for our purposes. Such programs may aim to alter the perceived reality by changing knowledge by providing more information or providing an impetus for changing behavior. Often changes in knowledge are easier to effect than changes in behavior. For example, even though most smokers are well aware that smoking is bad for their health, their own perceived reality, at least at an emotional level, is that they will not develop lung cancer. Sometimes the most important cognitive message of such a campaign is that treatment and cure is possible if the illness is diagnosed early enough. This is important in combating irrational fears that a diagnosis of cancer is a death sentence and thus to be avoided at all costs.

All three types of interventions must keep in mind the culture of the target population (Ilola, 1990). For example, an AIDS-prevention campaign would (or at least should) take a very different form if targeted at North American gay men, IV drug users, health care workers, or promiscuous

African heterosexual truck drivers. See Maibach and Parrott (1995) for a set of readings on psychological and communications considerations in designing health messages and J. D. Brown and Walsh-Childers (2002) for a review of health effects of media messages.

Stanford Five-City Multifactor Risk Reduction Project

A very clear and consistent finding from studies of public health social marketing campaigns is that mass media campaigns are most successful when used in conjunction with other types of intervention (see Solomon & Cardillo, 1985, for a discussion of the components of such campaigns). A good example of such a campaign is the extensive and relatively well controlled project conducted by Stanford University to reduce the instance of coronary heart disease and other factors (Farquhar et al., 1990; Schooler, Chaffee, Flora, & Roser, 1998; Schooler, Flora, & Farquhar, 1993; Schooler, Sundar, & Flora, 1996). This project involved three central California towns with a population of 12,000 to 15,000. Two of the towns received multimedia campaigns about coronary heart disease (CHD) over a 2-year period. One of those towns also received intensive interventions targeted at the high-risk population. These interventions involved both media messages and cooperation from the medical community. Health screenings were held, specific behavior-modification programs were set up, and people's attempted reduction of high-risk behaviors and characteristics was monitored.

Changes in both knowledge and behavior were monitored in the experimental towns and in the control town, which received no media campaign and no intervention. Results showed that media campaigns by themselves produced some increases in knowledge but only very modest, if any, changes in behavior and/or decreases in the overall percentage of at-risk people. Only when media campaigns were coupled with specific behavioral interventions and health monitoring were significant improvements and reduction of the numbers in the at-risk population seen. Similar results were found with other projects, such as a six-city study in Minnesota (Luepker et al., 1994).

Even more dramatic success came in the North Karelia project in rural Eastern Finland, which had one of the highest coronary heart disease (CHD) rates in the world. Along with media campaigns and medical intervention, environmental interventions were also instituted, including restrictions on smoking, selling more low-fat dairy foods, and substitution of mushrooms for fat in the local sausage. After $4\frac{1}{2}$ years of the project, there were dramatic reductions in systolic blood pressure and stroke incidence (McAlister, Puska, & Solonen, 1982). This project had local and national government cooperation and combined what Wallack, Dorfman,

Jernigan, and Themba (1993) called *downstream* and *upstream* marketing. Downstream efforts involve attempts to change consumers' behavior (stopping smoking, starting to exercise, seeking medical checkups, using designated drivers), while upstream efforts work at changing the conditions producing or encouraging the unhealthy behaviors (restricting tobacco sales to minors, stopping sale of high-fat meat, raising the drinking age, forcing insurance companies to pay for mammograms). Downstream marketing, which has been the predominant approach in social marketing, is often limited in what it can accomplish without some upstream changes as well (M. E. Goldberg, 1995).

AIDS Awareness Campaigns

One of the most urgent public health issues of the last generation has been HIV-AIDS. Worldwide, different nations and organizations have taken a variety of media approaches to try to increase general awareness and knowledge and to change risky behaviors, especially in target groups like gay men, intravenous drug users, and promiscuous heterosexuals. A content analysis of 127 AIDS-awareness PSAs in the United States televised in 1988 shows that most were directed at general audiences, rather than target audiences at high risk. They tended to use rational rather than emotional appeals and emphasized the acquisition of information rather than change of behaviors (Freimuth, Hammond, Edgar, & Monahan, 1990). A similar content analysis of 317 TV PSAs in 33 different countries from 1991 to 1994 found the major emphasis was on general facts and nonbehavioral content targeted at a general, poorly defined heterosexual audience (Johnson & Rimal, 1994).

Taking an experimental approach, Flora and Maibach (1990) measured people's cognitive involvement with the AIDS issue and exposed them to either a rationally based or an emotionally based PSA. Results showed that emotional appeals were more memorable than rational ones, especially for low-involvement people. Another study showed that information on prevention in conjunction with modeling and a chance for cognitive rehearsal of the prevention information was the most successful message (Maibach & Flora, 1993). Emotional appeals were also more effective than cognitive appeals in stimulating a desire to learn more about AIDS. For an analysis of Australian media messages about AIDS, see Tulloch, Kippax, and Crawford (1993). For an evaluation of the U.S. government's AIDS media campaign by the Center for Disease Control, see Ratzan, Payne, & Massett (1994).

Sometimes certain high-risk groups react differently to AIDS spots than the general public does (Baggaley, 1988). In general, prevention programs targeted at gay White men have been the most successful in changing risky behaviors (Coates, 1990; Stall, Coates, & Hoff, 1988; Witte, 1992), whereas the more general appeals and those targeted at other groups have been less successful. Especially in the developing world, changes in longstanding and deep-rooted social customs are required to slow the spread of AIDS. For example, in parts of central Africa, where AIDS is spread primarily from men to women by heterosexual intercourse, polygamy and multiple sex partners for men are condoned, and women have little social power to resist men's sexual advances or to insist on condom use. Such behaviors and attitudes may be extremely resistant to change, but will have to be altered before the spread of AIDS can be contained.

Although the use of PSAs and other media-based campaigns, especially if coupled with medical or environmental interventions and specific behavioral tips, can be useful in increasing knowledge and sometimes in changing behavior, the sell is a difficult one. Another very different use of media for prosocial ends comes in using entertainment media to convey these prosocial messages in the context of captivating fictional stories. We now turn to this type of media.

ENTERTAINMENT-EDUCATION MEDIA

Entertainment media may sometimes be explicitly and intentionally used for socially positive purposes within a society. Over 75 of such entertainment-education (E-E) campaigns have been implemented in at least 40 nations worldwide and are especially prevalent in developing countries (Sherry, 2002; Singhal & Rogers, 1999). Interestingly, none of these projects has occurred in the United States, and there is some reason to think they may be less successful in more media-saturated societies (Sherry, 2002). Nonetheless, some past projects have shown impressive success and this genre is gaining in popularity worldwide.

Sample E-E Programs

In many developing countries, radio and television have long been seen as tools for development and positive social change, rather than merely vehicles for entertainment. One of the earliest concerted efforts in this direction came in 1975–1982 from the giant Mexican network Televisa, which produced several series of programs, many in the very popular genre of telenovela (soap opera). These were designed to promote gender equality, adult literacy, sexual responsibility, and family planning (W. J. Brown, Singhal, & Rogers, 1989; Lozano, 1992; Rogers & Singhal, 1990; Singhal & Rogers, 1989b). The shows were very popular and viewers often requested the services promoted by the programs (Lozano, 1992).

Televisa's model of communicating prosocial messages through entertainment was emulated elsewhere. In 1987, Kenya aired the prosocial soap opera *Tushariane* ("*Let's Discuss*"), designed to promote family planning; it became the most popular show in the history of Kenyan TV (W. J. Brown & Singhal, 1990). The Nigerian soap opera *Cock Crow at Dawn* encouraged the adoption of modern agricultural practices (Ume-Nwagbo, 1986). Televisa's *Sangre Joven* ("*Young Blood*") telenovela of the early 1990s dealt with family planning, AIDS, and drug abuse. Jamaica produced a family planning radio soap opera, *Naseberry Street*, which reached 40% of the Jamaican population from 1985 to 1989 (Rogers & Singhal, 1990). The Peruvian Amazon's *Bienvenida Salud!* ("*Welcome, health!*") has combined a radio drama with popular music, local news, contests, and listener letters and testimonials since 1997 (Sypher, McKinley, Ventsam, & Valdeavellano, 2002). The Tanzanian radio soap opera *Twende na Wakati* ("*Let's Go with the Times*") featured a promiscuous truck driver who contracted HIV. His wife, then left him to set up her own business and was "rewarded" by not contracting AIDS. This program reached 55% of the population from 1993–1998, with 82% of those saying they had changed their behavior to reduce the chance of HIV infection (Rogers, Vaughan, Swalehe, Rao, Svenkerud, & Sood, 1999). See Box 11.8 for more African examples of media's effects far beyond entertainment.

Soul City.   One of the most ambitious recent projects has been the South African TV, radio, and public health campaign *Soul City* (Singhal & Rogers, 1999), which deals with the themes of HIV prevention, maternal and child health, domestic violence, and alcohol abuse. It uses a multifaceted approach. Its prime-time TV segment became South Africa's top-rated television show. The radio drama aired daily in eight different languages. Public health materials were widely distributed along with the broadcasts. *Soul City* was very successful in generating discussion and in furthering information-seeking, and also led to impressive increases in reported condom use and a commitment to tell one's partner of HIV infection. Before *Soul City*, only 3% agreed that one's HIV-positive status should not be kept secret from one's partner, but afterward 75% agreed the partner should be told.

Hum Log.   Another impressive commercial success was the Indian TV drama *Hum Log* ("*We People*"), which debuted in 1984. It became the most popular program in the history of Indian TV and also had substantial social impact (W. J. Brown & Cody, 1991; Singhal & Rogers, 1989a, 1989c). Although a commercial entertainment program, *Hum Log* also had the overt purpose of advancing the status of women, through dealing with such issues as wife battering, the dowry system, and political and social

---

BOX 11.8
STRIKING EXAMPLES OF PROSOCIAL MEDIA
FROM AFRICA

A popular comic book and video character in Zambia and several other African countries is 12-year-old Sara, a girl whose adventures include outwitting her greedy uncle who tries to steal her school fees, rescuing a friend about to be sexually molested, escaping from older women attempting genital mutilation, and making a smokeless cooking stove for her mother. The UNICEF-produced series has become very popular and provides a role model for empowering adolescent girls in societies that have not always valued education for girls (Bald, 1998).

After West African villagers in impoverished Sanankoroba, Mali, saw news on their battery-powered televisions of massive ice storm damage in Eastern Canada in January 1998, they took up a collection and sent about US$66 to their sister city of St.-Elisabeth, Quebec. Although the per capita income of St.-Elisabeth was about 75 times that of Sanankoroba, the Malians appreciated the Quebeckers' donations to them after floods in 1995 and 1997 and cited the Malian proverb that, "If you cannot share the meager resources you have today, you will not know how to part with a centime of the wealth you have tomorrow" (Friend in Need, 1998).

In another uplifting story from Mali, Malian singer Oumou Sangaré sings "More and more we live in a world ruled by individualism, a selfish world," and "Let us fight for women's literacy. Women, let us fight together for our freedom, so we can put an end to this social injustice." Sangaré's message combines traditional Malian music with a sort of blues style that is making her immensely popular worldwide and causing her traditional countrymen to seriously listen to a message they have long been closed to (Rothenberg, 1998).

---

equality of women and men. At the end of every episode, a famous Indian film actor gave a 30- to 50-second summary of the episode and appropriate guides to action. *Hum Log* encouraged women to work outside of the home and to make more of their own decisions.

Effects of E-E Programs

Evaluation research (W. J. Brown & Cody, 1991) found *Hum Log's* impact to be complex and not always what was predicted. For example, many women viewers identified with Bhagwanti, the family matriarch and traditional woman, rather than with her more independent daughters Badki and Chutki, at least in part because of concern over the difficulties that the younger women's more independent stance had brought to them. There is an interesting parallel between the effects of *Hum Log* and the 1970s U.S. sitcom *All in the Family,* where more traditional viewers identified with the bigoted Archie Bunker and found him to be a more positive figure than the producers had envisioned (Vidmar & Rokeach, 1974). This phenomenon of some viewers identifying with the intended negative role models has been observed in several nations and has come to be known as the "Archie Bunker effect," so named after the lead character in *All in the Family* (Singhal & Rogers, 1999).

E-E campaigns have shown impressive effects, if well implemented. The basic entertainment function provides interesting characters with whom the public develops parasocial relationships (Papa et al., 2000; Sood, 2002). The narrative form may be an especially good format for placing persuasive messages (Slater & Rouner, 2002). A good E-E program can increase a viewer/listener's sense of self-efficacy, one's beliefs about one's capabilities to exercise control over events that affect their lives (Bandura, 1997). These beliefs can then lead to prosocial behaviors like using condoms, seeking medical advice, or taking control over one's reproductive health. It can also contribute to a sense of collective efficacy, the belief in joint capabilities to forge individual self-interests into a shared agenda (Bandura, 1995). For example, when viewers of a *Soul City* story on wife-battering gather in front of a neighborhood batterer's home and bang their pans in censure, a behavior seen in the series, collective efficacy is achieved (Singhal & Rogers, 2002).

Conclusions. In considering the effectiveness of entertainment-education media in developing countries, Rogers and Singhal (1990; see also Singhal & Rogers, 1999, 2002) drew several conclusions:

1. Placing an educational message in an entertainment context can draw a mass audience and earn large profits, which thus support the prosocial campaign.
2. The educational message cannot be too blatant or hard sell or the audience will reject it.
3. The effect of the media message in such programs is enhanced by supplementary specific tips about behavior change.
4. The repetition of prosocial themes in a telenovela has a greater effect than a one-shot media PSA campaign. A continuing series like *Soul City* generally will have greater impact than a one-episode story on *ER*.
5. Prosocial campaigns are most successful if the media, government, commercial sponsors, and public health organizations work together. See Bouman (2002) for discussion of various management models for E-E campaigns.

Although no broad-based popular E-E campaigns have been promulgated in the United States, elements of E-E have appeared on American entertainment television on an occasional basis. Perhaps the earliest was the designated driver campaign of the later 1980s (Rosenzweig, 1999). Professor Jay Winsten of the Harvard School of Public Health worked with NBC and over 250 writers, producers, and TV executives over six months to try to incorporate what was then a new idea—the "designated driver"—into TV plot lines. By 1994, the designated driver message had appeared on 160 prime-time shows and had been the main topic of 25. Two-thirds of the public had noted the mention of designated drivers in TV shows and just over half of young adults reported they had served as a designated driver. By the late 1990s, the drunk-driving fatality rate had fallen by one-third from ten years earlier, in part almost surely due to greater use of designated drivers. Acceptance of this concept was due in part to a subtle entertainment-education campaign. See Box 11.9 for some additional recent examples.

BOX 11.9
PUBLIC HEALTH PRODUCT PLACEMENTS

On *Beverly Hills 90210* Steve brags about his flawless tan, but his girlfriend notices a suspicious mole on the back of his neck. Concerned about skin cancer, he later took a megaphone to the beach and shouted about the benefits of using sunscreen. On *ER* Dr. Mark Greene, concerned about overuse of antibiotics and later brutally honest after his brain surgery, walks into his hospital waiting room and tells the patients there not to expect antibiotics for the flu, after which half of them leave. Another episode of *ER* used a plot line about morning-after contraception; subsequent research showed that 6 million of the shows' 34 million viewers had learned about morning-after contraception from watching the show (Rosenzweig, 1999).

The first two of these plot lines were written by, or with the cooperation of, the Center for Disease Control, which since 1998 has had an entertainment-education program to assist teleplay writers in placing positive health messages in their entertainment scripts of popular TV shows. Viewers do find the information from such shows helpful. A Kaiser Family Foundation study found that one third of *ER* viewers reported learning something from the show that had been helpful in making health care decisions in their own families (Stolberg, 2001). Other embedded health messages included AIDS awareness themes on soap operas and pro-condom messages on the sitcom *Friends* (Brown & Walsh-Childers, 2002) and the teen-oriented shows *Felicity* and *Dawson's Creek* (Rosenzweig, 1999).

In examining explicit public health media campaigns, Flay and Burton (1990; see also Brown & Einsiedel, 1990) identified seven steps for public health media campaign to be maximally effective:

1. Develop and use high-quality messages, sources, and channels.
2. Disseminate effectively to the most appropriate target audience.
3. Gain and keep the attention of the audience.
4. Encourage favorable interpersonal communication about the issue after exposure to the message.
5. Work for behavior changes, as well as changes in awareness, knowledge, and attitudes.
6. Work for broader societal changes.
7. Obtain knowledge of campaign effectiveness through evaluation research.

Interestingly enough, all of these apply as well to E-E, and in fact these goals may often be better met through E-E than through traditional social marketing PSA campaigns. For example, people will attend more to gripping entertainment media than to PSAs and will talk more about them later. The audiences are potentially huge for these messages. Of course, there are ethical issues of concern, particularly in the case of messages not everyone would agree with. For example, if *ER* had a script strongly supporting or opposing abortion, large numbers of viewers would likely be incensed. Still, the E-E path is probably one that deserves a closer look in Western countries. Indeed, one study showed that popular and sympathetic gay characters like Will Truman on *Will and Grace* may do a lot toward increasing the broader society's acceptance of homosexuals (Bonds-Raacke, Cady, Schlegel, Harris, & Firebaugh, 2004).

CONCLUSION

A recurring theme throughout this chapter, indeed throughout the entire book, is that the effects of the media depend on more than the content. A perceived reality is constructed by viewers, readers, or listeners as their minds interact with the media message. Media exhortations to live a healthier lifestyle are more effective if combined with behavioral interventions with specific tips on lifestyle change and support for efforts to do so.

This idea is not unlike research on how children and adults survive traumatic life experiences in general (e.g., Leavitt & Fox, 1993). The ones who survive and grow, rather than suffer defeat and trauma, are those who have support in the rough times, those who can talk over the troubling events and have countervailing positive influences to partially balance the strong negative ones. It is almost a truism that television and other media may be a force for ill or good. Much writing and research has focused on the ill wind of TV or the Internet. Media are with us to stay, however; we cannot isolate our children from these influences. We can take steps to make that interaction a more positive, even rewarding, experience than it would be otherwise.

This chapter has examined some issues relating to values and the media. Questions of what is right and what is wrong lead to different answers in different contexts, but the questions are always there. As influential as television is in our lives, it becomes an obvious source to turn to for guidance on moral and ethical issues. How do our role models act? What are we taught is right? What are possible consequences of moral positions taken by media? How can television socialize values? In the case of U.S. media, we see a curious hybrid picture of considerable permissiveness in some areas (e.g., sexual behavior), almost puritanical restriction in others (e.g., birth control), and a sort of moderate mainstream value socialization in others. The glib protestations of those on the political far left and far right do not do the complex reality justice.

Returning to the question addressed early in this chapter, do media merely reflect the values of society or do they serve as a catalyst for changing those values? Clearly, they do in some sense mirror *somebody's* values, but that somebody may hardly be a typical media consumer. More importantly, they can and do serve as a catalyst for change. How this change occurs is of great importance but is far more difficult to study. The same processes discussed in earlier chapters, by which we respond to media and construct a world based on its teachings, also apply to values.

The cultivation theory approach of Gerbner and his colleagues (see chapter 2) has been particularly useful here (e.g., Gerbner et al., 2002; Signorielli & Morgan, 1990). Television and other media cultivate a system of values through the interaction of the viewer and the content presented. The social reality presented in media gradually becomes the reality for the public. Mechanisms of reinforcement, modeling, disinhibition, and classical conditioning are also at work. For example, some values held by the viewer are reinforced more than others. Certain values and those holding them are associated with very positive or negative stimuli and thus may be classically conditioned. Watching a trusted model act inconsistently with certain values may make those behaviors less negative for the viewer. may In fact, the media send many mixed messages on value issues, such as when PSAs stress using condoms and not smoking, on the one hand, and at the same time respected characters in dramas smoke and have casual unprotected intercourse. No wonder many young people show confusion about certain values. More and better research on the ways that media teach values is needed to further elucidate these issues.

BOX 11.10
REALITY SHOWS SHOW THE WORST SIDE OF REALITY

1. MTV's reality show *Jackass* features stunts like having a group of guys kick their friend in the groin for the amusement of the audience. (There were disclaimers of "Don't try this at home"). Another show featured diving in a sewage holding tank ("poo-diving"). *Jackass* was so popular that it became a movie in 2002.

2. *Fear Factor* has contestants perform stunts like eating live slugs or dunking their head into a tankful of snakes.

3. The *Survivor*-style reality shows so popular early in the new century featured such uplifting entertainment as placing groups of people in competition with each other to survive on a desert island. Daily votes of whom to "throw off the island" kept fans riveted for weeks. An African version *Big Brother Africa* was very popular but was condemned by government and religious leaders of several African nations for its explicit sexual content (Malawi bans *Big Brother Africa*, 2003). Perhaps the nadir of this genre was *Temptation Island*, where faithful couples were surrounded by beautiful opportunities to be unfaithful to their partner while the rest of us cheered them on. Various other countries produced their own variations on the same themes.

4. The show *Who Wants to Marry a Millionaire?* presented a handsome young man as a millionaire to be the object of several women's competing affections. The "punch line" was their reactions when the women found out he wasn't really a millionaire. On another occasion, producers were in some difficulty when inadequate background checks failed to discover one real life "hunk" being "sold" to competing women in fact had a criminal record for domestic battering.

Many have argued that the values communicated by such shows are distressing and disturbing. In some anxious people they may even trigger anxiety attacks (McCook, 2003). Some (e.g., Marling, 2002) have argued a class bias at work here: we like to watch lower-class "trailer park trash" demean themselves while we smugly sit back and watch and comfort ourselves that we would never stoop so low. Or have we already stooped that low by watching it?

In the last analysis, of course, we must remember that, given the economic realities of media, the values that sell the best will be what we see the most of. For example, the recent fad of the so-called "reality shows" offer a quite unrealistic, and many would say unsavory and even immoral, slice of life, yet they draw large numbers of viewers (see Box 11.10). This large audience size is, after all, the dominant "good" in most media.

CHAPTER **12**

Handling Media: Living With New Technologies and Communicating About Media

Q: What country in the world has the fastest rate of growth of cell phones?

A: Zimbabwe, with over 800% growth in 1999, compared to 24% in the U.S. and 70% in Europe. Developing countries with poor telephone infrastructure and long waiting lists for phone service have found cell phones much more reliable and attractive. In numerous countries like Botswana, Rwanda, Ivory Coast, Paraguay, and Venezuela, cell phone users outnumbered conventional phone users by 2000 (Romero, 2000).

Q: What was Mexican soap opera star Veronica Castro doing in Moscow in September 1992?

A: Being entertained by President Boris Yeltsin and Russian Parliament members. Her triumphal tour was in celebration of the success of the Mexican telenovela *The Rich Also Cry* in Russia. It had recently drawn 200 million daily viewers, 70% of the nation's population, making it the most watched TV series in the history of the world (Kopkind, 1993).

Q: How often do teens visit web sites with antisocial content?

A: According to Tarpley (2001), 44% have visited an adult sex site, 25% a site promoting hate groups, and 12% a site with information on how to buy a gun.

Q: What was the major impetus to turning the cattle ranches (fazendas) of southwestern Brazil's Pantanal into ecotourist vacation havens?

A: The 1994 Brazilian hit telenovela *Pantanal*, set in the Pantanal, the world's largest freshwater wetlands, which were up until that time largely empty and unknown to the outside world. (Grzelewski, 2002).

In this book we have examined the way that the perceived reality that we create from the media often deviates substantially from the real world.

Although media are not the only source of knowledge about the world, our perceived reality of what the world is like is often far more heavily influenced by the media than we realize. It greatly affects our attitudes and behavior when we implicitly assume that the world of the media faithfully reflects the real world.

One of the most difficult aspects of assessing the portrait of media versus reality in contemporary life is that technological advances are changing the face of media at an unprecedented, indeed almost alarming, rate. A generation ago mass communication meant print media (newspapers and magazines) and broadcast media (radio and TV). Although all four of those media are alive and well, albeit continually changing, the overall picture is more complex today. The traditional lines between mass communication and personal communication, on the one hand, are being blurred, as are the distinctions between media and entertainment. Is e-mail (personal or spam varieties) mass media? Are films on video or DVD and music downloaded off the Internet entertainment or mass media? The answers are not simple ones.

In this final chapter we begin by examining some of the new technologies that have transformed traditional media and given us totally new media, most notably the various types of computer-mediated communication. In the second half of the chapter, we turn our attention to various ways that we can actively respond to media. These include everything from individual expression of opinion to political strategies designed to induce change in media. Next, we look at the way that the reporting of news about the media in the press may affect the perceived reality constructed in the minds of the public. Finally, we conclude with some integrative thoughts on mass communication and the world it creates.

THE FUTURE AND NEW TECHNOLOGIES

The Reach of Media

Television.   No place on earth is beyond the reach of mass communication. For political reasons South Africa was for a long time the last large nation without TV, until 1976 (Mutz, Roberts, & van Vuuren, 1993). Mountainous Himalayan kingdoms of Nepal (1985) and Bhutan (1999) and the remote island nations of Cook Islands (1989), Fiji (1995), and St. Helena (1995) were among the last nations to welcome TV (Wheeler, 2001). Even the isolated valley town unable to receive TV as late as the 1970s is nonexistent today. Satellite dishes and VCRs running off generators now allow video experiences in places out of the normal reach of broadcast signals.

In the 1970s, a unique study was done in Canada to assess the effects of the introduction of television. Three towns in interior eastern British

Columbia were very similar except for the fact that one ("Multitel") received several Canadian and U.S. TV channels, another ("Unitel") received only one channel, and the third, because of its particular valley location, received no television signals ("Notel"). This study compared children and adults in the three towns before and after television was finally introduced to Notel. For example, children's creativity scores were higher before TV in Notel than in either (a) the other towns before TV or (b) any of the three towns after TV. See Macbeth (1996) for a summary of the findings and T. M. Williams (1986) for a collection of papers reporting results in more detail. For a similar though more recent study in a smaller place, see Charlton, Gunter, and Hannan (2002) for a study of the effects of the introduction of television to the remote South Atlantic island of St. Helena in 1995. This will probably be the last study of that sort which will ever be done because no such TV-less places still exist.

Some television markets have grown exponentially in recent years. For example, China is now by far the largest TV market, with over 350 million homes having access, thus reaching most of its 1.3 billion population. China moved from only 18 million people having access to TV in 1975 to one billion 20 years later. In contrast, the second-place U.S. had only 98 million homes with TV and third-place India 79 million (Thomas, 2003). The rapid growth of markets in developing countries will have far-reaching advertising implications in future decades.

Internet. Parallel changes are seen in other media. For example, in 1995 nearly 70% of Internet users lived in North America, but by 1999 the proportion had fallen below 50%, with a further drop to 33% by 2005 predicted. English was the language of about 80% of Internet users in 1996 but is projected to be the language of only about a third of users by 2005 (Lievrouw, 2000). Although Internet usage has grown exponentially in North America, it has grown even faster elsewhere, most spectacularly in China.

An important emphasis in future media research, as indeed in all social science research, will be on cross-cultural aspects. Virtually every society in the world is becoming increasingly multicultural, in part due to the communications revolution. We are all exposed to media communications from many different national and cultural sources, and it is necessary to understand how different cultures perceive the same message differently. For excellent collections of papers on comparative and cross-cultural media research, see Kamalipour (1999), Korzenny and Ting-Toomey (1992), Lull (1988), and Blumler, McLeod, and Rosengren (1992). In much of the world, watching television and film in another language dubbed or subtitled in your own is a common experience. For a discussion of how people process subtitles when they may not know the language of the media, see Box 12.1.

BOX 12.1
READING, IGNORING, OR NOT HAVING TO DEAL
WITH SUBTITLES

In much of the world a considerable amount of television is imported from some place where a different language is spoken. Thus, the program is either dubbed or subtitled in the local language. Dubbing allows one to hear one's own language, even though it does not match the lips of the characters on the screen. However, reading subtitles, while simultaneously processing the visual content and ignoring the sound track in an unfamiliar language, involves a set of cognitive skills that requires some practice to do effectively. Belgian psychologist Gery d'Ydewalle and his colleagues (e.g., d'Ydewalle, Praet, Verfaillie, & Van Rensbergen, 1991) did a series of studies measuring eye movements as indicators of people's relative attention to subtitles and visual content. They found that people look at subtitles in their own language and may find them distracting in cases where they know both the languages involved. Belgians are familiar with reading subtitles; most of their movies and much television is foreign and subtitled, sometimes bilingually in two subtitled parallel lines in French and Dutch (the country's two languages).

Movies and TV shows with subtitles can even be used to learn a language. For example, the Italian newsmagazine *L'Espresso* promoted itself by giving away "MovieTalk" CD-ROMS of old *Beverly Hills 90210* and *Columbo* episodes to use for English lessons. In addition to the original voicing, users had the option of pressing another button to hear a slower, less slurred precise voiceover (Stanley, 2000).

Subtitling, dubbing, and the original language can interact in some interesting ways in the mind of a multilingual viewer. For example, I remember once in Brazil seeing a Bergman film with lips moving in Swedish but dubbed in English and subtitled in Portuguese! On other occasions, I saw French Films subtitled in Portuguese; intermediate-level knowledge of both languages allowed me to pick up most of the story from simultaneously processing the French sound track and the Portuguese subtitles, although my mind was pretty exhausted after two hours!

The United States is unusual among nations in having virtually no subtitled television available. Presumably because so much domestic programming, virtually all in English, is available, US audiences have never had to become used to reading subtitles. Subtitled foreign films are shown, but only as art films to highly restricted audiences. The conventional industry wisdom, accurate or not, is that American audiences will not watch foreign language subtitled films or television. This largely untested assumption may exclude much high-quality and potentially popular television from U.S. screens.

New Technologies

Changes in Television. Changing technology is accelerating fundamental structural changes in television and other media. The slow but
sure decline in the audience percentage for network TV, which accounted
for over 90% of the audience as recently as 1978, and proliferating cable
channels and satellite technology are vastly increasing the number of offerings available. The psychological impact of all these choices is less clear;
it is not obvious how receiving 100 or even 500 channels will change one's
TV viewing. VCRs have greatly increased audience control in program selection and timing, as well as introducing the option of at least partially
avoiding commercials (Lindlof & Shatzer, 1990; Mares, 1998). Although the
days of the mass audience are not over (top-rated network TV shows are
still a very widely shared experience), the movement in the direction of
more precisely targeted audiences is probably unstoppable.

Pay-per-view television is beginning to catch on, especially for major
events like boxing matches, although growth has been slower that its proponents had hoped. High-definition television (HDTV) is on the horizon,
promising a whole new level of digital technology for television, if it can
pass the legislative and manufacturing hurdles. Machines like TiVo attach
to the TV and VCR and can be programmed to record programs of interest
to the viewer on whatever channel, although it sometimes runs into problems of space and difficulties in telling it exactly what to and what not to
record.

Interactive TV projects allow viewers, for example, to press one button
to see the original live feed and another to call up additional background
information during newscasts or sports events. Pressing yet another button
can bring up a close-up shot of an athlete during a ball game, whereas
another can provide an instant replay. Although around in some form since
the 1970s, interactive TV has not yet fully captured the public's interest, or
more to the point its willingness to pay for it. That will likely change with
improved technology and decreasing costs, however.

The opportunities for connecting one's computer, television, and music
system together will change the face of mass communication, and further
blur its distinctions from personal media and entertainment. For example,
you will be able to order a movie over the Internet and have it played on
your television at your convenience. The required trip to the video store
to rent a video or DVD may seem like a thing of the past in a few years.
Writeable CDs and DVDs will become cheaper and more usable.

Computer-mediated communication will be affecting video in new
ways no one would have thought possible years ago. For example, editing
devices may be installed that will "clean up" the language or content of
movies you watch, although these are artistically controversial (Box 12.2).

BOX 12.2
**MOVIE SANITIZERS: WELCOME INFLUENCE OR
ARTISTIC INTRUSION?**

There are now several options available or on the horizon for viewers who want to watch some movies without the full measure of violence, sex, or rough language. A Utah company called Cleanflicks offers cleaned-up versions of over 100 Hollywood films. A different approach is taken by MovieMask, ClearPlay, and Family Shield Technologies, all of which offer software loaded onto home computers or a box on the television. This software offers several levels of editing to remove as much or as little offending material as the viewer desires. Although most changes involve removing questionable material, sometimes other avenues are taken, such as when MovieMask gave Kate Winslet a digital corset for the nude sketching scene in *Titanic* or replaced the swords in *The Princess Bride* with what looked like light sabers from *Star Wars* (Lyman, 2002). Hollywood directors have joined the call against such editing, though the studios have not taken a position yet, being unsure whether or not they might want to enter this potentially lucrative market as well. Is this unfair tampering with an artistic work or a long-overdue option welcomed by parents? What do you think?

Although it does not immediately or obviously affect media content, one of the most significant changes in recent years is the consolidation of media ownership. Multiple holdings of TV networks, cable channels, movie studios, newspapers, magazines, TV and radio stations, publishing companies, Internet sites, and even sports teams are becoming common, especially as antitrust legislation was weakened in the U.S. and elsewhere in the early 21st century. See Box 12.3 for a current list of various parts of the largest media conglomerates.

Computer-Mediated Communication. Four types of computer-mediated communication, most often collectively called the "Internet" (M. Morris & Ogan, 1996; Strasburger & Wilson, 2002), are a part of the world all children grow up with now. Only a short time ago none of them even existed.

1. One-to-one asynchronous communication is traditional e-mail. Improving technology allows the sending of voice, video, and all sorts of written material as attachments to e-mail. The amount of material that can be instantaneously transmitted, and the numbers of receivers it can be transmitted to, is truly without precedent.

BOX 12.3
CONSOLIDATION OF MEDIA ENTERPRISES

In spite of the proliferation of television channels, radio stations, and print sources, the number of corporations producing this entertainment and news is actually surprisingly small. For example, the top four media conglomerates owned or controlled the following diverse holdings as of 2003 (Steyer, 2002).

Disney: ABC TV; ESPN, Disney Channel, ABC Family Channel, A & E, Lifetime, E!, Toon Disney; Walt Disney Pictures, Touchstone Pictures, Miramax; *Discover* magazine; Hyperion and Disney Publishing; various radio and TV stations, sports teams, music groups, and Internet sites

AOL Time Warner: AOL, *Time, Fortune, Sports Illustrated, People, Money, Entertainment Weekly, Parenting* magazines, Netscape, MapQuest, CompuServe, WB TV, Cinemax, HBO, CNN, TBS, TNT, Court TV, Cartoon Network, Comedy Central (part); Warner Brothers, Castle Rock Entertainment, New Line Cinema; Hanna-Barbera Productions, Atlanta Braves, Atlanta Hawks, Atlanta Thrashers; music labels Atlantic, Rhino, Elektra, Warner Bros., Columbia House

Viacom: CBS, UPN, MTV, VH-1, Nickelodeon, Comedy Central (part); Paramount Studios; Simon & Schuster publishers, Blockbuster Videos; many radio stations

NBC Universal: NBC, Vivendi, General Electric, Universal Studios, USA network, MSNBC.

Does this consolidation matter in terms of the news we receive and the choices we have? There is evidence it does. For example, in 1998 ABC news (owned by Disney) prepared a major investigative report on abuses of labor and safety practices at Walt Disney World theme park (Steyer, 2002). The story was killed by Disney executives (or self-censored by ABC) before it aired, as were other stories about large executive compensation (no one wanted to offend very well-paid Disney chairman Michael Eisner), lax screening procedures that allowed the hiring of pedophiles at the theme parks, and even a feature about the hit movie *Chicken Run,* produced by Disney rival DreamWorks (Mayer, 2000).

---

2. Many-to-many asynchronous communication involves listservers and electronic bulletin boards, where a receiver signs up for a service or logs on to a program to access messages from a particular group, usually focused on some specific topic.

3. If a user must seek out a site in order to asynchronously access information, it may involve one-to-one, many-to-one, or one-to-many source-receiver relationships, but most often involves visiting a web site. Although unknown much more than ten years ago, every conceivable organization, as well as many individuals, have their own web site now. The opportunities for disseminating and exchanging information are truly

---

BOX 12.4
THE RISE OF A BLOG

On January 20, 2003, University of North Carolina at Chapel Hill law professor Eric Muller started a blog called "Is That Legal?" After two weeks and few visitors, he almost shut it down. Then on February 4 North Carolina Congressman Howard Coble said in a radio interview that the internment of Japanese-Americans during World War II was justified. Muller, who just happened to have written a book on that topic with very different views, wrote a lengthy rebuttal on his blog, even though 15 newspapers showed little interest in the essay. Interest on the blog exploded as it did on several other legal and public-issues blogs linked to it. Muller and others directly challenged Coble's views that the internment was designed to protect the Japanese-Americans. Muller's blog went from 35 hits on the day of Coble's initial speech to almost 3,000 three days later. This allowed a far faster exchange of views than in most print media and far more detailed than possible on television or radio (Glenn, 2003).

---

unprecedented in human history. A sort of hybrid between web sites and listservers is the weblog (blog), a sort of open discussion group begun by an individual for discussion of a certain topic but accessible to anyone through the traditional search engines. See Box 12.4 for an example of how one blog exploded in growth after one incendiary comment by a legislator.

4. Finally, there is synchronous communication, which can be one-to-one, one-to-few, or one-to-many and includes chat rooms and instant messaging. These are very popular forms of communication among pre-teens and teens but also among most segments of society. Chat rooms are organized around certain themes and allow users, for the first time in history, to find people like themselves without the issue of physical location being an issue. If someone suffers from an extremely rare disease, for example, there is probably a chat room as well as a bulletin board to act as a support group.

Another capability which computers bring to traditional print and broadcast journalism is the ability to digitally alter photographs. With modern technology, a photograph can be so totally changed as to be completely unrecognizable. The ethical boundaries are fuzzy here. Although few would have problems with digitally cropping a photo to remove irrelevant background, how about digitally composing a photo to put people together who never were in that particular place at the same time? No doubt a national leader would object to an altered photo of himself shaking hands with a terrorist, but what about altering a student group shot for a university recruiting brochure to make it more ethnically diverse than the original photo was? This actually was an issue at the University of Wisconsin-Madison, where an African American student was digitally pasted into a photo of a football crowd scene to make it more ethnically diverse (Jacobson, 2001). Is this misrepresentation in a recruiting brochure? The student was in fact a UWM student and could have been at that football game, although in fact he wasn't. See Wheeler (2002) for a careful discussion of this issue.

The use of theories and research methodologies of mass communication to study such computer-mediated communication is a fairly recent phenomenon. See F. Williams, Strover, and Grant (1994) for some early possible theoretical perspectives on new media and Mundorf and Laird (2002) for more recent conceptualizing. For example, Papacharissi and Rubin (2000) examined people's uses and gratifications for Internet use. Ferguson and Perse (2000) compared the uses and gratifications involved in watching television and using the Internet. Mastro, Eastin, and Tamborini (2002) looked at how use of the Internet arouses users and how they can use that medium to arouse or calm themselves. Sometimes even technical aspects of the Internet can have measurable effects. For example, Sundar and Wagner (2002) found that the speed that an Internet image is downloaded affects physiological arousal; slower-loading images produce higher arousal, as measured by skin conductance, although this is also affected by how inherently arousing the downloaded image is.

There is disagreement in the literature about whether Internet use is associated with social isolation or loneliness (Cole, 2000; Kraut, et al., 1998; McKenna & Bargh, 1999). Overall, Internet use is typically more social than television viewing, in part due to social options like chat rooms and instant messaging. The strongest evidence for social isolation comes in the minority of the population who spend a very large number of hours online; effects of Internet use on social isolation are much weaker or nonexistent for moderate users. The question of Internet "addiction" was examined by LaRose, Lin, and Eastin (2003). They argue that the sort of compulsive Internet use often popularly characterized with the addiction metaphor can better be conceptualized as deficient self-regulation. People who extensively use the Internet at the expense of other activities and relationships are poorer than most people at monitoring and regulating their own behavior, although their behavior is not usually as disturbed as those who fit the clinical definition of addiction.

Numerous questions about computer-mediated communication remain. Why do people use e-mail and how does it complement traditional communication means like the telephone and writing? What do they get

BOX 12.5
MAKING FRIENDS ON-LINE

Are relationships which are formed on-line, through e-mail, chat rooms, or listservers inherently shallow, impersonal, and even hostile and dangerous, or do they allow a liberation from the confines of physical locality and superficial aspects like physical appearance? In a survey study of on-line relationships of people in a variety of newsgroups and Usenet hierarchies, Parks (1996) found that 60% of respondents reported making some sort of personal relationship on-line. Women were somewhat more likely than men to have such electronic friends, though age and marital status did not matter. Almost all had corresponded with their friend via e-mail and about a third each had used phone, letter, or face-to-face contact as well. These relationships developed in many of the same ways that traditional relationships do. In a study comparing self-disclosure online and face-to-face, McKenna and Green (2004) found that people shared more of their true selves online than face-to-face and liked an Internet partner more than a face-to-face partner. Of course, individual differences are important. People more strongly prefer online relationships if they are socially anxious or lonely or if their circumstances of current roles or relationships constrain face-to-face encounters. Far from keeping people from interacting personally, computers may thus sometimes enhance the development of friendships, free of the usual constraints of the first reactions to physical appearance and personal mannerisms. See Chenault (1998) for a thorough discussion of making personal friends and expressing emotion through computer-mediated communication.

from instant messaging and visiting chat rooms? How do they use listservers? How do they search web sites? How do they make friends on-line? See Box 12.5 for a closer look at the last question.

Most of this book has been concerned with the perceived reality that we construct through the interaction of our minds with the stimulus material from the TV, radio, magazines, or newspapers. If we want to actually change the media itself, however, we can sometimes do that as well. Although not a major focus of this book, this issue is worth examining briefly as a complement to our basic thesis.

INFLUENCING THE MEDIA

Very often, when we critically examine media, we are left with the feeling that there is much that we do not like, for whatever reason, but that there is little we can do about that state of affairs other than to choose not to use the medium (i.e., watch the program, read the paper). Just as we cognitively interact with the media in understanding it, so can we behaviorally interact with it to help effect change in desired ways. Commercial and political interests have long been doing this, and it behooves concerned and interested individual media consumers to learn to do likewise.

Individual Efforts

Individual complaints do have disproportionate impact, in that those who receive them assume that each complaint represents a similar view of many others who did not write. Certain types of letters are more effective than others. A reasoned, logically argued case has a lot more impact than an angry tirade. For example, one brand of club cocktails once advertised in *Ms* magazine with the slogan "Hit me with a Club." The company received over 1,000 letters of protest, arguing that the ad contained a suggestion of violence toward women. The company responded that such a connection was never intended or imagined, yet they were concerned enough by the letters to withdraw the ad (Will, 1987). Complaints do make a difference! Letters from Michigan homemaker Terry Rakolta and her supporters concerned about negative family values once caused Kimberly-Clark, McDonald's, and other sponsors to pull their ads from *Married With Children*.

Jamieson and Campbell (1992) suggested three types of arguments that are particularly effective when writing to a network, TV or radio station, or publication. First, a claim of inaccuracy or deception elicits immediate concern. Publishing or broadcasting inaccurate information is seldom intended and must be quickly corrected or balanced to avoid a loss of credibility and possible legal trouble as well. Second, a claim that an item violates community standards or general good taste causes concern. The press is very loath to offend, for example, with overly explicit sex, violence, or raunchy language. A sufficient number of people with such concerns may lead to the fear of loss of advertising dollars, the lifeblood of the enterprise. See Box 12.6 for an example of an ad that offended people and was withdrawn due to their complaints. Third, a claim of lack of balance or fairness is serious. This includes obvious concerns like lack of fairness in covering a political campaign or the use of an unfairly misleading ad, but also claims such as unfairly stereotyping some group or unfairly exploiting the cognitive immaturity of children to encourage them to request certain products from their parents.

Once in a great while the efforts of a single individual can result in policy change or the emergence of organizations to counter heavy media use to promote particular views. For example, in the 1960s John Banzhaf III persuaded the FCC that the Fairness Doctrine required television to

---

BOX 12.6
CASE STUDY OF A COMMERCIAL KILLED BY COMPLAINTS

A syndicated Ann Landers column (June 13, 1988) told of a test market commercial that was dropped due to calls and letters to the company. The ad opened with two teenage boys on a cliff overlooking the ocean. One challenges the other to a game, whereby both drive their cars toward the cliff and the one who jumps out first is a chicken. The boys start their race. The boy who made the dare at some point jumps out of his car. The other boy looks nervous and is shown panicking and pushing against the car door, which is stuck. We hear him screaming as his car goes over the cliff and crashes onto the rocks below, as the first boy watches in horror. Finally, the camera cuts to the ocean with a denim jacket and a pair of jeans floating on the water with a caption on a black screen: Union Bay—Fashion that Lasts.

The company's marketing director told Ann Landers that the ad was chosen for its impact and its dramatic quality. The director further said she believed that teens did not take ads very literally and would think that it was funny. However, after several complaints by phone and letter, the company withdrew the ad.

---

run antismoking ads to counter cigarette ads on TV at the time. (Tobacco ads were discontinued in the U.S. in 1971.) Pete Shields, who lost a son to a handgun homicide, and Sarah Brady, whose husband Jim was permanently brain-damaged in the assassination attempt on President Reagan in 1981, became active media users in gun control lobbying efforts. Millionaire heart-attack victim Phil Sokolof took out large newspaper ads pressuring big food corporations to change their practice of cooking in cholesterol-rich tropical oils. This campaign and the ensuing media coverage helped cause 12 large food corporations to begin using healthier oils within two years. Sokolof then turned his campaign on McDonald's to encourage them to reduce the fat content in their burgers (Dagnoli, 1990).

An excellent first outlet for media concerns is the editorial page of a local newspaper. Most are delighted to print letters to the editor or even guest columns. To find out about some larger media organizations and governmental and consumer agencies, search the Internet for web sites, which provide addresses, phone numbers, and e-mail addresses where agencies may be contacted.

Group Efforts

Individuals working together can often have more impact than isolated individuals. One corporate method is the *boycott*, whereby people refrain from buying some product or using some publication or station until changes are made. Even the threat of a boycott sends chills up the spines of advertisers, publications, or radio or TV stations. Newspapers have gone out of business when certain key economic interests have pulled their advertising. Convenience stores have stopped selling sex magazines in response to public complaints and the threat of a boycott. Nestle's changed its infant formula marketing campaign in response to public outcry and a boycott. Fear of adverse and organized public reaction is a major reason that U.S. television stations are so slow to accept condom ads, even in the age of the AIDS scare, when a majority of public opinion favors such ads.

In occasional cases a group may file legal action against a media organization. For example, when the FCC periodically reviews applications of radio and television stations for renewal, opportunity is available to challenge such renewal. Although the actual failure to renew a broadcasting license is extremely rare in the United States, such pressure may have substantial effects on subsequent station policy. For example, civil rights groups in the 1960s used this approach to force broadcasters to become more responsive to African American concerns in their communities. Sometimes the mere threat of legal or legislative action is enough to produce the desired change. For example, consumer groups like the now-defunct Action for Children's Television (ACT) have put pressure on the broadcast industry's National Association of Broadcasters (NAB) to limit the allowable number of minutes of commercials per hour on children's television. Their appeals to the FCC to regulate such numbers have led to the NAB limiting commercial time itself, a move it apparently considered preferable to government-mandated regulation.

Certain organizations have established themselves as watchdogs on certain kinds of issues. For example, the national Parent Teacher Association (PTA) has at different times monitored children's advertising and violent and sexual content on television. Resulting public awareness, as well as the latent threat of a boycott, has probably had some subtle effects. Many local citizens' groups protesting pornography have pressured convenience stores to stop selling sex magazines or put pressure on sponsors of very violent or sexual television programs. For example, a boycott of Pepsi in 1989 led to the company's cancellation of its sponsorship of a Madonna video and tour.

Sometimes follow-up monitoring is necessary, recognizing that unwanted regulation may sometimes be creatively circumvented. For example, the Children's Television Act of 1990 required TV stations to increase the number of hours of educational programming to children. In response to this, some stations redefined existing cartoons and syndicated sitcom reruns as educational. For example, in its license-renewal application, one station described *G.I. Joe* as "presenting a fight against an evil that has the capabilities of mass destruction of society" (School of Hard Knocks, 1992, p. 32). Truly educational shows like news shows for children ran at 5:30 in the morning, whereas newly defined "educational" programs like *The Jetsons* and *Leave It to Beaver* reruns retained the better time slots. By 1997, public dissatisfaction with such ruses pressured the FCC to clarify the 1990 law with an exact number of hours and clearer specification of what programming was considered educational (Steyer, 2002). However, after 2001 the pendulum again swung back in the free market, laissez faire direction.

Sometimes social science research itself may have an important impact on policy making. For example, the laboratory research finding that people could not perceive or be affected by backward audio messages (Box 4.7) led several states to withdraw pending legislation requiring record companies to put warning labels on album jackets (Vokey & Read, 1985). Research played a role in developing, and later modifying, the set of aged-based content ratings first used for TV programs in the United States in 1997 (Cantor, 1998a). The recent research on sexual violence (discussed in chapter 10) has tremendous potential impact on legal, policy, film-making, and even lifestyle issues. For a careful discussion of how research on sexual violence may be used to effect legal and policy change, see Penrod and Linz (1984) and Linz, Turner, Hesse, and Penrod (1984).

Before such research can have much impact on public opinion or public policy, however, the findings from that research must somehow be communicated to the world beyond the scientific community. This act in itself can often affect the perceived reality about that issue in the mind of the public.

COMMUNICATING MEDIA RESEARCH FINDINGS TO THE PUBLIC

In the reporting of science, the scientist's *truth* and the reporter's *news* are often quite different. For example, an editor may not consider a particular background feature story about pornography research as newsworthy because the paper has already carried two stories that week on that particular topic. The scientist looking at the same situation may not be convinced of the overlap, in that one was a story about citizens seeking a ban on sales of *Playboy* in convenience stores and the other was a story about a woman involved in acting in pornographic videos, neither of which at all overlaps with a report of behavioral research on the topic.

In their desire to fairly present all sides of an issue, journalists may emphasize controversy and thus (perhaps inadvertently) play up and legitimatize a fringe position given little credibility in the scientific community. As discussed in chapter 7, conflict and controversy are highly newsworthy. For example, subliminal advertising greatly intrigues and even alarms the general public, whereas the research community has long realized that its feared effects are vastly overrated or nonexistent (T. E. Moore, 1982; Pratkanis, 1992; Saegert, 1987). Such a topic may make good journalism, but it is bad science. The perceived reality of readers in response to such stories may be significantly at variance with the scientific reality.

Journalists and scientists use language in very different ways. As Tavris (1986) said:

> To the academician, the language of the reporter is excessively casual, trivial-
> izing, and simple-minded, if not downright wrong or silly. To the journalist,
> the language of the academicians is excessively passive, technical, and com-
> plicated, if not downright wordy or pompous. Academic language strives
> to be informative and accurate. To the reporter, though, the result sounds
> like nit-picking; it encumbers the research with so many qualifications and
> exceptions that the results seem meaningless. (p. 25)

It is not unusual to encounter the feeling that social science is an inferior, immature science. Not surprisingly, this feeling is common among journal-ists trained in science. More surprising, however, is that this view is also not unusual among social scientists themselves, some of whom see them-selves as doing work that is inferior to that of their colleagues in physics or biology. If many social scientists do not see themselves as true scientists, is it surprising that others do not so perceive them? This collective feeling of inferiority may stem from the fact that social science is by its very nature probabilistic, not deterministic. One can never predict for sure the effect on a particular person of seeing a violent movie, in the sense that one can predict with absolute certainty that $2 + 2 = 4$.

Researchers, including social science researchers, have not always been very successful at, or even interested in, communicating the results of their research to the public. Sometimes scientists who do so, such as Carl Sagan, are actually scorned by their professional colleagues (Ferris, 1997). They certainly are not rewarded by the academic profession, which primarily encourages obtaining research grants and publishing scholarly research papers. Even writing textbooks is held in relatively low esteem in terms of professional advancement (no professor ever writes a textbook before they have tenure!), and talking to the press and the public is often given no value at all, possibly even scorned. Professors and researchers receive no training at all in speaking with the press and often have no clue how to speak to reporters about their work in a way that gives the journalist something he or she can use in writing a story.

Still, social science stories hold much interest for many readers and even journalists. In a study by Dunwoody (1986), newspaper editors actually re-ported a preference for social science topics over those in physical science.

However, the reverse preference was found in reporters. Thus, there may often be a situation of an editor selecting a social science topic but assigning it to a reporter who has less interest in it and thus may not treat it as science, thereby resulting in more sloppy treatment than would be given a "real science" story. A recent study showed that neither journalists nor scientists believed that media do a good job communicating scientific information to the public (Chappell & Hartz, 1998). Indeed, sometimes the impression conveyed in the popular press is entirely opposite to the state of the research, as seen in chapter 9 in the study of popular press coverage of conclusions from media violence research (Bushman & Anderson, 2001). For a fascinating series of papers examining how the media report scientific research about media violence, see J. H. Goldstein (1986).

Throughout most of this book, we have focused on the perceived reality of the *receiver* of media input. It is even more magical to *appear* in the media, especially on television. Because it is a very intrusive medium, being on television makes someone either very excited or very uncomfortable or perhaps both. The importance seems to be more in the act of merely *being* on TV than in what one does there. People are very eager to look perfectly foolish singing a song or even exposing personally embarrassing information on a daytime talk show. Over the years we have seen shows of people in the real world, often doing very strange things (e.g., *Candid Camera, America's Funniest Home Videos, Survivor, Temptation Island*). It will be interesting to see if the use of camcorders and home videos removes some of the magic from being on TV, because children now grow up seeing themselves on the TV screen frequently. So far, however, the mystique still seems to be there.

CONCLUSION: WHAT IS MASS COMMUNICATION? (REVISITED)

For all sorts of reasons discussed in this chapter, it is becoming increasingly difficult to identify exactly where mass media stop and personal media begin or where the boundary between entertainment and mass media is. The advent of the VCR allows us to watch home movies using the technology of mass communication (television). Computer-mediated communication such as e-mail, the World Wide Web, listservers, and chat rooms have introduced totally new ways of communicating. The government of the city-state nation of Singapore initiated the National Information Infrastructure, a project to link all households in the country to a network of fiber-optic cables allowing high-speed exchanges of text, sound, video, and other information; there will also be a wireless communication network for mobile computer users. Similar projects are underway or are being seriously discussed elsewhere, including France, Japan, Germany, Canada, and the United States. Although great progress has been made, wiring up the poorest and most isolated segments of a society has usually proven more difficult and slower than expected.

Although electronic and, to a lesser extent, print media can be controlled by an authoritarian government, computers and VCRs are much more difficult to suppress. Computer bulletin boards and networks (Rafaeli & LaRose, 1993; Trevino & Webster, 1992) have been used to spread news during insurrections and revolution. Rebel groups worldwide routinely use videotaping of their activities to document actions against them and to recruit and motivate new members. When Boris Yeltsin and the democratic protesters took refuge in the Russian Parliament building during the abortive August 1991 coup in Moscow, they kept in touch with the world through fax and computer lines. These days rebel groups like Mexico's Zapatista rebels have to worry as much about keeping a modern arsenal of web pages and computerized address lists as they do an arsenal of weapons (see Box 12.7).

BOX 12.7
REBELLION ON THE WORLD WIDE WEB

Although the initial bloody rebellion by the Zapatista rebels in the southernmost Mexican state of Chiapas was fairly short-lived in 1994, the battle continues on the ground but also in cyberspace. The Zapatista National Liberation Army (EZLN) initially broadcast its revolutionary message on the Internet and has continued to use e-mail and web sites to communicate with each other and the public, usually without government censorship. The group's web site, Ya Basta! solicits funds for the group and provides updates on the local situation. Its leader, Subcomandante Marcos, writes communiques on his laptop computer plugged into the cigarette lighter of his truck. These messages are then transferred onto disks and put on the web site. Rebel use of the new technologies has forced the major Mexican TV networks like Televisa to give them more coverage, since the public is learning about the rebels from other sources anyway, including some Usenet groups like Chiapas95. In a careful comparison of newspaper and Internet news coverage of the Zapatistas, A. Russell (2001) concludes that each medium presents its unique approach to the rebel movement. She concludes that the Internet and Chiapas95 function similarly to newspapers in earlier, more partisan and less regulated days. Other radical groups worldwide, like the Irish Republican Army, the Islamic Hamas, and Peru's Sendero Luminoso (Shining Path), all have web sites and use e-mail communication (I. Vincent, 1996).

One of the first major manifestations of new communications technology appeared in the worldwide fax revolution of Chinese students in response to the 1989 Tiananmen Square massacre and subsequent government crack-down, where the estimated 10,000 fax numbers in China were jammed for weeks with reports from abroad about what had really happened in Beijing (Ganley, 1992). Much of the communication among those sending the fax messages was by e-mail. Taped newscasts out of Hong Kong (not yet part of China) circulated widely on the two million or more VCRs in China. The democratic uprising in China was suppressed but it will never again be possible to so totally isolate a society from the news of its own oppression. Indeed, the technology revolution is a major factor in the opening up of China in the last two decades. Electronic information in all its forms is not easily controlled.

Still, however, grandiose claims about new technologies revolutionizing the lives of everyone on the planet may be greatly overblown. In fact, there is reason to think that new communications technologies will only widen the gap between the rich and the poor. Consider, for example, Wresch's (1996) look at two Namibian men, one rich and one poor. The poor man, Negumbo, has no skills, no job, no electricity. Newspapers cost one tenth of his daily wage, on days that he manages to find work. Few in his neighbor-hood have TV, and it is all in English, a language he does not understand. His news sources are largely limited to one radio station that broadcasts in his language. He has traveled nowhere but his village in northern Namibia and the capital, Windhoek.

The rich man, Theo, is president of his own computer company, drives a BMW, speaks three languages, and is wired into the world via phone, e-mail, and the numerous CD-ROMs of information he receives daily. He also makes at least yearly trips to Germany and the United States and has a buyer in California who sends him a weekly shipment. He can come home and watch a movie on his VCR (but no Namibian movies—there aren't any) or watch American sitcoms or Mexican soap operas on his television. He can telephone to Europe or the United States but to hardly anyone outside the capital in his own country, because the local phone infrastructure is so bad.

Even as the information revolution wires Theo into more and more places, his countrymen becomes more and more isolated. Developing coun-tries like Namibia are becoming increasingly divided by information as well as income, and it is not at all clear that technology will bridge this gap anytime soon.

All of this brings us back to the question of why study the *psychology*, especially cognitive psychology, of the media? At heart media offer an experience that emerges from the interaction of our minds with the content of the communication. Media affect our minds: they give us ideas, change our attitudes, tell us what the world is like. These mental constructions (i.e., our perceived reality) then become the framework around which we interpret the totality of experience. Thus, media consumption and effects are very much cognitive phenomena.

In one sense, media production is a creation, a fabrication. But yet, as Picasso once said, "Art is a lie through which we can see the truth." The same is often true of media. Performing in media is action, pretending, taking a role, but as Oscar Wilde once said, "I love acting; It is so much more real than life." One might say the same about media. Life imitates art, and art imitates life. After a while, it becomes hard to tell which is which.

References

Abel, E. (1984). Television in international conflict. In A. Anno & W. Dissayanake (Eds.), *The news media and national and international conflict* (pp. 63–70). Boulder, CO: Westview Press.

Abel, G. G., Barlow, D. H., Blanchard, E. B., & Guild, D. (1977). The components of rapists' sexual arousal. *Archives of General Psychiatry, 34,* 895–903.

Abelman, R. (1989). From here to eternity: Children's acquisition of understanding of projective size on television. *Human Communication Research, 15,* 463–481.

Abernethy, A. M. (1992). The information content of newspaper advertising. *Journal of Current Issues and Research in Advertising, 14*(2), 63–68.

Abramson, P. R., & Hayashi, H. (1984). Pornography in Japan: Cross-cultural and theoretical considerations. In N. M. Malamuth & E. Donnerstein (Eds.), *Pornography and sexual aggression* (pp. 173–183). Orlando, FL: Academic Press.

Abramson, P. R., Perry, L., Seeley, T., Seeley, D., & Rothblatt, A. (1981). Thermographic measurement of sexual arousal: A discriminant validity analysis. *Archives of Sexual Behavior, 10*(2), 175–176.

Ahn, W.-K., Brewer, W. F., & Mooney, R. J. (1992). Schema acquisition from a single example. *Journal of Experimental Psychology: Learning, Memory, and Cognition, 18,* 391–412.

Alali, A. O., & Eke, K. K. (Eds.). (1991). *Media coverage of terrorism: Methods of diffusion.* Newbury Park, CA: Sage.

Alesandrini, K. L. (1983). Strategies that influence memory for advertising communications. In R. J. Harris (Ed.), *Information processing research in advertising* (pp. 65–82). Hillsdale, NJ: Lawrence Erlbaum Associates.

Allen, M., D'Alessio, D., & Brezgel, K. (1995). A meta-analysis summarizing the effects of pornography II: Aggression after exposure. *Human Communication Research, 22,* 258–283.

Allen, M., Emmers, T., Gebhardt, L., & Giery, M. A. (1995). Exposure to pornography and acceptance of rape myths. *Journal of Communication, 45*(1), 5–26.

Alperstein, N. (1991). Imaginary social relationships with celebrities appearing in television commercials. *Journal of Broadcasting and Electronic Media, 35,* 43–58.

Alvarado, M., Gutch, R., & Wollen, T. (1987). *Learning the media: An introduction to media teaching.* London: Macmillan.

Alwitt, L. F., Deighton, J., & Grimm, J. (1991). Reactions to political advertising depend on the nature of the voter-candidate bond. In F. Biocca (Ed.), *Television and political advertising: Psychological processes* (Vol. 1, pp. 329–350). Hillsdale, NJ: Lawrence Erlbaum Associates.

Amaral, R., & Guimarães, C. (1994). Media monopoly in Brazil. *Journal of Communication, 44*(4), 26–38.

Andersen, P. A., & Kibler, R. J. (1978). Candidate valence as a predictor of voter preference. *Human Communication Research, 5,* 4–14.

Anderson, C. A., & Bushman, B. J. (2001). Effects of violent video games on aggressive behavior, aggressive cognition, aggressive affect, physiological arousal, and prosocial behavior: A meta-analytic review of the scientific literature. *Psychological Science, 12,* 353–359.

Anderson, C. A., & Dill, K. E. (2000). Video games and aggressive thoughts, feelings, and behavior in the laboratory and in life. *Journal of Personality and Social Psychology, 78,* 772–790.

Anderson, C. A., & Morrow, M. (1995). Competitive aggression without interaction: Effects of competitive versus cooperative instructions on aggressive behavior in video games, *Personality and Social Psychology Bulletin, 21*(10), 1020–1030.

Anderson, D. R. (1985). Online cognitive processing of television. In L. F. Alwitt & A. A. Mitchell (Eds.), *Psychological processes and advertising effects* (pp. 177–199). Hillsdale, NJ: Lawrence Erlbaum Associates.

Anderson, D. R. (1998). Educational television is not an oxymoron. *The Annals of the American Academy of Political and Social Science, 557,* 24–38.

Anderson, D. R., Bryant, J., Wilder, A, Santomero, A, Williams, M., & Crawley, A. M. (2000). Researching *Blue's Clues*: Viewing behavior and impact. *Media Psychology, 2,* 179–194.

Anderson, D. R., Huston, A. C., Wright, J. C., & Collins, P. A. (1998). *Sesame Street* and educational television for children. In R. G. Noll and M. E. Price (Eds.), *A communications cornucopia: Markle Foundation essays on information policy.* (pp. 279–296). Washington, DC: Brookings Institution Press.

Anderson, D. R., & Burns, J. (1991). Paying attention to television. In J. Bryant & D. Zillmann (Eds.), *Responding to the screen: Reception and reaction processes* (pp. 3–25). Hillsdale, NJ: Lawrence Erlbaum Associates.

Anderson, D. R., & Field, D. E. (1991). Online and offline assessment of the television audience. In J. Bryant & D. Zillmann (Eds.), *Responding to the screen: Reception and reaction processes* (pp. 199–216). Hillsdale, NJ: Lawrence Erlbaum Associates.

Andreasen, M. S. (1990). Evolution of the family's use of television: Normative data from industry and academe. In J. Bryant (Ed.), *Television and the American family* (pp. 3–55). Hillsdale, NJ: Lawrence Erlbaum Associates.

Andreasen, M. S. (1994). Patterns of family life and television consumption from 1945 to the 1990s. In D. Zillmann, J. Bryant, & A. C. Huston (Eds.), *Media, children, and the family: Social scientific, psychodynamic, and clinical perspectives* (pp. 19–36). Hillsdale, NJ: Lawrence Erlbaum Associates.

Andsager, J. L., Austin, E. W., & Pinkleton, B. E. (2001). Questioning the value of realism: Young adults' processing of messages in alcohol-related public service announcements and advertising. *Journal of Communication, 51*(1), 121–142.

Appiah, O. (2002). Black and white viewers' perception and recall of occupational characters on television. *Journal of Communication, 52,* 776–793.

Apter, M. J. (1982). *The experience of motivation: The theory of psychological reversals.* San Diego, CA: Academic Press.

Arms, R. L., Russell, G. W., & Sandilands, M. L. (1979). Effects on the hostility of spectators of viewing aggressive sports. *Social Psychology Quarterly, 42,* 275–279.

Armstrong, E. G. (1993). The rhetoric of violence in rap and country music. *Sociological Inquiry, 63,* 64–84.

Armstrong, G. B., Neuendorf, K. A., & Brentar, J. E. (1992). TV entertainment, news, and racial perceptions of college students. *Journal of Communication, 42*(3), 153–176.

Atkin, C., & Arkin, E. B. (1990). Issues and initiatives in communicating health information. In C. Atkin & L. Wallack (Eds.), *Mass communication and public health* (pp. 13–40). Newbury Park, CA: Sage.

Atkin, C., Greenberg, B., & McDermott, S. (1983). Television and race role socialization. *Journalism Quarterly, 60*(3), 407–414.

Austin, E. W. (1993). Exploring the effects of active parental mediation of television content. *Journal of Broadcasting & Electronic Media, 37,* 147-158.

Austin, E. W. (2001). Effects of family communication on children's interpretation of television. In J. Bryant, & J. A. Bryant (Eds.), *Television and the American family.* (2nd ed., pp. 377–395). Mahwah, NJ: Lawrence Erlbaum Associates.

Austin, E. W., Bolls, P., Fujioka, Y., & Engelbertson, J. (1999). How and why parents take on the tube. *Journal of Broadcasting & Electronic Media, 43,* 175–192.

Austin, E. W., Pinkleton, B. E., & Fujioka, Y. (2000). The role of interpretation processes and parental discussion in the media's effects on adolescents' use of alcohol. *Pediatrics, 105,* 343–349.

Austin, E. W., Roberts, D. F., & Nass, C. I. (1990). Influences of family communication in children's television-interpretation processes. *Communication Research, 17,* 545–564.

Bacchetta, V. (1987). Brazil's soap operas: "Huge dramas where the country portrays itself." *Latinamerica Press, 19*(9), 5–6.

Bachen, C. M. (1998). Channel One and the education of American youths. *The Annals of the American Academy of Political and Social Science, 557,* 132–147.

Backer, T. E., Rogers, E. M., & Sopory, P. (1992). *Designing health communication campaigns: What works?* Newbury Park, CA: Sage.

Baggaley, J. P. (1988). Perceived effectiveness of interactional AIDS campaigns. *Health Education Research: Theory and Practice, 3,* 7–17.

Baggett, P. (1979). Structurally equivalent stories in movie and text and the effect of the medium on recall. *Journal of Verbal Learning and Verbal Behavior, 18,* 333–356.

Bald, M. (1998, May). Africa's wonderchild. *World Press Review, 45,* 22.

Ball, S., & Bogatz, G. A. (1970). *The first year of Sesame Street: An evaluation.* Princeton, NJ: Educational Testing Service.

Ball, S., & Bogatz, G. A. (1973). *Reading with television: An evaluation of The Electric Company*. Princeton, NJ: Educational Testing Service.

Ballard, M. E., & Coates, S. (1995). The immediate effects of homicidal, suicidal, and nonviolent heavy metal and rap songs on the mood of college students. *Youth & Society, 27*, 148–169.

Ballard, M. E., & Wiest, J. R. (1996). Mortal Kombat: The effects of violent video game play on males' hostility and cardiovascular responding. *Journal of Applied Social Psychology, 26*(8), 717–730.

Balter, R. (1999). From stigmatization to patronization: The media's distorted portrayal of physical disability. In L. L. Schwartz (Ed.), *Psychology and the media: A second look.* (pp. 147–171). Washington, DC: American Psychological Association.

Bancroft, J., & Mathews, A. (1971). Autonomic correlates of penile erection. *Journal of Psychosomatic Research, 15*, 159–167.

Bandura, A. (1965). Influence of models' reinforcement contingencies on the acquisition of imitative responses. *Journal of Personality and Social Psychology, 1*, 585–595.

Bandura, A. (1977). *Social learning theory*. Englewood Cliffs, NJ: Prentice-Hall.

Bandura, A. (1995). Exercise of personal and collective efficacy. In A. Bandura (Ed.), *Self-efficacy in changing societies* (pp. 1–45). New York: Cambridge University Press.

Bandura, A. (1997). *Self-efficacy: The essence of control*. New York: Freeman.

Bandura, A. (2001). Social cognitive theory of mass communication. *Media Psychology, 3*, 265–299.

Bandura, A. (2002). Social cognitive theory of mass communication. In J. Bryant and D. Zillmann (Eds.) *Media Effects.* (2nd ed., pp. 121–153). Mahwah, NJ: Lawrence Erlbaum Associates.

Bandura, A., Ross, D., & Ross, S. A. (1961). Transmission of aggression through imitation of aggressive models. *Journal of Abnormal and Social Psychology, 63*, 575–582.

Bandura, A., Ross, D., & Ross, S. A. (1963). Imitation of film-mediated aggressive models. *Journal of Abnormal and Social Psychology, 66*, 3–11.

Bandura, A., & Walters, R. H. (1963). *Social learning and personality development*. New York: Holt, Rinehart & Winston.

Barcus, F. E. (1980). The nature of television advertising to children. In E. L. Palmer & A. Dorr (Eds.), *Children and the faces of television: Teaching, violence, and selling* (pp. 273–285). New York: Academic Press.

Barcus, F. E. (1983). *Images of life on children's television*. New York: Prager.

Barnhurst, K. G., & Mutz, D. (1997). American journalism and the decline in event-centered reporting. *Journal of Communication, 47*(4), 27–53.

Baron, R. A. (1979). Heightened sexual arousal and physical aggression: An extension to females. *Journal of Research in Personality, 13*, 91–102.

Bartholomew, B. D., & Anderson, C. A. (2002). Effects of violent video games on aggressive behavior: Potential sex differences. *Journal of Experimental Social Psychology, 38*(3), 283–290.

Basil, M. D. (1994). Secondary reaction-time measures. In A. Lang (Ed.), *Measuring psychological responses to media* (pp. 85–98). Hillsdale, NJ: Lawrence Erlbaum Associates.

Basil, M., Schooler, C., & Reeves, B. (1991). Positive and negative political advertising: Effectiveness of ads and perceptions of candidates. In F. Biocca (Ed.), *Television and political advertising: Psychological processes* (Vol. 1, pp. 245–262). Hillsdale, NJ: Lawrence Erlbaum Associates.

Bateman, T. S., Sakano, T., & Fujita, M. (1992). Roger, me, and my attitude: Film propaganda and cynicism toward corporate leadership. *Journal of Applied Psychology, 77,* 768–771.

Bauserman, R. (1996). Sexual aggression and pornography: A review of correlation research. *Basic and Applied Social Psychology, 18,* 405–427.

Beagles-Roos, J., & Gat, I. (1983). Specific impact of radio and television on children's story comprehension. *Journal of Educational Psychology, 75,* 128–137.

Beeman, W. O. (1984). The cultural role of the media in Iran: The revolution of 1978–1979 and after. In A. Anno & W. Dissayanake (Eds.), *The news media and national and international conflict* (pp. 147–165). Boulder, CO: Westview Press.

Beentjes, J. W. J., & van der Voort, T. H. A. (1989). Television and young people's reading behaviour: A review of research. *European Journal of Communication, 4,* 451–477.

Beentjes, J. W. J., van Oordt, M. N., & van der Voort, T. H. A. (2002). How television commentary affects children's judgments on soccer fouls. *Communication Research, 29,* 31–45.

Belkin, L. (2001, March/April). Primetime pushers. *Mother Jones,* pp. 30–37.

Bellafante, G. (1995, March 27). Playing "Get the Guest." *Time,* 77.

Benedict, H. (1992). *Virgin or vamp: How the press covers sex crimes.* New York: Oxford University Press.

Bensley, L., & Van Eenwyk, J. (2001). Video games and real life aggression: Review of the literature. *Journal of Adolescent Health, 29*(4), 244–257.

Berelson, B. R., Lazarsfeld, P. F., & McPhee, W. N. (1954). *Voting.* Chicago: University of Chicago Press.

Berger, C. R. (1998). Processing quantitative data about risk and threat in news reports. *Journal of Communication, 48*(3), 87–106.

Berger, C. R. (2000). Quantitative depictions of threatening phenomena in news reports. *Human Communication Research, 26,* 27–52.

Berkowitz, L. (1965). Some aspects of observed aggression. *Journal of Personality and Social Psychology, 2,* 359–369.

Berkowitz, L. (1984). Some effects of thoughts on anti- and prosocial influences of media events: A cognitive neoassociation analysis. *Psychological Bulletin, 95,* 410–427.

Berry, G. L. (1980). Television and Afro-Americans: Past legacy and present portrayals. In S. B. Withey & R. P. Abeles (Eds.), *Television and social behavior* (pp. 231–247). Hillsdale, NJ: Lawrence Erlbaum Associates.

Berry, G. L., & Asamen, J. K. (Eds.). (1993). *Children and television: Images in a changing sociocultural world.* Newbury Park, CA: Sage.

Berry, V. T. (1992). From *Good Times* to *The Cosby Show:* Perceptions of changing televised images among black fathers and sons. In S. Craig (Ed.), *Men, masculinity, and the media* (pp. 111–123). Newbury Park, CA: Sage.

Best, J. (1999). *Random violence: How we talk about new crimes and new victims.* Berkeley, CA: University of California Press.

Bever, T., Smith, M., Bengen, B., & Johnson, T. (1975). Young viewers' troubling responses to TV ads. *Harvard Business Review, 53*(6), 109–120.

Bickham, D. S., Wright, J. C., & Huston, A. C. (2001). Attention, comprehension, and the educational influences of television. In D. G. Singer and J. L. Singer (Eds.), *Handbook of children and the media* (pp. 101–119). Thousand Oaks, CA: Sage.

Billings, A. C., & Eastman, S. T. (2003). Framing identities: Gender, ethnic, and national parity in network announcing of the 2002 Winter Olympics. *Journal of Communication, 53,* 569–585.

Biocca, F. (Ed.). (1991). *Television and political advertising, Vol. 1: Psychological processes.* Hillsdale, NJ: Lawrence Erlbaum Associates.

Bickham, D. S., Vandewater, E. A., Huston, A. C., Caplovitz, A. G., & Wright, J. C. (2003). Predictors of children's electronic media use: An examination of three ethnic groups. *Media Psychology, 5,* 107–137.

Bird, S. E. (Ed.). (1996). *Dressing in feathers: The construction of the Indian in popular culture.* Boulder, CO: Westview Press.

Bird, S. E. (1999). Gendered construction of the American Indian in popular media. *Journal of Communication, 49*(3), 61–83.

Bischoff, R. J., & Reiter, A. D. (1999). The role of gender in the presentation of mental health clinicians in the movies: Implications for clinical practice. *Psychotherapy, 36*(2), 180–189.

Bjerklie, D. (2002, August 12). Label reform. *Time,* Y4.

Bjerklie, D. (2003, July 28). *Time,* 73.

Blain, N., Boyle, R., & O'Donnell, H. (1993). *Sport and national identity in the European media.* Leicester, UK: Leicester University Press.

Blatt, J., Spencer, L., & Ward, S. (1972). A cognitive developmental study of children's reactions to television advertising. In E. A. Rubinstein, G. A. Comstock, & J. P. Murray (Eds.), *Television and social behavior: Television in everyday life: Patterns of use* (Vol. 4, pp. 452–467). Washington, DC: U.S. Government Printing Office.

Block, C. (1972). White backlash to Negro ads: Fact or fantasy? *Journalism Quarterly, 49*(2), 253–262.

Blumler, J. G. (1979). The role of theory in uses and gratifications research. *Communication Research, 6,* 9–36.

Blumler, J. G., McLeod, J. M., & Rosengren, K. E. (Eds.). (1992). *Comparatively speaking: Communication and culture across space and time.* Newbury Park, CA: Sage.

Blumler, J. G., & Katz, E. (Eds.). (1974). *The uses of mass communications: Current perspectives on gratifications research.* Beverly Hills, CA: Sage.

Blumler, J. G., & McQuail, D. (1969). *Television in politics: Its uses and influences.* Chicago: University of Chicago Press.

Boeckmann, K., & Hipfl, B. (1987). How can we learn about children and television? *Journal of Educational Television, 13,* 217–229.

Bogart, L. (1980). Television news as entertainment. In P. H. Tannenbaum (Ed.), *The entertainment functions of television* (pp. 209–249). Hillsdale, NJ: Lawrence Erlbaum Associates.

Bogart, L. (1981). *Press and public.* Hillsdale, NJ: Lawrence Erlbaum Associates.

Bogatz, G. A., & Ball, S. (1971). *The second year of Sesame Street: A continuing evaluation.* Princeton, NJ: Educational Testing Service.

Bogle, D. (1973). *Toms, coons, mulattoes, and bucks: An interpretive history of blacks in American films.* New York: Viking Press.

Boiney, J., & Paletz, D. L. (1991). In search of the model: Political science versus political advertising perspectives on voter decision making. In F. Biocca (Ed.), *Television and political advertising, Psychological processes* (Vol. 1, pp. 3–25). Hillsdale, NJ: Lawrence Erlbaum Associates.

Bollen, K. A., & Phillips, D. P. (1982). Imitative suicides: A national study of the effects of television news stories. *American Sociological Review, 47,* 802–809.

Bolls, P. D., & Lang, A. (2003). I saw it on the radio: The allocation of attention to high-imagery radio advertisements. *Media Psychology, 5,* 33–55.

Bolls, P. D., Lang, A., & Potter, R. F. (2001). The effects of message valence and listener arousal on attention, memory, and facial muscular responses to radio advertisements. *Communication Research, 28,* 627–651.

Bonds-Raacke, J. M., Cady, E. T., Schlegel, R., Harris, R. J., & Firebaugh, L. C. (2004). Remembering gay/lesbian characters: Can Ellen and Will improve attitudes toward homosexuals? Unpublished manuscript.

Bonds-Raacke, J. M., & Harris, R. J. (2004). Autobiographical memories of televised sporting events watched in different social settings. Unpublished manuscript.

Bordeaux, B. R., & Lange, G. (1991). Children's reported investment of mental effort when viewing television. *Communication Research, 18,* 617–635.

Borden, D. L., & Harvey, K. (Eds.). (1997). *The electronic grapevine: Rumor, reputation, and reporting in the new online environment.* Mahwah, NJ: Lawrence Erlbaum Associates.

Botta, R. A. (1999). Television images and adolescent girls' body image disturbance. *Journal of Communication, 49*(2), 22–41.

Bouman, M. (2002). Turtles and peacocks: Collaboration in entertainment-education television. *Communication Theory, 12,* 225–244.

Bower, A. (2002, May 6). Fast-food networks. *Time, 161,* Your Family page.

Brabant, S., & Mooney, L. (1986). Sex role stereotyping in the Sunday comics. *Sex Roles, 14*(3/4), 141–148.

Bradley, S. D., & Meeds, R. (2002). Surface-structure transformations and advertising slogans: The case for moderate syntactic complexity. *Psychology & Marketing, 19,* 595–619.

Breslow, L. (1978). Risk factor intervention for health maintenance. *Science, 200,* 908–912.

Bretl, D.J., & Cantor, J. (1988). The portrayal of men and women on U.S. television commercials: A recent content analysis and trends over 15 years. *Sex Roles, 18,* 595–609.

Brewer, W. F., & Nakamura, G. V. (1984). The nature and functions of schemas. In R. S. Wyer & T. K. Srull (Eds.), *Handbook of social cognition.* Hillsdale, NJ: Lawrence Erlbaum Associates.

Brockhoff, W. (1988, February). Magazine not negligent in running ad. *KSU Collegian, 92,* 2.

Brosius, H. B. (1993). The effects of emotional pictures in television news. *Communication Research, 20,* 105–124.

Brosius, H.-B., & Kepplinger, H. M. (1990). The agenda-setting function of television news: Static and dynamic views. *Communication Research, 17,* 183–211.

Brown, D., & Bryant, J. (1983). Humor in mass media. In P. E. McGhee & J. H. Goldstein (Eds.), *Handbook of humor research* (Vol. 2). New York: Springer-Verlag.

Brown, D., & Bryant, J. (1990). Effects of television on family values and selected attitudes and behaviors. In J. Bryant (Ed.), *Television and the American family* (pp. 227–251). Hillsdale, NJ: Lawrence Erlbaum Associates.

Brown, J. A. (1991). *Television "critical viewing skills" education: Major media literacy projects in the United States and selected countries.* Hillsdale, NJ: Lawrence Erlbaum Associates.

Brown, J. A. (1998). Media literacy perspectives. *Journal of Communication, 48*(1), 44–57.

Brown, J. D., & Campbell, K. (1986). Race and gender in music videos: The same beat but a different drummer. *Journal of Communication, 36*(1), 94–106.

Brown, J. D., & Einsiedel, E. F. (1990). Public health campaigns: Mass media strategies. In E. B. Ray & L. Donohew (Eds.), *Communication and health: Systems and applications* (pp. 153–170). Hillsdale, NJ: Lawrence Erlbaum Associates.

Brown, J. D., & Walsh-Childers, K. (2002). Effects of media on personal and public health. In J. Bryant and D. Zillmann (Eds.) *Media effects* (2nd ed., pp. 453–488). Mahwah NJ: Lawrence Erlbaum Associates.

Brown, N. R., & Siegler, R. S. (1992). The role of availability in the estimation of national populations. *Memory & Cognition, 20,* 406–412.

Brown, W. J., Basil, M. D., & Bocarnea, M. C. (2003). Social influence of an international celebrity: Responses to the death of Princess Diana. *Journal of Communication, 53,* 587–605.

Brown, W. J., & Cody, M. J. (1991). Effects of a prosocial television soap opera in promoting women's status. *Human Communication Research, 18,* 114–142.

Brown, W. J., & Singhal, A. (1990). Ethical dilemmas of prosocial television. *Communication Quarterly, 38,* 268–280.

Brown, W. J., Singhal, A., & Rogers, E. M. (1989). Pro-development soap operas: A novel approach to development communication. *Media Development, 36*(4), 43–47.

Brownstein, A. (2001, February 23), A battle over a name in the land of the Sioux. *The Chronicle of Higher Education,* A46–A49.

Bruce, S. (1990). *Pray TV: Televangelism in America.* London: Routledge.

Bruno, K. J., & Harris, R. J. (1980). The effect of repetition on the discrimination of asserted and implied claims in advertising. *Applied Psycholinguistics, 1,* 307–321.

Bryant, J. (1989). Viewers' enjoyment of televised sports violence. In L. A. Wenner (Ed.), *Media, sports, and society* (pp. 270–289). Newbury Park, CA: Sage.

Bryant, J. (Ed.). (1990). *Television and the American family.* Hillsdale, NJ: Lawrence Erlbaum Associates.

Bryant, J., Aust, C. F., Bryant, J. A., & Venugopalan, G. (2001). How psychologically healthy are America's prime-time television families? In J. Bryant, & J. A. Bryant (Eds.), *Television and the American family.* (2nd ed., pp. 247–270). Mahwah, NJ: Lawrence Erlbaum Associates.

Bryant, J., & Bryant, J. A. (2001). *Television and the American family* (2nd ed.). Mahwah, NJ: Lawrence Erlbaum Associates.

Bryant, J., & Raney, A. A. (2000). Sports on the screen. In D. Zillmann and P. Vorderer (Eds.), *Media entertainment: The psychology of its appeal* (pp. 153–174). Mahwah, NJ: Lawrence Erlbaum Associates.

Bryant, J., & Rockwell, S. C. (1994). Effects of massive exposure to sexually oriented prime-time television programming on adolescents' moral judgment. In D. Zillmann, J. Bryant, & A. C. Huston (Eds.), *Media, children, and the family: Social scientific, psychodynamic, and clinical perspectives* (pp. 183–195). Hillsdale, NJ: Lawrence Erlbaum Associates.

Bryant, J., Zillmann, D., & Raney, A. A. (1998). Violence and the enjoyment of media sports. In L. A. Wenner (Ed.), *MediaSport* (pp. 252–265). London: Routledge.

Bryant, J., & Zillmann, D. (Eds.). (2002). *Media effects* (pp. 453–488). Mahwah NJ: Lawrence Erlbaum Associates.

Buchholz, M., & Bynum, J. (1982). Newspaper presentation of America's aged: A content analysis of image and role. *The Gerontologist, 22,* 83–88.

Buckingham, D. (1993). *Children talking television: The making of television literacy.* London: Falmer.

Buckingham, D. (1996). Critical pedagogy and media education: A theory in search of a practice. *Journal of Curriculum Studies, 28*(6), 627–650.

Buckingham, D. (1998). Media education in the UK: Moving beyond protectionism. *Journal of Communication, 48*(1), 33–43.

Buerkel-Rothfuss, N. L., & Buerkel, R.A. (2001). Family mediation. In J. Bryant, & J. A. Bryant (Eds.). *Television and the American family* (2nd ed., pp. 355–376). Mahwah, NJ: Lawrence Erlbaum Associates.

Buerkel-Rothfuss, N. L., & Mayes, S. (1981). Soap opera viewing: The cultivation effect. *Journal of Communication, 31,* 108–115.

Bullard, S. (1998). Gangstawulf: Examining the allure of violence in lyric form. *Teaching Tolerance, 7*(1), 16–19.

Burke, R. R., DeSarbo, W. S., Oliver, R. L., & Robertson, T. S. (1988). Deception by implication: An experimental investigation. *Journal of Consumer Research, 14,* 483–494.

Bushman, B. J. (1998). Effects of television violence on memory of commercial messages. *Journal of Experiment Psychology: Applied, 4,* 291–307.

Bushman, B. J., & Anderson, C. A. (2001). Media violence and the American public: Scientific facts versus media misinformation. *American Psychologist, 56,* 477–489.

Bushman, B. J., & Anderson, C. A. (2002). Violent video games and hostile expectations: A test of the general aggression model. *Personality and Social Psychology Bulletin, 28,* 1679–1686.

Bushman, B. J., Baumeister, R. F., & Stack, A. D. (1999). Catharsis, aggression, and persuasive influences: Self-fulfilling or self-defeating prophecies? *Journal of Personality and Social Psychology, 76,* 367–376.

Bushman, B. J., & Phillips, C.M. (2001). If the television program bleeds, memory for the advertisement recedes. *Current Directions in Psychological Science, 10,* 43–47.

Busselle, R. W., & Shrum, L. J. (2003). Media exposure and exemplar accessibility. *Media Psychology, 5,* 255–282.

Cady, E. T., Harris, R. J., & Knappenberger, J. B. (2004). Using music to cue auto-biographical memory of different lifetime periods. Unpublished manuscript.

Calvert, S. L. (1988). Television production feature effects of children's comprehension of time. *Journal of Applied Developmental Psychology, 9,* 263–273.

Calvert, S. L. Kotler, J. A., Zehnder, S. M., & Shockey, E. M. (2003). Gender stereo-typing in children's reports about educational and informational television programs. *Media Psychology, 5,* 139–162.

Cameron, G. T., & Frieske, D. A. (1994). The time needed to answer: Measurement of memory response latency. In A. Lang (Ed.), *Measuring psychological responses to media* (pp. 149–164). Hillsdale, NJ: Lawrence Erlbaum Associates.

Canadian case. (1996, June 20). *Kansas State Collegian,* p. 2.

Cantor, J. (1991). Fright responses to mass media productions. In J. Bryant & D. Zillmann (Eds.), *Responding to the screen: Reception and reaction processes* (pp. 169–197). Hillsdale, NJ: Lawrence Erlbaum Associates.

Cantor, J. (1996). Television and children's fear. In T. M. Macbeth (Ed.), *Tuning in to young viewers: Social science perspectives on television* (pp. 87–115). Thousand Oaks, CA: Sage.

Cantor, J. (1998a). Ratings for program content: The role of research findings. *The Annals of the American Academy of Political and Social Science, 557,* 54–69.

Cantor, J. (1998b). *"Mommy, I'm scared": How TV and movies frighten children and what we can do to protect them.* San Diego: Harcourt Brace.

Cantor, J. (2002). Fright reactions to mass media. In J. Bryant and D. Zillmann (Eds.), *Media effects* (pp. 287–306). Mahwah, NJ: Lawrence Erlbaum Associates.

Cantor, J., Mares, M. L., & Hyde, J. S. (2003). Autobiographical memories of exposure to sexual media content. *Media Psychology, 5,* 1–31.

Cantor, J., & Nathanson, A. I. (1996). Children's fright reactions to television news. *Journal of Communication, 46*(4), 139–152.

Cantor, J., & Oliver, M. B. (1996). Developmental differences in responses to horror. In J. B. Weaver and R. Tamborini (Eds.), *Horror films: Current research on audience preferences and reactions* (pp. 63–80). Mahwah, NJ: Lawrence Erlbaum Associates.

Cantor, J., & Sparks, G. G. (1984). Children's fear responses to mass media: Testing some Piagetian predictions. *Journal of Communication, 34,* 90–103.

Cantor, J., & Wilson, B. J. (2003). Media and violence: Intervention strategies for reducing aggression. *Media Psychology, 5,* 363–403.

Cantor, J., Wilson, B. J., & Hoffner, C. (1986). Emotional responses to a televised nuclear holocaust film. *Communication Research, 13,* 257–277.

Cantor, M. G., & Cantor, J. M. (1986). American television in the international marketplace. *Communication Research, 13,* 509–520.

Carlson, M. (1990, September 10). A new ball game. *Time,* 40–41.

Carlson, M. (1996, August 5). The soap opera games. *Time,* 48.

Carlson, S. (2003, August 15). Can Grand Theft Auto Inspire Professors? *The Chronicle of Higher Education,* A31–A33.

Carlsson-Paige, N., & Levin, D. E. (1990). *Who's calling the shots? How to respond effectively to children's fascination with war play and war toys.* Philadelphia: New Society Publishers.

Carroll, J. S., Kerr, N. L., Alfini, J. J., Weaver, F. M., MacCount, R. J., & Feldman, V. (1986). Free press and fair trial: The role of behavioral research. *Law and Human Behaviour, 10*, 187–202.

Carveth, R., & Alexander, A. (1985). Soap opera viewing motivations and the cultivation process. *Journal of Broadcasting & Electronic Media, 29*, 259–273.

Cassata, B., Anderson, P., & Skill, T. (1980). The older adult in daytime serial drama. *Journal of Communication, 30*, 48–49.

Cassata, M., & Irwin, B. J. (1997). Young by day: The older person on daytime serial drama. In H. S. Noor Al-deen (Ed.), *Cross-cultural communication and aging in the United States* (pp. 215–230). Mahwah, NJ: Lawrence Erlbaum Associates.

Centerwall, B. S. (1989a). Exposure to television as a cause of violence. In G. Comstock (Ed.), *Public communication and behavior* (Vol. 2, pp. 1–58). New York: Academic Press.

Centerwall, B. S. (1989b). Exposure to television as a risk factor for violence. *American Journal of Epidemiology, 129*, 643–652.

Centerwall, B. S. (1992). Television and violence: The scale of the problem and where to go from here. *Journal of the American Medical Association (JAMA), 267*, 3059–3063.

Centerwall, B. S. (1993, Spring). Television and violent crime. *The Public Interest, 111*, 56–71.

Chaffee, S. H., & Choe, S. Y. (1980). Times of decision and media use during the Ford-Carter campaign. *Public Opinion Quarterly, 44*, 53–69.

Chandler, J. M. (1977, April). TV and sports: Wedded with a golden hoop. *Psychology Today*, 64–66, 75–76.

Chaffee, S. H., Nass, C. I., & Yang, S. M. (1990). The bridging role of television in immigrant political socialization. *Human Communication Research, 17*, 266–288.

Chamberlain, C. (2002, February 11). Gee, I can't be G. I. Joe. Abcnews.com.

Chappell, C. R., & Hartz, J. (1998, March 20). The challenge of communicating science to the public. *The Chronicle of Higher Education*, p. B7.

Charlton, T., Gunter, B., & Hannan, A. (Eds.). (2002). *Broadcast television effects in a remote community*. Mahwah, NJ: Lawrence Erlbaum Associates.

Check, J. V. P. (1985). *The effects of violent and nonviolent pornography*. Ottawa: Department of Justice for Canada.

Check, J. V. P. (1995). Teenage training: The effects of pornography on adolescent males. In L. Lederer & R. Delgado (Eds.), *The price we pay: The case against racist speech, hate propaganda, and pornography* (pp. 89–91). New York: Hill and Wang.

Check, J. V. P., & Guloien, T. H. (1989). Reported proclivity for coercive sex following repeated exposure to sexually violent pornography, nonviolent pornography, and erotica. In D. Zillmann & J. Bryant (Eds.), *Pornography: Research advances and policy considerations* (pp. 159–184). Hillsdale, NJ: Lawrence Erlbaum Associates.

Chen, M. (1994). *The smart parent's guide to kids' TV*. San Francisco: KQED Books.

Chenault, B. G. (1998, May). Developing personal and emotional relationships via computer-mediated communication. *CMC Magazine*, 1–19.

Christ, W. G., & Potter, W. J. (1998). Media literacy, media education, and the academy. *Journal of Communication, 48*(1), 5–15.

Christenson, P. G. (1992). The effects of parental advisory labels on adolescent music preferences. *Journal of Communication, 42*(1), 106–113.

Christenson, P. G., Henriksen, L., & Roberts, D. F. (2000). *Substance use in popular prime-time television.* Washington, DC: Office of National Drug Control Policy.

Christenson, P. G., & Roberts, D. F. (1983). The role of television in the formation of children's social attitudes. In M. J. A. Howe (Ed.), *Learning from television: Psychological and educational research* (pp. 79–99). London: Academic Press.

Christenson, P. G., & Roberts, D. F. (1998). *It's not only rock & roll: Popular music in the lives of adolescents.* Cresskill, NJ: Hampton Press.

Christianson, S., & Loftus, E. F. (1987). Memory for traumatic events. *Applied Cognitive Psychology, 1,* 225–239.

Church, G. J. (1996, January 29). Are we better off? *Time,* 38.

Cialdini, R. B. (2003). Crafting normative messages to protect the environment. *Current Directions in Psychological Science, 12*(4), 105–109.

Clark, C. (1969). Television and social controls: Some observation of the portrayal of ethnic minorities. *Television Quarterly, 8*(2), 18–22.

Clayman, S. E., & Heritage, J. (2002). Questioning Presidents: Journalistic deference and adversarialness in the press conferences of U.S. Presidents Eisenhower and Reagan. *Journal of Communication, 52,* 749–775.

Coakley, J. J. (1986). *Sport in society: Issues and controversies.* St. Louis, MO: Times Mirror/Mosby.

Coates, T. J. (1990). Strategies for modifying sexual behavior for primary and secondary prevention of HIV disease. *Journal of Consulting and Clinical Psychology, 58,* 57–69.

Colburn, D. (1997, October 13). Violent TV ads common on post-season baseball. *Manhattan Mercury* (*Washington Post* syndication), p. A7.

Cole, J. (2000). *Surveying the digital future.* Los Angeles: UCLA Center for Communication Policy.

Colfax, D., & Steinberg, S. (1972). The perpetuation of racial stereotypes: Blacks in mass circulation magazine advertisements. *Public Opinion Quarterly, 35,* 8–18.

Collins, A. M., & Loftus, E. F. (1975). A spreading activation theory of semantic processing. *Psychological Review, 82,* 407–428.

Collins, J. (1998, March 30). Talking trash. *Time,* 63–66.

Comstock, G. (1985). Television and film violence. In S. J. Apter & A. P. Goldstein (Eds.), *Youth violence: Programs and prospects.* New York: Pergamon Press.

Comstock, G., Chaffee, S., Katzman, N., McCombs, M., & Roberts, D. (1978). *Television and human behavior.* New York: Columbia University Press.

Comstock, J., & Strzyzewski, K. (1990). Interpersonal attraction on television: Family conflict and jealousy on primetime. *Journal of Broadcasting and Electronic Media, 34*(3), 263–282.

Condry, J. C. (1989). *The psychology of television.* Hillsdale, NJ: Lawrence Erlbaum Associates.

Conway, J. C., & Rubin, A. M. (1991). Psychological predictors of television viewing motivation. *Communication Research, 18,* 443–463.

Cook, G. (1992). *Discourse of advertising.* London: Routledge.

Cook, T. D., Appleton, H., Conner, R. F., Shaffer, A., Tabkin, G., & Weber, J. S. (1975). *Sesame Street revisited*. New York: Sage.

Coontz, S. (1992). *The way we never were: American families and the nostalgia trap*. New York: Basic Books.

Coontz, S. (1997). *The way we really are: Coming to terms with America's changing families*. New York: Basic Books.

Cooper, A. (1998). Sexuality and the Internet: Surfing into the new millennium. *CyberPsychology and Behavior, 1*(2), 187–193.

Corcoran, F. (1986). KAL 007 and the evil empire: Mediated disaster and forms of rationalization. *Critical Studies in Mass Communication, 3*, 297–316.

Corder-Bolz, C. R. (1980). Mediation: The role of significant others. *Journal of Communication, 30*, 106–118.

Court, J. H. (1977). Pornography and sex crimes: A re-evaluation in the light of recent trends around the world. *International Journal of Criminology and Penology, 5*, 129–157.

Court, J. H. (1982). Rape trends in New South Wales: A discussion of conflicting evidence. *Australian Journal of Social Issues, 17*, 202–206.

Court, J. H. (1984). Sex and violence: A ripple effect. In N. M. Malamuth & E. Donnerstein (Eds.), *Pornography and sexual aggression* (pp. 143–172). Orlando, FL: Academic Press.

Craig, R. (2000). Expectations and elections: How television defines campaign news. *Critical Studies in Media Communication, 17*, 28–44.

Crawley, A. M., Anderson, D. R., Wilder, A., Williams, M., & Santomero, A. (1999). Effects of repeated exposures to a single episode of the television program *Blue's Clues* on the viewing behaviors and comprehension of preschool children. *Journal of Educational psychology, 91*, 630–637.

Creedon, P. J. (Ed.) (1994). *Women, media, and sport: Challenging gender values*. Thousand Oaks, CA: Sage.

Crimmins, C. (1991, January). Sexism in cartoonland. *Working Mother*, 37–41.

Crockett, S. A., Jr. (2002, August 23). For young fans, the name of the video game is gore. Www.washingtonpost.com/wp-dyn/articles/A55183-2002Aug23.html

Croteau, D., & Hoynes, W. (1992). Men and the news media: The male presence and its effect. In S. Craig (Ed.), *Men, masculinity, and the media* (pp. 154–168). Newbury Park, CA: Sage.

Cumberbatch, G., & Negrine, R. (1991). *Images of disability on television*. London: Routledge.

Cumings, B. (1992). *War and television*. New York: Verso.

Cuperfain, R., & Clarke, T. K. (1985). A new perspective on subliminal perception. *Journal of Advertising, 14*(1), 36–41.

Cwalina, W., Falkowski, A., & Kaid, L. L. (2000). Role of advertising in forming the image of politicians: Comparative analysis of Poland, France, and Germany. *Media Psychology, 2*, 119–146.

Dagnoli, J. (1990, April). Sokolof keeps thumping away at food giants. *Advertising Age, 3*, 63.

Dall, P. W. (1988). Prime-time television portrayals of older adults in the context of family life. *The Gerontologist, 28*, 700–706.

Dan Quayle vs. Murphy Brown. (1992, June 1). *Time*, 50.

Davies, M. M. (1997). *Fake, fact, and fantasy: Children's interpretations of television reality*. Mahwah, NJ: Lawrence Erlbaum Associates.

Davis, D. K., & Baran, S. J. (1981). *Mass communication and everyday life: A perspective on theory and effects*. Belmont, CA: Wadsworth.

Davis, M. H., Hull, J. G., Young, R. D., & Warren, G. G. (1987). Emotional reactions to dramatic film stimuli: The influence of cognitive and emotional empathy. *Journal of Personality and Social Psychology, 52*, 126–133.

Davis, R. H. (1983). Television health messages: What are they telling us? *Generations, 3*(5), 43–45.

Davis, R. H., & Davis, J. A. (1985). *TV's image of the elderly*. Lexington, MA: Lexington Books/ D. C. Heath.

Day, D. M., & Page, S. (1986). Portrayal of mental illness in Canadian newspapers. *Canadian Journal of Psychiatry, 31*, 813–816.

Dearing, J., & Rogers, E. (1996). *Agenda setting*. Thousand Oaks, CA: Sage.

Demers, D. P., Craff, D., Choi, Y. H., & Pessin, B. M. (1989). Issue obtrusiveness and the agenda-setting effects of national network news. *Communication Research, 16*, 793–812.

Dermer, M., & Pyszczynski, T. A. (1978). Effects of erotica upon men's loving and liking responses. *Journal of Personality and Social Psychology, 36*, 1302–1309.

Dershowitz, A. (1985, May 25). These cops are all guilty. *TV Guide*, 4–7.

Desmond, R. (1987). Adolescents and music lyrics: Implications of a cognitive perspective. *Communication Quarterly, 35*(3), 276–284.

Desmond, R. J., Singer, J. L., & Singer, D. G. (1990). Family mediation: Parental communication patterns and the influences of television on children. In J. Bryant (Ed.), *Television and the American family* (pp. 293–309). Hillsdale, NJ: Lawrence Erlbaum Associates.

Detenber, B.H., & Reeves, B. (1996). A bio-informational theory of emotion: Motion and image size effects on viewers. *Journal of Communication, 46*(3) 66–84.

Dettwyler. K.A. (1995). Beauty and the breast: The cultural context of breast-feeding in the United States. In P. Stuart-Macadam & K. A. Dettwyler (Eds.), *Breastfeeding: Biocultural perspectives* (pp. 167–215). Hawthorne, NY: De Gruyter.

Devlin, L. P. (1987). Campaign commercials. In A. A. Berger (Ed.), *Television in society* (pp. 17–28). New Brunswick, NJ: Transaction Books.

Devlin, L. P. (1997). Contrasts in Presidential campaign commercials of 1996. *American Behavioral Scientist, 40*, 1058–1084.

D'Haenens, L. (2001). Old and new media: Access and ownership in the home. In S. Livingstone and M. Bovill (Eds.), *Children and their changing media environment: A European comparative study* (pp. 53–84). Mahwah, NJ: Lawrence Erlbaum Associates.

Diamond, D. (1987, June 13). Is the toy business taking over kids' TV? *TV Guide*, 4–8.

Diamond, E., & Noglows, P. (1987, June 20). When network news pulls its punches. *TV Guide*, 2–9.

Diamond, M., & Uchiyama, A. (1999). Pornography, rape, and sex crimes in Japan. *International Journal of Law and Psychiatry, 22*, 1–11.

Dietz, P. E., Harry, B., & Hazelwood, R. R. (1986). Detective magazines: Pornography for the sexual sadist? *Journal of Forensic Sciences, 31*(1), 197–211.

DiFranza, J. R., Richards, J. W., Jr., Paulman, P. M., Wolf-Gillespie, N., Fletcher, C., Jaffe, R. D., et al. (1991). RJR Nabisco's cartoon camel promotes Camel cigarettes to children. *Journal of the American Medical Association, 266,* 3149–3152.

DiFranza, J. R., & Tye, J. B. (1990). Who profits from tobacco sales to children? *Journal of the American Medical Association JAMA, 263,* 2784–2787.

DiLillo, D., Potts, R., & Himes, S. (1998). Predictors of children's risk appraisals. *Journal of Applied Developmental Psychology, 19,* 415–427.

Distefan, J. M., Gilpin, E. A., Sargent, J. D., & Pierce, J. P. (1999). Do movie stars encourage adolescents to start smoking? *Preventive Medicine, 28,* 1–11.

Dixon, T. L., & Linz, D. (2000). Overrepresentation and underrepresentation of African Americans and Latinos as lawbreakers on television news. *Journal of Communication, 50*(2), 131–154.

Dobrow, J. R. (1990). Patterns of viewing and VCR use: Implications for cultivation analysis. In N. Signorielli & M. Morgan (Eds.), *Cultivation analysis: New directions in media effects research* (pp. 71–84). Newbury Park, CA: Sage.

Dobrow, J. R., & Gidney, C. L. (1998). The good, the bad, and the foreign: The use of dialect in children's animated television. *The Annals of the American Academy of Political and Social Science, 557,* 105–119.

Dominick, J. R., & Rauch, G. E. (1972). The image of women in network TV commercials. *Journal of Broadcasting, 16,* 259–265.

Donnerstein, E. (1980). Aggressive erotica and violence against women. *Journal of Personality and Social Psychology, 39,* 269–277.

Donnerstein, E., & Berkowitz, L. (1981). Victim reactions in aggressive erotic films as a factor in violence against women. *Journal of Personality and Social Psychology, 41,* 710–724.

Donnerstein, E., Donnerstein, M., & Evans, R. (1975). Erotic stimuli and aggression: Facilitation or inhibition? *Journal of Personality and Social Psychology, 32,* 237–244.

Donnerstein, E., & Hallam, J. (1978). Facilitating effects of erotica on aggression against women. *Journal of Personality and Social Psychology, 36,* 1270–1277.

Donnerstein, E., Linz, D., & Penrod, S. (1987). *The question of pornography: Research findings and policy implications.* New York: Free Press.

Donnerstein, E., & Smith, S. L. (1997). Impact of media violence on children, adolescents, and adults. In S. Kirschner & D. A. Kirschner (Eds.), *Perspectives on psychology and the media* (pp. 29–68). Washington, DC: American Psychological Association.

Donohew, L., Helm, D., & Haas, J. (1989). Drugs and (Len) Bias on the sports page. In L. A. Wenner (Ed.), *Media, sports, and society* (pp. 225–237). Newbury Park, CA: Sage.

Doob, A. N., & Macdonald, G. E. (1979). Television viewing and fear of victimization: Is the relationship causal? *Journal of Personality and Social Psychology, 37,* 170–179.

Dorr, A. (1980). When I was a child I thought as a child. In S. B. Withey & R. P. Abeles (Eds.), *Television and social behavior* (pp. 191–229). Hillsdale, NJ: Lawrence Erlbaum Associates.

Dorr, A. (1982). Television and the socialization of the minority child. In G. L. Berry & C. Mitchell-Kernan (Eds.), *Television and the socialization of the minority child.* New York: Academic Press.

Dorr, A., Graves, S. B., & Phelps, E. (1980). Television literacy for young children. *Journal of Communication, 30,* 71–83.

Dorr, A., & Kunkel, D. (1990). Children and the media environment: Change and constancy amid change. *Communication Research, 17,* 5–25.

Dorr, A., & Kovaric, P. (1980). Some of the people some of the time—but which people? Televised violence and its effects. In E. Palmer & A. Dorr (Eds.), *Children and the faces of television* (pp. 183–199). New York: Academic Press.

Douglas, S. J. (1994). *Where the girls are: Growing up female with the mass media.* New York: Times Books.

Douglas, S. J. (1997, October 25). Mixed signals: The messages TV send to girls. *TV Guide,* 24–29.

Douglas, W. (2001). Subversion of the American television family. In J. Bryant, & J. A. Bryant. *Television and the American family* (2nd ed., pp. 229–246). Mahwah, NJ: Lawrence Erlbaum Associates.

Drabman, R. S., & Thomas, M. H. (1974). Does media violence increase children's toleration of real-life aggression? *Developmental Psychology, 10,* 418–421.

Drabman, R. S., & Thomas, M. H. (1976). Does watching violence on television cause apathy? *Pediatrics, 57,* 329–331.

Dubow, E. F., & Miller, L. S. (1996). Televised violence viewing and aggressive behavior. In T. M. Macbeth (Ed.), *Tuning in to young viewers: Social science perspectives on television* (pp. 117–147). Thousand Oaks, CA: Sage.

Duncan, M. C. (1992). Gender bias in televised sports [Special issue]. *Extra!, 27.*

Duncan, M. C., Messner, M. A., & Williams, L. (1990). *Gender stereotyping in televised sports.* Los Angeles: The Amateur Athletic Association of Los Angeles.

Dunwoody, S. (1986). When science writers cover the social sciences. In J. H. Goldstein (Ed.), *Reporting science: The case of aggression* (pp. 67–81). Hillsdale, NJ: Lawrence Erlbaum Associates.

DuRant, R. H., Rich, M., Emans, S. J., Rome, E. S., Allred, E., & Woods, E. R. (1997). Violence and weapon carrying in music videos: A content analysis. *Archives of Pediatric & Adolescent Medicine, 151,* 443–448.

Durkin, K. (1985a). Television and sex-role acquisition 1: Content. *British Journal of Social Psychology, 24,* 101–113.

Durkin, K. (1985b). Television and sex-role acquisition 2: Effects. *British Journal of Social Psychology, 24,* 191–210.

d'Ydewalle, G., Praet, C., Verfaillie, K., & Van Rensbergen, J. (1991). Watching subtitled television: Automatic reading behavior. *Communication Research, 18,* 650–666.

Easterbrook, G. (1989, February 20). *Satanic Verses* as Muslims see it. *Manhattan Mercury,* A5.

Eastman, H. & Liss, M. (1980). Ethnicity and children's preferences. *Journalism Quarterly, 57*(2), 277–280.

Eccles, A., Marshall, W. L., & Barbaree, H. E. (1988). The vulnerability of erectile measures to repeated assessments. *Behavior Research and Therapy, 26,* 179–183.

Edelstein, A. S. (1993). Thinking about the criterion variable in agenda-setting research. *Journal of Communication, 43*(2), 85–99.

Edwards, H. (1987). Race in contemporary American sports. In A. Yiannakis, T. McIntyre, M. Melnick, & D. Hart (Eds.), *Sport sociology: Contemporary issues* (pp. 194–197). Dubuque, IA: Kendall/Hunt.

Einsiedel, E. F. (1988). The British, Canadian, and U.S. pornography commissions and their use of social science research. *Journal of Communication, 38*(2), 108–121.

Eisenberg, D. (2002, September 2). It's an ad, ad, ad, ad world. *Time,* 38–41.

Elasmar, M. G. (Ed.). (2003). *The impact of international television: A paradigm shift.* Mahwah, NJ: Lawrence Erlbaum Associates.

Elliott, S. (2002, April 16a). Campaign spotlight: State Farm aims for where you live. *New York Times on the Web.* Retrieved April 16, 2002 from ads.nyt.com/ia.ad/ia-court08/courttv2.html/4-16-02.

Elliott, S. (2002, May 14b). The ad within the ad. *New York Times on the Web.* Retrieved May 14, 2002 from ads.nyt.com/ia.ad.

Englis, B. G. (1994). The role of affect in political advertising: Voter emotional responses to the nonverbal behavior of politicians. In E. M. Clark, T. C. Brock, & D. W. Stewart (Eds.), *Attention, attitude, and affect in response to advertising* (pp. 223–247). Hillsdale, NJ: Lawrence Erlbaum Associates.

Entman, R. (1990). Modern racism and the images of Blacks in local television news. *Critical Studies in Mass Communication, 7,* 332–345.

Entman, R. (1991). Framing U.S. coverage of international news: Contrasts in the narratives of the KAL and Iran Air incidents. *Journal of Communication, 42*(1), 6–27.

Entman, R. (1992). Blacks in the news: Television, modern racism, and cultural change. *Journalism Quarterly, 69,* 341–361.

Entman, R. (1993). Framing: Toward clarification of a fractured paradigm. *Journal of Communication, 43*(4), 51–58.

Entman, R. (1994a). Representation and reality in the portrayal of Blacks on network television news. *Journalism Quarterly, 71,* 509–520. (a)

Entman, R. (1994b). African Americans according to TV news. *Media Studies Journal, 8,* 29–38. (b)

Eron, L. D., & Huesmann, L. R. (1984). The control of aggressive behavior by changes in attitudes, values, and the conditions of learning. In *Advances in the study of aggression* (pp. 139–171). Orlando, FL: Academic Press.

Eron, L. D., Huesmann, L. R., Lefkowitz, M. M., & Walder, L. O. (1972). Does television violence cause aggression? *American Psychologist, 27,* 253–263.

Esslin, M. (1982). *The age of television.* San Francisco: Freeman.

Espinosa, P. (1997, Oct. 3). The rich tapestry of Hispanic America is virtually invisible on commercial TV. *The Chronicle of Higher Education,* B7–B8.

Eveland, W. P., Jr., Seo, M., & Marton, K. (2002). Learning from the news in campaign 2000: An experimental comparison of TV news, newspapers, and online news. *Media Psychology, 4,* 353–378.

Ex, C. T. G. M., Janssens, J. M. A. M., & Korzilius, H. P. L. M. (2002). Young females' images of motherhood in relation to television viewing. *Journal of Communication, 52*(4), 955–971.

Eysenck, H. J., & Nias, D. K. B. (1978). *Sex, violence, and the media.* New York: Harper.

Faber, R. J. (1992). Advances in political advertising research: A progression from if to when. *Journal of Current Issues and Research in Advertising, 14*(2), 1–18.

Fabes, R. A., & Strouse, J. S. (1984). Youth's perception of models of sexuality: Implications for sexuality education. *Journal of Sex Education and Therapy, 10*, 33–37.

Fabes, R. A., & Strouse, J. S. (1987). Perceptions of responsible and irresponsible models of sexuality: A correlational study. *Journal of Sex Research, 23*, 70–84.

Farhi, P. (2001, June). Nightly news blues. *American Journalism Review*, 32–37.

Farquhar, J. W., Fortmann, S. P., Flora, J. A., Taylor, B., Haskell, W. L., Williams, P. T., et al. (1990). Effects of communitywide education on cardiovascular disease risk factors: The Stanford five-city project. *Journal of the American Medical Association, 264*, 359–365.

Fejes, F. J. (1989). Images of men in media research. *Critical Studies in Mass Communication, 6*(2), 215–221.

Fejes, F. J. (1992). Masculinity as a fact: A review of empirical mass communication research on masculinity. In S. Craig (Ed.), *Men, masculinity, and the media* (pp. 9–22). Newbury Park, CA: Sage.

Fenigstein, A., & Heyduk, R. G. (1985). Thought and action as determinants of media exposure. In D. Zillmann & J. Bryant (Eds.), *Selective exposure to communication* (pp. 113–139). Hillsdale, NJ: Lawrence Erlbaum Associates.

Ferguson, D. A., & Perse, E. M. (2000). The World Wide Web as a functional alternative to television. *Journal of Broadcasting & Electronic Media, 37*, 31–47.

Ferrante, C. L., Haynes, A. M., & Kingsley, S. M. (1988). Image of women in television advertising. *Journal of Broadcasting & Electronic Media, 32*, 231–237.

Ferris, T. (1997, April 4). The risks and rewards of popularizing science. *The Chronicle of Higher Education.*

Feshbach, N. D. (1988). Television and the development of empathy. In S. Oskamp (Ed.), *Television as a social issue* (pp. 261–269). Newbury Park, CA: Sage.

Feshbach, N. D., & Feshbach, S. (1997). Children's empathy and the media: Realizing the potential of television. In S. Kirschner & D. A. Kirschner (Eds.), *Perspectives on psychology and the media* (pp. 3–27). Washington, DC: American Psychological Association.

Feshbach, S. (1955). The drive-reducing function of fantasy behavior. *Journal of Abnormal and Social Psychology, 50*, 3–11.

Feshbach, S. (1976). The role of fantasy in the response to television. *Journal of Social Issues, 32*, 71–85.

Feshbach, S., & Singer, R. (1971). *Television and aggression.* San Francisco: Jossey-Bass. *Final report of the attorney general's commission on pornography.* (1986). Nashville, TN: Rutledge Hill Press.

Fink, J. S. (1998). Female athletes and the media: Strides and stalemates. *Journal of Physical Education, Recreation, & Dance, 69*, 37–45.

Fisch, S. M. (2002). Vast wasteland or vast opportunity: Effects of educational television on children's academic knowledge, skills, and attitudes. In J. Bryant and D. Zillmann (Eds.), *Media effects* (pp. 397–426). Mahwah, NJ: Lawrence Erlbaum Associates.

Fisch, S. M., & Truglio, R. T. (Eds.) (2000). *"G" is for growing*: Thirty years of research on children and "Sesame Street." Mahwah, NJ: Lawrence Erlbaum Associates.

Fisch, S. M., Truglio, R. T., & Cole, C. F. (1999). The impact of *Sesame Street* on preschool children: A review and synthesis of 30 years' research. *Media Psychology, 1*, 165–190.

Fitch, M., Huston, A. C., & Wright, J. C. (1993). From television forms to genre schemata: Children's perceptions of television reality. In G. L. Berry & J. K. Asamen (Eds.), *Children and television: Images in a changing sociocultural world* (pp. 38–52). Newbury Park, CA: Sage.

Flay, B. R., & Burton, D. (1990). Effective mass communication strategies for health campaigns. In C. Atkin & L. Wallack (Eds.), *Mass communication and public health* (pp. 129–146). Newbury Park, CA: Sage.

Fleming, M. J., & Rickwood, D. J. (2001). Effects of violent versus nonviolent video games on children's arousal, aggressive mood, and positive mood. *Journal of Applied Social Psychology, 31*(10), 2047–2071.

Flora, J. A., & Maibach, E. W. (1990). Cognitive responses to AIDS information: The effects of issue involvement and message appeal. *Communication Research, 17*, 759–774.

Fonda, D. (2003, June 30). Baby, you can drive my car. *Time*, 46–48.

Ford, G. T., & Calfee, J. E. (1986). Recent developments in FTC policy on deception. *Journal of Marketing, 50*, 82–103.

Fore, W. F. (1987). *Television and religion: The shaping of faith, values, and culture.* Minneapolis, MN: Augsburg Publishing House.

Freimuth, V. S., Hammond, S. L., Edgar, T., & Monahan, J. L. (1990). Reaching those at risk: A content-analytic study of AIDS PSAs. *Communication Research, 17*, 775–791.

Friend in need. (1998, May). *World Press Review*, 32.

Fried, C. B. (1996). Bad rap for rap: Bias in reactions to music lyrics. *Journal of Applied Social Psychology, 26*, 2135–2146.

Fried, C. B. (1999). Who's afraid of rap: Differential reactions to music lyrics. *Journal of Applied Social Psychology, 29*, 705–721.

Friedrich-Cofer, L., & Huston, A. C. (1986). Television violence and aggression: The debate continues. *Psychological Bulletin, 100*, 364–371.

Fuchs, D. A. (1966). Election-day radio-television and Western voting. *Public Opinion Quarterly, 30*, 226–236.

Funabiki, J. (1992). Asian invasion cliches recall wartime propaganda. *Extra!, 5*(5), 13–14.

Funk, J. (1993a). Reevaluating the impact of video games. *Clinical Pediatrics, 32*, 86–90.

Funk, J. (1993b). Video games. *Adolescent medicine: State of the Art Reviews, 4*, 589–598.

Furnham, A., Gunter, B., & Walsh, D. (1998). Effects of programme context on memory of humorous television commercials. *Applied Cognitive Psychology, 12*, 555–567.

Furnham, A., Bergland, J., & Gunter, B. (2002). Memory for television advertisements as a function of advertisement-programme congruity. *Applied Cognitive Psychology, 16*, 525–545.

Fussell, J. A. (2000, September 21). Horror show. *Kansas City Star*, p. E1.

Gabbard, G. O., & Gabbard, K. (1999). *Psychiatry and the cinema* (2nd ed.). New York: Psychiatric Press.

Gamson, J. (1995, Fall). Do ask, do tell: Freak talk on TV, *The American Prospect*.

Gan, S. L., Zillmann, D., & Mitrook, M. (1997). Stereotyping effect of black women's sexual rap on white audiences. *Basic and Applied Social Psychology, 19*(3), 381–399.

Ganley, G. D. (1992). *The exploding political power of personal media*. Norwood, NJ: Ablex.

Gantz, W. (2001). Conflicts and resolution strategies associated with television in marital life. In J. Bryant, & J. A. Bryant. *Television and the American family* (2nd ed., pp. 289–316). Mahwah, NJ: Lawrence Erlbaum Associates.

Gardner, D. M., & Leonard, N. H. (1990). Research in deceptive and corrective advertising: Progress to date and impact on public policy. *Current Issues and Research in Advertising, 12*, 275–309.

Gardner, M. P., & Houston, M. J. (1986). The effects of verbal and visual components of retail communications. *Journal of Retailing, 62*, 64–78.

Garelik, G. (1985, April). The weather peddlers. *Discover*, 18–29.

Garramone, G. M. (1984). Voter responses to negative political ads. *Journalism Quarterly, 61*(2), 250–259.

Garramone, G. M. (1985). Effects of negative political advertising: The role of sponsor and rebuttal. *Journal of Broadcasting and Electronic Media, 29*(2), 147–159.

Garramone, G. M., Atkin, C. K., Pinkleton, B. E., & Cole, R. T. (1990). Effects of negative political advertising on the political process. *Journal of Broadcasting and Electronic Media, 34*, 299–311.

Garramone, G. M., Steele, M. E., & Pinkleton, B. (1991). The role of cognitive schemata in determining candidate characteristic effects. In F. Biocca (Ed.), *Television and political advertising: Psychological processes* (Vol. 1. pp. 311–328). Hillsdale, NJ: Lawrence Erlbaum Associates.

Gartner, M. (1991, July/August). Naming the victim. *Columbia Journalism Review*.

Geen, R. G. (1994). Television and aggression: Recent developments in research and theory. In D. Zillmann, J. Bryant, & A. C. Huston (Eds.), *Media, children, and the family: Social scientific, psychodynamic, and clinical perspectives.* (pp. 151–162). Hillsdale, NJ: Lawrence Erlbaum Associates.

Geen, R. G., & Quanty, M. B. (1977). The catharsis of aggression: An evaluation of a hypothesis. In L. Berkowitz (Ed.), *Advances in experimental social psychology* (Vol. 10, pp. 1–37). New York: Academic Press.

Geiger, S. F., & Reeves, B. (1991). The effects of visual structure and content emphasis on the evaluation and memory for political candidates. In F. Biocca (Ed.), *Television and political advertising: Psychological processes* (Vol. 1, pp. 125–143). Hillsdale, NJ: Lawrence Erlbaum Associates.

Geiger, S., & Reeves, B. (1993a). The effects of scene changes and semantic relatedness on attention to television. *Communication Research, 20*, 155–175.

Geiger, S., & Reeves, B. (1993b). We interrupt this program . . . Attention for television sequences. *Human Communication Research, 19*, 368–387.

Geiogamah, H., & Pavel, D. M. (1993). Developing television for American Indian and Alaska native children in the late 20th century. In G. L. Berry & J. K. Asamen (Eds.), *Children & television* (pp. 191–204). Newbury Park, CA: Sage.

Geis, F., Brown, V., Jennings, J., & Porter, N. (1984). TV commercials as achievement scripts for women. *Sex Roles, 10*(7/8), 513–525.

Gelb, B. D., & Zinkhan, G. M. (1985). The effect of repetition on humor in a radio advertising study. *Journal of Advertising, 14*(4), 13–20.

Gerbner, G. (1997). Gender and age in prime-time television. In S. Kirschner & D. A. Kirschner (Eds.), *Perspectives on psychology and the media* (pp. 69–94). Washington, DC: American Psychological Association.

Gerbner, G., & Gross, L. (1980). The violent face of television and its lessons. In E. Palmer & A. Dorr (Eds.), *Children and the faces of television: Teaching, violence, selling* (pp. 149–162). New York: Academic Press.

Gerbner, G., Gross, L., Morgan, M., & Signorielli, N. (1980). The mainstreaming of America: Violence profile No. 11. *Journal of Communication, 30*(3), 10–29.

Gerbner, G., Gross, L., Morgan, M., & Signorielli, N. (1981a). Health and medicine on television. *New England Journal of Medicine, 305*(15), 901–904.

Gerbner, G., Gross, L., Morgan, M., & Signorielli, N. (1981b). Scientists on the TV screen. *Society, 18*(4), 41–44.

Gerbner, G., Gross, L., Morgan, M., & Signorielli, N. (1982). Charting the mainstream: Television's contributions to political orientations. *Journal of Communication, 32*(2), 100–127.

Gerbner, G., Gross, L., Morgan, M., & Signorielli, N. (1984). Political correlates of television viewing. *Public Opinion Quarterly, 48,* 283–300.

Gerbner, G., Gross, L., Morgan, M., & Signorielli, N. (1986). Living with television: The dynamics of the cultivation process. In J. Bryant & D. Zillmann (Eds.), *Perspectives on media effects* (pp. 17–40). Hillsdale, NJ: Lawrence Erlbaum Associates.

Gerbner, G., Gross, L., Morgan, M., Signorielli, N., & Shanahan, J. (2002). Growing up with television: Cultivation processes. In J. Bryant & D. Zillmann (Eds.), *Media effects: Advances in theory and research* (2nd ed., pp. 43–67). Mahwah, NJ: Lawrence Erlbaum Associates.

Gerbner, G., Gross, L., Signorielli, N., & Morgan, M. (1980). Aging with television: Images on television drama and conception of social reality. *Journal of Communication, 30*(1), 37–47.

Gerbner, G., Gross, L., Signorielli, N., & Morgan, M. (1986). *Television's mean world: Violence profile No. 14–15.* Philadelphia: Annenberg School of Communication, University of Pennsylvania.

Gerbner, G. & Signorielli, N. (1979). *Women and minorities in television drama* (1969–1978). Philadelphia: Annenberg School of Communication, University of Pennsylvania.

Gettas, G. J. (1990). The globalization of *Sesame Street:* A producer's perspective. *Educational Technology Research and Development, 38*(4), 55–63.

Gibbons, J. A., Taylor, C., & Phillips, J. (2004). Gender and racial stereotypes in the mass media. In W. R. Walker (Ed.), *Cognitive technology: Transforming thought and society.* Jefferson, NC: McFarland & Co.

Gibbs, N. (1996, May 20). The screen test. *Time,* 31–32.

Gibson, B., & Maurer, J. (2000). Cigarette smoking in the movies: The influence of product placement on attitudes toward smoking and smokers. *Journal of Applied Social Psychology, 30,* 1457–1473.

Gibson, R., & Zillmann, D. (1994). Exaggerated versus representative exemplification in news reports: Perception of issues and personal consequences. *Communication Research, 21,* 603–624.

Gilboa, E. (2002). Global communication and foreign policy. *Journal of Communication, 52,* 731–748.

Giles, D. (2002). Parasocial interaction: A review of the literature and a model for future research. *Media Psychology, 4,* 279–305.

Giles, D. (2003). *Media psychology.* Mahwah, NJ: Lawrence Erlbaum Associates.

Gilly, M. C. (1988). Sex roles in advertising: A comparison of television advertisements in Australia, Mexico, and the United States. *Journal of Marketing, 52,* 75–85.

Glassner, B. (1999). *The culture of fear: Why Americans are afraid of the wrong things.* New York: Basic Books.

Glenn, D. (2003, June 6). Scholars who blog. *The Chronicle of Higher Education,* A14–A16.

Goldberg, B. (2002). *A CBS insider exposes how the media distort the news.* Washington, DC: Regnery.

Goldberg, M. (1988, February 20). Take two doses for Kildare and Casey and don't call me in the morning. *TV Guide,* 12–13.

Goldberg, M. E. (1995). Social marketing: Are we fiddling while Rome burns? *Journal of Consumer Psychology, 4,* 347–370.

Goldstein, J. H. (Ed.). (1986). *Reporting science: The case of aggression.* Hillsdale, NJ: Lawrence Erlbaum Associates.

Goldstein, J. H. (1998). Why we watch. In J. H. Goldstein (Ed.), *Why we watch: The attractions of violent entertainment* (pp. 212–226). New York: Oxford University Press.

Goldstein, J. H., & Arms, R. L. (1971). Effects of observing athletic contests on hostility. *Sociometry, 34,* 83–90.

Goldstein, S., & Ibaraki, T. (1983). Japan: Aggression and aggression control in Japanese society. In A. Goldstein & M. Segall (Eds.), *Aggression in global perspective.* New York: Pergamon Press.

Goldstein, W. (1998, April 10). Bad history is bad for a culture. *The Chronicle of Higher Education,* A64.

Gonzalez, D. (2001, January 25). Ladyville Journal: Listen, in Belize's jungles, it's the voice of Britain. *New York Times on the Web,* www.nytimes.com/2001/01/25/world/25BELI.html

Goodman, E. (1999, June 1). Our culture can make any woman anywhere feel insecure. *Manhattan Mercury,* A5.

Gorn, G. I., Goldberg, M. E., & Kanungo, R. N. (1976). The role of educational television in changing intergroup attitudes of children. *Child Development, 47,* 277–280.

Gornstein, L. (1997, April 13). Advertising finding its way into movies. *Manhattan Mercury,* C5.

Grabe, M. E., Lombard, M., Reich, R. D., Bracken, C. C., & Ditton, T. B. (1999). The role of screen size in viewer experiences of media content. *Visual Communication Quarterly, 6*(2), 4–9.

Graber, D. A. (1988). *Processing the news: How people tame the information tide.* New York: Longman.

Graber, D. A. (1989). Content and meaning: What's it all about? *American Behavioral Scientist, 33*, 144–151.

Graber, D. A. (1990). Seeing is remembering: How visuals contribute to learning from television news. *Journal of Communication, 40*(3), 134–155.

Graesser, A. C., & Bower, G. H. (Eds.). (1990). *Inferences and text comprehension.* San Diego: Academic Press.

Graves, S. B. (1980). Psychological effects of black portrayals on television. In S. B. Withey & R. P. Abeles (Eds.), *Television and social behavior* (pp. 259–289). Hillsdale, NJ: Lawrence Erlbaum Associates.

Graves, S. B. (1996). Diversity on television. In T. M. Macbeth (Ed.), *Tuning in to young viewers: Social science perspectives on television* (pp. 61–86). Thousand Oaks, CA: Sage.

Gray, P. (1998, January 19). Paradise found. *Time,* 63–68.

Greenberg, B. S. (1980). *Life on television.* Norwood, NJ: Ablex.

Greenberg, B. S. (1982). Television and role socialization. In D. Pearl, L. Bouthilet, & J. Lazar (Eds.), *Television and behavior: Ten years of scientific progress and implications for the eighties: Vol. 2. Technical Reviews.* Rockville, MD: NIMH.

Greenberg, B. S. (1986). Minorities and the mass media. In J. Bryant & D. Zillmann (Eds.), *Perspectives on media effects* (pp. 165–188). Hillsdale, NJ: Lawrence Erlbaum Associates.

Greenberg, B. S. (1988). Some uncommon television images and the Drench Hypothesis. In S. Oskamp (Ed.), *Television as a social issue* (pp. 88–102). Newbury Park, CA: Sage.

Greenberg, B. S. (1994). Content trends in media sex. In D. Zillmann, J. Bryant, & A. C. Huston (Eds.), *Media, children, and the family: Social scientific, psychodynamic, and clinical perspectives* (pp. 165–182). Hillsdale, NJ: Lawrence Erlbaum Associates.

Greenberg, B. S., & Atkin, C. (1982). Learning about minorities from television: A research agenda. In G. Berry & C. Mitchell-Kernan (Eds.), *Television and the socialization of the minority child* (pp. 215–243). New York: Academic Press.

Greenberg, B. S., & Brand, J. E. (1993). Television news and advertising in schools: The Channel One controversy. *Journal of Communication, 43*(1), 143–151.

Greenberg, B. S., & Brand, J. E. (1994). Minorities and the mass media: 1970s to 1990s. In J. Bryant & D. Zillmann (Eds.), *Media effects: Advances in theory and research* (pp. 273–314). Hillsdale, NJ: Lawrence Erlbaum Associates.

Greenberg, B. S., Brown, J. D., & Buerkel-Rothfuss, N. L. (1993). *Media, sex, and the adolescent.* Cresskill, NJ: Hampton Press.

Greenberg, B. S., & Busselle, R. W. (1996). Soap operas and sexual activity: A decade later. *Journal of Communication, 46*(4), 153–160.

Greenberg, B. S., & D'Alessio, D. (1985). Quantity and quality of sex in the soaps. *Journal of Broadcasting & Electronic Media, 29,* 309–321.

Greenberg, B. S., & Gantz, W. (Eds.). (1993). *Desert Storm and the mass media.* Cresskill, NJ: Hampton Press.

Greenberg, B. S., Heeter, C., Graef, D., Doctor, K., Burgoon, J. K., Burgoon, M., et al. (1983). Mass communication and Mexican Americans. In B. S. Greenberg, M. Burgoon, J. K. Burgoon, & F. Korzenny (Eds.), *Mexican Americans and the mass media* (pp. 7–34). Norwood, NJ: Ablex.

Greenberg, B. S., & Hofschire, L. (2000). Sex on entertainment television. In D. Zillmann and P. Vorderer (Eds.), *Media entertainment: The psychology of its appeal.* (pp. 93–111). Mahwah, NJ: Lawrence Erlbaum Associates.

Greenberg, B. S., Korzenny, F., & Atkin, C. (1979). The portrayal of the aging: Trends on commercial television. *Research on Aging, 1,* 319–334.

Greenberg, B. S., Ku, L., & Li, H. (1992). Parental mediation of children's mass media behaviors in China, Japan, Korea, Taiwan, and the United States. In F. Korzenny & S. Ting-Toomey (Eds.), *Mass media effects across cultures* (pp. 150–172). Newbury Park, CA: Sage.

Greenberg, B. S., Mastro, D., & Brand, J. E. (2002). Minorities and the mass media: Television into the 21st century. In J. Bryant & D. Zillmann (Eds.), *Media effects: Advances in theory and research* (2nd ed., pp. 333–351). Mahwah, NJ: Lawrence Erlbaum Associates.

Greenberg, B. S., Neuendorf, K., Buerkel-Rothfuss, N., & Henderson, L. (1982). The soaps: What's on and who cares? *Journal of Broadcasting, 26*(2), 519–535.

Greene, E., & Wade, R. (1987). Of private talk and public print: General pre-trial publicity and juror decision-making. *Applied Cognitive Psychology, 1,* 1–13.

Greene, K, Krcmar, M., Rubin, D. L., Walters, L. H., & Hale, J. L. (2002). Elaboration in processing adolescent health messages: The impact of egocentrism and sensation seeking on message processing. *Journal of Communication, 52,* 812–831.

Greenfield, P. M. (1984). *Mind and media.* Cambridge, MA: Harvard University Press.

Greenfield, P. M. & Beagles-Roos, J. (1988). Radio vs. television: The cognitive impact on different socioeconomic and ethnic groups. *Journal of Communication, 38*(2), 71–92.

Greenfield, P. M., Bruzzone, L., Koyamatsu, K., Satuloff, W., Nixon, K., Brodie, M., et al. (1987). What is rock music doing to the minds of our youth? A first experimental look at the effects of rock music lyrics and music videos. *Journal of Early Adolescence, 7,* 315–330.

Greenfield, P. M., Farrar, D., & Beagles-Roos, J. (1986). Is the medium the message? An experimental comparison of the effects of radio and television on imagination. *Journal of Applied Developmental Psychology, 7,* 201–218.

Greenfield, P. M., Yut, E., Chung, M., Land, D., Kreider, H., Pantoja, M., et al. (1993). The program-length commercial: A study of the effects of television/toy tie-ins on imaginative play. In G. L. Berry & J. K. Asamen (Eds.), *Children and television: Images in a changing sociocultural world* (pp. 53–72). Newbury Park, CA: Sage.

Greenwald, A. G., Spangenberg, E. R., Pratkanis, A. R., & Eskanazi, J. (1991). Double-blind tests of subliminal self-help audiotapes. *Psychological Science, 2,* 119–122.

Gregory, S. (2003, May 19). Lacrosse at 11! *Time,* (a).

Gregory, S. (2003, June 9). Taking it inside. *Time,* (b).

Griffiths, M. (1999). Violent video games and aggression: A review of the literature. *Aggression and Violent Behavior, 4*(2), 203–212.

Grimes, T. (1990). Audio-video correspondence and its role in attention and memory. *Educational Technology, Research, and Development, 38,* 15–25.

Grimes, T. (1991). Mild auditory-visual dissonance in television news may exceed viewer attentional capacity. *Human Communication Research, 17,* 268–298.

Grodal, T. (2000). Video games and the pleasures of control. In D. Zillmann & P. Vorderer (Eds.), *Media entertainment: The psychology of its appeal* (pp. 197–213). Mahwah, NJ: Lawrence Erlbaum Associates.

Gross, L. (1984). The cultivation of intolerance: Television, blacks, and gays. In G. Melischek, K. E. Rosengren, & J. Stappers (Eds.), *Cultural indicators: An international symposium* (pp. 345–364). Vienna: Austrian Academy of Sciences.

Grossman, D. (1996). *On killing: The psychological cost of learning to kill in war and society.* New York: Little Brown & Co.

Grossman, D. (1998, August 10). Trained to kill. *Christianity Today*, 1–8.

Grossman, D., & DeGaetano, G. (1999). *Stop teaching our kids to kill.* New York: Crown.

Grzelewski, D. (2002, November) Otterly fascinating. *The Smithsonian*, 100–108.

Gubash, C. (2002). U.S. woos Arabs with pop music. http://msnbc.com/news/784495.asp

Gunter, B. (1985). *Dimensions of television violence.* New York: St. Martin's Press.

Gunter, B. (1986). *Television and sex-role stereotyping.* London: John Libbey.

Gunter, B. (1987). *Poor reception: Misunderstanding and forgetting broadcast news.* Hillsdale, NJ: Lawrence Erlbaum Associates.

Gunter, B. (2001). *Media sex: What are the issues?* Mahwah, NJ: Lawrence Erlbaum Associates.

Gunter, B. (2003). *News and the net.* Mahwah, NJ: Lawrence Erlbaum Associates.

Gunter, B., Furnham, A., & Griffiths, S. (2000). Children's memory for news: A comparison of three presentation media. *Media Psychology, 2*, 119–146.

Gunter, B., & Levy, M. M. (1987). Social contexts of video use. *American Behavioral Scientist, 30*, 486–494.

Gunter, B., & Svennevig, M. (1987). *Behind and in front of the screen: Television's involvement with family life.* London: John Libbey.

Gunther, A. C. (1991). What we think others think: Cause and consequence in the third-person effect. *Communication Research, 18*, 355–372.

Gunther, A. C. (1995). Overrating the X-rating: The third-person perception and support for censorship of pornography. *Journal of Communication, 45*(1), 27–38.

Gunther, A. C., & Storey, J. D. (2003). The influence of presumed influence. *Journal of Communication, 53*, 199–215.

Gunther, A. C., & Thorson, E. (1992). Perceived persuasive effects of product commercials and public-service announcements: Third-person effects in new domains. *Communication Research, 19*, 574–596.

Guttmann, A. (1986). *Sports spectators.* New York: Columbia University Press.

Guttmann, A. (1998). The appeal of violent sports. In J. H .Goldstein (Ed.), *Why we watch: The attractions of violent entertainment* (pp. 1–26). New York: Oxford University Press.

Haberstroh, J. (1994). *Ice cube sex: The truth about subliminal advertising.* Notre Dame, IN: Cross Cultural Publications.

Hajjar, W. J. (1997). The image of aging in television commercials: An update for the 1990s. In H. S. Noor Al-deen (Ed.), *Cross-cultural communication and aging in the United States* (pp. 231–244). Mahwah, NJ: Lawrence Erlbaum Associates.

Halimi, S. (1998, August-September). Blood and celebrity. *Le Monde Diplomatique*. Reprinted in *World Press Review*, December 1998, 30–31.

Hallin, D. C. (1992). Sound bite news: Television coverage of elections, 1968–1988. *Journal of Communication, 42*(2), 5–24.

Hamilton, A. (1998, March 23). World watch. *Time Digital, 3*(1), 68–69.

Hamilton, W. L. (2003, March 30). Toymakers study troops, and vice versa. *The New York Times*.

Han, S., & Shavitt, S. (1994). Persuasion and culture: Advertising appeals in individualistic and collectivistic cultures. *Journal of Experimental Social Psychology, 30*, 326–350.

Hansen, C. H., & Hansen, R. D. (1990a). The influence of sex and violence on the appeal of rock music videos. *Communication Research, 17*, 212–234.

Hansen, C. H., & Hansen, R. D. (1990b). Rock music videos and antisocial behavior. *Basic and Applied Social Psychology, 11*(4), 357–369.

Hansen, C. H., & Hansen, R. D. (2000). Music and music videos. In P. Vorderer & D. Zillmann (Eds.), *Media entertainment: The psychology of its appeal* (pp. 175–196). Mahwah, NJ: Lawrence Erlbaum Associates.

Haridakis, P. M. (2002). Viewer characteristics, exposure to television violence, and aggression. *Media Psychology, 4*, 323–352.

Harris, R. J. (1981). Inferences in information processing. In G. H. Bower (Ed.), *The psychology of learning and motivation* (Vol. 15, pp. 82–128). New York: Academic Press.

Harris, R. J., Dubitsky, T. M., & Bruno, K. J. (1983). Psycholinguistic studies of misleading advertising. In R. J. Harris (Ed.), *Information processing research in advertising* (pp. 241–262). Hillsdale, NJ: Lawrence Erlbaum Associates.

Harris, R. J., Garner-Earl, B., Sprick, S. J., & Carroll, C. (1994). Effects of foreign product names and country-of-origin attributions on advertisement evaluations. *Psychology & Marketing, 11*, 129–144.

Harris, R. J., Hoekstra, S. J., Scott, C. L., Sanborn, F. W., Karafa, J. A., & Brandenburg, J. D. (2000). Young men's and women's different autobiographical memories of the experience of seeing frightening movies on a date. *Media Psychology, 2*, 245–268.

Harris, R. J., Jasper, J. D., Lee, B. J., & Miller, K. E. (1991). Consenting to donate organs: Whose wishes carry the most weight? *Journal of Applied Social Psychology, 21*, 3–14.

Harris, R. J., & Karafa, J. A. (1999). A cultivation theory perspective of worldwide national impressions of the United States. In Y. Kamalipour (Ed.), *Images of the U.S. around the world: A multicultural perspective* (pp. 3–17). Albany, NY: State University of New York Press.

Harris, R. J., Pounds, J. C., Maiorelle, M. J., & Mermis, M. M. (1993). The effect of type of claim, gender, and buying history on the drawing of pragmatic inferences from advertising claims. *Journal of Consumer Psychology, 2*, 83–95.

Harris, R. J., Schoen, L. M., & Hensley, D. (1992). A cross-cultural study of story memory. *Journal of Cross-cultural Psychology, 23*, 133–147.

Harris, R. J., & Scott, C. L. (2002). Effects of sex in the media. In J. Bryant & D. Zillmann (Eds.), *Media effects: Advances in theory and research* (pp. 307–331). Mahwah, NJ: Lawrence Erlbaum Associates.

Harris, R. J., Sturm, R. E., Klassen, M. L., & Bechtold, J. I. (1986). Language in advertising: A psycholinguistic approach. *Current Issues and Research in Advertising, 9,* 1–26.

Harris, R. J., Trusty, M. L., Bechtold, J. I., & Wasinger, L. (1989). Memory for implied versus directly asserted advertising claims. *Psychology & Marketing, 6,* 87–96.

Harrison, E. (1999, September). Branded into the scenery. *Los Angeles Times,* pp. 24–25.

Harrison, K. (1997). Does interpersonal attraction to thin media personalities promote eating disorders? *Journal of Broadcasting & Electronic Media, 41,* 478–500.

Harrison, K. (2000). The body electric: Thin-ideal media and eating disorders in adolescents. *Journal of Communication, 50*(3), 119–143.

Harrison, K., & Fredrickson, B. L. (2003). Women's sports media, self-objectification, and mental health in black and white adolescent females. *Journal of Communication, 53,* 216–232.

Harrison, K., & Cantor, J. (1997). The relationship between media exposure and eating disorders. *Journal of Communication, 47*(1), 40–67.

Harrison, K., & Cantor, J. (1999). Tales from the screen: Enduring fright reactions to scary media. *Media Psychology, 1,* 97–116.

Hart, R. P. (1994). *Seducing America: How television charms the modern voter.* New York: Oxford University Press.

Hart, R. P., & Jarvis, S. E. (1997). Political debate: Forms, styles, and media. *American Behavioral Scientist, 40,* 1095–1122.

Hartmann, D. P. (1969). Influence of symbolically modelled instrumental aggression and pain cues on aggressive behavior. *Journal of Personality and Social Psychology, 11,* 280–288.

Harvey, M., & Rothe, J. (1986). Videocassette recorders: Their impact on viewers and advertisers. *Journal of Advertising Research, 25*(6), 19–27.

Harwood, J., & Giles, H. (1992). "Don't make me laugh": Age representations in a humorous context. *Discourse & Society, 3,* 403–436.

Hass, R. G. (1981). Effects of source characteristics on cognitive responses and persuasion. In R. E. Petty, T. M. Ostrom, & T. C. Brock (Eds.), *Cognitive responses in persuasion* (pp. 141–172). Hillsdale, NJ: Lawrence Erlbaum Associates.

Hatfield, E., Cacioppo, J. T., & Rapson, R. L. (1992). Primitive emotional contagion. In M. S. Clark (Ed.), *Review of Personality and Social Psychology: Vol. 14. Emotions and Social Behavior.* Newbury Park, CA: Sage.

Hatfield, E., Cacioppo, J. T., & Rapson, R. L. (1993). Emotional contagion. *Current Directions in Psychological Science, 2,* 96–99.

Hausknecht, D., & Moore, D. L. (1986). The effects of time compressed advertising of brand attitude judgments. *Advances in Consumer Research, 13,* 105–110.

Hawkins, R. P., Kim, Y. H., & Pingree, S. (1991). The ups and downs of attention to television. *Communication Research, 18,* 53–76.

Hawkins, R. P., & Pingree, S. (1981). Uniform messages and habitual viewing: Unnecessary assumptions in social reality effects. *Human Communication Research, 7,* 291–301.

Hawkins, R. P., & Pingree, S. (1990). Divergent psychological processes in constructing social reality from mass media content. In N. Signorielli & M. Morgan (Eds.), *Cultivation analysis* (pp. 35–50). Newbury Park, CA: Sage.

Hawkins, R. P., Pingree, S., & Adler, I. (1987). Searching for cognitive processes in the cultivation effect: Adult and adolescent samples in the United States and Australia. *Human Communication Research, 13*, 553–577.

Hayes, D., & Birnbaum, D. W. (1980). Preschoolers' retention of televised events: Is a picture worth a thousand words? *Developmental Psychology, 16*, 410–416.

Hazlett, R. L., & Hazlett, S. Y. (1999). Emotional response to television commercials: Facial EMG vs. self-report. *Journal of Advertising Research, 39*(2), 7–23.

Healy, J. (1990). *Endangered minds: Why our children's don't think.* New York: Simon & Schuster.

Hearold, S. (1986). A synthesis of 1043 effects of television on social behavior. In G. Comstock (Ed.), *Public communication and behavior* (Vol. 1, pp. 65–133). Orlando, FL: Academic Press.

Heath, R. L., & Bryant, J. (1992). *Human communication theory and research: Concepts, contexts, and challenges.* Hillsdale, NJ: Lawrence Erlbaum Associates.

Heath, T. B., Mothersbaugh, D. L., & McCarthy, M. S. (1993). Spokesperson effects in high involvement markets. *Advances in Consumer Research, 20*, 704–707.

Heider, D. (2000). *White news: Why local news programs don't cover people of color.* Mahwah, NJ, Lawrence Erlbaum Associates.

Heintz-Knowles, K. E., (2001). Balancing acts: Work-family issues on prime-time TV. In J. Bryant & J. A. Bryant. *Television and the American family* (2nd ed., pp. 177–206). Mahwah, NJ: Lawrence Erlbaum Associates.

Heller, M. S., & Polsky, S. (1975). *Studies in violence and television.* New York: American Broadcasting Companies.

Herbert, B. (2002, November 28). The gift of mayhem. *The New York Times*, Op-ed.

Herman, E. S., & Chomsky, N. (1988). *Manufacturing consent: The political economy of the mass media.* New York: Pantheon.

Herman, E. S., & O'Sullivan, G. (1989). *The terrorism industry: The experts and institutions that shape our view of terror.* New York: Pantheon.

Herrett-Skjellum, J., & Allen, M. (1996). Television programming and sex-stereotyping: A met-analysis. In B. R. Burleson (Ed.), *Communication yearbook* (Vol. 19, pp. 157–185). Thousand Oaks, CA: Sage.

Hickey, N. (1996, August 3). No news is not good news: Has TV lost its taste for foreign affairs? *TV Guide*, 33–37.

Hicks, D. J. (1965). Imitation and retention of film-mediated aggressive peer and adult models. *Journal of Personality and Social Psychology, 2*, 97–100.

Hinck, E. A. (1992). *Enacting the Presidency: Political argument, Presidential debates, and Presidential character.* Westport, CT: Praeger.

Hirsch, P. M. (1980). The scary world of the nonviewer and other anomalies: A reanalysis of Gerbner et al.'s findings on cultivation analysis, part I. *Communication Research, 7*, 403–456.

Hirschberg, M. S. (1993). *Perpetuating patriotic perceptions: The cognitive function of the Cold War.* Westport, CT: Greenwood.

Hoekstra, S. J. (1998). Docudrama as psychobiography: A case study of HBO's "Stalin." *The Psychohistory Review, 26*, 253–264.

Hoekstra, S. J., Harris, R. J., & Helmick, A. L. (1999). Autobiographical memories about the experience of seeing frightening movies in childhood. *Media Psychology, 1,* 117–140.

Hoffner, C., & Buchanan, M. (2002). Parents' responses to television violence: The third-person effect, parental mediation, and support for censorship. *Media Psychology, 4,* 231–252.

Hoffner, C., Plotkin, R. S., Buchanan, M., Anderson, J. D., Kamigaki, S. K., Hubbs, L. A., et al. (2001). The third-person effect in perceptions of the influence of television violence. *Journal of Communication, 51*(2), 283–299.

Holbert, R. L., Pillion, O., Tschida, D. A., Armfield, G. G., Kinder, K., Cherry, K. L., & Daulton, A. R. (2003). *The West Wing* as endorsement of the U.S. Presidency: Expanding the bounds of priming in political communication. *Journal of Communication, 53*(3), 427–443.

Hong, S. T., & Wyer, R. S., Jr. (1989). Effects of country-of-origin and product-attribute information on product evaluation: An information-processing experiment. *Journal of Consumer Research, 16,* 175–187.

Hong, S. T., & Wyer, R. S., Jr. (1990). Determinants of product evaluation: Effects of the time interval between knowledge about a product's country of origin and information about its specific attributes. *Journal of Consumer Research, 17,* 277–288.

Hoover, S. M. (1988). *Mass media religion.* Newbury Park, CA: Sage.

Hoover, S. M. (1998). *Religion in the news: Faith and journalism in American public discourse.* Thousand Oaks, CA: Sage.

Hoover, S. M., & Lundby, K. (Eds.) (1997). *Rethinking media, religion, and culture.* Thousand Oaks CA: Sage.

Hopkins, R., & Fletcher, J. E. (1994). Electrodermal measurement: Particularly effective for forecasting message influence on sales appeal. In A. Lang (Ed.), *Measuring psychological responses to media* (pp. 113–132). Hillsdale, NJ: Lawrence Erlbaum Associates.

Hornik, R., & Yanovitzky, I. (2003). Using theory to design evaluations of communication campaigns: The case of the National Youth Anti-Drug Media Campaign. *Communication Theory, 13,* 204–224.

Hot Type (1998, February 20). *The Chronicle of Higher Education,* A22.

Howell, F., Miracle, A., & Rees, R. (1984). Do high school athletics pay? The effects of varsity participation on socioeconomic attainment. *Sociology of Sport Journal, 1*(1), 15–25.

Hoy, M. G., Young, C. E., & Mowen, J. C. (1986). Animated host-selling advertisements: Their impact on young children's recognition, attitudes, and behavior. *Journal of Public Policy and Marketing, 5,* 171–184.

Huesmann, L. R., & Eron, L. D. (1986). *Television and the aggressive child.* Hillsdale, NJ: Lawrence Erlbaum Associates.

Huesmann, L. R., Eron, L. D., Klein, R., Brice, P., & Fischer, P. (1983). Mitigating the imitation of aggressive behaviors by changing children's attitudes about media violence. *Journal of Personality and Social Psychology, 44,* 899–910.

Huesmann, L. R., Eron, L. D., Lefkowitz, M. M., & Walder, L. O. (1984). Stability of aggression over time and generations. *Developmental Psychology, 20,* 1120–1134.

Huesmann, L. R., Lagerspetz, K., & Eron, L. D. (1984). Intervening variables in the

TV violence-aggression relation: Evidence from two countries. *Developmental Psychology, 20,* 746–775.

Huesmann, L. R., Moise-Titus, J., Podolski, C. L., & Eron, L. D. (2003). Longitudinal relations between children's exposure to TV violence and their aggressive and violent behavior in young adulthood: 1977–1992. *Developmental Psychology, 39,* 201–221.

Hull, J. D. (1995, January 30). The state of the union. *Time,* 53–75.

Hurst, L. (1998, January 24). History repeats itself–again. *Toronto Star* (reprinted in *World Press Review* April 1998, 28–29.

Husson, W., Stephen, T., Harrison, T. M., & Fehr, B. J. (1988). An interpersonal communication perspective on images of political candidates. *Human Communication Research, 14,* 397–421.

Huston, A. C., Donnerstein, E., Fairchild, H. H., Feshbach, N. D., Katz, P., Murray, et al. (1992). *Big world, small screen: The role of television in American society.* Washington, DC: American Psychological Association.

Huston, A. C., & Wright, J. C. (1987). The forms of television and the child viewer. In G. A. Comstock (Ed.), *Public communication and behavior* (Vol. 2, pp. 103–159). New York: Academic Press.

Huston, A. C., Anderson, D. R., Wright, J. C., Linebarger, D. L., & Schmitt, K. L. (2001). *Sesame Street* viewers as adolescents: The recontact study. In S. M. Fisch & R. T. Truglio (Eds.), *"G" is for growing: Thirty years of research on children and* Sesame Street (pp. 131–144). Mahwah, NJ: Lawrence Erlbaum Associates.

Huston, A. C., & Wright, J. C. (1998). Television and the informational and educational needs of children. *The Annals of the American Academy of Political and Social Science, 557,* 9–23.

Huston, A. C., Wright, J. C., Rice, M. L., Kerkman, D., & St. Peters, M. (1990). The development of television viewing patterns in early childhood: A longitudinal investigation. *Developmental Psychology, 26,* 409–420.

Hutcheon, D. (2002, July/August). Mixing up the world's beat. *Mother Jones,* 74–75.

Iiyama, P., & Kitano, H. H. L. (1982). Asian-Americans and the media. In G. L. Berry & C. Mitchell-Kernan (Eds.), *Television and the socialization of the minority child* (pp. 151–186). New York: Academic Press.

Ilola, L. M. (1990). Culture and health. In R. W. Brislin (Ed.), *Applied cross-cultural psychology* (pp. 278–301). Newbury Park, CA: Sage.

Intons-Peterson, M. J., & Roskos-Ewoldsen, B. (1989). Mitigating the effects of violent pornography. In S. Gubar & J. Hoff-Wilson (Eds.), *For adult users only.* Bloomington, IN: Indiana University Press.

Intons-Peterson, M. J., Roskos-Ewoldsen, B., Thomas, L., Shirley, M., & Blut, D. (1989). Will educational materials reduce negative effects of exposure to sexual violence? *Journal of Social and Clinical Psychology, 8,* 256–275.

Iyengar, S., & Simon, A. (1993). News coverage of the Gulf Crisis and public opinion. *Communication Research, 20,* 365–383.

Iyer, E., & Banerjee, B. (1993). Anatomy of green advertising. *Advances in Consumer Research, 20,* 494–501.

Jackson, D. Z. (1989, January 22). Calling the plays in black and white. *The Boston Globe*, pp. A30–A33.

Jacobson, J. (2001, March 16). In brochures, what you see isn't necessarily what you get. *The Chronicle of Higher Education*, pp. A41–42.

Jacoby, J., & Hoyer, W. D. (1987). *The comprehension and miscomprehension of print communication: A study of mass media magazines.* Hillsdale, NJ: Lawrence Erlbaum Associates.

Jacques, W. W., & Ratzan, S. C. (1997). The Internet's World Wide Web and political accountability: New media coverage of the 1996 Presidential debates. *American Behavioral Scientist, 40*, 1226–1237.

Jakes, J. (1985, November 2). What? A successful media campaign without TV spots and Phil Donohue? *TV Guide*, 12–15.

Jamieson, K. H. (1992). *Packaging the Presidency: A history and criticism of Presidential campaign advertising.* (2nd ed.). New York: Oxford University Press.

Jamieson, K. H., & Campbell, K. K. (1992). *The interplay of influence: News, advertising, politics, and the mass media.* (3rd ed.). Belmont, CA: Wadsworth.

Jamieson, K. H., & Waldman, P. (1997). Mapping campaign discourse: An introduction. *American Behavioral Scientist, 40*, 1133–1138.

Jamieson, K. H., & Waldman, P. (2003). *The press effect: Politicians, journalists, and the stories that shape the political world.* New York: Oxford University Press.

Janis, I. L. (1980). The influence of television on personal decision making. In S. B. Withey & R. P. Abeles (Eds.), *Television and social behavior* (pp. 161–189). Hillsdale, NJ: Lawrence Erlbaum Associates.

Jennings, J., Geis, F., & Brown, V. (1980). Influence of television commercials on women's self-confidence and independent judgment. *Journal of Personality and Social Psychology, 38*(2), 203–210.

Jhally, S., & Lewis, J. (1992). *Enlightened racism: The Cosby Show, audiences, and the myth of the American dream.* Boulder, CO: Westview Press.

Johnson, D., & Rimal, R. N. (July, 1994). Analysis of HIV/AIDS television public service announcements around the world. Paper presented at International Communication Association meeting, Sydney, Australia.

Johnson, J. D., Adams, M. S., Ashburn, L., & Reed, W. (1995). Differential gender effects of exposure to rap music on African American adolescents' acceptance of teen dating violence. *Sex Roles, 33*, 597–606.

Johnson, J. D., Jackson, L. A., & Gatto, L. (1995). Violent attitudes and deferred academic aspirations: Deleterious effects of exposure to rap music. *Basic and Applied Social Psychology, 16*, 27–41.

Johnson, J. G., Cohen, P., Smailes, E. M., Kasen, S., & Brook, J. S. (2002). Television viewing and aggressive behavior during adolescence and adulthood. *Science, 295*, 2468–2471.

Johnson-Cartee, K. S., & Copeland, G. A. (1991). *Negative political advertising: Coming of age.* Hillsdale, NJ: Lawrence Erlbaum Associates.

Johnson-Cartee, K. S., & Copeland, G. A. (1997). *Manipulation of the American voter: Political campaign commercials.* New York: Praeger.

Johnsson-Smaragdi, U. (1983). *TV use and social interaction in adolescence: A longitudinal study.* Stockholm: Almqvist & Wiksell International.

Johnston, C. B. (2001, Winter). Screened out. *Wooster*, 51–53.

Joiner, T. E., Jr. (1999). The clustering and contagion of suicide. *Current Directions in Psychological Science, 8*, 89–92.

Jones, A. (1994, March 10). Crimes against women: Media part of problem for masking violence in the language of love. *USA Today*.

Jones, K. (1997). Are rap videos more violent? Style differences and the prevalence of sex and violence in the age of MTV. *Howard Journal of Communication, 8*, 343–356.

Jordan, A. B. (2001). Public policy and private practice. In D. G. Singer & J. L. Singer (Eds.), *Handbook of children and the media* (pp. 651–662). Thousand Oaks, CA: Sage

Jowett, G. S. (1993). Toward a propaganda analysis of the Gulf War. In B. S. Greenberg & W. Gantz (Eds.), *Desert Storm and the mass media* (pp. 76–98). Cresskill, NJ: Hampton Press.

Jowett, G. S., & Linton, J. M. (1989). *Movies as mass communication* (2nd ed.). Newbury Park, CA: Sage.

Joy, L. A., Kimball, M. M., & Zabrack, M. L. (1986). Television and children's aggressive behavior. In T. M. Williams (Ed.), *The impact of television: A natural experiment in three communities* (pp. 303–360). Orlando, FL: Academic Press.

Just, M., Crigler, A., & Wallach, L. (1990). Thirty seconds or thirty minutes: What viewers learn from spot advertisements and candidate debates. *Journal of Communication, 40*(3), 120–133.

Kahle, L. R., & Homer, P. M. (1985). Physical attractiveness of the celebrity endorsers: A social adaptation perspective. *Journal of Consumer Research, 11*, 954–961.

Kaid, L. L. (1997). Effects of the television spots of images of Dole and Clinton. *American Behavioral Scientist, 40*, 1085–1094.

Kaid, L. L., & Boydston, J. (1987). An experimental study of the effectiveness of negative political advertisements. *Communication Quarterly, 35*, 193–201.

Kaid, L. L., Gerstle, J., & Sanders, K. R. (Eds.). (1991). *Mediated politics in two cultures: Presidential campaigning in the United States and France*. New York: Prager.

Kaid, L. L., & Holtz-Bacha, C. (Eds.). (1995). *Political advertising in Western democracies: Parties and candidates on television*. Thousand Oaks, CA: Sage.

Kaid, L. L., & Johnston, A. (1991). Negative versus positive television advertising in U.S. Presidential campaigns, 1960–1988. *Journal of Communication, 41*(3), 53–64.

Kamalipour, Y. (Ed.). (1999). *Images of the U.S. around the world: A multicultural perspective*. Albany, NY: SUNY Press.

Kane, M. J. (1996). Media coverage of the post Title IX female athlete. *Duke Journal of Gender Law & Policy, 3*, 95–127.

Kardes, F. R. (1992). Consumer inference: Determinants, consequences, and implications for advertising. In A. A. Mitchell (Ed.), *Advertising exposure, memory, and choice*. Hillsdale, NJ: Lawrence Erlbaum Associates.

Kassarjian, H. (1969). The Negro and American advertising: 1946–1965. *Journal of Marketing Research, 6*, 29–39.

Kelly, H. (1981). Reasoning about realities: Children's evaluations of television and books. In H. Kelly & H. Gardner (Eds.), *Viewing children through television*. San Francisco: Jossey-Bass.

Kenrick, D. T., Gutierres, S. E., & Goldberg, L. L. (1989). Influence of popular erotica on judgments of strangers and mates. *Journal of Experimental Social Psychology, 25,* 159–167.

Kern-Foxworth, M. (1994). *Aunt Jemima, Uncle Ben, and Rastus: Blacks in advertising, yesterday, today, and tomorrow.* Westport, CT: Praeger.

Kessler, R. C., Downey, G., Milavsky, J. R., & Stipp, H. (1988). Clustering of teenage suicides after television news stories about suicides: A reconsideration. *American Journal of Psychiatry, 145,* 1379–1383.

Key, W. B. (1974). *Subliminal seduction.* New York: Signet.

Key, W. B. (1976). *Media sexploitation.* New York: Signet.

Key, W. B. (1981). *The clam-plate orgy.* New York: Signet.

Key, W. B. (1989). *The age of manipulation.* New York: H. Holt.

Kher, U. (2003, January 27). How to sell XXXL. *Time,* 43–36.

Kiesler, S. (Ed.) (1997). *Culture of the Internet.* Mahwah, NJ: Lawrence Erlbaum Associates.

Kilbourne, J. (1995). Slim hopes: Advertising and the obsession with thinness [Video]. Northampton, MA: Media Education Foundation.

Kilbourne, W. E., Painton, S., & Ridley, D. (1985). The effect of sexual embedding on responses to magazine advertisements. *Journal of Advertising, 14*(2), 48–56.

Kimball, M. M. (1986). Television and sex-role attitudes. In T. M. Williams (Ed.), *The impact of television: A natural experiment in three communities* (pp. 265–302). Orlando, FL: Academic Press.

King, C. M. (2000). Effects of humorous heroes and villains in violent action films. *Journal of Communication, 50*(1), 5–24.

King, K. W., & Reid, L. N. (1990). Fear arousing anti-drinking and driving PSAs: Do physical injury threats influence young people? *Current Issues and Research in Advertising, 12,* 155–175.

Kintsch, W. (1977). On comprehending stories. In P. Carpenter & M. Just (Eds.), *Cognitive processes in comprehension.* Hillsdale, NJ: Lawrence Erlbaum Associates.

Kirkpatrick, D. D. (2003, May 19). Shaping cultural tastes at big retail chains. *The New York Times* online. Retrieved May 18, 2003 from nytimes.com/2003/05/18/business/18 MART.html

Kirsch, S. J. (1998). Seeing the world through Mortal Kombat-colored glasses: Violent video games and the development of a short-term hostile attribution bias. *Childhood: Global Journal of Childhood Research, 5*(2), 177–184.

Kline, S. (1992). *Out of the garden: Toys, TV, and children's culture in the age of marketing.* New York: Verso.

Knill, B. J., Pesch, M., Pursey, G., Gilpin, P., & Perloff, R. M. (1981). Still typecast after all these years? Sex role portrayals in television advertising. *International Journal of Women's Studies, 4,* 497–506.

Knobloch, S. (2003). Mood adjustment via mass communication. *Journal of Communication, 53,* 233–250.

Kolbe, R. H., & Muehling, D. D. (1992). A content analysis of the fine print in television advertising. *Journal of Current Issues and Research in Advertising, 14*(2), 47–61.

Koolstra, C. M., & Van der Voort, T. H. A. (1996). Longitudinal effects of television on leisure-time reading. *Human Communication Research, 23,* 4–35.

Kopkind, A. (1993, May/June). From Russia with love and squalor. *Utne Reader*, pp. 80–89.

Korzenny, F., & Ting-Toomey, S. (Eds.). (1992). *Mass media effects across cultures.* Newbury Park, CA: Sage.

Kosicki, G. M. (1993). Problems and opportunities in agenda-setting research. *Journal of Communication, 43*(2), 100–127.

Kotler, J. A., Wright, J. C., & Huston, A. C. (2001). Television use in families with children. In J. Bryant & J. A. Bryant (Eds.), *Television and the American family.* (2nd ed., pp. 33–48). Mahwah, NJ: Lawrence Erlbaum Associates.

Kottak, C. P. (1990). *Prime-time society: An anthropological analysis of television and culture.* Belmont, CA: Wadsworth.

Krafka, C. L., Linz, D., Donnerstein, E., & Penrod, S. (1997). Women's reactions to sexually aggressive mass media depictions. *Violence Against Women, 3*(2), 148–181.

Kraft, R. N., Cantor, P., & Gottdiener, C. (1991). The coherence of visual narratives. *Communication Research, 18,* 601–616.

Kraus, S. (Ed.). (1962). *The great debates.* Bloomington, IN: Indiana University Press.

Kraus, S. (Ed.). (1977). *The great debates: 1976, Ford vs. Carter.* Bloomington, IN: Indiana University Press.

Kraus, S. (1988). *Televised presidential debates and public policy.* Hillsdale, NJ: Lawrence Erlbaum Associates.

Kraus, S. (1996). Winners of the first 1960 televised Presidential debate between Kennedy and Nixon. *Journal of Communication, 46*(4), 78–96.

Kraut, R., Patterson M., Lundmark, V., Kiesler, S., Mukopadhyay, T., & Scherlis, W. (1998). Internet paradox: A social technology that reduces social involvement and psychological well-being? *American Psychologist, 53,* 1017–1031.

Krcmar, M., & Cooke, M. C. (2001). Children's moral reasoning and their perceptions of television violence. *Journal of Communication, 51*(2), 300–316.

Krcmar, M., & Curtis, S. (2003). Mental models: Understanding the impact of fantasy violence on children's moral reasoning. *Journal of Communication, 53*(3), 460–478.

Krcmar, M., & Greene, K. (1999). Predicting exposure to and uses of television violence. *Journal of Communication, 49*(3), 24–45.

Krohn, F. B., & Suazo, F. L. (1995). Contemporary urban music: Controversial messages in hip-hop and rap lyrics. *ETC.: A Review of General Semantics, 52,* 139–155.

Kubey, R. (1980). Television and aging: Past, present, and future. *Gerontologist, 20,* 16–35.

Kubey, R. (1986). Television use in everyday life: Coping with unstructured time. *Journal of Communication, 36,* 108–123.

Kubey, R. (1992). A critique of *No Sense of Place* and the homogenization theory of Joshua Meyrowitz. *Communication Theory, 2,* 259–271.

Kubey, R., & Csikszentmihalyi, M. (1990). *Television and the quality of life: How viewing shapes everyday experience.* Hillsdale, NJ: Lawrence Erlbaum Associates.

Kuiper, K. (1995). *Smooth talkers: The linguistic performance of auctioneers and sportscasters.* Mahwah, NJ: Lawrence Erlbaum Associates.

Kunkel, D. (1988). Children and host-selling television commercials. *Communication Research, 15*(1), 71–92.

Kunkel, D. (1998). Policy battles over defining children's educational television. *The Annals of the American Academy of Political and Social Science, 557*, 39–53.

Kunkel, D., Cope-Farrar, K., Biely, E., Farinola, W., & Donnerstein, E. (2001). *Sex on TV 2: A biennial report to the Kaiser Family Foundation.* Menlo Park, CA: Henry J. Kaiser Family Foundation.

Kunkel, D. & Gantz, W. (1992). Children's television advertising in the multichannel environment. *Journal of Communication, 42*(3), 134–152.

Kutchinsky, B. (1973). The effect of easy availability of pornography on the incidence of sex crimes: The Danish experience. *Journal of Social Issues, 29*(3), 163–181.

Kutchinsky, B. (1991). Pornography and rape: Theory and practice? *International Journal of Law and Psychiatry, 14*, 47–64.

Labi, N. (1999, April 19). Classrooms for sale. *Time*, 44–45.

Labi, N. (2002, December 16). The new Funday School. *Time*, 60–62.

Lacayo, R. (2003, May 19). Hear of glass. *Time*, 57.

Lambert, W. E., & Klineberg, O. (1967). *Children's views of foreign peoples: A cross-national study.* New York: Appleton-Century-Crofts.

Lang, A. (1990). Involuntary attention and physiological arousal evoked by structural features and emotional content in TV commercials. *Communication Research, 17*, 275–299.

Lang, A. (1991). Emotion, formal features, and memory for televised political advertisements. In F. Biocca (Ed.), *Television and political advertising: Psychological Processes* (Vol. 1, pp. 221–243). Hillsdale, NJ: Lawrence Erlbaum Associates.

Lang, A. (Ed.). (1994a). *Measuring psychological responses to media.* Hillsdale, NJ: Lawrence Erlbaum Associates.

Lang, A. (1994b). What can the heart tell us about thinking? In A. Lang (Ed.), *Measuring psychological responses to media* (pp. 99–112). Hillsdale, NJ: Lawrence Erlbaum Associates.

Lang, A. (2000). The limited capacity model of mediated message processing. *Journal of Communication, 50*, 46–70.

Lang, A., Geiger, S., Strickwerda, M., & Sumner, J. (1993). The effects of related and unrelated cuts on television viewers' attention, processing capacity, and memory. *Communication Research, 20*, 4–29.

Lang, A., Potter, R. F., & Bolls, P. D. (1999). Something for nothing: Is visual encoding automatic? *Media Psychology, 1*, 145–163.

Lang, G. E., & Lang, K. (1984). *Politics and television re-viewed.* Beverly Hills, CA: Sage.

Lang, K., & Lang, G. E. (1968). *Politics and television.* Chicago: Quadrangle Books.

Lapchick, R., & Rodriguez, A. (1990). Professional sports: The 1990 racial report card. *Center for the Study of Sport in Society Digest, 2*(2), 4–5.

LaRose, R., Lin, C. A., & Eastin, M. S. (2003). Unregulated Internet usage: Addiction, habit, or deficient self-regulation? *Media Psychology, 5*, 225–253.

Larson, J. F. (1984). *Television's window on the world: International affairs coverage on the U.S. networks.* Norwood, NJ: Ablex.

Larson, J. F. (1986). Television and U.S. foreign policy: The case of the Iran hostage crisis. *Journal of Communication, 36*(4), 108–130.

Larson, J. F., McAnany, E. G., & Storey, J. D. (1986). News of Latin America on network television, 1972–1981: A northern perspective on the southern hemisphere. *Critical Studies in Mass Communication, 3,* 169–183.

Larson, M. S. (1989). Interaction between siblings in primetime television families. *Journal of Broadcasting and Electronic Media, 33*(3), 305–315.

Larson, M. S. (2001a). Sibling interaction in situation comedies over the years. In J. Bryant & J. A. Bryant (Ed.), *Television and the American family* (2nd ed., pp. 163–176). Mahwah, NJ: Lawrence Erlbaum Associates.

Larson, M. S. (2001b). Interactions, activities, and gender in children's television commercials: A content analysis. *Journal of Broadcasting & Electronic Media, 45,* 41–56.

Lasisi, M. J., & Onyehalu, A. S. (1992). Cultural influences of a reading text on the concept formation of second-language learners of two Nigerian ethnic groups. In R. J. Harris (Ed.), *Cognitive processing in bilinguals* (pp. 459–471). Amsterdam: Elsevier/North Holland.

Lasswell, H. D. (1927). *Propaganda technique in the world war.* New York: Knopf.

Lasswell, H. D. (1935). *World politics and personal insecurity: A contribution to political psychiatry.* New York: McGraw-Hill.

Lau, R. R. (1986). Political schemata, candidate evaluations, and voting behavior. In R. R. Lau & D. O. Sears (Eds.), *Political cognition* (pp. 95–126). Hillsdale, NJ: Lawrence Erlbaum Associates.

Lavine, H., Sweeney, D., & Wagner, S. H. (1999). Depicting women as sex objects in television advertising: Effects on body dissatisfaction. *Personality and Social Psychology Bulletin, 25,* 1048–1058.

Lawlor, S. D., Sparkes, A., & Wood, J. (1994, July). *When Lawrence came out: Taking the funnies seriously.* Paper presented at Annual Conference of the International Communication Association, Sydney, Australia.

Lazarsfeld, P. F. (1941). Remarks on administrative and critical communications research. *Studies in Philosophy of Social Science, 9,* 2–16.

Lazarsfeld, P. F., Berelson, B., & Gaudet, H. (1948). *The people's choice.* New York: Columbia University Press.

Leavitt, L. A., & Fox, N. A. (Eds.). (1993). *The psychological effects of war and violence on children.* Hillsdale, NJ: Lawrence Erlbaum Associates.

Lee, C. C. (1980). *Media imperialism reconsidered.* Beverly Hills, CA: Sage.

Lee, H. (2000, March 10). Reggae power. *Libération.* Reprinted in *World Press Review,* June 2000, 37.

Lee, M. A., & Solomon, N. (1991). *Unreliable sources: A guide to detecting bias in news media.* New York: Carol Publishing Group.

Lefkowitz, M. M., Eron, L. D., Walder, L. O., & Huesmann, L. R. (1977). *Growing up to be violent: A longitudinal study of the development of aggression.* New York: Pergamon.

Legrain, P. (2003, May 9). Cultural globalization is not Americanization. *The Chronicle of Higher Education,* B7–B10.

Lemar, J. (1977). Women and blacks on prime-time television. *Journal of Communication, 27,* 70–80.

Lemert, J. B., Wanta, W., & Lee, T. T. (1999). Party identification and negative advertising in a U.S. Senate election. *Journal of Communication, 49*(2), 123–134.

Leone, R. (2002). Contemplating ratings: An examination of what the MPAA considers "too far for R" and why. *Journal of Communication, 52*, 938–954.

Lever, J., & Wheeler, S. (1993). Mass media and the experience of sport. *Communication Research, 20*, 125–143.

Levin, I. P., & Gaeth, G. J. (1988). How consumers are affected by the framing of attribute information before and after consuming the product. *Journal of Consumer Research, 15*, 374–378.

Levy, M. R. (1982). Watching TV news as para-social interaction. In G. Gumpert & R. Cathcart (Eds.), *Inter/media* (2nd ed., pp. 177–187). New York: Oxford University Press.

Levy, M. R. (1987). Some problems of VCR research. *American Behavioral Scientist, 30*, 461–470.

Levy, M. R., & Windahl, S. (1984). Audience activity and gratifications: A conceptual clarification and exploration. *Communication Research, 11*, 51–78.

Lewy, G. (1978, February). Vietnam: New light on the question of American guilt. *Commentary, 65*, 29–49.

Leyens, J., Camino, L., Parke, R., & Berkowitz, L. (1975). The effects of movie violence on aggression in a field setting as a function of group dominance and cohesion. *Journal of Personality and Social Psychology, 32*, 346–360.

Lichter, S. R. (2001). A plague on both parties: Substance and fairness in TV election news. *Harvard Journal of Press/Politics, 6*(3), 8–30.

Lieberman, T. (2000, May/June). You can't report what you don't pursue. *Columbia Journalism Review*, 44–49.

Liebert, R. M., & Sprafkin, J. (1988). *The early window: Effects of television on children and youth* (3rd ed.). New York: Pergamon.

Liebes, T., & Livingstone, S. M. (1992). Mothers and lovers: Managing women's role conflicts in American and British soap operas. In J. G. Blumler, J. M. McLeod, & K. E. Rosengren (Eds.), *Comparatively speaking: Communication and culture across space and time* (pp. 94–120). Newbury Park, CA: Sage.

Lievrouw, L. A. (2000). Babel and beyond: Languages on the Internet. *ICA News, 28(3)*, 6–9.

Lightdale, J. R., & Prentice, D. A. (1994). Rethinking sex differences in aggression: Aggressive behavior in the absence of social roles. *Personality and Social Psychology Bulletin, 20*(1), 34–44.

Lindlof, T. R., & Shatzer, M. J. (1990). VCR usage in the American family. In J. Bryant (Ed.), *Television and the American family* (pp. 89–109). Hillsdale, NJ: Lawrence Erlbaum Associates.

Linz, D. (1985). *Sexual violence in the mass media: Effects on male viewers and implications for society.* Unpublished doctoral dissertation, University of Wisconsin, Madison.

Linz, D., & Donnerstein, E. (1988). The methods and merits of pornography research. *Journal of Communication, 38*(2), 180–184.

Linz, D., & Donnerstein, E. (1992, September 30). Research can help us explain violence and pornography. *Chronicle of Higher Education*, B3–B4.

Linz, D., & Donnerstein, E., & Adams, S. M. (1989). Physiological desensitization and judgments about female victims of violence. *Human Communication Research, 15*, 509–522.

Linz, D., Donnerstein, E., Bross, M., & Chapin, M. (1986). Mitigating the influence of violence on television and sexual violence in the media. In R. Blanchard (Ed.), *Advances in the study of aggression* (Vol. 2, pp. 165–194). Orlando, FL: Academic Press.

Linz, D., Donnerstein, E., & Penrod, S. (1984). The effects of multiple exposures to filmed violence against women. *Journal of Communication, 34*(3), 130–147.

Linz, D., Donnerstein, E., & Penrod, S. (1987). The findings and recommendations of the Attorney General's Commission on Pornography: Do the psychological "facts" fit the political fury? *American Psychologist, 42,* 946–953.

Linz, D., Fuson, I. A., & Donnerstein, E. (1990). Mitigating the negative effects of sexually violent mass communications through preexposure briefings. *Communication Research, 17,* 641–674.

Linz, D., & Malamuth, N. (1993). *Pornography.* Newbury Park, CA: Sage.

Linz, D., Turner, C. W., Hesse, B. W., & Penrod, S. D. (1984). Bases of liability for injuries produced by media portrayals of violent pornography. In N. M. Malamuth & E. Donnerstein (Eds.), *Pornography and sexual aggression* (pp. 277–304). Orlando, FL: Academic Press.

Liotti, M., Murray, J. P., & Ingmundson, P. (in press). Children's brain activations while viewing televised violence revealed by fMRI. *Human Brain Mapping.*

Lippert, B. (2003, January-February). What's wrong with this picture? *My Generation,* 48–52.

Loftus, E. F., & Burns, T. E. (1982). Mental shock can produce retrograde amnesia. *Memory & Cognition, 10,* 318–323.

Loftus, E. F., & Ketcham, K. (1994). *The myth of repressed memory.* New York: St. Martin's Press.

"Lolita in Japan." (1997, April 6). *Manhattan Mercury,* p. A7.

Lombard, M., Reich, R. D., Grabe, M. E., Bracken, C. C., & Ditton, T. B. (2000). Presence and television: The role of screen size. *Human Communication Research, 26,* 75–98.

Lombard, M., Snyder-Duch, J., & Bracken, C. C. (2002). Content analysis in mass communication: Assessment and reporting of intercoder reliability. *Human Communication Research, 28,* 587–604.

Long, D. L., & Graesser, A. C. (1988). Wit and humor in discourse processing. *Discourse Processes, 11,* 35–60.

Longford, L. (Ed.). (1972). *Pornography: The Longford Report.* London: Coronet.

Longmore, P. K. (1985, Summer). Screening stereotypes: Images of disabled people. *Social Policy,* pp. 31–37.

Lovdahl, L. T. (1989). Sex role messages in television commercials: An update. *Sex Roles, 21,* 715–724.

Lowery, S., & DeFleur, M. L. (1983). *Milestones in mass communication research.* New York: Longman.

Lowry, D. T., Love, G., & Kirby, M. (1981). Sex on the soap operas: Patterns of intimacy. *Journal of Communication, 31,* 90–96.

Lowry, D. T., Nio, T. C. J., & Leitner, D. W. (2003). Setting the public fear agenda: A longitudinal analysis of network TV crime reporting, public perceptions of crime, and FBI crime statistics. *Journal of Communication, 53*(1), 61–73.

Lowry, D. T., & Towles, D. E. (1989). Soap opera portrayals of sex, contraception, and sexually transmitted diseases. *Journal of Communication, 39*(2), 76–83.

Lozano, E. (1992). The force of myth on popular narratives: The case of melodramatic serials. *Communication Theory, 2,* 207–220.

Luebke, B. (1989). Out of focus: Images of women and men in newspaper photographs. *Sex Roles, 20*(3/4), 121–133.

Luepker, R. V., et al. (1994). Community education for cardiovascular disease prevention: Risk factor changes in the Minnesota Heart Health Program. *American Journal of Public Health, 84,* 1383–1393.

Luke, C. (1987). Television discourse and schema theory: Toward a cognitive model of information processing. In M. E. Manley-Casimir & C. Luke (Eds.), *Children and television: A challenge for education* (pp. 76–107). New York: Praeger.

Lull, J. (Ed.). (1988). *World families watch television.* Newbury Park, CA: Sage.

Luscombe, B. (2000, October 9). Laugh track. *Time,* 102.

Lyman, R. (2002, September 19). Hollywood balks at high-tech sanitizers. *The New York Times on the Web.*

Lyons, J. S., Anderson, R. L., & Larson, D. B. (1994). A systematic review of the effects of aggressive and nonaggressive pornography. In D. Zillmann, J. Bryant, & A. C. Huston (Eds.), *Media, family, and children: Social, scientific, psychodynamic, and clinical perspectives* (pp. 271–310). Hillsdale, NJ: Lawrence Erlbaum Associates.

Macbeth, T. M. (1996). Indirect effects of television: Creativity, persistence, school achievement, and participation in other activities. In T. M. Macbeth (Ed.) *Tuning in to young viewers: Social science perspectives on television* (pp. 149–219). Thousand Oaks, CA: Sage.

MacFarland, D. T. (1990). *Contemporary radio programming strategies.* Hillsdale, NJ: Lawrence Erlbaum Associates.

Maibach, E., & Flora, J. A. (1993). Symbolic modeling and cognitive rehearsal: Using video to promote AIDS prevention self-efficacy. *Communication Research, 20,* 517–545.

Maibach, E., & Parrott, R. L. (1995). *Designing health messages.* Thousand Oaks, CA: Sage.

Maier, S. (1994, January). India's awakening? *World Press Review, 41,* 29.

Malamuth, N. M. (1981). Rape fantasies as a function of exposure to violent sexual stimuli. *Archives of Sexual Behavior, 10,* 33–47.

Malamuth, N. M. (1984). Aggression against women: Cultural and individual causes. In N. M. Malamuth & E. Donnerstein (Eds.), *Pornography and sexual aggression* (pp. 19–52). Orlando, FL: Academic Press.

Malamuth, N. M. (1996). Sexually explicit media, gender differences, and evolutionary theory. *Journal of Communication, 46*(3), 8–31.

Malamuth, N. M., & Check, J. V. P. (1980a). Penile tumescence and perceptual responses to rape as a function of victim's perceived reactions. *Journal of Applied Social Psychology, 10,* 528–547.

Malamuth, N. M., & Check, J. V. P. (1980b). Sexual arousal to rape and consenting depictions: The importance of the woman's arousal. *Journal of Abnormal Psychology, 89,* 763–766.

Malamuth, N. M., & Check, J. V. P. (1983). Sexual arousal to rape depictions: Individual differences. *Journal of Abnormal Psychology, 92,* 55–67.

Malamuth, N. M., Check, J. V. P., & Briere, J. (1986). Sexual arousal in response to aggression: Ideological, aggressive, and sexual correlates. *Journal of Personality and Social Psychology, 50,* 330–340.

Malamuth, N. M., Feshbach, S., & Heim, M. (1980). Ethical issues and exposure to rape stimuli: A reply to Sherif. *Journal of Personality and Social Psychology, 38,* 413–415.

Malamuth, N. M., Haber, S., & Feshbach, S. (1980). Testing hypotheses regarding rape: Exposure to sexual violence, sex differences, and the "normality" of rapists. *Journal of Research in Personality, 14,* 121–137.

Malamuth, N. M., Heim, M., & Feshbach, S. (1980). Sexual responsiveness of college students to rape depictions: Inhibitory and disinhibitory effects. *Journal of Personality and Social Psychology, 38,* 399–408.

Malamuth, N. M., & Impett, E. A. (2001). Research on sex in the media: What do we know about effects on children and adolescents? In D. Singer & J. Singer (Eds.), *Handbook of children and the media.* Newbury Park, CA: Sage.

Malawi, bans. *Big Brother Africa.* (2003, August 6). BBC News. News.bbc.co.uk

Mankiewicz, F., & Swerdlow, J. (1978). *Remote control: Television and the manipulation of American life.* New York: Ballantine.

Manrai, L. A., & Gardner, M. P. (1992). Consumer processing of social ideas advertising: A conceptual model. *Advances in Consumer Research, 19,* 15–20.

Mares, M. L. (1998). Children's use of VCRs. *The Annals of the American Academy of Political and Social Science, 557,* 120–131.

Mares, M. L., & Woodard, E. H. (2001). Prosocial effects on children's social interactions. In D. G. Singer & J. L. Singer (Eds.), *Handbook of children and the media* (pp. 183–205). Thousand Oaks, CA: Sage.

Marling, K. A. (2002, May 28). They want their mean TV. *New York Times.* Retrieved May 28, 2002 from www.nytimes.com/2002/05/26/arts/television/26MARL.html

Martin, M. C. (1997). Children's understanding of the intent of advertising: A meta-analysis. *Journal of Public Policy and Marketing, 16,* 205–216.

Martz, L. (1998, May). Defending the most basic freedom. *World Press Review, 45,* 14–16.

Mastro, D. E., Eastin, M. S., & Tamborini, R. (2002). Internet search behaviors and mood alterations: A selective exposure approach. *Media Psychology, 4,* 157–172.

Mastro, D. E., & Greenberg, B. S. (2000). The portrayal of racial minorities on prime-time television. *Journal of Broadcasting & Electronic Media, 44,* 690–703.

Matabane, P. W. (1988). Television and the black audience: Cultivating moderate perspectives on racial integration. *Journal of Communication, 38*(4), 21–31.

Matas, M., Guebaly, N., Harper, D., Green, M., & Peterkin, A. (1986). Mental illness and the media: Part II. Content analysis of press coverage of mental health topics. *Canadian Journal of Psychiatry, 31,* 431–433.

Mattussek, M. (1995, April 3). Tuning in hate. *Der Spiegel.* (Reprinted in *World Press Review,* June 1995).

Mayer, J. (2000, August 14). Bad news: What's behind the recent gaffes at ABC? *The New Yorker.* pp. 30–36.

Mayerson, S. E., & Taylor, D. A. (1987). The effects of rape myth pornography on women's attitudes and the mediating role of sex role stereotyping. *Sex Roles, 17*, 321–338.

McAlister, A. L., Puska, P., & Salonen, J. T. (1982). Theory and action for health promotion: Illustrations from the North Karelia project. *American Journal of Public Health, 72*, 43–50.

McAnany, E. G. (1983). Television and crisis: Ten years of network news coverage of Central America, 1972–1981. *Media, culture and society, 5*(2), 199–212.

McCauley, C. (1998). When screen violence is not attractive. In J. H. Goldstein (Ed.), *Why we watch: The attractions of violent entertainment* (pp. 144–162). New York: Oxford University Press.

McCombs, M.E. (1994). News influence on our pictures of the world. In J. Bryant & D. Zillmann (Eds.). *Media effects: Advances in theory and research* (pp. 1–16). Hillsdale, NJ: Lawrence Erlbaum Associates.

McCombs, M. E., & Ghanem, S. (2001). The convergence of agenda setting and framing. In S. D. Reese, O. Gandy, & A. Grant (Eds.). *Framing in the new media landscape*. Mahwah, NJ: Lawrence Erlbaum Associates.

McCombs, M. E., & Gilbert, S. (1986). News influence on our pictures of the world. In J. Bryant & D. Zillmann (Eds.), *Perspectives on media effects* (pp. 1–15). Hillsdale, NJ: Lawrence Erlbaum Associates.

McCombs, M. E., & Reynolds, A. (2002). News influence on our pictures of the world. In J. Bryant & D. Zillmann (Eds.), *Media effects: Advances in theory and research* (2nd ed., pp. 1–18). Mahwah, NJ: Lawrence Erlbaum Associates.

McCombs, M. E., & Shaw, D. L. (1993). The evolution of agenda-setting research: Twenty-five years in the marketplace of ideas. *Journal of Communication, 43*(2), 58–67.

McCombs, M. E., Shaw, D. L., & Weaver, D. (Eds.). (1997). *Communication and democracy: Exploring the intellectual frontiers in agenda-setting theory.* Mahwah, NJ: Lawrence Erlbaum Associates.

McCook, A. (2003, April 17). "Fear Factor" TV show may be too scary for some. Reuters Health on the Web.

McCool, J. P., Cameron, L. D., & Petrie, K. J. (2001). Adolescent perceptions of smoking imagery in film. *Social Science & Medicine, 52*, 1577–1587.

McDermott, S., & Greenberg, B. (1985). Parents, peers, and television as determinants of black children's esteem. In R. Bostrom (Ed.), *Communication yearbook 8.* Beverly Hills, CA: Sage.

McDonnell, J. (1992). Rap music: Its role as an agent of change. *Popular Music and Society, 16*, 89–108.

McGhee, P. (1979). *Humor: Its origin and development.* San Francisco: Freeman.

McGinn, D. (2002, November 11). Guilt free TV. *Newsweek*, 53–59.

McGuire, W. J. (1974). Psychological motives and communication gratification. In J. G. Blumler & E. Katz (Eds.), *The uses of mass communications: Current perspectives on gratifications research* (pp. 167–196). Beverly Hills, CA: Sage.

McGuire, W. J. (1985). The myth of massive media impact: Savagings and salvagings. In G. Comstock (Ed.), *Public communication and behavior* (Vol. 1). New York: Academic Press.

McIntyre, P., Hosch, H. M., Harris, R. J., & Norvell, D. W. (1986). Effects of sex and attitudes toward women on the processing of television commercials. *Psychology and Marketing, 3,* 181–190.

McKenna, K. Y. A., & Bargh, J. A. (1999). Causes and consequences of social interaction on the Internet: A conceptual framework. *Media Psychology, 1,* 249–269.

McKenna, K. Y. A., & Green, A. S. (2004). Getting social online. In R. Walker (Ed.), *Cognitive technology: Transforming thought and society.* Jeffersen, NC: McFarland.

McKenzie-Mohr, D., & Zanna, M. P. (1990). Treating women as sexual objects: Look to the (gender schematic) male who has viewed pornography. *Personality and Social Psychology Bulletin, 16,* 296–308.

McNeal, J. U. (1998). Tapping the three kids' markets. *American Demographics, 20*(4), 36–41.

McNeal, J. U. (1999). *The kids' market: Myths and realities.* Ithaca, NY: Paramount Market.

Meadowcroft, J. M., & Reeves, B. (1989). Influence of story schema development on children's attention to television. *Communication Research, 16,* 352–374.

Médioni, G. (2002, April 11). Stand up, Africa! *L'Express.* Reprinted in *World Press Review,* July 2002, 34–35.

Melton, G., & Fowler, G. (1987). Female roles in radio advertising. *Journalism Quarterly, 64*(1), 145–149.

Mendelsohn, H. A. (1966). Election-day broadcasts and terminal voting decisions. *Public Opinion Quarterly, 30,* 212–225.

Merikle, P. M. (1988). Subliminal auditory messages: An evaluation. *Psychology & Marketing, 5,* 355–372.

Merikle, P. M., & Cheesman, J. (1987). Current status of research on subliminal advertising. *Advances in Consumer Research, 14,* 298–302.

Merikle, P. M., & Skanes, H. E. (1992). Subliminal self-help audiotapes: A search for placebo effects. *Journal of Applied Psychology, 77,* 772–776.

Merritt, S. (1984). Negative political advertising: Some empirical findings. *Journal of Advertising, 13,* 27–38.

Merskin, D. (1998). Sending up signals: A survey of Native American media use and representation in the mass media. *Howard Journal of Communication, 9,* 333–345.

Mesmer, T., Baskind, I., & Lerdau, E. (1998, October). Reflecting on an alliance. *Américas, 50*(5), 52–55.

Messaris, P. (1994). *Visual literacy—Image, mind, and reality.* Boulder, CO: Westview Press.

Messaris, P. (1997). *Visual persuasion: The role of images in advertising.* Thousand Oaks, CA: Sage.

Messaris, P. (1998). Visual aspects of media literacy. *Journal of Communication, 48*(1), 70–80.

Messner, M. A., Duncan, M. C., & Jensen, K. (1993). Separating the men from the girls: The gendered language of televised sports. *Gender & Society, 7,* 121–137.

Meyer, P. (1990). News media responsiveness to public health. In C. Atkin & L. Wallack (Eds.), *Mass communication and public health: Complexities and conflicts* (pp. 52–57). Newbury Park, CA: Sage.

Meyrowitz, J. (1985). *No sense of place: The impact of electronic media on social behavior.* New York: Oxford University Press.

Meyrowitz, J. (1998). Multiple media literacies. *Journal of Communication, 48*(1), 96–108.

Mielke, K. W., & Chen, M. (1983). Formative research for *3-2-1 Contact:* Methods and insights. In M. J. A. Howe (Ed.), *Learning from television: Psychological and educational research* (pp. 31–55). London: Academic Press.

Mills, J. (1993). The appeal of tragedy: An attitude interpretation. *Basic and applied social psychology, 14,* 255–271.

Mills, J. S., Polivy, J., Herman, C. P., & Tiggemann, M. (2002). Effects of exposure to thin media images: Evidence of self-enhancement among restrained eaters. *Personality and Social Psychology Bulletin, 28,* 1687–1699.

Moeller, S. D. (1999). *Compassion fatigue: How the media sell disease, famine, war, and death.* New York: Routledge.

Moisy, C. (1997, Summer). Myths of the global information village. *Foreign Policy,* 78–87.

Mok, T. (1998). Getting the message: Media images and stereotypes ad their effect on Asian Americans. *Culture Diversity and Mental Health, 4,* 185–202.

Moore, D. L., Hausknecht, D., & Thamodaran, K. (1986). Time compression, response opportunity, and persuasion. *Journal of Consumer Research, 13,* 85–99.

Moore, T. E. (1982). What you see is what you get. *Journal of Marketing, 46*(2), 38–47.

Moore, T. E. (1988). The case against subliminal manipulation. *Psychology & Marketing, 5,* 297–316.

Morgan, M. (1982). Television and adolescents' sex-role stereotypes: A longitudinal study. *Journal of Personality and Social Psychology, 43*(5), 947–955.

Morgan, M. (1989). Television and democracy. In I. Angus & S. Jhally (Eds.), *Cultural politics in contemporary America* (pp. 240–253). New York: Routledge.

Morgan, M. (1990). International cultivation analysis. In N. Signorielli & M. Morgan (Eds.), *Cultivation analysis: New directions in media effects research* (pp. 225–247). Newbury Park, CA: Sage.

Morgan, M., & Gerbner, G. (1982). TV professions and adolescent career choices. In M. Schwarz (Ed.), *TV and teens: Experts look at the issues* (pp. 121–126). Reading, MA: Addison-Wesley.

Morgan, M., & Shanahan, J. (1991). Television and the cultivation of political attitudes in Argentina. *Journal of Communication, 41*(1), 88–103.

Morgan, M., & Shanahan, J. (1992). Comparative cultivation analysis: Television and adolescents in Argentina and Taiwan. In F. Korzenny & S. Ting-Toomey (Eds.), *Mass media effects across cultures* (pp. 173–197). Newbury Park, CA: Sage.

Morgan, M., & Shanahan, J. (1995). *Democracy tango: Television, adolescents, and authoritarian tensions in Argentina.* Cresskill, NJ: Hampton Press.

Morgan, M., & Signorielli, N. (1990). Cultivation analysis: Conceptualization and methodology. In N. Signorielli & M. Morgan (Eds.), *Cultivation analysis: New directions in media effects research* (pp. 13–34). Newbury Park, CA: Sage.

Morgan, S. E., Palmgreen, P., Stephenson, M. T., Hoyle, R. H., & Lorch, E. P. (2003), Associations between message features and subjective evaluations of the sensation value of antidrug public service announcements. *Journal of Communication, 53*(3), 512–526.

Moritz, M. J. (1995). The gay agenda: Marketing hate speech to the mainstream media. In R. K. Whillock and D. Slayden (Eds.), *Hate speech* (pp. 55–79). Thousand Oaks, CA: Sage.

Morley, D. (1986). *Family television: Cultural power and domestic leisure.* London: Comedia.

Morley, D. (1988). Domestic relations: The framework of family viewing in Great Britain. In J. Lull (Ed.), *World families watch television* (pp. 22–48). Newbury Park, CA: Sage.

Morris, J. S. (1982). Television portrayal and the socialization of the American Indian child. In G. L. Berry & C. Mitchell-Kernan (Eds.), *Television and the socialization of the minority child* (pp. 187–202). New York: Academic Press.

Morris, M., & Ogan, C. (1996). The Internet as mass medium. *Journal of Communication, 46*(1), 39–50.

Mosher, D. L., & Maclan, P. (1994). College men and women respond to X-rated videos intended for male or female audiences: Gender and sexual scripts. *Journal of Sex Research, 31*, 99–113.

Moskalenko, S., & Heine, S. J. (2003). Watching your troubles away: Television viewing as a stimulus for subjective self-awareness. *Personality and Social Psychology Bulletin, 29*, 76–85.

Most famous Canadian (1996, February). *World Press Review, 43*, 33.

Mowlana, H. (1984). The role of the media in the U.S.-Iranian conflict. In A. Arno & W. Dissayanake (Eds.), *The news media in national and international conflict* (pp. 71–99). Boulder, CO: Westview Press.

Mowlana, H., Gerbner, G., & Schiller, H. (Eds.). (1993). *Triumph of the image: The media's war in the Persian Gulf—A global perspective.* Boulder, CO: Westview Press.

Muehling, D. D., & Kolbe, R. H. (1999). A comparison of children's and prime-time fine-print advertising disclosure practices. In M. C. Macklin & L. Carlson (Eds.), *Advertising to children: Concepts and controversies* (pp. 143–164). Thousand Oaks, CA: Sage.

Mundorf, N., Drew, D., Zillmann, D., & Weaver, J. (1990). Effects of disturbing news on recall of subsequently presented news. *Communication Research, 17*, 601–615.

Mundorf, N., & Laird, K. R. (2002). Social and psychological effects of information technologies and other interactive media. In J. Bryant & D. Zillmann (Eds.), *Media effects* (2nd ed., pp. 583–602). Mahwah, NJ: Lawrence Erlbaum Associates.

Mundorf, N., Weaver, J., & Zillmann, D. (1989). Effects of gender roles and self-perceptions on affective reactions to horror films. *Sex Roles, 20*, 655–673.

Murnen, S. K., & Stockton, M., (1997). Gender and self-reported sexual arousal in response to sexual stimuli: A meta-analytic review. *Sex Roles, 37*, 135–153.

Murphy, S. T. (1998). The impact of factual versus fictional media portrayals on cultural stereotypes. *Annals of the American Academy of Political and Social Science, 560*, 165–178.

Murray, J. P. (1999). Studying television violence: A research agenda for the 21st century. In J. K. Asamen & G. L. Berry (Eds.), *Research paradigms, television, and social behavior* (pp. 369–410). Thousand Oaks, CA: Sage.

Murray, J. P. (2001, October). TV violence and brainmapping in children. *Psychiatric Times, 18*(10).

Mutz, D. C., Roberts, D. F., & van Vuuren, D. P. (1993). Reconsidering the displacement hypothesis. *Communication Research, 20*, 51–75.

Myers, P. N., Jr., & Biocca, F. A. (1992). The elastic body image: The effect of television advertising and programming on body image distortions in young women. *Journal of Communication, 42*(3), 108–133.

North Korean movies' propaganda role. (2003, August 18). BBC News online Retrieved August 18, 2003 from news.bbc.co.uk

Naked Capitalists. (2001, May 20). *New York Times.* Cited in *Kansas State Collegian*, February 5, 2002.

Nathanson, A. I. (1999). Identifying and explaining the relationship between parental mediation and children's aggression. *Communication Research, 26*, 124–143.

Nathanson, A. I., Wilson, B. J., McGee, J., & Sebastian, M. (2002). Counteracting the effects of female stereotypes on television via active mediation. *Journal of Communication, 52*, 922–937.

Nathanson, A. I., & Yang, M. S. (2003). The effects of mediation content and form on children's response to violent television. *Human Communication Research, 29*, 111–134.

National Television Violence Study, Vols. 1–2. (1997). Thousand Oaks, CA: Sage.

Naughton, J. (1998, January 9). Colleges eye restrictions on promotions by brewing companies. *The Chronicle of Higher Education*, A57.

Nell, V. (2002). Why young men drive dangerously: Implications for injury prevention. *Current Directions in Psychological Science, 11*, 75–79.

Nelson, J. P., Gelfand, D. M., & Hartmann, D. P. (1969). Children's aggression following competition and exposure to an aggressive model. *Child Development, 40*, 1085–1097.

Neuendorf, K. A. (2002). *The content analysis guidebook.* Thousand Oaks, CA: Sage.

Newhagen, J. E., & Reeves, B. (1991). Emotion and memory responses for negative political advertising: A study of television commercials used in the 1988 Presidential election. In F. Biocca (Ed.), *Television and political advertising: Psychological processes* (Vol. 1, pp. 197–220). Hillsdale, NJ: Lawrence Erlbaum Associates.

Newhagen, J. E., & Reeves, B. (1992). The evening's bad news: Effects of compelling negative television news images on memory. *Journal of Communication, 42*(2), 25–41.

Nias, D. K. B. (1983). The effects of televised sex and pornography. In M. J. A. Howe (Ed.), *Learning from television: Psychological and educational implications* (pp. 179–192). London: Academic Press.

Nimmo, D., & Savage, R. L. (1976). *Candidates and their images.* Pacific Palisades, CA: Goodyear.

Nisbett, R. E. (2003). *The geography of thought: How Asians and Westerners think differently . . . and why.* New York: The Free Press.

Noe, D. (1995). Parallel worlds: The surprising similarities (and differences) of country-and-western and rap. *The Humanist, 55*, 20–23.

Noll, A. M. (1996). *Highway of dreams: A critical view along the information superhighway*. Mahwah, NJ: Lawrence Erlbaum Associates.

Norris, J., George, W. H., Davis, K. C., Martell, J., & Leonesio, R. J. (1999). Alcohol and hypermasculinity as determinants of men's empathic responses to violent pornography. *Journal of Interpersonal Violence, 14*, 683–700.

Numbers. (1997, September 29). *Time*, 23.

Numbers. (1998, January 19). *Time*, 19. (a)

Numbers. (1998, February 2). *Time*, 17. (b)

Numbers. (1999, May 31). *Time*, 29. (a)

Numbers. (2001, June 4). *Time*, 25.

Numbers. (2002, October 14). *Time*, 29.

Nussbaum, J. F., & Robinson, J. D. (1986). Attitudes toward aging. *Communication Research Reports, 1*, 21–27.

O'Bryant, S. L., & Corder-Bolz, C. R. (1978). The effects of television on children's stereotyping of women's work roles. *Journal of Vocational Behavior, 12*, 233–244.

O'Connor, J. J. (1990, February 20). Cartoons teach children, but is the lesson good? *New York Times*, p. B1.

Ohbuchi, K., Ikeda, T., & Takeuchi, G. (1994). Effects of violent pornography upon viewers' rape myth beliefs: A study of Japanese males. *Psychology, Crime, & Law, 1*, 71–81.

Oliver, M. B. (1993). Adolescents' enjoyment of graphic horror. *Communication Research, 20*, 30–50.

Oliver, M. B. (1994). Portrayals of crime, race, and aggression in "reality-based" police shows: A content analysis. *Journal of Broadcasting and Electronic Media, 38*, 179–192.

Oliver, M. B., & Fonash, D. (2002). Race and crime in the news: Whites' identification and misidentification of violent and nonviolent criminal suspects. *Media Psychology, 4*, 137–156.

Olson, D. R. (1994). *The world on paper*. New York: Cambridge University Press.

Olweus, D. (1979). The stability of aggressive reaction patterns in human males: A review. *Psychological Bulletin, 85*, 852–875.

Orecklin, M. (2003, May 19). There's no escape. *Time*.

Orman, J. (1992). Conclusion: The impact of popular music in society. In K. J. Bindas (Ed.), *America's musical pulse: Popular music in twentieth-century society* (pp. 281–287). Westport, CT: Praeger.

Paik, H., & Comstock, G. (1994). The effects of television violence on antisocial behavior: A meta-analysis. *Communication Research, 21*, 516–546.

Paletz, D. L. (1988). Pornography, politics, and the press: The U.S. attorney general's commission on pornography. *Journal of Communication, 38*(2), 122–136.

Paletz, D. L., & Schmid, A. P. (Eds.). (1992). *Terrorism and the media*. Newbury Park, CA: Sage.

Palmgreen, P. (1984). Uses and gratifications: A theoretical perspective. In R. N. Bostrom (Ed.), *Communication Yearbook 8* (pp. 20–55). Newbury Park, CA: Sage.

Panee, C. D., & Ballard, M. E. (2002). High versus low aggressive priming during video game training: Effects of violent action during game play, hostility, heart rate, and blood pressure. *Journal of Applied Social Psychology, 32*, 2458–2474.

Panitt, M. (1988, June 4). In India, they'll trash a station . . . or worship an actor. *TV Guide*, 44–45.

Papa, M. J., Singhal, A., Law, S., Pant, S., Sood, S., Rogers, E. M., et al. (2000). Entertainment-education and social change: An analysis of parasocial interaction, social learning, collective efficacy, and paradoxical communication. *Journal of Communication, 50*(4), 31–55.

Papacharissi, Z., & Rubin, A. (2000). Predictors of Internet use. *Journal of Broadcasting and Electronic Media*, 175–196.

Parke, R., Berkowitz, L., Leyens, J., West, S., & Sebastian, R. (1977). Some effects of violent and non-violent movies on the behavior of juvenile delinquents. In L. Berkowitz (Ed.), *Advances in social psychology* (Vol. 10). New York: Academic Press.

Parks, M. R. (1996). Making friends in cyberspace. *Journal of Communication, 46*(1), 80–97.

Payne, D. (2003, February 21). In your face. *The Chronicle of Higher Education*, A6–A8.

Pechmann, C., & Stewart, D. W. (1988). Advertising repetition: A critical review of wearin and wearout. *Current Issues and Research in Advertising, 11*, 285–329.

Peck, J. (1992). *The gods of televangelism: The crisis of meaning and the appeal of religious television*. Cresskill, NJ: Hampton Press.

Pecora, N. O. (1997). *The business of children's entertainment*. New York: Guilford.

Penrod, S., & Linz, D. (1984). Using psychological research on violent pornography to inform legal change. In N. M. Malamuth & E. Donnerstein (Eds.), *Pornography and sexual aggression* (pp. 247–265). Orlando, FL: Academic Press.

Peracchio, L. A., & Luna, D. (1998). The development of an advertising campaign to discourage smoking initiation among children and youth. *Journal of Advertising, 27*(3), 49–56.

Percy, L., & Rossiter, J. R. (1983). Mediating effects of visual and verbal elements in print advertising upon belief, attitude, and intention responses. In L. Percy & A. Woodside (Eds.), *Advertising and consumer psychology* (pp. 171–186). Lexington, MA: Lexington Books.

Perkins, K. P. (1997, October). It would take a miracle of sorts to save "Nothing Sacred." *Manhattan Mercury*, A7.

Perlmutter, D. D. (2000). Tracing the origin of humor. *Humor, 13*, 457–468.

Perloff, R. M. (1989). Ego-involvement and the third person effect of television news coverage. *Communication Research, 16*, 236–262.

Perloff, R. M. (2002). The third-person effect. In J. Bryant & D. Zillmann (Eds.), *Media effects: Advances in theory and research* (2nd ed., pp. 489–506). Mahwah, NJ: Lawrence Erlbaum Associates.

Percy, L., & Lautman, M. R. (1994). Advertising, weight loss, and eating disorders. In E. M. Clark, T. C. Brock, & D. W. Stewart (Eds.), *Attention, attitude, and affect in response to advertising* (pp. 301–311). Hillsdale, NJ: Lawrence Erlbaum Associates.

Perse, E. M. (1986). Soap opera viewing patterns of college students and cultivation. *Journal of Broadcasting & Electronic Media, 30*, 175–193.

Perse, E. M. (2001). *Media effects and society*. Mahwah, NJ: Lawrence Erlbaum Associates.

Perse, E. M., & Rubin, R. B. (1989). Attribution in social and parasocial relationships. *Communication Research, 16,* 59–77.

Petty, R. E., Priester, J. R., & Briñol, P. (2002). Mass media attitude change: Implications of the Elaboration Likelihood model of persuasion. In J. Bryant & D. Zillmann (Eds.), *Media effects* (2nd ed., pp. 155–198). Mahwah, NJ: Lawrence Erlbaum Associates.

Pewewardy, C. D. (1999). The deculturalization of indigenous mascots in U.S. sports culture. *The Educational Forum, 63,* 342–347.

Pezdek, K., & Hartman, E. F. (1983). Children's television viewing: Attention and comprehension of auditory versus visual information. *Child Development, 54,* 1015–1023.

Pezdek, K., Lehrer, A., & Simon, S. (1984). The relationship between reading and cognitive processing of television and radio. *Child Development, 55,* 2072–2082.

Pezdek, K., & Stevens, E. (1984). Children's memory for auditory and visual information on television. *Developmental Psychology, 20,* 212–218.

Pfau, M., Mullen, L. J., Deidrich, T., & Garrow, K. (1995). Television viewing and the public perception of attorneys. *Human Communication Research, 21,* 307–330.

Phillips, D. P. (1977). Motor vehicle increase just after publicized suicide stories. *Science, 196,* 1464–1465.

Phillips, D. P. (1984). Teenage and adult temporal fluctuations in suicide and auto fatalities. In H. S. Sudak, A. B. Ford, & N. B. Rushforth (Eds.), *Suicide in the young* (pp. 69–80). Boston: John Wright.

Phillips, D. P., & Carstensen, L. L. (1986). Clustering of teenage suicides after TV news stories about suicides. *New England Journal of Medicine, 315,* 685–689.

Phillips, K. (1993, January–February). How *Seventeen* undermines young women. *Extra!, 6*(1), 14.

Picard, R. G. (1993). *Media portrayals of terrorism: Functions and meaning of news coverage.* Ames, IA: Iowa State University Press.

Pierce, M. C., & Harris, R. J. (1993). The effect of provocation, race, and injury description on men's and women's perception of a wife-battering incident. *Journal of Applied Social Psychology, 23,* 767–790.

Pingree, S., & Hawkins, R. (1981). U.S. programs on Australian television: The cultivation effect. *Journal of Communication, 31*(1), 97–105.

Pingree, S., & Thompson, M. E. (1990). The family in daytime serials. In J. Bryant (Ed.), *Television and the American family* (pp. 113–127). Hillsdale, NJ: Lawrence Erlbaum Associates.

Pinkleton, B. E. (1998). Effects of print comparative political advertising on political decision-making and participation. *Journal of Communication, 48*(4), 24–36.

Pitkanen-Pulkkinen, L. (1981). Concurrent and predictive validity of self-reported aggressiveness. *Aggressive Behavior, 7,* 97–110.

Pitta, P. (1999). Family myths and the TV media: History, impact, and new directions. In L. L. Schwartz (Ed.), *Psychology and the media: A second look* (pp. 125–145). Washington, DC: American Psychological Association.

Ploghoft, M. E., & Anderson, J. A. (1982). *Teaching critical television viewing skills: An integrated approach.* Springfield, IL: Charles C Thomas.

Pollard, P. (1995). Pornography and sexual aggression. *Current Psychology: Developmental, Learning, Personality, Social, 14*(3), 200–221.

Pollitt, K. (1991, June 24). Naming and blaming: Media goes wilding in Palm Beach. *The Nation.*

Poniewozik, J. (2001, May 28). What's wrong with this picture? *Time,* 80–82.

Pope, H. G., Jr., Phillips, K. A., & Olivardia, R. (2000). *The Adonis complex: The secret crisis of male body obsession.* New York: The Free Press.

Postman, N. (1982). *The disappearance of childhood.* New York: Delacorte.

Postman, N. (1985). *Amusing ourselves to death.* New York: Viking Penguin.

Potter, W. J. (1986). Perceived reality and the cultivation hypothesis. *Journal of Broadcasting & Electronic Media, 30,* 159–174.

Potter, W. J. (1988). Perceived reality in television effects research. *Journal of Broadcasting & Electronic Media, 32,* 23–41.

Potter, W. J. (1989). Three strategies for elaborating the cultivation hypothesis. *Journalism Quarterly, 65,* 930–939.

Potter, W. J. (1991a). Examining cultivation from a psychological perspective: Component subprocesses. *Communication Research, 18,* 77–102.

Potter, W. J. (1991b). The relationships between first- and second-order measures of cultivation. *Human Communication Research, 18,* 92–113.

Potter, W. J. (1993). Cultivation theory and research: A conceptual critique. *Human Communication Research, 19,* 564–601.

Potter, W. J. (2001). *Media literacy* (2nd ed.). Thousand Oaks, CA: Sage.

Potter, W. J., & Tomasello, T. K. (2003). Building upon the experimental design in media violence research: The importance of including receiver interpretations. *Journal of Communication, 53,* 315–329.

Potter, W. J., & Warren, R. (1998). Humor as camouflage of television violence. *Journal of Communication, 48*(2), 40–57.

Potts, R. Doppler. M., & Hernandez, M. (1994). Effects of television content on physical risk-taking in children, *Journal of Experimental Child Psychology, 58,* 321–331.

Potts, R., & Martinez, I. (1994). Television viewing and children's beliefs about scientists. *Journal of Applied Developmental Psychology, 15,* 287–300.

Potts, R., & Sanchez, D. (1994). Television viewing and depression: No news is good news. *Journal of Broadcasting & Electronic Media,* 79–90.

Potts, R., & Swisher, L. (1998). Effects of televised safety models on children's risk taking and hazard identification. *Journal of Pediatric Psychology, 23,* 157–163.

Powers, R. (1984). *Supertube: The rise of television sports.* New York: Coward-McCann.

Pratap, A. (1990, August 13). Romance and a little rape. *Time,* 69.

Pratkanis, A. R. (1992). The cargo-cult science of subliminal persuasion. *Skeptical Inquirer, 16,* 260–272.

Pratkanis, A. R., & Aronson, E. (1992). *Age of propaganda: The everyday use and abuse of persuasion.* New York: W. H. Freeman.

Pratkanis, A. R., & Greenwald, A. G. (1988). Recent perspectives on unconscious processing: Still no marketing applications. *Psychology & Marketing, 5,* 339–355.

Preston, E. H. (1990). Pornography and the construction of gender. In N. Signorielli & M. Morgan (Eds.), *Cultivation analysis* (pp. 107–122). Newbury Park, CA: Sage.

Preston, I. L. (1975). *The great American blow-up: Puffery in advertising and selling.* Madison, WI: University of Wisconsin Press.

Preston, I. L. (1994). *The tangled web they weave: Truth, falsity, & advertisers.* Madison, WI: University of Wisconsin Press.

Preston, I. L., & Richards, J. I. (1986). Consumer miscomprehension as a challenge to FTC prosecutions of deceptive advertising. *The John Marshall Law Review, 19,* 605–635.

Price, M. E. (Ed.) (1998). *The V-chip debate: Content filtering from television to the Internet.* Mahwah, NJ: Lawrence Erlbaum Associates.

Price, V., & Czilli, E. J. (1996). Modeling patterns of news recognition and recall. *Journal of Communication, 46*(2), 55–78.

Pritchard, D., & Hughes, K. D. (1997). Patterns of deviance in crime news. *Journal of Communication, 47*(3), 49–67.

Provenzo, E. F., Jr. (1991). *Video kinds: Making sense of Nintendo.* Cambridge, MA: Harvard University Press.

Quackenbush, D. M., Strassberg, D. S., & Turner, C. W. (1995). Gender effects of romantic themes in erotica. *Archives of Sexual Behavior, 24,* 21–35.

Quinsey, V. L., Chapman, T. C., & Upfold, D. (1984). Sexual arousal to nonsexual violence and sadomasochistic themes among rapists and on sex offenders. *Journal of Consulting and Clinical Psychology, 52,* 651–657.

Rabinovitch, M. S., McLean, M. S., Markham, J. W., & Talbott, A. D. (1972). Children's violence perception as a function of television violence. In G. A. Comstock, E. A. Rubinstein, & J. P. Murray (Eds.), *Television and social behavior: Vol. 5. Television's effects: Further explorations.* Washington, DC: U.S. Government Printing Office.

Rader, B. G. (1984). *In its own image: How television has transformed sports.* New York: The Free Press.

Rafaeli, S., & LaRose, R. J. (1993). Electronic bulletin boards and A "public goods" explanation of collaborative mass media. *Communication Research, 20,* 277–297.

Rainville, R., & McCormick, E. (1977). Extent of covert racial prejudice in pro football announcers' speech. *Journalism Quarterly, 54*(1), 20–26.

Raju, P. S., & Lonial, S. C. (1990). Advertising to children: Findings and implications. *Current Issues and Research in Advertising, 12,* 231–274.

Ramirez Berg, C. (1990). Stereotyping in films in general and of the Hispanic in particular. *Howard Journal of Communication 2,* 286–300.

Raney, A. A. (2002). Moral judgment as a predictor of enjoyment of crime drama. *Media Psychology, 4,* 305–322.

Raney, A. A., & Bryant, J. (2002). Moral judgment and crime drama: An integrated theory of enjoyment. *Journal of Communication, 52*(2), 402–415.

Ratzan, S. C., Payne, J. G., & Massett, H. A. (1994). Effective health message design: The America Responds to AIDS campaign. *American Behavioral Scientist, 38,* 294–309.

Rawson, H. (2003, June/July). The road to freedom fries. *American Heritage, 12.*

Real, M. R. (1989). Super Bowl football versus World Cup soccer: A cultural-structural comparison. In L. A. Wenner (Ed.), *Media, sports, and society* (pp. 180–203). Newbury Park, CA: Sage.

Reeve, D. K., & Aggleton, J. P. (1998). On the specificity of expert knowledge about a soap opera: An everyday story of farming folk. *Applied Cognitive Psychology*, *12*, 35–42.

Reeves, B., & Nass, C. (1996). *The media equation: How people treat computer, television, and the new media like real people and places*. New York: Cambridge University Press.

Reeves, B., Thorson, E., Rothschild, M., McDonald, D., Hirsch, J., & Goldstein, R. (1985). Attention to television: Intrastimulus effects of movement and scene changes on alpha variation over time. *International Journal of Neuroscience*, *25*, 241–255.

Reid, P. T. (1979). Racial stereotyping on television: A comparison of the behavior of black and white television characters. *Journal of Applied Psychology*, *64*(5), 465–489. *Report of the Special Committee on Pornography and Prostitution* (Vol. 1, 1985). Ottawa: Minister of Supply and Services.

Rice, M. L., Huston, A. C., & Wright, J. C. (1986). Replays as repetitions: Young children's interpretation of television forms. *Journal of Applied Developmental Psychology*, *7*, 61–76.

Rice, M. L., Huston, A. C., Truglio, R., & Wright, J. C. (1990). Words from Sesame Street: Learning vocabulary skills while viewing. *Developmental Psychology*, *26*, 421–428.

Rich, F. (1997, Dec. 26). Mental illness still needs a spokesman. *Manhattan Mercury*, A7.

Richards, J. I. (1990). *Deceptive advertising*. Hillsdale, NJ: Lawrence Erlbaum Associates.

Richardson, G. W., Jr. (2001). Looking for meaning in all the wrong places: Why negative advertising is a suspect category. *Journal of Communication 51*(4), 775–800.

Riffe, D., & Freitag, A. A. (1997). A content analysis of content analyses: Twenty-five years of Journalism Quarterly. *Journalism and Mass Communication Quarterly*, *74*, 873–882.

Riffe, D., Lacy, S., & Fico, F. G. (1998). *Analyzing media messages: Using quantitative content analysis in research*. Mahwah, NJ: Lawrence Erlbaum.

Riggle, E. D. B., Ellis, A. L., & Crawford, A. M. (1996). The impact of "media contact" on attitudes toward gay men. *Journal of Homosexuality*, *31*(3), 55–69.

Riggs, M. (1992, June 15). *Color adjustment* [documentary]. New York: PBS.

Rimmer, L. (2002, July 21). Brand-new day. *Scotland on Sunday*. Reprinted in *World Press Review*, October 2002, 36–37.

Ritchie, D., Price, V., & Roberts, D. F. (1987). Reading and television: A longitudinal investigation of the displacement hypothesis. *Communication Research*, *14*, 292–315.

Roberts, D. F. (2000). Media and youth: Access, exposure, and privatization. *Journal of Adolescent Health*, *27S*(2), 8–14.

Roberts, D. G., & Christenson, P. G. (2001). Popular music in childhood and adolescence. In D. G. Singer & J. L. Singer (Eds.), *Handbook of children and the media* (pp. 395–413). Thousand Oaks, CA: Sage.

Roberts, D. F., Henriksen, L., & Christenson, P. G. (1999). *Substance use in popular movies and music*. Washington, DC: Office of National Drug Control Policy.

Roberts, D. F., & Maccoby, N. (1985). Effects of mass communication. In G. Lindzey & E. Aronson (Eds.), *Handbook of social psychology* (3rd ed.). New York: Random House.

Robertson, T. S., & Rossiter, J. R. (1974). Children and commercial persuasion: An attribution theory analysis. *Journal of Consumer Research, 1*(1), 13–20.

Robertson, T. S., Rossiter, J. R., & Gleason, T. C. (1979). *Televised medicine advertising and children.* New York: Praeger.

Robinson, J. D. (1989). Mass media and the elderly: A uses and dependency interpretation. In J. F. Nussbaum (Ed.), *Life-span communication* (pp. 319–337). Hillsdale, NJ: Lawrence Erlbaum Associates.

Robinson, J. D., & Skill, T. (2001). Five decades of families on television: From the 1950s through the 1990s. In J. Bryant & J. A. Bryant. *Television and the American family* (2nd ed., pp. 139–162). Mahwah, NJ: Lawrence Erlbaum Associates.

Robinson, J. P., & Davis, D. K. (1990). Television news and the informed public: An information-processing approach. *Journal of Communication, 40*(3), 106–119.

Robinson, M. J., & Sheehan, M. A. (1983). *Over the wire and on TV: CBS and UPI in Campaign 80.* New York: Sage.

Robinson, T. N., Saphir, M. N., Kraemer, H. C., Varady, A., & Haydel, K. F. (2001). Effects of reducing television viewing on children's request for toys: A randomized control trial. *Journal of Developmental and Behavioral Pediatrics, 22,* 179–184.

Robinson, T. N., Wilde, M. L., Navracruz, L. C., Haydel, F., & Varady, A. (2001). Effects of reducing children's television and video game use on aggressive behavior. *Archives of Pediatric and Adolescent Medicine, 155,* 17–23.

Rogers, E. M., Dearing, J. W., & Bregman, D. (1993). The anatomy of agenda-setting research. *Journal of Communication, 43*(2), 68–84.

Rogers, E. M., & Singhal, A. (1989). Estrategias de educacion entretenimiento [Strategies for educating through entertainment]. *Chasqui, 31,* 9–22.

Rogers, E. M., & Singhal, A. (1990). The academic perspective. In C. Atkin & L. Wallack (Eds.), *Mass communication and public health* (pp. 176–181). Newbury Park, CA: Sage.

Rogers, E. M., Vaughan, P. W., Swalehe, R. M. A., Rao, N., Svenkerud, P., & Sood, S. (1999). Effects of an entertainment-education radio soap opera on family planning behavior in Tanzania. *Studies in Family Planning, 30*(3), 193–211.

Rojahn, K., & Pettigrew, T. F. (1992). Memory for schema-relevant information: A meta-analytic resolution. *British Journal of Social Psychology, 31,* 81–109.

Rolandelli, D. R., Wright, J. C., Huston, A. C., & Eakins, D. (1991). Children's auditory and visual processing of narrated and nonnarrated television programming. *Journal of Experimental Child Psychology, 51,* 90–122.

Romer, D., Jamieson, K. H., & DeCoteau, N. (1998). The treatment of persons of color in local television news: Ethnic blame discourse or realistic group conflict. *Communication Research,* 286–305.

Romer, D., Jamieson, K. H., & Aday, S. (2003). Television news and the cultivation of fear of crime. *Journal of Communication, 53,* 88–104.

Romero, S. (2000, December 19). A cell phone surge among world's poor in Haiti. *New York Times,* from http://www.nytimes.com/2000/12/19/technology/19CELL.html

Rosenbaum, J., & Prinsky, L. (1987). Sex, violence, and rock'nroll: Youth's perception of popular music. *Popular Music and Society, 11*, 79–90.

Rosenberg, T. (2003, July 3). In Colombia, muckrakers have become scarce. Retrieved July 3, 2003 from http://www.nytimes.com

Rosencrans, M. A., & Hartup, W. W. (1967). Imitative influences of consistent and inconsistent response consequences to a model on aggressive behavior in children. *Journal of Personality and Social Psychology, 7*, 429–434.

Rosengren, K. E. (1992). The structural invariance of change: Comparative studies of media use (some results from a Swedish research program). In J. G. Blumler, J. M. McLeod, & K. E. Rosengren (Eds.), *Comparatively speaking: Communication and culture across space and time* (pp. 140–178). Newbury Park, CA: Sage.

Rosengren, K. E., Wenner, L. A., & Palmgreen, P. (Eds.). (1985). *Media gratifications research: Current perspectives.* Newbury Park, CA: Sage.

Rosenkoetter, L. I. (1999). The television situation comedy and children's prosocial behavior. *Journal of Applied Social Psychology, 29*, 979–993.

Rosenzweig, J. (1999). Can TV improve us? *The American Prospect, 45*, 58–63.

Ross, J. (1992, August). The cola war's new front. *World Press Review, 39*, 45.

Rössler, P., & Brosius, H.-B. (2001). Do talk shows cultivate adolescents' view of the world? A prolonged-exposure experiment. *Journal of Communication, 51*(1), 143–163.

Rotfeld, H. J. (1988). Fear appeals and persuasion: Assumptions and errors in advertising research. *Current Issues and Research in Advertising, 11*, 21–40.

Rothenberg, D. (1998, June 5). The sounds of global change: Different beats, new ideas. *The Chronicle of Higher Education*, B8.

Rothenbuhler, E. W. (1988). The living room celebration of the Olympic games. *Journal of Communication, 38*(4), 61–81.

Roy, A., & Harwood, J. (1997). Underrepresented, positively portrayed: Older adults in television commercials. *Journal of Applied Communication Research, 25*, 39–56.

Rubin, A. M. (1981). An examination of television viewing motivations. *Communication Research, 8*, 141–165.

Rubin, A. M. (1983). Television uses and gratifications: The interactions of viewing patterns and motivations. *Journal of Broadcasting, 27*, 37–51.

Rubin, A. M. (1984). Ritualized and instrumental television viewing. *Journal of Communication, 34*(3), 67–77.

Rubin, A. M. (2002). The uses-and-gratifications perspective of media effects. In J. Bryant & D. Zillmann (Eds.), *Media effects: Advances in theory and research* (2nd ed., pp. 525–548). Mahwah, NJ: Lawrence Erlbaum Associates.

Rubin, A. M., & Perse, E. M. (1987). Audience activity and television news gratifications. *Communication Research, 14*, 58–84.

Rubin, A. M., & Perse, E. M. (1988). Audience activity and soap opera involvement. *Human Communication Research, 14*, 246–268.

Rubin, A. M., Perse, E. M., & Powell, R. A. (1985). Loneliness, parasocial interaction, and local television news viewing. *Human Communication Research, 12*, 155–180.

Rubin, A. M., Perse, E. M., & Taylor, D. S. (1988). A methodological examination of cultivation. *Communication Research, 15*, 107–134.

Rubin, A. M., & Windahl, S. (1986). The uses and dependency model of mass communication. *Critical Studies in Mass Communication, 3,* 184–199.

Rubin, D. C. (1995). *Memory in oral traditions: The cognitive psychology of epic, ballads, and counting-out rhymes.* New York: Oxford University Press.

Rubin, D. M., & Cummings, C. (1989). Nuclear war and its consequences on television. *Journal of Communication, 39*(1), 39–58.

Rubin, R. B., & McHugh, M. P. (1987). Development of parasocial interaction relationships. *Journal of Broadcasting & Electronic Media, 31,* 279–292.

Rumelhart, D. E. (1980). Schemata: Building blocks of cognition. In R. J. Spiro, B. C. Bruce, & W. F. Brewer (Eds.), *Theoretical issues in reading comprehension* (pp. 33–58). Hillsdale, NJ: Lawrence Erlbaum Associates.

Russell, A. (2001). Chiapas and the news: Internet and newspaper coverage of a broken cease fire. *Journalism, 2,* 197–220.

Russell, D. E. H. (1998). *Dangerous relationships: Pornography, misogyny, and rape.* Thousand Oaks, CA: Sage.

Russo, J. E., Metcalf, B. L., & Stevens, D. (1981). Identifying misleading advertising. *Journal of Consumer Research, 8,* 119–131.

Russo, V. (1981). *The celluloid closet: Homosexuality in the movies.* New York: Harper & Row.

Saegert, J. (1987). Why marketing should quit giving subliminal advertising the benefit of the doubt. *Psychology & Marketing, 4,* 107–120.

Sagarin, B., Britt, M. A., Heider, J. D., Wood, S. E., & Lynch, J. E. (2004). Intrusive technology. In R. Walker (Ed.), *Cognitive technology: Transforming thought and society.* Jefferson, NC: McFarland.

Salamon, J. (2001, March 13). When it comes to TV, coveted adolescents prove to be unpredictable. *New York Times,* p. E1.

Salomon, G. (1979). *Interaction of media, cognition, and learning.* San Francisco: Jossey-Bass.

Salomon, G. (1983). Television watching and mental effort: A social psychological view. In J. Bryant & D. Anderson (Eds.), *Children's understanding of television* (pp. 181–198). New York: Academic Press.

Salomon, G. (1984). Television is "easy" and print is "tough": The differential investment of mental effort in learning as a function of perceptions and attributions. *Journal of Educational Psychology, 76,* 647–658.

Salomon, G. (1987). Television and reading: The roles of orientations and reciprocal relations. In M. E. Manley-Casimir & C. Luke (Eds.), *Children and television* (pp. 15–33). New York: Praeger.

Sapolsky, B. S. (1984). Arousal, affect, and the aggression-moderating effect of erotica. In N. M. Malamuth & E. Donnerstein (Eds.), *Pornography and sexual aggression* (pp. 85–113). Orlando, FL: Academic Press.

Sapolsky, B. S., & Molitor, F. (1996). Content trends in contemporary horror films. In J. B. Weaver and R. Tamborini (Eds.), *Horror films: Current research on audience preferences and reactions* (pp. 33–48). Mahwah, NJ: Lawrence Erlbaum Associates.

Sargent, J. D., Beach, M. L., Dalton, M. A., Mott, L. A., Tickle, J. J., Ahrens, M. B., et al. (2001). Effect of seeing tobacco use in films on trying smoking among adolescents: Cross sectional study. *British Medical Journal, 323,* 1394–1397.

Schachter, S., & Singer, J. E. (1962). Cognitive, social, and physiological determinants of emotional state. *Psychological Review, 69*, 379–399.

Schaefer, H. H., & Colgan, A. H. (1977). The effect of pornography on penile tumescence as a function of reinforcement and novelty. *Behavior Therapy, 8*, 938–946.

Schement, J. R., Gonzalez, I. N., Lum, P., & Valencia, R. (1984). The international flow of television programs. *Communication Research, 11*, 163–182.

Schenk-Hamlin, W. J., Procter, D. E., & Rumsey, D. J. (2000). The influence of negative advertising frames on political cynicism and politician accountability. *Human Communication Research, 26*, 53–74.

Schleuder, J., McCombs, M. E., & Wanta, W. (1991). Inside the agenda-setting process: How political advertising and TV news prime viewers to think about issues and candidates. In F. Biocca (Ed.), *Television and political advertising: Psychological processes* (Vol. 1, pp. 265–309). Hillsdale, NJ: Lawrence Erlbaum Associates.

Schlinger, M. J., & Plummer, J. (1972). Advertising in black and white. *Journal of Marketing Research, 9*, 149–153.

Schmitt, K. L., Anderson, D. R., & Collins, P. A. (1999). Form and content: Looking at visual features of television. *Developmental Psychology, 35*, 1156–1167.

Schmitt, K. L., Woolf, K. D., & Anderson, D. R. (2003). Viewing the viewers: Viewing behaviors by children and adults during television programs and commercials. *Journal of Communication, 53*, 265–281.

Schneider, A. (1998, January 9). Advising Spielberg: A career studying the *Amistad* rebellion. *The Chronicle of Higher Education*, A12.

Schneider, J. A. (1987). Networks hold the line. In A. A. Berger (Ed.), *Television in society* (pp. 163–172). New Brunswick, NJ: Transaction Books.

Schneider, K. C., & Schneider, S. B. (1979). Trends in sex roles in television commercials. *Journal of Marketing, 43*(3), 79–84.

Schneider, S. L., & Laurion, S. K. (1993). Do we know what we've learned from listening to the news? *Memory & Cognition, 21*, 198–209.

Scholfield, J., & Pavelchak, M. (1985). *The Day After:* The impact of a media event. *American Psychologist, 40*, 542–548.

School of hard knocks. (1992, October 12). *Time*, 31–32.

Schooler, C., Chaffee, S. H., Flora, J. A., & Roser, C. (1998). Health campaign channels: Tradeoffs among reach, specificity, and impact. *Human Communication Research, 24*, 410–432.

Schooler, C., Flora, J. A., & Farquhar, J. W. (1993). Moving toward synergy: Media supplementation in the Stanford five-city project. *Communication Research, 20*, 587–610.

Schooler, C., Sundar, S. S., & Flora, J. (1996). Effects of the Stanford Five-City Project Media Advocacy Program. *Health Education Quarterly, 23*(3), 346–364.

Schulkind, M. D., Hennis, L. K., & Rubin, D. C. (1999). Music, emotion, and autobiographical memory: They're playing your song. *Memory & Cognition, 27*, 948–955.

Schuman, H., & Presser, S. (1981). *Questions and answers in attitude surveys: Experiments on question form, wording, and context.* New York: Academic Press.

Schumann, D. W., Petty, R. E., & Clemons, D. S. (1990). Predicting the effectiveness of different strategies of advertising variation: A test of the repetition-variation hypotheses. *Journal of Consumer Research, 17*, 192–202.

Schumann, D. W., & Thorson, E. (Eds.) (1999). *Advertising and the World Wide Web.* Mahwah, NJ: Lawrence Erlbaum Associates.

Schwarz, N., & Brand, J. F. (1983). Effects of salience of rape on sex role attitudes, trust, and self-esteem in non-raped women. *European Journal of Social Psychology, 13,* 71–76.

Seefeldt, C. (1977). Young and old together. *Children Today, 6*(1), 22.

Seggar, J. F., Hafen, J., & Hannonen-Gladden, H. (1981). Television's portrayal of minorities and women in drama and comedy drama, 1971–1980. *Journal of Broadcasting, 25*(3), 277–288.

Seifart, H. (1984). Sport and economy: The commercialization of Olympic sport by the media. *International Review for the Sociology of Sport, 19,* 305–315.

Selnow, G. W. (1997). *Electronic whistle-stops: The impact of the Internet on American politics.* New York: Praeger.

Shaheen, J. G. (1984). *The TV Arab.* Bowling Green, OH: Bowling Green State University Popular Press.

Shaheen, J. G. (1992). The Arab stereotype: A villain without a human face. *Extra!, 5*(5), 26.

Shaheen, J. G. (1997). *Arab and Muslim stereotyping in American popular culture.* Washington, DC: Georgetown University Center for Muslim-Christian Understanding.

Shaheen, J. G. (2001). *Reel bad Arabs: How Hollywood vilifies a people.* New York: Olive Branch Press.

Shain, R., & Phillips, J. (1991). The stigma of mental illness: Labeling and stereotyping in the news. In L. Wilkins & P. Patterson (Eds.), *Risky business: Communicating issues of science, risk, and public policy* (pp. 61–74). Westport, CT: Greenwood Press.

Shanahan, J., & McComas, K. (1999). *Nature stories.* Cresskill, NJ: Hampton Press.

Shanahan, J., Morgan, M., & Stenbjerre, M. (1997). Green or brown? Television's cultivation of environmental concern. *Journal of Broadcasting & Electronic Media, 41*(3), 305–323.

Shanteau, J. (1988). Consumer impression formation: The integration of visual and verbal information. In S. Hecker & D. W. Stewart (Eds.), *Nonverbal communication in advertising* (pp. 43–57). Lexington, MA: Lexington.

Shanteau, J., & Harris, R. J. (Eds.). (1990). *Organ donation and transplantation: Psychological and behavioral factors.* Washington, DC: American Psychological Association.

Shapiro, M. A. (1991). Memory and decision processes in the construction of social reality. *Communication Research, 18,* 3–24.

Shapiro, M. A., & Chock, T. M. (2003). Psychological processes in perceiving reality. *Media Psychology, 5,* 163–198.

Sheikh, A. A., Prasad, V. K., & Rao, T. R. (1974). Children's TV commercials: A review of research. *Journal of Communication, 24*(4), 126–136.

Sherman, B. L., & Dominick, J. R. (1986). Violence and sex in music videos: TV and rock 'n' roll. *Journal of Communication, 36*(1), 79–93.

Sherry, J. L. (2001). The effects of violent video games on aggression: A meta-analysis. *Human Communication Research, 27,* 409–431.

Sherry, J. L. (2002). Media saturation and entertainment-education. *Communication Theory, 12*, 206–224.

Shimp, T. A., & Gresham, L. G. (1983). An information-processing perspective on recent advertising literature. *Current Issues and Research in Advertising, 5*, 39–75.

Shoemaker, P. J., Chang, T., & Brendlinger, N. (1987). Deviance as a predictor of newsworthiness: Coverage of international events in U.S. media. *Communication Yearbook, 10*, 348–365.

Shoemaker, P. J., Danielian, L. H., & Brendlinger, N. (1987). Deviant acts, risky business, and U.S. interests: The newsworthiness or world events. *Journalism Quarterly, 68*, 781–795.

Shrum, L. J. (2001). Processing strategy moderates the cultivation effect. *Human communication Research, 27*, 94–120.

Shrum, L. J. (2002). Media consumption and perceptions of social reality: Effects and underlying processes. In J. Bryant & D. Zillmann (Eds.), *Media effects: Advances in theory and research* (2nd ed., pp. 69–95). Mahwah, NJ: Lawrence Erlbaum Associates.

Shrum, L. J., & Bischak, V. D. (2001). Mainstreaming, resonance, and impersonal impact: Testing moderators of the cultivation effect for estimates of crime risk. *Human communication Research, 27*, 187–215.

Siegel, A. N. (1956). Film-mediated fantasy aggression and strength of aggressive drive. *Child Development, 27*, 365–378.

Sigesmund, B. J. (2003, July 3). XXX-ceptable. Retrieved July 3, 2003 from www.msnbc.com/m/pt/printthis_main.asp?storyID-934252

Signorielli, N. (1989). The stigma of mental illness on television. *Journal of Broadcasting and Electronic Media, 33*, 325–331.

Signorielli, N. (1990). Television's mean and dangerous world: A continuation of the Cultural Indicators perspective. In N. Signorielli & M. Morgan (Eds.), *Cultivation analysis: New directions in media effects research* (pp. 85–106). Newbury Park, CA: Sage.

Signorielli, N. (1993). Television, the portrayal of women, and children's attitudes. In G. L. Berry & J. K. Asamen (Eds.), Children & television: Images in a changing sociocultural world (pp. 229–242). Newbury Park, CA: Sage.

Signorielli, N. (2001). Television's gender role images and contribution to stereotyping. In D. G. Singer & J. L. Singer (Eds.), *Handbook of children and the media* (pp. 341–358). Thousand Oaks, CA: Sage.

Signorielli, N., & Morgan, M. (Eds.). (1990). *Cultivation analysis: New directions in media effects research*. Newbury Park, CA: Sage.

Signorielli, N., & Morgan, M. (2001). Television and the family: The cultivation perspective. In J. Bryant & J. A. Bryant. *Television and the American family* (2nd ed., pp. 333–351). Mahwah, NJ: Lawrence Erlbaum Associates.

Silk, M. (1995). *Unsecular media: Making news of religion in America*. Urbana, IL: University of Illinois Press.

Simmons, R. (2002). *Odd girl out: The hidden culture of aggression in girls*. New York: Harcourt.

Simon, R. J., & Fejes, F. (1987). Real police on television supercops. In A. A. Berger (Ed.), *Television in society* (pp. 63–69). New Brunswick, NJ: Transaction Books.

Simons, R. F., Detenber, B. H., Cuthbert, B. N., Schwartz, D. D., & Reiss, J. E. (2003). Attention to television: Alpha power and its relationship to image motion and emotional content. *Media Psychology, 5*, 283–301.

Singer, D. G., & Singer, J. L. (1983). Learning how to be intelligent consumers of television. In M. J. A. Howe (Ed.), *Learning from television: Psychological and educational research* (pp. 203–222). London: Academic Press.

Singer, D. G., & Singer, J. L. (1998). Developing critical viewing skills and media literacy in children. *The Annals of the American Academy of Political and Social Science, 557*, 164–179.

Singer, D. G., Singer, J. L., & Zuckerman, D. M. (1981). *Getting the most out of TV.* Santa Monica, CA: Goodyear.

Singer, D. G., Zuckerman, D. M., & Singer, J. L. (1980). Helping elementary school children learn about TV. *Journal of Communication, 30*(3), 84–93.

Singer, J. L., & Singer, D. G. (1976). Can TV stimulate imaginative play? *Journal of Communication, 26*, 74–80.

Singer, J. L., & Singer, D. G. (1981). *Television, imagination, and aggression: A study of preschoolers.* Hillsdale, NJ: Lawrence Erlbaum Associates.

Singer, J. L., & Singer, D. G. (1998). *Barney & Friends* as entertainment and education. In J. K. Asamen & G. Berry (Eds.), *Research paradigms, television, and social behavior* (pp. 305–367). Thousand Oaks, CA: Sage.

Singer, M. (1984). Inferences in reading comprehension. In M. Daneman & P. A. Carpenter (Eds.), *Reading research: Advances in theory and practice* (Vol. 6). New York: Academic Press.

Singer, M. I., Slovak, K., Frierson, T., & York, P. (1998). Viewing preferences, symptoms of psychological trauma, and violent behaviors among children who watch television. *Journal of the American Academy of Child and Adolescent Psychiatry, 37*(10), 1041–1048.

Singhal, A., & Rogers, E. M. (1989a). Prosocial television for development in India. In R. E. Rice & C. Atkin (Eds.), *Public communication campaigns* (2nd ed., pp. 331–350). Newbury Park, CA: Sage.

Singhal, A., & Rogers, E. M. (1989b). Entertainment-education strategies for family planning. *Populi, 16*(2), 38–47.

Singhal, A., & Rogers, E. M. (1989c). *India's information revolution.* New Delhi: Sage.

Singhal, A., & Rogers, E. M. (1999). *Entertainment-Education: A communication strategy for social change.* Mahwah, NJ: Lawrence Erlbaum Associates.

Singhal, A., & Rogers, E. M. (2002). A theoretical agenda for entertainment-education. *Communication Theory, 12*, 117–135.

Sintchak, G., & Geer, J. (1975). A vaginal plethysymograph system. *Psychophysiology, 12*, 113–115.

Skill, T. (1994). Family images and family actions as presented in the media: Where we've been and what we've found. In D. Zillmann, J. Bryant, & A. Huston (Eds.), *Media, children, and the family: Social scientific, psychodynamic, and clinical perspectives.* (pp. 37–50). Hillsdale, NJ: Lawrence Erlbaum Associates.

Skill, T., Robinson, J., & Wallace, S. (1987). Family life on primetime television: Structure, type, and frequency. *Journalism Quarterly, 64*(2/3), 360–367, 398.

Skill, T., Lyons, J. S., & Larson, D. (1991, November). *Television and religion: Content analysis of the portrayal of spirituality in network primetime fictional programs.* Summary report to the American Family Association, Tupelo, MS.

Skill, T., & Wallace, S. (1990). Family interactions on prime-time television: A descriptive analysis of assertive power interactions. *Journal of Broadcasting and Electronic Media, 344*(3), 243–262.

Skill, T., Wallace, S., & Cassata, M. (1990). Families on prime-time television: Patterns of conflict escalation and resolution across intact, nonintact, and mixed-family settings. In J. Bryant (Ed.), *Television and the American family* (pp. 129–163). Hillsdale, NJ: Lawrence Erlbaum Associates.

Slater, D., & Elliott, W. R. (1982). Television's influence on social reality. *Quarterly Journal of Speech, 68,* 69–79.

Slater, M. D. (1990). Processing social information in messages: Social group familiarity, fiction versus nonfiction, and subsequent beliefs. *Communication Research, 17,* 327–343.

Slater, M. D. (2003). Alienation, aggression, and sensation seeking as predictor of adolescent use of violent film, computer, and website content. *Journal of Communication, 53*(1), 105–121.

Slater, M. D., & Rouner, D. (2002). Entertainment-education and elaboration likelihood: Understanding the process of narrative persuasion. *Communication Theory, 12,* 173–191.

Smith, R., Anderson, D. R., & Fischer, C. (1985). Young children's comprehension of montage. *Child Development, 56,* 962–971.

Smith, S. L., & Donnerstein, E. (1998). Harmful effects of exposure to media violence: Learning of aggression, emotional desensitization, and fear. In R. G. Geen & E. Donnerstein (Eds.), *Human aggression: Theories, research, and implications for social policy* (pp. 167–202). San Diego: Academic Press.

Smith, T. M. (1998). *The myth of green marketing: Tending our goats at the edge of apocalypse.* Toronto, Canada: University of Toronto Press.

Snyder, L., Roser, C., & Chaffee, S. (1991). Foreign media and the desire to emigrate from Belize. *Journal of Communication, 41*(1), 117–132.

Soap operas. (1981, September 28). *Newsweek,* 65.

Soley, L. (1983). The effect of black models on magazine ad readership. *Journalism Quarterly, 60*(4), 686–690.

Solomon, D. S., & Cardillo, B. A. (1985). The elements and process of communication campaigns. In T. A. van Dijk (Ed.), *Discourse and communication* (pp. 60–68). Berlin, Germany: de Gruyter.

Sommerfeld, J. (2002, September 17). Most weight-loss ads too good to be true, report shows. MSNBC online news.

Sommers-Flanagan, R., Sommers-Flanagan, J., & Davis, B. (1993) What's happening on music television? *Sex Roles, 28,* 745–753.

Sood, S. (2002). Audience involvement and entertainment-education. *Communication Theory, 12,* 153–172.

Spangler, L. C. (1989). A historical overview of female friendships in prime-time television. *Journal of Popular Culture, 22*(4), 13–23.

Spangler, L. C. (1992). Buddies and pals: A history of male friendships on prime-time television. In S. Craig (Ed.), *Men, masculinity, and the media* (pp. 93–110). Newbury Park, CA: Sage.

Sparks, G. G. (1986). Developmental differences in children's reports of fear induced by the mass media. *Child Study Journal, 16*(1), 55–66.

Sparks, G. G., Pellechia, M., & Irvine, C. (1999). The repressive coping style and fright reactions to mass media. *Communication Research, 26,* 176–192.

Sparks, G. G., & Sparks, C. W. (2000). Violence, mayhem, and horror. In D. Zillmann & P. Vorderer (Eds.), *Media entertainment: The psychology of its appeal* (pp. 73–91). Mahwah, NJ: Lawrence Erlbaum Associates.

Sparks, G. G., & Sparks, C. W. (2002). Effects of media violence. In J. Bryant & D. Zillmann (Eds.), *Media effects* (pp. 269–285). Mahwah, NJ: Lawrence Erlbaum Associates.

Spencer, J. W., Seydlitz, R., Laska, S., & Triche, E. (1992). The different influences of newspaper and television news reports of a natural hazard on response behavior. *Communication Research, 19,* 299–325.

Sperber, M. (2001). *Beer and circus: How big-time college sports is crippling undergraduate education.* New York: Henry Holt.

Sprafkin, J. N., Gadow, K. D., & Abelman, R. (1992). *Television and the exceptional child: A forgotten audience.* Hillsdale, NJ: Lawrence Erlbaum Associates.

Springwood, C. F., & King, C. R. (Eds.). (2001). *Team spirits: The Native American mascots controversy.* Lincoln, NE: University of Nebraska Press. (a)

Springwood, C. F., & King, C. R. (2001, November 1). "Playing Indian": Why Native American mascots must end. *The Chronicle of Higher Education,* B13–14.

Stall, R. D., Coates, T. J., & Hoff, C. (1988). Behavioral risk reduction for HIV infection among gay and bisexual men. *American Psychologist, 43,* 878–885.

Stanley, A. (2000, September 14). Rome journal. *New York Times.*

Stayman, D. M., & Kardes, F. R. (1992). Spontaneous inference processes in advertising: Effects of need for cognition and self-monitoring on inference generation and utilization. *Journal of Consumer Psychology, 1,* 125–142.

Stein, J. (1997a, September 22). The God squad. *Time.*

Stein, J. (1997b, December 15). Tall men behaving badly. *Time,* 91–92.

Stein, J. (1998, February 2). And they get held up again. *Time,* 79.

Stephens, N., & Stutts, M. A. (1982). Preschoolers' ability to distinguish between television programming and commercials. *Journal of Advertising, 11,* 16–26.

Stephenson, M. T. (2003). Examining adolescents' responses to antimarijuana PSAs. *Human Communication Research, 29,* 343–369.

Stewart, D. W., Pavlou, P., & Ward, S. (2002). Media influences on marketing communications. In J. Bryant & D. Zillmann (Eds.), *Media effects* (2nd ed., pp. 353–396). Mahwah, NJ: Lawrence Erlbaum Associates.

Steyer, J. P. (2002). *The other parent: The inside story of media's effect on our children.* New York: Atria Books.

Stodghill, R. (1998, June 15). Where'd you learn that? *Time,* 52–59.

Stolberg, S. G. (2001). C.D.C. injects dramas with health messages. Retrieved July 11, 2001 from www.nytimes.com/2001/06/26/health/26CDC.html

Stone, G. (1987). *Examining newspapers: What research reveals about America's newspapers.* Newbury Park, CA: Sage.

Stonehill, B. (1995, Spring). Hearts, smarts, and sparkle. *Los Angeles Times.* Reprinted in *Connect, 9,* 4.

Stout, D. A., & Buddenbaum, J. M.. (Eds.). (1996). *Religion and mass media: Audiences and adaptations*. Thousand Oaks, CA: Sage.

Strasburger, V. C. (1995). *Adolescents and the media: Medical and psychological impact*. Thousand Oaks, CA: Sage.

Strasburger, V. C., & Donnerstein, E. (1999). Children, adolescents, and the media: Issues and solutions. *Pediatrics, 103*, 129–139.

Strasburger, V. C., & Wilson, B. J. (2002). *Children, adolescents, and the media*. Thousand Oaks, CA: Sage.

Strate, L. (1992). Beer commercials: A manual on masculinity. In S. Craig (Ed.), *Men, masculinity, and the media* (pp. 78–92). Newbury Park, CA: Sage.

Straubhaar, J. D., Heeter, C., Greenberg, B. S., Ferreira, L., Wicks, R. H., & Lau, T. Y. (1992). What makes news: Western, socialist, and Third-world newscasts compared in eight countries. In F. Korzenny & S. Ting-Toomey (Eds.), *Mass media effects across cultures* (pp. 89–109). Newbury Park, CA: Sage.

Strayer, D., Drews. F. A., & Johnston. W. A. (2004). Distracted while driving. In R. Walker (Ed.). *Cognitive psychology: Transforming thought and society*. Jefferson, NC: McFarland.

Strobel, W. P. (1997). *Late-breaking foreign policy: The news media's influence on peace operations*. Washington, DC: Institute of Peace Press.

Strouse, J. A., & Fabes, R. A. (1985). Formal vs. informal sources of sex education: Competing forces in the sexual socialization process. *Adolescence, 78*, 251–263.

Stutts, M. A., & Hunnicutt, G. G. (1987). Can young children understand disclaimers in television commercials? *Journal of Advertising, 16*(1), 41–46.

Stutts, M. A., Vance, D., & Hudelson, S. (1981). Program-commercial separators in children's television: Do they help a child tell the difference between *Bugs Bunny* and *The Quik Rabbit? Journal of Advertising, 10*(2), 16–48.

Subervi-Velez, F. A., & Colsant, S. (1993). The television worlds of Latino children. In G. L. Berry & J. K. Asamen (Eds.), *Children & television*. (pp. 215-228). Newbury Park, CA: Sage.

Suggs, W. (1999, May 14). A color line on the gridiron? *The Chronicle of Higher Education*, A49–50.

Suleiman, M. W. (1988). *The Arabs in the mind of America*. Brattleboro, VT: Amana Books.

Sullivan, B. (2003, August 6). Has the spam dam really burst? Msnbc.com.

Suls, J. M. (1983). Cognitive processes in humor appreciation. In P. E. McGhee & J. H. Goldstein (Eds.), *Handbook of humor research: Basic issues* (Vol. 1, pp. 39–57). New York: Springer-Verlag.

Sundar, S. S. & Wagner, C. B. (2002). The world wide wait: Exploring physiological and behavioral effects of download speed. *Media Psychology, 4*, 173–206.

Surlin, S. H. (1974). Bigotry on air and in life: The Archie Bunker case. *Public Telecommunications Review, 212*, 34–41.

Sutton, M. J., Brown, J. D., Wilson, K. M., & Klein, J. D. (2002). Shaking the tree of knowledge for forbidden fruit: Where adolescents learn about sexuality and contraception. In J. D. Brown, J. R. Steele, & K. Walsh-Childers (Eds.), *Sexual teens, sexual media* (pp. 25–55). Mahwah, NJ: Lawrence Erlbaum Associates.

Sypher, B. D., McKinley, M., Ventsam, S., & Valdeavellano, E. E. (2002). Fostering reproductive health through entertainment-education in the Peruvian Amazon: The social construction of *Bienvenida Salud! Communication Theory, 12,* 192–205.

Tamborini, R. (1991). Responding to horror: Determinants of exposure and appeal. In J. Bryant & D. Zillmann (Eds.), *Responding to the screen: Reception and reaction processes* (pp. 305–328). Hillsdale, NJ: Lawrence Erlbaum Associates.

Tamborini, R. (1996). A model of empathy and emotional reactions to horror. In J. B. Weaver, III, and R. Tamborini (Eds.), *Horror films: Current research on audience preferences and reactions* (pp. 103–123). Mahwah, NJ: Lawrence Erlbaum Associates.

Tamborini, R., & Choi, J. (1990). The role of cultural diversity in cultivation research. In N. Signorielli & M. Morgan (Eds.), *Cultivation analysis: New directions in media effects research* (pp. 157–180). Newbury Park, CA: Sage.

Tamborini, R., & Stiff, J. (1987). Predictors of horror film attendance and appeal: An analysis of the audience for frightening films. *Communication Research, 14,* 415–436.

Tamborini, R., Stiff, J., & Heidel, C. (1990). Reacting to graphic horror: A model of empathy and emotional behavior. *Communication Research, 17,* 616–640.

Tamborini, R., Stiff, J., & Zillmann, D. (1987). Preference for graphic horror featuring male versus female victimization: Individual differences associated with personality characteristics and past film viewing experiences. *Human Communication Research, 13,* 529–552.

Tan, A. S. (1986). Social learning of aggression from television. In J. Bryant & D. Zillmann (Eds.), *Perspectives on media effects* (pp. 41–55). Hillsdale, NJ: Lawrence Erlbaum Associates.

Tannen, D. (1990). *You just don't understand: Women and men in conversation.* New York: Ballantine Books.

Tannen, D. (1994). *Talking 9 to 5: Women and men in the workplace: Language, sex and power.* New York: Avon Books.

Tannen, D. (1998). *The argument culture: Stopping America's war of words.* New York: Ballantine Books.

Tannenbaum, P. H. (1971). *Emotional arousal as a mediator of communication effects* (Technical reports of the Commission on Obscenity and Pornography, Vol. 8). Washington, DC: U.S. Government Printing Office.

Tannenbaum, P. H. (1980). Entertainment as vicarious emotional experience. In P. H. Tannenbaum (Ed.), *The entertainment functions of television* (pp. 107–131). Hillsdale, NJ: Lawrence Erlbaum Associates.

Tapper, J. (1995). The ecology of cultivation: A conceptual model for cultivation research. *Communication Theory, 5,* 36–57.

Tarpley, T. (2001). Children, the Internet, and other new technologies. In D. G. Singer & J. L. Singer (Eds.), *Handbook of Children and the Media* (pp. 547–556). Thousand Oaks, CA: Sage.

Taruskin, R. (2001, Dec. 10). Music's dangers and the case for control. *New York Times,* www.nytimes.com/2001/12/09/arts/music.09TARU,html? ex= 1009010548&ei=1&en=268782b4008ae6a6

Tate, E., & Surlin, S. (1976). Agreement with opinionated TV characters across culture. *Journalism Quarterly, 53*(2), 199–203.

Tavris, C. (1986). How to publicize science: A case study. In J. H. Goldstein (Ed.), *Reporting science: The case of aggression* (pp. 23–32). Hillsdale, NJ: Lawrence Erlbaum Associates.

Tavris, C. (1988). Beyond cartoon killings: Comments on two overlooked effects of television. In S. Oskamp (Ed.), *Television as a social issue* (pp. 189–197). Newbury Park, CA: Sage.

Taylor, C. (2003, June 16). Spam's big bang! *Time*, 50–53.

Taylor, C. R., Lee, J. Y., & Stern, B. B. (1995). Portrayals of African, Hispanic, and Asian Americans in magazine advertising. *American Behavioral Scientist, 38*, 608–621.

Taylor, P. (2000, Nov-Dec). The new political theater. *Mother Jones*, 30–33.

Taylor, S. (1982). The availability bias in social perception and interaction. In D. Kahneman, P. Slovic, & A. Tversky (Eds.), *Judgment under uncertainty: Heuristics and biases* (pp. 190–200). Cambridge, England: Cambridge University Press.

Teplin, L. A. (1985). The criminality of the mentally ill: A dangerous misconception. *American Journal of Psychiatry, 142*, 593–599.

Tewksbury, D. (1999). Differences in how we watch the news. *Communication Research, 26*, 4–29.

Tewksbury, D. (2003). What do Americans really want to know? Tracking the behavior of news readers on the Internet. *Journal of Communication, 53*(4), 694–710.

Thaler, P. (1994). *The watchful eye: American justice in the age of the television trial.* New York: Praeger.

The Faustian bargain (1997, Sept. 6). *The Economist.* Reprinted in *World Press Review,* Nov., 1997, pp. 12–13.

Thomas, B. (2003, January). What the world's poor watch on TV. *Prospect.* Reprinted in *World Press Review,* March 2003, 30–33.

Thomas, S. (1986). Gender and social-class coding in popular photographic erotica. *Communication Quarterly, 34*(2), 103–114.

Thompson, T. L., & Zerbinos, E. (1995). Gender roles in animated cartoons: Has the picture changed in 20 years? *Sex Roles, 32*, 651–673.

Thomsen, S. R., McCoy, J. K, Gustafson, R. L., & Williams, M. (2002). Motivations for reading beauty and fashion magazines and anorexic risk in college-age women. *Media Psychology, 4*, 113–135.

Thorndyke, P. W. (1984). Applications of schema theory in cognitive research. In J. R. Anderson & S. M. Kosslyn (Eds.), *Tutorials in learning and memory* (pp. 167–192). San Francisco: Freeman.

Thorson, E. (1990). Consumer processing of advertising. *Current Issues and Research in Advertising, 12*, 197–230.

Thorson, E. (1994). Using eyes on screen as a measure of attention to television. In A. Lang (Ed.), *Measuring psychological responses to media* (pp. 65–84). Hillsdale, NJ: Lawrence Erlbaum Associates.

Thorson, E., Christ, W. G., & Caywood, C. (1991). Selling candidates like tubes of toothpaste: Is the comparison apt? In F. Biocca (Ed.), *Television and political advertising: Psychological processes* (Vol. 1, pp. 145–172). Hillsdale, NJ: Lawrence Erlbaum Associates.

Tickle, J. J., Sargent, J. D., Dalton, M. A., Beach, M. L., & Heatherton, T. F. (2001). Favourite movie stars, their tobacco use in contemporary movies, and its association with adolescent smoking. *Tobacco Control, 10,* 16–22.

Tinic, S. (1997). United Colors and untied meanings: Benetton and the commodification of social issues. *Journal of Communication, 47*(3), 3–25.

Tinsley, H. E. A., & Weiss, D. J. (2000). Interrater reliability and agreement. In H. E. A. Tinsley & S. D. Brown (Eds.), *Handbook of applied multivariate statistics and mathematical modeling.* (pp. 95–124). San Diego, CA: Academic Press.

Toney, G. T., & Weaver, J. B. (1994) Effects of gender and gender role self-perceptions on affective reactions to rock music videos. *Sex Roles, 30,* 567–583.

Took, K. J., & Weiss, D. S. (1994). The relationship between heavy metal and rap music and adolescent turmoil: Real or artifact? *Adolescence, 29,* 613–621.

Toplin, R. B. (1995). *History by Hollywood: The use and abuse of the American past.* Urbana, IL: University of Illinois Press.

Tower, R. B., Singer, D. G., & Singer, J. L. (1979). Differential effects of television programming on preschoolers' cognition, imagination, and social play. *American Journal of Orthopsychiatry, 49,* 265–281.

Trevino, L. K., & Webster, J. (1992). Flow in computer-mediated communication: Electronic mail and voice mail evaluation and impacts. *Communication Research, 19,* 539–573.

Tuchman, G. (1978). *Making news: A study in the construction of reality.* New York: Free Press.

Tuchman, G. (1987). Mass media values. In A. A. Berger (Ed.), *Television in society* (pp. 195–202). New Brunswick, NJ: Transaction Books.

Tuchman, S., & Coffin, T. E. (1971). The influence of election nights television broadcasts in a close election. *Public Opinion Quarterly, 35,* 315–326.

Tulloch, J., Kippax, S., & Crawford, J. (1993). *Television, sexuality, and AIDS.* Sydney, Australia: Allen & Unwin.

Tunstall, J. (1977). *The media are American.* New York: Columbia University Press.

Tversky, A., & Kahneman, D. (1973). Availability: A heuristic for judging frequency and probability. *Cognitive Psychology, 5,* 207–232.

Tversky, A., & Kahneman, D. (1974). Judgment under uncertainty: Heuristics and biases. *Science, 185,* 1124–1131.

Tye, J. B., Warner, K. E., & Glantz, S. A. (1987, Winter). Tobacco advertising and consumption: Evidence of a causal relationship. *Journal of Public Health Policy,* pp. 492–508.

Ume-Nwagbo, E. N. E. (1986). "Cock Crow at Dawn": A Nigerian experiment with television drama in development communication. *Gazette, 37*(4), 155–167.

U.S. Commission on Obscenity and Pornography. (1970). *The report of the Commission on Obscenity and Pornography.* New York: Bantam.

Vaid, J. (1999). The evolution of humor: Do those who laugh last? In D. H. Rosen & M. C. Luebbert (Eds.), *Evolution of the psyche: Human evolution, behavior, and intelligence* (pp. 123–138). Westport, CT: Praeger Publishers.

Valente, J. (1997, March 2). Do you believe what newspeople tell you? *Parade,* 4–6.

Valkenburg, P. M. (2001). Television and the child's developing imagination. In

D. G. & J. L. Singer (Eds.), *Handbook of children and the media* (pp. 121–134). Thousand Oaks, CA: Sage.

Valkenburg, P. M. & Beentjes, J. W. J. (1997). Children's creative imagination in response to radio and television stories. *Journal of Communication, 47*(2), 21–38.

Valkenburg, P. M., & Cantor, J. (2001). The development of a child into a consumer. *Journal of Applied Developmental Psychology, 22,* 61–72.

Valkenburg, P. M., & Janssen, S. C. (1999). Who do children value in entertainment programs? A cross-cultural investigation. *Journal of Communication, 49*(2), 3–21.

Valkenburg, P. M., & van der Voort, T. H. A. (1994). Influence of TV on daydreaming and creative imagination: A review of research. *Psychological Bulletin, 116,* 316–339.

van der Voort, T. H. A. (1986). *Television violence: A child's eye view.* Amsterdam: North-Holland.

van der Voort, T. H. A., & Valkenburg, P. M. (1994). Television's impact on fantasy play: A review of research. *Developmental review, 14,* 27–51.

Van Evra, J. P. (1997). *Television and child development.* (2nd ed.). Mahwah, NJ: Lawrence Erlbaum Associates.

Vidmar, N., & Rokeach, M. (1974). Archie Bunker's bigotry: A study in selective perception and exposure. *Journal of Communication, 24*(1), 35–47.

Vincent, I. (1996, June 11). Rebel dispatches on the Net. *World Press Review, 43,* 23–24.

Vincent, R. C., Davis, D. K., & Boruszkowski, L. A. (1987). Sexism on MTV: The portrayal of women in rock videos. *Journalism Quarterly, 64*(4), 750–755.

Vokey, J. R., & Read, J. D. (1985). Subliminal messages: Between the devil and the media. *American Psychologist, 40,* 1231–1239.

Volgy, T. J., & Schwarz, J. E. (1980). TV entertainment programming and sociopolitical attitudes. *Journalism Quarterly, 57,* 150–155.

von Feilitzen, C., Strand, H., Nowak, K., & Andren, G. (1989). To be or not to be in the TV world: Ontological and methodological aspects of content analysis. *European Journal of Communication, 4,* 11–32.

Vorderer, P., & Knobloch, S. (2000). Conflict and suspense in drama. In D. Zillmann & P. Vorderer (Eds.), *Media entertainment: The psychology of its appeal* (pp. 59–72). Mahwah, NJ: Lawrence Erlbaum Associates.

Vorderer, P. Wulff, H. J., & Friedrichsen, M. (Eds.). (1996). *Suspense: Conceptualizations, theoretical analyses, and empirical explorations.* Mahwah, NJ: Lawrence Erlbaum Associates.

Wahl, O. F. (1995). *Media madness: Public images of mental illness.* New Brunswick, NJ: Rutgers University Press.

Walker, J. R., & Bellamy, R. V., Jr. (2001). Remote control devices and family viewing. In J. Bryant & J. A. Bryant. *Television and the American family* (2nd ed., pp. 75–89). Mahwah, NJ: Lawrence Erlbaum Associates.

Walker, M., Langemeyer, L., & Langemeyer, D. (1992). Celebrity endorsers: Do you get what you pay for? *Journal of Consumer Marketing, 9,* 69–76.

Wallack, L. (1990). Improving health promotion: Media advocacy and social marketing approaches. In C. Atkin & L. Wallack (Eds.), *Mass communication and public health* (pp. 147–163). Newbury Park, CA: Sage.

Wallack, L., Dorfman, L., Jernigan, D., & Themba, M. (1993). *Media advocacy and public health.* Newbury Park, CA: Sage.

Walma van der Molen, J. H., & van der Voort, T. H. A. (2000). The impact of television, print, and audio on children's recall of the news. *Human Communication Research, 26,* 3–26.

Walsh-Childers, K., Gotthoffer, A., & Lepre, C. R. (2002). From "just the facts" to "downright salacious": Teens' and women's magazines coverage of sex and sexual health. In J. D. Brown, J. R. Steele, & K. Walsh-Childers (Eds.), *Sexual teens, sexual media* (pp. 153–171). Mahwah, NJ: Lawrence Erlbaum Associates.

Walters, R. H., & Willows, D. C. (1968). Imitative behavior of disturbed and nondisturbed children following exposure to aggressive and nonaggressive models. *Child Development, 39,* 79–89.

Wanta, W. (1997). *The public and the national agenda: How people learn about important issues.* Mahwah, NJ: Lawrence Erlbaum Associates.

Ward, S., Wackman, D., & Wartella, E. (1977). *How children learn to buy: The development of consumer information-processing skills.* Beverly Hills, CA: Sage.

Wartella, E. (1980). Individual differences in children's responses to television advertising. In E. L. Palmer & A. Dorr (Eds.), *Children and the faces of television: Teaching, violence, and selling* (pp. 307–322). New York: Academic Press.

Wartella, E., Heintz, K. E., Aidman, A. J., & Mazzarella, S. R. (1990). Television and beyond: Children's video media in one community. *Communication Research, 17,* 45–64.

Wartella, E., & Jennings, N. (2001). Hazards and possibilities of commercial TV in the schools. In D. G. Singer & J. L. Singer (Eds.), *Handbook of children and the media* (pp. 557–570). Thousand Oaks, CA: Sage.

Watkins, B. (1988). Children's representations of television and real-life stories. *Communication Research, 15,* 159–184.

Watt, J. H., Mazza, M., & Snyder, L. (1993). Agenda-setting effects of television news coverage and the effects delay curve. *Communication Research, 20,* 408–435.

Weaver, J. (2002, August 21). Is this an ad or what? Http://msnbc.com/news/796647.asp

Weaver, J. (2003a). A hot 'hispanicized' consumer market. Retrieved May 14, 2003 from www.msnbc.com/news/912895.asp?0cv=CB20

Weaver, J. (2003, July 7b). College students are avid gamers. Retrieved July 18, 2003 from Msnbc.com.

Weaver, J. (2003, July 24c). Teens tune out TV, log on instead. Retrieved July 25, 2003 from Msnbc.com.

Weaver, J. B. III. (1991). Responding to erotica: Perceptual processes and dispositional implications. In J. Bryant & D. Zillmann (Eds.), *Responding to the screen* (pp. 329–354). Hillsdale, NJ: Lawrence Erlbaum Associates.

Weaver, J. B. III, Masland, J. L., & Zillmann, D. (1984). Effects of erotica on young men's aesthetic perception of their female sexual partners. *Perceptual and Motor Skills, 58,* 929–930.

Weaver, J. B. III, & Tamborini, R. (Eds.). (1996). *Horror films: Current research on audience preferences and reactions.* Mahwah, NJ: Lawrence Erlbaum Associates.

Weaver, J. B. III, & Wakshlag, J. (1986). Perceived vulnerability to crime, criminal victimization experience, and television viewing. *Journal of Broadcasting & Electronic Media, 30,* 141–158.

Webster, J. G., & Wakshlag, J. (1985). Measuring exposure to television. In D. Zillmann & J. Bryant (Eds.), *Selective exposure to communication* (pp. 35–62). Hillsdale, NJ: Lawrence Erlbaum Associates.

Weigel, R. H., Loomis, J., & Soja, M. (1980). Race relations on prime time television. *Journal of Personality and Social Psychology, 39*(5), 884–893.

Weimann, G., & Brosius, H.-B. (1991). The newsworthiness of international terrorism. *Communication Research, 18,* 333–354.

Weiss, A. J., & Wilson, B. J. (1998). Children's cognitive and emotional responses to the portrayal of negative emotions in family-formatted situation comedies. *Human Communication Research, 24,* 584–609.

Weisz, M. G., & Earls, C. M. (1995). The effects of exposure to filmed sexual violence on attitudes toward rape. *Journal of Interpersonal Violence, 10,* 71–84.

Wenner, L. A. (1989). The Super Bowl pregame show: Cultural fantasies and political subtext. In L. A. Wenner (Ed.), *Media, sports, & society* (pp. 157–179). Newbury Park, CA: Sage.

Wenner, L. A., & Gantz, W. (1998). Watching sports on television: Audience experience, gender, fanship, and marriage. In L. A. Wenner (Ed.), *MediaSport* (pp. 233–251). New York: Routledge.

Wenner, L. A., & Gantz, W. (1989). The audience experience with sports on television. In L. A. Wenner (Ed.), *Media, sports, & society* (pp. 241–269). Newbury Park, CA: Sage.

Wernick, R. (1996, August). Let's hear it for the lowly sound bite! *Smithsonian, 27*(5), 62–65.

Weston, M. A. (1996). *Native Americans in the news: Images of Indians in the twentieth century press.* Westport, CT: Greenwood.

Weymouth, L. (1981, January-February). Walter Cronkite remembers. *Washington Journalism Review,* p. 23.

Whannel, G. (1992). *Fields in vision: Television sport and cultural transformation.* London: Routledge.

What's so funny? (1997, December 20). *The Economist.* Reprinted in *World Press Review,* March 1998, 18–19.

What's up, doc? (1995, February 5). *Manhattan Mercury,* A7.

Wheeler, D. L. (2001, January 5). Embracing technology and spirituality, at the top of the world. *The Chronicle of Higher Education,* A64.

Wheeler, T. H. (2002). *Phototruth or photofiction? Ethics and media imagery in the digital age.* Mahwah, NJ: Lawrence Erlbaum Associates.

Whillock, R. K. (1997). Cyber-politics: The on-line strategies of '96. *American Behavioral Scientist, 40,* 1208–1225.

White, L. A. (1979). Erotica and aggression: The influence of sexual arousal, positive affect, and negative affect on aggressive behavior. *Journal of Personality and Social Psychology, 37,* 591–601.

Wicks, R. H. (2001). *Understanding audiences: Learning to use the media constructively.* Mahwah, NJ: Erlbaum.

Wilcox, B. L. (1987). Pornography, social science, and politics: When research and ideology collide. *American Psychologist, 42,* 941–943.

Wilhoit, G. C., & de Bock, H. (1976). "All in the Family" in Holland. *Journal of Communication, 26*(1), 75–84.

Will, E. (1987). Women in media. *The Other Side, 23*(4), 44–46.

Williams, B. (1979, November). *Report of the Departmental Committee on Obscenity and Film Censorship.* London: Her Majesty's Stationery Office. Command 7772.

Williams, B. A., & Delli Carpini, M. X. (2002, April 19). Heeeeeeere's democracy! *The Chronicle of Higher Education,* B14–B15.

Williams, F., Strover, S., & Grant, A. E. (1994). Social aspects of new media technologies. In J. Bryant & D. Zillmann (Eds.), *Media effects: Advances in theory and research* (pp. 463–482). Hillsdale, NJ: Lawrence Erlbaum Associates.

Williams, T. M. (Ed.). (1986). *The impact of television.* Orlando, FL: Academic Press.

Willwerth, J. (1993, February 15). It hurts like crazy. *Time,* 53.

Wilson, B. J. (1987). Reducing children's emotional reactions to mass media through rehearsed explanation and exposure to a replica of a fear object. *Human Communication Research, 14,* 3–26.

Wilson, B. J. (1989). Desensitizing children's emotional reactions to the mass media. *Communication Research, 16,* 723–745.

Wilson, B. J. (1991). Children's reactions to dreams conveyed in mass media programming. *Communication Research, 18,* 283–305.

Wilson, B. J., & Cantor, J. (1987). Reducing fear reactions to mass media: Effects of visual exposure and verbal explanation. In M. McLaughlin (Ed.), *Communication yearbook 10* (pp. 553–573). Newbury Park, CA: Sage.

Wilson, B. J., Colvin, C. M., & Smith, S. L. (2002). Engaging in violence on American television: A comparison of child, teen, and adult perpetrators. *Journal of Communication, 52*(1), 36–60.

Wilson, B. J., Hoffner, C., & Cantor, J. (1987). Children's perceptions of the effectiveness of techniques to reduce fear from mass media. *Journal of Applied Developmental Psychology, 8,* 39–52.

Wilson, B. J., Linz, D., Donnerstein, E., & Stipp, H. (1992). The impact of social issue television programming on attitudes toward rape. *Human Communication Research, 19,* 179–208.

Wilson, B. J., Smith, S. L., Potter, W. J., Kunkel, D., Linz, D., Colvin, C. M., et al. (2002). Violence in children's television programming: Assessing the risks. *Journal of Communication, 52*(1), 5–35.

Wilson, B. J., & Weiss, A. J. (1992). Developmental differences in children's reactions to a toy advertisement linked to a toy-based cartoon. *Journal of Broadcasting & Electronic Media, 36,* 371–394.

Wilson, B. J., & Weiss, A. J. (1993). The effects of sibling coviewing on preschoolers' reactions to a suspenseful movie sequence. *Communication Research, 20,* 214–248.

Wilson, C. C. II., & Gutierrez, F. (1995). *Race, multiculturalism, and the media: From mass to class communication.* Thousand Oaks, CA: Sage.

Wilson, J. R., & Wilson, S. L. R. (1998). *Mass media/Mass culture* (4th ed.). New York: McGraw-Hill.

Wilson, S. N. (2000). Raising the voices of teens to change sex education. *SIECUS Report, 28*(6), 20–24.

Wilson, W. (1999). *The psychopath in film*. Washington, D.C.: University Press of America.

Windahl, S. (1981). Uses and gratifications at the crossroads. In G. C. Wilhoit & H. de Bock (Eds.), *Mass communication review yearbook* (Vol. 2, pp. 174–185). Newbury Park, CA: Sage.

Winn, M. (1977). *The plug-in drug: Television, children, and the family*. New York: Viking Penguin.

Winn, M. (1987). *Unplugging the plug-in drug*. New York: Penguin Books.

Witte, K. (1992). Preventing AIDS through persuasive communications. In F. Korzenny & S. Ting-Toomey (Eds.), *Mass media effects across cultures* (pp. 67–86). Newbury Park, CA: Sage.

Wittebols, J. H. (1991). The politics and coverage of terrorism: From media images to public consciousness. *Communication Theory, 1*, 253–266.

Wober, J. M. (1978). Televised violence and paranoid perception: The view from Great Britain. *Public Opinion Quarterly, 42*, 315–321.

Wober, J. M. (1986). The lens of television and the prism of personality. In J. Bryant & D. Zillmann (Eds.), *Perspectives on media effects* (pp. 205–231). Hillsdale, NJ: Lawrence Erlbaum Associates.

Wober, J. M., & Gunter, B. (1986). Television audience research at Britain's Independent Broadcasting Authority, 1974–1984. *Journal of Broadcasting & Electronic Media, 30*, 15–31.

Wood, J. M., & Duke, N. K. (1997). Inside *Reading Rainbow*: A spectrum of strategies for promoting literacy. *Language Arts, 74*, 95–106.

Wood, W., Wong, F. Y., & Chachere, J. G. (1991). Effects of media violence on viewers' aggression in unconstrained social interaction. *Psychological Bulletin, 109*, 371–383.

Wresch, W. (1996). *Disconnected: Haves and have-nots in the information age*. New Brunswick, NJ: Rutgers University Press.

Wright, C. R. (1986). *Mass communication: A sociological perspective* (3rd ed.). New York: Random House.

Wright, J. C., Kunkel, D., Pinon, M., & Huston, A. C. (1989). How children reacted to televised coverage of the space shuttle disaster. *Journal of Communication, 39*(2), 27–45.

Wright, J. C., St. Peters, M., & Huston, A. C. (1990). Family television use and its relation to children's cognitive skills and social behavior. In J. Bryant (Ed.), *Television and the American family* (pp. 227–251). Hillsdale, NJ: Lawrence Erlbaum Associates.

Wroblewski, R., & Huston, A. C. (1987). Televised occupational stereotypes and their effects on early adolescence: Are they changing? *Journal of Early Adolescence, 7*, 283–297.

Wulf, S. (1996, July 29). An old sweet song. *Time*, 67–69.

Wyer, R. S., & Collins, J. E. (1992). A theory of humor elicitation. *Psychological Review, 99*, 663–688.

Yalch, R. F. (1991). Memory in a jingle jungle: Music as a mnemonic device in communicating advertising slogans. *Journal of Applied Psychology, 76*, 268–275.

Yanovitzky, I., & Bennett, C. (1999). Media attention, institutional response, and health behavior change: The case of drunk driving, 1978–1996. *Communication Research, 26,* 429–453.

Yates, E., Barbaree, H. E., & Marshall, W. L. (1984). Anger and deviant sexual arousal. *Behavior Therapy, 15,* 287–294.

Yorke, D., & Kitchen, P. (1985). Channel flickers and video speeders. *Journal of Advertising Research, 25*(2), 21–25.

Young, B. M. (1991). *Television advertising and children.* New York: Oxford University Press.

Zechmeister, E. B., & Johnson, J. E. (1992). *Critical thinking: A functional approach.* Pacific Grove, CA: Brooks-Cole.

Zelizer, B. (1992). CNN, the Gulf War, and journalistic practice. *Journal of Communication, 42*(1), 66–81.

Zhao, X., & Gantz, W. (2003). Disruptive and cooperative interruptions in prime-time television fiction: The role of gender, status, and topic. *Journal of Communication, 53,* 347–362.

Zielinska, I. E., & Chambers, B. (1995). Using group viewing of television to teach preschool children social skills. *Journal of Educational Television, 21,* 85–99.

Zill, N. (2001). Does *Sesame Street* enhance school readiness? Evidence from a national survey of children. In S. M. Fisch & R. Truglio (Eds.), *"G" is for "growing": Thirty years of research on children and* Sesame Street (pp. 115–130). Mahwah, NJ: Lawrence Erlbaum Associates.

Zillmann, D. (1978). Attribution and mis-attribution of excitatory reactions. In J. H. Harvey, W. J. Ickes, & R. F. Kidd (Eds.), *New directions in attribution research* (Vol. 2). Hillsdale, NJ: Lawrence Erlbaum Associates.

Zillmann, D. (1980). Anatomy of suspense. In P. H. Tannenbaum (Ed.), *The enter- tainment functions of television* (pp. 133–163). Hillsdale, NJ: Lawrence Erlbaum Associates.

Zillmann, D. (1983). Transfer of excitation in emotional behavior. In J. T. Cacioppo & R. E. Petty (Eds.), *Social psychophysiology* (pp. 215–240). New York: Guilford Press.

Zillmann, D. (1984). *Connections between sex and aggression.* Hillsdale, NJ: Lawrence Erlbaum Associates.

Zillmann, D. (1991a). Television viewing and physiological arousal. In J. Bryant & D. Zillmann (Eds.), *Responding to the screen: Reception and reaction processes* (pp. 103–133). Hillsdale, NJ: Lawrence Erlbaum Associates.

Zillmann, D. (1991b). Empathy: Affect from bearing witness to the emotions of others. In J. Bryant & D. Zillmann (Eds.), *Responding to the screen: Reception and reaction processes* (pp. 135–167). Hillsdale, NJ: Lawrence Erlbaum Associates.

Zillmann, D. (1991c). The logic of suspense and mystery. In J. Bryant & D. Zillmann (Eds.), *Responding to the screen: Reception and reaction processes* (pp. 281–303). Hillsdale, NJ: Lawrence Erlbaum Associates.

Zillmann, D. (1996). The psychology of suspense in dramatic exposition. In P. Vorderer, H. J. Wulff, & M. Friedrichsen (Eds.), *Suspense: Conceptualizations, the- oretical analyses, and empirical explorations* (pp. 199–231). Mahwah, NJ: Lawrence Erlbaum Associates.

Zillmann, D. (2000). Humor and comedy. In D. Zillmann & P. Vorderer (Eds.) *Media entertainment* (pp. 37–57). Mahwah, NJ: Lawrence Erlbaum Associates.

Zillmann, D. (2002). Exemplification theory of media research. In J. Bryant & D. Zillmann (Eds.), *Media effects* (2nd ed., pp. 19–42). Mahwah, NJ: Lawrence Erlbaum Associates.

Zillmann, D., & Bryant, J. (1982). Pornography, sexual callousness, and the trivialization of rape. *Journal of Communication, 32*(4), 10–21.

Zillmann, D., & Bryant, J. (1983). Selective-exposure phenomena. In D. Zillmann & J. Bryant (Eds.), *Selective exposure to communication* (pp. 1–10). Hillsdale, NJ: Lawrence Erlbaum Associates.

Zillmann, D., & Bryant, J. (1984). Effects of massive exposure to pornography. In N. M. Malamuth & E. Donnerstein (Eds.), *Pornography and sexual aggression* (pp. 115–141). Orlando, FL: Academic Press.

Zillmann, D., & Bryant, J. (1988a). Pornography's impact on sexual satisfaction. *Journal of Applied Social Psychology, 18,* 438–453.

Zillmann, D., & Bryant, J. (1988b). Effects of prolonged consumption of pornography on family values. *Journal of Family Issues, 9,* 518–544.

Zillmann, D., & Bryant, J. (1988c). A response to Linz and Donnerstein. *Journal of Communication, 38*(2), 185–192.

Zillmann, D., & Bryant, J. (Eds.). (1989). *Pornography: Research advances and policy considerations.* Hillsdale, NJ: Lawrence Erlbaum Associates.

Zillmann, D., & Bryant, J. (1991). Responding to comedy: The sense and nonsense in humor. In J. Bryant & D. Zillmann (Eds.), *Responding to the screen: Reception and reaction processes* (pp. 261–279). Hillsdale, NJ: Lawrence Erlbaum Associates.

Zillmann, D., Bryant, J., Comisky, P. W., & Medoff, N. J. (1981). Excitation and hedonic valence in the effect of erotica on motivated intermale aggression. *European Journal of Social Psychology, 11,* 233–252.

Zillmann, D., Bryant, J., & Sapolsky, B. S. (1979). The enjoyment of watching sport contests. In J. H. Goldstein (Ed.), *Sports, games, and play: Social and psychological viewpoints* (pp. 297–355). Hillsdale, NJ: Lawrence Erlbaum Associates.

Zillmann, D., & Mundorf, N. (1987). Image effects in the appreciation of video rock. *Communication Research, 14,* 316–334.

Zillmann, D., & Weaver, J. B. (1996). Gender-socialization theory of reactions to horror. In J. B. Weaver & R. Tamborini (Eds.), *Horror films: Current research on audience preferences and reactions* (pp. 81–101). Mahwah, NJ: Lawrence Erlbaum Associates.

Zillmann, D., & Weaver, J. B., III. (1997). Psychoticism in the effect of prolonged exposure to gratuitous media violence on the acceptance of violence as a preferred means of conflict resolution. *Personality and Individual Differences, 22,* 613–627.

Zillmann, D., & Weaver, J. B., III. (1999). Effects of prolonged exposure to gratuitous media violence on provoked and unprovoked hostile behavior. *Journal of Applied Social Psychology, 29,* 145–165.

Zillmann, D., Weaver, J. B., Mundorf, N., & Aust, C. F. (1986). Effects of opposite-gender companion's affect to horror on distress, delight, and attraction. *Journal of Personality and Social Psychology, 51,* 586–594.

Zinkhan, G. M., Qualls, W. J., & Biswas, A. (1990). The use of blacks in magazine and television advertising: 1946 to 1986. *Journalism Quarterly, 67*, 547–553.

Zoglin, R. (1991, March 11). It was a public relations rout too. *Time, 150*, 56–57.

Zoglin, R. (1995, January 30). Talking trash. *Time, 154*, 77–78.

Zohoori, A. R. (1988). A cross-cultural analysis of children's TV use. *Journal of Broadcasting & Electronic Media, 32*(1), 105–113.

Zuckerman, M. (1994). *Behavioral expressions and psychobiological bases of sensation seeking.* New York: Cambridge University Press.

Zuckerman, M. (1996). Sensation seeking and the taste for vicarious horror. In J. B. Weaver & R. Tamborini (Eds.), *Horror films: Current research on audience preferences and reactions* (pp. 147–160). Mahwah, NJ: Lawrence Erlbaum Associates.

Author Index

A

Abel, E., 199
Abel, G. G., 306
Abelman, R., 22, 36
Abernethy, A. M., 96
Abramson, P. R., 292, 302
Adams, M. S., 184
Adams, S. M., 309
Aday, S., 216
Adler, I., 28
Aggleton, J. P., 36
Ahn, W. K., 36
Ahrens, A. B., 143
Aidman, A. J., 292
Alali, A. O., 220
Alesandrini, K. L., 106
Alexander, A., 297
Alfini, J. J., 212
Allen, M., 26, 306, 314
Allred, E., 182
Alperstein, N., 103
Alvarado, M., 145
Alwitt, L., 251
Amaral, R., 252
Anderson, C. A., 256, 279, 281, 367
Anderson, D. R., 7, 25, 36, 40, 131, 133, 135
Anderson, J. A., 147
Anderson, P. A., 247
Anderson, P. T., 81
Anderson, R. A., 314
Anderson, R. L., 292
Andreasen, M. S., 7
Andren, G., 40
Andsager, J. L., 339

Appiah, O., 69
Appleton, H., 131
Apter, M. J., 46
Arkin, E. B., 335
Armfield, G. G., 254
Arms, R. L., 170
Armstrong, E. G., 184
Armstrong, G. B., 70
Aronson, E., 95
Ashburn, L., 184
Atkin, C., 54, 69, 80, 250, 335
Aust, C. F., 154, 268, 321
Austin, E. W., 148, 149, 339

B

Bacchetta, V., 252
Bachen, C. M., 136
Backer, T. E., 335
Baggaley, J. P., 343
Baggett, P., 126
Bald, M., 346
Ball, S., 69, 131, 132
Ballard, M. E., 183, 281
Balter, R., 83
Bancroft, J., 293
Bandura, A., 22, 27, 28, 50, 260, 263, 271, 281, 347
Banerjee, B., 114
Baran, S. J., 19
Barbaree, H. E., 292, 306
Barcus, F. E., 68
Bargh, J. A., 360
Barlow, D. H., 306

443

Barnhurst, K. G., 196
Baron, R. A., 305, 306
Bartholomew, B. D., 281
Basil, M. D., 25, 33, 250
Baskind, I., 150
Bateman, T. S., 23
Baumeister, R. F., 275, 303
Bauserman, R., 303, 314
Beach, M. L., 143
Beagles-Roos, J., 24, 126
Bechtold, J. I., 108, 112
Beeman, W. O., 197
Beentjes, J. W. J., 126, 128, 170
Belkin, L., 121
Bellafante, G., 155
Bellamy, R. V., Jr., 325
Benedict, H., 313
Bengen, B., 139
Bennett, C., 337
Bensley, L., 281
Berelson, B. R., 251
Berger, C. R., 216
Bergland, J., 106
Berkowitz, L., 264, 272, 273, 306, 312
Berry, G. L., 67
Berry, J., 212, 256
Best, V. T., 62
Bever, T. G., 139
Bickham, D. S., 36
Biely, E., 290, 295
Billings, A. C., 173
Biocca, F. A., 64, 250
Bird, S. E., 72
Birnbaum, D. W., 126
Bischak, V. D., 28, 29
Bischoff, R. J., 88
Biswas, A., 67
Bjerklie, D. M., 114, 317
Blain, N., 175
Blanchard, E. B., 306
Blatt, J., 139
Block, C., 67
Blumler, J. G., 31, 250, 354
Blut, D., 311
Bocarnea, M. C., 33
Bogart, L., 2, 11, 200
Bogatz, G. A., 69, 131, 132
Bogle, D., 67
Boiney, J., 251
Bollen, K. A., 217
Bolls, P. D., 25, 39, 102, 106, 148

Bonds-Raacke, J. M., 80, 167, 349
Bordeaux, B. R., 125
Borden, D. L., 145
Boruszkowski, L. A., 55, 60
Botta, R. A., 64
Bouman, M., 347
Bower, A., 138
Bower, G. H., 35, 108
Boydston, J., 250
Boyle, R., 175
Brabant, S., 58
Bracht, N., 342
Bracken, C. C., 20, 51
Bradley, S. D., 96
Brand, J. E., 54, 68, 69, 71, 72, 136, 306
Brandenburg, J. D., 268, 276
Bregman, D., 34
Brendlinger, N., 194
Brentar, J. E., 70
Breslow, L., 341
Bretl, D. J., 55
Brewer, W. F., 35, 36
Brezgel, K., 314
Brice, P., 283
Briere, J., 306
Briñol, P., 104, 250
Britt, M. A., 121
Brockhoff, W., 262
Brook, J. S., 278
Brosius, H, B., 29, 188, 211, 220
Bross, M., 311
Brown, D., 45, 321
Brown, J. A., 145, 146
Brown, J. D., 60, 287, 290, 292, 295, 297,
    335, 342, 348, 349
Brown, N. R., 211
Brown, V., 64
Brown, W. J., 33, 70, 344, 346
Brownstein, A., 74
Bruce, S., 333
Bruno, K. J., 108, 113
Bryant, J., 6, 19, 30, 34, 45, 47, 135,
    156, 170, 171, 272, 276, 292, 297,
    299, 300, 305, 306, 309, 310, 314,
    321
Bryant, J. A., 6, 321
Buchanan, M., 25
Buchholz, M., 80, 81
Buckingham, D., 146
Buddenbaum, J. M., 328
Buerkel, R. A., 147

Buerkel-Rothfuss, N. L., 67, 147, 290, 292, 295, 297
Bullard, S., 286
Burke, R. R., 108, 112
Burns, J., 40
Burns, T. E., 211, 270
Burton, D., 335, 349
Bushman, B. J., 107, 256, 275, 279, 281, 303, 367
Busselle, R. J., 216
Bynum, J., 80, 81

C

Cacioppo, J. T., 154
Cady, E. T., 80, 185, 349
Calfee, J. E., 109
Calvert, S. L., 36, 55
Cameron, G. T., 25
Cameron, L. D., 143
Camino, L., 264
Campbell, K., 60
Campbell, K. K., 191, 192, 362
Cantor, J., 55, 64, 138, 149, 187, 257, 260, 272, 284, 291, 356
Cantor, J. M., 37
Cantor, M. G., 37
Cantor, P., 36
Cardillo, B. A., 342
Carlaw, R., 342
Carlson, M., 164, 229
Carlson, S., 141, 142
Carlsson-Paige, N., 141, 142
Carroll, C., 98
Carroll, J. S., 212
Carstensen, L. L., 217
Carveth, R., 297
Cassata, M., 80, 81, 321, 322
Caywood, C. B., 245
Centerwall, B.S., 264
Chachere, J. G., 26, 256, 285
Chaffee, S. H., 31, 32, 69, 250, 342
Chamberlain, C., 62
Chambers, B., 131
Chang, T., 194
Chapin, M., 311
Chapman, T. C., 306
Chappell, C. R., 367
Charlton, T., 354
Check, J. V. P., 25, 287, 292, 301, 306, 310, 312
Cheesman, J., 116

Chen, M., 133, 135, 149, 325
Chenault, B. G., 361
Cherry, K. L., 254
Chock, T. M., 51
Choe, S. Y., 250
Choi, Y, H., 188
Choi, J., 29
Chomsky, N., 220
Christ, W. G., 145, 245
Christenson, P. G., 10, 122, 131, 143, 151, 181, 182, 316
Christianson, S. A., 211, 270
Chung, M., 141
Church, G. J., 7
Cialdini, R. B., 340
Clark, C., 65
Clarke, T. K., 116
Coakley, J. J., 173, 178
Coates, S., 183
Coates, T. J., 344
Cody, M. J., 70, 345, 346
Coffin, T. E., 232
Cohen, P., 278
Colburn, D., 286
Cole, C. F., 129, 131, 132
Cole, J., 360
Cole, R. T., 250
Colfax, D., 66
Colgan, A. H., 292
Collins, A. C., 246
Collins, J., 155
Collins, J. E., 45
Collins, P. A., 40
Colsant, S., 71
Colvin, C. M., 255, 271
Comiskey, P. W., 305
Comstock, G., 69, 250, 251, 256, 303
Comstock, J., 322
Conner, R. F., 131
Conway, J. C., 33, 34
Cook, G., 106
Cook, T. D., 131
Cooke, M. C., 271
Coontz, S., 158, 320
Cooper, A., 288
Cope-Farrar, K., 290, 295
Copeland, G. A., 250, 251
Corcoran, F., 203
Corder-Bolz, C. R., 64
Court, J. H., 301, 302
Craff, D., 188

Craig, R., 230
Crawford, A. M., 80
Crawford, J., 343
Crawley, A. M., 135
Creedon, P. J., 174
Crigler, A., 248
Crimmins, C., 58
Crockett, S. A., Jr., 280
Croteau, D., 55
Crow, R., 342
Csikszentmihalyi, M., 1
Cumberbatch, G., 83
Cumings, B., 220
Cummings, C., 193
Cuperfain, R., 116
Curtis, S., 271
Cuthbert, B. N., 25, 40
Cwalina, W., 250, 253
Czilli, E. J., 209

D

Dagnoli, J., 363
D'Alessio, D., 314
Dall, P. W., 80
Dalton, M. A., 143
Danielian, L. H., 194
Daulton, A. R., 254
Davies, M. M., 51
Davis, B., 55
Davis, D. K., 19, 55, 60, 222
Davis, H., 56
Davis, J. A., 80, 82
Davis, J. H., 56
Davis, K. C., 306
Davis, M. H., 44, 276
Davis, R. H., 61, 80, 82
Day, D. M., 84
Dearing, J. W., 34, 50, 188
DeBock, H., 70
DeCoteau, N., 68
DeFleur, M. L., 19
DeGaetano, G., 255, 256, 282
Deighton, J., 251
DelliCarpini, M. X., 188
Demers, D.P., 188
Dermer, M., 300
Dershowitz, A., 87
DeSarbo, W. S., 108, 112
Desmond, R. J., 149, 183
Detenber, B. H., 25, 40, 51

Dettwyler, K. A., 57
Devlin, L. P., 246
D'Haenens, L., 7
Diamond, D., 140
Diamond, M., 302
Diedrich, T., 87
Dietz, P. E., 316
DiFranza, J. R., 124, 143, 144
Dill, K. E., 281
Distefan, J. M., 143
Ditton, T. B., 51
Dixon, T. L., 68, 71
Dobrow, J. R., 55
Dominick, J. R., 55, 56
Donnerstein, E., 7, 23, 255, 256, 268, 285, 287, 290, 295, 305, 306, 309, 312, 314, 315
Donnerstein, M., 305
Donohew, L., 176
Doob, A. N., 30
Doppler, M., 28
Dorfman, L., 342, 343
Dorr, A., 42, 125, 139, 145, 147, 273, 292
Douglas, W., 321
Douglas, S. J., 58
Downey, G., 217
Drabman, R. S., 268
Drew, D., 209
Drews, F. A., 41
Dubitsky, T. M., 108
Dubow, E. F., 256, 285
Duke, N. K., 134
Duncan, M. C., 173
Dunwoody, S., 366
DuRant, R. H., 182
Durkin, K., 54, 63
d'Ydewalle, G., 355

E

Eakins, D., 40
Earls, C. M., 309
Easterbrook, G., 210
Eastin, M. S., 12, 360
Eastman, H., 69
Eastman, S.T., 173
Eccles, A., 292
Edelstein, A. S., 188
Edgar, T., 343
Edwards, H., 175
Einsiedel, E. F., 311, 349
Eisenberg, D. M., 119, 120, 121

Eke, K. K., 220
Elasmar, M. G., 37
Elliott, S., 98, 119
Elliott, W. R., 30
Ellis, A. L., 80
Elmer, P., 342
Emans, S. J., 182
Emmers, T., 26, 306, 314
Engelbertson, J., 148
Englis, B. G., 247
Entman, R. M., 35, 68, 203
Eron, L. D., 264, 270, 272, 277, 278,
   283, 284
Eskenazi, J., 116
Espinoza, P., 70
Esslin, M., 39, 41
Evans, R., 305
Eveland, W. P., Jr., 25
Ex, C. T. G. M., 64
Eysenck, H. J., 303, 310

F

Faber, R. J., 250
Fabes, R. A., 292
Fairchild, H. H., 255, 256, 285
Falkowski, A., 250, 253
Farhi, P., 187, 189
Farinola, W., 290, 295
Farquhar, J. W., 342
Farrar, D., 24
Fehr, B. J., 247
Fejes, F. J., 63, 86
Feldman, V., 212
Fenigstein, A., 275
Ferguson, D. A., 360
Ferrante, C. L., 55, 57
Ferreira, L., 225
Ferris, T., 366
Feshbach, N. D., 44, 255, 256, 285
Feshbach, S., 44, 272, 274, 275, 301, 306, 312
Fico, F. G., 20
Field, D. E., 25, 40
Fink, J. S., 173
Finnegan, J., 342
Firebaugh, L. C., 80, 349
Fisch, S. M., 129, 135
Fischer, C., 36
Fisher, P., 283
Fitch, M., 42, 51, 52
Flay, B. R., 335, 349

Fleming, M. J., 281
Fletcher, C., 124, 143, 144
Fletcher, J. E., 25
Flora, J. A., 342, 343
Folsom, A. R., 342
Fonash, D., 210
Fonda, D., 103
Ford, J. T., 109
Fore, W. F., 103, 333
Fortmann, S. P., 342
Fowler, G., 55
Fox, N. A., 349
Frederickson, B. L., 175
Freimuth, V. S., 343
Freitag, A. A., 20
Fried, C. B., 184
Friedrich-Cofer, L., 285
Friedrichsen, M., 45
Frierson, T., 258
Frieske, D. A., 25
Fuchs, D. A., 232
Fujioka, Y., 148
Fujita, M., 23
Funabiki, J., 75
Funk, J., 255
Furnham, A., 102, 106, 126
Fuson, I. A., 311
Fussell, J. A., 101

G

Gabbard, G. O., 88
Gabbard, K. L., 88
Gadow, K. D., 22
Gaeth, G. J., 113
Gamson, J., 154, 155
Gan, S. L., 183
Ganley, G., 145, 369
Gantz, W., 59, 138, 140, 167, 207, 325
Gardner, D. M., 112
Gardner, M. P., 106, 335, 336
Garelik, G., 190
Garner-Earl, B., 98
Garramone, G. M., 247, 249, 250
Garrow, K. L., 87
Gartner, M., 314
Gat, I. E., 126
Gatto, L., 184
Gaudet, H., 251
Gebhardt, L., 26, 306, 314
Geen, R. G., 256, 275

Geer, J., 292
Geiger, S., 36, 40, 251
Geiogamah, H., 73
Geis, F., 64
Gelb, B. D., 102
Gelfand, D. M., 263
George, W. H., 306
Gerbner, G., 24, 28, 29, 50, 51, 54, 55, 67, 81, 207, 251, 253, 269, 319, 350
Gerstle, J., 253
Gettas, G. J., 129
Ghanem, S., 35
Gibbons, J. A., 210
Gibbs, N., 225
Gibson, B., 119
Gibson, R., 211
Gidney, C. L., 55
Giery, M. A., 26, 306, 314
Gilbert, S., 34
Gilboa, E., 217, 218
Giles, D., 34
Giles, H., 82, 103, 191
Gilly, M. C., 57
Gilpin, E. A., 143
Gilpin, P., 57
Glantz, S. A., 143
Glassner, B., 213, 216, 256
Glenn, D., 359
Goldberg, B., 198
Goldberg, L. L., 299
Goldberg, M., 85
Goldberg, M. E., 69, 335, 336, 343
Goldberg, N., 68
Goldstein, J. H., 170, 270, 275, 367
Goldstein, R., 25
Goldstein, S., 302
Goldstein, W., 223
Gonzalez, D., 32
Gonzalez, I. N., 37
Goodman, E., 53
Gorn, G. I., 69
Gornstein, L., 118
Gottdiener, C., 36
Gotthoffer, A., 287
Grabe, M. E., 51
Graber, D. A., 209, 211
Graesser, A. C., 35, 45, 108
Grant, A. E., 360
Graves, S. B., 54, 68, 69, 147
Gray, P., 134
Green, M., 84

Greenberg, B. S., 29, 54, 68, 72, 80, 131, 136, 149, 207, 225, 290, 292, 295, 297
Greene, A. S., 360
Greene, E., 212
Greene, K., 276, 339
Greenfield, P. M., 24, 125, 127, 141
Greenwald, A. G., 116
Gregory, S., 160
Gresham, L. G., 105, 106
Griffiths, M., 281
Griffiths, S., 126
Grimes, T., 209
Grimm, J., 251
Grodal, T., 280
Gross, L., 24, 28, 29, 50, 51, 251, 253, 269, 319, 350
Grossman, D., 255, 256, 263, 282
Grzelewski, D., 352
Gubash, C., 185
Guebaly, N., 84
Guild, D., 306
Guimaraes, C., 252
Guloien, T. H., 310
Gunter, B., 30, 54, 102, 106, 126, 191, 211, 222, 272, 292, 314
Gunther, A. C., 26, 316
Gustafson, R. L., 65
Gutch, M., 145
Gutierres, S. E., 299
Guttman, A., 157, 158, 162, 170

H

Haas, J., 176
Haber, S., 301
Haberstroh, J., 115
Hafen, J., 67
Hajjar, W. J., 80
Hale, J. L., 339
Halimi, S., 10
Hallam, J., 305
Hallin, D. C., 196, 225, 233
Hamilton, W. L., 141, 142, 280
Hammond, S. L., 343
Han, S., 99
Hannan, A., 354
Hannonen-Gladden, H., 67
Hansen, C. H., 181, 183, 184, 316
Hansen, R. D., 181, 183, 184, 316
Haridakis, P. M., 276
Harper, D., 84

Harris, R. J., 35, 36, 64, 80, 98, 108, 112, 113, 167, 185, 259, 265, 268, 276, 292, 314, 326, 337, 339, 349
Harrison, K., 22, 64, 174, 259
Harrison, L., 92
Harrison, T. M., 247
Harry, B., 316
Hart, R. P., 236
Hartman, E. F., 24, 126
Hartmann, D. P., 263, 273
Hartup, W. W., 263
Hartz, J., 367
Harvey, K., 145
Harvey, M., 9
Harwood, J., 80, 82
Haskell, W. L., 342
Hass, R. G., 103
Hatfield, E., 154
Hausknecht, D., 107
Hawkins, R. P., 28, 30, 40
Hayashi, H., 302
Haydel, K. F., 147, 284
Hayes, D., 126
Haynes, A. M., 55, 57
Hazelwood, R. R., 316
Hazlett, R. L., 25
Hazlett, S. Y., 25
Healy, J., 128, 131
Hearold, S., 273
Heath, R. L., 19, 30, 34
Heath, T. B., 103
Heatherton, T. F., 143
Heeter, C., 225
Heidel, C., 264
Heider, D., 68
Heider, J. D., 121
Heim, M., 306, 312
Heine, S. J., 48
Heintz, K. E., 292
Heintz-Knowles, K. E., 321, 322
Heller, M. S., 272
Helm, D., 176
Helmick, A. L., 259
Henderson, L., 67
Hennis, L. K., 185
Henriksen, L., 122, 143, 151, 182
Hensley, D. L., 36
Herbert, B., 124
Herman, E. S., 220
Herman, C. P., 65
Hernandez, M., 28

Herrett-Skjellum, J., 26
Hesse, B. W., 365
Heyduk, R. G., 275
Hicks, D. J., 263
Hinck, E. A., 235
Hirsch, J., 25
Hirsch, P. M., 30
Hirschberg, M. S., 209
Hoekstra, S. J., 222, 259, 268, 276
Hoff, C., 344
Hoffner, C., 25, 259, 284
Hofschire, L., 290
Holbert, R. L., 254
Holtz-Bacha, C., 251
Homer, P. M., 103
Hong, S. T., 98
Hoover, S. M., 332, 333, 335
Hopkins, R., 25
Hornik, R., 336
Hosch, H., 64
Houston, M. J., 106
Howell, F., 175
Hoy, M. G., 139
Hoyer, W. D., 109
Hoyle, R. H., 339
Hoynes, W., 55
Hubbs, L. A., 25
Hudelson, S., 139
Huesmann, L. R., 264, 270, 272, 277, 278, 283, 284
Hughes, K. D., 194
Hull, J. D., 9
Hull, J. G., 44, 276
Hunnicutt, G. G., 140
Hurst, L., 234
Husson, W., 247
Huston, A. C., 7, 36, 40, 42, 51, 52, 64, 85, 130, 131, 149, 153, 255, 256, 285
Hutcheon, D., 180
Hyde, J. S., 291

I

Ibaraki, T., 302
Iiyama, P., 75
Ikeda, T., 306
Ilola, L. M., 341
Impett, E. A., 314
Ingmundson, P., 260
Intons-Peterson, M. J., 311
Irvine, C., 259

Irwin, B. J., 80
Iyengar, S., 207
Iyer, E., 114

J

Jackson, D. Z., 175
Jackson, L. A., 184
Jacobs, D. R., Jr., 342
Jacobson, J., 360
Jacoby, J., 109
Jacques, W. W., 254
Jaffe, R. D., 124, 143, 144
Jakes, J., 226
Jamieson, K. H., 35, 68, 191, 192, 216, 230,
    236, 238, 240, 243, 245, 249, 251
Janis, I., 36, 38
Janssen, S. C., 124
Janssens, J. M. A. M., 64
Jarvis, S. E., 236
Jasper, J. D., 337
Jennings, J., 64, 120
Jensen, K., 173
Jernigan, D., 342, 343
Jhally, S., 69, 70
Johnson, D., 243
Johnson, J. D., 184
Johnson, J. G., 278
Johnson, T., 139
Johnson-Cartee, K. S., 250, 251
Johnsson-Smaragdi, U., 148
Johnston, A., 249
Johnston, C. B., 225
Johnston, W. A., 41
Joiner, T. E., Jr., 217
Jones, A., 313
Jones, K., 182
Jordan, A. B., 7, 9, 10
Jowett, G. S., 12, 206
Joy, L. A., 264
Just, M., 248

K

Kahle, L. R., 103
Kahneman, D., 212, 300
Kaid, L. L., 249, 250, 251, 253
Kamalipour, Y., 326, 354
Kamigaki, S. K., 25
Kane, M. J., 173
Kanungo, R. N., 69

Karafa, J. A., 268, 276, 326
Kardes, F. R., 108
Kasen, S., 278
Kassarjian, H., 66
Katz, E., 31
Katz, P., 255, 256, 285
Katzman, N., 69, 250, 251
Kenrick, D. T., 299
Kepplinger, H. M., 188
Kerkman, D., 130
Kern-Foxworth, M., 66, 68
Kerr, N. L., 212
Kessler, R. C., 217
Ketcham, K., 340
Key, W. B., 21, 116
Kher, U., 53
Kibler, R. J., 247
Kiesler, S., 12, 145, 360
Kilbourne, J., 53, 56, 57
Kilbourne, W. E., 116
Kim, Y. H., 40
Kimball, M. M., 64, 264
Kinder, K., 254
King, C. M., 47, 273
King, C. R., 73
King, K. W., 101
Kingsley, S. M., 55, 57
Kintsch, W., 38
Kippax, S., 343
Kirby, M., 314
Kirkpatrick, D. D., 336
Kirsch, S. J., 281
Kitano, H. H. L., 75
Kitchen, P., 9
Klassen, M. L., 108
Klein, J. D., 287
Klein, R., 283
Kline, S., 141
Klineberg, O., 54
Knappenberger, J. B., 185
Knill, B. J., 57
Knobloch, S., 44, 181
Kolbe, R. H., 106, 140
Koolstra, C. M., 128
Kopkind, A., 352
Korzenny, F., 80, 354
Korzilius, H. P. L. M., 64
Kosicki, G. M., 34
Kotler, J. A., 7, 55
Kottak, C., 7, 166
Kovaric, P., 273

Kraemer, H. C., 147
Krafka, C. L., 309
Kraft, R. N., 36
Kraus, S., 235, 237, 254
Kraut, R., 360
Krcmar, M., 271, 276, 339
Kreider, H., 141
Krohn, F. B., 183
Ku, L., 149
Kubey, R. L., 1, 31, 34, 81, 325
Kuiper, K., 158
Kunkel, D., 133, 138, 140, 145, 153, 255, 290, 292, 295
Kutchinsky, B., 301, 303

L

Labi, N., 120, 335
Lacayo, R., 200
Lacy, S., 20
Lagerspetz, K., 264, 270, 277
Laird, K. R., 145, 360
Lambert, W. E., 54
Land, D., 141
Lang, A., 22, 25, 36, 39, 51, 102, 106, 250
Lang, G. E., 208, 232
Lang, K., 208, 232
Lange, G., 125
Langenmeyer, D., 103
Langenmeyer, L., 103
Lapchick, R., 175
LaRose, R. J., 360, 368
Larson, D. B., 292, 314, 317, 329, 329
Larson, J. F., 197, 217, 219
Larson, M. S., 141, 322
Lasisi, M., 36
Laska, S., 24
Lasswell, H., 21
Lau, R. R., 247
Lau, T. Y., 225
Laurion, S. K., 209
Lautman, M. R., 56
Lavine, H., 64
Law, S., 347
Lawlor, S. D., 79
Lazarsfeld, P. F., 19, 251
Leavitt, L. A., 349
Lee, B. J., 337
Lee, C. C., 37
Lee, H. C., 180
Lee, J. Y., 68

Lee, M. A., 4, 5, 188, 203, 205, 207
Lee, T. T., 250
Lefkowitz, M. M., 264, 272, 277, 284
Legrain, P., 37
Lehrer, A., 24, 126
Leitner, D. W., 216
Lemar, J., 64
Lemert, J. B., 250
Leonard, N. H., 112
Leone, R., 13
Leonesio, R. J., 306
Lepre, C. R., 287
Lerdau, E. R., 150
Lever, J., 158
Levin, D. E., 141, 142
Levin, I. L., 113
Levy, M. R., 9, 30, 191
Lewis, J., 69, 70
Lewy, G., 200
Leyens, J., 264, 272
Li, H., 149
Lichter, S. R., 230
Lieberman, T., 203
Liebert, R. M., 7, 262
Liebes, T., 325
Lievrouw, L. A., 354
Lightdale, J. R., 281
Lin, C. A., 360
Lindlof, T. R., 356
Linebarger, D. L., 7, 131
Linton, J. M., 12
Linz, D., 23, 68, 71, 255, 268, 292, 309, 312, 314, 315, 365
Liotti, M., 260
Lippert, B., 82
Liss, M., 69
Livingstone, S. M., 325
Loftus, E. F., 211, 246, 270, 340
Lombard, M., 20, 51
Long, D. L., 45
Longford, L., 311
Longmore, P. K., 83
Lonial, S. C., 139
Loomis, J., 67
Lorch, E. P., 339
Lovdahl, L. T., 55
Love, G., 314
Lowery, S., 19
Lowry, D. T., 216, 314
Lozano, E., 344
Luebke, B., 55

Luepker, R. V., 342
Luke, C., 36
Lull, J., 354
Lum, P., 37
Luna, D., 339
Lundby, K., 335
Lundmark, V. C., 360
Luscombe, B., 165
Lyman, R., 357
Lynch, J. E., 121
Lyons, J. S., 292, 314, 317, 328, 329

M

Macbeth, T. M., 354
Maccoby, N., 19, 342
MacCourt, R. J., 212
Macdonald, G. E., 30
MacFarland, D. T., 127
Maclan, P., 291, 292
Maibach, E., 342, 343
Maier, S., 308
Maiorellle, M. J., 112
Malamuth, N. M., 25, 287, 292, 301, 305, 306,
   312, 314, 315
Markham, J. W., 267
Marling, K. A., 351
Marshall, W. L., 292, 306
Martell, J., 306
Martin, M. C., 139
Martinez, I., 29
Marton, K., 25
Martz, L., 201
Masland, J. L., 299
Massett, H. A., 343
Mastro, D. E., 12, 54, 68, 72, 360
Matabane, P. W., 69
Matas, M., 84
Mathews, A., 293
Mattussek, M., 154
Maurer, J., 119
Mayer, J., 358
Mayerson, S. E., 306
Mayes, S., 297
Mazza, M., 188
Mazzarella, S. R., 292
McAlister, A. L., 342
McAnany, E. G., 219
McCarthy, M. S., 103
McCauley, C., 273, 284
McComas, K., 29

McCombs, M. E., 34, 35, 50, 69, 188, 209, 246,
   250, 251
McCook, A., 351
McCool, J. P., 143
McCormick, E., 175
McCoy, J. K., 65
McDermott, S., 69
McDonald, D., 25
McDonnell, J., 183
McGee, J., 65
McGhee, P., 45
McGuire, W. J., 19, 33
McHugh, M. P., 33
McIntyre, P., 64
McKenna, K. Y. A., 360, 361
McKenzie-Mohr, D., 299
McKinley, M., 345
McLean, M. S., 267
McLeod, J. M., 354
McNeal, J. U., 138
McPhee, W. N., 251
McQuail, D., 250
Meadowcroft, J. M., 38
Medioni, G., 180
Medoff, N. J., 305
Meeds, R., 96
Melton, G., 55
Mendelsohn, H. A., 232
Merikle, P. M., 116
Mermis, M., 112
Merritt, S., 249
Merskin, D., 72
Mesmer, T., 150
Messaris, P., 145
Messner, M. A., 173
Metcalf, B. L., 108, 112
Meyer, P., 195
Meyrowitz, J., 30, 31, 145, 227
Mielke, K. W., 135
Milavsky, J. R., 217
Miller, K. E., 337
Miller, L. S., 256, 285
Mills, J., 44, 65
Miracle, A., 175
Mitrook, M., 183
Mittelmank, M. B., 342
Moeller, S. D., 190
Moise-Titus, J., 270, 272, 278
Moisy, C., 204
Mok, T., 75
Molitor, F., 310

Monahan, J. L., 343
Mooney, L., 58
Mooney, R. J., 36
Moore, D. L., 107
Moore, T. E., 116, 366
Morgan, M., 24, 28, 30, 50, 51, 251, 253, 269, 319, 350
Morgan, S. E., 339
Moritz, M. J., 80
Morley, D., 325
Morris, J. S., 72
Morrow, M., 281, 357
Mosalenko, S., 48
Mosher, D. L., 291, 292
Mothersbaugh, D. L., 103
Mott, L. A., 143
Mowen, J. C., 139
Mowlana, H., 197, 207
Muehling, D. D., 106, 140
Mukopadhyay, T., 360
Mullen, L. J., 87
Mundorf, N., 145, 154, 209, 268, 316, 360
Murnen, S. K., 292
Murphy, S. T., 90
Murray, D. M., 346
Murray, J. P., 255, 256, 260, 285
Mutz, D. C., 128, 196, 353
Myers, P. N., Jr., 64

N

Nakamura, G. V., 35
Nass, C. I., 31, 125, 149
Nathanson, A. I., 65, 147, 149, 187
Naughton, J., 168
Navracruz, L. C., 284
Negrine, R., 83
Nelson, J. P., 263
Neuendorf, K. A., 20, 67, 70
Newhagen, J. E., 211, 250, 270
Nias, N. K. B., 303, 310
Nimmo, D., 247
Nio, T. C. J., 216
Nisbett, R. E., 99
Noe, D., 184
Noll, A. M., 12, 145
Norris, J., 306
Norvell, W., 64
Nowak, K., 40
Nussbaum, J. F., 80

O

O'Bryant, S. L., 64
O'Connor, J. J., 68
O'Donnell, H., 175
Ogan, C., 357
Ohbuchi, K., 306
Olivardia, R., 61
Oliver, M. B., 154, 210, 256, 258, 259, 307
Oliver, R. L., 108, 112
Olson, D. R., 125
Olweus, D., 284
Onyehalu, A. S., 36
Orecklin, M., 121
Orman, J., 179
O'Sullivan, G., 220

P

Page, S., 84
Paik, H., 256
Painton, S., 116
Paletz, D. L., 220, 251, 311
Palmgreen, P., 31, 32, 50, 339
Panee, C. D., 281
Panitt, M., 32
Pant, S., 347
Pantoja, M., 141
Papa, M. J., 347
Papacharissi, Z., 360
Parke, R., 264, 272
Parks, M. R., 361
Parrott, R. L., 342
Patterson, M., 360
Paulman, P. M., 124, 143, 144
Pavel, D. M., 73
Pavelchak, M., 43, 193, 258
Pavlou, P., 93
Payne, D., 121
Payne, J. G., 343
Pechmann, C., 102
Peck, J., 333
Pecora, N. O., 140
Pellechia, M., 259
Penrod, S. D., 23, 268, 309, 311, 365
Peracchio, L. A., 339
Percy, L., 56, 106
Perkins, K. P., 330
Perlmutter, D. D., 45
Perloff, R. M., 25, 57, 121, 222, 316
Perry, L., 292

Perse, E. M., 21, 27, 30, 33, 34, 51, 191, 278, 285, 297, 360
Pesch, M., 57
Pessin, B. M., 188
Peterkin, A., 84
Petrie, K. J., 143
Pettigrew, T. F., 35
Petty, R. E., 104, 250
Pewewardy, C. D., 73
Pezdek, K., 24, 126
Pfau, M., 87
Phelps, E., 147
Phillips, D. P., 217
Phillips, J., 84, 210
Phillips, K., 56, 61, 107
Picard, R. G., 220
Pierce, J. P., 143
Pierce, M. C., 265
Pillion, O., 254
Pingree, S., 28, 30, 40, 325
Pinkleton, B. E., 148, 247, 250, 339
Pinon, M., 153
Pitkanen-Pulkkinen, L., 277
Pitta, P., 321
Ploghoft, M. E., 147
Plotkin, R. S., 25
Plummer, J., 67
Podolski, C. L., 270, 272, 278
Polivy, J., 65
Pollard, P., 307, 310
Pollitt, K., 314
Polsky, S., 272
Pope, H. G., Jr., 61
Porter, N., 64
Postman, N., 30, 334
Potter, W. J., 28, 30, 43, 51, 52, 145, 146, 255, 272, 273
Potter, R. F., 25, 39
Potts, R., 28, 29, 48, 137
Pounds, J. C., 112
Powell, R. A., 33, 191
Powers, R., 158
Praet, C., 355
Prasad, V. K., 139
Pratap, A., 308
Pratkanis, A. R., 95, 115, 116, 366
Prentice, D. A., 281
Presser, S. L., 30
Preston, E. H., 29
Preston, I. L., 108, 110
Price, M. E., 283

Price, V., 128, 209
Priester, J. R., 104, 250
Prinsky, L., 183
Pritchard, D., 194
Procter, D. E., 250
Provenzo, E. F., Jr., 255
Pursey, G., 57
Puska, P., 342
Pyszczynski, T. A., 300

Q

Quackenbush, D. .M., 292
Qualls, W. J., 67
Quanty, M. B., 275
Quinsey, V. L., 306

R

Rabinovitch, M. S., 267
Rader, B. G., 156, 158, 163, 178
Rafaeli, S., 368
Rainville, R., 175
Raju, P. S., 139
Ramirez-Berg, C., 71
Raney, A. A., 156, 170, 276
Rao, N., 345
Rao, T. R., 139
Rapson, R. L., 154
Ratzan, S. C., 254, 343
Rauch, G. E., 55, 56
Rawson, H. J., 98
Read, J. D., 117, 365
Real, M. R., 151, 159
Reed, W., 184
Rees, R., 175
Reeve, D. K., 36
Reeves, B., 25, 38, 40, 51, 125, 211, 250, 251, 270
Reich, R. D., 51
Reid, L. N., 101
Reid, P. T., 67
Reiss, J. E., 25, 40
Reiter, A. D., 88
Reynolds, A., 34, 50, 188, 209
Rice, M. L., 36, 130
Rich, F., 85
Rich, M., 182
Richards, J. I., 108, 112
Richards, J. W., Jr., 124, 143, 144
Richardson, G. W., Jr., 249

Rickwood, D. J., 281
Ridley, D., 116
Riffe, D., 20
Riggle, E. D. B., 80
Riggs, M., 68
Rimal, R. N., 343
Rimmer, L., 118
Ritchie, D., 128
Roberts, D. F., 7, 8, 10, 19, 69, 122, 128, 131, 143, 149, 151, 181, 182, 250, 251, 353
Robertson, T. S., 108, 112, 139
Robinson, J. D., 80, 82, 321, 322
Robinson, J. P., 222
Robinson, M. J., 236
Robinson, T. N., 147, 284
Rockwell, S. C., 297, 300
Rodriguez, A., 175
Rogers, E. M., 34, 50, 188, 335, 344, 345, 347
Rojahn, K., 35
Rokeach, M., 70, 347
Rolandelli, D. R., 40
Rome, E. S., 182
Romer, D., 68
Romer, S., 216
Romero, S., 352
Rosenbaum, J., 183
Rosenberg, T., 201
Rosencrans, M. A., 263
Rosengren, K. E., 31, 32, 354
Rosenkoetter, L. I., 136
Rosenzweig, J., 348
Roser, C., 32, 342
Roskos-Ewoldsen, B., 311
Ross, D., 27, 263
Ross, J., 104
Ross, S. A., 27, 263
Rossiter, J. R., 106, 139
Rossler, P., 29
Rotfeld, H. J., 101
Rothblatt, A., 292
Rothe, J., 9
Rothenberg, D., 346
Rothenbuhler, E. W., 167
Rothschild, M., 25
Rouner, D., 347
Roy, A., 80, 82
Rubin, A. M., 30, 32, 34, 50, 51, 191, 319, 360
Rubin, D. C., 185
Rubin, D. L., 339

Rubin, D. M., 193
Rubin, R. B., 33, 34
Rubinstein, E. A., 255, 256, 285
Rumelhart, D. A., 35
Rumsey, D. J., 250
Russell, A., 368
Russell, D. E. H., 288
Russell, G. W., 170
Russo, J. E., 108, 112
Russo, V., 78

S

Saegert, J., 116, 366
Sagarin, B., 121
Sakano, T., 23
Salamon, J., 138
Salomon, G., 125
Salonen, J. T., 342
Sanborn, F. W., 268, 276
Sanchez, D., 48
Sanders, K. R., 253
Sandilands, M. L., 170
Santomero, A., 135
Saphir, M. N., 147
Sapolsky, B. S., 171, 305, 310
Sargent, J. D., 143
Savage, R. L., 247
Schachter, S., 152
Schaefer, H. H., 292
Schement, J. R., 37
Schenk-Hamlin, W. J., 250
Scherlis, W., 360
Schiller, H., 207
Schlegel, R. J., 80, 349
Schleuder, J., 246
Schlinger, M. J., 67
Schmid, A. P., 220
Schmitt, K. L., 7, 40, 131
Schneider, A., 223
Schneider, J. A., 30
Schneider, K. C., 57
Schneider, S. B., 57
Schneider, S. L., 209
Schoen, L. M., 36
Scholfield, J., 43, 193, 258
Schooler, C., 250, 342
Schulkind, M. D., 185
Schuman, H., 30
Schumann, D. W., 120
Schwartz, D. D., 25, 40

Schwarz, J. E., 29
Schwarz, N., 306
Scott, C. L., 268, 276, 292, 314
Sebastian, M., 65
Sebastian, R., 264, 272
Seefeldt, C., 81
Seeley, D., 292
Seeley, T., 292
Seggar, J. F., 67
Seidlitz, R., 24
Seifart, H., 164
Selnow, G. W., 253
Seo, M., 25
Shaffer, A., 131
Shaheen, J. G., 76, 77
Shain, R., 84
Shanahan, J., 24, 28, 30, 50, 51, 253, 269, 319, 350
Shanteau, J., 106, 337, 339
Shapiro, M. A., 28, 29, 51
Shatzer, M. J., 356
Shavitt, S., 99
Shaw, D. L., 34, 35, 188
Sheehan, M. A., 236
Sheikh, A. A., 139
Sherry, J. L., 281, 344
Shimp, T. A., 105, 106
Shirley, M., 311
Shockey, E. M., 55
Shoemaker, P. J., 194
Shrum, L. J., 28, 30, 216
Siegel, A. N., 274
Siegler, R. S., 211
Sigesmund, B. J., 288, 289
Signorielli, N., 24, 28, 29, 50, 51, 54, 55, 67, 84, 251, 252, 253, 269, 319, 350
Silk, M., 333
Simmons, R., 256
Simon, A., 207
Simon, J., 86
Simon, S., 24, 126
Simons, R. F., 25, 40
Singer, D.G., 127, 145, 147, 149
Singer, J. E., 152
Singer, J. L., 127, 145, 147, 149
Singer, M., 35
Singer, M. I., 258
Singer, R., 275
Singhal, A., 344, 345, 347
Sintchak, G., 292
Skanes, H. E., 116

Skill, T., 81, 317, 321, 328, 329
Slater, M. D., 90, 276, 347
Slater, D., 30
Slovak, K., 258
Smailes, E. M., 278
Smith, M., 139
Smith, R., 36
Smith, S. L., 256, 271
Smith, T. M., 114
Snyder, L., 32, 188
Snyder-Duch, J., 20
Soja, M., 67
Soley, L., 67
Solomon, D. S., 342
Solomon, N., 4, 5, 188, 203, 205, 207
Sommerfeld, J., 109
Sommers-Flanagan, J., 55
Sommers-Flanagan, R., 55
Sood, S., 345, 347
Sopory, P., 335
Spangenberg, E. R., 116
Spangler, L. C., 62
Sparkes, A., 79
Sparks, C. W., 256, 257, 275, 278
Sparks, G. G., 256, 257, 259, 272, 275, 278
Spencer, J. W., 24
Spencer, L., 139
Sperber, M., 162
Sprafkin, J. N., 7, 22, 262
Sprick, S. J., 98
Springwood, C. F., 73
St.Peters, M., 130, 149
Stack, A. D., 275, 303
Stall, R. D., 344
Stanley, A., 355
Stayman, D. M., 108
Steele, M. E., 247
Stein, J., 175, 176, 286, 330
Steinberg, S., 66
Stenbjerre, M., 29
Stephen, T., 247
Stephens, N., 139
Stephenson, M. T., 339
Stern, B. B., 68
Stevens, D., 108, 112
Stevens, E., 24, 126
Stewart, D. W., 93, 102
Steyer, J. P., 4, 144, 188, 203, 246, 358, 365
Stiff, J., 264, 284
Stipp, H., 217, 312

Stockton, M., 292
Stodghill, R., 287
Stolberg, S. G., 348
Stone, G., 11
Stonehill, B., 199
Storey, J. D., 26, 219
Stout, J. M., 328
Strand, H., 40
Strasburger, V. C., 4, 5, 7, 140, 143, 179, 180, 183, 203, 255, 256, 280, 285, 287, 290, 299, 314, 357
Strassberg, D. S., 292
Strate, L., 63
Straubhaar, J. D., 225
Strayer, D., 41
Strickwerda, M., 36
Strobel, W. P., 202, 204, 218, 220, 222
Strouse, J. S., 292
Strover, S., 360
Strzyzewski, K., 322
Sturm, R. E., 108
Stutts, M. A., 139, 140
Suazo, F. L., 183
Suleiman, M. W., 76
Sullivan, B., 92, 121
Suls, J. M., 45
Summer, J., 36
Sundar, S. S., 342, 360
Surlin, S. H., 70
Sutton, M. J., 287
Svenkerud, P., 345
Svennevig, M., 321
Swalele, R. M. A., 345
Sweeney, D., 64
Swerdlow, J., 21
Swisher, L., 28, 137
Sypher, B. D., 345

T

Tabkin, G., 131
Takeuchi, G., 306
Talbott, A. D., 267
Tamborini, R., 12, 29, 154, 264, 268, 276, 284, 305, 360
Tan, A. S., 27, 260, 285
Tannen, D., 59, 62, 192
Tannenbaum, P., 44, 153, 273
Tapper, J., 30
Tarpley, T., 352
Taruskin, R., 182

Tate, E., 70
Tavris, C., 170, 171, 366
Taylor, B., 342
Taylor, C., 92, 120, 210
Taylor, C. R., 68
Taylor, D. A., 306
Taylor, D. S., 30
Taylor, P., 239
Taylor, S., 120, 210, 300
Teplin, L. A., 84
Tewksbury, D., 191, 212
Thaler, P., 87
Thamodaran, K., 107
Themba, M., 342, 343
Thomas, B., 354
Thomas, L., 311
Thomas, M. H., 268
Thomas, S., 61
Thompson, M. E., 325
Thompson, T. L., 55
Thomsen, S. R., 65
Thorndyke, P. W., 35
Thorson, E., 25, 40, 105, 120, 245, 316
Tickle, J. J., 143
Tiggeman, M., 65
Ting-Toomey, S., 354
Tinic, S., 105
Tinsley, H. E. A., 20
Tomasello, T. K., 272
Toney, G. T., 55
Took, K. J., 55
Toplin, R., 221
Trevino, L. K., 368
Triche, E., 24
Truglio, R. T., 129, 132
Trusty, M. L., 112
Tschida, D. A., 254
Tuchman, G., 199, 318
Tuchman, S., 232
Tulloch, J., 343
Tunstall, J., 37
Turner, C. W., 292, 365
Tversky, A., 212, 300
Tye, J. B., 143

U

Uchiyama, A., 302
Ume-Nwagbo, E. N. E., 345
Upfold, D., 306

V

Vaid, J., 45, 46
Valdeavellano, E. E., 345
Valencia, R., 37
Valente, J., 187
Valkenburg, P. M., 124, 126, 128, 138
Van Eenwyk, J., 281
Van Evra, J., 31
Van Oordt, M. N., 170
Vance, D., 139
VanderVoort, T. H. A., 128, 170, 210, 271
VanRensbergen, J., 355
VanVuuren, D. P., 128, 353
Varady, A., 147, 284
Vaughan, P. W., 345
Ventsam, S., 345
Venugopalan, G., 321
Verfaillie, K., 355
Vidmar, N., 70, 347
Vincent, I., 368
Vincent, R. C., 50, 55
Vokey, J. R., 117, 365
Volgy, T. J., 29
Von Feilitzen, C., 40
Vorderer, P., 44, 45

W

Wackman, D., 139
Wade, R., 212
Wagner, C. B., 360
Wagner, S. H., 64
Wahl, O. F., 84
Wakshlag, J., 21, 30, 40, 269
Walder, L. O., 264, 272, 277, 284
Waldman, P., 35, 230, 236, 238, 240, 243, 245, 249
Walker, J. R., 325
Walker, M., 103
Wallace, S., 321, 322
Wallach, L., 248
Wallack, L., 335, 342, 343
Walma van der Molen, J. H., 210
Walsh, D., 102
Walsh-Childers, K., 287, 335, 342, 348
Walters, L. H., 339
Walters, R. H., 27, 263
Wanta, W., 34, 35, 246, 250
Ward, S., 93, 139
Warner, K. E., 143

Warren, G. G., 44, 276
Warren, R., 273
Wartella, E., 120, 139, 292
Wasinger, L., 112
Watkins, B., 126
Watt, J. H., 188
Weaver, D., 35
Weaver, F. M., 212
Weaver, J., 12, 70, 100, 280
Weaver, J. B., III, 6, 30, 55, 154, 209, 263, 268, 269, 275, 276, 299, 305, 310, 314
Weber, J. S., 131
Webster, J., 21, 40, 368
Weigel, R. H., 67
Weimann, G., 220
Weiss, A. J., 139, 148
Weiss, D. J., 20
Weiss, D. S., 55
Weisz, M. G., 309
Wenner, L. A., 32, 163, 167
Wernick, R., 196
West, S., 264, 272
Weston, M. A., 72
Weymouth, L., 200
Whannel, G., 158
Wheeler, S., 158
Wheeler, D. L., 353
Wheeler, T. H., 360
Whillock, R. K., 254
White, L. A., 305
Wicks, R. H., 35, 225, 244
Wiest, J. R., 281
Wilcox, B. L., 255, 256, 285, 311
Wilde, M. L., 284
Wilder, A., 135
Wilhoit, G. C., 70
Will, E., 362
Williams, B. A., 188
Williams, F., 360
Williams, L., 173
Williams, M., 65, 135
Williams, P. T., 342
Willow, D. C., 263
Willwerth, J., 84
Wilson, B. J., 36, 65, 139, 140, 143, 148, 179, 180, 183, 203, 255, 259, 271, 284, 312, 357
Wilson, J. R., 10, 11, 92, 110, 116, 118
Wilson, K. M., 287
Wilson, S. L. R., 10, 11, 92, 110, 116, 118
Wilson, S. N., 288
Wilson, W., 84

Windahl, S., 30, 32, 50
Winn, M., 21, 131
Witte, K., 344
Wittebols, J. H., 220
Wober, M., 30
Wolf-Gillespie, N., 124, 143, 144
Wollen, T., 145
Wong, F. Y., 26, 256, 285
Wood, J., 79, 134
Wood, P. D., 342
Wood, S. E., 121
Wood, W., 26, 256, 285
Woodard, E. H., 133
Woods, E. R., 182
Woolf, K. D., 40
Wright, C. R., 4
Wright, J. C., 7, 36, 40, 42, 51, 52, 130, 131, 149, 153
Wroblewski, R., 64, 85
Wulf, S., 151, 156, 165
Wulff, H. J., 45
Wyer, R. S., 45, 98

Y

Yalch, R. F., 185
Yang, M. S., 148
Yang, S. M., 31

Yanovitsky, I., 336, 337
Yates, E., 306
York, P., 258
Yorke, D., 9
Young, B. M., 139
Young, C. E., 139
Young, R. D., 44, 276
Yut, E., 141

Z

Zabrack, M. L., 264
Zanna, M. P., 299
Zehnder, S. M., 55
Zelizer, B., 207
Zerbinos, E., 55
Zhao, X., 59
Zielinska, I. E., 131
Zill, N., 131
Zillmann, D., 6, 19, 25, 44, 45, 47, 152, 170, 172, 183, 209, 211, 212, 263, 268, 273, 275, 276, 284, 292, 299, 300, 305, 306, 309, 310, 314
Zinkhan, G. M., 67, 102
Zoglin, R., 154, 207
Zohoori, A. R., 31
Zuckerman, D. M., 147, 255, 256, 285
Zuckerman, M., 276

Subject Index

A

Abolitionism and media, 226
Advertising, 92–123
  alcohol advertising and sports, 168
  cognition and marketing,
    105–113
  deceptive advertising, 108–113
  drugs, prescription, 122
  ethics in, 101, 103–104
  "Green advertising," 114
  history, 93–94
  in schools, 119–120
  on the Internet, 120–122
  political advertising, 245–251
  product placements, 118–119, 348
  psychological appeals in, 95–105
  regulation of, 144
  subliminal advertising, 115–116
  to children, 138–144
  types of, 94–95
African Americans, media portrayals of,
  66–70
Agenda-setting theory, 34–35
Aging adults, 80–83
Alcohol, values about, 326–327
All in the Family, 347
Amistad, 223
Asian Americans, media portrayals of,
  74–75
Arabs and Arab Americans
  media portrayals of, 7
  Radio Sawa appeal to, 185
Arousal, sexual, 292–293
Attention, 40

B

Backward messages in music,
  comprehension of, 117
Beer commercials, messages of masculinity
  in, 63
Belize, 32
Benetton, United Colors campaign, 105
Blacks, *see* African Americans
Blogs, 359
Brazil
  Olympics coverage, 166
  politics, ideology, and media, 252
Breast-feeding, 56–57

C

Captive marketing, 121
Catharsis, 274–275, 303
Cell phone as distraction while driving, 41
Censorship, 5–6, 200–204
Channel One, 135–136
Children and media, 124–150
  advertising to children, 138–144
  and sexual media, 291
  media literacy, 144–149
  prosocial children's TV, 127–137
  use of different media, 125–127
Christian television, *see* religious television
Classical conditioning
  in advertising, 113–115
  desensitization, 267–268
College students, media portrayals of, 89
Computer-mediated communication, 12–13,
  357–361, 367–370, *see also* Internet

Content analysis, 19–20
Contraception, 297–299
Creativity and media, 127
Crime coverage, effects of, 212–217
Cultivation theory, 28–30, 251–253, 269, 350

D

Debates, televised presidential, 235–237
Deception in advertising, 108–113
Desensitization in response to viewing
    violent media, 267–268
Disabilities, media portrayals of person
    with, 83–84
Disclaimers in advertising, 139–140
Disorders, psychological, media portrayals
    of persons with, 84–85
Docudrama, 221–223
Drugs
    advertising of prescription drugs, 122
    illicit drugs in sports, 176

E

Effects of media
    models, 21–22
    strength of, 26–27, 278, 285
    types of, 22–26
Elaboration Likelihood Model, 104
Election of 2000 (U.S.), coverage of, 242–245
Electronic vs. print media, 3
Emotion and media, 151–155
    sports, 171–172
Empathy, 43–44, 276
Entertainment-Education media, 344–349
ER, 348
Exposure research, 21

F

Families, 320–327
    composition of families in media, 321–322
    family relations, 323
    influence of TV on, 325
    solidarity values, 322–325
Farmers and rural life in media, 88–89
Fear
    appeals in advertising, 100–101
    responses to violence, 257–260
Fifties (1950s), 320
Food styling, 110

Football, 162–163
Foreign names for products, 98
Foreign policy, news reporting effects on,
    217–220
Framing of political candidates, 238–240

G

Gay men, media portrayals of, 78–80
Gender bias in sports, 172–175

H

Health media campaigns, see Social
    Marketing
Hero worship and sports, 175–178
Hispanics, see Latinos
Homosexuals, see Gay Men and Lesbians
Horror films, 307–310
Hum Log, 345–347
Humor
    in advertising, 102
    psychology of, 45–48

I

Identification with media characters, 42–43
Imperialism, cultural, 37
India, 32, 308
Influencing media, 361–365
    group efforts, 363–365
    individual efforts, 362–363
Internet
    advertising on, 120–122
    growth of, 354, 367–370
    uses of, 357–361
Iran hostage crisis 1979–1981, 197
Iraq War 2003, 207–208
Islam, 77, 210

J

Japan, pornography in, 302
Journalism, science, 365–367

L

Landmine avoidance, teaching through
    comic books, 150
Latinos
    advertising to, 100
    media portrayals of, 70–72

Lawrence, in "For Better or For Worse," 79
Lawyers and the law in media, 86–87
Lesbians, media portrayals of, 78–80
Limited capacity model, 39
Literacy, media, 144–149, 282–284, 311–312

M

Magazine use, 11–12
Men, media portrayals of, 60–65
Mental illness, *see* Disorders, psychological
Minority portrayals, 65–78
    stages of, 65–66
Modeling effects of viewing violence,
    260–264
Mood management through media, 48
Murphy Brown and Dan Quayle, 296
Music, popular, 178–186
    African pop music, 180
    as memory cue, 185–186
    backward messages in, 117
    content of lyrics, 181–183
    effects of, 183–184
    MTV, 179
    uses and gratifications of, 180–181

N

Namibia
    radio in, 11
    rich versus poor in, 369–370
Native Americans, media portrayals of,
    72–74
News coverage, 187–245
    as creating a perceived reality, 199–208
    characteristics of newsworthy events,
        191–198
    effects of, 208–220
    limits of media influence, 222–224
    manipulation of, 200–208
    memory for, 209–211
    political news, 225–245
    religion and the news, 330–333
    responses to crime coverage, 212–217
    sexual details in, 294–294
    violent images, 265
Newspaper use, 10–11
Nielsen ratings, 20
North Korean cinema, 49
Nuclear war
    as entertainment TV, 43
    news coverage, 193

O

Occupations, media portrayals of, 85–89
Older adults, *see* Aging
Olympic Games, 163–166
Overview of book, 14–17

P

Parental mediation of television, 147–149,
    283–284
Patriotic appeals, 99–100
Perceived reality, 48–52, 271–272
Perfectionism and sports fanship, 172
Persian Gulf War 1991, coverage of, 205–207
Police officers in media, 86
Polling, public opinion, 232
Politics, 225–254
    campaign coverage, 228–235
    candidates' use of media, 237–242
    debates, televised presidential, 235–237
    election of 2000, coverage of, 242–245
    moderation, TV as cultivator of political,
        251–253
    political advertising, 245–251
Pornography, *see* Sex in media
Pornography commissions 1970, 1986,
    310–311
Product placements, 118–119, 348
Pseudo-events, 240–241
Psychologists and psychiatrists in media,
    87–88
Public Service Announcements (PSAs),
    see also Social Marketing
    for AIDS, 177, 343–344

R

Racial bias in sports coverage, 174–175
Radio use, 9–10
Rape, *see* Sexual Violence
Ratings, MPAA, 13, 283
Reading in competition with TV, 128
Reality shows, 351
Religion, 328–335
    effects of TV on, 334–335
    in TV series, 328–329
    religion and news, 330–333
    religious professionals, portrayals of,
        329
    religious television, 333–334

Research frameworks, 19–27
Risks, misperceptions from news reporting,
    212–217

S

Schema theory, 35–39
Science shows for children, 135
Sensation-seeking, 276
Sensitization as response to media violence,
    264–267
Sesame Street, 129–132
Sex in media, 287–316
    content analyses, 288–292
    effects of viewing, 292–304
    in advertising, 113–115
    prevailing tone, 303–304
    promiscuity and U.S. Presidents,
        234
    scientific theory and ideology, 315
    sex crimes, 294, 301–303, 312–314
    sexual values, 293–299
    sexual violence, 305–314
Sexes, portrayals of, 54–65
    effects of portrayals, 63–65
Simpson, O. J., trial of, 199
Simpsons, 329
Singapore, 32
Slasher movies, 307–310
Social cognitive theory, 27–28
Socialization theories, 30–31
Social marketing, 335–344
    audience factors, 338–339
    obstacles to, 336–338
    positive effects of, 339–341
    public health media campaigns,
        341–344
Soul City, 345–347
Sports and media, 155–178
    history of, 156–157
    how TV has changed, 157–166
    psychological issues in, 166–178
Stanford Five-City Multifactor Risk
        Reduction Project, 342–343
Stereotyping of groups in media,
        53–91
Subliminal messages, 113–117
Subtitles in film and TV, 355
Suicides, media as trigger, 217
Suspense, 44–45
Suspension of disbelief, 41–42

T

Talk shows on TV, 154–155
Teen shows on TV, 136–137
Television
    use by groups, 6–9
    stages of impact, 8
    technological advances, 356–357
    worldwide growth, 353–354
Testimonials in advertising, 103–104, 176
Theories of mass communication research,
        27–39
Third-person effect, 25
Tobacco
    advertising and role modeling, 142–144
    values about, 326–327
Toys and television, 140–142

U

Uses and gratifications theory, 31–34

V

V-chip, 282–283
Values and media, 317–335
    alcohol and tobacco, 326–327
    economic, 326
    family, 320–325
    religion, 328–335
    sexual, 293–299
    Wal-Mart as values gatekeeper, 336
Vamp and virgin narratives of reporting
        rape, 312–314
Video games, violence, 280–282
Vietnam War
    in movies, 266
Violence, 255–286
    effects of viewing, 257–275
    longitudinal studies, 277–279
    public perception of research, 279–280
    sexual violence, 305–314
    sports violence, 170–171
    video games, 280–282
    who watches it, 275–276

W

Wal-Mart and values, 336
Weather forecasts, 190
Weight loss, 57
Women, media portrayals of, 54–60